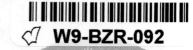

Oracle Press™

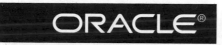

Oracle Designer/2000 Handbook

Dr. Paul Dorsey
Peter Koletzke

Osborne **McGraw-Hill**

Berkeley New York St. Louis San Francisco
Auckland Bogotà Hamburg London Madrid
Mexico City Milan Montreal New Delhi Panama City
Paris São Paulo Singapore Sydney Tokyo Toronto

Osborne **McGraw-Hill**
2600 Tenth Street
Berkeley, California 94710
U.S.A.

For information on translations or book distributors outside the U.S.A., or to arrange bulk purchase discounts for sales promotions, premiums, or fundraisers, please contact Osborne/**McGraw-Hill** at the above address.

Oracle Designer/2000 Handbook

234567890 DOC 9987

ISBN 0-07-882229-7

Publisher
Brandon A. Nordin

Acquisitions Editor
Wendy Rinaldi

Project Editor
Emily Rader

Copy Editor
Judy Ziajka

Technical Editor
Christine Hall

Proofreaders
Rhonda Holmes
Linda Medoff
Paul Medoff

Computer Designer
Jani P. Beckwith

Illustrator
Lance Ravella

Series Design
Jani P. Beckwith

Indexer
Caryl Lee Fisher

About the Authors...

Dr. Paul Dorsey is president of Dulcian, Inc., a consulting firm that specializes in data warehousing and system development of Oracle-based systems. One of the founding members of Oracle's Ambassador 2000 program, he is vice president of the New York Oracle Users Group and president of the International Ad Hoc Query SIG. He is one of the top presenters at Oracle user conferences, having won best paper awards for both the International Oracle User Week and East Coast Oracle conference.

Peter Koletzke is an independent consultant who specializes in Oracle Designer/2000 and Developer/2000 work. He also teaches Oracle subjects and is the head of the relational database track for Columbia University's Computer Technology and Applications program. In addition, Peter is on the Board of Directors of the New York Oracle Users Group and is a frequent contributor to Oracle development newsletters and users group conferences.

Contents

PART 2
Development Phases

PART 3
Other Designer/2000 Activities

Designer/2000 Contents at a Glance

The following list provides the starting page numbers for material on the main Designer/2000 tools and utilities. Only the page numbers for the overviews and for the explanations of techniques are listed. In addition to these locations, you will find discussions of how these tools are used in system development in the chapters on the development phases.

Tool or Utility	Description	Location
Data Diagrammer	Overview	38
	Introduction	355
Database Design Wizard	Overview	51
	Introduction	322
Dataflow Diagrammer	Overview	36
	Introduction	203
	More Features	269
Designer/2000 window	Introduction	58
	How to bypass	571
Entity Relationship Diagrammer	Overview	35
	Introduction	119
	How to create an autolayout	222
	More Features	252
Forms Generator	Overview	44
	Introduction	465
Function/Attribute Matrix utility	Overview	216
	Introduction	261
Function Hierarchy Diagrammer	Overview	35
	Introduction	272
Generate Default Links utility	Introduction	432
Generate Reference Tables utilities	Introduction	433
Generate Summary Usages utility	Introduction	391
Graphics Generator	Overview	44
	Introduction	496
Matrix Diagrammer	Overview	50
	Introduction	281
Module Data Diagrammer	Overview	40
	Introduction	422
Module Logic Navigator	Overview	39
	Introduction	381
Module Structure Diagrammer	Overview	41
	Introduction	409

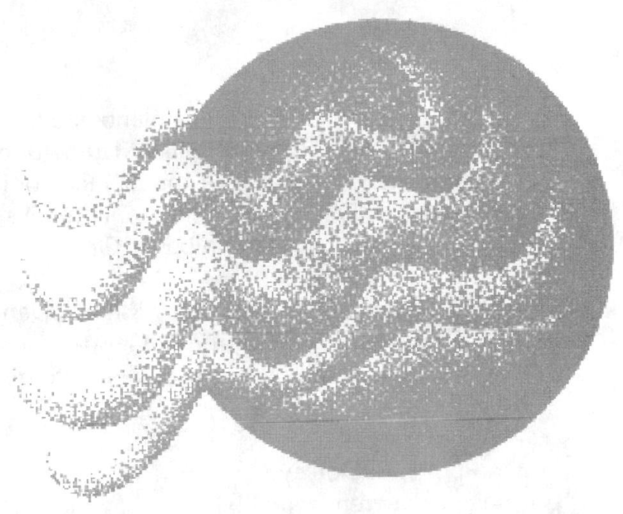

Acknowledgments

Deciding to write a book is the easy part. Actually starting and, more importantly, finishing the process is another story. Although there are only two authors' names on the cover of this book, it would have been impossible to accomplish this work without the help and support of many other people throughout the months of deadlines, schedule juggling, missed sleep, and a complete lack of a social life. The fact that you are reading this is a tribute to their patience and perseverance.

Many thanks to Christine Hall of Detroit Edison, who became much more than a technical editor. She was a major contributor to the book. Without her astute insights sprinkled with humorous comments, which cheered us on as we worked, this book would be something far less than it is.

A special mention must go to Caryl Lee Fisher who helped write, edit, and re-edit the manuscript, and re-edit the manuscript, and re-edit the manuscript. . .

Love and gratitude to Katherine Duliba, my wife, for contributing the section on business process re-engineering that we include in the Analysis chapter and for putting up with me throughout this arduous process.

Also thanks to many other people who have, by design or inadvertently, contributed ideas to this book, including Ian Fisher and Dai Clegg of Oracle Corporation, for their support; Eyal Aronoff, who contributed the ideas surrounding the political environment of a project; Bonnie O'Neil, for her ideas concerning business rules; Michael Hillanbrand II, for his information on database security and thoughtful comments; Mike Martin, for his thoughts on process-centric versus data-centric analysis; Tony Ziemba, for innumerable ongoing conversations and support; Erik Enger, for his contributions to the sections on the Designer/2000 generators; and Jim Phipps of Oracle Corporation, for his valuable insights on the Analysis phase.

Many thanks to Wendy Rinaldi, Daniela Dell'Orco, Judy Ziajka, and especially Emily Rader, of Osborne McGraw-Hill for all their efforts and support on this project.

And finally, heartfelt apologies to my dog, Popper, for having neglected him for the last six months.

Paul Dorsey
Lawrenceville, NJ
September, 1996

In a theatrical show, the actors provide their talent to the production and enjoy, as well as suffer, the spotlight. The show could not exist as a vehicle for the actors, however, without the backstage personnel in charge of lighting, scenery, costumes, and stage management. These people contribute to the show their hard work, expertise, and creativity, but receive little or no public recognition.

Writing a book is much like mounting a theatrical show. (I speak from experience, because my previous career was as a stage manager and lighting technician.) The authors of this book are like actors who are in the spotlight, and the book itself is like the production. There were also numerous "backstage" people who assisted in "raising the curtain" and "lighting the lights" of this book. Since we cannot list all of these as co-authors, it is appropriate to at least mention their contributions and offer gratitude and thanks for their efforts.

I greatly appreciate the efforts of all involved at Osborne/McGraw-Hill: Wendy Rinaldi, acquisitions editor; Daniela Dell'Orco, editorial assistant; Emily Rader, project editor; and our unknown (but all important) friends in production. Thanks also to Judy Ziajka, our copy editor on the book. At the start of this project, we set quite an ambitious schedule, and all at OMH dedicated themselves to work many hours to finish it. Particular thanks to Emily, who went out of her way to speed us needed copies of review material. How could we not meet our deadlines when all these people were giving up so much personal time to meet theirs?

Ian Fisher, Vice President of Designer/2000 Product Marketing for Oracle UK, assisted us by supplying us with an early copy of Designer/2000 1.3. Without that jump-start, we would have lagged behind our early deadlines by a few weeks. Thanks Ian.

Our technical reviewer, Chris Hall, provided astute, uncompromising, and accurate opinions and judgments of the work-in-progress. She put much time into carefully reviewing the drafts and caught some potentially embarrassing typos and unclear sentences.

Many thanks go to Titus Bocseri and Dr. Zhongsu Chen, for base material on the Forms and Reports generators. Their hard work, timeliness, enthusiasm, and expertise was of key importance to the Build chapter.

Caryl Lee Fisher cheerfully endured the daily phone calls and more frequent e-mail. Her phone was rarely silent and most of the traffic was related to this book. Caryl Lee was really the authors' stage manager, as she organized our work and focused us on the proper tasks at the proper times with gentle reminders. All that hard work and commitment is greatly appreciated.

My wife, Anne, as well as my parents and brother, bore with the difficult schedule that I imposed on myself. They also provided momentary diversions when the work started to be too intense, and listened empathetically to me while I explained each step of the book production process. I now understand the reasons why everyone who writes a book must recognize their family's assistance.

Finally, thanks to all my major teachers of the last 30 years from whom I learned much: Gilbert, Todd, Art, and Sai. Hopefully the torch is passed without diminishing its flame.

Peter Koletzke
New York City, NY
September, 1996

Introduction

12-Step Program for Traditional System Development

1. *Think up a really cool acronym.*
2. *Figure out a mission-critical system that fits the acronym.*
3. *Convince the CIO that you need a bunch of money to build the system.*
4. *Divert most of the money to other projects that have used up their funding.*
5. *Assign a couple of junior developers to build the system when it is discovered that everyone else is too busy.*
6. *Hire a team of consultants who have never done anything like this because they will give you a good rate.*
7. *Tell the consultants not to bother gathering system requirements because you know what the users want.*
8. *Hire a new consulting team because the first one hasn't made enough progress.*
9. *Just start coding because the project is way behind schedule.*
10. *Don't bother with documentation, since no one reads that stuff anyway.*
11. *Have your cousin from out of town do user acceptance testing.*
12. *Write a system work request to propose what you actually accomplished. Backdate it and declare victory.*

The process of designing and building automated information systems is greatly influenced by the software tools used to assist in the process. Systems analysts, designers, and developers turn to Computer-Aided Software Engineering (CASE) programs to capture information about business requirements, create a design for the data structures to fulfill those requirements, and generate front-end and server program code. Since CASE tools automate much of the manual, repetitive, and error-prone work needed for system development, they can, when properly used, greatly increase the productivity of those who produce the systems, as well as the accuracy of the design and robustness of the implementation. These tools become such an important part of the mechanics of creating systems that it is impossible to separate the process from the tools.

Designer/2000, Oracle Corporation's CASE product now at version 1.3, represents an unparalleled achievement in Oracle's ability to support all phases of traditional, as well as alternative, System Development Life Cycle methods. One such method is presented in Richard Barker's Oracle CASE books, which serve as excellent overviews. Unfortunately, these books are often misused by developers who follow them dogmatically, or mistakenly believe that the books, together with the Designer/2000 product, form a complete development methodology. These books were never really intended to serve as complete methodology guides, as each step in the development life cycle really deserves its own book.

The Purpose of this Book

This book represents the first development method fully integrated with Oracle's Designer/2000 product. Its purpose is to show the practical steps and methodological phases of producing software, in addition to specific ways in which the Designer/2000 tool can support them. Our work here has two objectives. The first is to revise and expand on the CASE method. We have gone into more detail than have the original CASE books, added more deliverables, and restructured the whole process. The second objective is to describe how Designer/2000 can best be used to support our revised CASE method.

We call this revised method the *CASE Application Development Method* (CADM). This book represents a serious departure from traditional books about the System Development Life Cycle and traditional books about software products. It is an integration of these two distinct types of books. Rather than saying, "this is a book on how to build systems" or "this is a book about how to use Designer/2000," we say "this is a book about how to build systems using Designer/2000." We have combined the best industry practices for system development with the best integrated CASE tool on the market—Oracle's Designer/2000.

One of the main goals of this book is to present a development process that tracks the path of a business requirement from its original source, typically gathered during Analysis, to its eventual implementation in the system. We wanted to formulate a process that would guard against encountering the scenario in which a user shows up at the end of a project with interview notes gathered six months earlier, points to a paragraph, and says, "We wanted this in our system and it's not here. You signed off on this. Where is it?" In order to avoid this frightening scenario, our entire development process is driven by business requirements. This book discusses the methodology itself—what you need to think about, talk about, and do as you progress through the System Development Life Cycle.

Another goal of this book is to include a very strong quality assurance component with virtually every aspect of every phase of the development process. It doesn't matter that you have a great application development method if the developers don't follow it carefully. The key to the success of CADM is making sure that each phase is correctly completed prior to moving on to the next.

The book also contains information on what tools Designer/2000 can support in each of the phases and how it supports them. It supplies details, not found in other sources, for effective use of the tools, and explains what information is important to gather at each stage. The book also mentions how this information flows from one phase to another in the development process. Interspersed in these discussions, as well as discussions of the methodology itself, are tips and techniques for productive work in the tool.

Organization of This Book

This book is divided into three parts. Part 1 contains an overview of the CADM methodology and of Designer/2000 in Chapters 1 and 2, respectively. Part 2 (Chapters 3–12) provides details on each phase of the methodology, as well as on the Designer/2000 tools and utilities that support each phase. Each phase is discussed in one or two chapters, although discussions of the Implementation and Maintenance phases are combined in one chapter.

The CADM life cycle we present in this book progresses in a linear way from one phase to another. We recognize, however, that system development is not a simple, linear process. The scope of a project can change at any time. New user requirements can be discovered anywhere in the process, even in the Test phase. In addition, quality-control checks can fail. In general, reality always creeps into our theoretically clean process. Therefore, Chapter 11 includes a large section on how to respond to the unexpected.

Part 3 contains information on several Designer/2000 features you use throughout the methodology phases. In particular, Chapter 13 outlines application system and repository administration, and Chapter 14 introduces the Application Programmatic Interface.

Since many Designer/2000 tools and utilities are used in more than one phase, discussion of a particular tool may be spread across more than one chapter. You can refer to the "Designer/2000 Contents at a Glance" following the table of contents if you are interested in where in the book to find the major discussions of a particular tool or utility.

Why Use Designer/2000?

Designer/2000 is the best integrated CASE product on the market. Its capabilities greatly influence the CADM process. Designer/2000's ability to track data and process information in a single repository makes it an invaluable aid. In addition to its built-in breadth and depth, Designer/2000 offers User Extensibility and the Application Programmatic Interface (API). These features allow you to extend the capabilities of Designer/2000 to support aspects that the Oracle product designers chose not to implement in the core product or that are specific to your working environment.

In general, Designer/2000 promises to make application system development more accurate and flexible, as shown in the following table. This is because Designer/2000 provides a way to capture and manage the often voluminous data associated with a new or current system. The data can be so unmanageable that systems designers end up ignoring or overlooking key business needs or spending too much time developing the system and, along the way, lose sight of the requirements.

Development Aspect	With Designer/2000	Without Designer/2000
System development	Structured	Usually ad hoc
Maintenance costs	Low	High
Generation of database code	Automated (low cost)	Manual (high cost)
Front-end code generation	Partially automated	Manual
System documentation	Mostly stored in the repository	Ad hoc

Why CASE Projects Fail

CASE tools have historically been viewed as a waste of time and resources, because project leaders who bought into the concept could not support the huge learning curve required for their staff. If time was not devoted solely to learning the tools and how they were supposed to work, the project was delayed significantly or failed totally. Due to these early negative experiences, a stigma was attached to the word "CASE," and many companies would not touch it. Oracle (as well as other CASE vendors) has therefore reworked the idea and totally expunged the word "CASE" from documentation and discussions of the current product. Designer/2000 is, nonetheless, a CASE tool, and while the product is much deeper and easier to use than previous versions, the learning curve is still significant. Ignoring this fact may cause projects to fail.

Another major reason for the failure of CASE projects was that CASE users who did not understand the software development process relied on the product to lead them through the life cycle, one step at a time. While this is somewhat possible in the current version of Designer/2000, it was not and still is not possible to expect the CASE tool to do all the driving. After all, CASE is "Computer-Aided" not "Computer-Driven" Software Engineering. A CASE tool should not be confused with a methodology. The methodology, rather than the tool, defines our procedures.

Determining the Methodology

When developing a system, care and attention must be given to the development methodology. One of the important influences on a methodology is the tool selected for the task. In particular, CASE tools have the strongest impact on the development method because of their direct influence on all phases of the project. As we just mentioned, the danger is that the CASE tools *become* the methodology. If the tools perform many of the development tasks, it is easy to assume that they support and drive all development tasks. This tool-driven methodology encourages developers to miss essential steps in the development process because those steps are not explicitly handled by the tool.

We all would like an easy, "don't have to think about it" design process. We would like check lists, detailed deliverables, and precise standards. We would also like to give up our responsibility of having to think about what we are doing. In reality, though, this will never work, because every system is different, and developing systems is an intellectual exercise. Developers must ask the following questions:

- Is there a theoretically sound plan that will take the project where it should go?
- How will we know when a task or phase has been accomplished?
- How will we measure success?

These are the kinds of questions that must be asked at each phase. Unfortunately, it is far too easy to be blinded by the work plan, the delivery deadline, and the demands for immediate results.

Where Does CADM Fit?

After writing this book, we recognized that, after all, CADM is a traditional System Development Life Cycle (SDLC) approach. Our experience has been that developers and users are more satisfied with the finished product when the analysis and design are carefully done. Most of us have worked on systems where failures have been of biblical proportions. These failures usually happen because shortcuts are taken and the proper methodology is not followed or performed with enough care. Designer/2000 helps us to do better analysis and design by providing a unified repository to store most of the analysis and design information.

While CADM does not emphasize prototyping, there is nothing to say that small prototypes cannot also be included as part of the Analysis and Design phases in order to show proof of concept. Prototyping can occur throughout the system's life cycle in order to better communicate the overall vision of the system to users. This gives users useful feedback about how the completed system eventually will look before a significant amount of money is spent building it. In the Pre-Design phase, we suggest that developers produce a prototype so that users can experience the look and feel of the system. Then, by the time the system is ready to be built, the users have helped the system evolve through its life cycle.

At the risk of looking like traditionalists (i.e., non-forward-thinking radicals) who are bucking the trend toward the rapid prototyping environment, we strongly advocate a traditional SDLC, but one that is done better, faster, more efficiently, and with better organization. We believe that Analysis should be done carefully and correctly. When it is, valuable time and money can be saved by not having to redo what should have been done right the first time.

When we first started writing this book, we envisioned a much smaller work. Now that we've finished it, we have to acknowledge that even though it is larger than we originally thought it would be, it is merely an overview of the application development process. Time and time again, we found ourselves wanting to write more about a topic, but the practical limitations of the project prohibited this. We do not claim that this book is a complete treatment of how to use Designer/2000 to build systems, as that would take many volumes. However, we do feel that it is a complete overview of our vision of the best way to build systems using Designer/2000.

PART 1

Getting Started

CHAPTER 1

Introduction to System Design Methodology

A poorly planned project will take five times as long as anticipated. A well-planned project will take only three times as long as anticipated.

The key to a successful system design project lies in the coordination of several critical success factors—namely the right people, the right technology/tools, and the right method. An effective combination of these three factors is necessary for system success. This is not just a how-to book about the Designer/2000 tool, nor is it a college textbook on systems analysis and design. Rather, this book serves as a guide for systems developers on how to successfully build systems using the Designer/2000 tool based on actual project experiences of the authors.

You will be exploring each step in the system development process in detail in the following chapters. This chapter presents short summaries of all of the steps to give you an idea of the individual phases. The detailed steps will be easier to follow if you first have a broad understanding of the entire process. The next chapter gives an overview of the Designer/2000 tools and explains their role in system development.

Overview of CASE Application Development Method (CADM)

There is no magic about the System Development Life Cycle (SDLC). It has been documented in every book on analysis and design for the last 20 years. With the exception of a few radical shifts such as prototyping methodology in the mid 1980s, there hasn't been a fundamental shift in the SDLC since it was described decades ago. Essentially, it boils down to the fact that all methodologies, regardless of whether they are developed in-house or purchased by a software project management or consulting firm, address a structure to plan, analyze, design, build, and implement business applications. What differentiates them is their level of detail, techniques, and their integration with people, processes, and technology.

Since the Designer/2000 product is an Oracle product, many readers of this book will be familiar with the SDLC steps known as the *CASE* method and outlined by Richard Barker in CASE Method: Tasks and Deliverables, (Case Method: Tasks and Deliverables: Addison-Wesley, 1990). Richard Barker was one of the driving influences behind Oracle's CASE products and the CASE methodology. He spearheaded the development of the CASE tool.

We will use the same major phases and terms utilized by Barker as a starting point. However, to achieve the objectives of this book, we found it necessary to modify and enhance the CASE method. No explicit assumption is made that the reader is familiar with Barker's method; but for those readers already familiar with it, we hope that our remaining consistent with Barker's terminology will help avoid confusion.

The basic phases in Barker's method are Strategy, Analysis, Design, Build, Documentation, Transition, and Production. We found the basic steps of the CASE method too broad. What this book attempts to do is lay out the goals, deliverables, and methods for evaluating the success and completion of each phase. Not all tasks in the various phases of the CASE method are supported by the Designer/2000 tool. A list of the basic phases of our revised development method and what tasks each supports is presented in Table 1-1.

We have added the transition steps of Pre-Analysis and Pre-Design to the basic methodology and have included Test, Implementation, and Maintenance in the overall process. We have named this revised method CASE Application Development Method (CADM). Also, because of its importance in today's development environment, a section on business process re-engineering has been

Revised CASE Design Phases	Supported by Designer/2000	Not Supported by Current Version of Designer/2000	Can Be Supported by Designer/2000 with User Extensibility
Strategy	Strategy ERD Process flows	Strategy document Cost-benefit analysis Workplan	
Analysis	Analysis ERD Function hierarchy Dataflow diagrams	User interviews Prototypes Storyboards	System requirements Report audit
Design	Basic modules	Complex modules	Design specifications
Build	Basic modules	Complex modules	
Test		Automated testing	Test plan and execution
Implementation	Rollout plan		
Maintenance	Versioning		

TABLE 1-1. *Simplified CADM Development Phases and What Designer/2000 Supports in Each Step*

included in this book. Prototyping concepts have been employed throughout the process, although the book does not advocate a strict prototyping methodology.

Strategy

In the Strategy phase, the entire focus is on the business. The goal of the Strategy phase is to gain a clear understanding of the business area's goals, objectives, processes, direction, and needs in order to structure and document the vision of a project. This "vision document" has been referred to as a project charter, project definition document, and scope document, depending upon your organization's preference. For our purposes, we will call it the strategy document. The *strategy document* outlines the scope of a project and defines an agreement about what the project is committed to deliver. It also includes the estimated budget, time frame, resources, controls, and standards within which the project must be completed. It is the foundation for moving forward and preparing detailed plans.

Strategy is the most often neglected phase of a systems project. The strategy document is usually quite brief and not well thought out. Barker states very clearly that "the objective of the strategy phase is to produce, with user management, a set of business models, a set of recommendations and an agreed plan for information systems development."

Many analysts view Strategy as a protective step. It is used to limit later finger pointing and enable analysts to justify cases in which they went over budget.

Preparing the strategy document is a complex step that must be completed before going forward. Development of business models requires understanding of the organization. A few meetings with top management are not usually sufficient. In the Strategy phase, one of the goals is to intimately understand the business. The system requirements are going to change over the course of the project. (Has there ever been a project during which user needs did not evolve?) By thoroughly understanding the business, the analyst will be prepared to evolve with the project.

At the completion of the Strategy phase, it is important to deliver a high-quality strategy document that includes the following parts: a strategy ERD, a top-level requirements document, an analysis of the political environment, a work flow plan, strategy-level process flows, and a strategy evaluation. For this overview, we have described only some of the sections. A complete list and discussion of all parts of the strategy document can be found in Chapter 3.

Strategy ERD

The purpose of the strategy ERD is to identify the primary data or main entities of a business area. The strategy ERD serves to demonstrate a preliminary understanding of the business area. There should be little thought at this point in the process as to how the system will eventually be implemented. The only goal is to capture the users' needs at the highest level.

Strategy ERDs should focus on readability rather than on relational theory. Good drawing and naming techniques, such as those proposed by David Hay (a consultant who works with Group R, an Oracle consulting firm) should be used. All you are trying to do is draw a picture. It is not necessary to completely fill in all Designer/2000 element entities with descriptions; nicely named relationships and a few key columns are sufficient.

Keep strategy ERDs small enough to be useful. Several small models of 10 to 20 entities each are better than one complicated (and intimidating) model.

Strategy Document

A comprehensive strategy document is essential to the success of a project. Although most of the system requirements are gathered during the Analysis phase, the key system requirements should be included in the strategy document. The keys to a good strategy document are planning and organization. The main goal of this document is to scope the project—to identify and describe high-level requirements. The "real" requirements document comes later. Another goal is to sell the system. A cost-benefit analysis of the system should be included.

Business and Formal Sponsorship

The systems analyst needs to be aware of the political environment within the organization in which he or she is working. The existing political environment can have a major impact on how the project phases proceed. This environment, including its players and methods for resolving potential conflicts, should be documented by the analyst.

High-Level Work Plan

A high-level work plan identifies the major phases, activities, milestones, key deliverables, resources and duration of the project. The work plan outlines the steps to be followed as the system goes forward and can largely be boilerplate text. It should be clear to the reader not only how long things will take but also that the plan will produce the desired results. Personnel requirements and deliverables should be included in the work plan.

Strategy-Level Process Flows

Business process flows are typically defined as part of the Analysis phase. However, the key business processes should be identified and modeled at this point as process flows.

Strategy Evaluation

The evaluation of the strategy requires input from both users and developers. Unfortunately, users may not understand the process of development well enough to evaluate whether or not the Strategy phase has been properly completed. Therefore, it is important to educate users as necessary so they can effectively evaluate the project strategy. The challenge on the side of the developers is to not delude themselves that the strategy is complete when it isn't. Developers must understand the basics of the system they are developing.

At its core, the strategy document is a contract. There must be a meeting of the minds if the contract is to make sense and be honored. Developers must understand the needs and direction of the business; and users must have confidence that the developers have grasped a level of understanding sufficient to move forward. The strategy document is the vehicle for making this mutual understanding possible.

Pre-Analysis

The goals of Pre-Analysis are to plan the analysis process and to begin to set standards. Users and developers together must develop a strategy that ensures that the analysis will be performed correctly. Therefore, the first step is to decide on the goals of the Analysis phase.

Barker describes Analysis as expanding Strategy to "ensure business accuracy, feasibility and a sound foundation for Design." However, Analysis is more than this. The goal of Analysis is to capture all user specifications for the project and to completely detail all business processes that will be involved in the system design.

Analysis therefore focuses on the user rather than on the system. It attempts to figure out what the users want and how their business works. Later, items can be declared out of scope or budget. At this point, there is no reason to argue with users about their requirements. The only goal is to understand these requirements.

The pre-analysis document should include the following: analysis plan, plan for implementing CASE analysis standards, and pre-analysis evaluation.

Analysis Plan

Before Analysis can begin, there must be an analysis plan. Steps and deliverables must be included. "Analysis" is not a well-defined word. Different analysts explain this step very differently. The developer must include a statement of the scope of the analysis.

Plan for Implementing CASE Analysis Standards

The developer must specify how CASE analysis standards will be implemented. How will the CASE tool be used? What fields will be filled in and with what information? How will entities and attributes be named? How detailed will the descriptions be? Will functions be numbered or named? What will be ignored? These are some of the many questions that must be answered before the project can go forward into Design.

Pre-Analysis Evaluation

Pre-Analysis is finished when everyone agrees that there is an appropriate plan for gathering all system requirements. As with other phases, both users and developers have to agree that the Pre-Analysis phase is complete.

Assessment of the analysis plan is similar to that of an ERD. To "break" an ERD, you try to come up with a data example that the model can't handle. In Pre-Analysis evaluation, it is helpful to have users try to come up with requirements that the process will not gather. For example, in one system a veteran on-site developer asked: "We have requirements hard-coded in our old C routines that must make it into the new system; how will we find out about those?" Because of that one question, the analysis plan was expanded.

Analysis

The goal of the Analysis phase is to capture all of the user specifications for the project and to completely detail all business processes that will be involved. This is the most important step in systems design. We will discuss the Analysis phase in Chapters 5 and 6.

The ERD and function hierarchy are built with the user directly and indirectly through the requirements document; good analysts do not just work with the user for an hour and then come back three months later with a product that they developed on their own.

The existing business processes, the legacy system, and the users themselves are all sources of the requirements information. The amount of information gathered will be so large that its management is a task in itself. A thorough requirements document can easily fill several thousand pages.

The analysis document consists of the following parts: analysis ERD, process flows (logical), requirements document, and analysis evaluation.

Analysis ERD

The goal of the analysis ERD is to completely represent as many business rules as possible. Any rules that cannot be represented in the model must be written down. In Analysis, the focus is still on the user, so there is no need to worry about how the system will be implemented.

Process Flows (Logical)

The developer needs to document logical process flows. What are the tasks? Who performs them? What tasks precede other tasks? Process flows modeling major business transactions attempt to answer these questions, with one flow chart used for each business transaction. The Oracle Process Modeller tool is the ideal tool for this task.

Requirements Document

The requirements document is a critical aspect of the Analysis phase. A missing or inadequate requirements document can lead to client dissatisfaction and, ultimately, system failure. A requirements document must include the following:

- **Detailed business objectives and critical success factors for each business area that the system will support**
- **Legacy system documentation** Unless it is a new system, the existing legacy system should be modeled. A small Oracle database that tracks existing files, fields, applications, and menu screens is easy to build and is a great help in making sure that the new system does not lose any legacy system functionality. The legacy documentation database should be mapped to the new system database and function hierarchy to ensure functional and data completeness of the new system.

- **Requirements list** A list of all requirements elicited directly from users and other sources. User interviews should be structured so that user requirements are easily identified and assigned to functional areas. Each interview should generate a document that is returned to the user for sign-off.
- **A report audit** Developers need to know which reports in the current system will be brought forward into the new system.
- **Process flows for all major business functions**
- **Function hierarchy** An analysis function hierarchy should capture all basic business functions. This will not be mapped to modules, so the only goals here are completeness and readability.
- **Business rules** The developer needs to take all system requirements and distill them down to business rules. Business rules are represented in two places. One is in the analysis ERD. Not even all data-level business rules can be reflected in the ERD, however. Therefore, these requirements need to be tracked in text and, in the Build phase, translated into database triggers.
- **Requirements mapped to the function hierarchy** To prove completeness of the function hierarchy, all requirements from the detailed requirements list should be mapped to the function hierarchy. Any functions not representing a user need should be reexamined and, usually, dropped. Requirements that cannot be mapped to existing functions require the creation of new functions.

The completed document can then be used as a cross-check to ensure that the proposed data and function models are complete. A requirements document of this type greatly increases the likelihood of system design success.

The importance of the requirements document is evident in the following example of a situation in which no requirements document was originally planned. The client wanted a requirements document and also pushed for documentation of system requirements. Unfortunately, the senior consulting staff was not responsive to the client's requests. They fought the construction of a full list of all the project's requirements. They felt that creation of such a document would be a duplication of effort because the CASE tool already allows for descriptions for each function. However, this was not enough for the client. The client wanted a list of everything from detailed requirements to process flows. This client tired of the consultants coming onto the site and taking information directly from users and putting it into the functional models and ERDs. This tactic made it impossible for the information to be cross-checked. The project manager could not track who authorized what functions, especially when information, such as the source and topic, that could have been noted in the CASE tool was left out. Development effort was spent on complex ERD modeling when some of the data being modeled was not even required for the system. Furthermore, duplicate functions were hard to find, while exactly who needed a certain function could only be inferred from the description of the function.

With a requirements document, it is possible to cross-reference requirements by entity model, function model, and source. Then a tool can be constructed that enables both user and analyst to validate the information transfer. By mapping system requirements to the Designer/2000 deliverables, the ERDs and functional hierarchies can be cross-checked. Analysts can receive the users' and management's approval on the requirements and model them in a way that achieves the appropriate goal. Without the requirements document, it can only be hoped that individuals can keep all of the requirements in their head while they validate the ERDs and functional hierarchies.

The requirements document should include the following: analysis function hierarchy, legacy system documentation, business rules, and requirements mapped to the function hierarchy.

Analysis Evaluation

The first question in analysis evaluation is whether the set of requirements is complete—and the answer is always no; there is always something overlooked. If requirements are sorted by detailed function and shown to users, users frequently will find something new at this point. In-house systems people should also spend time evaluating the requirements. They frequently know more about what really goes on at the detail level than many users. Finally, it is up to the developers to make sure that system-level requirements are specified. Response time, accuracy, and volatility are all factors that users frequently take for granted but which have profound impacts on the design.

The next question is whether the ERD is correct. A correct, logical ERD is a third normal-form representation of as many data-relation business rules as possible. Any data-related business rules that cannot be represented in the ERD can be represented in a non-ERD supportable business rules document. The developer must ensure that the ERD can support all of the organization's business transactions. The way to accomplish this is to take the most complex examples of everything stored and make sure this data can be represented. People often think that their model is correct until someone attempts to put data into it. Every data business rule must be captured in the ERD. Any rule that can't be modeled should be written as trigger specs that accompany the ERD.

The final question in analysis evaluation is whether the function hierarchy is correct. The purpose of the function hierarchy is to show the business process and make sure all system requirements are on schedule for implementation. The function hierarchy is used mainly for organizational purposes. If all major business functions are represented, all requirements are mapped to at least one function, and each function has at least one system requirement associated with it, the analysis evaluation is finished.

Business Process Re-engineering

Business process re-engineering (BPR) is a radical redesign of the underlying way an organization performs tasks. When redesigning a system, it is frequently a good opportunity to not just replace an existing legacy system or automate a manual process, but also to think about what changes can be made to the underlying business processes in order to make them faster, more efficient, and better meet the needs of the organization. BPR is not a phase of the traditional system development process but can be added to broaden the scope of the proposed system.

In any project, one very important issue that must be considered carefully is how much the new system being built will change the existing system and the way business is done. For example, the automated teller machine (ATM) fundamentally re-engineered the way people interact with banks. World Wide Web (WWW) applications have re-engineered the way customers interact with companies.

However, re-engineering efforts need not be so drastic. Katherine Duliba has studied the way that companies re-engineer their business and has developed the taxonomy shown in Table 1-2. She notes that when a new system is built, re-engineering is not an all or nothing proposition. There exist gradations of re-engineering reflecting the amount and types of changes made to the existing system. In the table, the Xs represent what is being re engineered at each step.

The columns in this table provide a list of the elements that can change in the re-engineering process:

- **Process** The way business is done
- **Software** The software used to perform the task
- **Interface** The user interface, such as changing from text to GUI or WWW
- **Hardware** The hardware used to perform the task
- **Data** The data, such as restructuring data from flat files into a relational database
- **People** The individuals who perform various parts of the task being re-engineered

	Process	Software	Interface	Hardware	Data	People
Reaffirm						
Repackage			X			
Rehost				X		
Rearchitect		X	X	X	X	
Re-engineer	X	X	X	X	X	X

TABLE 1-2. *Business Process Re-engineering Taxonomy*

The rows of the table indicate the amount of change from smallest to most radical:

- **Reaffirm** Make an explicit decision to do nothing, an alternative that should always be considered.
- **Repackage** Change the user interface, for example, from a character interface to a GUI or Web-based interface.
- **Rehost** Fundamentally change the hardware platform, for example, by moving from a centralized mainframe environment to a client/server environment.
- **Rearchitect** Change everything within the core technology not explicitly affecting the way business is done.
- **Re-engineer** Change all of the factors mentioned above while moving from the old system to the new one.

It is also necessary to look at the scope of the change within an organization. Changes can be implemented at the individual, departmental, divisional, or organization level. The more severe the change and the greater the scope, the greater the potential benefits and the greater the potential risks. More severe changes have greater up-front costs and lower immediate returns with a longer life cycle. Less severe changes have lower up-front costs, more proportionally immediate returns, and a shorter life cycle. All of these factors must be taken into consideration when business process re-engineering is performed.

Pre-Design

In the phase between Analysis and Design, the rest of the project is planned. Only after Analysis does the developer know exactly what the system is required to do. As the process moves from Analysis into Design, several steps need to be taken. Some people firmly believe that these steps belong in Analysis; others vigorously assert that they should be in Design. To avoid controversy, this book includes them as steps in the transitional, Pre-Design phase.

The Pre-Design phase includes the following: design plan, process flows (physical), design standards, screen concept prototype, and pre-design evaluation.

Design Plan

The plan for the Design phase must move comfortably from logical design to physical design. The plan should start with the logical process flows. The plan should then specify the results of consultation with the users regarding what will be part of the new system and what will remain as a manual process. The next step in the plan should be to iteratively develop prototypes of the system with screen designs that are supported by physical level process flows; when the developers are satisfied that they have a strong design, they should go back to the functional hierarchy and redo it at the physical level. Next, the designers should identify elemental functions in preparation for generation of modules.

Process Flows (Physical)

Physical process flows differ from logical process flows in that logical flows model the business whereas physical flows model the proposed system. The development of physical process flows is the first attempt at a functional system design. These process flows describe the way the new system will work functionally. They are modified throughout the Design phase as the system design matures.

Design Standards

Design standards describe the layout of the proposed system. Decisions must be made concerning the following:

- Screen layout, including colors, fonts and buttons
- Navigation tools, including menus and buttons

- Help
- Documentation
- Functionality
- Coding standards
- Naming conventions

One of the best strategies for developing design standards is to create several archetypal applications and then to reverse engineer the standards into Designer/2000 templates. Archetypal applications should include the following types:

- Simple, single table
- Master-detail
- Complex

This task must be performed knowing how Designer/2000 will generate applications. The goal is to produce standards that are easily generated by Designer/2000.

Screen Concept Prototype

The developer should create a screen prototype. This prototype is a major deliverable that will validate the design standards and the analysis. Screen design prototypes, sometimes called *storyboards*, implement the physical process flows and design standards. Through prototypes, users can evaluate the ability of the system to meet their needs. The storyboard does not need to access data, although some functionality is helpful when trying to get users to understand the design strategy.

Pre-Design Evaluation

In pre-design evaluation, the focus shifts from the user to the system. Systems professionals should have a greater say in this phase than should the users. Users should feel comfortable with the design plan; but systems people are the ones who will have to implement it, so their influence should be greater than that of the users.

The Pre-Design phase is complete when users are happy with the screen prototypes and process flows. Both users and developers should approve the design standards and design plan.

Design

The Design phase is where the blueprints are drawn for building the system. Every detail should be laid out before generation. The vision of iterative development using CASE is still a fantasy for large projects. So much time is spent preparing modules for generation and cleaning up after generation that it is important to have a clear picture of the system before the first generation.

The Design phase is divided into two parts: database design and application design, which will be discussed in Chapters 8 and 9, respectively.

Database Design

Database design involves the designing of the tables and columns along with the detailed specification of domains and check constraints on the columns. Also, database design includes the denormalization of the database to improve performance along with the associated triggers to support that denormalization. You do not have to worry about more physical level issues such as striping and tablespace layout. Those final parts of the design work occur in the Build phase.

Design Data Model

The design data model is the final physical design of the data base. Here is where any necessary denormalization takes place. Low-level details should be considered; and table designs should be rigorously, logically tested with sample data before implementation.

The data model must be built with the assistance of the database administrator (DBA). The time is over for any shoulder-shrugging comments that "we will worry about this later." It is later *now*. Not only must the system encapsulate the user needs, but it must work in the real world. Here is where the best and most experienced DBA talent should be used. If good in-house talent is not available, this is a cost-effective place to hire a consultant. The main downside to using an outside consultant is that a consultant will not have to live with the design day-in and day-out. Therefore, if possible, the in-house DBA should be the main driver of this effort.

Application Design

In addition to the design of specific applications and reports, application design involves decision making about what product (for example, Visual Basic, Forms, HTML, or C++) will be used for those designs.

Screen Design

Screen designs should be built according to what will realistically be generated using Designer/2000. Efficient system design is predicated upon staying as close as possible to what Designer/2000 will generate. There is no point in showing users a prototype that will be inferior to the final system.

Design Book

Each module to be generated should have a set of information associated with it. Beyond the information associated with the tool, each module has functions that should be documented. The goal here is to generate a folder for each application that fully describes that application. This folder acts as the primary unit testing document. The tester need only ensure that the application meets the specifications listed in the folder. In addition, the physical process flows should be a part of the design book to assist in system testing.

Design Evaluation

Design is complete when the design documents can be handed over to another team to build, with each application having its own screen (or report) design, list of detailed functionality, and create-retrieve-update-delete (CRUD) report.

Build

The Build phase involves two areas: the database and applications. If all of the preceding steps have been performed carefully and thoroughly, this phase should proceed smoothly. Database building involves direct generation using Designer/2000. All triggers and data structures can be kept within the physical model in Designer/2000, so the building of the database is a straightforward operation.

About the only specific work to be done at this point is final decision making regarding tablespace sizes and physical disk locations. Also, a final decision needs to be made as to how many copies of the database will be used. A *database* is a self-contained Oracle environment. It is common practice to use three (develop, test, and production). However, this book advocates five databases, which are described in more detail in the Pre-Design phase discussion in Chapter 7.

Before building applications, you need a sample database to test whether the applications are working properly. It is possible and common to build systems without this sample database. However, in those cases, you may spend a great deal of time figuring out where errors are coming from and how fast the system will run with real data. This book thus strongly advocates the use of sample data, described in detail in the discussion of the Build phase in Chapter 10.

Application building should rely on the use of templates whenever possible. After generation, application modifications should be stored in application-specific templates to aid in regeneration. This effort minimizes the need for additional modifications after regeneration.

Before you finish the Build phase, you must subject the system to a first-pass unit-level test. You should be sure to perform this testing while building the application because the application will at that point still be fresh in your mind. Then immediately pass the system to a tester to check that the system meets the design book specifications and that functionality from the user standpoint is working properly.

Documentation

Documentation should be an ongoing process occurring throughout the system development process. It should accompany the first prototype that the user sees. Documentation should not simply be a separate step at the end of the process.

There are two main types of documentation: system documentation and user documentation. Both of these types should be prepared throughout all development phases.

We all know the nightmare stories of developers who come in to modify an existing system for which there is no documentation. In the worst cases, the system not only has no system documentation, but also no source code for the applications. Let us resolve not to inflict this situation on future developers. By preparing careful system and user documentation throughout the life cycle of the project, developers are not left with a major task at the end. In addition, frequently little or no client money is left at this point to pay to extend the development process further.

Just as the applications of a system are tested, the documentation should also go through a testing process. Testing the system itself is impossible before the system documentation is written because there will be nothing to test against. The point is that no system is finished until both system and user documentation are completed satisfactorily.

Test

Test is one of the most important but usually most poorly conducted phases in the system design process. The key to proper testing is to use multiple tests. No single test, no matter how carefully conducted, will find all of the errors in a system. It is better to perform several different tests less carefully; these usually catch more errors at less cost to the organization.

By the time you reach the Test phase of the development process, you should not need to audit the logical or physical design of the database. This should already have been done at the end of the Analysis and Design phases. The first goal at this stage is to audit the correctness of the applications: do they meet the requirements?

To achieve this goal, you must perform unit-level tests application by application. The testing process should be meticulous, using test data, automated testing scripts, code walkthroughs, and interviews with the system developer. You also must perform overall database-level checks, including the following processes:

- Run a test deck (large amount of sample data) through the applications.
- Perform a consistency check on the database by running many procedures.
- Compare report output from the new system with that from the old system.
- Build small simple forms applications to help visually inspect the data.
- Run SELECT DISTINCT on all columns in all tables to check for valid data values.

The second goal of the Test phase is to perform user acceptance testing. Give users the applications to work with and perform real (not sample) transactions using the new system. Perform a final validation check on the user interface. This process is discussed in more detail in Chapter 11.

Implementation

At some point, the finished system needs to be turned over to the users and brought into production (after user training on the new system, of course, has taken place). There are various schools of thought on Implementation. The first is the "big bang" approach. The second is phased implementation.

The big bang approach entails pulling the plug on the old system and bringing up the new system and insisting that everyone use it. In this approach, there is no turning back. If you use this approach, it is critical that the system is well tested.

The advantage of this approach is that is it cheaper to do everything at once and not have parallel systems running simultaneously. In theory, this approach involves much less work because it forces 100 percent commitment from the entire organization. Some large consulting firms advocate the big bang approach. However, this book does not, in general, advocate its use.

The major disadvantage of the big bang approach is that there is no way to test a system so extensively that a developer can guarantee that it will work. However, if you really have confidence in your system, this approach can save time and money—so long as you are willing to assume the risks.

The second, more common, approach is phased implementation. Various portions of the new system are brought up one at a time, either by subject or by class of users. In most cases, running the new system in parallel with the legacy system requires double entry into both systems while the bugs are being worked out. Such an approach is clearly more costly than the big bang approach, but if something goes wrong, there is always the legacy system to fall back on.

Other important parts of the Implementation phase include devising an implementation schedule and a user training strategy. How will users be trained? Options include training manuals, classes, and the creation of a computer-based training system (CBT). However, for all but the largest organizations, the creation of a CBT is too slow and much too costly to be effective. As the system evolves and changes, modification of the CBT is expensive and time consuming.

Another consideration at the Implementation phase is the help desk strategy. How will support be provided for users of the new system? The help desk strategy may include the following:

- One centralized person who is trained to provide support
- Several designated experts on portions of the new system who receive extra training
- User manuals
- E-mail or telephone support

The help desk strategy should be thoroughly considered before the new system is up and running.

Maintenance

Even when a system is "finished" and brought into production, it is still in a state of flux. There will, of course, be some problems with any new system along with the need for user enhancements, requests for changes in the way the system functions, the need for new reports, missing fields, and so on. The major goal of the Maintenance phase is to provide a process for screening, ranking, and then handling these problems and changes in the system. It is necessary to recognize that changes not only affect the database and applications, but also must be reflected in the system and user documentation and training. The people involved in the help desk functions must also be kept apprised of any changes.

Versioning is the key to efficient system maintenance. You can't just make changes to the system one by one and implement them throughout the system.

These uncontrolled changes are potentially dangerous for the integrity of the production system. Changes must also proceed through a process that includes testing and quality assurance (QA).

Finally, changes are not cheap to make. To minimize costs, desired changes should be bundled along with all associated documentation and help desk updates. Because projects often are large and can take months or even years to complete, it is likely that by the time the Implementation phase is reached, the system requirements will have changed from those determined in the Analysis phase.

Conclusion

This chapter has provided an overview of the basic CASE methodology phases along with others that this book proposes should be added to the system development process. If all of the phases are completed carefully and thoroughly, the likelihood of system success is greatly increased. Part 2 provides more details and specific information on the methodology.

As you proceed through this book, you will learn how you can integrate Designer/2000 with the extended CASE methodology presented here, which we call CADM. This information should make the development process for a system using Designer/2000 faster, easier, more efficient, and more effective. The ultimate result will be satisfied developers, clients, and users.

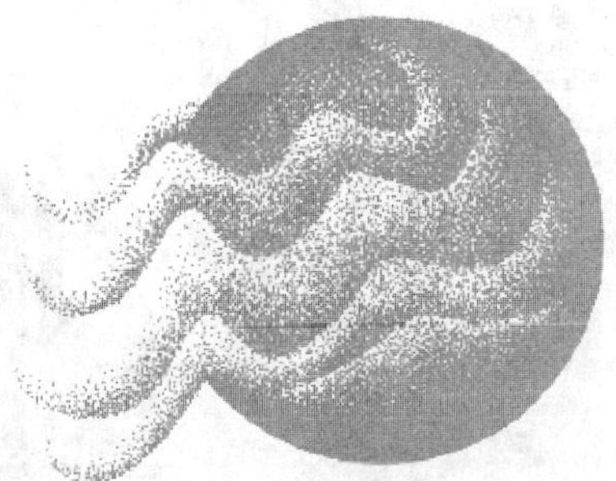

CHAPTER 2

Introduction to Designer/2000

Designer/2000—A CASE Odyssey. So what will we call it in 2001?

As you may have gathered from the preceding chapter, you need to capture an enormous amount of information for successful system development. Missing information can cause a project to fail or, at least, not fulfill some of the intentions of the system. In addition, ignored information on requirements or lost business rules have the potential to cause inaccuracies that can seriously affect business. It is therefore critical to the success of a system that you store the information on the system in a place where it can easily be retrieved and modified. Traditionally, before the advent of CASE tools, this place has been paper documents and human memory (people's heads). This method was probably successful in some cases, and companies were able to deal with the flood of paper that emanated from the analysis and design processes. However, modifications to the system after implementation meant relying on documentation inside existing programs or in system documentation (if that was ever created).

The original intention of CASE tools was to assist in managing system information so information technologists could effect system upgrades by referring to the documentation stored in a central place online. Therefore, one major component of a CASE tool is the *repository*, or central storage place. The other is the front-end products that allow users to enter and query data in this repository.

Designer/2000 follows the traditional component setup. It contains a repository, implemented using Oracle's relational database management system—currently Oracle7. The repository consists of database objects that store information on the system you are analyzing, designing, and producing. Since the repository is contained in a standard Oracle database, it has all the benefits and considerations of a multiuser system: security, connectivity, concurrency, and so on. The biggest benefit, of course, is that an entire team of developers can access the definitions and work on a common model. The Designer/2000 front-end component contains many screens and utilities to manipulate the repository data. In addition, Oracle provides a method for you to develop front-end products to access the repository outside the Designer/2000 tools.

Oracle Designer/2000 supports a broad range of tasks and is considered an *integrated CASE (I-CASE)* tool because it supports work in the Strategy, Analysis, and Design phases as well as finished code generation for the Build phase. Not very many products accomplish all of these tasks. Many CASE products stop with the Analysis (and sometimes Design) phases; these type of products are known as *upper CASE* products because they cover activities only in the top part of the System Development Life Cycle (SDLC). Designer/2000 will take you through the full System Development Life Cycle and generate fully working and bug-free forms, reports, and menus in addition to the SQL code needed to create the database objects.

This chapter discusses the major aspects of the repository and the front-end tools to give you an idea of the scope of the product as well as an overview of the different areas in which you will work while using Designer/2000. Subsequent chapters describe the methodology for system development and the specific use of Designer/2000 to support each of these steps.

No matter what your experience with previous versions of Oracle CASE tools, you should work through the book-based tutorial that Oracle provides with the product before you proceed further in this book. The tutorial will give you good hands-on practice with the tools. The discussions in this book assume that you have either completed the tutorial or have had some experience with the Designer/2000 interface.

The Repository

The repository consists of the tables and views you use to interface with the data and the procedural code to manage them. It essentially stores the details of the system you are developing. Later in this chapter you will learn how to access these items. First, though, you will learn the basic concepts behind the repository.

Makeup of the Repository

The repository is contained in the schema or domain area of a single user (the *repository owner*) in the Oracle database. Therefore, before installing Designer/2000, you either create a new user account or choose an existing user account that will own all the tables and code for the repository. The repository owner then grants access to its tables to existing Oracle users who also need to be Designer/2000 users and creates synonyms in their accounts. This procedure sets up the *repository users* who will be able to manipulate the *repository objects* such as entity and table definitions.

What the Repository Stores

The repository holds *meta-data*—or data about data—as definitions of objects or elements you are using to create the system design. These may include entities and their attributes or tables and their columns, all of which have individual aspects, called properties, that define them. For example, a table definition includes a name, short name (or alias), tablespace name, storage parameters, and various text descriptions. Each of these items is a property of the table, and all of these properties together make up its definition. There is a hierarchy of elements, with the top level being the application system that contains all objects for a certain system development project or part of a project.

Application System

Repository users create one or more application systems (if they have rights to do so) and grant access on the application system level to other repository users. The application system *owner* (creator) can *share* objects into their application system from another application system if the owner of that application system gives share access to that user. The shared objects appear as part of that application system although they may not be changed. Therefore, the elements you work on in an application system are those that are directly owned by the system and also those that other application systems share with that system.

Elements

The application system owns two types of elements: primary access controlled (PAC) elements, which exist on the highest level of the element hierarchy under the application system, and secondary access controlled (SAC) elements, which depend on and are owned by the PAC elements. Figure 2-1 shows an example of this relationship. In this example, a table definition is a PAC, and column definitions for that table are SACs, as are the indexes and primary key constraints.

Associations

An *association* is a special type of repository element (a SAC) that relates one element to another. An association, for example, may specify a link between ENTITY1 and FUNCTION8. The repository stores this association, in this case a Function Entity Usage, as a separate definition and links it to the two elements.

Properties

Each element definition has a set of properties that describe it. The set of properties for a type of element is always the same, but the values for the properties differ for each instance of a definition. Table 2-1 shows two tables that have the same properties, but different values for each.

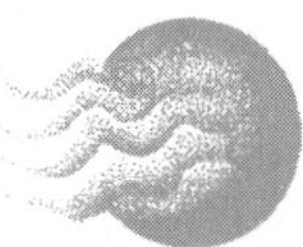

NOTE

Keep in mind that meta-data is not the actual data structure. For example, table definitions in the repository are not actual tables in the database. Rather they only contain the information needed to create actual tables that may or may not exist. The repository stores the table element and its property values, but no table exists in the database until you run a TABLE CREATE statement to create it. This is an important, but not necessarily obvious, concept.

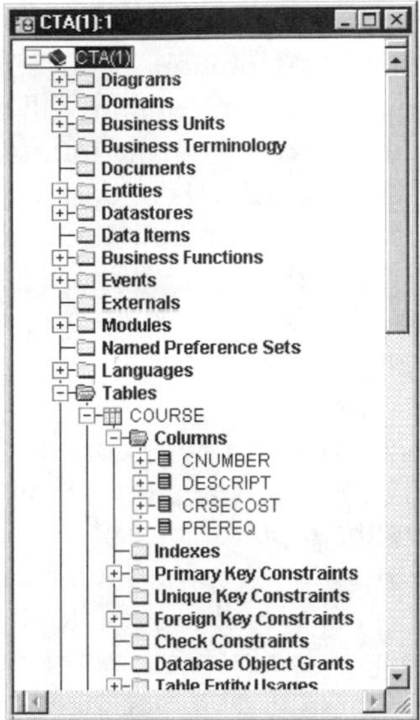

FIGURE 2-1. *Application system hierarchy*

What the Repository Looks Like

At the lowest level, the repository consists of a handful of tables and a large number of procedure packages stored in the database in PL/SQL (Oracle's procedural language extension of SQL). These tables have many views (most are named with a CI_ prefix) defined for them that correspond roughly to the elements and associations in the application system. For example, a view called CI_TABLE_DEFINITIONS shows the

Property	STUDENT Table	INSTRUCTOR Table
Name	STUDENT	INSTRUCT
Alias	STUD	INST
Description	Student profile and registration information	Instructor profile and hire information
Start Rows	500	10
End Rows	500,000	1,000

TABLE 2-1. *Sample Properties of Two Different Table Definitions*

properties of a table element, and you can perform a SQL query on this element to get information on a particular table definition.

The Designer/2000 online help system contains full explanations for all these views under the topic "Application Programmatic Interface." Additionally, the documentation shipped with Designer/2000 contains diagrams representing these views and their relationships. If you refer to both these sources, you can usually determine what view to use for a particular element. This topic is discussed further in Chapter 14, which describes the Designer/2000 Application Programmatic Interface (API).

The API PL/SQL code packages that access the repository tables correspond roughly to the views themselves. You can write code to access a particular definition for Insert, Update, Delete, or Select by calling the package that corresponds to the view where the repository displays that definition. For example, the CI_TABLE_DEFINITIONS view has a corresponding PL/SQL package called CIOTABLE_DEFINITION. This package allows you to safely manipulate the table definition repository data through your own code. The online help system also has documentation on this system of PL/SQL packages, which Chapter 14 will discuss further.

Quick Tour of the Designer/2000 Front End

The best feature about Designer/2000 is that while there are many methods you can use to access the repository, you do not need to rely on those methods for most tasks, because the front-end tools Oracle provides will do the job. This section describes the major tools and utilities in Designer/2000 to give you a sense of the scope of the product. This chapter assumes that you are familiar with the diagrams and the System Development Life Cycle phases in which they are used. Those phases and their diagrams and tasks are discussed in detail in subsequent chapters.

Front-end Programs

You work with Designer/2000's front-end tools under an MS (Microsoft) Windows (Windows 3.1, Windows 95, or Windows NT) platform. You can generate code for other platforms, but the front end itself has a standard Windows interface (written in C++) with toolbars, menus, and dialog boxes. In the past, Oracle used the current Forms and Reports tool set to present the CASE interface; for example, Oracle CASE used Forms 4.0 for the screens to manipulate the table definitions. This strategy tied the tools to the releases of what is now Developer/2000, and the decision was made to break that tie. Therefore, the current Designer/2000 tools do not use the Developer/2000 front-end and run only on the Windows interface platforms. Designer/2000 provides many different front-end programs, but they all fall into two categories of interface styles: diagrammers and repository utilities.

Diagrammers

The diagrammer is one of the major interface paradigms that Designer/2000 uses to store system analysis and design information in the repository. Diagramming tools are available to enter many element definitions, so you, as the repository user, can interact with the repository in a visual way. The diagrammers work directly with the repository objects, so when you draw an entity, for example, in an entity relationship diagram, Designer/2000 inserts that entity definition directly in the repository. This procedure works the same way for all objects, so you can define the object in one diagram and use the same object in another diagram of that type or of a different but compatible type. For example, you can diagram the same function elements on the Function Hierarchy Diagrammer, Process Modeller, and Dataflow Diagrammer.

The repository stores the diagram itself as an object with associations to the objects on the diagram. You can view these diagram definitions by using the Repository Object Navigator, but you need to access the diagrammers themselves to make changes to the layout. The Repository Object Navigator also provides a way to edit the properties of an element. In addition, you can access these properties of the diagrammed objects directly in the diagrammer itself. This feature allows you to easily change or refine the definition of an object without leaving the diagrammer.

Repository Utilities

The other major interface type that Designer/2000 supplies for entering or manipulating data is that of the Repository utilities. These are all nondiagrammatic interfaces that use GUI dialog boxes, object navigators, and properties windows to assist you in entering repository data. Some utilities actually insert the data for you. For example, Designer/2000 provides a utility to convert your existing entity definitions into table definitions. It inserts repository information for tables based on the entities you have already defined. You can modify the rough table definitions that this utility produces and refine them manually, but the utility does a large amount of work for you.

Some Repository utilities only cross-check data rather than insert new data. Others archive application systems, create files of sets of objects that can be managed with other repositories, delete and version application systems, and so on. Designer/2000 also provides utilities to manage the repository and its users; assist in installing, upgrading and checking the repository; backup and restore the repository objects; and extend the set of repository elements.

Components of Designer/2000

Designer/2000 has five major components consisting of diagrammer and utility front-end programs:

- Process Modeller
- Systems Modeller
- Systems Designer
- Generators
- Repository utilities (including the Design Wizards)

These components correspond to the areas on the Designer/2000 window launchpad application—the starting point for all Designer/2000 work—shown in Figure 2-2.

The first four component categories correspond roughly with and support the major System Development Life Cycle phases. The last component category involves Designer/2000–specific activities. Table 2-2 summarizes the correspondence between phases and components. The following sections describe these categories and the tools they provide.

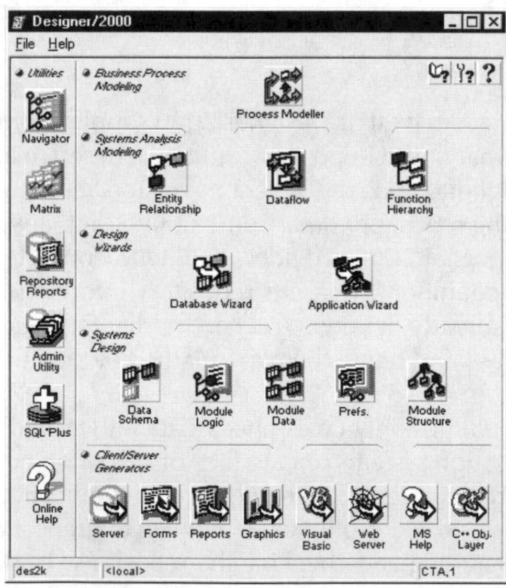

FIGURE 2-2. *Designer/2000 window*

Major System Development Phase	Designer/2000 Component
Strategy	Process Modeller, Systems Modeller
Analysis	Process Modeller, Systems Modeller
Design	Systems Designer, Repository utilities (Database and Application Design Wizards)
Build	Generators
All phases	Repository utilities

TABLE 2-2. *System Development Phases and Designer/2000 Components*

Process Modeller

The Process Modeller component consists of one diagrammer, the Process Modeller, which Oracle abbreviates as BPM for Business Process Modeller. This tool displays processes and flows as well as the organization units that perform them. You can use this tool to assist you in business process re-engineering, which can be a full phase or part of a phase in some system development life cycles. It also supports work in the Strategy and Analysis phases. You use the Process Modeller to conceptually show and possibly redefine what happens in the current system or what will happen in a new system.

One unique aspect of this diagrammer is that you can use it to create a diagram that represents the departments or groups in a company and show which processes, dataflows, and datastores each owns. In addition, you can drill down from a high-level process to a lower level and diagram the subprocesses that compose it. This tool also lets you diagram the data flowing between processes and data stores. There is no facility for detailing the data (for example, entities and attributes that make up a flow or store), because the purpose of this tool is to create a visual representation of existing or new business activities, the flows of data, and the organizational units that own them.

Another unique aspect of this diagrammer is that you can use it to show external triggering events from and outcomes to processes in your business area. Using this concept of triggers and outcomes, you can show that some external process or source is providing the stimulus for one of your processes (*triggers*), and conversely, which processes in your business area provide data (*outcomes*) to targets outside it.

The diagrams you produce in the Process Modeller are capable of multimedia enhancement, so you can show, for example, an animated flow from one process to another. In addition, you can embed video and sound clips to emphasize or clarify a point or process. You can also link to external programs, so you could, for example, run a slide show from a presentation program to help clarify a particular process, or show a spreadsheet or graph of sales representing activities in another process. You can also simulate the time sequence of a series of business processes by assigning time parameters to the processes and flows and then "running" the diagram to give you an idea of the events that occur simultaneously and the processes that may be bottlenecks in the system. All these assist in communicating your understanding and intention to the customer, client, or user.

Figure 2-3 shows a sample session in the Process Modeller.

Systems Modeller

The tools in the Systems Modeller category perform activities related to the Strategy and Analysis phases of the life cycle. You use three tools to diagram the data and processes or functions that make up a system:

- Function Hierarchy Diagrammer
- Entity Relationship Diagrammer
- Dataflow Diagrammer

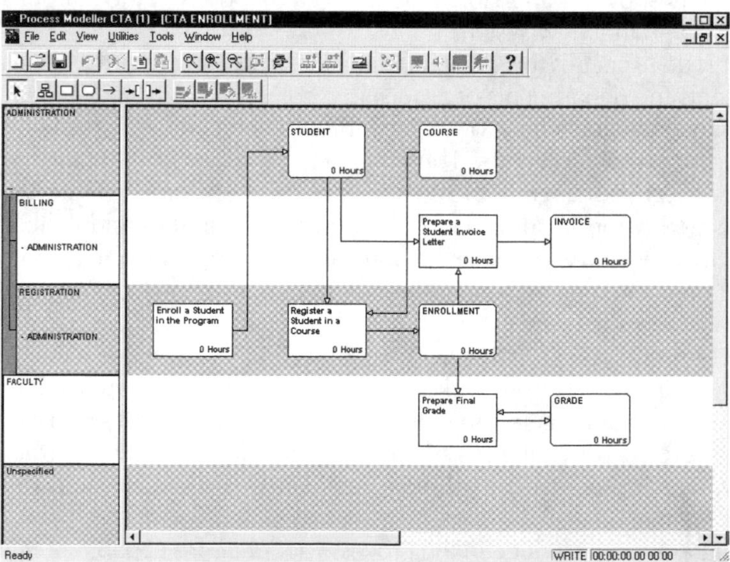

FIGURE 2-3. *Process Modeller session*

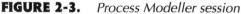

Function Hierarchy Diagrammer (FHD)

The Function Hierarchy Diagrammer lets you show the different levels of system processes or functions (terms that Designer/2000 treats as synonymous) in your system in one diagram. You can tell at a glance from this type of diagram the decomposition of functions and, consequently, what is the lowest level and what is the highest level in a series of processes. This tool frees you from the need to define flows as you would do in the Process Modeller and Dataflow Diagrammer.

Once you have represented the data by creating entity and attribute definitions in the ER Diagrammer or elsewhere, you can use this tool to declare which data elements you wish to associate with each process. Designer/2000 calls this association of data and functions the *data usage,* which also includes not only the data elements but the actions that will be performed on them (Insert, Update, Delete, Select). This concept is used later in the Systems Designer tools as well. You can create, reposition, and *level* (decompose) functions in this diagrammer or just redisplay the same functions you created and diagrammed in the Dataflow Diagrammer or Process Modeller diagram.

Figure 2-4 shows a sample session with the Function Hierarchy Diagrammer.

Entity Relationship (ER) Diagrammer

The ER Diagrammer shows entities with their attributes and relationships that represent the logical model of the data. As with the other diagrammers, once the

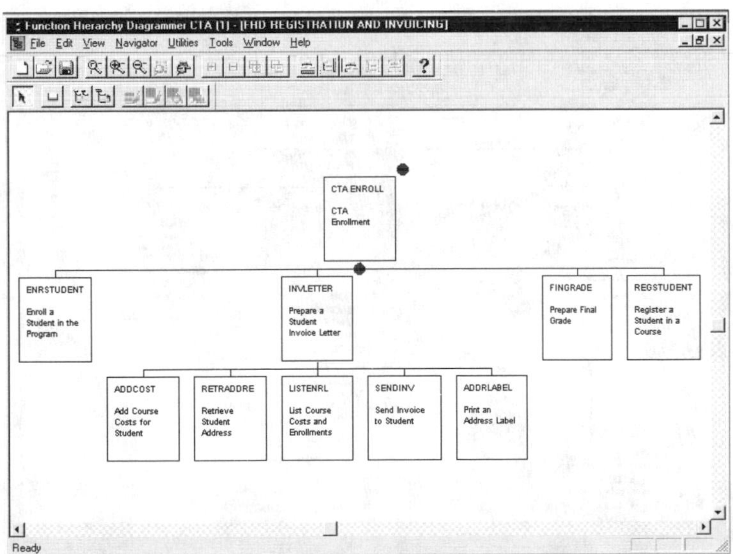

FIGURE 2-4. *Function Hierarchy Diagrammer session*

definitions for an element—in this case, an entity—are in the repository, you can produce different diagrams to show all or some of them in different layouts. The entities you create here are the source for the function data usage associations in the Function Hierarchy Diagrammer (FHD), so you typically use the ER Diagrammer at the same time as the FHD or before you associate the functions on the FHD with entities.

The ER Diagrammer has a rich set of symbols and provides support for subtype/supertype entities and arc (mutually exclusive) relationships. The entity and attribute definitions that this tool diagrams are separate from the definitions of the physical (design-level) elements or tables. Therefore, you can have two different data models in your system—a logical one and a physical one. This fulfills a typical need to keep these two models separate because typically they have slightly different contents.

Figure 2-5 shows a sample Entity Relationship Diagrammer session.

Dataflow Diagrammer (DFD)

The Dataflow Diagrammer allows you to display functions, dataflows, and stores as does the Process Modeller. It displays the same information as the Process Modeller but in a different type of diagram that may be more familiar to analysts and users.

One of the features of the Dataflow Diagrammer that is missing from the Process Modeller is the association of the data elements—entities and

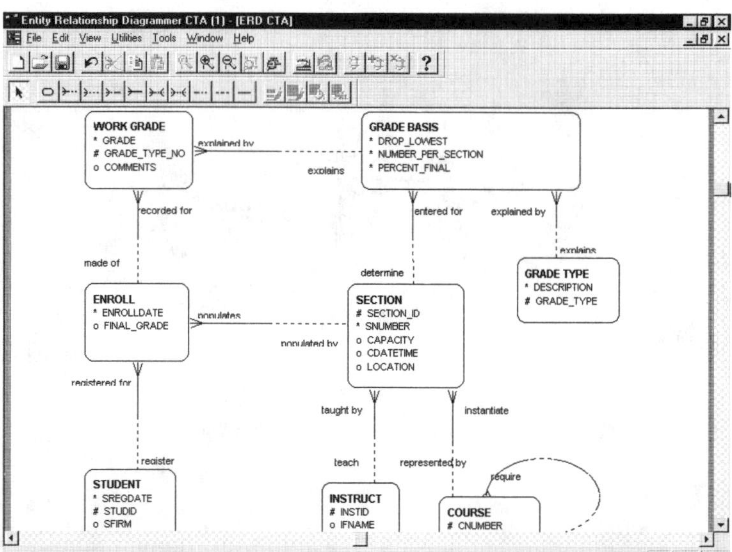

FIGURE 2-5. *Entity Relationship Diagrammer session*

attributes—with functions, flows, and stores. You can also represent entities that are external to your system in this diagram and show data flowing in and out of these entities. This representation is similar in concept to the triggers and outcomes in the Process Modeller, but this diagrammer lets you define the actual data elements (entities and attributes) that are flowing to and from your system to those externals.

Since this diagrammer is so similar to the Process Modeller, the decision about which one to use is really a matter of personal choice. You can use either diagrammer to define and display processes in the Strategy and Analysis phases, but if you choose the Process Modeller, you will need to seriously consider using the Function Hierarchy Diagrammer or Matrix Diagrammer to fill in data usages.

Figure 2-6 shows a sample Dataflow Diagrammer session.

Systems Designer

Designer/2000 provides numerous Systems Designer tools. These tools are typically used in the Design phase and are applied to the wide range of activities performed to define the physical system. The Design Wizards are Repository utilities you can use to move information from the logical (entities, attributes, functions) to the "physical" (tables, columns, modules) design elements. Once you do this, the elements are available for editing and diagramming in the Systems Designer tools.

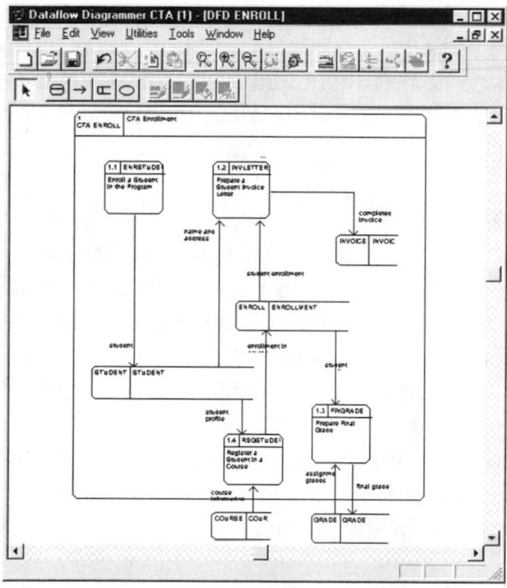

FIGURE 2-6. *Dataflow Diagrammer session*

Alternatively, you can create the elements directly in the Systems Designer tools whether or not you have created logical Systems Modeller elements. This approach is useful for rapid prototyping because you can skip the Analysis phase or, at least, not move the data from the Analysis phase to the Design phase. You can then quickly produce sample screens and reports after entering only the table and column information.

Whatever the source of the objects you use in this category of tools, the output of the work provides the basis for the generator tools. Therefore, you spend time ensuring that the data here is complete and accurate and truly represents the analysis work. These tools provide what you need to denormalize the data structures, modify the names of elements such as tables and columns, fill out any necessary PL/SQL code modules, design the modules (forms and reports) that make up the application, and perform other design activities.

Designer 2000 provides the following system design tools:

- Data Diagrammer
- Module Logic Navigator
- Module Data Diagrammer
- Preferences Navigator
- Module Structure Diagrammer

One purpose of all of these tools is to enable you to create definitions sufficient and complete enough for the generators. In addition, you can use them as design workplaces where you can experiment with design options. The definitions in the elements created here can serve as system documentation and assist in system upgrading and maintenance.

Data Diagrammer (DD)

The Data Diagrammer shows and allows you to enter definitions for *relations*: tables, views, and snapshots. You can also define columns and constraints including primary and foreign keys. This diagrammer could easily be confused with the Entity Relationship Diagrammer because it shows boxes with names, columns, and relationships. There is a small difference in symbols, but the biggest difference is that in the Data Diagrammer these symbols represent physical design objects that you will actually implement in the finished system; whereas in the Entity Relationship Diagrammer, the symbols represent only the logical data structures, which may or may not be exactly the same as the physical ones.

In the Data Diagrammer, you create or retrieve existing tables, views, and snapshots with their relationships and columns to form the diagram. As in the other diagrammers, you can change the properties of the objects on the diagram within the tool itself. For example, you could change the datatype of an existing column in a table definition by displaying the properties of that column and making the change without leaving the diagrammer.

Figure 2-7 shows the Data Diagrammer in action.

Module Logic Navigator (MLN)

When you move to the Design phase, you create *modules*—normally, forms or reports—for groups of functions defined in the Analysis phase. These modules can also be PL/SQL code—packages, procedures, functions, cursors—that you will eventually create on the database side or client side. This diagrammer helps you create the PL/SQL modules themselves. It has three different methods for storing the code in the module; you choose which method to use based on your knowledge of the PL/SQL language and how you want the actual code stored. This diagrammer is not so much a visual "link the boxes" tools as it is a means of visualizing the structure and components of your PL/SQL code.

Figure 2-8 shows a sample Module Logic Navigator session.

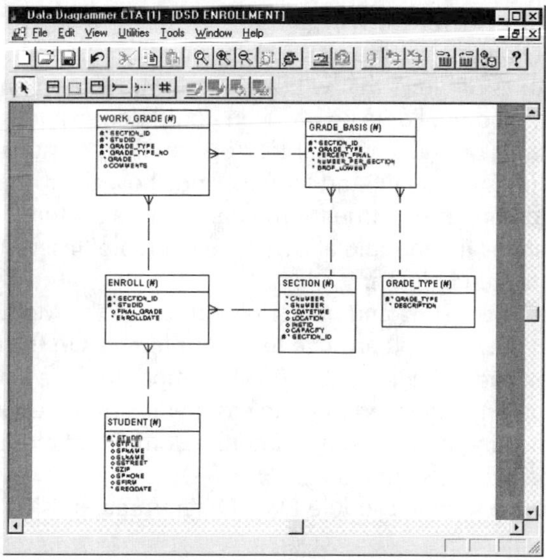

FIGURE 2-7. *Data Diagrammer session*

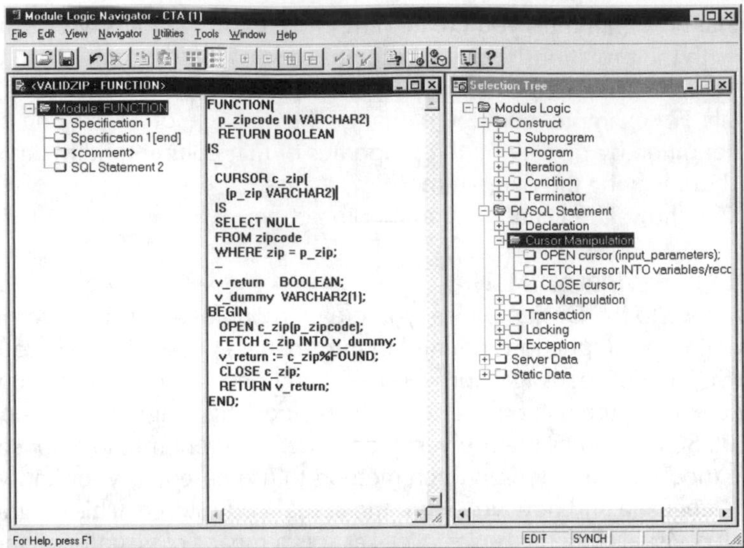

FIGURE 2-8. *Module Logic Navigator session*

Module Data Diagrammer (MDD)

The Module Data Diagrammer shows the data usages for a module. It enables you to see the actual tables or views that will be in a form or report and how those tables relate in that module. For example, you could define a master-detail form that has a lookup table on the master table. You can then create a module diagram for all three tables (master, detail, and lookup) and show their relationships within that module. In addition, as was true for the data usages for functions, you can specify what operations the module allows on each table (Insert, Update, Delete, Select) and even on each column.

One of the most interesting and powerful features of the Module Data Diagrammer is that the way you arrange the data elements in the diagram determines the look and behavior of the finished module. This feature makes changing the layout of the finished module easy: you simply reposition the tables or the borders, indicating new windows, and the completed module will have major changes when you generate it again.

Figure 2-9 shows a sample Module Data Diagrammer session.

Preferences Navigator

When Designer/2000 generates modules, it relies on a large number (more than 450) of user-defined settings when making decisions as to how to produce the

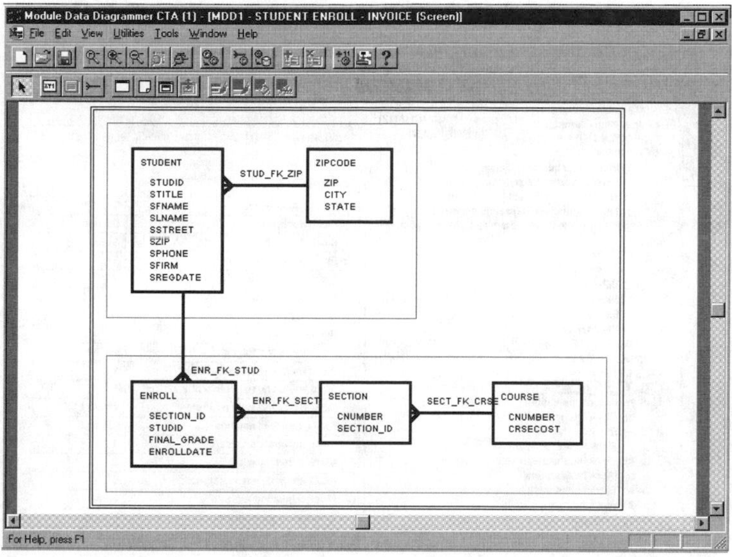

FIGURE 2-9. *Module Data Diagrammer session*

finished code. You can change these settings, or *preferences*, using the Preferences Navigator, which Oracle abbreviates as GPN for Generator Preferences Navigator. The Designer/2000 generators rely on these preference values when forming the user interface and internal code for a particular module. For example, one preference might specify the type of decoration or box the generator puts around a radio group, and another might specify where the label for that radio group appears.

You can set preferences on different levels, from the application down to the individual table in the module. These preference values become part of the application system in Designer/2000, and all modules in the system can use them or override them on an individual basis.

Figure 2-10 shows the interface for the Preferences Navigator. Note that it is similar to the Developer/2000 tools, with navigator and properties windows.

Module Structure Diagrammer (MSD)

The Module Structure Diagrammer shows the module networks that display how a module links to other modules in the application. This diagrammer represents the system of navigation the user will employ to get from one module to another. The application menu system or navigation command buttons in the forms or reports will be the actual mechanism for this navigation; and this diagrammer shows the links between modules that provide this mechanism. In addition, PL/SQL code

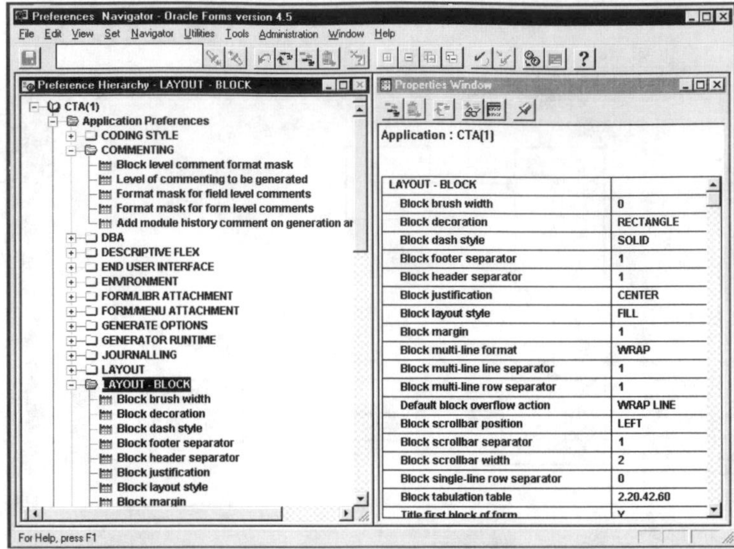

FIGURE 2-10. *Preferences Navigator session*

modules can call other modules as well as be called by other modules. All of those calls show as module networks in this tool.

Figure 2-11 shows the Module Structure Diagrammer.

Generators

The code generators in Designer/2000 are Repository utilities that are highly functional and feature-full and can give you complete, bug-free code that you can use immediately in the Build phase of the System Development Life Cycle. While it is true that you can realize many of the benefits of Designer/2000 without even using the code generators, the ability to produce working applications is one of the main strengths of the product. The strategy is to complete the module data diagrams and their data usages; specify the language in which you wish to generate the application; and run the generator utilities. You can classify the collection of generators in two types: the Server Code Generator and the front-end product generators. The following briefly describes, and shows a sample screen for, each of those so you can get the flavor of what they do.

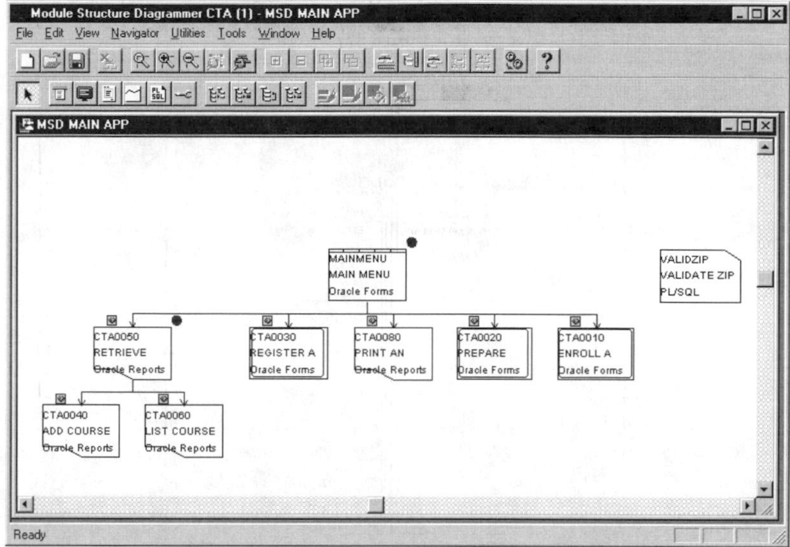

FIGURE 2-11. *Module Structure Diagrammer session*

Server Generator

The Server Generator is a repository utility that produces the SQL scripts you use to create database objects. You create the database definitions in the repository for database objects such as tables, columns, views, snapshots, sequences, PL/SQL code, tablespaces, role grants, and even the database itself. When you run this utility, you specify the objects for which you want the script, and the Server Code Generator creates the scripts to create the objects. Generally, you run this script under the user account that owns the application tables, and Designer/2000 lets you run the script from within the tools so you can test your generated module.

Figure 2-12 shows one of the dialog boxes in the Server Generator.

Common Features of the Front-end Product Generators

There are front-end product generators for Oracle Forms, Reports, Graphics; Visual Basic; Oracle WebServer; MS Help; and C++ Object Layer. They have different outputs according to the language you are generating, but the dialog boxes you fill in are all similar. Each produces a working program using the preferences you set in the Preferences Navigator, the module definition you set in the Module Data Diagrammer, and for some, a product-specific *template* (or starting file) supplied

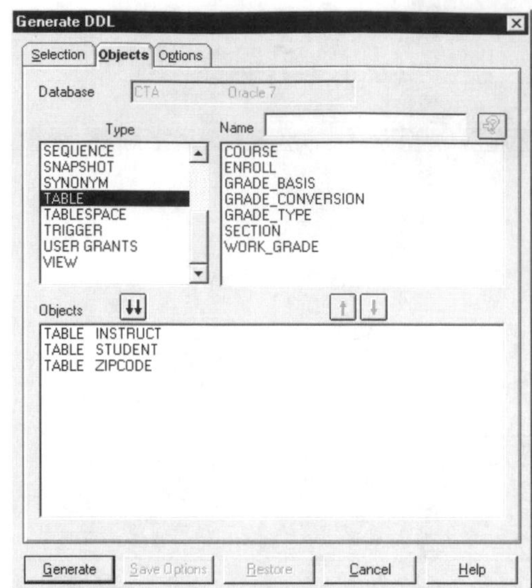

FIGURE 2-12. *Server Generator dialog box*

with Designer/2000 or one that you have created with particular interface items. The Forms, Reports, and Graphics generators are different from the other front-end generators because they do not require an outside compile or install process: when they are done, you have completely finished and runnable code. The other generators require you to go to the development tool specific to the language to compile the finished product.

Generally, Designer/2000 hides the complexity in the generator itself and presents you with just a few options to fill in during the generator session, but some dialog boxes presented in the generators are more detailed than others. Regardless of the complexity of the dialog boxes, in all cases you can modify the templates and module definitions and, in some cases—for Forms, Reports, Visual Basic, Help, and WebServer—change the preferences to greatly tailor the resulting application. The following sections briefly explore the specifics for each front-end product generator.

Forms, Reports, and Graphics Generators

Although they are three separate generators, the Oracle Forms, Reports, and Graphics Generators present you with the same kinds of dialog boxes to work on a particular module that you define or refine in the Module Data Diagrammer. Each generator allows you to fill in specific properties that apply only to that generation session, such as the template name. Figure 2-13 shows a sample dialog box from the Forms generator. The Reports and Graphics generators are simpler but similar in concept and in the items you fill in. Designer/2000 ships with the full development and runtime tools for Developer/2000 products, so you can modify and run the generated application modules.

Visual Basic Generator

The generator for Visual Basic (VB) is also simpler than the Forms Generator, but it works similarly on a particular module to create the code using Visual Basic. You can take the code from this generator and load it into the Visual Basic 4.0 development tool (a separate product) to create the finished application and executable. Figure 2-14 shows a Visual Basic Generator dialog box.

WebServer Generator

The WebServer Generator creates PL/SQL packages from modules that you define in the Module Data Diagrammer. You run these PL/SQL scripts on an Oracle WebServer (a separate product) to create the Web application. The WebServer then

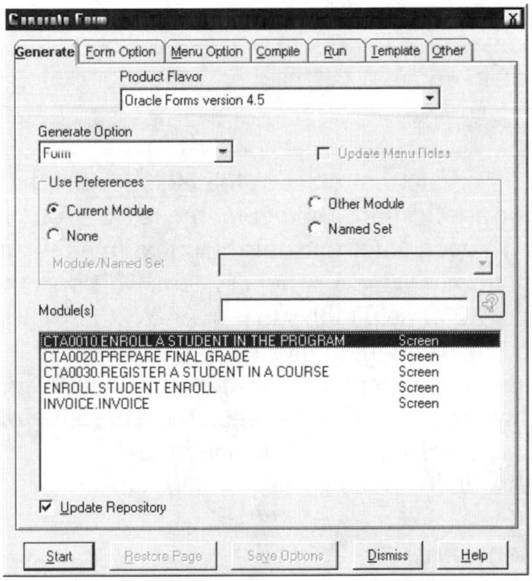

FIGURE 2-13. *Forms Generator dialog box*

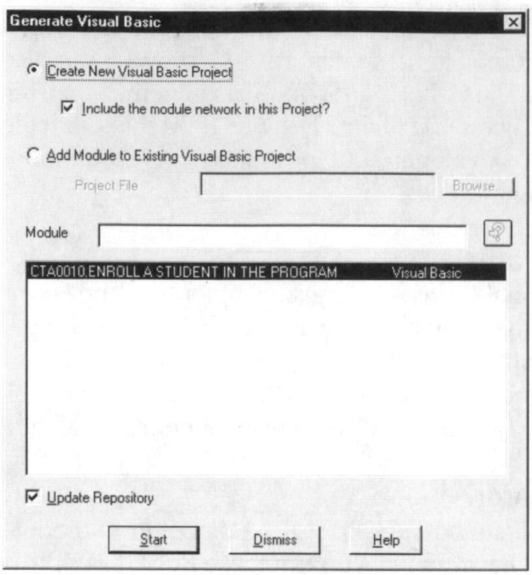

FIGURE 2-14. *Visual Basic Generator dialog box*

creates the HTML code needed to present data according to the PL/SQL application code you ran. Figure 2-15 shows a WebServer Generator dialog box.

MS Help Generator

The MS Help Generator creates help files in MS Help format that attach to your Forms and Visual Basic applications. You enter the text as you create the modules and table definitions. The generator puts this help text in a file and creates the links and jumps you expect from a Windows help system. This system is an alternative to the traditional Designer/2000 help tables that query text from the database and present it in a called form. These help files can save on database activity because they are solely file based and compiled as part of the runtime application.

Note that this utility produces files that need the MS Help compiler (a separate product) to generate the WinHelp-format finished files.

Figure 2-16 shows a dialog box for the MS Help Generator.

C++ Object Layer Generator

The C++ Object Layer Generator creates C++ class definitions and code you can use to access the relational database objects in an object-oriented way. The entities you enter in the Systems Modeller tools form the basis for the classes, which include both the data and the functions acting on that data. The Designer/2000 C++ Generator gives you code you incorporate into your C++ application to

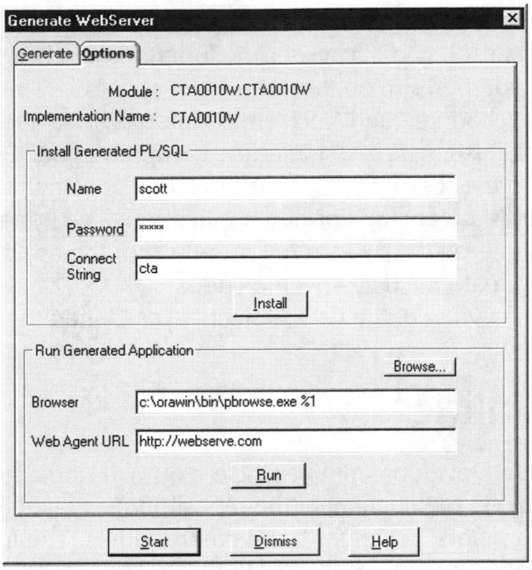

Generate WebServer

Generate | Options

Module : CTA0010W.CTA0010W

Implementation Name : CTA0010W

Install Generated PL/SQL

Name scott

Password *****

Connect String cta

Install

Run Generated Application

Browse...

Browser c:\orawin\bin\pbrowse.exe %1

Web Agent URL http://webserve.com

Run

Start Dismiss Help

FIGURE 2-15. *WebServer Generator dialog box*

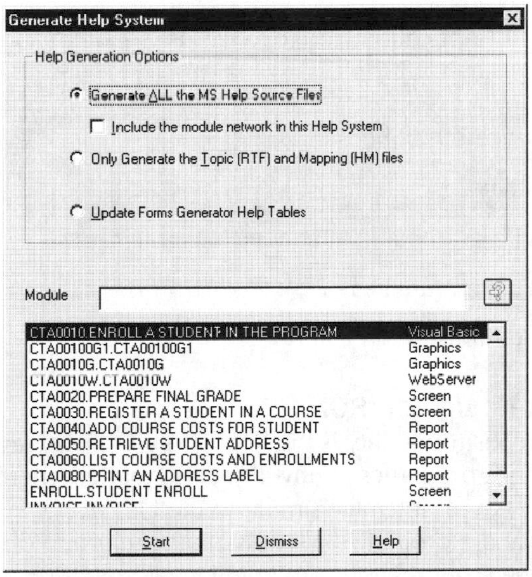

Generate Help System

Help Generation Options

Generate ALL the MS Help Source Files

Include the module network in this Help System

Only Generate the Topic (RTF) and Mapping (HM) files

Update Forms Generator Help Tables

Module

CTA0010.ENROLL A STUDENT IN THE PROGRAM	Visual Basic
CTA00100G1.CTA00100G1	Graphics
CTA0010G.CTA0010G	Graphics
CTA0010W.CTA0010W	WebServer
CTA0020.PREPARE FINAL GRADE	Screen
CTA0030.REGISTER A STUDENT IN A COURSE	Screen
CTA0040.ADD COURSE COSTS FOR STUDENT	Report
CTA0050.RETRIEVE STUDENT ADDRESS	Report
CTA0060.LIST COURSE COSTS AND ENROLLMENTS	Report
CTA0080.PRINT AN ADDRESS LABEL	Report
ENROLL.STUDENT ENROLL	Screen

Start Dismiss Help

FIGURE 2-16. *MS Help Generator dialog box*

provide access to the data in the tables created by those entities. It produces both the classes for the data itself and classes for the functions (such as Select, Insert, Update, and Delete) you perform on that data.

As with the VB, WebServer, and MS Help generators, you need to do some work outside of Designer/2000, including compiling your Designer/2000–generated classes with the rest of the C++ code you write elsewhere and linking it with the C++ libraries to create the finished application. The benefit of this utility is that you can concentrate on the C++ code for the rest of the application and rely on Designer/2000 to create the data-specific code.

Figure 2-17 shows a view of the C++ Object Layer Generator interface.

Repository Utilities

Throughout the System Development Life Cycle, you will find a need for various utilities to check, change, or supplement the repository work you do in the Designer/2000 diagrammers, generators, and other utilities. The following sections explore the major repository utilities that fulfill this need:

- Repository Object Navigator
- Matrix Diagrammer
- Repository Reports
- Database and Application Design Wizards
- Table to Entity Retrofit
- Reverse engineering utilities
- Reconcile utility
- Application Programmatic Interface
- Application system utilities
- Repository Administration Utility

Repository Object Navigator (RON)

The most universal repository utility is the Repository Object Navigator. It allows you to view and change properties of any object no matter where you created it. As Figure 2-18 shows, it has an interface similar to the Developer/2000 products, with a navigator window and a properties window. You can group objects together and apply properties to the group as you can do in Developer/2000.

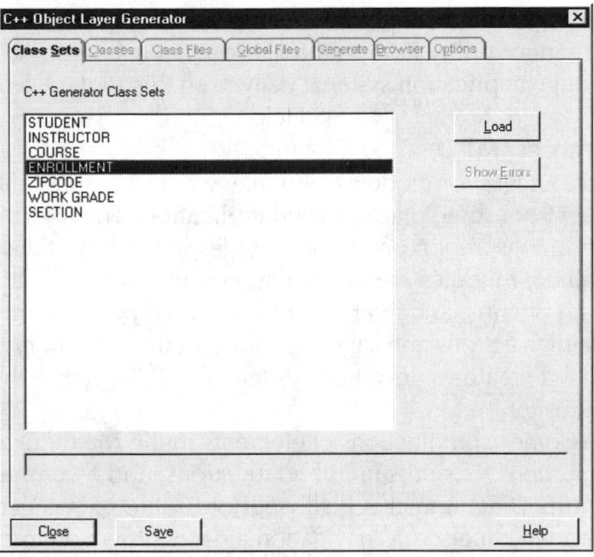

FIGURE 2-17. *C++ Object Layer Generator dialog box*

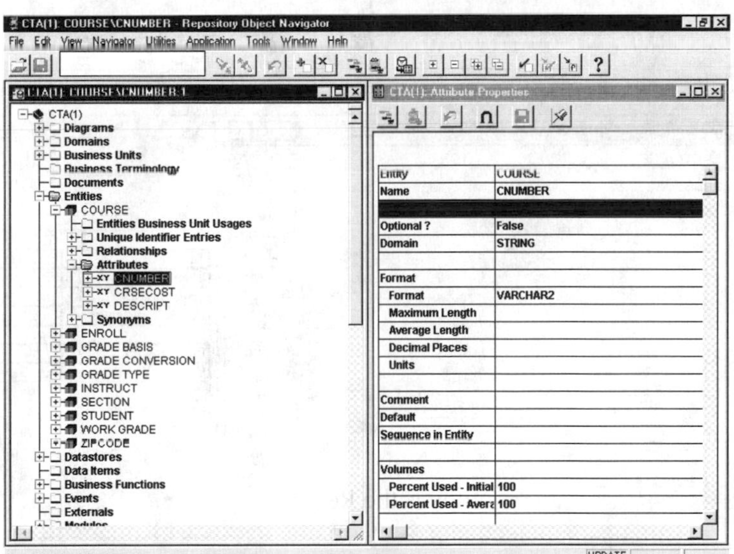

FIGURE 2-18. *Repository Object Navigator*

RON also serves as the focal point for all other tools and utilities as you can start any diagrammer or utility from its menu. You can access some utilities, such as those that manage application systems, only from this tool.

Matrix Diagrammer (MXD)

As you create data usages for modules, you may want to ensure that all data can be entered or queried from some place in your application. The Matrix Diagrammer can, among other things, report on the data usages in your modules so you can, at a glance, determine if modules are missing. It presents the information in a table format with rows, columns, and intersection values. You can examine and change the values at the intersections and save the values in the repository. The diagrammer is like a create-retrieve-update-delete (CRUD) report that is connected directly to the repository.

You can show other combinations of elements in the Matrix Diagrammer, such as entities and functions, business units and functions, and assumptions and modules. The Matrix Diagrammer is highly customizable so you can look at the data in almost any way; it also has navigation aids to allow you to diagram a large system and quickly go to any section you desire.

Figure 2-19 shows a sample Matrix Diagrammer session.

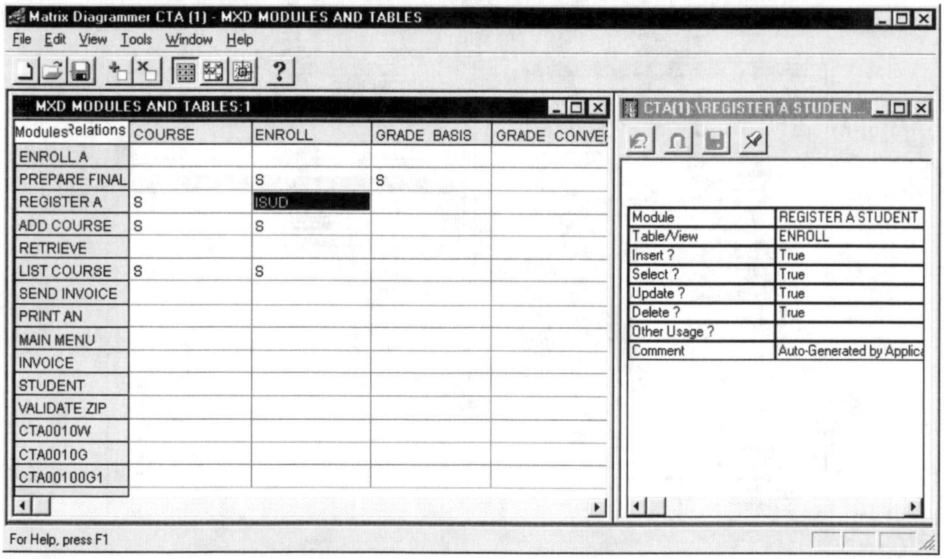

FIGURE 2-19. *Matrix Diagrammer session*

Repository Reports

You can view all object definitions in the Repository Object Navigator and the intersection of objects with the Matrix Diagrammer; however, you might want to just print out a report on a particular set of elements such as all tables in your system. You can write your own report using your preferred reporting tool or use one of the over 150 predefined reports that Designer/2000 offers for displaying objects in the database. Repository Reports organizes and presents these predefined reports with variable parameters you can enter to define the output. This utility, like a few of the others, displays a hierarchy and a properties window, as Figure 2-20 shows.

Database and Application Design Wizards (DDW and ADW)

When you move from Analysis to Design in Designer/2000, you have to transfer definitions from the logical to the physical, entities to tables, attributes to columns, relationships to foreign key columns and constraints, functions to modules, and so on. The Design Wizards assist with this move and give you a rough-cut application and database definitions that you can refine. The Wizards also save you much of the repetitive and error-prone work that needs to be done in this transition and, although they may not be able to guess exactly what you have in mind, there are ways to make the results of the utilities closely match your needs.

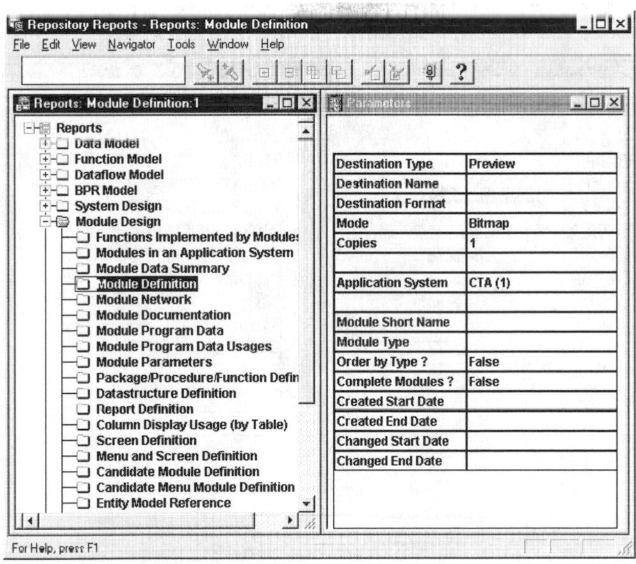

FIGURE 2-20. *Repository Reports session*

The Database Design Wizard (DDW) copies the entity and attribute definitions to tables and columns in the design area. It can resolve many-to-many, subtype-supertype, and arc relationships, so you can implement them as relational database tables. It can create columns based on the attributes in the entities and foreign key constraints based on the relationships between entities. You can run this utility more than once and modify or create particular elements that were not defined properly or completely the first time you ran it. The logical elements will remain in the application, so you will have many more objects in your application system after the utility runs. Figure 2-21 shows a DDW dialog box.

The Application Design Wizard (ADW) combines functions to form modules and links modules together based on the function hierarchy. It uses a well-documented set of rules to perform the combination and produces both the modules and the menus (module structures). The *candidate modules* you create as output from this utility are subject to your approval and modification before they become working modules. Figure 2-22 shows an ADW dialog box.

Table to Entity Retrofit

Consider the situation in which you have created a table definition without defining an entity. If you have a full system of entities for the existing tables, you will probably want to keep this system complete and be sure that all tables should

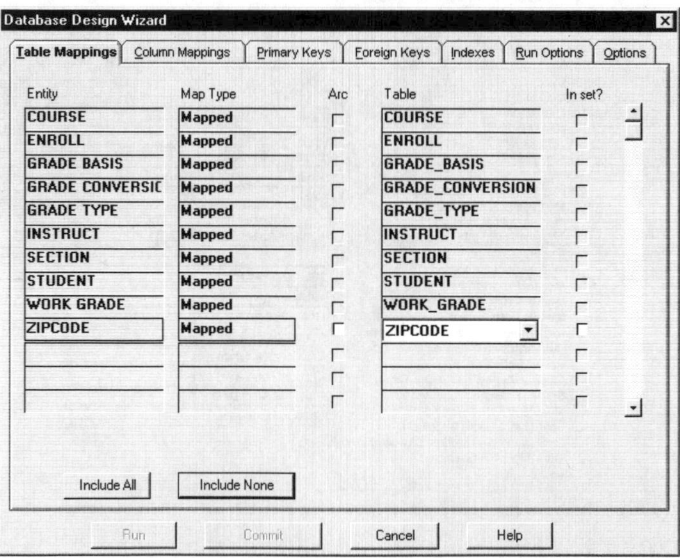

FIGURE 2-21. *Database Design Wizard dialog box*

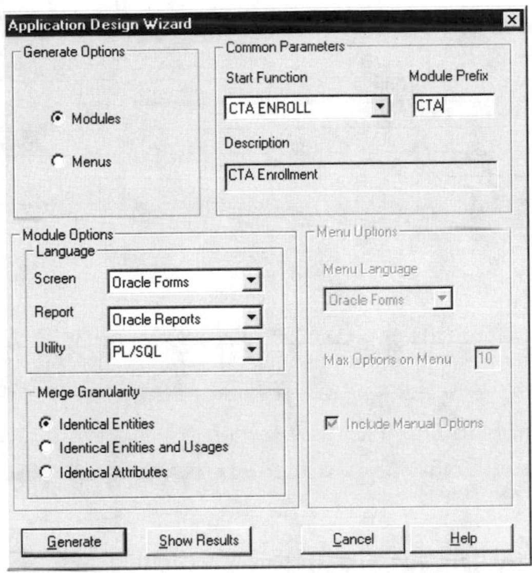

FIGURE 2-22. *Application Design Wizard dialog box*

also have an entity definition. The Table to Entity Retrofit repository utility assists you with this task. It takes existing tables that do not have a base entity and creates entities and attributes for them.

This utility is extremely useful if you need to create definitions in Designer/2000 for existing database objects (for example, from a legacy system). You run the Reverse Engineer Database Objects utility to obtain table and other definitions. Then you run the Table to Entity Retrofit utility to create entity and attribute definitions for the table and column definitions. Figure 2-23 shows the Table to Entity Retrofit screen.

Reverse Engineering Utilities (Database and Modules)

You can *reverse engineer* database objects and code that exists outside Designer/2000 to create repository definitions. Reverse engineering is sometimes known as *design recovery,* although that term connotes a problem that needs immediate solution (maybe not so inappropriate after all). These utilities provide a method for moving existing applications into the repository so you can make changes, diagram the system, or document the parts of the application.

The Reverse Engineer Database Objects utility examines existing database objects such as tables, views, and sequences in the local or remote Oracle databases and creates the proper Designer/2000 objects. You can then include these objects in the appropriate diagrams or use them to create new modules or,

Table to Entity Retrofit

Table Name	Entity Name	Entity Short Name	Entity Plural
COURSE	COURSE	CRSE	COURSE
SECTION	SECTION	SECT	SECTION

Candidate Tables | Reverse Engineer | Cancel | Help

FIGURE 2-23. *Table to Entity Retrofit screen*

with the Table to Entity Retrofit utility, create a logical schema of entities from tables. You can run this utility multiple times against different databases to reverse engineer a system implemented in a multi-database environment. Figure 2-24 shows a Reverse Engineer Database Objects dialog box.

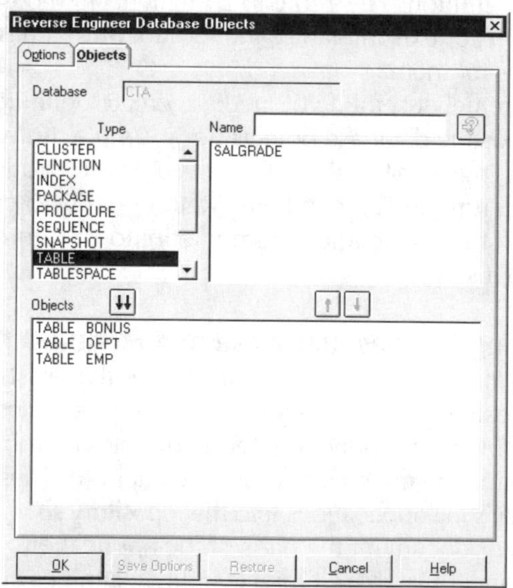

FIGURE 2-24. *Reverse Engineer Database Objects dialog box*

The Forms and Reports reverse engineering utilities take existing Developer/2000 files (with .FMB and .RDF extensions) and create modules in the Designer/2000 repository. This operation creates the module definition so you can supplement or rework it in preparation for generating the form or report. This operation also gives you a way to document the Forms and Reports modules that make up your system. There is no facility to reverse engineer a menu, however. Figure 2-25 shows the dialog box for the Reverse Engineer Form utility, which is similar to the Reverse Engineer Report utility (not shown).

Reconcile Utility

The Reconcile utility compares existing database objects against their definitions in Designer/2000. You can select a report to help you synchronize the repository with the database or a DDL script that you run to synchronize the database with the repository. This utility is extremely useful if someone makes changes to the database without first entering them in the repository. It is also good to ensure that changes to the repository have also been made to the database. You run this utility multiple times if you have a distributed database since this utility works on one database at a time. Figure 2-26 shows a Reconcile utility dialog box.

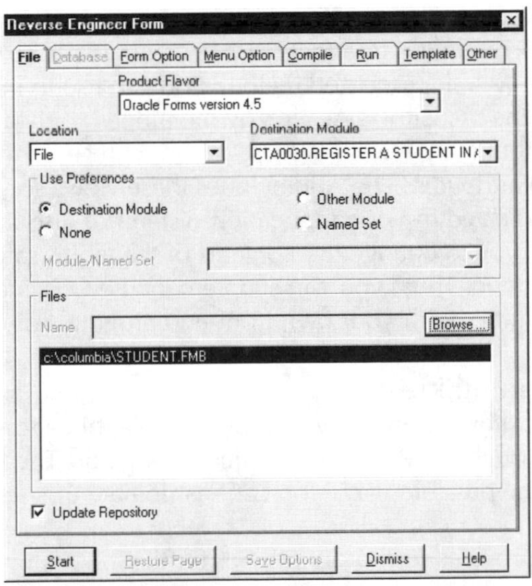

FIGURE 2-25. *Reverse Engineer Form utility dialog box*

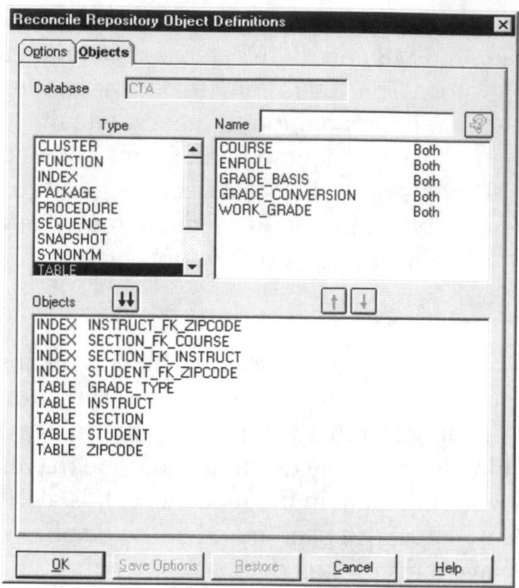

FIGURE 2-26. *Reconcile utility dialog box*

Application Programmatic Interface (API)

The Application Programmatic Interface, or API, is not really so much a utility with a dialog screen as a documented method you can use to insert data into and modify data within the repository. As already mentioned, only a few tables store the repository data, but many views of these tables represent the actual objects, such as entities and attributes. The API includes these views so you can examine the definitions you created in your application systems. It also includes the PL/SQL packages that allow you to change the contents of the tables safely outside of the Designer/2000 front end. Thus, you can supplement the Designer/2000 diagrammers and utilities with your own front-end programs or code.

Application System Utilities

There are other repository utility activities specific to application systems that you can perform through the Repository Object Navigator. The following list will give you a taste of the possible ways you can manipulate the repository within Designer/2000.

Designer/2000 provides repository utilities for the following tasks:

- *Sharing objects* between application systems, leaving a read-only copy of an object in an application system from another application system.

- *Copying objects* from one application system to another, creating an exact copy of the object that is both readable and modifiable.
- *Transferring ownership* of objects from one application system to another, giving the other application system the readable and writeable copy and leaving the original system with a shared copy that is read-only.
- *Granting access* to your application system to another repository user, indicating what actions another user is allowed: Select, Insert, Update, Delete, Share, or Administrate, or some combination.
- *Archiving and restoring* application systems, creating an export file that you can transfer to another repository instance.
- *Renaming, deleting, versioning, and transferring ownership* of the application system itself.
- *Loading, unloading, checking in, and checking out* objects to work on them in other application systems or repositories.
- *Performing other actions* on objects, such as creating attribute usages for functions, updating attributes or columns in a domain for which the definition has changed, and creating module data usages.

Repository Administration Utility (RAU)

You use the Repository Administration Utility to manage the repository itself, with all its application systems. You can use this utility to install, upgrade, and back up an instance of the repository and to grant and revoke repository user access. In addition, you can add properties to existing elements or even add new types of elements to the repository through a facility called *user extensibility*. This facility allows you to place site-specific objects in your application systems that are not normally included in Designer/2000. The first step you take after installing the front-end tools, in fact, is to use this utility to create the repository owner and install the repository data structures and code. Figure 2-27 shows this utility's opening screen.

The Designer/2000 Interface

As already mentioned, you are strongly urged to complete the book-based tutorial Oracle provides with Designer/2000 to at least become familiar with the product's organization and how you accomplish tasks. Nevertheless, this section discusses briefly how to work with the Designer/2000 tools on an operator level. You can be more productive if you know how the tools are organized and if you master a few simple techniques. All diagrammers and utilities have certain aspects in common, and you use common techniques to interface with them. When you learn about

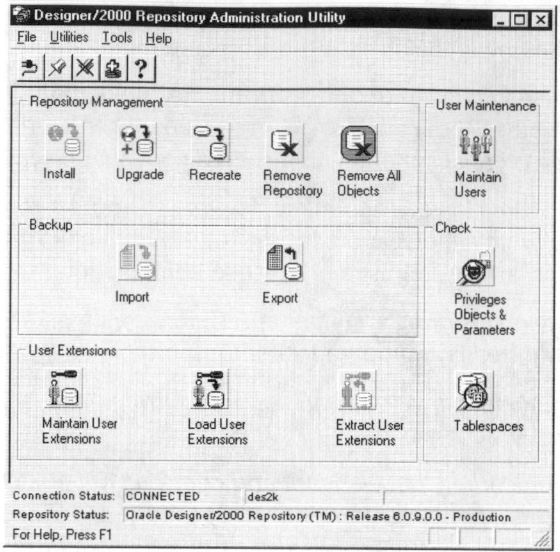

FIGURE 2-27. *Repository Administration utility dialog box*

each diagrammer in later chapters, these techniques will allow you to focus on the specifics for that diagrammer instead of on basic features and techniques that are common to all Designer/2000 tools.

The Designer/2000 Window

After you install Designer/2000, you will see an icon in the Designer/2000 group labeled "Oracle Designer 2000." You click (or somehow activate) this icon to start the Designer/2000 window application, as mentioned before (see Figure 2-2). When this utility starts, you log in to the Oracle database where the repository resides and choose an application system. If you will be creating a new application system, you cancel the dialog box that asks for the application system. If you have not created any application systems, the buttons in this window will be disabled except for those for utilities such as Repository Object Navigator (RON).

Starting the Designer/2000 Window

To start The Designer/2000 window, log into Oracle, and load a particular application system automatically, use the command line (in the icon properties):

DES2K*XX* *user/password@database*/A:*appsys,version*/S

where *XX* is the version number of Design/2000; *user/password@database* is the login string; *appsys* is the application system name; and *version* is the version number.

If you leave off the version number, you will get a prompt for the application system when Designer/2000 starts. If you omit the "/S" (suppress splash screen), you will get Designer/2000 logo splash screen. For example, SCOTT, who has a password of TIGER, will log into a repository in the database called DESIGNER and load the application system EMPDEPT version 1. He uses:

```
DES2K13 SCOTT/TIGER@DESIGNER /A:EMPDEPT,1 /S
```

Since you need an application system to hold your objects, you can choose RON, select **File→New** from the menu, and fill in the application system name. After you press the Save (commit changes) button, Designer/2000 will create the new application system. You then work in this context until you choose Change Application System from any File menu.

The Designer/2000 window has buttons for all major diagrammers and repository utilities as well as links to the help system. You can choose the Help button here and drop the question mark icon on any other button to see the help topic for that tool. The Help menu also has selections that let you look at the changes in the new version and the table of contents for the help system. There is also a button for Help that loads the contents page of the Designer/2000 main help system. The SQL*Plus button will start up that tool and log you in automatically. It appears in the Utilities section but is not specifically a Designer/2000 tool or utility, although Designer/2000 uses it heavily in the installation and upgrade process.

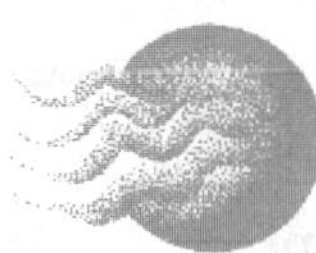

NOTE

The status line of the major diagrammers and utilities contains information worth noticing. For example, the Designer/2000 window status line contains the application system name and version number as well as the name of the user who is logged in at that moment.

Help System

Two words apply to the Designer/2000 help system: use it! The help system contains conceptual overviews of each tool, instructions on how to use each tool generally, and detailed step-by-step procedures for completing tasks. Designer/2000's scope is so extensive, and its features increase so quickly, that printed manuals attempting to cover the same information would (and have) quickly become obsolete. In addition, well-designed help files are much easier to search for topics in and find the correct information in than any printed manual—and these are well-designed help files.

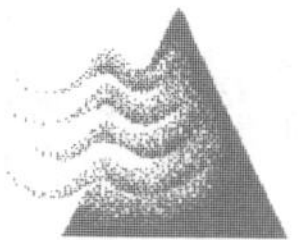

TIP

Spend five or ten minutes at your earliest convenience exploring the Designer/2000 help system. The interface is familiar to users of any Windows product and it is arranged logically by product and component category. For example, when you select Contents from the Help menu in the Designer/2000 window, you will load the main contents topic. This page is available from any other help topic by pressing the Top Level button. The contents topic contains one link for each of the major tools and diagrammers and is arranged in the order of the component types (e.g., Process Modeller, Systems Modeller, Systems Designer, etc.). The time you use to explore this system will be well spent, because you will be able to find help easier when you have key work to do.

No matter what your opinion of help files generally, you should give the Designer/2000 help system a chance. For example, suppose you have not touched the tools in several months and have forgotten how to create a dog-leg (angle) relationship line for an ERD, since the procedure is a bit different than that for other Windows drawing tools. You open the help system, navigate to the ER Diagrammer (or just choose Help-Contents from the ER Diagrammer), and search for "dog-leg"—problem solved.

Designer/2000 also has cue cards that act as step-by-step tutors on how to perform selected actions such as creating an entity relationship diagram. This feature is great when you are learning the tools as well as later, when you need to refresh your mind regarding a task you have not done for some time.

In addition, Designer/2000 has a "?" button on the toolbar for each major tool. These buttons change the cursor to the "What's This" arrow and question mark. When you click this special cursor on an object on the screen, the help system will load and jump to a topic appropriate to the object. This is great when you don't know what something is called and therefore cannot look it up in the help system index.

Diagrammer Interface

The diagrammer tools—named with the word "diagrammer"—all have a look and feel that is essentially the same. (Note, however, that although the Matrix Diagrammer is called a diagrammer, it is better categorized as a utility.) The standard features of diagrammers work essentially the same way in all cases and can be divided into four categories:

- Application window
- Mouse actions
- Menu system
- Toolbars

Application Window

The main application (Multiple Document Interface, or MDI) window for each diagrammer may contain multiple windows for different diagrams as you can open more than one diagram at the same time. Since you can have many diagrams of the same repository objects, each showing the objects in a different way, you might want to display these diagrams side by side in different windows. In addition, you can display different views of the same diagram in different windows.

Figure 2-28 shows the standard Windows interface features that appear in the MDI window: the diagram window with a title bar, scroll bars to move the working view, page breaks, and a drawing area; the dialog and object properties window; the MDI window title that shows the name of the diagrammer, application, and diagram; a status bar for messages from Designer/2000; a menu bar for the pull-down menu system; and Windows icons for minimizing, maximizing, and closing the diagrammer window.

Mouse Actions

Designer/2000 is a graphical user interface (GUI) product and relies heavily on the mouse or pointer to respond to dialog boxes, change cursor focus, draw symbols in the diagrammers, and navigate the screen. In fact, you can respond to some dialog boxes and perform some navigation only with the mouse; the keyboard will not work. If you are not comfortable with the mouse as an input device, you might want to practice on other programs or games so you will not falter when you need to accomplish something in Designer/2000.

You use the mouse in the diagrammers to move objects around on the screen and place new objects in the desired position. In addition, if you double-click the mouse on an object in the diagrammer, Designer/2000 displays the Properties window for that object to allow you to make changes to those properties directly in

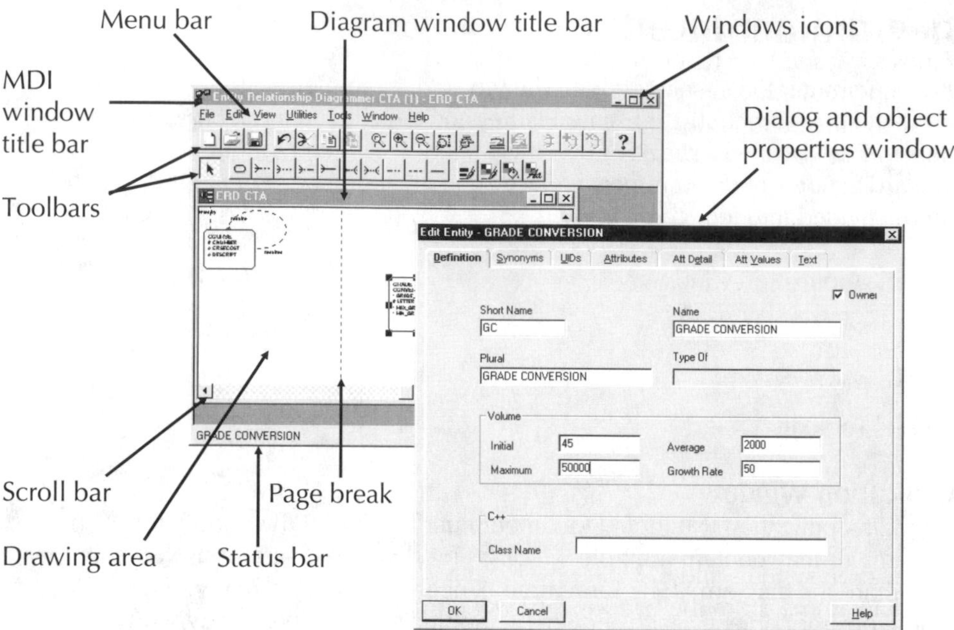

FIGURE 2-28. *Diagrammer window anatomy*

the diagrammer. Single-clicking on a diagram object selects it so you can resize it by dragging the borders or move it by dragging the object itself; holding the control button while clicking selects multiple items, and holding the mouse button while dragging a selection box around items selects all those items when you release the mouse button. These are all standard Windows drawing actions.

Menu System

All diagrammers have similar functions that you need to perform to manipulate the diagram as a whole, and most of these are available from the menu system and toolbar. The following sections examine the common pull-down menus and their functions.

File Menu The file concept does not really apply directly to the diagrams in Designer/2000 because they are saved in the repository, but the File menu is a standard GUI feature, and the definition of the File items can be stretched to fit repository objects. **New** creates a new diagram; **Open** presents a list of existing diagrams of that type in the repository so you can load one into the drawing area;

Close unloads a displayed diagram; **Save** and **Save As** save the diagram to the repository; and **Delete** removes a diagram from the repository after you choose a diagram from a list in the dialog box.

The File menu also includes **Summary Information**, where you can enter information regarding the diagram as in Figure 2-29. This item creates a title block on the diagram that contains the information you indicate with check marks in the dialog box. Once you click OK on this dialog box, the title block will appear in the upper-left corner of the drawing, but you can reposition it if you wish.

Change Connection and **Change Application System** in the File menu allow you to change the user account or application system you are connected to. Although you can also accomplish this in the Designer/2000 window (launch pad screen), you would need to exit and restart the diagrammer before the change took effect.

The File menu also has **Print**, **Print Preview**, and **Print Setup** options, which open standard dialog boxes for printing to the printer. **Print Setup** also lets you change the page orientation so you can use a landscape (sideways) layout instead of portrait (straight-up) layout.

The last items in this menu are a list of recently opened diagrams from all application systems and the **Exit** option, to close the diagrammer. You can also exit the diagrammer from the window title bar (upper-left corner) or close icon (upper-right corner).

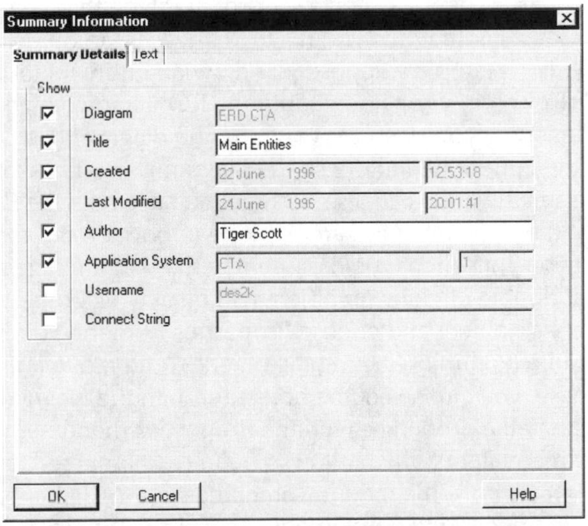

FIGURE 2-29. *Summary Information dialog box*

Edit Menu **Redo** undoes the last main change in the diagram. **Cut**, **Copy**, **Paste**, and **Delete** work on selected objects the same as they do in all Windows programs; but you have to remember that **Cut** removes the object from the diagram, not from the repository, and **Delete** deletes it from the diagram and the repository. **Paste Link** inserts an object that you have pasted onto the clipboard from another application. The object then appears in your diagram, but its source is the application that produced it in the first place. You can use this option to insert graphics or logos or a legend of symbols into your diagram using symbols that the diagrammer otherwise does not support.

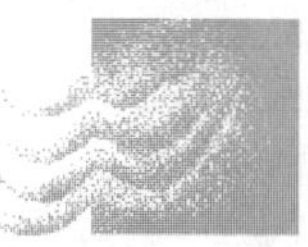

CAUTION
Delete in the diagrammers means "remove from the diagram and the repository." Cut means "remove from the diagram only." There is a warning dialog that appears when you indicate you want to Delete, but keep in mind what it means when you answer it.

Select All and **Select Same Type** let you select objects on the screen; the latter selects only the types of objects you have previously selected. **Select Elements** allows you to select all objects of a certain type: for example, all entities. **Navigate To** lets you select one object from a list of objects of a certain type. This option is useful if your diagram is large and you cannot quickly locate a particular object.

Include is the menu choice you use to put an object onto your diagram that already exists in the repository. **Include** displays a list of object types, and you choose one of these to display a list of objects of that type that you can include. You can choose **Consolidate** when you make changes to an object on a diagram from another tool. For example, suppose you draw an entity relationship diagram and include ENTITY1 on it. Then you go into the RON and change the name to ENTITY_1. The next time you open the diagram, the diagrammed object will be out of sync with the current definition, so the diagrammer will ask if you want to consolidate. This same situation can also occur if you have both the ER Diagrammer and RON open at the same time and are working in both on the same object. The menu choice lets you consolidate before opening the diagram again.

Normally, just double-clicking an object will display its Properties window. You can also select an object and choose **Properties** from the Edit menu. This approach is useful if you think selecting the object could move it around on the diagram. In this case, you can select the object through the **Navigate To** menu item and then display the properties with the **Properties** menu item.

The **Domains** menu item (which allows you to define named datatype and values objects) appears on some menus (sometimes in the **Elements** menu item) to allow you to add and modify domain objects. This feature is useful in the ER Diagrammer and Data Diagrammer as attributes and columns, respectively, need domains and, if they do not already exist, could be created here.

Preferences displays a screen that allows you to modify the display characteristics of the diagram. Each diagrammer is slightly different, but you can specify the colors, fonts, included objects, and grid size characteristics. Figure 2-30 shows the preferences for the ER Diagrammer. One trick to selecting a new color or font is clicking an object you wish to change to select it, and then clicking a color or font toolbar button. You can also set the grid size and specify whether you want to snap, or force, objects into grid lines. This feature is useful for keeping lines straight, but you will probably want to set the grid size smaller than the default value.

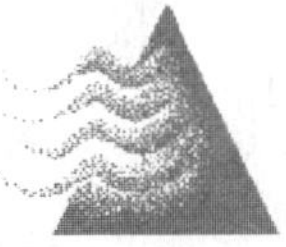

TIP

Press the Save button in the Preferences dialog to hold these preferences between sessions of the diagrammer or utility. If you set preferences and do not press Save, those preferences will not be there when you reopen that tool. Also, the preferences are saved for each tool individually, so you may have to make the same choice in different tools.

Insert New Object, **Links**, and **Object** handle the Object Linking and Embedding (OLE) of objects from other applications into the current one. These options are related to the **Paste Link** option mentioned before; **Paste Link** handles a link from the clipboard, whereas these options handle links directly from other applications.

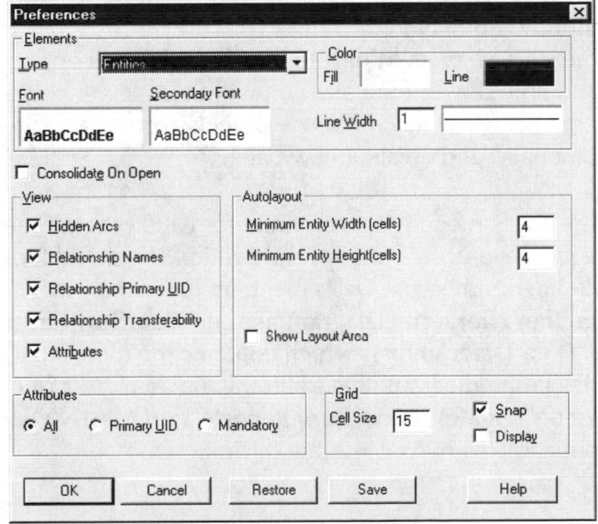

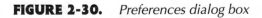

FIGURE 2-30. *Preferences dialog box*

View Menu One powerful feature of the diagrammers is that you can look at a diagram in many different ways. **Zoom In** and **Zoom Out** move the view closer or farther from the diagram in a preset percentage. **Zoom Reset** restores the last view before you zoomed. **Zoom Area** prompts you to draw out an area and then fills the window with that area.

Best Fit Selection (or **Area**) and **Best Fit Diagram** also let you change how much of the diagram you view. If you use **Best Fit Selection** (or **Area**) after selecting an object or set of objects, the window will be filled with those items. If you choose **Best Fit Diagram**, the window will fill, if possible, with the entire diagram.

Grid displays a set of lines on the screen with the grid size you specify in the Preferences dialog box. This grid helps you line up objects and can also be printed.

Standard Toolbar, **Drawing Toolbar**, and **Status Bar** turn those window items on or off. If you check them, they will be displayed; otherwise, they are hidden.

Utilities Menu The Utilities menu varies depending on the diagrammer you are using and includes the actions that the particular diagrammer performs on its objects. There are specific discussions on these menu items in subsequent chapters. However, a number of diagrammers do have in common an **Autolayout** selection that redraws the diagram in a new configuration (Designer/2000's best guess). If you keep pressing this button, you may (or may not) achieve the diagram layout you want without making manual modifications. **Previous Layout** restores the last autolayout layout, but it will not return to the layout if **Autolayout** did not produce it. You can specify some preferences that affect the Autolayout feature. Some diagrammers also have an **Autolayout to New Area** (or **Same Area**) option that lets you select an area for the autolayout layout.

Most diagrammers also have a **Minimise Number of Pages** option that reduces the spread across multiple pages if the diagram will fit on fewer pages. This option fixes the situation that occurs when you move objects around and they get too close to the edge of a page and create a new page.

Tools Menu The Tools menu is also different for each diagrammer, but the menus all have the same purpose—to allow navigation to related tools. For example, in the ER Diagrammer, the Tools menu includes the other Systems Modeller tools: **Function Hierarchy Diagrammer** and **Dataflow Diagrammer**. It also includes the **Data Diagrammer**, which contains the tables that may be related to the entities in the diagram. In addition, you can access utilities such as **Repository Object Navigator**, **Repository Reports**, and **Matrix Diagrammer**, all of which are applicable to objects used in this diagrammer.

Window Menu The Window menu includes the standard list of open windows as well as choices for tiling, cascading, and arranging the icons of the open windows. In addition, a **New Window** choice enables you to create another window with the same diagram as the active diagram. So you can look at two different parts of the same diagram at once.

Help Menu **Help→Contents** displays the applicable contents page, and **Cue Cards** loads a menu of related cue card tutorial windows. **Search for Help On**, **How to Use Help**, and **About** respectively display the help topic search window, help on the help system, and a window with information on the version number of this tool.

Toolbars

The button toolbars are an extension of the menu system and show the major features you need to access most frequently. To show the purpose of a button, all buttons include icons and display bubble help when you hold the mouse over a button. There are two main toolbars: the standard toolbar and the drawing toolbar.

The following illustration shows the standard toolbar buttons. These represent menu items: File buttons for New, Open, and Save; Edit buttons for Undo, Cut, Copy, and Paste; View buttons for Zoom Reset, Zoom In, Zoom Out, Best Fit Selection (or Zoom to Selection), and Best Fit Diagram; and diagrammer-specific buttons (such as the ones for the ER Diagrammer in the next illustration; you'll learn more about these in subsequent chapters). This toolbar also provides a "What's This" help button that you press to display the question mark cursor, which you can click on an item to display context-sensitive help for that item.

There is also a toolbar below the standard toolbar for drawing functions. The next illustration shows the ER Diagrammer drawing toolbar. This toolbar provides sets of buttons for functions not on the menu: Select, so the mouse cursor can select an item by drawing around it; object buttons where you select and then draw the object on the drawing surface; and visual palette buttons such as Line Width, Line Color, Fill Color, and Font. The visual palette buttons are not available until you select an item by clicking the mouse on it.

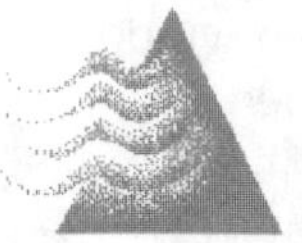

TIP
Although the default location of these toolbars is one on top of the other, you can actually drag and drop them anywhere. If you click and hold the mouse button on a nonbutton region within the outline of the toolbar, you can reposition the toolbar anywhere on the screen. If you drop the toolbar in the toolbar area at the top or side of the window, it will attach to the MDI window itself. If you drop it outside the toolbar, it will become a floating toolbar that you can move around inside or outside the window. This sort of toolbar is handy for maximizing the space in the drawing area because moving the toolbar out of its normal location leaves that much more area for the drawing.

Utilities Interface

Just as the diagrammers have a common interface, the utilities also look and act in similar ways. There are two types of utilities: those that use a full window and those that use only a pop-up window.

Full-Window Utilities

Repository Object Navigator, Repository Administration, Repository Reports, Preferences Navigator, and Matrix Diagrammer (which is really more of a utility than a diagrammer) are all full-window utilities. They each appear in an MDI window and present a Windows interface similar to the diagrammers.

Some of these utilities use object navigator (hierarchy) displays like the one in Figure 2-1. These allow you to get to a node quickly: you find the object type, open the type by clicking the + button, and then find the object in the list under the type. You may have to open up more subnodes before finding the object you need, but the hierarchy should assist you in the search.

The companion to the Object Navigator window is the Properties window. Once you find an object in the hierarchy and select it, the Properties window displays the properties for that object, as shown in Figure 2-31. You may have to explicitly display the Properties window by selecting it from the Windows menu. Chapter 3 explores the Object Navigator and Properties window in more depth while discussing the Repository Object Navigator.

Pop-up Window Utilities

Pop-up window (dialog box) utilities start from another diagrammer or utility such as Repository Object Navigator and the Designer/2000 window. The generators

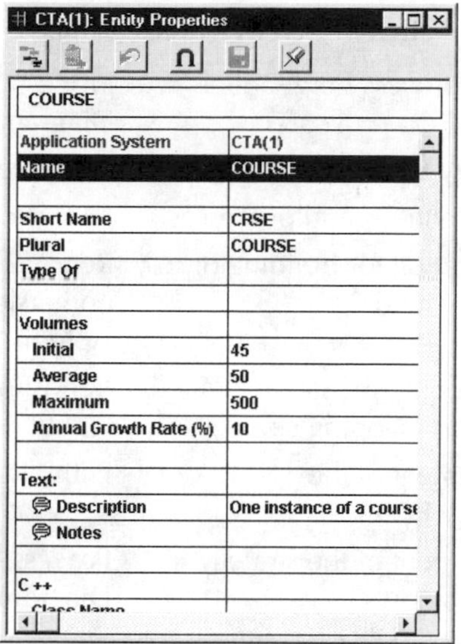

FIGURE 2-31. *Entity Properties window*

and the Reconcile and reverse engineering utilities are all in this category of utilities. Figure 2-13 shows the window for one of these utilities: the Forms Generator.

All of these utilities appear in one window and may have tab folder dialog boxes with a collection of standard Windows controls: text boxes, list items, check boxes, and radio groups. There is usually one button that starts an action, one to cancel or dismiss the dialog box, and one to display help on the fields in the dialog box.

How the Designer/2000 Tools Fit into the System Development Life Cycle

You have now seen all the major tools and utilities in Designer/2000. Although the main intention of the rest of this book is to explain how Designer/2000 supports the System Development Life Cycle, it is appropriate in this section to summarize where each tool fits into the SDLC. Table 2-3 shows the phases, some of the main activities and deliverables, and tools that support them.

Phase	Major Activity or Deliverable	Tools
Strategy	Initial process flow model	Process Modeller or Dataflow Diagrammer
	Strategy ERD	Entity Relationship Diagrammer
Pre-Analysis	List of entities and processes	Repository Reports
	Preparation for building on strategy models	Repository Object Navigator (to version the application system)
	User requirements to function mapping strategy	Repository Administration Utility
Analysis (both parts)	Refinement of the strategy ERD	Entity Relationship Diagrammer
	Refinement of the strategy process flows	Process Modeller or Dataflow Diagrammer
	Attachment of the entity usages to processes	Matrix Diagrammer
	Performance of additional functional decomposition	Function Hierarchy Diagrammer
	Analysis document with all repository objects	Repository Reports
	BPR process flows (for business process re-engineering)	Process Modeller
	Post-BPR ERD	Entity Relationship Diagrammer
	Functional overview of re-engineered business processes	Function Hierarchy Diagrammer
Pre-Design	Designation of functions as manual or automated	Function Hierarchy Diagrammer
	Design phase process flows	Process Modeller or Dataflow Diagrammer
	Preparation to build on analysis model	Repository Object Navigator (to version the application system)

TABLE 2-3. *Methodology Phases, Major Activities or Deliverables, and Designer/2000 Tools*

Phase	Major Activity or Deliverable	Tools
	Screen and report prototypes	Generators
	GUI standards	Preferences Navigator
	Refinement of templates	Developer/2000 Forms, Reports, Graphics; Visual Basic
Database Design	Physical database design: rough cut of tables, views, indexes, and so on	Database Design Wizard
	Refinement of rough-cut design	Data Diagrammer and Repository Object Navigator
Application Design	Application design: rough cut of modules	Application Design Wizard
	Refinement of rough-cut design	Module Data Diagrammer, Module Structure Diagrammer, Module Logic Navigator, Preferences Navigator, Matrix Diagrammer
Build	Refinement of module design during application building	All tools mentioned in Application Design phase
	Completed application modules	Forms, Reports, Graphics, Visual Basic, WebServer, MS Help, C++ generators
	Refinement of database design	All tools mentioned in Database Design phase
	Completed database objects creation scripts	Data Diagrammer, Repository Object Navigator, and Server Generator
Test	Cross-check for design completeness	Matrix Diagrammer
Implementation	Lists of completed modules	Repository Reports

TABLE 2-3. *Methodology Phases, Major Activities or Deliverables, and Designer/2000 Tools* (continued)

Phase	Major Activity or Deliverable	Tools
	System documentation	Repository Reports
Maintenance	Addition to system functionality or bug fixes	Appropriate utility or tool depending on the fix
All Phases	Management of repository data and users	Repository Object Navigator and Repository Administration Utility
	Display of repository contents	Repository Reports, Repository Object Navigator

TABLE 2-3. *Methodology Phases, Major Activities or Deliverables, and Designer/2000 Tools* (continued)

Conclusion

You have now been introduced to the important concepts behind the data in the repository and seen the major diagrammers and utilities that you use to access this data. The repository holds the definitions of all objects you create in the various phases of the System Development Life Cycle. This data helps you build systems that meet the business needs of the users. It serves as the basis for the database and application code that creates a reality from the virtual elements in the repository. The Designer/2000 front-end tools provide easy entry points into the repository, as well as give structure to the development process. Now it is time to delve into the details of the methodology phases and, for each phase, to see how to harness the power of Designer/2000.

PART 2

Development Phases

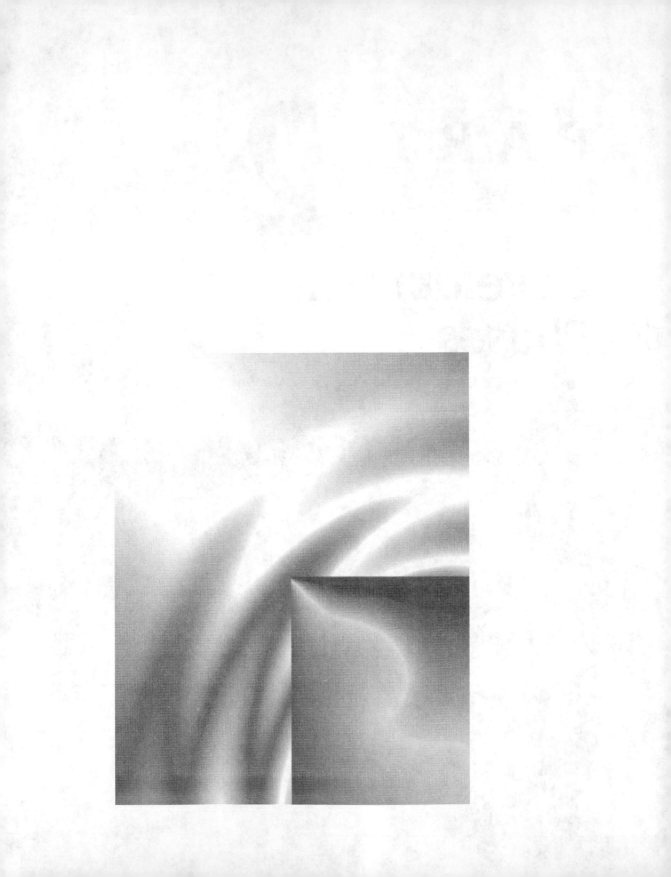

CHAPTER 3

Strategy

Why do we have to do a strategy document? Can't we just start coding?

The first step in CADM is strategy. The goal of the Strategy phase is to gain an overall idea of what the system you are about to design should do and to define the scope of the project. This chapter presents an in-depth view of the Strategy phase. It provides an overview of this phase and describes its key deliverable, the strategy document, in detail. It then discusses how to implement the Strategy phase in Designer/2000.

Overview of the Strategy Phase

The purpose of the Strategy phase is to formulate a basic description of the overall scope of the project and how the project will proceed. It is a contract between the ultimate users of the system and the people who will analyze, design, and build the system.

Spending an adequate amount of time on the strategy portion of the project is critical. Ideally, you should spend as much time as management will allow. A better understanding of what the project is committed to deliver will reduce confusion and help keep the project on course. The more that is known about the underlying business goals and requirements early on, the less likely it is that there will be surprises during the Analysis phase or that the scope of the project will change dramatically. It is not necessary that every specific system requirement be reported at this phase, but all necessary information should be gathered. The more analysis that can be incorporated into the Strategy phase, the better. If the analyst has done a careful and thorough job in the Strategy phase, the Analysis phase will proceed more smoothly.

On some projects, problems arise when different individuals on the project team and within the organization think about the project in different ways. For example, in a data warehouse project, the systems people may focus on the migration of the legacy system information; but top management may not see this as a goal or interest, and it may not fit in with the company's overall vision for the system.

Without a clear and common vision, a project can be sidetracked and months of work can be lost; or a system may be built that does not meet the core requirements. Development team after development team may come and go if they do not obtain a consensus of understanding among individuals involved at all levels as to the vision and goals of the project. There are many talented technical consultants who can write code and programs galore; but without a solid overall plan and goal, these efforts are wasted.

Rarely does anyone in a systems environment advocate cutting corners on data structures or applications without considering the impact on the system. However, there is a tendency to look upon strategic planning and methodology as an easy place to reduce costs. In the long run, this is a huge mistake and usually greatly increases the length of time for project completion.

The first part of the Strategy phase is to develop a strategy plan. This plan will help answer questions such as the following:

- What will the strategy document contain?
- Who will be interviewed?
- What committees will be involved in the project?
- What will the deliverables be?
- How long will the entire systems project take?

Several weeks may be necessary to produce an effective strategy plan. The development team needs the user to buy into the entire project and procedure. The plan for the strategy document should include criteria for determining when the Strategy phase is finished, what the expected deliverables are, and who ultimately approves the strategy part of the project before it proceeds to the next phase.

One useful aspect of the Strategy phase from both user and development team perspectives is that the users can contract with the development team to complete the work in this phase without committing to the full implementation of the project. Because it is impossible to accurately estimate the costs and resources necessary for completion of a project until the end of the Strategy phase (and, in most cases, the end of Analysis phase), completing the Strategy phase gives both the development team and the users a much better idea of what the proposed project will entail. The Strategy phase must be completed in order for both client and development team to have a good enough grasp of what needs to be done in order to make a decision to proceed.

Deliverables

The main deliverable for the Strategy phase is the strategy document. The strategy document is a high-level, focused description of the proposed system. It acts as a contract between the development team and the user organization. The strategy document should precisely describe the scope of the proposed system and, in broad strokes, lay out the plan of how to accomplish the project.

The intended audience for this document includes the user-side project leader, everyone on the development team, and any area managers who need to be involved in system development. It should not be written for one specific person. Frequently, the strategy document is presented to a management committee for sign-off. In small- and medium-sized companies, this committee often is the board of directors. Therefore, there may need to be several versions of the document for different audiences. A broader version might be suitable for the development team. For other audiences one or more sections may need to be removed, altered, or expanded.

Goals of the Strategy Document

The strategy document has the following goals:

- To communicate to management and all people involved in the project just what the project entails.
- To act as a sales tool for the development team. The strategy document proves the need for and importance of the project, clearly explaining why the project is cost-benefit efficient and demonstrating that the proposed plan makes sense, is feasible, and is the best plan to get the job done.
- To serve as a contract between the development team and users.
- To assess the scope of the project, list the promised deliverables, lay out the assumptions and limitations of the project, and limit the liability of the development team to what is agreed upon.
- To provide a baseline for the proposed system, specifying the rights and obligations of both analyst and user, including the right of the analyst to rethink the project when changes in the scope of the project occur or the stable allocation of resources is altered. The document should make it clear that any major changes will affect the deliverable dates.
- To provide a reference point and mechanism for handling conflicts that may arise.

The Strategy Document

The strategy document should be as complete and detailed as possible to ensure that both the user and the development team have a clear understanding of what is expected. It should not only list conclusions but should draw the reader through a logically coherent argument that demonstrates how the conclusions were arrived at. It should provide an audit trail back to the source documents.

Gathering information for the Strategy phase is done mostly through interviewing. Interviews are usually conducted with individuals reasonably high up in the organization since these individuals have the authority to allocate the money and resources to the project. Interview notes should be given unique document name/number identifiers, such as the person's name and the date of the interview. These notes should be kept in a binder and can be referred to by footnote in the strategy document. Using one's own interview document as a reference helps to make the writing tighter and less cumbersome. Instead of repeatedly writing "according to so and so" or "so and so said," footnotes can be used to reference statements in the original interview notes. All paragraphs in the strategy document should include footnotes citing the original interview notes. Since all interview notes will have been approved by the people being interviewed, the analyst has a defensible strategy document.

The strategy document should include the following sections, each of which this chapter discusses in detail:

I. Executive summary: The *executive summary* is a short overview of the entire strategy document and includes an executive summary abstract. Each section is then expanded in the complete strategy document.

II. Legacy System Description: History, Current System

III. Related Projects

IV. Business and Financial Sponsorship

V. Motivation

VI. Project Scope

VII. Solution: System, ERD, Process Flow

VIII. Cost-Benefit Analysis

IX. Project Organization and Staffing

X. Workplan

XI. Business Impact

XII. Conclusion

I. Executive Summary

The executive summary is not just an introduction to the strategy document. It is a self-contained document and should be written to be read on its own. It should completely describe all of the salient features of the strategy document. The executive summary represents the project team's current understanding of the total project.

Consider the following anecdote, perhaps apocryphal, about a study of National Science Foundation research grant proposal applications. These proposals reflect important research projects and are typically hundreds of pages long. Millions of dollars in grant money are distributed based on decisions made regarding the worthiness of the proposals these documents describe. The study found that the average amount of time spent making a decision on an application was fifteen minutes.

The point of this story for a systems environment is that much of what is written is not read carefully, if at all. How much time is a busy executive realistically going to spend reading a document? The executive summary should convince the user that they want to buy into the project as outlined, whether the costs are a few thousand dollars or several million. The executive summary defines the scope, solution, development method, costs, and benefits.

How long should this document be? This decision often depends on the style of the manager being addressed. Some want two pages, others want only one. Still others may want a more detailed five-to-ten-page document. The executive summary should *never* be more than ten pages. If, for some reason, the system being designed is so large that the summary exceeds ten pages, this document should have its own summary. Also, depending on the audience for this document, certain sections that appear in the larger strategy document (such as a description of the legacy system) can be added or removed as necessary.

A good deal of time and thought should go into the executive summary. Just because it is a short document does not mean that it should be tossed off quickly. As the analyst's understanding of the project matures, the executive summary should be refined and revised. Since some of the information in the executive summary must be extracted from the whole strategy document, it may be necessary to complete some work on the project before a useful executive summary can be written. Revisions may need to be made as often as every few days.

After you draft the executive summary document, you can expand it and add parts of it to other sections of the strategy document as you write it. It is perfectly acceptable to reuse paragraphs from the executive summary document elsewhere in the overall strategy document.

Executive Summary Abstract

The *executive summary abstract* is a quick-and-dirty summary of 100 to 200 words that forms the first paragraph of the executive summary. It should begin with a sentence of 25 words or less stating what the project intends to accomplish. This step serves as an internal validity check. If the project goal can't be stated clearly in 25 words or less, the analyst doesn't clearly understand the project and is not ready to write the strategy document. This statement serves as the core requirement for the system being designed.

Here is an example first sentence of an executive summary for a data warehouse project: "The proposed data warehouse will provide data structures adequate for replacing all existing production reporting and any ad hoc report requested in the last 6 months." If the project is very large or diverse, it may be necessary to break the 25 words or less rule; however, with a laundry list of several goals, it is very easy to lose sight of the core goal.

The remainder of the abstract condenses the executive summary into a few key sentences.

Business and Financial Sponsorship

Every project of any magnitude needs to have the appropriate commitment from the organization to accomplish its goals. The existing political environment within an organization strongly influences how the project phases (especially the Analysis phase) take place. The project team needs to carefully document the following:

- Who the players are
- The relative stakes in the project of each player and department
- The individual needs and requirements of each player and department
- The mechanism for conflict resolution, including who has ultimate authority

Motivation

The motivation section should consist of one or two paragraphs describing the underlying business need for the proposed project. Like the executive summary abstract, this section should also begin with a brief—25 words or less—explanation of why the project was undertaken: for example, "The existing system is inadequate and must be replaced within six months. We want to add new products that the current system cannot handle." The motivation section must present a clear, concise, direct, and compelling statement of the user's reasons for wanting a system developed.

Here is an example of a motivation section directed to the management team of a large financial company in the Northeast that was building a new trading system: "The existing system is an antiquated COBOL system held together by patches. It is only a matter of time until there is a catastrophic program failure causing an interruption in business. New products cannot be added to the system, which is preventing us from entering new markets. The existing system is incapable of expanding into new geographic regions. Management is considering trying to support 24-hour trading. The old system cannot support this at all. The longer we wait, the more this will cost our company." This statement justified a multimillion dollar expenditure.

Solution

The solution section should be no more than one or two paragraphs long. It should briefly describe what the analysts intend to build, the basic vision of the overall system architecture, and how the system will work. It should summarize the solution section of the overall strategy document, described later in this chapter.

Cost-Benefit Analysis

The benefits versus costs section is devoted to estimating the cost of the project and the resources required to complete the project. It is important for the development team to have a clear and accurate picture of the resources (hardware, software, personnel) that the user will have to provide and to present this in the document.

An ethical question arises in estimating costs. Users may be so used to being mislead regarding the amount of time and money required for system development projects that they may automatically double or triple low estimates. This is a tricky issue. If the development team is honest about the time and money required, the user, who may assume that the numbers are low, may feel that the costs are unreasonable. On the other hand, if the cost estimate is low and the project ends up way over budget and late, the development team will have a very unhappy user. We believe that the best advice is to be as realistic as possible. Let your conscience be your guide. It is rare that a project does not go over budget; but if the development team has been honest with the user, budget overruns can be handled amicably.

This section of the document should also spell out exactly what deliverables the user will get. This can be a list of the hard and soft benefits that the finished project will provide, as discussed in more detail later in this chapter.

Conclusion

End the executive summary with a few concluding sentences, not with numbers. Expectations for a formal business document include a conclusion. Part of the goal of the executive summary document is to communicate to the user that the development team is well-organized and can be trusted to do the job completely.

II. Legacy System

Describe the legacy system, including both the history of the legacy system and its current status.

History of the Current System

It is important to understand how the existing system was created. Without a thorough understanding of the legacy system, it is not possible to redesign the system. Find out about previous attempts at system redesign. If possible, talk to people who were involved in the original system design; you will gain important information regarding the legacy system.

Include a walkthrough of the existing system and its development history in this section. The likelihood is high that this is not the first attempt to fix a system problem or design a new system. To avoid repeating past mistakes, examine the remains of earlier projects and any existing half-built structures. Documentation and analyses of these previous failures may help pinpoint the reasons for failures and help you avoid the same pitfalls. This information is well worth the time needed to gather it and incorporate it into the strategy document.

Some individuals in the business re-engineering community would advocate that a thorough review of the legacy system is unnecessary and would hamper the completion of a quality re-engineering effort. The fallacy of this logic stems from the fact that, particularly with older systems, there will be system requirements embedded in the legacy system that will not be discovered any other way. A review of the legacy system is merely another source of requirements. To ignore this potentially valuable resource would be a mistake.

Description of the Current System

A new system can't be intelligently designed without a thorough description of the underlying system. Obtaining this information will require talking to more than one person. The analyst needs to understand more than just the functional aspects of the system. He or she needs to observe the system in use to get a sense of the supporting data structures (for a computer system), inputs, outputs, how the system is used, who uses it, what they use it for, the business reason for the system, and so on. Without a baseline measure, you will not be able to discuss benefits of the new system.

This section should include an overview of the existing hardware and software.

Frequently neglected aspects of the legacy system are the reports generated by the existing system. Often, even after re-engineering, reports may be similar to those generated by the legacy system. The strategy document should list the numbers and types of reports and provide examples. These reports will be completely explored in the Analysis phase.

III. Related Projects

With rare exceptions, projects do not exist in isolation. The following questions must be considered in the Strategy phase of any project:

- How is the system being developed going to interface with existing systems?
- How and when will this integration be accomplished?

It is critical to consider how the integration with existing systems will affect the amount of time needed for the new system development.

NOTE
Interfacing with existing systems can take longer than the design of the system being developed.

This is true even when interfacing with an existing Oracle system. Non-Oracle database integration can take even longer because of the difficulties of dealing with different platforms. Also, in general, interfacing with packaged software takes longer than interfacing with in-house systems.

Sometimes, particularly in large systems projects, multiple teams will be working on different portions of development. In these cases, clear delineation of scope, interfacing, and deliverables is critical to project success. Trying to coordinate multiple teams on a project is exceedingly difficult and usually results in finger pointing and infighting when something goes wrong. This usually causes the project to fail. Having multiple teams, particularly from different areas, should be avoided whenever possible. However, having one team subcontract another team to fill in expertise where it is needed is acceptable.

IV. Business and Financial Sponsorship

It is not politically correct to have a section in the strategy document called "political environment." However, from the developer's perspective, the political environment of the organization needs to be taken into account and documented. A complete description of the existing political environment is a critical piece of the strategy document.

Political Environment

The political situation within an organization will influence the way any system is built. The political environment is just as important as the fundamental strategy requirements for the system. Just like changes in the scope of an ongoing project, a change in the political environment can cause the entire project to be rethought from the ground up.

Examples of changes in the political environment that can affect a project include personnel changes, department head changes, and the addition or elimination of a department involved in the project. A new person in a position of authority may have an entirely different agenda than his or her predecessor. A substantive upset in the balance of power among the players or departments can also cause a fundamental shift in project goals. Unless a way to handle these changes from the project perspective is carefully spelled out, the whole project may be in jeopardy should a change in the political environment occur. For example, if a main department head changes mid project, the entire project may be pulled off track, and it may not be until another major organizational change occurs that the project gets back on track.

The best way to collect the necessary information on the political environment is to ask questions. Find out who the players are whose needs should be met. Define the organizational areas that the system affects. Create an organizational chart that includes all the people involved and goes high enough in the organization for its various branches to meet at a central person with ultimate decision-making power.

The deliverables in this section include the following:

- Organizational chart
- List of the names, titles, and relationships of players
- Strategy-level requirements for each of the players or a description of how the needs of various players differ (each section may need to be developed with each player using a problem/definition format)
- Conflict-resolution structure

Conflict Resolution

The approval process needs to be carefully spelled out and the following questions answered:

- How will it be determined when a particular deliverable is finished?
- How will changes in scope or deliverables be handled?
- What will be the sign-off process for each phase of the project?

When there are differences of opinion in spite of the above, there must be a process for resolving the conflict. Usually, the best way to resolve conflicts on a project is to hold a joint application development (JAD) session. At this meeting, all of the parties are brought together to lay out all of the pertinent issues and forge a consensus. If a consensus cannot be reached, there should be a clear mechanism for a higher authority to arbitrate the final decision. All those involved should have agreed to this process before proceeding. This is another example of the importance of regarding the strategy document as a contract between the user and the analyst. These issues are often not stated explicitly but are truly salient and material portions of the contract. Everyone involved needs to understand and buy into the process as a whole in order for the project to be successfully completed.

V. Motivation

The motivation section justifies the need for the project. The information you gathered in your interviews should include all the evidence you need. However, like a good journalist, a good systems analyst does not depend upon one source. The ultimate authority is the person with the overall responsibility for the project and the person or persons to whom the development team reports. The line of authority should be clear. If others present differing opinions regarding the project, it is the responsibility of the analyst to dig further and report these in the strategy document. It is important to keep the user informed at all stages of the project.

VI. Project Scope

Even though scope issues will enter into other parts of the strategy document, scope is such an important topic that it should be dealt with specifically. Scope can be limited by any number of factors:

- **Access to users** In one project, the scope was limited by who the development team was allowed to interview. That limitation of access restricted the quality of the analysis and, therefore, also restricted what the development team could deliver.
- **Subject area** One portion of a system may need to be replaced without making modifications to other portions of an existing system.
- **Interface with existing systems** This interface can restrict scope. For example, building an inventory management system is one project. Hooking that system into an existing purchase order (PO) system is a separate project.
- **Technical limitations** Developers may supply database design and application resources but not technical hardware, networking, or custom-written Windows DLLs.
- **Role of the developers** This can be restricted to analysis and development and may not include training or user documentation.

Negotiation of scope depends upon the needs of the users as well as the capabilities of the development team. It is important that the scope of a project is specifically laid out, including what is within the scope and, often more importantly, a declaration of what is out of scope and will not be delivered.

VII. Solution

The solution section should summarize all aspects of the system to be built and include a strategy ERD and process flow diagrams.

Proposed System

The discussion of the proposed system should lay out, specifically and in depth, what the development team will do for the user. This is not the place to discuss costs. This section should discuss the following:

- **Hardware requirements** What equipment will be required to complete the project? Is a client/server environment to be assumed?
- **Software requirements** What software will be needed? What licenses will be needed? Does existing software need to be upgraded?
- **Deliverables** List the deliverables that are planned: for example, applications, reports, documentation, training, maintenance agreements.
- **Knowledge transfer** This is relevant when an outside consulting team does the development. An important deliverable is that the consulting team provide a knowledge transfer to the in-house developers that will enable them to perform maintenance and enhancements throughout the lifetime of the new system.

Strategy ERD

Depending on the complexity of the business area and the level of knowledge of the project team and users, it may or may not be appropriate to include a strategy ERD as part of the strategy document. However, this diagram should be created anyway, if only for the purpose of helping to focus the analysts' thinking.

At the Strategy level, the ERD should identify the key entities and their relationships to provide an overall perspective of the business area data. For example, for a purchase order, the key entities might be vendors, approved items, purchase order, customer, and so on. This is not the place to confirm whether an entity is a lookup table or to define the cardinality of relationships.

In addition to the diagram itself, the strategy ERD must include narrative definitions of each entity. These definitions should be clear and concise. Errors in

ERDs frequently occur because the analyst does not have a clear understanding of the entities being modeled. These definitions should come from the business users.

Entities in an ERD are not merely descriptions. They represent items of particular significance and interest to an organization about which they need to keep information. Demographic information, for example, is not an entity. The naming of an entity is a key factor in the success of an ERD. Good names of entities facilitate communication of the business area information requirements. Critical to the success of an ERD are precise and accurate entity definitions. This is an iterative process which may take some time. Good definitions of the relationships between entities are important because they reflect business rules.

The process for creating a strategy ERD is as follows:

1. Identify and name the major entities. At this point, the name is only relevant from a communications perspective. It is pointless to disagree over names before clear, concise definitions are written.
2. Define relationships among entities.
3. Write the best possible entity definitions.
4. Write the best possible relationship definitions.
5. Finalize the entity names.

From these steps, often the best entity names will emerge.

The entity definition always represents something in the real world. These definitions are crucial to the accuracy of the diagram. Entity descriptions should never start with "information on . . ." nor should they describe the attributes of the entity. The entity must be a noun. For example, the entity description of an employee could be "a warm, breathing body that works here." Each instance of that entity (row in the table) therefore represents "a warm breathing body that works here." When entities are dependent, the description should include a reference to the parent entity. For example, a description of a purchase order detail might be "the quantity of a specific item purchased using a specific purchase order." Entities should always be discussed as things that exist in the real world.

A problematic aspect of many ERDs is the naming of intersection entities. For example, "student-class" has a many-to-many relationship. To handle such entities, create an artificial intersection entity called "enrollment." The definition of enrollment is "the act of a specific student taking a specific class." Therefore, each row in the table represents one specific student taking one specific class. Thinking of the intersection often guides the description.

To help others understand the ERD, generate tables and include sample data to clarify the way information is reflected in the diagram structure. The strategy ERD should not have many entities; strategy ERDs should be limited to 10-20 entities.

The diagram should fit on one 8½-by-11-inch page. If the project consists of multiple modules, each should have its own ERD broken down by subject area. It is acceptable to have the same entity reflected on multiple diagrams.

Process Flow Diagram

A process flow is a diagram that shows business processes and their interactions. In the Strategy phase, process flows are used to demonstrate to the user that the development team fully understands the business processes within the scope of the project. At this stage, process flows do not need to be overly detailed unless more detail is needed to satisfy the user. Most of the work of creating a process flow is figuring out how the business processes interact and fit together, which usually takes place in the Analysis phase.

A strategy-level process flow can still be used to communicate the scope of the project. For example, for a purchase order (PO) system, the strategy-level process flow will show what is being included and what is not. Will the system track the distribution of goods by matching the distribution against the PO when the goods arrive? Is this tracking part of another system? Does the system include the PO authorization process? These questions can be answered by looking at the process flow diagram for the proposed PO system. If an existing system will be changed significantly, it is usually appropriate to deliver before and after process flow diagrams.

VIII. Cost-Benefit Analysis

The strategy document needs to show that the benefits of the proposed system will outweigh its costs.

Benefits

How can benefits be quantified? For a re-engineering project, the cost-benefit analysis is fairly straightforward. For example, before re-engineering, a report may take 14 person days to produce, and after re-engineering, the same report may take only one minute to produce. Such a benefit is easy to document, and the advantages of time saved are obvious.

How can a value be placed on new flexibility within a system? One can look at the number of new reports generated by the legacy system in the last six months. If the legacy system took 10 to 12 person days to do what the new system can do in 1 or 2, then improvements in productivity can be realistically estimated and reflected as benefits of the new system.

Three types of benefits can be examined:

- **Process improvements** Time saved in completing tasks
- **System modification efficiencies** Changes to the system, improving performance, new reports, and so on

- **Ethereal improvements** Executive information systems, ability to expand product line or market segment, ad hoc query tools, data warehouse, and so on

How can a value be placed on these types of benefits? One way is to ask managers and users of the system what they perceive the value to be. For example, a manager can be asked, "If we could give you a new benefit—namely, bringing in a service bureau to perform ad hoc querying—what would you be willing to pay per month for that benefit?" or "In your functional area, how much would you pay for a fixed contract price to perform a specific task?" By asking people in all functional areas related to the proposed project questions like these, it is possible to estimate the value of possible benefits delivered by the proposed system.

Costs

The cost section should provide the user with a detailed account of the estimated monetary costs of developing the proposed system as well as the internal resources needed to complete and support the project. Costs can be estimated by phase. For example, the estimate for the Analysis phase should be pretty solid; however, estimates for the Design and Build phases will be less precise since there are many more unknowns in those phases at this stage of development. The true costs are never fully known until the system has been in production for one or two years.

The following should be included in the costs:

- Number of person hours required of internal systems and business people by level
- Cost of external consultants by level, based on hourly or daily rates
- Expected number of hours per day for each phase of the project
- Expected hardware costs
- Cost of software licenses
- Networking costs
- Cabling costs
- Number of person hours of internal user resources required

This last item is crucial to the successful completion of any project. The user needs to have a clear understanding of the need for a person or persons from his or her organization on the development team. These resources should be identified by name: for example, "We need 25 hours with Joe, 10 hours with Susan . . ." and so on. The individuals must be chosen carefully since they will function as the liaison between the analysts and the users. They may be required to devote their full time to the project until it is completed. The liaison person or persons should attend all team meetings and work side by side with the analysts building the requirements documents, designing screen shots, and so on. Their participation in all aspects of system development also helps overcome the us-them attitude of user and analyst and promote a more collaborative effort.

The input from the liaison person will play a major role in steering the direction of the project. When the project is completed, this person will be a more valuable employee to the company since the person will gain an understanding of systems development in general as well as being an expert on the new system. A rule of thumb in selecting this person is that if the user won't miss the person, he or she is probably the wrong person for the job.

Once again, it is important to keep in mind that the analyst and the user are building a contract. There must be a meeting of minds. The user is not just agreeing to pay the analyst but also must be willing to allocate the necessary internal resources to the project. The analyst must be firm about this commitment of resources from the user. For example, if the analyst needs 10 to 15 hours of time from several top executives, this time must be set aside. If the resources are not made available or the user attempts to substitute lower-level employees, the analyst must indicate that this places the entire project at risk. These cheaper internal resources then become "pseudousers," and all the analyst can guarantee is that these pseudousers will be happy with the results. If the user is not willing to spare the appropriate employees, then the whole system development process is in jeopardy. If the analyst cannot get the right resources, then the analyst needs to report that the proposed system may not be deliverable.

IX. Project Organization and Staffing

Identification of the different roles of people working on a project is a frequently overlooked step. There are numerous roles associated with a CADM project:

- **Project Leader** This person coordinates all of the other roles and acts as a liaison with the business management in the organization where the project is being done. One of the main responsibilities of the project leader is to make sure that the project plan is being followed. He/she needs to communicate to the project team what steps should be followed and how these steps fit into the overall design plan.

- **Systems Architect** This is the technical leader of the project who makes sure that the applications and underlying data are coordinated.

- **Business Analyst** a) *Process Analyst*: This person extracts and analyzes the system requirements with the focus on analysis and representation of business processes.

b) *Data Analyst*: This individual keeps track of and analyzes entity relationships used by the business.

- **Logical Data Modeller** This person is responsible for the complete analysis ERD representing all of the business requirements.
- **Physical Data Modeller** This individual understands the performance considerations associated with determining the formal data structures.
- **Designer/2000 expert** This person is responsible for helping implement the project in the software tool.
- **Repository Manager** This person takes care of data security and working with different areas of the Designer/2000 repository.
- **GUI Design Standards Developer** This person determines the project's GUI design standards by understanding the limitations of what Designer/2000 can easily generate.
- **Application Designer** This individual supervises the overall user interface design of the application.
- **Application Tuner** This individual ensures that applications are correctly tuned.
- **Data Tester** This individual ensures that the database meets system requirements.
- **Application Tester** This individual ensures that the applications meet system requirements.
- **Reporting Designer** This person designs production and ad-hoc reporting requirements.
- **QA person** This person is responsible for the overall quality assurance for the project and ensures that things are done according to the specifications that were laid out.
- **PL/SQL Programmer** This person takes care of complex database and application level triggers.
- **Application Developer** This individual is familiar with Forms and Reports or whatever application tool is being used.
- **Network Administrator** If necessary, this person takes care of network considerations and the underlying physical network of the project.
- **Systems Administrator** This person supports the operating systems and other systems software.
- **DBA** This person handles backups and recovery, and manages database instances.

- **Data Migration Expert** This person managees the process of migrating data from the Legacy system to the new database structures.
- **Users** It is important to have users on the development team from each functional area, preferably full time. These individuals should sit in on all meetings throughout the life cycle of the project.

Clearly, many of these roles can and will be performed by the same person. The question arises: How big of a team is desirable? As F. Brooks described in *The Mythical Man-Month: Essays on Software Engineering* (Reading, MA: Addison-Wesley, 1975), a surgical team model is the best approach. This means that there is one key person supported by as many others as necessary to keep that person productive. On a system development team, a few people do all of the "real" work. Others on the team do support work. We consider it irresponsible and unethical to use high-level development talent for tasks such as typing in entity descriptions or taping together ERDs. The underlying staffing principles here include the following:

- There should be various levels of talent on any team.
- Always use the cheapest, lowest-level talent possible for any task.
- Never use low-level talent on complex tasks except for training purposes.
- Use key people to perform key tasks.

On normal, straightforward, low-level development tasks, an expert analyst may be able to complete these tasks in half the time needed by a lower-level analyst. For complex tasks, an expert developer/analyst can often accomplish a task in one tenth of the time needed by a novice developer, assuming that the novice developer could do the task at all. Using the surgical metaphor again, a first year medical student can suture up a minor cut but no matter how much time the student is given, he or she cannot perform brain surgery. That can only be done by a brain surgeon. Likewise, complex systems tasks require top-level talent.

For the following tasks, it is particularly important to use top-level talent:

- **Design of the logical ERD** Lower-level talent can do requirements analysis and the first cut of the logical ERD, but the final version requires much expertise.
- **Audit of the logical ERD** This requires a separate highly skilled data modeller other than the ERD designer. It can be a consultant brought in specifically for this purpose.
- **Design of the physical database** Physical database design is its own specialty.

- **Audit of the physical ERD** The same level talent applies to this audit as to design of the logical ERD.
- **Application design** Person responsible for the overall user interface for all applications.
- **GUI standards development** GUI applications are very different from older, character-based applications.
- **DBA** Once the database is set up, this job can be passed to a maintenance DBA.
- **Internal control system design** This is crucial to the project success, particularly on financial systems which need to stand up to rigorous financial audits.
- **Change control system** Once the system is in place, an experienced person needs to handle how changes are made and managed.

X. Workplan

The strategy document should include a high-level workplan. Other, more detailed workplans will be developed during each phase of the project. At this point, the workplan should be painted in broad strokes from a top management perspective. Top management wants to know about the deliverables. The workplan should lay out the tasks to be performed for each major phase of the project. Management will not know when analysis is finished unless a requirements document is generated. The analyst should make sure to generate deliverables at each project point for management to review.

The strategy document should not simply list promises, but should tell management what specifically will be delivered, and when, for the entire project. The user should have a clear picture of what the analyst intends to do and how the user will be kept informed of the project's progress. The analyst needs to instill confidence in the user that the proposed process will enable the project to be completed successfully. The user must buy into the process as well as the end result. For example, during the Strategy phase, one deliverable should be the written project plans as they are done. The user should approve each workplan.

The workplan should be an iterative, negotiated document. The first cut should be an appropriate plan based on the strategy already laid out. This plan is a refinement of the contract between the analyst and user. Each should have a clear idea of this agreement.

What should the workplan look like? It should not simply be a Microsoft Project document. A one-page chart should be included as part of the workplan, but this alone is not enough. The full workplan should describe each major process step and the accompanying deliverables in narrative form. This plan will let management know how the analyst intends to accomplish the various phases of the whole project. Management must agree to each part of the workplan.

How should the number of hours be calculated? To do this, the analyst must internally generate another level of detail. Time tends to be notoriously underestimated. Each portion and subportion of the project must be thought through carefully. Although this level of detail is not overly relevant for the strategy document, it is useful to have if the user wants to know how the numbers were derived. Common errors to avoid are a tendency to leave out some time-consuming steps and to underestimate how long tasks will take. This more detailed document can be shown to the key user to back up information in the strategy document.

Writing the workplan requires the analyst to make many assumptions. At this stage of the project, he or she may not know enough to go into great detail. There is still much to find out about the user-site terrain, politics, pitfalls, and so on. It is important to lay out assumptions of the size of the problem and anticipated access to resources. These factors have a direct impact on the workplan portion of the Strategy phase. It is also important to include, as a line item, unexpected disasters. These might include key resource people becoming unavailable for whatever reason and interviews that produce radically differing versions of what needs to be done. Don't underestimate the cost of unexpected disasters. If the development team has already completed a project for this user in the same area, he or she can allocate 20 percent of the overall project cost for unexpected disasters. The project team can perform a risk analysis to estimate the disaster percentage potential. If this is not possible or this is the first project for a particular user, the development team should plan for 100 percent of the overall project cost for unexpected disasters.

At this stage, the workplan should outline the major phases and deliverables of the project. This can be done with Microsoft Project to produce a one-page document, the goal of which is to educate the user regarding the methods for building the system. The primary goal at this stage continues to be to build the user's confidence in the project team's ability to convert a vision into reality. The workplan should be as detailed as the user wants. The analyst can gauge the level of detail wanted from the user feedback.

XI. Business Impact

How can business impact be determined at the Strategy phase? The analyst will need to hypothesize, "If we had the proposed system in place, what would it do for us?" Obviously, the answer will vary greatly from project to project.

When redesigning a legacy system, whether or not business process re-engineering occurs as well, the business impact will be clear: the user will get a more flexible system that can more easily respond to changes in business.

Traditional systems are much less user and analyst friendly, though management is often unaware of this. A new report in Designer/2000 takes a day or two to design and build, whereas the same report may take days or even weeks to generate using the legacy system.

The following common outcomes of implementing a Designer/2000 system affect business:

- Designer/2000 provides a centralized storage place for many of the system requirements.
- A coherent strategy exists in that all information stored in the Designer/2000 repository is linked to the applications.
- When data is changed, it can be automatically updated in many of the applications depending on how well the applications are generated and what percent of the applications can be generated through Designer/2000. This outcome influences the flexibility of the system with respect to regeneration.

A new Designer/2000 system is more user friendly than a legacy system. Having a centralized storage place ready in case the underlying technology changes is very useful. For example, as the work environment changes from a client/server environment to a Web server environment, by using Designer/2000 the user is better positioned to take advantage of an entirely different architecture.

On the database side, the environment is shifting to the object-oriented environment used by Oracle, and database designs are becoming increasingly object oriented. Designer/2000 will be staying on top of the latest developments in Oracle's DBMS, and a shorter time will be needed to implement changes in a Designer/2000 environment. If the legacy system is not even relational, there will be a level of improvement in moving to a relational environment and yet another level of improvement in moving to Designer/2000. If business process re-engineering is performed, even greater efficiencies can be realized, as discussed in Chapter 6.

The bottom line is that the business impact should meet the needs outlined in the motivation section. The new system should provide a solution to the stated business problems. The analyst should go back to the motivation section and make sure each need is addressed one by one and discuss how the new system will support each need.

XII. Strategy Document Conclusions

The strategy document should have a structured conclusion summarizing all of the sections outlined in the preceding paragraphs.

In general, the strategy document should be as detailed as possible. The more analysis that can be included, the better. In reality, however, until the analysis is completed and confirmed with the users, the development team will have an incomplete vision of the full scope of the project. The full scope really can't be understood until the Design phase is complete.

Application Partitioning

It's no secret that smaller applications are much easier to build than larger ones. The number of things to consider increases exponentially as the size of the application increases. A small application with a suite of modules that operates on perhaps ten different database tables can be easily built by a couple of developers in a few weeks. A suite of modules running on 30–50 tables will require the efforts of a 5–10 person development team for several months. A large effort involving several hundred modules operating on a few hundred tables can consume whatever resources are applied to it and may take a year or more, if it is ever completed.

The idea is to break the system into several independent development efforts. There is some cost to partitioning, though. For every portion of a large system that is built, you need to consider how that partition will interface with the other partitions. The system should be partitioned in such a way that the interfaces between partitions are as simple as possible. It is necessary to find a happy medium between many small systems with horrendous interfacing problems and a few large partitions with minor interface problems but that have all the other problems associated with larger systems. In the past, the tendency has been to create very large systems. Our experience has been that projects are usually not sufficiently partitioned.

How should the partitioning be done? Optimally, partitioning should be done by subject area. The main criteria to use in selecting application partitions is that it should be possible for the partition to be put into production, independent of the other partitions. In most businesses, systems can be partitioned by accounting cycles, such as purchase and acquisition, sales and distribution, or payroll.

Partitioning need not only take place during the Strategy phase. It is possible to partition your system at any point in the CADM process. In fact, the appropriate way of partitioning may not be evident until the end of the Analysis phase. At the end of every phase, the development team should audit the correctness of any system partitioning.

What we are describing in this book is the process for a complete system design involving a complete replacement of a legacy system or a new system development effort. Frequently, the scope of a project is inconsistent with the full CADM process. For example, in one project that the authors worked on, the mandate was to replace the front-end of an existing character-based application. Going back to the users and starting over with a complete Analysis phase was not an option. To further complicate matters, there were other applications outside the scope of this project currently using the same data structures. Finally, a cursory review of the database revealed serious design flaws in the database.

Developing the workplan for this project was quite challenging. The Analysis phase was abbreviated and only involved interfacing with existing systems personnel. An audit of the logical ERD and database was performed without a requirements document. We had to rely on the in-house developers to act as "human surrogates" for a requirements document. The rest of the workplan followed the model proposed in this book.

The main point is that, in many cases, the scope of the project may not include full Analysis and Design phases. At the beginning of any project, the analyst needs to evaluate what changes are appropriate to CADM in order to take into account the starting point of the project.

Modifications for Smaller Systems

A full-blown strategy document is appropriate only in very large projects costing a million dollars or more. However, the Strategy phase can certainly be pared down to suit smaller projects. You can stratify the size of the projects being discussed, as follows:

- **Type 1** Multimillion dollar projects requiring person years of effort taking place over months or years.
- **Type 2** Medium-sized projects, including stand-alone systems such as payroll and purchasing systems, and systems requiring integration with existing systems.
- **Type 3** Small projects that are short term and require limited budget and resources.

(Note that any project requiring integration with an existing system can be viewed as one size larger. In other words, a small project requiring integration with a functioning system should be considered a medium-sized project, and so on.)

For very small projects, the Strategy and Analysis phases are combined. For example, when building a help desk system, all that is necessary is a few-page write-up indicating the project scope and cost estimate, a strategy ERD, and perhaps a process flow diagram. The result will be a strategy document with some analysis and design specifications all rolled into one. From this, the project can move to a rapid prototyping environment. With the sophistication of existing tools such as Designer/2000, the application can be built so quickly that if it is not satisfactory, it can be rebuilt and quickly moved through the refinement process. Descriptions of the legacy system and political environment also are not necessary for small projects.

For medium-sized systems, a strategy document still is necessary. However, not as much time needs to be spent on this since there will be fewer users to interview. Also, since the project is smaller in scope with less money involved, you will not need to justify the plans as carefully at this stage as would be necessary in a large project. For small and medium projects, an executive summary is needed only if the strategy document is more than ten pages long. Legacy system and political environment descriptions may or may not be needed, depending on the specific situation.

Within this book, most of the information pertains to projects of type 1 in the preceding list. However, modifications of the proposed methodology for small- and medium-sized projects will be mentioned at the end of each phase, as in this section.

Strategy Document Example

The following example of a strategy document uses a small project as an example because the documentation for a large project can be very long. Nevertheless, this small project illustrates the concepts being discussed.

The example project calls for redesign of a legacy human resources system. This example was chosen because every organization needs to keep track of its employees on some level. The organization in this example is XYZ Company.

The following paragraphs present the strategy document for the proposed project.

I. Executive Summary

Using Designer/2000 and Developer/2000, we propose to re-engineer the data structure and applications for the XYZ Staff ID database.

The XYZ Staff ID database is in need of redesign. The current system is based on a Forms 3.0 application interface; and the database design has some conceptual flaws that require either applications or users to add the same information multiple times into the database. This flawed database structure will increase the overall cost and maintenance of the project because the applications will be harder to write.

We propose to not only convert Forms 3.0 to 5.0, but use this opportunity to re-engineer the database and clean up its structure.

II. Legacy System Description

The existing system is an Oracle Version 6.0 database with a Forms 3.0 front-end. The data structure has some conceptual flaws, and the Forms 3.0 front-end will require serious reworking to bring it up to modern standards.

III. Related Projects

This is a stand-alone system that has no need to interface with any other project.

IV. Business and Financial Sponsorship

This is an important project, but unfortunately, its value is not obvious. Funding will come from general department resources. Therefore, the Staff ID database project will have to be piggybacked onto other projects that have greater political priority.

In this case, we can use this project to set up and design our GUI and Designer/2000 standards. Also, we can use the project as a watershed for the application development process using Designer/2000.

V. Motivation

The existing system has numerous conceptual flaws. For example, people are assigned to organizations in three different places in the data structure. Three different intersection tables connect individuals and organizations, so if one individual's relationship spans more than one of these tables, that information must be stored redundantly.

The current character-based application needs to be converted to a GUI environment. Since we are now moving to a GUI Designer/2000 environment, we need to set up standards, methodology, and CASE templates and document how applications will be designed in the future.

VI. Project Scope

In this project, we will only make essential modifications to the underlying database structure to minimize the cost of data conversion. We will develop the structure of a Designer/2000–based methodology and GUI design standards. Then we will build a Developer/2000–based front-end to support required functionality. We will not support any ad hoc reporting or query capability, or interfacing with any other XYZ systems.

VII. Solution

We propose to complete this project in two phases. Phase I will determine XYZ's GUI design and application development standards, lay out the application and development methodology, and perform some prototyping on the Staff ID database. In phase II, we will apply these standards to the problem of re-engineering the Staff ID database.

We will deliver a re-engineered Staff ID database and a set of applications that will act as the front-end of that database. Of course, if we change the data structure, we will have to make some modifications to the Reports 2.5 application that generates the XYZ phone book.

ERD

Figure 3-1 shows the basic data model for the XYZ Staff ID system based on preliminary discussions with management. The diagram indicates that individuals can have multiple relationships of different types within an organization and that

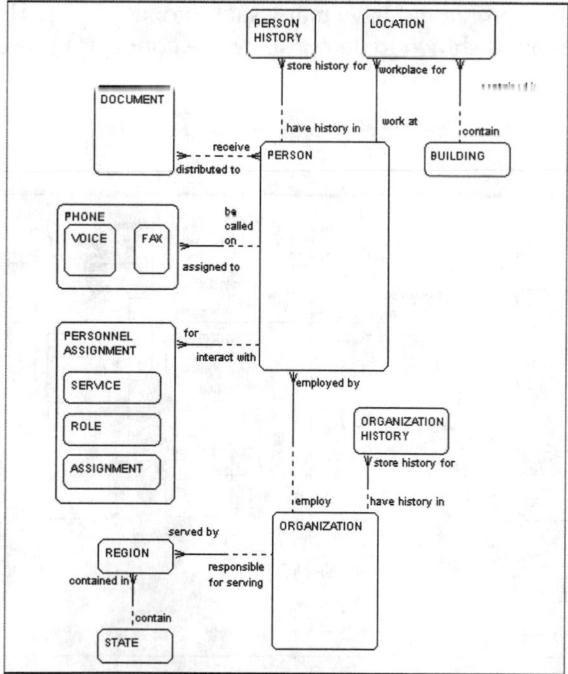

FIGURE 3-1. *Strategy ERD*

individuals can have multiple phones. The diagram also indicates that we will be tracking changes over time (history) for both people and organizations.

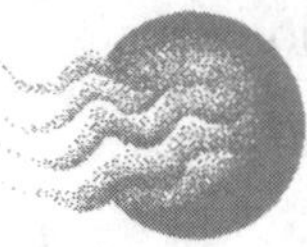

NOTE
In the diagram in Figure 3-1, the many-to-many relationship between persons and documents is not resolved, but the many-to-many relationship between persons and organizations is resolved. If this relationship had not been resolved, the diagram would be less clear. Also note that this diagram is limited because a phone cannot be shared by people and any particular phone must be of only one type. However, for a strategy ERD, this is okay since it is just trying to capture the high-level business requirements: that is, that individuals can have only one phone.

Process Flow Diagram

One of the principal process flows associated with the system is the hiring of employees. This process is represented in Figure 3-2.

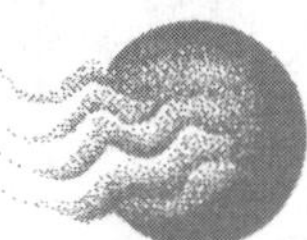

NOTE
This system would have many such process flows. This one simple example is shown to demonstrate the concept. Process flows are discussed in more detail in Chapter 6.

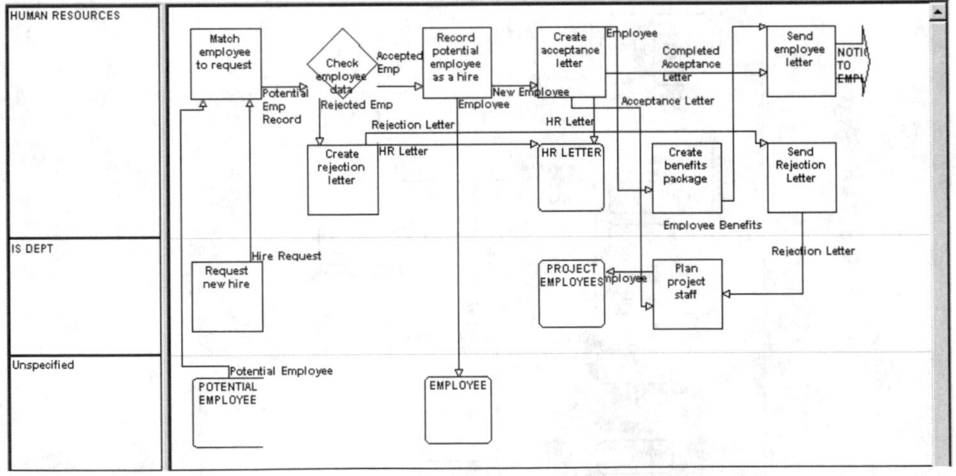

FIGURE 3-2. *Strategy process flow*

VIII. Cost-Benefit Analysis

The benefits of the new system for XYZ are listed next, along with the associated costs for the development of the proposed system.

Benefits

- Almost all applications will be generated using Designer/2000 so changes to the model can be propagated to the applications through a straightforward regeneration process.
- When phase I is complete, a validated Designer/2000-based development methodology will be in place that can be used for other application development projects.
- A solid set of GUI standards enforcing a consistent look and feel throughout all GUI applications will also be in place.
- The new system will be much more user friendly, requiring significantly less time in data entry and user training.
- At the end of phase II, the underlying data structure will be much more logically organized. This logical organization will decrease future development time because applications will be simpler to develop and the data structure will be easier for developers to use.

Costs

Both phases I and II are heavily dependent upon whether we use off-the-shelf GUI development standards already built or standards custom designed for XYZ. Assuming the first option, using GUI standards similar to those built for other users with minimal rework required, we estimate the cost of phases I and II to be approximately $50,000 per phase. This assumes a time and materials contract and represents our best estimate of cost based on currently available information.

IX. Project Organization and Staffing

The proposed system will require two developers and one project manager for the duration of the project. One person from the Human Resources department will be required half-time on the project development team.

In addition, time will be required from middle and upper management in the Human Resources area to periodically review the project status.

X. Workplan

We will complete the project in two phases. Time estimates are best guesses based on past experience and current information.

Phase I

1. Prototype application suite to validate GUI standards (1 to 10 days). Building the prototype is a simple, one-day task. If our GUI standards are not satisfactory, we will need to spend additional time modifying these standards to suit your needs.
2. Set Designer/2000 preferences (5 to 10 days). There are 450 preferences to set.
3. Create Designer/2000 template (5 to 10 days). As we dig this far into the generation process, there will be a clear need to re-engineer the template.

Phase II

1. Redesign database (5 days).
2. Create storyboard application (3 to 10 days). We will build the whole application as quick screen shots so you will have an idea how it will look. If you are not satisfied with our first try, extra time will be required to redo the storyboard.
3. Build detailed design book (2 to 5 days). For each application, we will need to describe how it functions. The level of complexity of the applications will determine how long this phase will take.
4. Module design within Designer/2000 (10 days). We are guessing that we will have 50 modules to build. This will take some time.
5. Generate and modify modules (10 days).
6. Engineer changes into templates (5 to 10 days). The time needed for this step will depend on the number of modifications required for each module. Only complex modules will need significant template modification.
7. Build system documentation (5 days). Most system documentation will already be included in the design book or can be generated using Designer/2000. We are allocating a week for cleanup and quality assurance (QA).

8. Build user documentation (5 to 10 days). With user feedback, this step always takes longer than originally planned.
9. Testing and QA (5 to 10 days). We will audit the applications to ensure that they meet the design specifications of the design book.

XI. Business Impact

Because the scope of this project is so small, the business impact was discussed under Benefits (see Section VIII).

XII. Strategy Document Conclusions

By setting up GUI and design standards that can be used for future system development and restructuring the existing database, we will make the XYZ Staff ID system more efficient and user friendly.

When Is the Strategy Phase Complete?

How do you determine when the Strategy phase is finished? A rule of thumb is that it is finished when all major players believe it is finished. This consensus is formalized when everyone involved signs the strategy document. There are no objective criteria for determining completion. However, it is important to gather and verify as much information from both users and in-house systems staff as possible. If the analyst does not get an approval from the primary user, then the definition of whether or not the system is complete is ambiguous. The analyst must put in writing that if access to the proper individuals is denied, he or she cannot be held responsible for the outcome of the total project.

It is up to the analyst to write a complete strategy document that covers all sections of the project. This should be a joint effort with the user community. This contract is executed when all parties sign, thus binding both analysts and users to the stated scope and deliverables.

The Strategy Phase in Designer/2000

Designer/2000 supports all the diagramming work you perform in the Strategy phase as the following table shows.

Activity or Deliverable	Designer/2000 Tool
Create strategy process flow diagram	Process Modeller
Create strategy ERD	ER Diagrammer

These two diagrammers represent the functions and data in the system and are excellent tools for communicating with users and the development team, and checking whether your understanding of what the system should do is complete and accurate.

The discussion here of the methods you use to work with these diagrammers assumes that you have read the section, "The Designer/2000 Interface" in Chapter 2. These diagrammers use the Designer/2000 standard interface described in that section, and you start both from the Designer/2000 window, also discussed in that section.

Process Modeller

The objective of the Process Modeller in the Strategy phase is to produce a complete high-level picture of the system for communication to management or users. The Process Modeller lets you diagram the processes and flows of data to and from other processes and data stores. Additionally, the Process Modeller shows the organization units (org units) that perform the processes and own the stores, which is a valuable piece of information and one to which nontechnologists can instantly relate.

This tool is useful as a business process re-engineering (BPR) diagrammer, where you show the current system and propose new methods for completing the tasks. In the Strategy phase, however, you are not so much concerned with BPR as with accurately identifying the current system or proposed new system, and this tool works quite well for both purposes. Note that while this tool stores quite a few details about the data stores or flows, it does not represent the data usage (the entity and attributes they consist of). The strength of this tool is in the non–data process details it stores and its display of the organization units.

Basic Techniques

Working with the Process Modeller is similar to working with the other diagrammers. You use similar menu and toolbar sets and the same kind of mouse actions. This discussion, therefore, concentrates on what is different about this diagrammer and assumes that you understand the material in the section "The Designer/2000 Interface" in Chapter 2. Be sure to use the help system and cue cards for detailed information on how to perform an action when you need more information or a reminder on something that momentarily may have slipped your mind.

Opening a Diagram You open a diagram the same way as in the other diagrammers (using **File→Open** or the Open button). The diagram will appear in the Process Modeller window as in Figure 3-3. If you need to create a new diagram, you select the New button (or choose from the File menu) and identify the root (or base) process, which is the process that the diagram represents. The root process contains all the processes you will diagram and is not actually visible in the diagram itself. It is similar to the outer process in a dataflow diagram—all processes are within it—although the dataflow diagram (DFD) actually shows the process box in the diagram. The root process can be any process that you have already defined or, if the process does not exist, one that you create at that point by pressing the Create New Root Process button. The process definition box will pop up and give you a chance to enter the short definition and label for this new process. Then the drawing area will appear with one organization unit: Unspecified.

Drawing Objects You place an object on the diagram in one of two ways: you create it by selecting the corresponding button in the drawing toolbar and drawing it on the screen, or you retrieve an existing object from the repository with the menu sequence **Edit→Include→Process Step**. (If you were including an object other than a process step, you would select that type from the **Edit→Include** menu instead of **Process Step**.) A list of elements will appear, and you can choose one or

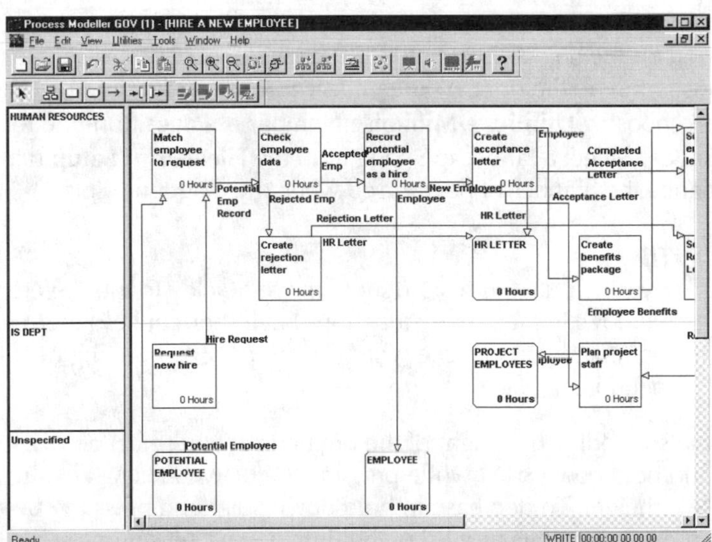

FIGURE 3-3. *Process Modeller diagram*

more from that list. (Hold down the CTRL key and click to make multiple selections.) If the element is a function, you can include the flows as well by checking the Include Flows check box. When you draw an object such as a process, store, trigger, or outcome in the Process Modeller, you have to choose an org unit to drop it into; the org unit represents the owner or source of that element. In addition, flows require an object on either end, so you click one process or store and hold the mouse button while dragging the mouse to another before releasing the button.

You can create org units the same way you create other objects. When you select the appropriate button and click in the org unit area, a new *swim lane* representing the organization unit appears. You can create subunits of a unit by selecting the button and clicking within an existing org unit. This will make the new org unit a child of the one you dropped it into. If you just want to create a new org unit on the top level, drop it on the Unspecified unit. There are menu choices to hide or display the child org units of a parent: **View→Drill Up Organization** when you have the parent selected to hide the child units and **View→Drill Down Organization** when you have the parent selected to also show the child units. When the parent has children, it will have an ellipsis (. . .) in the lower-left corner to signal you that children exist. You use the Unspecified org unit for objects that have no single owner or an unknown owner.

When you drop an object onto the diagram or move an existing object, it will snap to a certain location determined by an invisible grid. You cannot change the size of that grid, although you can change the size of all objects in the Preferences window by choosing **Edit→Preferences** as in Figure 3-4. The size of the org unit is variable based on the objects you put in it. The width expands as soon as you move objects farther to the right. You can decrease the width if no objects occupy the space by choosing **Utilities→Minimise Number of Pages** from the menu. In addition, you can select a landscape page from the **File→Print Setup** dialog box. This will change the number of pages used when the diagram prints.

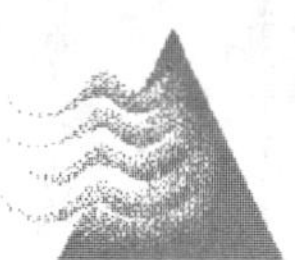

TIP
Pressing CTRL-F is a shortcut to move quickly to the Preferences window. In fact, many functions have shortcut keys identified with them, and you can see which key to press by looking next to the menu item.

You can also modify the height of the org units. If you select an org unit label on the left and hold down SHIFT while pressing the DOWN ARROW key, the org unit will increase in height. To decrease it, hold down SHIFT and press the UP ARROW key. You can move org units around by holding down CTRL and pressing the UP or DOWN ARROW key.

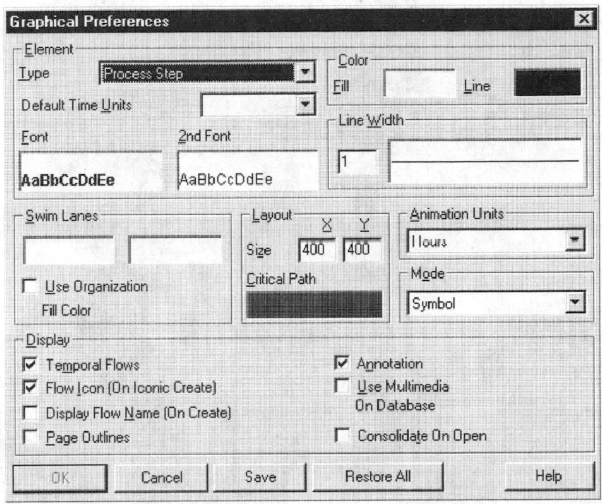

FIGURE 3-4. *Preferences window*

You will find that if you provide alternating colors for the org units, the diagram is easier to read, because the eye can follow one color horizontally to see what the org unit owns. You accomplish this on the **Edit→Preferences** screen in the swim lanes area by clicking on the swim lane color. You can also specify in this same area that the swim lanes take the color of the corresponding org unit title box.

You should practice this and other basic techniques so the activities do not slow you down when you are creating a diagram.

Naming Objects You normally follow some naming convention when creating the objects in the Process Modeller. One common standard is the use of phrases in mixed case starting with verbs (since they represent an action) as the process names: for example, "Request new employee hire." The names of the flows themselves are usually nouns, because they represent "things," in lowercase format: for example, "employee profile." The names of data stores are usually either uppercase or mixed-case nouns that are the same or similar to the names of the flows that go into them: for example, "Employee." Triggers and outcomes are named like processes as they are events that imply action. If you change your mind and need to change the name of an object (or even its type) after you create it, you can display the Properties window (by double-clicking the object) and select the Specific tab as in Figure 3-5.

Using the Symbol Set The set of symbols you use in the Process Modeller, as shown in Figure 3-6, is relatively small. A *process step* represents a process or

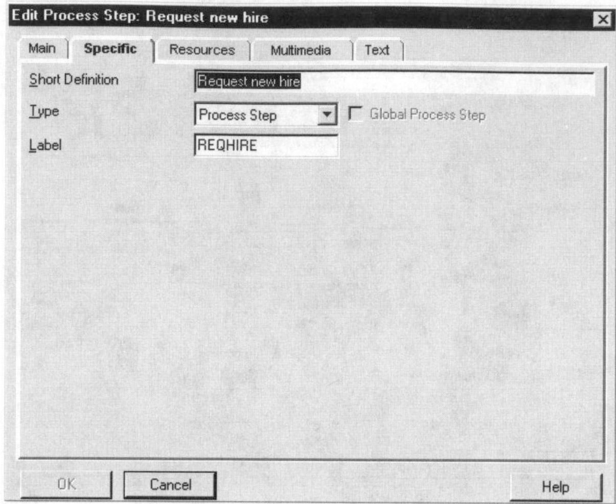

FIGURE 3-5. *Specific property tab*

function, a *flow* shows the data flowing from one process to another or to a store, a *store* symbolizes a collection of data that is not moving in a flow but is stored somewhere, a *trigger* is an event that starts a process from a source external to the system, and an *outcome* is an event that sends data outside the system or triggers a process outside the system.

These symbols have different types to represent details that you might want to specify for an object. For example, a process could be a type of process step, decision point, data entry, or report. Since the type of the object is one of its properties, you can obtain a report later on the objects and their types. In addition, the type determines how the symbol appears in Enhanced Symbol mode.

You can display the diagram in three modes: *Symbol,* which shows boxes and flows but no distinction between types of objects as in Figure 3-7; *Enhanced Symbol,* which shows the objects with distinctive symbols for different types as in Figure 3-8; and *Iconic,* which shows the objects as small pictures as in Figure 3-9. As mentioned before, the main container for objects in this diagrammer represents the owner of the objects: the organization unit.

Performing Functional Decomposition The Process Modeller allows you to perform *functional decomposition,* which breaks down a process (function) into its component processes. Each diagram represents one base process and the detail processes that comprise it. For each process displayed, you can create a separate diagram that represents the processes that make it up. For example, you may have

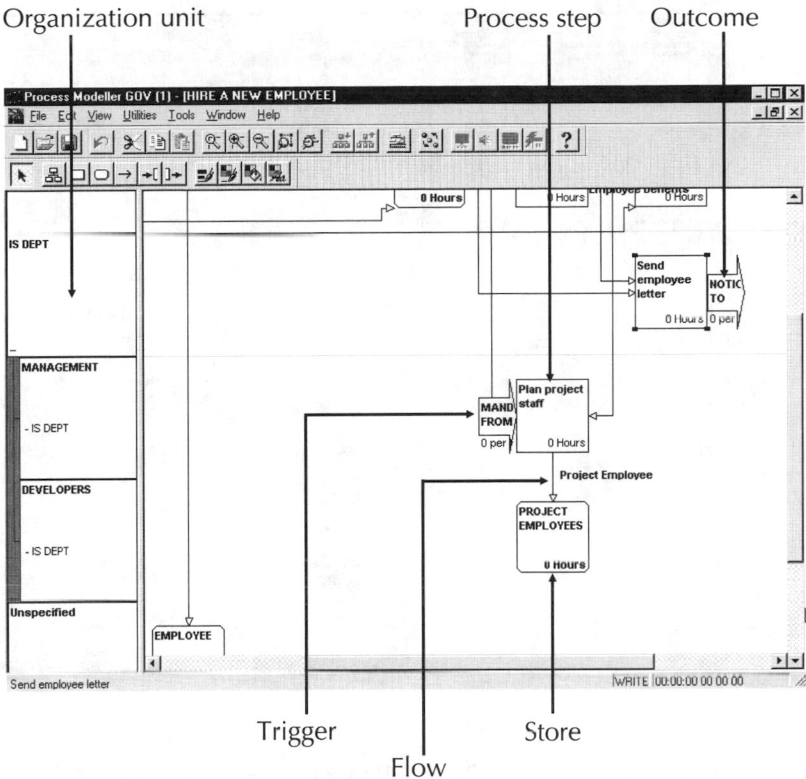

FIGURE 3-6. *Process Modeller symbol set*

a process called "Hire new employee" that has a dataflow to another process on the same diagram. You may want to break the process into the steps that compose it, so you create another diagram that has the process you want to decompose as its root process. In effect, you drill down into the details of a process. The diagram you create in this way is a separate diagram, but it is linked to the upper-level one. Thus, if you select the process and choose **File→Open Down** from the menu, the next level of diagram opens in the Process Modeller window. If you are in a lower-level diagram, you can select **File→Open Up**, and the upper-level diagram will open regardless of whether or not it is currently open.

Properties Text Tab The Text tab for the element properties (process, flow, or store) gives you a place to enter notes and descriptions to document the object. You can choose among several categories of text to place here and you can cut, copy, and paste between them with the CTRL-X, CTRL-C, and CTRL-V keys,

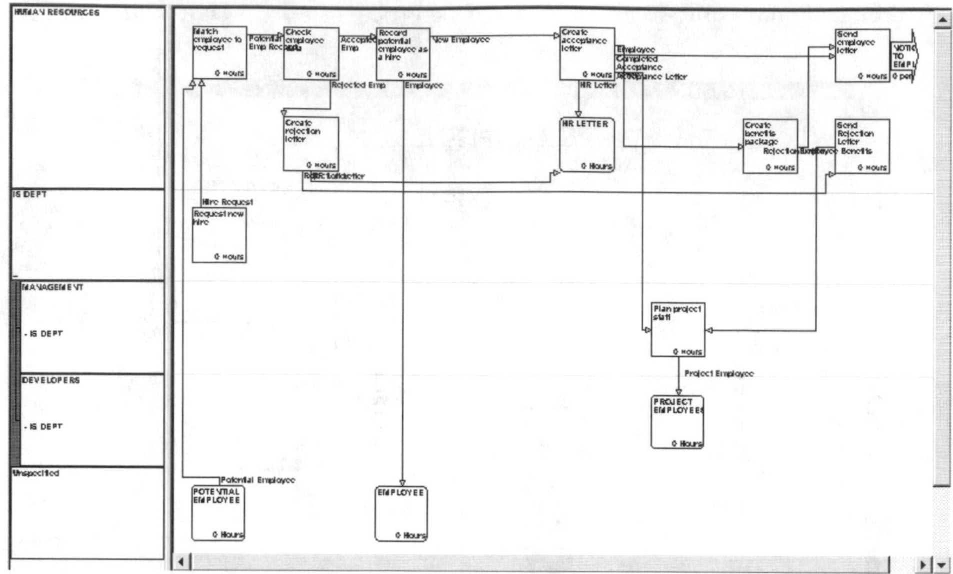

FIGURE 3-7. *Symbol mode*

respectively. These text items serve as documentation only, and they are available for reports on the objects in the diagram.

Advanced Techniques

The techniques discussed in the preceding paragraphs will enable you to use the basic functionality of the Process Modeller and will probably suffice for the Strategy phase. If you want to enhance your diagram or add pizzazz to it for a presentation, however, you need to apply some advanced techniques.

Allocating Time and Costs One distinctive feature of the Process Modeller diagrammer over the others in the Designer/2000 tool set is that it allows you to assign expected resource usage time and cost, in various units, to each process, flow, and store. The Main tab for these objects (shown in Figure 3-10) has time and cost information that you can change and modify. This information is available for reports (such as an Activity Based Costing report in Repository Reports). The information also affects how the diagram runs if you animate it; the times you assign to the processes and flows determine how long each item is active in the animation. You can also use the Resources tab to note the resources required or the quality factor for a process, flow, or store.

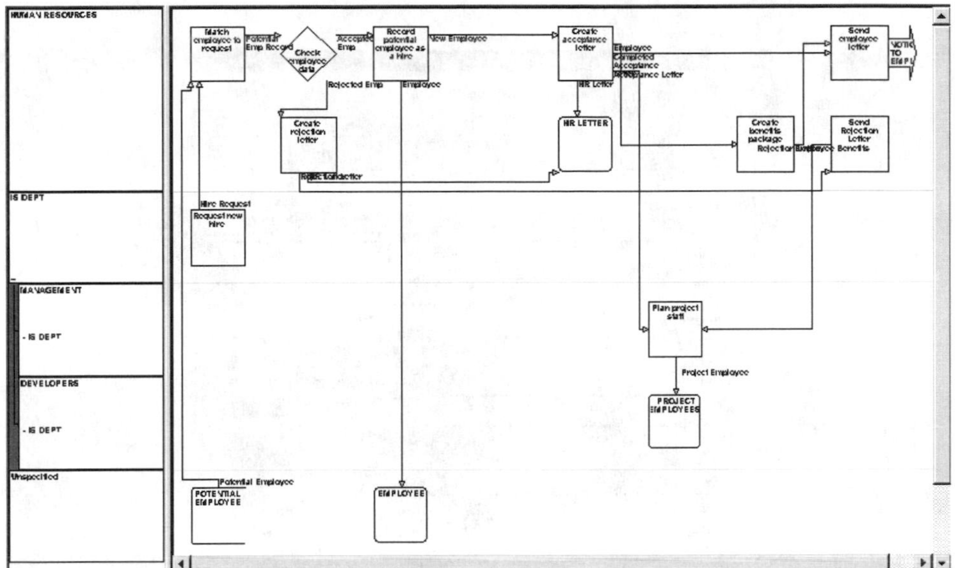

FIGURE 3-8. *Enhanced Symbol mode*

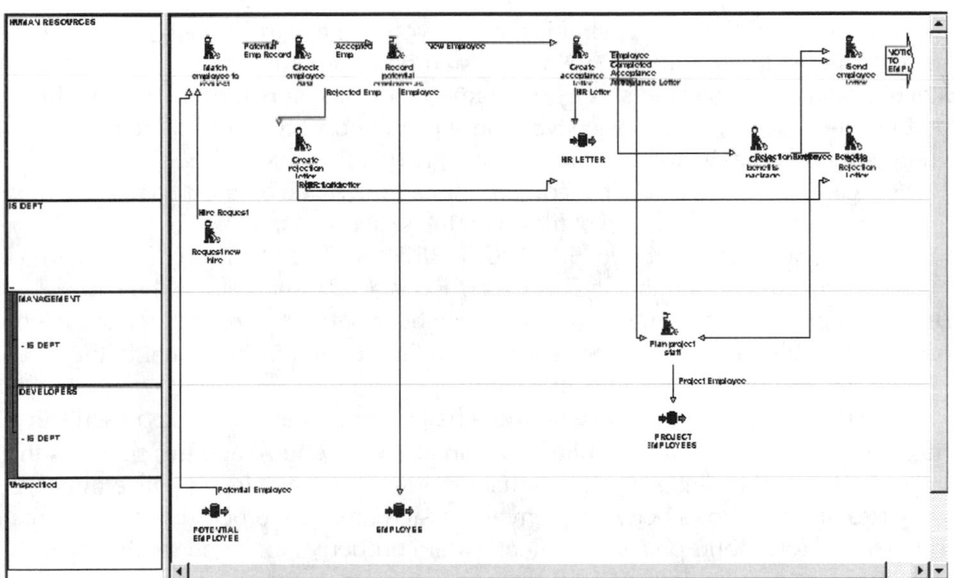

FIGURE 3-9. *Iconic mode*

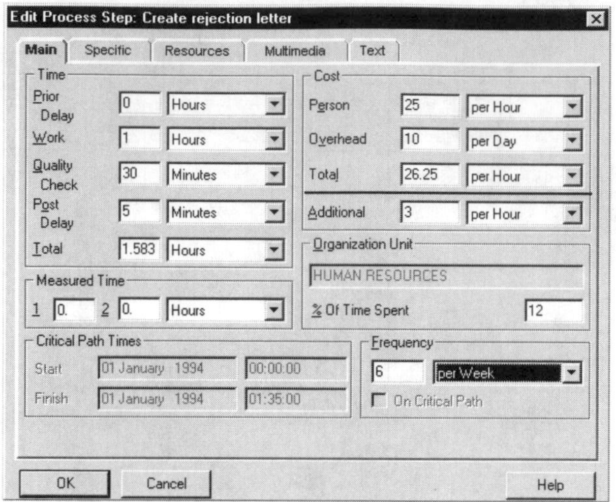

FIGURE 3-10. *Main tab for specifying time and cost*

Creating Multimedia Presentations One powerful feature of the Process Modeller is its multimedia capabilities, which you can assign for each item using the Multimedia tab (Figure 3-11). You can start other programs by adding an Execution String property to specify the name of the program to run. This enables the Execute Program button whenever you select the object in the diagrammer, so when you press that button, the program assigned to the object runs.

You can also select a starting icon for animation. This icon must have the suffix "1" and must be part of a group of files with the suffixes "2" and "3" for the animation to work (for example, BIKE1.ICO, BIKE2.ICO, BIKE3.ICO). If you define an icon name and ensure that the necessary icons are present (or use the icons Oracle supplies), when you press the Animate button, the Process Modeller cycles through icon files 1, 2, and 3 and repeats for a time period proportional to the amount defined on the Main properties tab.

You declare what actual time period a half second of animation represents in the animation options dialog (**Utilities→Animation→Options**) and this specifies the proportion of real business time to animation time. For example, you have three processes and two flows between them and assign times for processes of two hours and flows of four hours on each element's Main property tab. If you set the animation options dialog Time Step amount to two hours, when you animate the

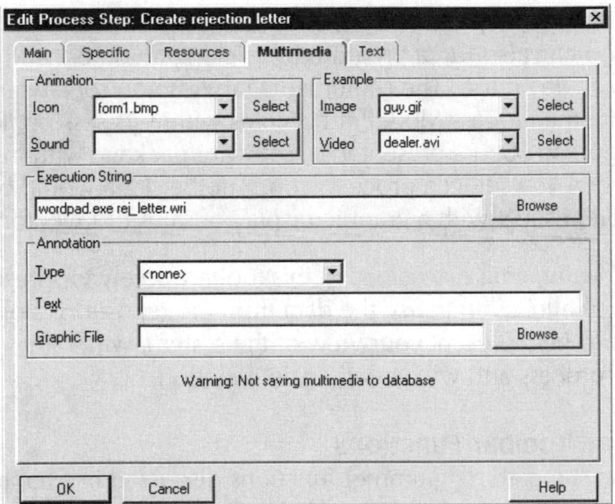

FIGURE 3-11. *Multimedia tab dialog box*

diagram, each process will take a half second and each flow will take one second. By watching the animated diagram, you will get an idea of the time (although compressed in duration) that the business process takes to complete each of its steps. This can help you identify bottlenecks in the process flows that need to be improved.

Other multimedia capabilities define Image, Sound, and Video properties on the Multimedia tab. If you have defined an image viewer, sound player, and video player program in the **File→Configuration→Basic** menu item, you can attach an image, sound, or video clip (or all three) to this object. Then when you select the object in the Process Modeller, the corresponding button on the toolbar will be enabled, and you can "play" the object. This feature allows you to use a video clip or picture file to represent a process to help explain it to an audience. These image, sound, and video clips can be stored in the database if you have the resources and if you have checked the proper box in the **File→Configuration→Advanced** dialog box (or in the **Edit→Preferences** dialog box).

The Multimedia tab also provides a group of annotations you can attach to an object. The annotation is a text or graphic (.BMP or .DIB file) or both, that appears on the diagram next to the object (in all view modes) to explain it. To display any annotations, you must turn on the Annotation preference (**Edit→Preferences**). Annotations are useful tools for including text and images that describe your objects on a diagram.

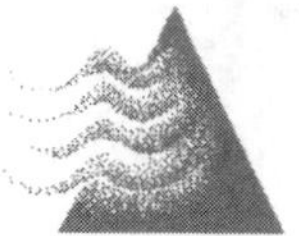

TIP

You can also run a program by clicking an object and clicking the Execute button. The Multimedia tab lets you specify another program that the Process Modeller executes within its session. For example, you can open a presentation software package with a slide show when you select a process icon. Another idea would be to run a spreadsheet with a graphic display of sales or inventory.

Clearly, the multimedia extensions of this tool are solely for presentation purposes, but they allow you to use the data from the repository along with multimedia files to help present your view of the system, which may assist in the communication process and will, surely, gain attention.

Other Menu and Toolbar Functions

In addition to the standard diagrammer functions discussed in Chapter 2 and the Drill Up/Down Organization and Open Up/Down functions mentioned earlier in this chapter, the Process Modeller menu contains some other items. The toolbar buttons, other than those on the drawing toolbar, that are not part of the standard set handle some of the new menu features, providing multimedia execution buttons and Drill Up/Down buttons. The Tools, Window, and Help menus all have the expected items.

File Menu As mentioned in Chapter 2, you can include summary information in the diagram definition and also include it on the diagram as a title block. Choose the **Summary Information** item from the File menu and check the items you want on the title block.

The File menu also includes additional menu items for **Configuration→Basic** and **Configuration→Advanced**. The Configuration - Basic window (see Figure 3-12) lets you specify up to five programs that will attach to the Tools menu. This gives you a way to run a program directly from the Process Modeller without having to go back to the operating environment to call it. The other areas in the basic configuration window allow you to indicate which directories contain the files the Process Modeller needs for Iconic mode and multimedia capabilities and what commands (programs) you use to edit and preview these icon, sound, image, and video files.

The Configuration - Advanced window, shown in Figure 3-13, allows you to specify preferences for how the Process Modeller lays out symbols in this diagrammer for the whole application system. These preferences apply globally, and after you make any changes here you need to exit and reenter the Process Modeller for them to take effect.

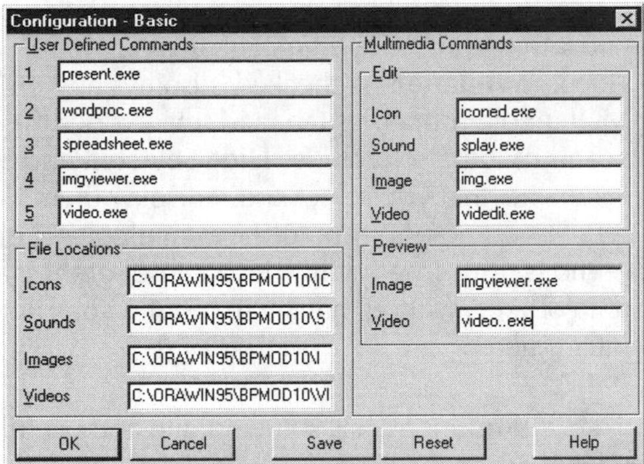

FIGURE 3-12. *Configuration - Basic window*

Edit Menu The only nonstandard button in the Edit menu is the **Element** item, which allows you to go to an element's Property window without selecting **Edit→Properties** on the menu or double-clicking. This option provides a quick way to go to a particular element and is useful on large diagrams where you may not be able to find the element easily.

Configuration - Advanced
Default Icons
Process Step bubble1.bmp
Store dollar1.bmp
Flow bike1.bmp
Miscellaneous
Use Element Preference Set
Icon Data File
Browse
Application Preferences
Use 3D Controls
Fill Label On Create
Use Multimedia On Database
Consolidate On Diagram Open
Flow Icon On Iconic Create
Display Flow Name
Obstruction Routing
OK
Cancel
Help

FIGURE 3-13. *Configuration - Advanced window*

View Menu The View menu contains several nonstandard items in addition to **Drill Up/Down Organization** and the **Symbol**, **Enhanced Symbol**, and **Iconic** view modes already described. **Annotation**, if checked, displays any object annotations you defined on the Multimedia properties tab, and Image does the same for images defined for elements. This menu also includes **Hide Selected** and **Show Hidden** options, which hide elements that you select and redisplay them, respectively. These options are useful if you do not want to show all elements on a particular diagram to someone who is concerned only with a subset of the objects; you can temporarily hide certain objects without having to modify your diagram and then redisplay them at a later time.

Utilities Menu The Utilities menu has some unique and useful items, including options for the following:

- The **Animation** submenu manages animation as it is running.
- The **Multimedia** submenu starts a multimedia event (Image, Sound, Video, Program) for an element if that element has an event defined. These options are also activated by the multimedia toolbar buttons.
- **Restore Graphical Preferences** restores the default set of preferences saved for a diagram after you have made changes to the preferences.
- **Update Selected** updates properties of all elements in a group that you select by dragging a selection box around them or holding down CTRL and clicking to select multiple items.
- **Calculate Critical Path** and **Reset Critical Path** manage the critical paths of elements that affect the amount of time the whole process will take. Any changes made to a component of the critical path affect the duration of the process.
- **Export Data** exports data to another format and creates a file with element information you can import into a spreadsheet or another program so you can print or manipulate the data.

Where Does This Information Go?

The objects you enter in the Process Modeller show up again when you create other function diagrams using the Dataflow Diagrammer and Function Hierarchy Diagrammer. They also flow through the SDLC into the Analysis and Design phases and appear in the Repository Object Navigator with the names shown in Table 3-1.

You can use the functions created here as process steps in the Function Hierarchy Diagrammer or Dataflow Diagrammer. The flows and stores can be worked into your dataflow diagram as well. The resource allocation information and business unit assignments are relevant only in the context of this diagrammer,

Process Modeller Element	Repository Element and Use in SDLC
Datastores	Datastores; cross-checks for data usage on functions
Organization units	Business units; used to group modules for the module network structure in the Design phase
Process steps	Business Functions; used by the Application Design Wizard to create modules
Triggers and Outcomes	Events—also called "Function/Events - Triggering" as a subnode of Business Functions; used to document which functions cause which others to begin
Flows	Dataflows (Source and Destination) subnodes under Business Functions and under Datastores; used to cross-check data usage in functions and generate parameters to the modules derived from these functions

TABLE 3-1. *Process Modeller Elements and Repository Elements*

but you can report on them using the BPR modeller node in the Repository Reports tool. The business unit assignments will actually assist the Application Design Wizard when it determines how to group functions into modules later in the life cycle.

Entity Relationship Diagrammer

Whereas the Process Modeller concerns itself with the functional side of the business area, the Entity Relationship Diagrammer (ER Diagrammer) concentrates on the data side and on the details of the data. The data represented here is essentially logical; that is, there may not be actual *physical* tables or data structures that handle the entities on a one-to-one basis. An entity represents one instance or occurrence of an object, so an EMPLOYEE entity would appear on the diagram as a box representing one employee. In addition, the entity relationship diagram normally contains the attributes or details for each entity. Relationships appear on the entity relationship diagram as lines with "crows feet" or forks to represent the "many" side of a relationship and as a single line for the "one" side of a relationship. You show the optionality of a relationship using dotted lines for an optional relationship and solid lines for a mandatory (required) relationship.

In the Strategy phase, it is important to be complete in identifying entities, but it may not be necessary to identify all attributes of those entities. In fact, you could show the entity relationship diagram with no attributes at all to get a sense from the user as to whether or not the entity side is complete. The diagram at this stage need not be complex or normalized, but all business entities should appear on it.

Relationships are as important as the entities. Designer/2000 treats relationships as attributes that describe the entity (on the many side or, in the case of a one-to-one relationship, on one of the one sides). Therefore, you do not create a separate attribute for the many side (foreign key) entity to represent the link to the unique identifier of the other entity. The relationship itself serves as an attribute, and when you create tables from those entities, the relationship creates a column on the foreign key side. Figure 3-14 shows an Entity Relationship Diagrammer session.

Basic Techniques

The ER Diagrammer, like the Process Modeller, follows many of the common Designer/2000 interface standards mentioned in Chapter 2. However, there are particular considerations for entity relationship diagrams, and this section discusses the specific way Designer/2000 handles the objects or elements in the diagram. As

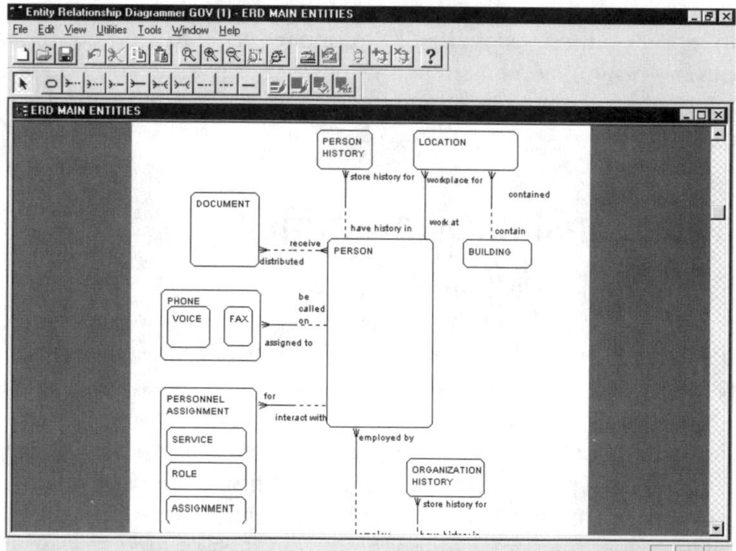

FIGURE 3-14. *Entity Relationship Diagrammer window*

before, this discussion provides the information you need to grasp the tool quickly, but you should consult the online help system and cue cards for assistance with actions that you find obscure.

Opening a Diagram You open a diagram in the ER Diagrammer in the same way as in any other Designer/2000 diagrammer: by using the **File→Open** menu choice or the Open button. If you want to create a new diagram, you just click the New button or choose **File→New** from the menu. Either method opens a new window with a drawing surface that you can fill with new objects. You can change the diagram orientation (landscape or portrait) in the **File→Print Setup** dialog box, and can create extra pages by dragging any item off of the existing page. If you have blank pages, you can choose **Utilities→Minimise Number of Pages**, and the diagrammer will reduce the number of pages as best it can.

Drawing Objects You place objects on the diagram either by creating them with the drawing toolbar buttons or retrieving existing objects with the **Edit→Include** menu item. If you use the latter method to include existing entities, you can include the relationships between those entities at the same time. As with all diagrammers, once the objects exist in the repository, you can arrange them on any number of diagrams with different sets of other elements. When you save the diagram, Designer/2000 saves references to the repository elements but leaves the base objects alone.

Creating objects with the ER Diagrammer is as simple as clicking the toolbar button for the element you want to create and drawing it on the surface. If you are creating a relationship, you have to select the correct relationship button and click once on an existing entity to start the relationship, and once more on an existing entity to end it. When placing a new entity, you can click the entity button once and then click in the drawing area once (or drag out a box and release the mouse button) to place the entity. You can resize the entity directly on the drawing surface by selecting it and dragging its corner or side in or out.

If you need to create a subtype, draw the new entity within its supertype entity. An alert box will notify you that the subtype is now part of the supertype. If you want to create an arc (mutually exclusive) relationship, select all end labels on the side of the relationships where you want the arc to appear and select **Utilities→Create Arc**. If you want to delete a relationship from an arc, select the arc, select the relationship, and choose **Utilities→Remove From Arc** on the menu.

You create recursive ("pig's ear") relationships by clicking the appropriate relationship button, clicking one side of the entity, and then clicking another side of the same entity. The "from" and "to" ends will go to the same entity.

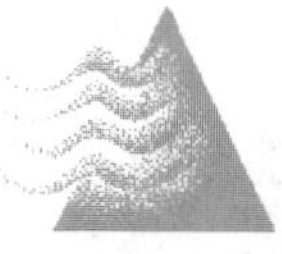

TIP

Remember that when you create a relationship, you need to draw the relationship in the order it appears on the button. Therefore, if you choose the >----- (many-to-one) relationship from the toolbar, the first entity you drop it on will be the "many" side, and the second will be the "one" side.

Usually you should avoid unnecessary angled, or *dog-leg,* relationship lines as they can make the diagram difficult to follow, but if you need one, select the relationship and hold down SHIFT as you click the mouse in the middle of the line and then drag the line. You can release the SHIFT key any time after the extra point appears. To eliminate that point, hold the SHIFT key and click the dog-leg point once.

You can use the Autolayout feature described in Chapter 2 in the section "The Designer/2000 Interface" to cycle through a random set of layouts. The Previous Layout button returns you to the last Autolayout setup. You might consider some system other than the random one: for instance, the traditional "crows fly south and east" system. This system places all relationship lines so the many sides are on the left and top of the relationship lines. This places the entities with the most frequency in the upper-left corner and those with the lowest frequency in the lower-right corner. You might choose another format, but some conscious system for arranging the entities will make your diagram easier to read.

Relationship names never seem to end up in the right place and sometimes need manual moving and resizing. You can resize the invisible box that contains a relationship name by clicking the name so you see the four corners and reshaping this box. This technique is useful if you want the relationship name to run over to more than one line. If it consists of more than one word and space is tight, you can make the box less wide but high enough for as many lines as you need. The clearest position for relationship names is close to the entity they describe. Double-check your diagram to be sure each relationship is clearly next to only one relationship and entity. If you can't tell which entity and relationship a name belongs to, select the name and the relationship will also be selected.

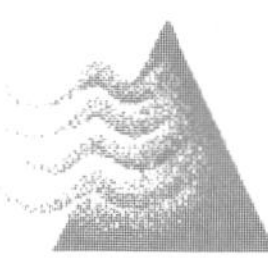

TIP

One technique that is useful with all elements is to modify the grid size (using **Edit→Preferences**) and turn Snap on. Then the objects you place and lines you draw will "snap" to the grid lines (invisible or not), and you will find creating straight lines much easier to do. **Edit→Preferences** also lets you display the grid, which will help you line up entities and relationships. The grid will print if it is displayed when you start printing the diagram.

Naming Objects Whenever you create a new element anywhere in Designer/2000, you have to assign a name and certain other characteristics to it. Entities require a name, short name, and plural name. If you do not fill in the latter two, Designer/2000 will fill them in with its best guess. Usually, this is fine, but keep in mind whenever you create an entity that the plural name is used as the table name. Therefore, if you do not like plural table names, you will not like Designer/2000's best guess in filling in this property, and you will want to specify the plural name explicitly using whatever you want as the table name. One common standard is to name entities with a word or short phrase that is a singular noun (because an entity is "a thing of significance").

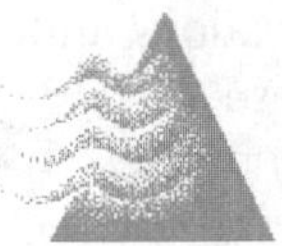

TIP
When filling in the new entity window, if you want the plural entity name to be the same as the normal entity name, you can select the text, press CTRL-C to copy, navigate to the plural name field, and press CTRL-V to paste. These edit keys (along with CTRL-X for cut) are available in most text-editing boxes.

Relationship names require a bit of thought when you first create them. When you draw relationships in the ER Diagrammer, you fill in the "from" name (the side of the relationship that starts it) and the "to" name (the side of the relationship that ends it). In addition to the name, you have to know the cardinality (one-to-many or many-to-many) and optionality (required or not) of the relationship. Also, you should understand how to read the entity relationship diagram.

Reading the Entity Relationship Diagram The entity relationship diagram is a communication tool as well as an analysis tool. The diagrams you produce say much about the business you are modeling, so if you will be cross-checking the model with users or clients, it is essential that you read or write everything that the diagram represents. Since people can readily understand the concept of an entity, most of your explanation should concern the relationships, which can represent sometimes complex business rules. You can use any system you want to name your relationships, but the traditional Oracle CASE method system uses this syntax:

Each *A* [may | must] be *relationship_name* [one and only one | one or more] *B*

A is the name of the entity on the from end of the relationship, *relationship_name* is the name of the relationship on the diagram, and *B* is the entity on the to end of the relationship. You choose one of the may/must and one-and-only-one/one-or-more pairs to represent the optionality of the from end and cardinality of the to end, respectively. For example, using the entity relationship diagram in Figure 3-15, you would construct the following narrative:

> "Each organization may be responsible for serving one or more regions; each region must be served by one and only one organization."

Notice that you need two sentences to fully describe the relationship because the relationship is two-sided. Also, both of the phrases start with "each" to clarify that the entity you are describing is a singular thing. The syntax makes both cardinality and optionality completely explicit and provides a standard and unconfusing way to read and understand the relationships. You may be tempted to say something like "There is a one-to-many relationship between organizations and regions," or "Each organization has many regions." The problem with these statements is that they do not clarify the exact relationship; they do not indicate that there are two sides to the relationship; and they do not explain which is the many side nor if it is mandatory or not.

Although this syntax is not mandatory, you should consider adopting it, because when Designer/2000 lists relationships on reports, it constructs the sentences using this template.

Using the Symbol Set There are only two main symbols in the ERD, as Figure 3-16 shows: entities and relationships. Entities can have subtypes (entities within them) that use the same entity symbols as the supertype. Relationships can have different cardinality and optionality values, but they are all essentially just lines

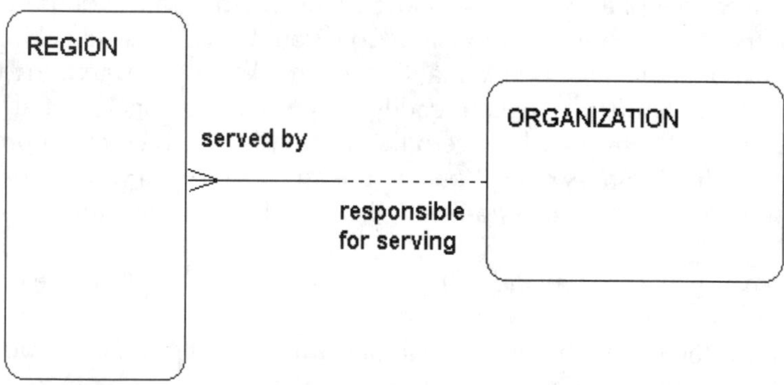

FIGURE 3-15. *Sample relationship*

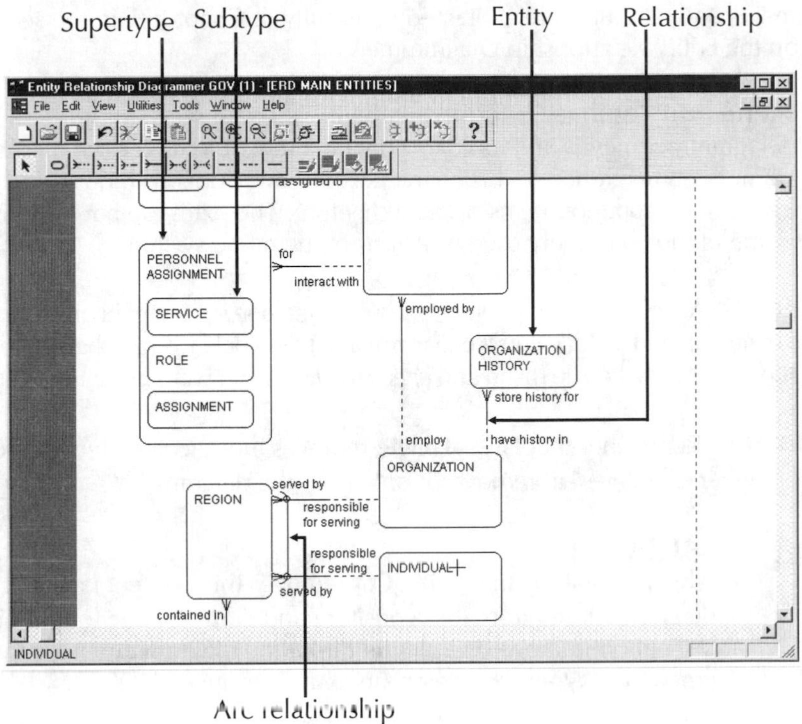

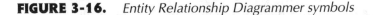

FIGURE 3-16. *Entity Relationship Diagrammer symbols*

between entities. Arc relationships appear as two or more relationships joined by a curved line symbol representing a mutually exclusive relationship.

Using Attributes and Domains A normal entity relationship diagram contains all attributes for all entities as well as designations of the datatypes and optionality. In addition, you can use *domains* to assist in creating attributes. A domain is a named collection of properties for attributes and columns, including datatype, size, decimal places, derivation (calculation expression), and the set of valid values. When you attach a domain to an attribute, the attribute takes on all characteristics of that domain. This makes defining the attribute easier and allows you to change all attributes in a domain by changing the domain definition and running a utility to propagate the changes.

You create the attribute definitions for an entity in the Entity property window. In the Strategy phase, you do not necessarily need to go into attribute details.

Domains and attributes are explained more fully in Chapter 6, in the section "More on the Entity Relationship Diagrammer."

Other Menu and Toolbar Functions

The ER Diagrammer menus and toolbars contain a few other items not discussed in Chapter 2 nor yet mentioned in this chapter. The View, Tools, Window, and Help menus contain the common items discussed before. The extra toolbar buttons handle some of the commonly used functions in the menu system.

File Menu As mentioned in Chapter 2, you can include summary information in the diagram definition and include it in the diagram as a title block. Choose the **Summary Information** item from the File menu and check the items you want in the title block.

Edit Menu Remember that **Edit→Delete** removes the selected element from the repository whereas **Edit→Cut** removes it only from the diagram.

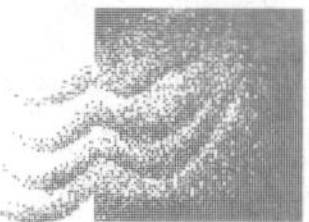

CAUTION

It bears repeating that **Edit→Cut** removes the element from the diagram but not from the repository and **Edit→Delete** (or pressing the DEL button) removes the element from the diagram and from the repository. When you delete an entity, Designer/2000 also deletes all attributes and attached relationships.

Utilities Menu The Utilities menu provides a number of ERD-specific functions. Before you use any of the layout choices, you should save your diagram because, although you can return to the last Autolayout, you cannot return to the original layout if you do not like any of the random layouts you use. If you have saved the diagram, you can always close the diagram without saving and reopen it in its original form.

The Utilities menu offers these options:

- **Autolayout** and **Previous Layout** change the diagram layout to a neatly drawn but random one and restore the previous Autolayout, respectively.

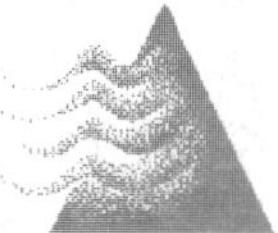

TIP

The first time you press the Autolayout button, you will not be able press Previous Layout to return to the previous layout but you can select **Edit→Undo** from the menu to go back to the last layout. After you press Autolayout the second time, the Previous Layout button will be available, so you can return to the previous layouts.

- **Autolayout to New Area** prompts you to use the mouse to draw an area as the target for the automatically laid out elements.
- **Autolayout to Same Area** repeats the Autolayout process in the same area you chose for the Autolayout to New Area function.
- **Minimise Number of Pages**, as already mentioned, reduces the number of pages Designer/2000 uses to show the diagram.
- **Rescale Diagram** resizes elements and fonts to fit on the number of pages you specify. This option is useful for diagrams migrated from CASE version 5.1 and can also be useful in an automatic layout.
- **Create Arc**, **Add to Arc**, and **Remove from Arc** let you create and modify arcs. These are also toolbar buttons, although the menu item may be enabled before the button is.
- **Table/Entity Retrofit** creates entity definitions from table definitions. This option is useful when you reverse engineer an existing system in the Design and Analysis phases in Designer/2000 as discussed in Chapter 5.
- **Update All Attributes within Domains** propagates changes in domains to attributes associated with those domains. Chapter 6 discusses this utility further.
- **Database Design Wizard** creates design objects (for example, tables and columns) from the analysis objects (for example, entities and attributes). Chapter 7 gives more details on this utility.
- **Generate C++ Classes** runs the C++ Object Layer Generator to create modules of this type. Chapter 10 explains how this works.
- **Function/Attribute Matrix** assigns attributes to functions if there are already entity usages for those functions. Chapter 5 discusses this utility in the context of the Dataflow Diagrammer.
- **Convert ERD 1.1 Diagrams** is helpful if you migrate the repository from Oracle CASE version 5.0 or 5.1 to Designer/2000. It converts the entity relationship diagrams to the new format.

Where Does This Information Go?

The entity, attribute, and relationship information in the strategy ERD carries over into the Analysis phase, where you modify and add to the definitions. No other diagrammers share these elements, although the Process Modeller, Dataflow Diagrammer, and Function Hierachy Diagrammer allow you to attach entity and attribute *usages*—which define the data sources for the process (function), flow, or

Strategy and Analysis Data Element	Design Data Element
Entity	Table
Attribute	Column
Primary unique identifier	Primary key constraint
One-to-many relationship	Foreign key constraint and foreign key column
Many-to-many relationship	Intersection table and foreign key constraints
Arc and subtype/supertype relationships	Single tables or multiple tables with special columns to link them

TABLE 3-2. *Strategy and Analysis Data Elements and Their Design Data Element Counterparts*

store—to their elements. In the Design phase, the elements transform from logical Analysis phase elements into the physical Design data objects, as Table 3-2 shows.

In addition, the table definition can reference the entity or entities it was created from. This is called a *table entity usage* and defines a link from the table to the entity for documentation and reverse engineering purposes.

Conclusion

At the end of the Strategy phase, the strategy document is delivered to the user for sign off. However, some issues may remain. What happens if the underlying strategy document needs to be changed after the Strategy phase has begun? This is an important issue since it involves fundamental changes in the structure of the system. In this case, the project team needs to take the change in strategy and walk it through the entire development process to determine its impact on the remainder of the project. This situation can result in considerable added expense and requires a rethinking of all system life-cycle deliverables. Try to avoid "scope creep." One way to avoid surprises is to work closely with the users during the development of all strategy document sections.

This chapter discussed all aspects of the Strategy phase, and it introduced the two Designer/2000 tools that can assist you greatly in this phase toward identifying and drawing process flows and entity relationships: the Process Modeller and ER Diagrammer. You will return to these tools briefly in the Analysis phase. The next chapter, though, will explore the Pre-Analysis phase and how Designer/2000 can help you perform the activities in this phase.

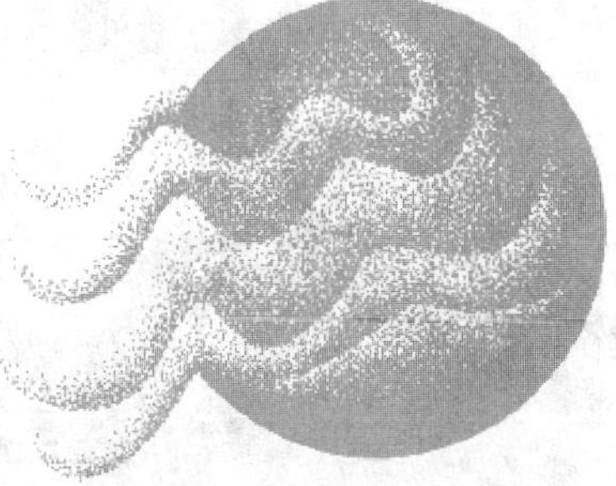

CHAPTER 4

Pre-Analysis

You're traveling through yet another project. A project of sight and sound but no mind. A journey into a wondrous land whose boundary is the budget. You are now entering the Analysis Zone. Apologies to Rod Serling.

In the Pre-Analysis phase, the goals are to plan the analysis process and to begin establishing analysis standards for Designer/2000. The deliverables for Pre-Analysis are the analysis plan and the plan or specifications for the continued use of Designer/2000. Since the goal of Analysis is to gather and organize all of the substantive user requirements, the analysis plan, when executed, should result in an understanding of what the business does and what kind of automated support it can use.

Overview of the Pre-Analysis Phase

The Analysis phase breaks logically into two parts: information gathering and requirements analysis. Within the information-gathering portion of Analysis, techniques for getting at user requirements include interviews, questionnaires, electronic bulletin boards, and joint application development (JAD) sessions, along with reviews of the legacy system, the report audit, and user and system documentation.

In requirements analysis, we extract the system requirements from the information gathered and place them in an organized structure. This can be done at both the unit level and, ultimately, at the system level. For example, at the unit level, after each interview, an ERD sketch, small function hierarchy, and or mini-process flow can be generated specific to that interview. Once some quantity of information has been gathered, some system-level requirements analysis can begin. In requirements analysis, the information from the various sources is synthesized in an effort to create the analysis ERD, analysis process flows, and overall function hierarchy.

As this synthesis takes place, gaps in the information are discovered along with conflicting information and inconsistent requirements. Therefore, the analyst must go back to the users and ask more questions and do more information gathering, which must then be integrated into what was collected previously. Thus the two aspects of the whole analysis process are not completely discrete or linear. There is a need to move back and forth between gathering the information and analyzing it.

Because of this need to alternate between gathering and analyzing business requirements, an essential aspect of the analysis plan is flexibility. As the project progresses through the Analysis phase, new sources of requirements become evident. The analysis plan needs to have a built-in mechanism for ongoing review to ensure that any opportunities for other areas of analysis are found, incorporated into the plan, and provisions made for resolving conflicts and inconsistencies, usually through JAD sessions. Of course, it is impossible to predict all possible new sources or areas of information that might be discovered; however, when creating the analysis budget, count on the likelihood that some unforeseen factors will arise.

The developers are the primary users of the analysis plan. The plan will serve as a guide through the Analysis phase. Other users of the analysis plan include the project leaders and the person in charge of quality assurance.

Within CADM, the Pre-Analysis phase is a transitional period between Strategy and Analysis in which the project team initiates and performs the preparation work and obtains approval to proceed with Analysis. The objectives of Pre-Analysis are:

- To develop a detailed workplan and schedule for the Analysis phase
- To reconfirm the project environment (standards, political environment, project staffing and organization, and conflict resolution)
- To define data collection strategies
- To define the format, structure, and contents of the requirements document

It is difficult to discuss the analysis plan without also thoroughly discussing all of the analysis topics. This chapter lays out the structure of the analysis plan without going into depth regarding how each part of the plan will be executed. Details of how to execute the analysis plan are deferred until their appropriate sections in Chapters 5 and 6.

Information Gathering

No single source of information for user requirements is sufficient. The analysis plan should account for multiple sources and information gathering methods. Interviews should be conducted with both high-level management and low-level system users. The analyst should walk through the existing business processes with employees at different levels and, if relevant, observe how the work is done.

A thorough audit of the legacy system should also be planned. Code walk-throughs of the legacy system will be required to determine the business rules implemented in the code.

The analysis plan should estimate the number of individuals that need to be interviewed and how much time should be spent with each one. It may be useful to conduct some of the actual interviews at this point. Doing some actual analysis as part of the Pre-Analysis phase will allow the analyst to better estimate the time required for the Analysis phase.

User-Supplied Requirements

Consider the following means of gathering information from people for inclusion in the analysis plan:

- Interviews
- Questionnaires
- Electronic bulletin boards
- Joint application development (JAD) sessions

The question, of course, arises, "Who should be interviewed or surveyed?" Never count on a single source of information. Whether this single source is an individual, a committee, or a group, all of the necessary information will not be elicited from one place. Interviews conducted with groups can be effective, but the group itself has a dynamic of its own. Each individual in the group should be interviewed individually as well.

You should interview users who have experience with the legacy system or will need to use the new system. These users can supply details regarding processes, data requirements, system functionality, and constraints.

To be successful, the analyst should talk to a variety of users. Some very important sources of information are the architects or maintainers of the legacy system. They often know more about how the system actually functions in their specific business environment than the users. Systems people, managers, and rank-and-file users may also have valuable input.

Interviews

Interviewing is a complex and important step. Open-ended interviews with users are the traditional requirements analysis method most commonly employed. In these interviews, one or more analysts sit down with one or more users. Such interviews are probably the most important source of user requirements in the design of a new system.

Interviewing managers is just as important as interviewing actual system users. Managers sometimes have a broader vision and better understanding of the overall process. They are often more open to re-engineering, although they may have less understanding of the day-to-day operations and decisions faced by the end users.

Legacy system developers can often make important contributions to the gathering of user requirements. Since they are very familiar with the existing system, they can provide information about requirements that are hard-coded in the legacy system.

Analysis cannot be performed without talking to representatives from all of the groups mentioned here. Talking to only one group results in an incomplete analysis. The workplan should allocate time for interview planning (including identifying candidates, setting the date, and developing questions), the conduct of the interview, and post-interview documentation and confirmation.

Questionnaires

Open-ended interviews require skilled interviewers and generate a considerable amount of information that is difficult to collate and analyze. This can be a very labor-intensive process. Using questionnaires is less labor intensive and less expensive. If carefully designed, questionnaires don't even need to be administered in person; they can be administered by mail or e-mail.

Analysis and collation of information from questionnaires is inexpensive. However, the creation of high-quality interviewing instruments is difficult. Inexpertly created interview questionnaires will generate misleading results.

JAD Sessions

A joint application development (JAD) session is a specific type of analysis and development interview. In a JAD session, you bring together several interested parties and attempt to move the project forward. JAD sessions are usually run with someone acting as a facilitator and can be very effective for solving specific analysis and design problems.

JAD sessions bring together many people at once, so they are very expensive and require extensive planning. A JAD session should always have a very specific agenda. If not run well, JAD sessions can degenerate into forums for venting opinions and for political posturing; run correctly, they can help forge a consensus among parties with differing needs.

Legacy System Review

In formulating the analysis plan, you must thoroughly review the legacy system. Unless the new system will be so radically different that the current system is irrelevant, a legacy system review is necessary. This review should include the elements discussed here.

Code Walkthrough

Business requirements are embedded within the legacy code. The analyst either needs to personally walk through the legacy system code or work with the legacy system developers to determine user requirements embedded in the code.

Report Audit

A report audit is a review and analysis of all the reports generated by the legacy system. The analyst should plan to perform a report audit to determine what reports will be retained, discarded, or changed from those generated by the original system.

User Walkthrough

The analyst must sit down with users and have them walk through actual business transactions in the legacy system. This will allow the analyst to see what parts of the system are being used and how they are used.

User and System Documentation Review

A review of the user documentation can frequently bring to light user requirements not found in any other source. The user documentation may discuss user requirements that, if the system is mature, may have been assumed for so long that no one mentions them. Similarly, a review of the system documentation, if it exists, can help uncover system requirements.

Requirements Analysis

All of the information gathering mechanisms generate pages of notes that must be analyzed. Each document must be read; and the relevant user requirements must be extracted for further processing. The number of requirements varies and serves as the backbone of the Analysis phase.

Designer/2000 has an element called Objectives which, at first glance, seems like it would suffice for storing requirements. However, there is really a difference between requirements and objectives. Nevertheless, Designer/2000 has no separate element type specifically for requirements. In addition to storing the requirements, you need to store the associations from requirements to other repository elements such as functions. One method you can use outside the repository is to build the tables for the requirements and associations to existing repository elements as the ERD in Figure 4-1 shows.

Alternatively, you can create a new Designer/2000 repository element, called Requirements, by employing the User Extensibility feature. If you also add extensions for the association elements needed to link these to the existing elements, such as functions, the system can be implemented entirely in Designer/2000. The implementation of these extensions in Designer 2000 is discussed at the end of this chapter in the section "Repository Administration Utility (RAU)."

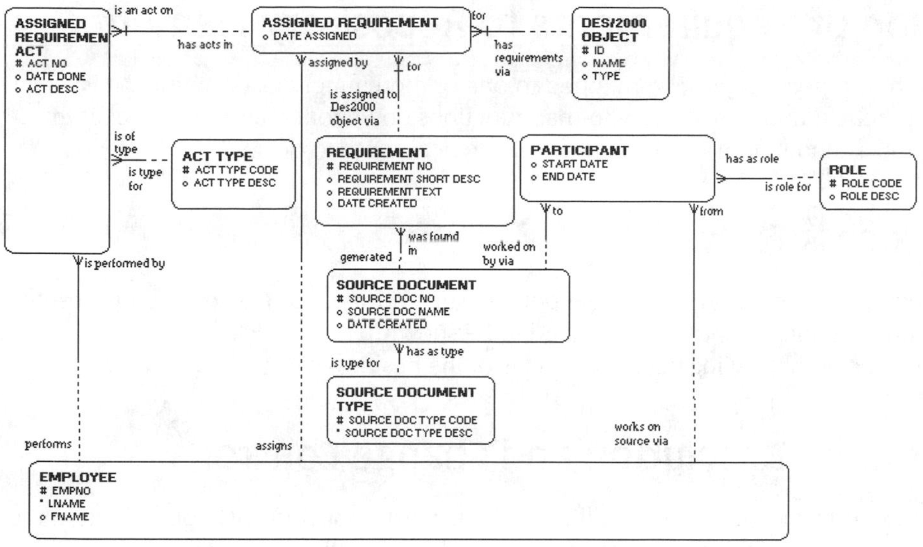

FIGURE 4-1. *Entity relationship diagram for tracking requirements*

Analysis ERD

The analysis ERD attempts to capture as many of the data-related business rules as possible in a diagram. No consideration is given to performance or to the feasibility or implementation of a rule. The only goal is to fairly represent the business requirements. Data-related business rules that cannot be implemented in the ERD are stated as text.

There is some disagreement among analysts as to the correct scope of an analysis ERD. Many analysts advocate a higher-level approach that ignores many details. Others take performance and other aspects of physical implementation into consideration when designing their ERD. Whatever approach you decide to take, it is essential that the approach is well documented and adhered to by all members of the design team.

Function Hierarchy

In Pre-Analysis, the function hierarchy serves to organize user requirements into functional areas. Little attempt should be made at this point to identify functions that will actually map to application modules.

Map of Requirements to Repository Elements

Each requirement must be mapped to one or more functions or entities. It is impractical and unnecessary to map functions down to the attribute level at this point, although it may sometimes make logical sense to do so.

Process Flows

Detailed process flows that show both existing business processes and proposed changes under the new system need to be shown. These process flows must be very specific, showing detailed aspects of the business.

Conflict Resolution and Change Control

Rules and procedures for handling conflicts must be specifically spelled out in the analysis plan—including a mechanism for dealing with conflicting user requirements.

The analysis plan should specify the procedures for making changes when new sources of requirements are found or when other changes need to be made to the analysis plan.

The Analysis Plan

The analysis plan describes the analysis document including the structure and format of the analysis document and how information will be gathered, tracked, and analyzed. It should describe each step in the analysis process in detail. Everything from who will be interviewed to the final format of the ERD and what the process flows will look like must be decided. For example, how will feedback to interview notes be given? Will notes be compiled at every meeting or weekly? At what point will user sign-off be required? The analysis plan should include answers to these questions in order to give the client a clear picture of what the analysis process will entail.

The analysis plan should provide estimates for a legacy system review, listing the resources needed, time estimates, and a description of interim deliverables. In addition, a process flow diagram should show how information will be gathered during the Analysis interviews and how other information-gathering activities will be organized and coded.

Naming Conventions

As items are added to the function hierarchy, analysis ERD, and process flows, decisions must be made about naming them. It is necessary to figure out what will be the standard for naming various objects. In general, the principle is to facilitate communication back to the users. There is nothing wrong with extremely verbose names for repository objects and extensive descriptions. Terse, obscure abbreviations have no place in Analysis. However, you may want to use some to minimize the amount of typing for the Design phase. It is appropriate to periodically print out a combined list of repository objects to ensure that abbreviations are applied consistently.

A standard that is frequently employed is to use no abbreviations at all for any words within Analysis. For example, the field representing "Employee Last Name" would be called EMPLOYEE_LAST_NAME. However, it is better to employ a limited set of abbreviations where they will not obscure the meaning of the objects. For example, you might want, as an organization, to create a table like the following:

company	COM
contract	CON
department	DEPT
division	DIV
employee	EMP

If such a limited set of abbreviations is going to be used, the list should be relatively small—no more than 100 abbreviations. These should be limited to only the most commonly used terms. It must be carefully enforced that these are the only abbreviations used and that they are applied consistently throughout the design process. Any word not on the approved abbreviation list must be spelled out completely. As with any standard, a precise definition of the standard is not as important as the meticulous application of the standard. The person with the role of repository manager should enforce this.

Analysis Plan Example

This section presents an example of an analysis plan for the redesign of a small legacy system. This small project will make relatively minor modifications to the legacy system. The primary Analysis phase focus in this project is a thorough analysis of the legacy system.

Since this is a very small application with relatively few requirements, the requirements document will be a simple narrative with appropriate sections for each module within the system. A real analysis plan, however, may be dozens of pages long. Because the example system is so small, the information gathering process can be relatively informal. A rule of thumb is that the bigger the system, the more formal the requirements gathering process should be.

Sample Analysis Plan

To complete the analysis plan, we will do the following:

By looking at the data structures, we will determine the data-related business requirements.

By looking at the applications, we will determine the required functionality that the applications must support.

We will interview users of the system to find out what changes they want in the current system.

NOTE
Keep in mind that, even with a small system, it is necessary to interview more than one user at more than one level within the organization.

We will write up the user requirements and give them to the users for sign-off.

As part of our analysis, we will prepare a preliminary storyboard and prototype of the revised application. Because we have a working legacy system database, we can prototype the new system against the working database using live production data.

We will pass the storyboard and prototype to users for feedback.

We will redesign the storyboard and prototype to reflect user feedback.

We will declare the Analysis phase complete when the users approve the revised storyboard and prototype.

Workplan

Here are our time estimates for completing the analysis plan:

- Legacy system analysis (2 days)
- User interviews (1 day)

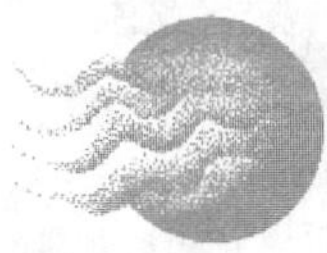

NOTE
Depending upon user availability, user interviews may take more than one calendar day.

- Analysis and write-up of information (2 days)
- Presentation of analysis to users for feedback (1 day)
- Preparation of storyboard and prototype (3 days)
- Presentation of storyboard and prototype to users for sign-off (1 day)

Modifications for Smaller Systems

For a small project, the entire Pre-Analysis phase may not be required, assuming the strategy document provided sufficient detail to move right into Analysis. However, for medium-sized projects, a Pre-Analysis transition phase is recommended. The main reason for performing a careful analysis is to have an audit trail of points leading up to the building of the system. It is just as important to know that the user requirements have been met in a medium-sized system as it is in a large one.

As mentioned earlier, most analysts skip Pre-Analysis, even for large projects. An important statistic from many business studies going back to the 1960s and 1970s should be kept in mind: *Approximately 80 percent of all projects fail.*

One common reason for these failures is the taking of shortcuts in the methodology. Consider one real-life example of a project that started out without a lot of structure. By the end of the Analysis phase, the analysts were able to impose some structure along with a strong Pre-Design phase plan. During the Design phase, however, the project leader changed as a result of an organizational shift. Corners were cut in this phase. Although this did not result in the catastrophic failure of the project, the scope was drastically pared down, and what was delivered did not meet user expectations, mainly because important elements were skipped in the earlier stages.

The lesson to be learned here is that it is critical to the success of any project to stay methodologically sound throughout CADM. There is always a danger in believing that a project is not as big as it really is and skipping crucial steps. This is especially true when the system being designed must be integrated with an existing system.

When is the Pre-Analysis Phase Complete?

The Pre-Analysis phase can be considered complete when the lead developer, lead client, and any other primary clients are satisfied with the proposed analysis process. The project team members should feel confident that they have the right level of detail to proceed with the Analysis phase.

Pre-Analysis is one of the most difficult phases in which to assess completion, mainly, as mentioned at the beginning of this chapter, because the analysis plan must be flexible and may be changed throughout the analysis process. Practically, though, you should begin Analysis as soon as the project leader and management approve the analysis plan.

The analysis plan written in the Pre-Analysis phase should lay out the entire Analysis phase, from information gathering to the completion of the analysis document.

The Pre-Analysis Phase in Designer/2000

Since Pre-Analysis is basically a preparation phase, you need to perform or consider only a limited number of activities in Designer/2000. These are outlined in Table 4-1.

This section describes the Designer/2000 utilities used in Pre-Analysis and the features you need at this stage. You will find the tools discussed here handy for the Designer/2000 work you do throughout the CADM phases.

This discussion assumes that you have read Chapter 2 and know the basics of how to use the common features of the diagrammers and utilities. You should also familiarize yourself with the extensive online help system and cue cards so you can obtain step-by-step help in performing common operations.

Repository Object Navigator (RON)

The major function of the Repository Object Navigator utility, in general, is to allow you to access and manipulate the properties of any element in the repository.

Activity or Deliverable	Designer/2000 Tool
Spot-check the strategy definitions	Repository Object Navigator
Version the application system	Repository Object Navigator
Produce reports on the strategy repository definitions	Repository Reports
Provide a structure to handle system requirements data	Repository Administration Utility

TABLE 4-1. *Pre-Analysis Activities and Designer/2000 Tools*

You use the Repository Object Navigator in the Pre-Analysis phase to view the element definitions you created in the Strategy phase and add any missing information easily and quickly. You also use it to create a new version of the application system created in the Strategy phase that will be the basis for the Analysis phase. Its main interface consists of an Object Hierarchy window (the same style as those in the Developer/2000 design tools) and a Properties window that give you quick access to the properties you defined for elements in the diagrammers or other utilities. Figure 4-2 shows these two windows.

Although diagrams appear as elements in the Object Hierarchy window, you cannot actually create, delete, or manipulate them, but you can inspect the elements that they include.

RON also gives you access to all other utilities and tools from its menu system. It serves as a common launch point outside the Designer/2000 window and has many user-friendly aspects, such as allowing you to drag and drop elements between application systems and group similar elements to change all properties in a single update operation.

Basic Techniques

Since the Repository Object Navigator is in the category of repository utilities, you interact with it in a different way than with the diagrammers. The main operations you perform here concern activity in the two windows shown in Figure 4-2.

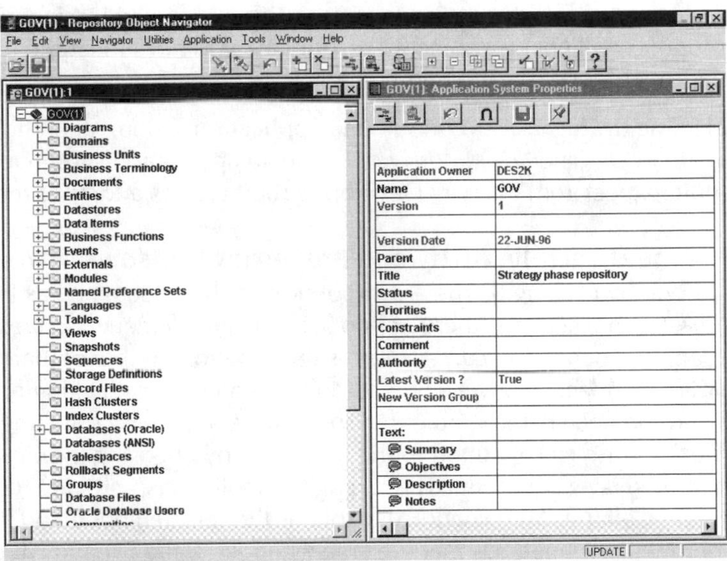

FIGURE 4-2. *Repository Object Navigator Object Hierarchy and Properties windows*

Arranging the Screen You start a typical session in RON by maximizing the window and opening the application system (using **File→Open**), if it is not already on the screen. You then select **Window→Tile Vertically** (being sure the Object Hierarchy window is active, so that window appears on the left). This procedure arranges the screen as in Figure 4-2 and gives you the largest view of each window, which reduces the likelihood that you will need to move the windows around later in the session, an activity that may be fun to some, but one that really just minimizes productivity. All other actions in RON at this point consist of finding and changing properties using the two windows.

Note that if you are accustomed to the workings of the Developer/2000 Object Navigators and Properties window, you will find some similarities in the workings of RON's Object Hierarchy and Properties windows, but there are differences. Don't assume common mechanisms between Developer/2000 and Designer/2000. Here are some Developer/2000 interface features that are different in Designer/2000:

- Designer/2000 does not provide right-click pop-up menus anywhere in the Object Hierarchy window.
- In Designer/2000, you can't copy or move many objects in the Object Hierarchy; for example, you can't copy columns between tables, although you can copy tables.
- When you copy properties in the Properties window in Designer/2000, all properties will not be copied automatically; you have to explicitly select the properties before you copy them.
- Selecting the highest-level node (the application system) and clicking Create in Designer/2000 does not create an application system as you would expect from the way Developer/2000 creates a form or report.

Working in the Object Hierarchy and Properties Windows You expand a hierarchy node by clicking on the **+** symbol next to the node name as Figure 4-3 shows. If no **+** symbol appears, there are no subordinate elements, so you do not need to expand the node. You can also press the **+** button on the toolbar or select from the Navigator menu. Conversely, you collapse a node by clicking on the – symbol next to the node name. You can also collapse a node by selecting the node and pressing the – (Collapse) button in the toolbar or by choosing the Collapse menu item in the Navigator menu. The menu and toolbar also provide the options **Expand All** and **Collapse All**. Expand All expands the selected node and all subnodes below it. If a node has many elements under it, the Expand All process can take some time and will fill your Object Hierarchy window with all the subnodes and their element instances. Therefore, use **Expand All** with care. **Collapse All** collapses all nodes under the selected node.

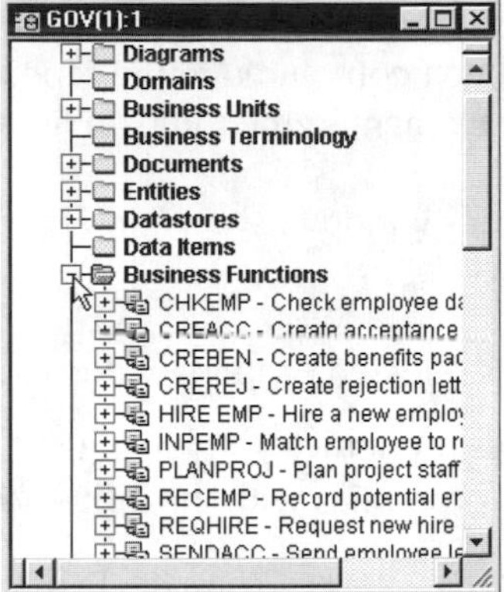

FIGURE 4-3. *Expanding an Object Hierarchy node*

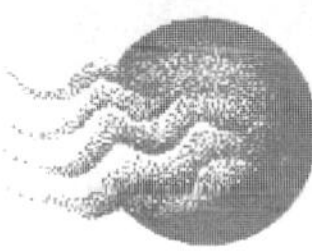

NOTE

The icon picture next to the element in the hierarchy denotes the element type. The help system for RON has a chart with all element icons and their meanings. Do an index search for Icons, and choose Icons from the list that appears. Then click the topic link for Element Type Icon.

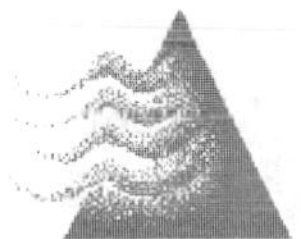

TIP

You can quickly load a particular diagram from the RON Hierarchy by double-clicking on the icon next to the name under the Diagrams node. If the appropriate diagrammer is not open at the time, it will load and open the diagram you clicked. If the diagrammer is open, focus will shift to the diagrammer, where you can perform **File→Open** to open the diagram.

The next step is to find the element you wish to modify or inspect. Expand subnodes in order until you find the element. When you select the element in the Object Hierarchy, its properties appear in the Properties window. The Properties window uses colors to tell you the status of each property. Although you can change these colors through **Edit→Preferences**, the default colors are as follows:

- Normal: Black
- Error; Mandatory: Red
- Modified: Blue
- Shared; Noneditable: Green

Additionally, if the Save button is enabled (not grayed out), the changes in the Properties window have not been committed to the repository. Press the Save button or navigate to another element in the Object Hierarchy to commit the previous element's changes.

The buttons in the Properties window, shown in Figure 4-4, perform the following actions:

- *Copy Properties* saves selected property values to the clipboard.
- *Paste Properties* pastes properties you have just copied to the clipboard. You can view pasted properties with the **Edit→View Copied Properties** menu item.
- *Undo* restores the values that were already in the repository for the element.
- *Union/Intersect* displays all properties or properties in common, respectively, if you select more than one type of element in the Object Hierarchy.
- *Save* commits the changes to the repository.
- *Pin* freezes the display of the element's properties to allow you to navigate to another element, open another Properties window (by selecting **Window→New Properties Window** on the menu), and compare the two (frozen and new) Properties windows side by side.

You will find RON useful throughout your work in the CADM life cycle, from the birth of the application system to its versioning and completion. The more familiar you become with the various methods and buttons in the Object Hierarchy and Properties windows, the easier your work will be later.

The properties that you can change (those not in green) have various display characteristics. All require you to select the property in the list and edit it in the edit area at the top of the window, shown in Figure 4-4. Some properties are fixed list items that you choose by clicking the down arrow at the right side of the edit area. Other properties allow you to type anything in the edit area. Still others (the ones with balloon icons) let you press the balloon icon on the right side of the edit area and open up TextPad (or an editor of your choice as set in the **Edit→Preferences** dialog box). TextPad is a plain text editor that lets you cut, copy, and paste text to and from other editors and itself. Figure 4-5 shows the use of TextPad to edit a description property. Notice that the RON menu has been replaced by a menu for TextPad. When you close TextPad, the normal RON menu returns.

To set properties for many elements at the same time, you can select elements in the Object Hierarchy window by holding down the CTRL key and clicking the elements you need or holding down SHIFT and clicking to select a range of elements

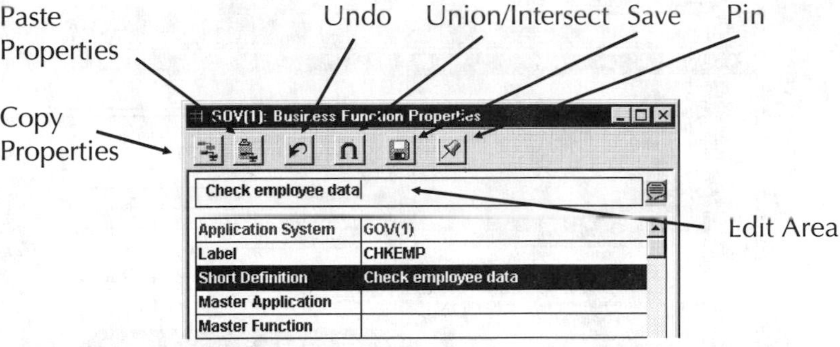

FIGURE 4-4. *Properties window buttons and edit area*

from the list. The Properties window will contain a list of all common properties, and it will display *** if the selected objects have different property values for that property. You can then set a property in this grouped window, and all selected objects will have that value. Figure 4-6 shows a grouped list of elements and the Properties window that applies to it.

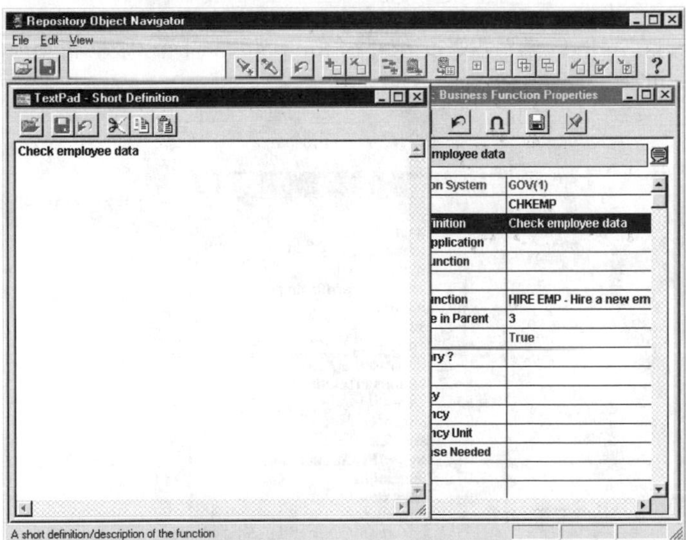

FIGURE 4-5. *TextPad editing a description property*

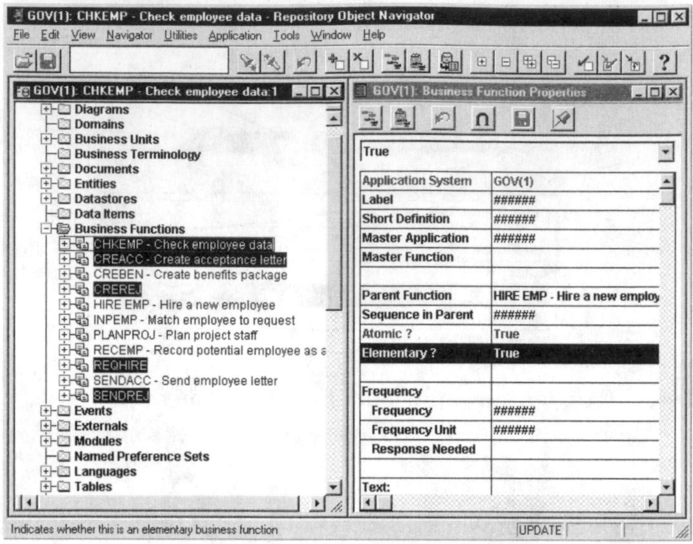

FIGURE 4-6. *Grouped elements and the Properties window*

A technique you can use to help you view the Object Hierarchy items is to split the screen. You do this by dragging the bar at the top-right corner of the navigator down. This splits the screen vertically. You can split the screen horizontally by dragging the bar in the lower-left corner of the navigator inward. Figure 4-7 shows a drag bar splitting the screen.

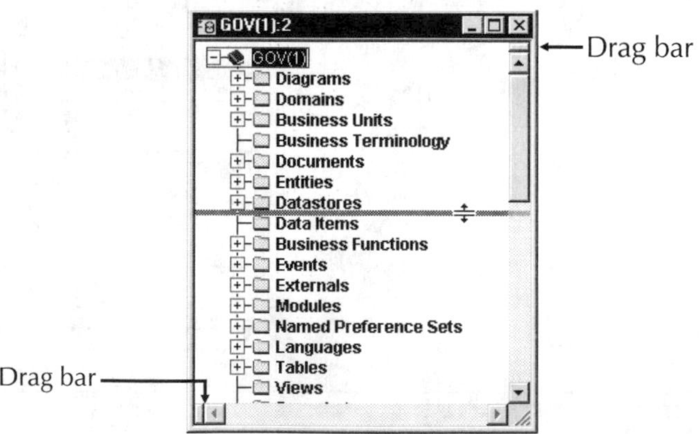

FIGURE 4-7. *Drag bars for splitting the navigator view*

Finding Objects in the Object Hierarchy If you know the name of the element you want to find in the Object Hierarchy, you can select the application system name at the top of the hierarchy and type the name or part of the name in the find area next to the Save button. Then click the Find Next button directly to the right of this area. The cursor will jump to an element with that name if there is a match. If you know the element type but not the exact name, it will be easier to open the hierarchy nodes until you find it. Note that the order of the PAC (highest-level) nodes is, by default, as follows:

1. Diagrams from all phases
2. Analysis objects
3. Design objects
4. User-extension-defined objects (such as Assumptions and Problems)
5. User defined sets created to help move objects between repositories (you will learn more about these later)

This order, called *Type Sequence,* is the order these elements might be used in system development. Another ordering, called *Type Name*, just alphabetizes the nodes without regard to the development sequence. You can choose which order you prefer in the View menu: **Sort by Type Sequence** or **Sort by Type Name**.

Jumping to Other Objects Designer/2000 provides a handy technique for jumping to an object defined somewhere else. For example, suppose you have a Person table that is based on the Person entity, and this table is associated with the entity under the table definition node Entity Table Usages. Figure 4-8 shows this table and usage. The blue arrow next to the entity name indicates that this is a referenced element that has a definition elsewhere. If you click the blue arrow or press the Go To Referenced Object button, the selection will jump to the source element that contains the definition.

This same effect occurs when you have a shared object, denoted by an open-hand icon, and you click this icon. This operation opens the application system that the object is shared from and highlights the object in that system.

You can also set a mark (like a bookmark) so you can return to a particular selected object. Just select the object and click the Mark button (check mark symbol). You can then move to any other object definition and click the Return to Mark button, and the selection will jump back to the marked object. Figure 4-9 shows a mark being set, and Figure 4-10 shows the selection returning to the mark.

The functions of the Go To Referenced Object, Mark, and Return to Mark buttons also appear in the Navigator menu.

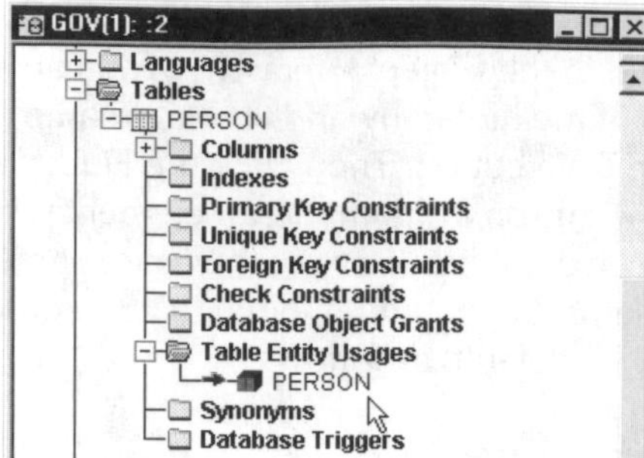

FIGURE 4-8. *Table Entity Usage node with a reference to an entity*

Other Menu and Toolbar Functions

You have seen the main toolbar and menu actions. Designer/2000 offers a few more features on its pull-down menus. In addition to the options discussed in this section, the Window menu contains the normal choices as well as those mentioned for tiling and opening a new Properties window, and the Help menu contains all the usual choices.

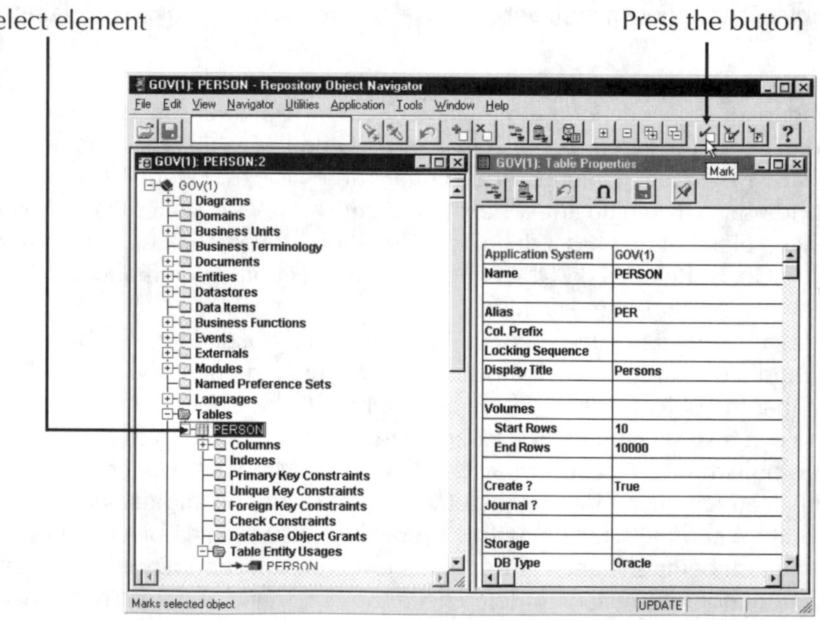

FIGURE 4-9. *Setting a mark*

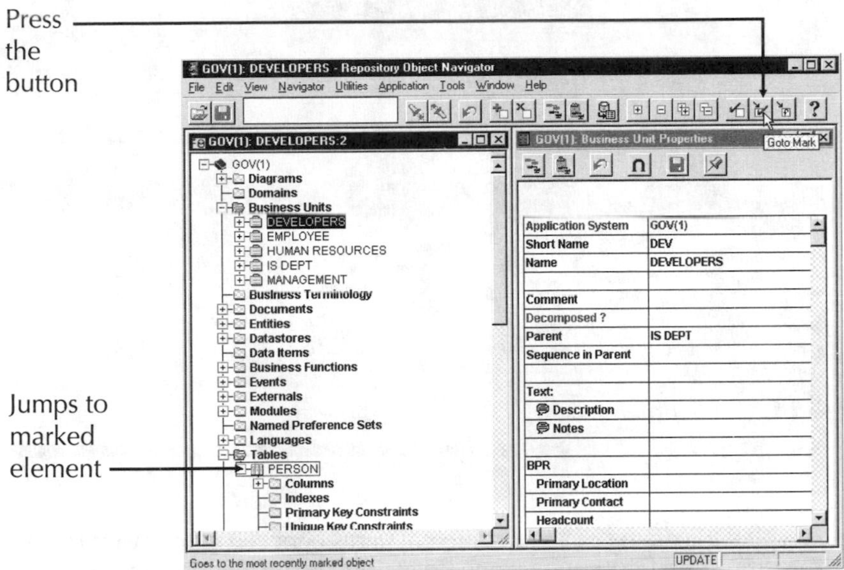

FIGURE 4-10. *Returning to the mark*

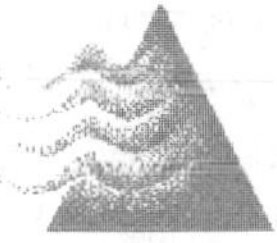

TIP

You may have questions about the meaning of some element types you see in the Object Hierarchy. The help button in the toolbar can get you help for a particular element quickly and easily. Just click the help button; the cursor will change to the What's This cursor which you can drop (by clicking) on the element type in question. The help system will open and load the topic that refers to that element.

File Menu The **New**, **Open**, and **Close** items on the RON File menu refer to the application system. The only way to create a new application system is through **File→New**. You can open more than one application system at the same time to share, copy, or transfer ownership of element definitions among them. You can also open the same application system in more than one Object Hierarchy window using **File→Open**. **Save** on this menu refers to committing changes you made to properties or objects in the application system.

When you open an application system, the Filter dialog appears as in Figure 4-11. This dialog box lets you specify the elements that RON displays for this application system. You can set a preference (using **Edit→Preferences**) to not display this dialog box if you always want to see application systems in the same

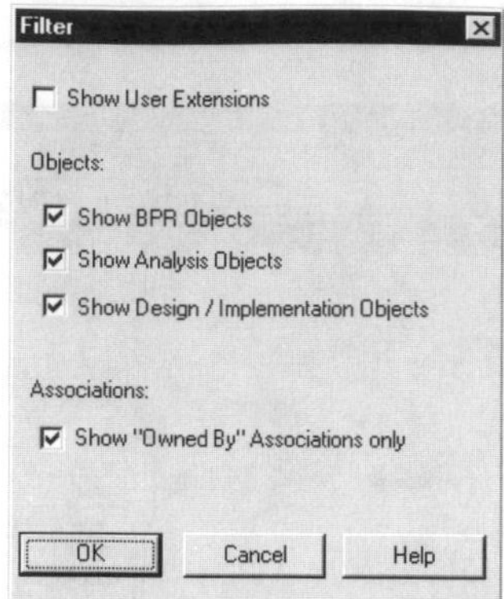

FIGURE 4-11. *Filter dialog box*

way, or to display the dialog box with different items checked if you want to be able to change the selections but typically use certain settings.

The File menu also includes **Load**, **Unload**, and **Unload for Exchange** options that let you copy definitions of some or all objects to a flat file that you can bring into another repository or application system or (in the case of the Exchange product) another CASE tool. Load allows you to bring in element definitions from an external repository through a specially formatted flat file. **Check Out** lets you place elements into another application system and lock elements that are checked out. **Check In** brings the checked-out elements back in. **Unlock Set** releases the lock on a *user-defined set*: a set of objects you have named and that you can check out or lock against changes. You will learn more about **Load/Unload**, **Check In/ Check Out**, and user-defined sets in Chapter 13.

Edit Menu You can use the Edit menu to create or delete an object. You can also use the Create (green **+**) button to create objects and the Delete (red **x**) button to delete objects. You select a node of the type of object you wish to create and press the Create button or select the **Edit→Create** menu item. Deleting an element is just a matter of selecting it in the Object Hierarchy window and clicking the Delete button or selecting the **Edit→Delete** menu item. If the object has child objects or associations, you will not be able to delete it unless you use the **Force Delete** option on the Utilities menu, which deletes all child and association objects as well. The **Undo** option does the same thing as the Undo button: it reverses the last action unless the last action was a delete or commit (save) operation. The Undo button in the Properties window differs slightly in that it affects only properties you have changed in that window.

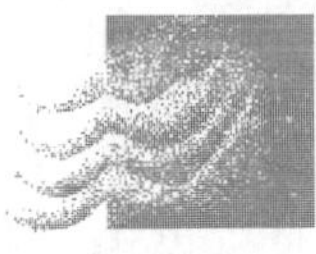

CAUTION

Remember that Designer/2000 commits work in RON implicitly when you move the cursor selection from a changed object to another in the Object Hierarchy. Therefore, if you create a new object and select another object before filling in all the required properties, the implicit commit will take place and fail because the required properties are missing. At that point you can fill in the missing properties or delete the object before moving on.

The **Copy** and **Paste Properties** options are available on this menu as well as on the toolbar in the Properties window and on the application toolbar. As mentioned, you can examine copied properties by using the **View Copied Properties** selection.

The Preferences menu option lets you set up the RON environment; you can specify such settings as the font and colors, the initial application loaded by default, whether the Filter dialog box (where you specify what elements are displayed) appears when you open an application, the date format, and the text editor (if you want to use something other than TextPad). Figure 4-12 shows one of the settings tabs in the Preferences dialog box.

View Menu The View menu contains the options for ordering the Object Hierarchy elements. It also contains the **Requery** option for requerying the database (also provided as a toolbar button). You may need to requery if element definitions are changed in another diagrammer or utility after RON is opened. You can select a particular node before pressing the Requery button, and RON will retrieve all definitions of that node and all the subnodes. You can also select just one object to requery if you want to speed up the query.

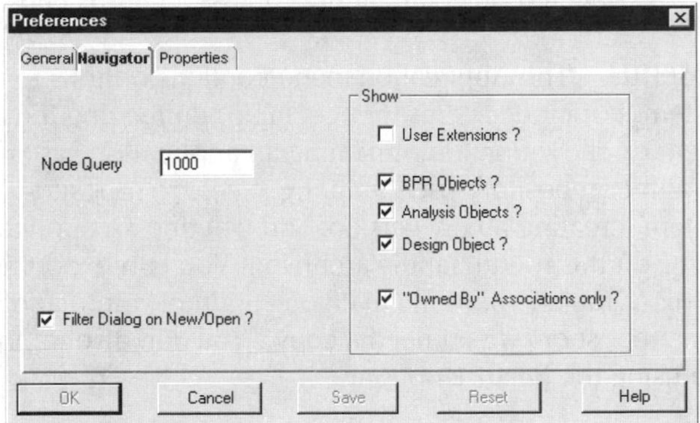

FIGURE 4-12. *Preferences dialog box*

Navigator Menu The only item on the Navigator menu not already mentioned is **Find**. This option displays a dialog box in which you can type a name (using the wildcard % if desired) and optionally specify the parent object and one or more types of objects to find. This option is a bit more flexible than the Object Hierarchy Find field.

Utilities Menu Using the Utilities menu, along with the Application and Tools menus, you can access virtually every utility and diagrammer in Designer/2000. The Utilities menu lets you choose the repository utilities, some of which are not available elsewhere. There are five categories of items, listed here, which let you perform several tasks:

- **Design Wizards** These load the Database Design Wizard and the Application Design Wizard.
- **Generators** These load one of the eight code generators. **Generate Reference Tables** is also in this category, and it lets you create the actual tables that hold the online help, reference codes, and code controls.
- **Reverse engineering utilities** These create definitions in the repository for database objects, Forms, and Reports. **Table to Entity Retrofit** performs reverse engineering of tables to entities, and **Reconcile** checks the objects in an existing database against the object definitions in the repository.
- **Utilities for association elements and domain members** These load the data usage associations for Functions and Modules and update columns and attributes in a domain if the domain has changed.
- **Utilities for cross-application element definitions** These copy, share, or transfer ownership of elements between application systems. **Force Delete** deletes the selected object, including all associations and child objects.

Application Menu The Application menu contains options to maintain the application system. It includes items for freezing or unfreezing the application system to prevent or allow updates, renaming an application system, transferring ownership to another repository user, granting access to repository users to this application system, creating a new version, and deleting an application system.

The last items on this menu handle archiving. You can export an application system to a .DMP (Oracle Export) file that you can import into another repository (or into the same repository if you need a copy). You can also import the .DMP file from this menu using the **Restore** option.

Tools Menu The Tools menu gives you access to all diagrammers and major utilities in Designer/2000. It serves as an alternative to the Designer/2000 window that starts all tools. You can also load SQL*Plus, and RON will log you in automatically.

RON Features to Spot-Check Your Strategy Work

You use Repository Object Navigator in the Pre-Analysis phase to spot-check the entities and processes in your strategy ERD and process model. You may ask, "Why use RON when the diagrammers also show the element definitions as well as the diagrams themselves?" The answer is that the Repository Object Navigator is essential when you are comparing a number of element definitions because you can group elements together and view the same or different properties—an operation that is possible nowhere else in the tools except in the Process Modeller for a limited number of properties. You can quickly move from one definition to another without the screen redraw overhead that the diagrammers impose. You can also view element definitions side by side in different Properties windows to compare and copy and paste between them.

For example, in RON you might perform a cross-check of the entities that you are diagramming in the ER Diagrammer. You can view their definitions in RON and be sure you are happy with the name, short name, and plural name for each entity. You can also fill in text information in the Description and Notes properties easier in RON than in the ER Diagrammer.

TIP

One approach you might consider is to ignore the entity properties when you are creating the entities in the ER Diagrammer because otherwise you have to perform another operation to open the Properties window for each entity. Then use RON in the Pre-Analysis phase to fill in the details in preparation for the reports and versioning tasks. This approach can speed your work in the ER Diagrammer and still provide complete entity definitions. You can use a similar strategy in other diagrammers for other elements throughout your System Development Life Cycle work.

RON Features to Create a New Version

The other essential activity that RON assists with during Pre-Analysis is the creation of a new version of the application system. Versioning an application system in Designer/2000 creates a complete copy of the application system, increments the version number, and freezes the old copy so you cannot make changes, although you can view it. Designer/2000 cannot version individual elements or groups of elements, so application system versioning is the only way to create an online copy of the strategy elements.

The reason you perform versioning at this stage is that you will (probably) radically change the element definitions—even rename or divide them—in

Analysis, and you need the copy that supports the strategy discussions and document. Although you could explicitly freeze the application system so no one could make changes, you will have to start a completely new application system for the Analysis phase, and you will possibly need to reenter all your initial strategy definitions if you do that.

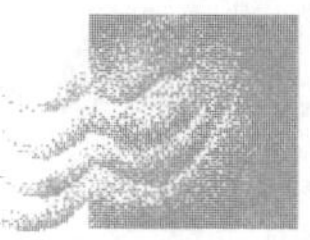

CAUTION

When you delete an application system, there is no way to restore it unless you have a backup.

Suppose you have versioned an application system called PRODAPP by selecting **Application→New Version** in the RON menu to freeze version 1 and create a copy called version 2. The version number appears after the application system name in most dialog boxes and window titles; for example, PRODAPP(1) indicates application system version 1. When you open an application system, you can set a preference (via **Edit→Preferences**) to display all the versions in the Open dialog box. At this point, you can't change or add to version 1, but you can do anything to version 2.

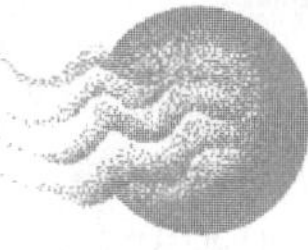

NOTE

If you have an application system that you wish to delete and it is not a second version of a previous version, the operation could take some time if the application system has many elements. Designer/2000 checks dependencies as it deletes the elements and uses database resources more heavily than usual, so the operation could affect system performance while the delete takes place. Therefore, you probably will not want to delete application systems frequently, and careful planning in the initial stages can reduce the need to do so.

An alternative to versioning is to make a backup copy of the application system and export it. You can do this in RON by choosing **Archive** from the Application menu. This procedure loads the element definitions and all other details on the application system, including the diagrams, into temporary extract tables (which have names with an XT_ prefix). Once the utility has copied the element definitions into these tables, you can select **Application→Export** and create an export (.DMP) file. This file is in standard Oracle export format, so you can import it (through RON's **Utilities→Restore** menu item) into another repository or just use it to back up the application system. This file is a complete snapshot of all data including diagrams, and it can hold all the strategy information in a form that cannot be changed.

The benefit of this alternative over creating a new version is that you do not take up space in the repository for a new application system, and you still have data to support your Strategy phase. The drawback is that the application system is, in effect, offline so you cannot easily query it or reprint its definitions or diagrams. Since you are building on the strategy elements in the one online application system, strategy details will be "lost" there, and you will have to restore the original application system to retrieve the details. Still, there are site-specific reasons for using this approach.

Repository Reports

Repository Reports is a repository utility that lets you view the element definitions in particular formats. You can run more than 150 pre-built reports (using the Developer/2000 Reports tool) with this utility. Since you have diagrammed the Entity Model and Process Model at this point, reports to start with might be the Entity Definition (and other reports in the Data Model group) and Dataflow Definition (and other reports in the Dataflow Model or BPR Model group). You will see how to find these and other reports and groups and how to get around the Repository Reports interface. Again, Chapter 2 contains the basics of the Designer/2000 interface, and if you are new to the object navigator window methods, a review of the section on the Repository Object Navigator might help you.

Basic Techniques

The Repository Reports interface is similar to that of the Repository Object Navigator. It uses the paradigm of the object navigator for its Reports window and also displays a Parameters window (like the Properties window in RON), as Figure 4-13 shows. Therefore, you follow the same procedure after opening the tool as for RON: you maximize the window and tile the windows vertically (using **Window→Tile Vertically**) while the Reports window is active (so it appears on the left). You also expand and contract nodes and use the Find box and menu choice in the same way as in RON. The Mark and Go To Mark buttons and Navigator menu items also work exactly the same as in RON.

Running a report is a three-step process:

1. Find the report to run.
2. Fill in its parameters.
3. Press the Execute button and examine the output.

The following sections explain these steps.

Finding a Report The list of reports is so extensive that you need some assistance in finding the correct one. Designer/2000 gives you three ways to look at the list of reports: **Group**, **Object Type**, and **Report Name**. You can switch between these views by selecting the appropriate choice from the View menu. A given node

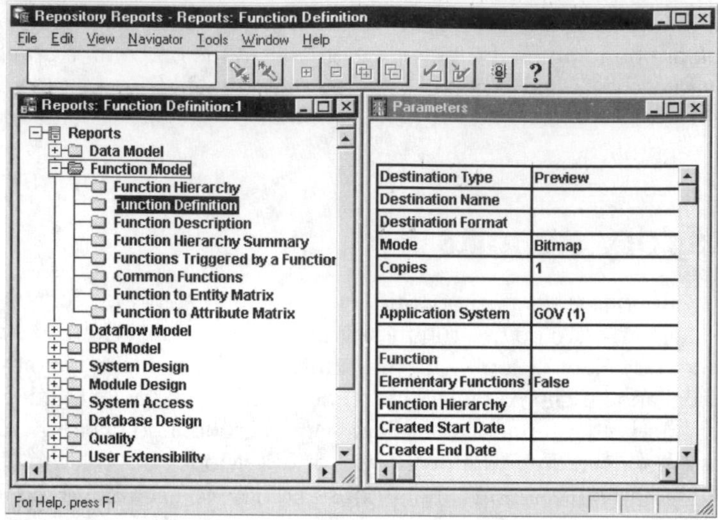

FIGURE 4-13. *Repository Reports windows*

may have the same report listed as another node. Therefore, if you are viewing by object type, the Function to Attribute Matrix report will appear under both the Attribute and Function nodes.

Group displays reports by project life cycle phase or area, as in Figure 4-14. This view is a good choice if you want to see what other reports are available in a particular section. For example, suppose you know that you want to list Attributes so you look under the Data Model node. You find the Attribute Definition report there but also see other reports that might be useful at this stage of the CADM life cycle and might supplement the attribute report.

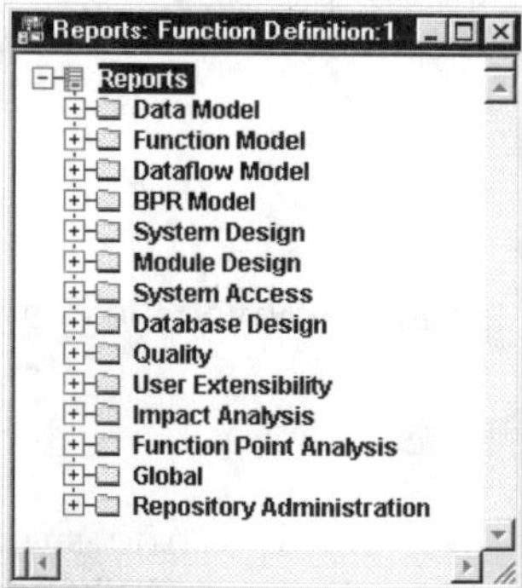

FIGURE 4-14. *Report listing by group*

Object Type displays reports by element type. Reports in this category are potentially the easiest to find as you will probably know the type of element you need to report on. For example, if you are looking for a list of entities, you can find a number of reports under the Entities node to choose from. Figure 4-15 shows some of the Object Type nodes.

The **Report Name** view of the reports is merely an alphabetical listing of all reports in Designer/2000. This is the best method for finding the report you want if you have a copy in front of you with the name of the report or can remember the exact name (or at least the first word or two in the name). Figure 4-16 shows a list of reports by report name. Note that the filename of the report appears after the report name. This feature is useful if you need to change the report in some way.

As mentioned previously, you might want a listing of the entities and processes you diagrammed in the Strategy phase. Use the reports Entity Definition (and other reports in the Data Model group) and Dataflow Definition (and other reports in the Dataflow Model or BPR Model group) as a starting point for the Pre-Analysis work.

While the set of reports Designer/2000 provides is extensive, it is possible the report you want is just not available. You will find some suggestions for handling this situation later in this chapter in the section "What to Do If the Report You Want Is Not Pre-Built."

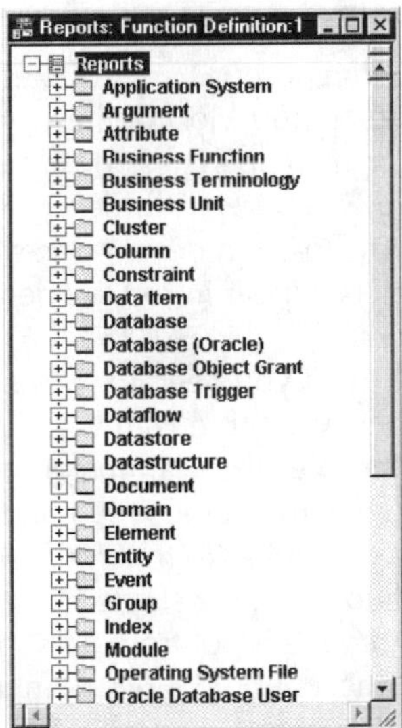

FIGURE 4-15. *Report listing by object type*

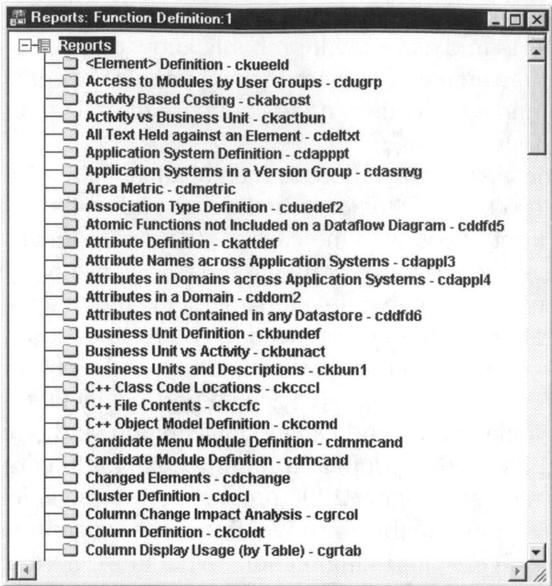

FIGURE 4-16. *Reports listed by report name*

Filling In Parameters Each report has a set of parameters you enter to specify the elements that will be in the output. Most of these are specific to the report and are well documented in the online help system. Just press F1 after selecting a report. This procedure opens the help system report index, where you can select the particular report you are running to see a description of the report and its parameters. Required parameters appear in red (by default); these must be entered before you run the report.

You can use the wildcard "%" if you need to specify a range of elements in any parameter. For example, to specify a Table Name parameter to indicate that you want all tables, you could enter % as that parameter value. Similarly, to report on all tables with PERS somewhere in the name, you can specify a parameter value of %PERS%. Note that this syntax is similar to that for SQL query conditions, but you cannot enter a complex condition—only a single exact value or a single value with a wildcard. Some parameters require input from a list of values (as in RON), some require typed input, and some accept both types of input (for example, the Entity parameter of the Entity Definition report, shown in Figure 4-17).

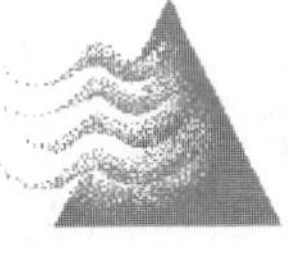

TIP

You can include a certain subset of elements on a particular report even if they do not have a similar name. Some reports include a parameter for the name of a diagram on which the elements appear. For example, the Entity Definition report includes an ERD parameter, which lists the existing reports. If you select one, Designer/2000 uses it as the source for the entities it reports on. Thus, suppose a diagram called ERD PERSON contains the entities PERSON, ORGANIZATION, and PURCHASE_ORDER. You can fill in the name of the diagram in the ERD parameter, and the report will include only the entities in that diagram. Note that the wildcard % works here too, so if you have similarly named diagrams and specify the wildcarded name in this parameter, Designer/2000 will report on all entities on all diagrams with names that meet the parameter condition.

Running and Examining a Report The last step after finding the proper report and filling in its parameters is to run and examine the report. Running a report is as simple as clicking Run Report button or choosing **File→Run**. If you retained the default Preview value in the Destination Type parameter, the report will appear on the screen in the Developer/2000 Reports Previewer window. This window has buttons for navigating the report and printing it. If you specified a different destination, the report will go there directly.

The Output Window

To output to a file, you fill in properties as listed in Table 4-2. These settings produce a file in the directory you are using as the default for Designer/2000.

Parameters

%PERS%

Destination Type	Preview
Destination Name	
Destination Format	
Mode	Bitmap
Copies	1
Application System	GOV (1)
Entity	%PERS%
ER Diagram	
Created Start Date	
Created End Date	
Changed Start Date	
Changed End Date	

FIGURE 4-17. *Filling in a report parameter value*

Parameter	Value
Destination Type	File
Destination Name	*FILENAME*.LIS (substituting the name of the report and using the .LIS extension so the report will appear in the Output window)
Mode	Character

TABLE 4-2. *Parameter Values for Printing to a File*

when you are printing to a file, be sure to designate the Oracle Reports ASCII Driver in the print dialog box that appears.

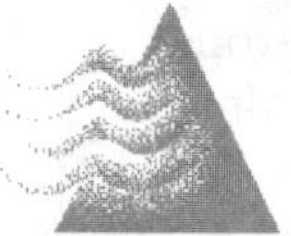

TIP
Create a separate directory for Designer/2000 work and make this the working directory by navigating to the Properties window for the Win 95, Win 3.1, or Win NT icon or program item that runs Designer/2000. Then all files you create from Repository Reports or other utilities will be written into this directory.

If you open the Output window (using **Window→Output Window**), you will see a list of files that Designer/2000 produced or any other files with the .LIS extension in the working directory. Double-clicking the filename (or selecting **File→Open**) in this navigator loads the report into the default text editor, where you can view, edit, or print it. Figure 4-18 shows the Output window. You may have to run a report to a file to make the file list refresh if you open this window before running any reports. You can delete files from this window by selecting them and choosing **Edit→Delete**.

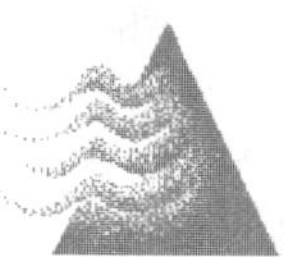

TIP
The reports engine may perform better if you start the Developer/2000 Reports server outside Designer/2000. This procedure will cause Oracle Reports to start faster. The file to run is R25SRV32.EXE (for NT and Win 95) or R25SRV.EXE (for Win 3.x) in the \ORAWIN95\BIN\ directory (or wherever your Oracle executables were installed).

What to Do If the Report You Want Is Not Pre-Built

If you can't find a repository report that fulfills your needs, you do either of two things: you can find a report that is close to your needs and modify it as necessary,

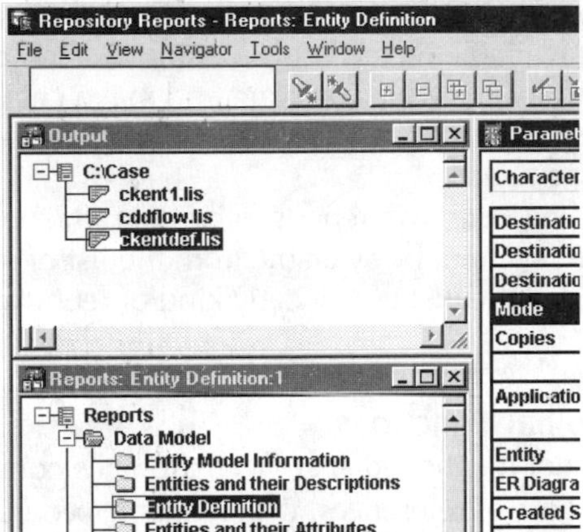

FIGURE 4-18. *Reports Files Output window*

or you can write your own report from scratch using Developer/2000 Reports, SQL*Plus, or some other reporting tool.

Modifying Existing Reports All repository reports are Reports Designer files (.RDF) that you can modify in the Developer/2000 Reports Designer. You can find all report files in the \ORAWIN95\REPADM10\SRW directory. Designer/2000 prints the name of the file in the bottom margin of the report, as well as in the **View by Report Name** mentioned before. If you have not printed or previewed the file onscreen, you can find the filename in the Report window report description after selecting **View→View by Report Name** from the menu. Then you can run Reports Designer directly from the Tools menu and navigate to the SRW directory to open and modify the file.

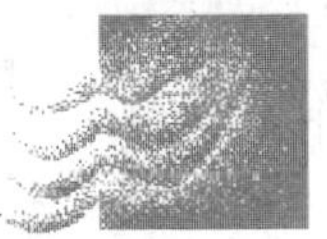

CAUTION
If you are modifying existing reports, be sure to keep a backup copy. Some reports are complex, and changing one small object in them can cause major complications. Also, you should not attempt to modify an existing report unless you are very familiar with the way Reports Designer works.

Writing Your Own Reports If you are proficient with a reporting tool, you can use it to create reports on the views in the repository. The repository views are discussed fully in Chapter 14, but note here that you will have to decipher the relationships between views and the meaning of their columns. This is not an insurmountable task, but it may require some time in the beginning. If you decide to use Oracle Reports (available on the Tools menu), you can copy an existing repository report that is close to what you want and make changes to it. You can also use SQL*Plus—also available on the Tools menu—to create reports that do not have complex formatting needs.

The drawback to using your own reports, other than the need to figure out the data sources, is that they will not be available from the list of repository reports. The benefit is that you can create basically any kind of report you wish from the repository elements.

Other Menu and Toolbar Functions

The only menu choice not mentioned apart from the ones common to all Designer/2000 tools is **Edit→Preferences**, which enables you to change settings such as the font, color, initial application, and date format.

Mapping System Requirements to Repository Elements

Pre-Analysis involves planning and making decisions about what will happen in the Analysis phase. One of the decisions you have to make is how to map system requirements to elements so you can cross-check later in the CADM life cycle to ensure that your design fulfills these requirements. This mapping traditionally is a manual process, if it occurs at all: someone compares the requirements list with the list of system features to ensure completeness. You can also use the table structure proposed earlier to store the requirements and tie them to the repository definitions. In addition, you can use Designer/2000.

How Designer/2000 Handles System Requirements

Designer/2000 does not provide a Requirements PAC element, but it does provide a Documents PAC element where you can store the details of documents pertinent to the life cycle, such as the system requirements document. You can also store the document text itself in this definition in plain text format as well as associations to any other repository element. This procedure will not fulfill the need to map requirements to functions and other elements, but it can provide a list of project documents and a central storage location for certain documents.

Designer/2000 also includes an Objectives element where you can store information on objectives, which you can interpret as requirements. Objectives is actually an element that Oracle created as an extension to the normal set of objects and that has associations to elements for Critical Success Factors, Business Functions, Key Performance Indicators, and Modules. You can use this element to store the text of your requirement and use the associations provided to map to these elements.

User Extensions to Designer/2000

Another method for implementing a system to store requirements is to use Designer/2000's User Extensibility feature to create your own element. User extensions are additional elements, associations, or properties you define as parts of the repository. You create these in the Repository Administration Utility (RAU) and then enter data into them through RON or the Matrix Diagrammer or your own front-end tool or utility such as SQL*Plus. Since the extended objects become part of the repository, you can create reports on them in the same way as you create reports on predefined objects. Although they are not available in Designer/2000 utilities or diagrammers other than RON, they allow you to customize your application with items that Designer/2000 does not give you by default.

Choosing Between User Extensions and a Table-Based System

In some cases, the features that Designer/2000 provides may not meet the needs of your particular situation. For example, you may want to customize the way Designer/2000 handles project- or company-specific elements, and you will find yourself asking, "How do I accomplish this with Designer/2000?" How do you decide whether to use a system of database tables or to extend the repository to include these features? Although no one can say categorically which is the better approach in every situation, if you know the benefits and drawbacks of each, you will be better prepared to decide what will work best. Table 4-3 lists the major characteristics you should consider.

The other factor that will affect your choice of method is your knowledge of what is involved in implementing the solution in each case. This discussion assumes that you or a colleague knows how to implement a relational database table solution, so it only offers insights into the process of creating user extensions to Designer/2000 using the Repository Administration Utility.

Repository Administration Utility (RAU)

The Repository Administration Utility (RAU) manages the repository tables and user accounts and allows you to easily install, upgrade, back up, and restore the repository data and its code. In addition, it provides the means to extend the Designer/2000 repository with elements and properties that you define. The RAU interface is a bit different than that of the other diagrammers and utilities, but it is similar to the Designer/2000 window—the launch pad for all tools that you get when you click the Designer/2000 icon—because you just click a button to activate a function. RAU has groups of buttons for the following task areas, as Figure 4-19 shows:

Repository Management	User Maintenance
Backup	
User Extensions	Check (database objects)

Feature	Table-Based Solution	Designer/2000 User Extension Solution
Ease of creating of data structures	Familiar process to relational database developers	Developers need to learn the extension process.
Data structure creation process	Can generate table scripts in Designer/2000 or manually write them	Does not use scripts, only definitions in the Designer/2000 Repository Administration Utility.
Limitations on size and number of extensions	Unlimited	100 extra association types, 100 extra elements, unlimited text types, and 10 extra properties per element.
Front-end for loading data	Needs to be developed, but applications can be generated from Designer/2000 since they use standard SQL and table concepts	Can use RON and Matrix Diagrammer as is; if something more is needed, it must be developed outside the Designer/2000 generators and the Designer/2000 API must be accessed, a process that requires more programming than standard SQL.
Data maintenance	No ties to Designer/2000 data repository; if Designer/2000 data changes, changes will not automatically cascade to tables	Provided by Designer/2000's repository.
Reporting capabilities	Reports must be created manually or through Designer/2000	Reports must be created manually.
Data sharing with other application systems	Nearly impossible	Built-in feature because the data is in the repository.
Support of application system import/export	None	Built in.
Support of checkin/checkout and load/unload	None	Built in.

TABLE 4-3. *Differences in Implementing User Extensions Inside and Outside Designer/2000*

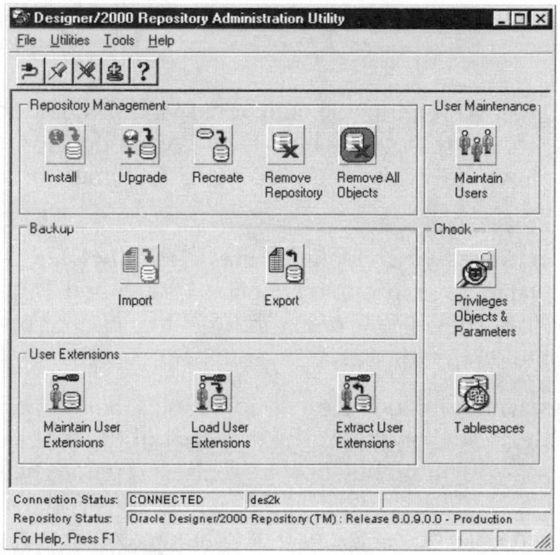

FIGURE 4-19. *Repository Administration Utility screen*

Chapter 13 discusses the management aspects of RAU. This section describes the RAU in general and the User Extensions facility in detail as you may wish to use it to maintain the system requirements mappings—a decision you would make in the Pre-Analysis phase.

Elements, Associations, and Text Types

An example of how to create the requirements system with the RAU User Extensibility feature is described later in this chapter. First, though, you will find it useful to review the makeup of the repository data. These discussions refer to the *meta-model*, or the "model of the system model," and how to relate it to elements and associations in the Repository Object Navigator (RON). Keep in mind that the discussion pertains to element and association *types*, not *instances*. For example, it refers to the Entity element type, which RON represents as the Entity node in its hierarchy. This type can have many instances, which RON represents as the entities themselves: for example, PERSON, ORGANIZATION, and PHONE. Think of a type as a biological species—like a domestic cat—and an instance as an individual living being—like Maya, the cat—who belongs to that species and shares common traits called aspects (claws, whiskers, ears, and so on) with others of the same species. Also keep in mind that the discussion does not refer to the tables or views where Designer/2000 stores or presents these items, but only to the concepts about and structures for the data.

All structures for the data in the repository can be divided into three main conceptual types:

- *Element types,* which include Functions, Modules, Entities, Tables, and Columns. These are both the high-level PAC nodes (for example, Tables) and some lower-level nodes (for example, Columns for those tables) you see in RON.
- *Association types,* which include Function Entity Data Usage, Function Attribute Data Usage, Module Function Usage, and Table Entity Usage. These are lower-level SAC nodes in RON that appear under an element and link it to other elements.
- *Text types,* which include Description, Notes, Select Text, and Where/Validation Condition. These appear in RON as properties of an element or association, but they are really a separate type.

Additionally, certain aspects describe or characterize each type: properties or text type usage. Table 4-4 shows which aspects belong to which types. RON represents properties as the rows that appear in the Properties window. Text type usage indicates the kind of text you are storing for an Element or Association—such as Description, Notes, or Where/Validation Condition—and RON shows the text type usages also as rows in the Properties window even though they are stored apart from the element instance. Text types use text type usages to indicate which element types use them.

Figure 4-20 shows this system of types, properties, and text usages. Note that this figure represents only the top-level structures, and there is an implied one-to-many relationship from each of the diagrammed structures to an actual instance of that structure. For example, the diagram represents Element Type, which Table would instantiate. Other examples of Element Type instances include entities, columns, attributes, functions, and dataflows.

Type	**Properties**	**Text Type Usages**
Element type	Yes	Yes
Association type	Yes	Yes
Text type	No	Yes (to represent which elements use it)

TABLE 4-4. *Types and Their Aspects*

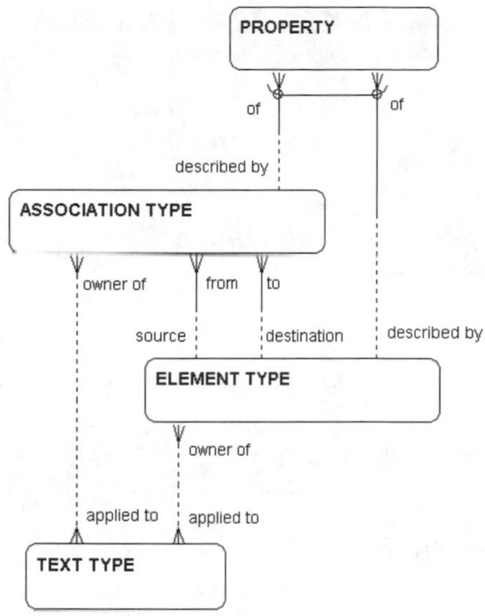

FIGURE 4-20. *The repository types meta-model*

Element Types The User Extension area in the Repository Administration Utility makes these concepts clearer. Figure 4-21 shows the list of element types with extensible properties for the Entity element.

Notice that no properties other than Name and the user-extensible properties (such as Usrx0 and Usrx1) appear because they cannot be modified, but RON displays them for each instance of the element type as in Figure 4-22. The properties and element types with an asterisk (*) next to them in Figure 4-21 are *published* items—meaning they have been fully incorporated into the repository with views and procedure packages to represent them. If you create a new element type, you automatically assign Name and Comment properties and can also define some or all of the Usrx properties that are not normally displayed in RON. Once you publish the definition, the element type and properties appear in RON. You'll see an example of this later.

In RAU, you can also look at the details of element and property definitions. Figure 4-23 shows the Entity element type definition, and Figure 4-24 shows the Name property definition of the Entity type. These figures show examples of the details you will fill in when you create your own element types and properties.

The element type also has text types linked to it that represent one side of the many-to-many relationship between Text Type and Element Type in Figure 4-20. Figure 4-25 shows the Entity element with its list of text types (CDIDSC and

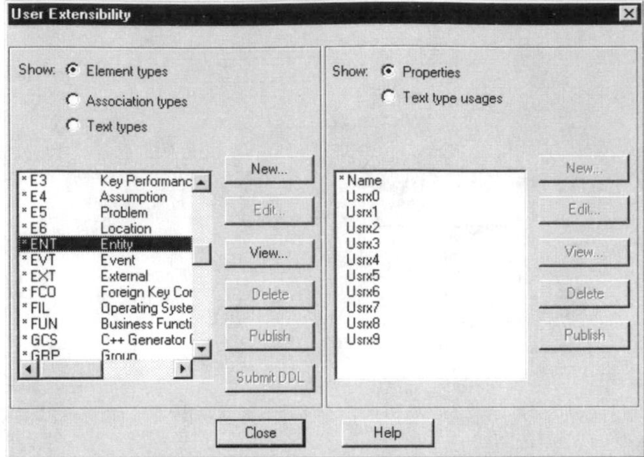

FIGURE 4-21. *Element types and properties in RAU*

CDINOT). You can extend the definition of an element by adding text type usages to its list. The new text types will appear in the RON Properties window as properties although they are really text types.

GOV(1): Entity Properties

Application System	GOV(1)
Name	ASSIGNMENT
Short Name	ASGN
Plural	ASSIGNMENT
Type Of	PERSONNEL ASSIGNMENT
Volumes	
Initial	2
Average	2000
Maximum	5000
Annual Growth Rate (	10
Text:	
Description	A person at a task.
Notes	
C ++	
Class Name	

FIGURE 4-22. *Entity properties in RON*

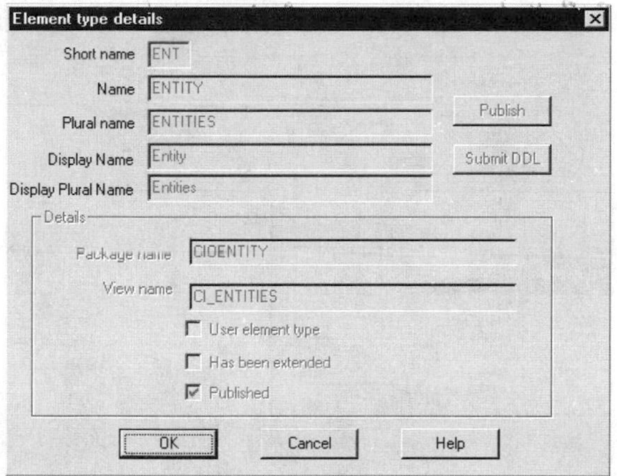

FIGURE 4-23. *Entity element type definition*

Association Types Association types denote a relationship or link between two element types. These act the same as element types because they have properties and text types usages as their aspects. The definitions look a bit different

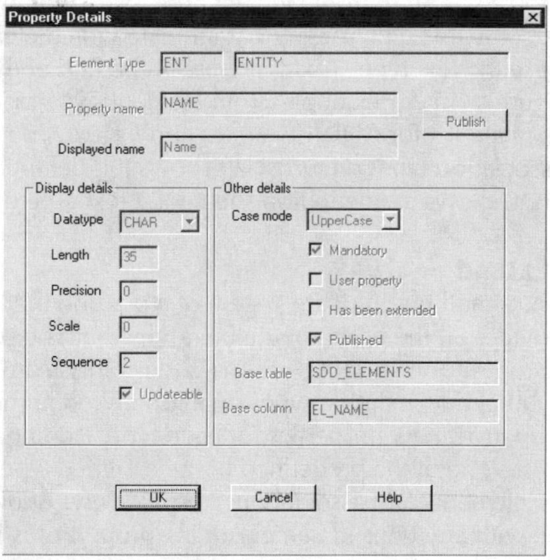

FIGURE 4-24. *Name property definition*

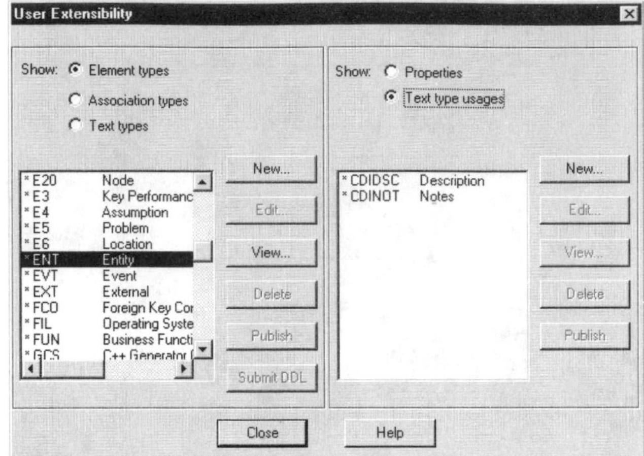

FIGURE 4-25. *Entity element with its text types*

because they include the definition of the elements that they relate. Figure 4-26 shows the definition window for an association type for Function Entity Usage, and Figure 4-27 shows the corresponding RON Properties window.

Text Types Text types differ from element and association types in that they have no properties, only text type usages that indicate which element and association types use the text type. Text types are at the end of the many-to-many relationships in Figure 4-20 (for example, from Element Type to Text Type). Figure 4-28 shows the text type list for CDINOT Notes and its text type usages, which are all element and association types. Figure 4-29 shows the definition sheet for this text type. Figure 4-30 shows the definition sheet for a text type usage of a text type.

What You Can Extend

Using this somewhat small but intricate system of types and their aspects, Designer/2000 provides all the nodes in the hierarchy that you see in RON. You can customize the repository with RAU's User Extensibility feature to add up to 100 entirely new element and association types or an unlimited number of text types; you can also add up to 10 new properties for each type. Adding element and association types uses one of the predefined but unassigned types named E0 to E99 and A0 to A99, for elements and associations, respectively. Adding text types defines a new type with any unused name. Adding properties is just a matter of defining a new name and datatype for one or more of the 10 unassigned Usrx

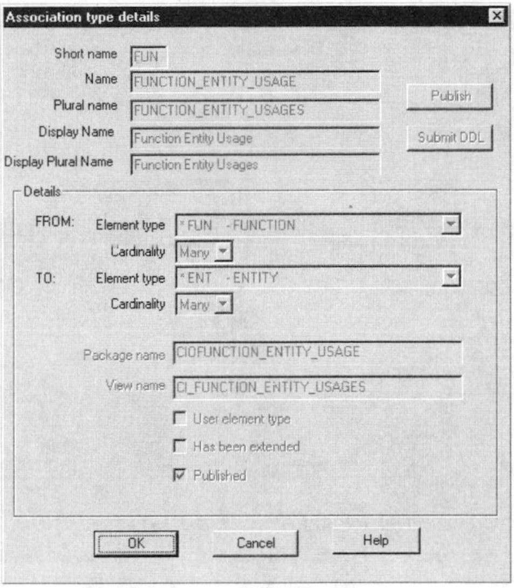

Association type details

Short name: FUN
Name: FUNCTION_ENTITY_USAGE
Plural name: FUNCTION_ENTITY_USAGES
Display Name: Function Entity Usage
Display Plural Name: Function Entity Usages

Publish
Submit DDL

Details
FROM: Element type: *FUN - FUNCTION
Cardinality: Many
TO: Element type: *ENT - ENTITY
Cardinality: Many

Package name: CIOFUNCTION_ENTITY_USAGE
View name: CI_FUNCTION_ENTITY_USAGES

User element type
Has been extended
Published

OK
Cancel
Help

FIGURE 4-26. *Definition of the Function Entity Usage association type*

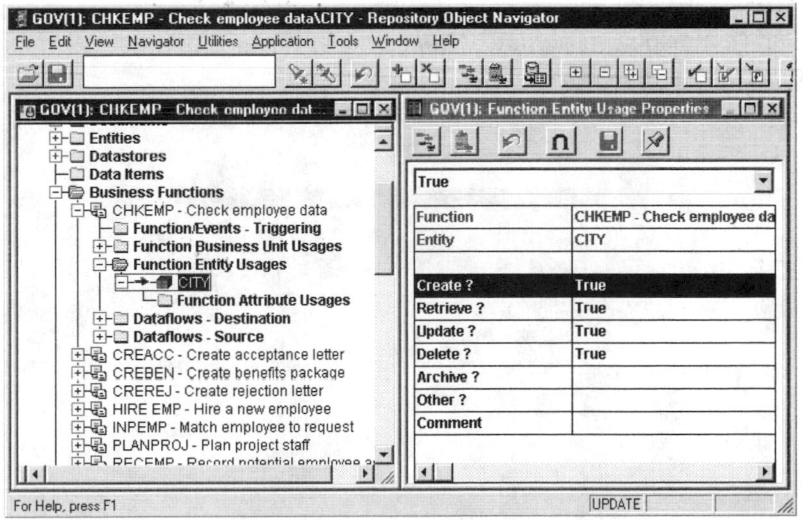

FIGURE 4-27. *RON Properties window for Function Entity Usage*

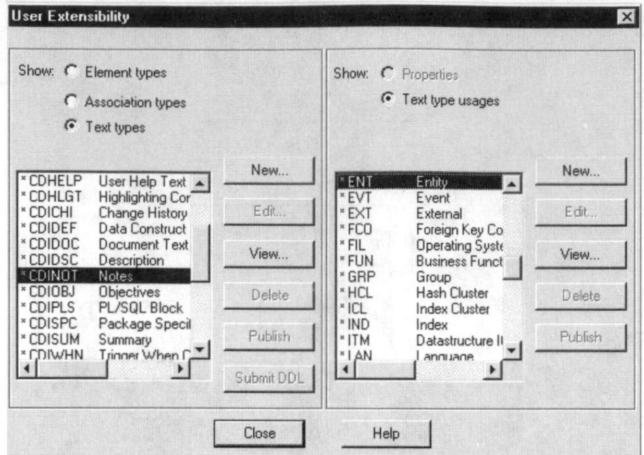

FIGURE 4-28. *Text type list for CDINOT and its text type usages*

properties (called User-Defined Property 0 through User-Defined Property 9) already attached to each item but not shown in RON.

If you decide to define extra properties for an existing element or association, remember that the properties you see in RAU are only the extensible ones (and Name and Comments), so be sure a property does not already exist that matches the one you need.

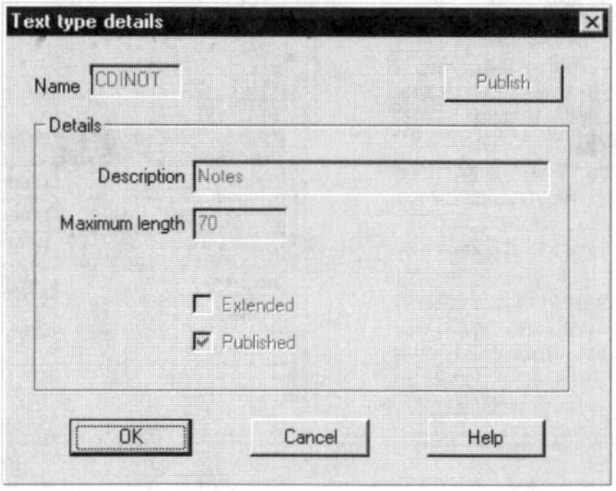

Text type details
Name CDINOT
Publish
Details
Description Notes
Maximum length 70
Extended
Published
OK
Cancel
Help

FIGURE 4-29. *Text type definition*

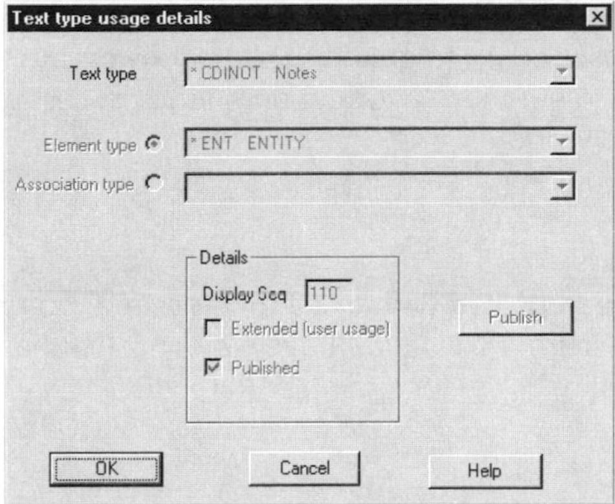

FIGURE 4-30. *Definition of a text type usage for a text type*

TIP

The repository stores audit information on each definition in properties that you may or may not see. In RON, choose **Edit→Preferences** from the menu. Then click the Properties tab where there is a check box for Show Audit Properties. If that is checked, you will be able to see for each property list the name of the person who created and changed the element and when these actions occurred.

How to Define User Extensions in RAU

As shown in Figure 4-19 earlier in this chapter, RAU provides three tools in the User Extensions area to accomplish the following:

- *Maintain User Extensions* for creating, changing, and viewing user extensions
- *Load User Extensions* for bringing user extensions into the repository from an export file created with the next utility
- *Extract User Extensions* for creating the export file that stores the user extensions

The last two tools are used only for importing and exporting the extended definitions and are well documented in the help system. You use the first tool to perform the main work of creating and modifying user extensions.

Steps for Creating a User Extension

Following are the steps you use to create a user extension. Remember that you can press the Help button to get more information on the process and details on particular steps as you work.

1. **Make a Plan**

Make a plan of the steps you will take and, if desired, draw an ERD of the new items like the one in Figure 4-31. If you have elements that have a relationship or link, define an association type (for example, REQUIREMENT FOR FUNCTION).

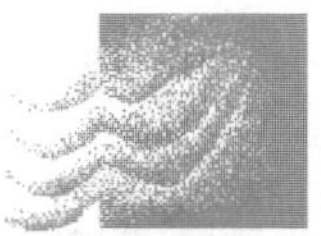

CAUTION

When you publish a new type or property, you will change all application systems in the repository, and the extension is not reversible.

Use care when you publish user extensions. If you make a mistake when defining a new element, you can define a new extension under a different name and not use the type that is in error, but you cannot delete the old extension. Also, you can use the Designer/2000 API to change some characteristics of user-defined properties after you have published them. (See Chapter 14 for more information.)

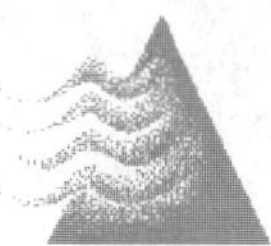

TIP

Perform a full-user repository export to create a .DMP file via RAU before publishing. If you make a mistake, you can delete the repository and import the .DMP file to restore the original state of the repository—all RAU tasks.

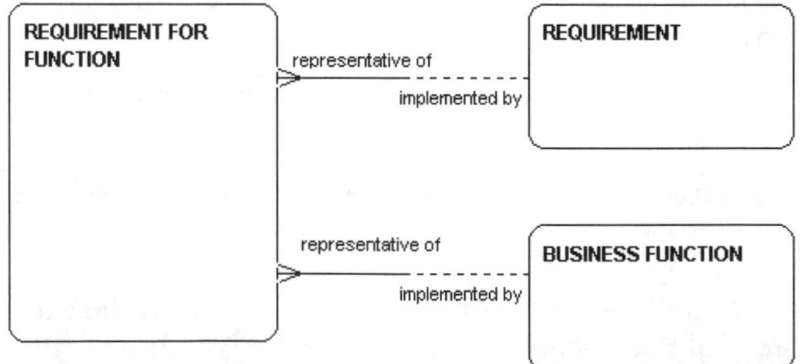

FIGURE 4-31. *ERD of proposed element and association*

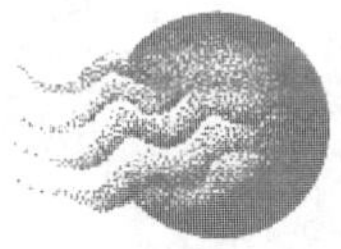

NOTE

If you export an application system to another repository that does not have your user extensions installed, you have to also export the user extensions using RAU. You then import these user extensions into the other repository with RAU as well.

2. Define the New Objects

Click the Maintain User Extensions button in RAU. If you want to create a new type (element, association, or text), choose the appropriate type on the list on the top left side. Click the left-hand New button to reach the definition screen and fill in all items there. Click OK and do not publish yet. Note that element and association types are automatically named with a letter and number (like E7). You should not change these names so you can clearly identify these items as user-extensions when you look at the list. This reference name will not be visible anywhere other than in this utility (and in the base table, of course). Elsewhere, you will refer to the new item by the name you define. Be sure to define properties for new element and association types as discussed next. Figure 4-32 shows the definition window for the new Requirements element type.

For the Requirements example, you would define a new association type for User Req to Function using a similar process. When you define an association type, you have to state the cardinality from it to each of the elements it links. Specify the cardinality carefully—you usually want many-to-many associations so the link will appear under both elements.

FIGURE 4-32. *Definition of the Requirements element type*

After defining the types, you can assign names to the extendible Usrx properties. Choose the element from the list on the left. Then select the Usrx property you want to rename on the right and choose Edit. Fill in the items on the next screen and click OK; do not publish yet.

If you want to create a new text type usage, choose the type you want to add it to on the left and select Text Type Usages on the right. Click the New button and fill in the definition sheet that appears. Click OK and do not publish yet. For the Requirements example, we will not define any additional text types.

3. Publish It

You cannot reverse the extension once you have published, so ensure that the new items you are adding are accurate and spelled correctly. Also be sure that you have backed up the repository so you can restore it if needed after the extension process. Click the Publish button for each type when you have completed your check. If you are defining a new type, you will be prompted to indicate whether you also want to publish unpublished properties. The answer to this is OK. Then you will be prompted as to whether you want to run the data definition language (DDL) script to generate the views and packages. This is not an optional step, but you can perform it later with the Submit DDL button if you wish.

4. Reconcile Grants

The last step in the process is to update the grants and synonyms for repository users so they can see and use the new extensions. Click the Recreate button in the RAU Repository Management area. Choose Full Recompile, and RAU will run scripts to update user access so users can use the new elements or properties.

You will now have new elements and properties in your repository. Check RON for the new node or property in an element. If you also defined an association, you will not see that node until you create an element of one of the types. Figure 4-33 shows the new Requirement PAC with an association node under one of its instances. Be sure you specify that you want to see user extensions in the Hierarchy window by selecting that check box in the **Edit→Preferences** dialog box before you open the application system. Alternatively, you can check that check box when the Filter dialog box shows for the **File→Open** procedure.

The Requirements Mapping System

If you wanted to implement the system requirements activity in the repository, you would follow the same steps for each of the two new types: Requirement (element) and Requirement for Function (association). The association function ties the new Requirement element type to the existing Business Function element type. In

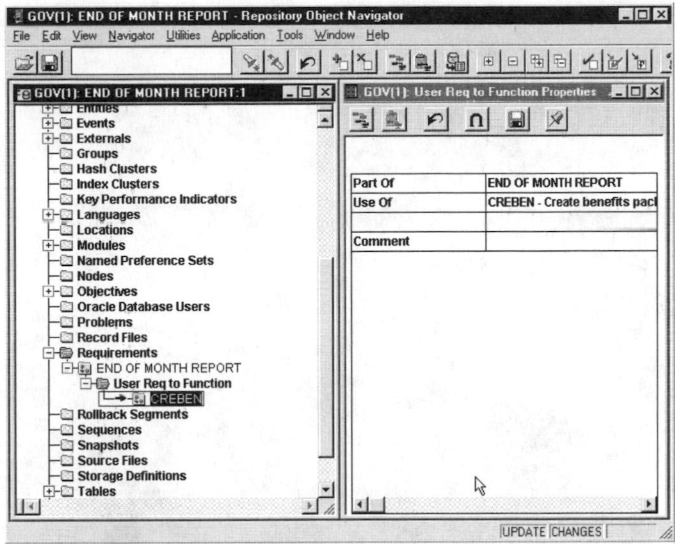

FIGURE 4-33. *New Requirement PAC*

addition, you could expand on this idea to fully implement the ERD in Figure 4-1 as user extensions to the repository.

Conclusion

In Pre-Analysis, you determine how to gather all of the necessary system requirements. First, you must consider all of the possible sources of requirements, as well as how to go about gathering those requirements. Next, you need to decide how all of this information will coherently be integrated into a set of system requirements. The key to a successful Analysis phase is a carefully thought-out analysis plan.

The main objective of the Analysis phase is to produce a complete set of system requirements; and the Pre-Analysis phase is where you plan how you will realize that objective in the best and most efficient way. Designer/2000 supports this planning by allowing you to check your strategy document diagram elements to ensure that you can build on the strategy elements but still keep copies of the source, and helping you produce reports of the work you did in the Strategy phase. You will now move into the Analysis phase and learn about the tasks you need to perform as well as how Designer/2000 supports and integrates this work.

CHAPTER 5

Analysis: Part 1—Information Gathering

Gather ye requirements while ye may. The old system is still a flying. And the same project that's on time today, tomorrow will be dying. Apologies to Robert Herrick (1591-1674).

Analysis is the process of gathering system requirements. At this point in the system development process, the analyst should have the following idea uppermost in mind: "It is not possible to meet a user's need that was never discovered."

Consider this real-world example of lost requirements. The Analysis phase was almost finished when the analysts were approached by one of the client's legacy system programmers and told the following: "There are elements written into the programs that allow us to do some types of business in New Jersey and not in Pennsylvania. Most of the users are unaware of this. Where are these requirements being written down?" In this case, the confusion occurred because the project leader had not thought through the Analysis phase completely prior to its execution.

It is very easy to just begin talking to people and gathering data. However, the analyst must constantly keep in mind the following questions:

- How will the system designers find out everything they need to know to complete the project?
- Are the resources adequate?
- Will the analysis process truly generate all system requirements?

The goal at this point is straightforward: namely, to execute the analysis plan. However, throughout the Analysis phase, the analysts need to think very carefully about the process that was outlined in Pre-Analysis.

As mentioned in Chapter 4, Analysis consists of two parts: information gathering and requirements analysis. Information gathering activities such as conducting interviews, implementing questionnaires, holding JAD sessions, and reviewing the legacy system are performed first. After information gathering is complete, the requirements analysis portion of the Analysis phase begins where all of this information is collated and analyzed while, at the same time, inconsistencies among requirements are identified and resolved and a coherent statement of the new system requirements is formulated.

Overview of Information Gathering

Analysts traditionally follow a two-step process:

1. They talk to users in order to understand what they want and need.
2. They build ERDs, function hierarchies, and prototypes.

Steps 1 and 2 must be linked together, however. Creating a transition step—the delivery of the requirements document—provides a means to cross-check the functional models and ERDs, and not just directly with the users, but with a document the users approved weeks ago, about which they said, "Yes, that is the way we want it done."

This extra step also gives the users something to compare with the system function hierarchy and ERD. They first compare what they want done with their requirements list. Then they compare this requirements list (which they have already approved) to what is in the ERD, function hierarchy, and any prototypes that have been made.

During information gathering, the analysis team should be focused on determining the system requirements. If the information gathered is incomplete or inaccurate or does not reflect the users' needs, the system to be implemented will be a failure. It is important to spend an adequate amount of time to gather this information completely and effectively. In general, information gathering tasks require both a strict information gathering process and a separate unit analysis process.

Devices such as prototypes, screen shots, preliminary database models, and storyboarded applications are appropriate only insofar as they serve as vehicles to communicate back to the users what the analysts understand their needs to be.

This feedback to the users should be done at the unit level, interview by interview and user by user. For example, in an individual user interview, the analyst tries to collect as much information as possible. Then the analyst examines the information gathered and generates informal ERDs, process flows, or other appropriate representations to effectively feed back to the user, in an organized way, what was learned in the interview. Ideally, this unit analysis activity takes place with the help and hands-on support of the user. Unfortunately, sometimes users have neither the time nor the inclination to be this involved in the system development process.

After the unit analysis is performed, the information is passed back to the user for approval of both the interview notes and whatever analysis of the interview was performed. Until the user signs off, the interview is not complete.

The analysis process can then proceed. The analysis plan prescribes various information gathering activities that need to be performed in a particular sequence and the degree of parallelism of these activities. Each information gathering task follows the same process. Information gathering and unit analysis are described in the remainder of this chapter.

Eliciting Requirements from the Users

This section discusses the various methods of gathering the information necessary to understand the business area and identify requirements. These methods include:

- Interviews
- Questionnaires
- Electronic bulletin boards
- Joint application development (JAD) sessions

Interviews

Interviews that are conducted carefully can go a long way toward eliciting the necessary system requirements. The standard procedure for gathering user requirements is to interview the business users at the client site. This may sound like a straightforward and simple task, but the methods used to obtain and organize the information can greatly affect the results.

Open-Ended Interviews

Open-ended interviews consist of one or more analysts and interviewers sitting down with a user and asking questions. One of the authors of this book did a doctoral dissertation on the topic of user interviews that sought to measure how much information was discussed. Hundreds of hours of video tape of actual interviews between analysts and users were analyzed to determine the answer to this question: how is it that good analysts are able to elicit up to ten times as much information as inexperienced ones?

Some of what was discovered was consistent with the advice typically given to analysts. However, much of what was found contradicted conventional wisdom. It is critical to constantly keep in mind the nature of the analyst-user interaction and the purpose of the interview: namely, to understand the business and identify requirements. This can be supported in several ways: through good questions and comments, productive feedback, and a pre-existing structure for the information to be gathered.

When conducting interviews, it is very useful to bring a person other than the interviewer to act as a scribe for the interview. In this way, the interviewer can concentrate on the questions being asked and on providing appropriate feedback as discussed later in this section. A logical choice for this role is a junior analyst. He or she will gain experience in how to conduct an interview. The senior analyst can then review the write-up of the interview shown to the user for final sign-off.

Question Syntax Is Irrelevant Much has been written in various fields about the syntax of the questions asked in an interview and how this affects the information gathered. These studies typically stipulate that questions must be open-ended so as not to bias the feedback, and they conclude that careful attention must be paid to the exact words and syntax of the questions in order to get the most accurate answers. These conclusions were reached by looking at standardized exams, police interviews, psychiatric interviews, and teacher-student interactions.

However, there is a substantive difference between the interactions in the standard research settings and those in a system development environment. The goal in system development is to give and receive information. The relationship between interviewer and user is *cooperative*, not adversarial, and there is no attempt to coerce or trick the person being interviewed. Both the analyst and the person being interviewed are working toward a common goal. Therefore, the syntax of the questions asked is completely irrelevant in this setting.

In the author's doctoral dissertation research, the amount of information and users' perceptions of the information transferred were precisely measured, along with the user satisfaction when the syntax of the questions was altered. In contrast to the results of the other research, this study found no appreciable differences in the responses to questions regardless of the syntax. For example, it didn't matter which of the following two questions the interviewer asked:

"Do you want a printer?" (yes/no question)

"How would you like to handle your printing needs?" (open-ended question)

Not only were open-ended questions no better at eliciting the desired information, but there was a statistically significant greater probability that the user would not understand these more complex questions.

The issue then remained: if the syntax didn't make a difference, what did matter in conducting a successful interview? The conclusion reached was that certain interviewer behaviors and strategies were the key factors.

Listen, Then Talk The most important factor observed from the hours of interview tapes was that the interviewers who were most successful placed themselves in a mode to receive information and stayed locked into this mode. Their primary goal was to listen, not give information. To do this, they displayed several key behaviors, some of which are covered in the literature on active listening:

- They asked good questions.
- They gave encouraging nonverbal feedback (such as note taking, head nodding, and "uh-huhs").

- They let the user say what he or she wanted to say without interruption until finished.

Interview questions should be designed to open up topics for the user to talk about. The comment "Let's talk about printing" could elicit the same feedback as yes/no or complex questions about printing. The important point is for the interviewer to always keep in mind the specific setting and situation of the interview in the business environment. The nature of this interaction is that information can go only one way at a time. Someone must be giving information, and someone must be receiving information. If both the analyst and user are trying to give information at the same time, then no one is listening.

Use Feedback Good listening behavior, however, is not enough. Attentive listening and "uh-huhs" do not communicate to unhappy users that they have been heard and understood. The most successful interviewers repeated back what they had heard, using statements like "Let me see if I understand what you are saying" or "From what I've heard, this is what you are looking for." These interviewers were able to get much more information from the users. There was a direct correlation between using these feedback strategies and getting more information. Finally, a key question that must always be asked is "Is there anything you would like to add?" This makes the person being interviewed feel that the interviewer has heard and thought about what has been said and forces acknowledgment that the user has no more to say.

Use Power Carefully Another important issue in conducting successful interviews is that of power. In a typical interview situation, there is a clear delineation of who is in the position of power. This is not the case in an analyst-user relationship. The optimal arrangement is a relative parity in power positions between the interviewer and the user. In general, the user needs to feel comfortable enough to talk about what needs to be discussed. If a user is insecure, it is the job of the interviewer to put the user at ease. Ways that this can be accomplished include conducting the interview on the user's turf (for instance, in the user's office) and using nonverbal cues. Nonverbal cues may include note taking, head nodding, body position, and voice volume. These cues can be used to manipulate the power structure of the situation to suit the needs of the interviewer.

For example, if the user isn't letting the interviewer get a word in edgewise, the interviewer can take control by standing and walking to the white board or using paper and drawing or reviewing what has been discussed. This puts the interviewer in the place of highest power since all attention will be focused on the person at the board. At that point, the interviewer owns the situation and is in control. Less-severe power gaining measures include controlling the actual volume (voice level) of talk. Also, the interviewer can remain in an information receiving mode but encourage an alternation of discussion between him or herself and the user. If done correctly, this can make for a very effective interview. Body position can also influence the power balance. If the interviewer is sitting in a relaxed pose, this is a higher power stance and tends to put the user in a weaker position.

In the opposite situation where the user is reluctant to talk, the interviewer needs to give the user more power. This can be done with body language: for example, the interviewer can sit up in an attentive pose waiting to receive information. Gentle cues ("Tell me about. . .") and questions can draw out the reticent user and extract the necessary information.

A related issue to that of power in analyst-user interviews is that of gender. Because of deeply rooted social norms and perceptions within society, the gender of the interviewer and user may play a role in the success of the interaction. The interviewer simply needs to be aware of this and make slight adjustments in the power structure of the interaction. If a male interviewer is dealing with a female user accustomed to a male boss, he may want to speak quietly and take lots of notes to facilitate better transfer of information. Conversely, a female interviewer with a male user accustomed to being in control may want to use more power-increasing strategies in her interviewing.

Protect Against Bias One factor to be very careful about in interviewing but which can be quite difficult to detect is interviewer bias. Consider the results of a study done in the 1930s concerning the reasons for homelessness among people. Some of the interviewers sent out were temperance workers; they reported that the main cause of homelessness among the subjects they interviewed was alcohol. Other interviewers were socialists; they reported that the cause of homelessness among their subjects was economic conditions in society. These interviewers were not conducting open-ended interviews. Even though they were using precisely written questionnaires, their own biases influenced the way they asked the questions, thus influencing the responses.

The potential for bias on the part of the interviewer in an open-ended interview is even greater. The only effective way to guard against bias is to use several different analysts who will hopefully have different biases. By analyzing all of their information, a balanced picture of user requirements can be obtained.

Another way to help prevent interviewer bias is to send two analysts to conduct an interview with one user. In this way, their individual biases will have less effect. An added benefit of this strategy is that one analyst can be assigned to interview the user from a data-centric perspective and the other from a more process-centered perspective.

Structure Your Information Retrieval So that as many requirements as possible are uncovered and the validity of the information is explored as thoroughly possible, three topics must be addressed during user interviews:

- What each user does
- How each user does what he or she does
- What each user needs to do his or her job

It is also important to discuss these topics, which don't relate directly to the user's current system:

- Improvements that the new system could supply
- Topics outside the range of the user's immediate job function

When asking what users do, the analyst should have them list their tasks. For each task noted, the analyst then should determine the process flow. The process flow for a task is simply how people do their jobs. Each task further refines into subtasks. These subtasks will probably turn into functions when the information is entered into Designer/2000. In most cases, a task becomes a screen function if the user needs to create, update, or delete information. A task becomes a report function if the user needs to retrieve the information on the screen or on paper. If the user performs quality checks on the data, the task might become an integrity constraint.

The third topic, what users needs to do their jobs, includes determining what functions and data users need. The decisions a user makes during the day are often critical issues when determining the requirements of the system.

After the first three topics have been covered with the user, what the user needs in the new system can be addressed. Now that *how* the existing system works has been detailed, areas for improvement can be discussed.

Finally, the analyst should ask the user for comments that do not relate directly to the user's tasks and job. These not only shed light on processes that might affect the user indirectly; but they may open up ideas for future work. For example, a person might explain that checks are never issued on time. This may be out of scope for the current project, but an attempt to work on this related project could be made in the future.

Following this interview procedure will allow you to question users in a way that stimulates discussion. Users discuss what they do every day with co-workers and friends. In most cases, you will not get a constructive response if you ask a person, "What are the requirements of the new system from your point of view?" It is much better to put the system in perspective and have the users tell you what they do, how they do it, and what they need to do.

Group Questions into Categories A skilled interviewer may be able to elicit a great deal of information, but without some type of format or structure, the value of the information is greatly diminished. A skilled analyst organizes his or her questions into related topics.

These structurally related questions typically start with a structural identifier. The interviewer introduces topic A and then provides contextual structural cues relating to the question to reduce the probability that the question will be misunderstood. In this fashion, subtopics A.1, A.2, and so on can be covered in depth. The interviewer builds a tree of information with three types of questions:

- **Validation questions** For instance, "Is this what you are saying? Have I got this right?"
- **Horizontal questions** For instance, "You've told me about A1 and A2. Is there an A3? Are there other areas about A that we need to discuss?"
- **Vertical questions** For instance, "Tell me about A.1. Is A.1 important? How should we handle things associated with A.1?"

The skilled analyst is able to organize information as it is being gathered into a structural hierarchy. The analyst begins with a list of questions and moves both horizontally and vertically through the topics. The responses can be organized into a tree structure where one topic (such as A) is the parent, and each parent topic has children (A1, A2, A3). These children are siblings and follow a horizontal format. Each child can then be further broken down into more layers of subtopics in a vertical format (A1.1 A1.2, and so on). Each horizontal and vertical topic is explored until a termination point is reached on every set of siblings in the tree. This point is reached when the answer to the question "Is there anything you would like to add?" is "no." In writing up this information, horizontal and vertical lines can be drawn at the appropriate termination points to indicate that the topic has been exhausted.

Work from an Information Template Having an internal information template has been found to be one of the key factors in distinguishing an experienced systems person from an inexperienced one. A large body of research on schema theory suggests that learning and comprehension of new information is strongly affected by whatever pre-existing related information the learner brings to the task. This can work both ways in an analyst-user interview. The experienced analyst brings a whole range of information on system development and business applications to the interview. At his or her disposal will be many detailed questions about various types of systems that will help shape the interview and get at the desired information. Users, for their part, bring knowledge of their business and what they want the new system to be able to do. Also, they may have some expectations regarding the questions the interviewer will ask. If there is a conflict between the existing schemas of the analyst and the user, the appropriate information may be difficult to obtain.

At the highest subject level, the analyst's internal template, or schema, may be the following question: "If I'm going to build a system, what are the hardware and software requirements?" For an inexperienced analyst, this might be the whole template. A more experienced analyst would have a much more extensive, complete, and detailed set of questions to ask.

For example, to get at the system requirements for performance, a good analyst would know to ask the following questions:

1. What is the acceptable time lag for each transaction?
2. How up-to-date must information be in each context? For example, for trend analysis, work on a data warehouse that is updated monthly might be adequate. For a customer billing inquiry, information may have to be up to the second.
3. What is the cost of the system going down for 1 minute, 10 minutes, 1 hour, 4 hours, 1 day, etc?
4. How many transactions per hour will the system need to support?
5. How many users will be on the system at one time?

The more complex the structural template the analyst brings to the interview, the more likely he or she is to get all the necessary information to eventually create a system that successfully meets the users' needs. The ultimate goal is to get the maximum amount of information on the user's business, existing system, desired changes, and hoped-for aspects and features of the new system.

In reviewing the research video tapes in the author's doctoral study, three levels of analysts emerged based upon their interviewing procedures:

- **Inexperienced** These interviewers took notes and did a lot of head nodding and saying "uh-huh" but elicited only a fraction of the potential information from the client.
- **Intermediate** These interviewers followed up on particular threads of information by asking some questions but let the conversation wander. If the interviewer was lucky, the appropriate information was elicited, but it was disorganized, which made it easy to miss important points.
- **Experienced** These analysts walked into interviews with an information template in their heads that allowed them to work through a systematic

hierarchical structure of information retrieval. The user can provide a great deal of information, but the information given will not be generated in a structured format unless the interviewer provides this structure.

For example, the skilled interviewer will already have identified three important areas (A, B, and C) that need to be discussed and will begin by saying, "Tell me about A." From that prompt, topics A1, A2, and A3 will emerge. For each area, the experienced interviewer will lead the user through the information in a structured fashion, and at some appropriate point, the interviewer will review each point with the user to ensure that all the relevant information is elicited.

The interview procedure allows the analyst to develop a list of requirements and show each user what he or she said. It gives the analyst a document that can be given back to each user. The analyst can say "This is what you told me," and ask "Do I have it right?" Recording the details is important in big projects, where many ideas that may seem little at the time may fall through the cracks. The requirements document is used to explain to the user "You want the existing system with these changes. We understand the existing system does these things." It does not get any simpler; the analyst has just outlined the scope of the project with the user's own words.

Techniques of the Good Interviewer To summarize, in order to be a successful interviewer, you should use these four important techniques:

- Go into the interview with an internal template of topics and questions relevant to the specific business situation.
- Ask the kinds of questions designed to elicit the maximum amount of information in a structured format.
- Listen actively and effectively, providing useful verbal and non-verbal feedback.
- Provide a hierarchical structure within which the information can be elicited and organized.

When all these elements are in place, the information you gather from the interviews will provide a solid base from which to start system development and will go a long way toward ensuring that users are entirely satisfied with the finished product. In addition, carefully documented and reported user interviews can be invaluable in determining the source of potential problems with the finished product and ways to solve them.

Questionnaires

Unlike open-ended interviews, the question syntax in questionnaires greatly influences their effectiveness. In questionnaires, significantly different results can be obtained depending upon the wording of the questions. The order of both questions and response selections can also affect responses. Items listed first tend to be selected more often. For instance, if asked "Which online service would you rather have access to: CompuServe, Prodigy, or America Online?" more users would choose CompuServe simply because it is listed first.

If questionnaires are administered face to face, the issues of bias mentioned for interviews should be taken into consideration.

A potential problem with questionnaires is not asking the right questions. Ask any teacher or professor how difficult it is to write tests and exams. Think back to the last few times you received a questionnaire in the mail where the questions did not make sense. When composing questions, you must consider the complete range of people who will be answering them. Questions appropriate for managers may not be appropriate for end users. You may need to develop different questionnaires for different classes of system users.

In developing questionnaires, you should subject the questions to extensive testing. Present sample questions to a few users face to face to ensure that users interpret the questions the way you intended.

Once questionnaires have been designed and distributed, the results need to be analyzed. The analysis of the answers is a complex task that requires a skilled statistician.

Electronic Bulletin Boards

Computers have changed the way we communicate within organizations. They have made communication with management much easier across the organization and have, in general, increased the amount of communication within a given organization.

Unfortunately, this communications channel is underused to support requirements analysis. There are several ways that it can be used in this capacity. Electronic information can facilitate various portions of the analysis process as well as other phases within CADM. Two are presented here.

Electronic bulletin boards can be used for discussion among users about the system being designed. For example, an electronic bulletin board can be set up to debate the features that the new system toolbar should include and whether the organization should go to the expense of including a user-customizable toolbar. Such an electronic bulletin board, where any user could post messages, would be simple to set up. All messages would be visible to everyone using the bulletin board. There already exist numerous products to support such bulletin boards. They should be applied where appropriate.

The second way electronic information can be used to assist in the gathering of user requirements is by giving users direct access to the list of requirements being compiled. Users can review and respond to specific items on the list. A Web server application can be set up to access the Designer/2000 repository. This would allow users to see the listed functions and their associated requirements and enable them to suggest new requirements or comment on existing requirements.

Joint Application Development (JAD) Sessions

A JAD session utilizes a workshop setting where business and technology professionals participate in the planning, analysis and design of a system development effort. JAD sessions produce the best results when the number of participants does not exceed twenty. JAD sessions should be attended by representatives from all interested groups. The organizers should ensure that the group is reasonably balanced in terms of user level.

In order to be effective, JAD sessions must have some specific purposes and goals. They should not be used for general application development work. They are very expensive and usually not very efficient.

A JAD session is an inherently political event that may often involve more political posturing than problem solving. Avoid holding a JAD session to discuss a topic when there is no decision to be made. In such a case, the main function of the session will simply be to allow users to feel as though they have been heard. Often, the outcome of these unfocused JAD sessions is the appointment of a steering committee to perform the work that the JAD session was supposed to accomplish.

If you are going to hold a JAD session, it must have a precise agenda and goal. The more precise the focus, the more successful the JAD session is likely to be. To keep JAD sessions from wasting time, a useful strategy is to schedule them before lunch. Participants are sharper and more focused in the morning, and after one or one and a half hours, they will be ready to leave. In the authors' experience, nothing useful has ever happened in a JAD session after the first one and a half hours.

A successful JAD session must have a trained and experienced facilitator whose job it is to work with the project team in developing the purpose, scope, and deliverable in advance of the session. The facilitator must manage the group dynamics, enforce the ground rules and adhere to the agenda. The purpose, scope, anticipated delvierables and the agenda should be documented and distributed to all participants well before the scheduled meeting time. The approximate amount of time allocated to each agenda topic should be indicated.

JAD sessions are useful when conflicting user requirements are encountered. A JAD session is the best place to resolve such conflicts. If there are very strong concerns, the proposed session can be used to communicate these concerns to all groups.

An additional function of a JAD session can be to convince obstinate individual users who believe they speak for a large number of other users that they may be mistaken. The JAD session can be a vehicle for overcoming the objections of one or more individuals by demonstrating a general consensus on a particular issue.

Legacy System Review

Most systems projects are not brand-new stand-alone systems. They are often upgrades or replacements of existing systems. Therefore, an understanding of those systems being modified or replaced is key to the success of the new system. The analyst should perform a legacy system review that includes the following steps to adequately document the existing system:

- Code walkthrough
- Report audit
- User walkthrough
- Review of user and system documentation

Just as you should learn what user requirements are from multiple sources, you should examine the legacy system from several viewpoints to elicit the necessary requirements. When interviewing users, it is possible, and necessary, to interview more than one, and a requirement forgotten by one user is likely to be mentioned by another. You will not have these multiple opportunities in the legacy system review. Each step in the legacy system review may be the only chance for the analysts to learn about a particular requirement. Therefore, it is important to assign highly skilled and responsible people to the legacy system review.

Code Walkthrough

The legacy system frequently will contain data and application requirements that are embedded in the underlying legacy code. Particular attention should be paid to the following areas of code in trying to discover these requirements:

- Data validation
- Code that generates redundant or summary fields
- Code that supports data and application security

- Complex application logic

Code walkthroughs are difficult to accomplish if you are not intimately acquainted with the application. Thus, they are best done with a legacy system developer or supporter. If the code has not been maintained or well documented and no legacy system developers are available, a code walkthrough may not be worth doing at all.

Report Audit

A report audit is where you ask the user to verify that they actually use each report they receive. A report audit is a cheap and easy way to determine reporting needs. During the first part of the Analysis phase, you should look at the existing reports produced by the current system. The following information should be gathered as a part of this process:

- Determine the user requirements associated with the reports: what kind of information do the system users need and use?
- Determine the reporting requirements for the new system.
- Determine how the existing reports will need to be modified.

Just because a report has been produced for ten years, analysts should not assume that it is still being read. When users are asked what information they are concerned about, they invariably will leave out important information. The system analyst needs to look carefully at the reports generated by the system and how they are used by individuals in the organization.

The users should be given copies of all the relevant existing reports and asked to rank them using a scale such as this:

- **Level 1: Mission Critical** This report must be converted and in production on day 1.
- **Level 2: Very Useful** If possible, this report should be available on day 1; it has high priority for implementation.
- **Level 3: Useful** Users would like to have this report in the new system.
- **Level 4: Marginally Useful** This report may be used.
- **Level 5: Not Useful**

For all reports marked levels 1 through 3, users should use a marking pen to indicate the information that is specifically useful to them. Frequently, reports have multiple parts. Some users may look only at the summary or for a trend or sample of detail information. It may be possible to decrease the amount of information in reports to make them more concise. Some reports may have been designed for one particular user or class of users that is no longer relevant, but the system keeps churning out the reports anyway. The cost of doing this in the existing system is small, but the cost of writing a useless report in the new system is prohibitive.

The report audit needs to be completed by a large number of users. Unless the total number of users is very small, the audit should be completed by 10 to 20 users per reporting area (such as payroll, accounting, human resources, top management.) There should be representatives from each reporting area in the audit group. The developer also needs to be aware of the different constituencies for which each report is relevant.

The results of the audit can be written in a spreadsheet with the report names listed on the left and the users and user group names across the top. For each report, the priority number (1 to 5) assigned to the report by each user or group should be shown. The users should be asked to look at reports ranked 1 through 3 in more detail and identify the information from those reports that they want in the new system and anything that may be unnecessary.

After all this information is collected, the analyst must decide which reports to incorporate into the new system. The implications of this decision used to be huge, because putting a report into production used to take two to three person weeks. With modern reporting tools or report generation using Designer/2000, this process now takes one to two days or less. The authors, for example, once developed nine production reports in one day.

At the end of this process, the analyst should have three binders of reports:

- First-priority reports that must go into the new system
- Reports that the developer will attempt to implement in phase 1 of the new system
- Reports without broad enough appeal to be included in the new system

Keep in mind that the first two binders may include new reports not yet in production. These binders should also include facsimiles of the actual reports or prototypes.

The cost-benefit tradeoff for straightforward reports has also changed over time. Costs have been greatly reduced because of products such as Oracle Reports, with its Lexical Parameter Facility. Reports with similar layouts can be combined into a single report. Using the lexical parameters, the system can support the passing of flexible parameters to the report. With this facility, what originally looked like 200 different reports, each requiring a day or two of effort, becomes 10 reports requiring two or three days effort, with the added advantage that changes to the underlying data structure can be implemented very quickly across the entire reporting environment.

The analyst therefore needs to sort and group the designated reports to support the users' reporting needs. It is not necessary to worry about the total number of reports. As mentioned in the preceding paragraph, there may be permutations of other existing reports. It is easier to start with more reports and not be restricted to just the essential ones. Using a combination of Designer/2000 and Oracle Reports, the analyst should have the ability to support the major reporting requirements of a substantial reports system with about one month of effort.

User Walkthrough

How a user actually uses a system may differ markedly from the way the system was designed to be used. Users are notorious for figuring out workarounds to support functionality that the system was never designed to deliver. Similarly, functionality that was designed into the system may not be as important as was originally thought and may be rarely or never used.

There is no reason to reproduce all of the functionality of the legacy system if it is not all used. For example, a reporting system may include a flexible ad hoc reporting engine that allows users to filter and break for subtotals on many fields in the database. In practice, however, the users may consider only a handful of fields, thus making a large part of the functionality of the system irrelevant.

Sometimes, the only way for analysts to find out what users actually do is to sit down with them and watch them do it. These user walkthroughs should be conducted with different users at different levels. Often, the users themselves can help the analysts select individuals who are doing interesting things with the system or who are often sought out for help with the existing system.

Here are some specific areas that analysts should target during system walkthroughs:

- Ask users to identify any workarounds and how they are performed.
- Ask questions designed to find out whether existing system features are being used as they were intended. For instance, if the system includes an employee or customer name field, ask whether this field is used for any purpose other than the stated one.
- Ask what all of the uses are for a particular screen.

User and System Documentation Review

Of course, a thorough reading of the legacy system documentation and any user documentation, where it exists, is a given. These sources will frequently point to other user requirements not mentioned elsewhere. The analyst will not get accurate or complete information on the legacy system by simply talking to users. Users often don't know how the system is designed or even how all of its functions work.

When legacy system documentation is missing or inadequate, the analysts must reconstruct it as best they can. The legacy system documentation should be organized into three sections:

- **Data structure** The data structure section should include documentation of files and of the file structure, if the database is relational. Also, a physical ERD should be included as well as a logical ERD if these exist. Finding an ERD for a legacy system is a rare occurrence. However, even when the system is not a physical system, the analyst should try to reverse engineer a physical ERD.
- **Fields** The analyst needs to know the purpose of all the fields in tables and files. Ideally, descriptions of all existing fields should exist for the legacy system. If these descriptions do not exist, the analyst should build them before proceeding. If fields are redundant and used only for processing, it is sufficient to identify and describe only the significant data fields.
- **Where each field comes from** For simple systems, a matrix can be constructed to show how a specific data element from a specific screen is populated. A simple spreadsheet or application that becomes a master-detail report can be used for this purpose.

It is also important to find out the following information on the legacy system:

- How do data elements on the screen (the user interface) map to data elements in the database?
- How are business transactions performed?
- What business rules are embedded in the data structure?

It is not always possible to count on the logical, consistent mapping and file structures that developers now expect in relational databases. Fields aren't necessarily just one thing; they may serve multiple purposes. For example, a system may include a salesperson ID field, but during data migration, you may discover that although this field usually contains a salesperson ID, sometimes transactions not credited to a specific sales person are credited to a department, and a null employee entry is made in the salesperson ID field. Consequently, the field may contain either a real employee or an unassigned employee.

On one system, we discovered that most customer transactions were associated with only one or two products, though a small number of deals with customers are associated with a dozen or more products. The legacy system analysts designed a user interface that supports a small number of transactions, and the tables used for these transactions are also used for financial reporting due to their similar structure.

The point is that the analyst needs to go into some depth in a legacy system to find out all the different ways in which information is placed in a particular field.

The analyst should also track performance characteristics of the legacy system. How long do reports take to run? How fast is the user response in performing various tasks? The new system should at least outperform the old one. It is important to find out from the users what their performance concerns are and where performance matters less. Rank the performance issues and determine the most frequent user actions so that the new system can be more efficient.

Determining the processes embedded in the legacy system code is as important as finding out the business rules. Process-oriented people will often forget about business rules, but both aspects are important to overall project success. By observing how users actually use the existing system, analysts can get a better idea of how users will interact with the new system. A new system that is replacing a legacy system must duplicate only the business functionality of the legacy system that the users deem necessary to support their business.

The documentation of the legacy system is best handled with a small ad hoc database. The ad hoc system must track the legacy system's fields, files, modules, and data structures. The appropriate structure for this system will change from system to system.

Note that programs need not be documented at the field level. The cost to achieve that level of detail outweighs the added benefits. This ERD is used to map the main functionality of the old system to the new system. It is used to make sure that no legacy-supported business function is missed in the design of the new system. The diagram is also used to map legacy fields to the new system attributes.

Security

It is necessary to determine the sensitivity of the information that will comprise the system. For most information, we want to have some security to prevent unauthorized manipulation of the information. In other places, we must also worry about unauthorized retrieval of information.

At this point in the information-gathering process, the goal is to determine not only the security requirements but also the costs of a security breach. The likelihood of such a breach must also be assessed. This involves the possible motivations of individuals to breach security. For example, in a banking wire transfer system, a breach of security would allow someone the ability to initiate fraudulent wire transfers. Preventing unauthorized access to systems is particularly important where financial data is concerned. A list of a company's clients might be of great interest to a competitor. However, information concerning how much a company has paid for office supplies in the last six months is of little interest.

As with other areas of system requirements, it is necessary to ask the opinions of numerous individuals at different levels within the organization to determine security requirements. In contrast to other areas of information gathering, typically the best information concerning security can be obtained from middle and upper management rather than end users because of their broader perspective on the role of information in the organization.

It is easy for users to blithely say that they want all data to be completely secure from unauthorized access or manipulation. However, there is always a cost associated with the implementation of security. No system is completely secure. It is necessary to determine the desired level of security for a specific system and the possible costs to the organization of a security failure.

Unit-Level Analysis

Chapter 6 discusses in detail the analysis of the requirements you collect. Within information gathering, you must extract the relevant system requirements from all of the interview and legacy system data you have collected. The goal at this stage is only to understand—not to comment on, filter, dispute, or synthesize the information. As discussed in the "Interviews" section, the analysts should be locked into information receipt mode.

The information collected must, however, be placed into a useful format for the Analysis phase to proceed further. To that end, you must perform unit-level analysis. User interviews will have generated many interview notes. These interview notes may suggest process flows, data models, and elements that may eventually be included in a function hierarchy.

The interview notes from each user should focus on the tasks the user must accomplish. The process flows, the tasks per user, and what information the user needs should be recorded. To allow easy cross-checking of the data, the source should also be noted with each requirement. Listing each requirement, its business function, and its source will make the project flow more smoothly. Again, it is vital that all system requirements be uncovered. Knowing who said that the system must have certain features or functions enables the team to resolve conflicting needs. It also helps the analyst weigh the information of each user, since some users know more about certain areas than others. The user who is an expert in policy management, for example, may only be able to guess what an underwriter would require to make a decision.

For each interview, create the appropriate business models (ERD, process model, function hierarchy) as well as any narrative descriptions to support the models. What is needed is both a graphical and narrative method to communicate to the user that the analyst has understood what was said and at the same time educate the user about some of the diagrams used by systems people—specifically, data models and process flows. This process can give novice analysts conducting interviews some experience in performing data and process analysis.

Possible feedback to the user may be as simple as a review of the notes taken during the interviews, in narrative form. For a more complex response, the analyst can map the interview to a function hierarchy. The best solution may be a combination of the two. The notes can be written, and a structured document can be generated using Word for Windows to put the information into a hierarchy. If desired, this Word document can be loaded into the Designer/2000 function hierarchy using a C program to read the file and load the data into the repository.

A copy of the user-feedback report should go for sign-off to each user interviewed. This sign-off is the ultimate feedback since this will be the information that goes into the requirements document.

Modifications for Smaller Systems

You don't need to make any modifications whatsoever for smaller systems for this part of the analysis process. Information gathering is essential to any project. All that is different for a smaller project is the amount of information gathered. Procedures, interview notes, user feedback, sign-off, and so on should all be conducted in the same manner no matter how small the system.

When Is Information Gathering Complete?

Information gathering is an ongoing process throughout the System Development Life Cycle. However, it is easy to fall into the trap of "analysis paralysis," which can stall a project indefinitely. Often, what harms a project at this point is not the information that has been gathered, but information that has not been kept track of properly after it has been gathered. Nothing is more infuriating to users than having a second or even a third group of analysts ask them the same questions. If a user ever asks, "Don't you people ever talk to each other?" you can conclude that the information gathering process is flawed.

Being meticulous in all aspects of the information gathering process is an important attribute. Obtaining requirements from so many different sources will, of course, result in some duplication of effort. However, the cost of missing an essential requirement is much higher than the cost of collecting a few requirements more than once.

The Analysis Phase in Designer/2000: Information Gathering

Designer/2000 offers you considerable support in the Analysis phase, and you can produce many of the main deliverables directly from the tools and diagrammers. Table 5-1 lists the diagrammers and utilities that are most useful for the information gathering part of the Analysis phase.

The rest of this chapter discusses how you can use each of these Designer/2000 tools to complete the work for these activities. Some tools have already been introduced in previous chapters, but this chapter briefly mentions how they apply to this phase. As usual, you are strongly encouraged to review the introduction to the Designer/2000 interface in Chapter 2 if you have not had hands-on experience with this interface and to consult the Designer/2000 help system for information on the diagrammers and utilities if you need additional instruction.

Activity or Deliverable	Designer/2000 Tool
Interview documents: process flows	Process Modeller or Dataflow Diagrammer
Interview documents: ERD	Entity Relationship Diagrammer
Legacy System ERD	Reverse Engineer Database Objects utility, Table to Entity Retrofit utility, Entity Relationship Diagrammer
Legacy system report audit	Repository Administration Utility (with user extensions to add a property to the Modules element)

TABLE 5-1. *Analysis Activities and Designer/2000 Tools: Information Gathering*

Process Modeller and Entity Relationship Diagrammer in Information Gathering

During the interviewing process, you gather information about requirements, data, and process flows in the organization. You may find it useful to immediately diagram some of these processes or data entities as a visualization of the information you have gathered. Such diagrams can help you to solidify your understanding and communicate this understanding to your interviewees. The idea is to quickly translate your notes from the interviewing process into diagrams right after the interviews. You can also do this outside Designer/2000 initially and then, after checking your diagrams with users or business experts, spend more time carefully entering the information during the requirements analysis stage of the Analysis phase.

Alternatively, you can use Designer/2000s diagrammers to create the first-cut diagrams that you use to communicate with the users in the unit-level analysis work. The Designer/2000 Process Modeller and Entity Relationship Diagrammer can fulfill this need for a set of rough diagrams as you can quickly enter and move elements around on the screen. While these may not be the ultimate in drawing tools, the graphical features are rich enough for you to create these first-cut diagrams easily and efficiently. The benefit of using the Designer/2000 tools is that when you are done, even if the diagrams are not perfectly accurate, you will have some information in the repository that can serve as a basis for the next part of the Analysis phase: requirements analysis.

Completeness and correct decomposition of the process flow models and exact representation of entities are not your main concerns in this part of the Analysis phase. Rather, you should concentrate on the ideas and concepts of the functions and data. You do not want the process of drawing the interview flows and ERDs to take you away from the work of gathering information and checking it with the people you are interviewing.

Chapter 3 discussed the Process Modeller in some depth, and you should be able to use that information to complete the process flows to represent the knowledge you gained from interviews. You should also find the discussion of the Entity Relationship Diagrammer in Chapter 3 sufficiently detailed to enable you to show the entities and relationships themselves on the diagram.

Dataflow Diagrammer

You use the Dataflow Diagrammer (DFD) for a purpose similar to that of the Process Modeller: to diagram the functions, flows, and stores in the system you are analyzing. Although the symbols and methods are a bit different, you work with the same repository objects in both. This diagrammer is really just an alternative to the Process Modeller in this part of Analysis and helps you diagram the process flows you harvest from the interviewing sessions.

Note that although the following discussion explores the DFD fully, you do not need to go into great depth in the dataflow diagram in the information gathering step of the Analysis phase. The purpose of the process flow diagrams in the initial stages of the life cycle, whether you create them in the Process Modeller or the Dataflow Diagrammer, is to document your initial understanding of the user's requirements and to communicate this understanding to the clients and users. You use the Dataflow Diagrammer or Process Modeller more heavily in the next step of the Analysis phase when you analyze the requirements in depth.

Differences Between the Dataflow Diagrammer and Process Modeller

Because the Dataflow Diagrammer and Process Modeller seem to accomplish the same task, you may need help in determining which one to use. Table 5-2 lists the major differences (other than symbol sets) between the these two diagrammers.

As you can see from this table, one major benefit of the Dataflow Diagrammer is that you can attach entity and attribute usages to processes, flows, and stores in the Properties dialog box, whereas in the Process Modeller you cannot. This may or

Task	Process Modeller	Dataflow Diagrammer
Represent organization units on the diagram	Yes	No
Distinguish different types for processes, flows, and stores	Yes	Processes only
Define triggering events and outcomes	Yes	No
Run other programs from the diagram	Yes	No
Attach multimedia and text annotations to diagram elements	Yes	No
Animate the diagram and show process timing	Yes	No
Represent entities external to the system	No	Yes
Attach data usages to processes, flows, and stores	No	Yes
Use a numbering system to indicate function hierarchy levels	No	Yes

TABLE 5-2. *Differences Between the Process Modeller and Dataflow Diagrammer*

may not be a deciding factor; you will need to weigh the differences between these two diagrammers to decide which one to use. You may also need to base your decision on standards in your corporate environment or the company for which this project is being done. Your own background is a consideration as well; if you are accustomed to dataflow diagrams, you may decide to stay with that tool, although learning the new features of the Process Modeller should not be an insurmountable task. If you have no experience in either tool, you might seriously consider the Process Modeller for the extended set of features and presentation capabilities it offers; all you lose by making that decision is the data usage mapping—which you can perform in the Function Hierarchy Diagrammer—and the representation of external entities.

Keep in mind that, whatever your choice of diagrammer, you can always use the other diagrammer to create a new diagram and include (with the **Edit→Include** menu option) existing elements no matter where you first defined them.

The following discussion details some of the operational aspects of the Dataflow Diagrammer that differ from the common diagramming techniques mentioned in Chapter 2. This discussion also mentions how the Dataflow Diagrammer differs from the Process Modeller in specific techniques or features.

Figure 5-1 shows a sample Dataflow Diagrammer session.

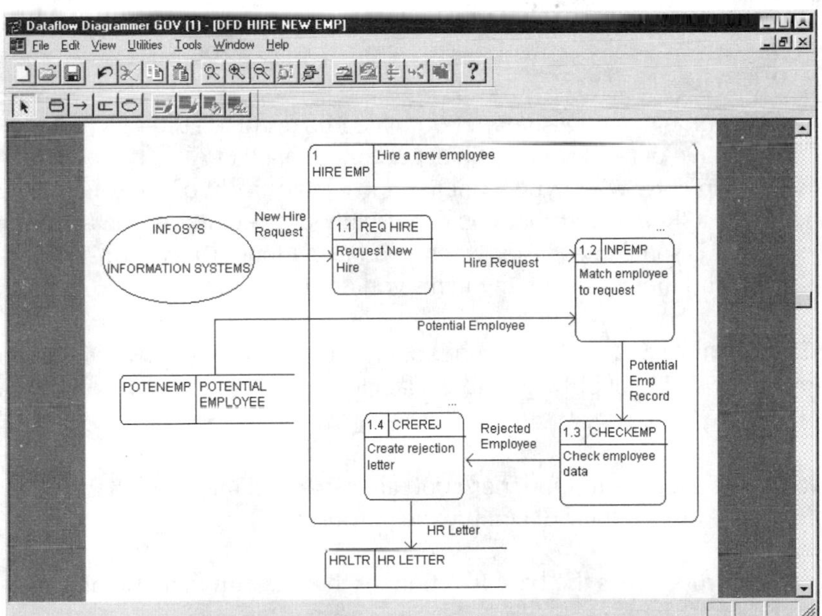

FIGURE 5-1. *Dataflow Diagrammer session*

Basic Techniques

The Dataflow Diagrammer uses the same basic techniques as the other Designer/2000 diagrammers for opening, saving, and creating a new diagram. When you select **File→New** from the menu, you have to choose a function on which to base the diagram as you do in the Process Modeller. This function serves as a frame to contain all child functions (subfunctions) and is called a *frame function.* You can create a new function at this point with the Create Function button or choose an existing process. The process you choose will appear as a rounded box on the screen (as do all processes) with a name, number, and description. Remember that Designer/2000 makes no distinction between a process and a function. Therefore, while you may think in terms of modelling processes, Designer/2000 calls these processes Business Functions in the repository.

Drawing Objects Except for the frame function, which Designer/2000 draws when you create the diagram, you draw all elements in the diagram by clicking the corresponding button in the drawing toolbar and dragging the item within the drawing area. With functions, you can just click the drawing area to create a default-sized box. If the element you wish to diagram is already in the repository (from another dataflow diagram or another diagrammer), you can select **Edit→Include** from the menu and choose the type of item and then one or more existing items of that type. If you are including functions, you can include the dataflows automatically by checking a box in the Include Function dialog box.

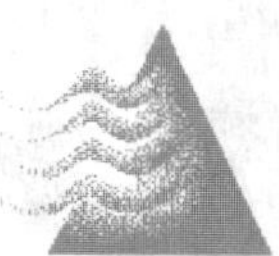

TIP

Some of the Designer/2000 dialog boxes (like **Edit→Include** boxes) have buttons such as Select All and UnSelect All. These will speed up entry when you want to choose all or most of the selections in the list. Remember that you can usually deselect items one at a time, so it is sometimes faster when you have a long list to choose Select All and then deselect any items you do not need.

Using the Symbol Set The number of symbols in the Dataflow Diagrammer is quite small, consisting of only functions, dataflows, datastores, and externals, as shown in Figure 5-2.

Functions Functions in Designer/2000 are separated into the following categories according to their diagrammatic purpose:

- *Frame function* is the base function for the diagram that contains the child functions.

- *Common function* is a copy of a function from this or another application system. You define this function on the Common tab in the Properties window for the function. This function copies the label of its source function.
- *Local function* is a function within the frame function.
- *Global function* is a function outside the frame function.

These categories of functions all have the same symbol in the DFD, and you distinguish them mainly by position. The categories are distinct from the types of processes that the Process Modeller handles. In that tool, you can assign a process as one of the following types: Process Step, Decision Point, Data Entry, or Report. The specified type becomes a property of that process and further refines its meaning.

You can display a function's Properties window by double-clicking on the function symbol in the diagram. The Definition tab of this window has a check box for a property called *Elementary*. An elementary function must be completed

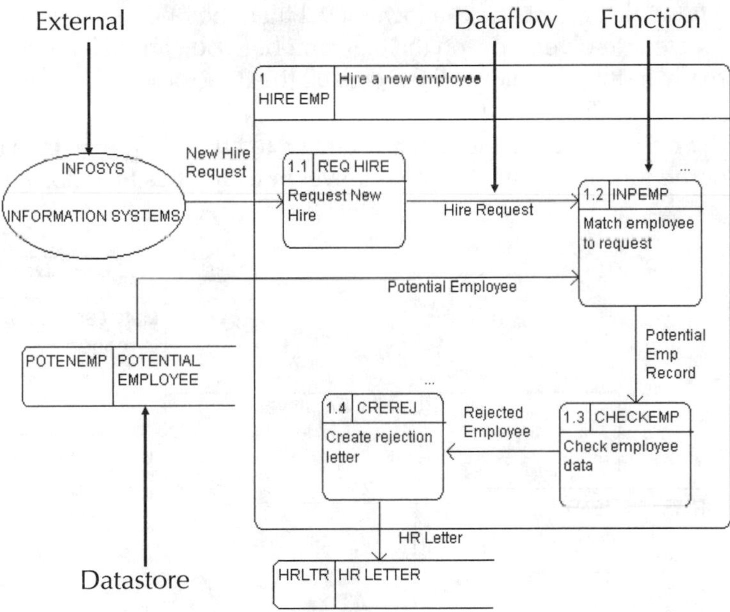

FIGURE 5-2. *Dataflow Diagrammer symbol set*

successfully and, if it is not successful, all changes made by that function must be reversed completely. Designer/2000 uses this property in the Design phase of the life cycle when it groups functions into candidate modules.

You can also assign a property of *Atomic* to a function in the Definition tab. A function with the Atomic property is at its lowest level of decomposition. Designer/2000 places a check mark in this box if you have not broken the function down into any component functions. This property does not appear in the Process Modeller Properties window.

If you have created functions on a lower level than a function on the diagram, that parent function will have an ellipsis (. . .) in the upper-right corner. The ellipsis indicates that you can choose **Open→Down** from the File menu to display a diagram, its children, or subfunctions. It is not necessary to have an existing lower-level diagram; it is only necessary that the lower-level elements exist.

Dataflows Flows (or dataflows) in Designer/2000 are single directional, with one source and one target. You can represent a two-way flow in the Dataflow Diagrammer with two one-way flows in opposite directions. This technique enables you to specify separate names, properties, and data usages for each direction.

Resolved flows link elements on a lower level than the one in the diagram. You cannot create a resolved flow on the diagram, but you can include one from a definition already in the repository (entered using the Repository Object Navigator, for instance). Designer/2000 indicates resolved flows with a dashed line, as in Figure 5-3. The dashed line indicates that you have to choose **Open→Down** (in the File menu) for the function to see the lowest level in which this flow appears.

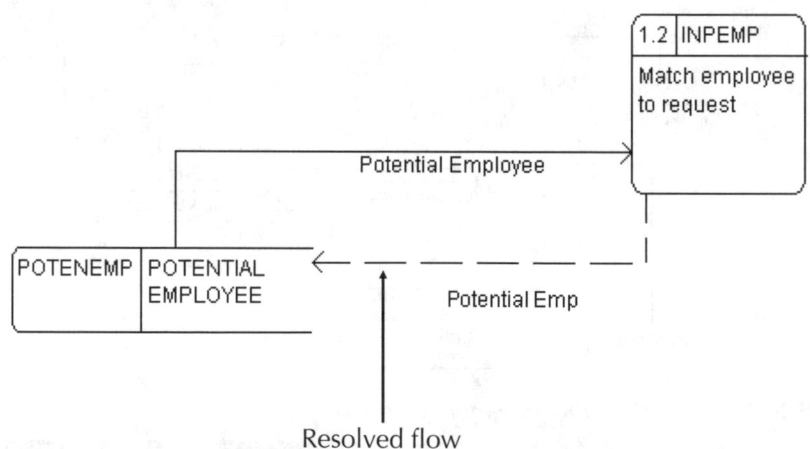

FIGURE 5-3. *Resolved flow in the DFD*

The DFD makes a distinction between normal dataflows and *global flows,* which link to a global function. Therefore, when you choose **Edit→Include** from the menu, you see separate types for Global Flows and Dataflows, as shown here:

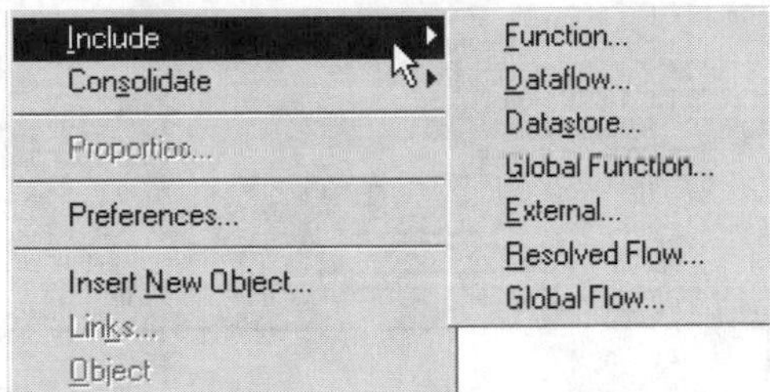

The Dataflow Diagrammer also allows you to type in your own classification (type) for the flow in the Properties window. This is a free-form field, and there is no fixed list to choose from. The Process Modeller also allows you to classify flows and to assign a flow a type from a fixed list of options: Flow, Data Flow, Temporal Flow, and Material Flow. The DFD and Process Modeller classification types appear as separate properties in the repository.

You can *split* flows to create new flows or elements from existing ones. You split a flow to add a new (or include an existing) datastore in a flow between a global and local function, indicating that the data is stored before the next process takes over. All you do is select the flow and the store (if there is one) and click the Split Dataflow button (or select **Utilities→Split Dataflow** from the menu).

You also can *divide* a flow to add a new flow to which you will assign part of the data usage. For example, you might have Dataflow1 to which Entity1.Attribute1 and Entity1.Attribute2 are assigned. You could create another flow from this one and assign Entity1.Attribute 2 to it (which would de-assign Attribute2 from the original flow). This feature is useful when you want to send part of the data from one flow to another destination. The procedure is as easy as selecting the flow and clicking the Divide Dataflow button (or selecting **Utilities→Divide Dataflow** from the menu). You will see a dialog box, where you can specify the elements that you want to move to the new flow, and then the DFD will draw a new flow that you can move to another element. Figure 5-4 shows the Divide Dataflow Contents dialog box.

Datastores Datastores are simple elements with just a few properties. The only trick you can pull with them is to create them on the fly between processes with the Split Dataflow feature just mentioned. The Dataflow Diagrammer Properties window lets you assign one of the following types to a datastore: Computer, Manual, or Transient. Assigning a type is useful for grouping stores later and for reporting purposes. The Process Modeller classifies datastores using the following

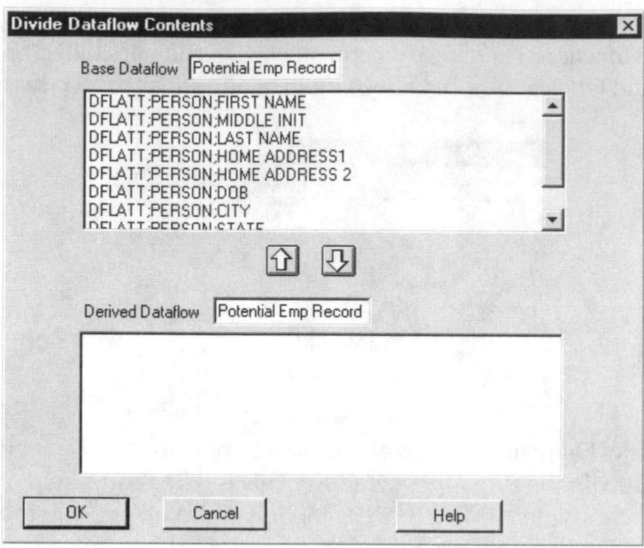

FIGURE 5-4. *Divide Dataflow Contents dialog box*

types: Store, Material Store, and Data Store. The Process Modeller store type and Dataflow Diagrammer datastore type appear as separate properties in the repository.

Externals Externals also have only a few properties. You might want to designate the organization unit or data entity from this application system with which the external entity is associated. Externals may also be organization units or entities from another application system that are shared with this application system and so fulfill the definition that an external identifies something outside the scope of the hierarchy that will have data flowing to or from it.

Naming Elements The way you name the elements on the diagram is up to you, but consistency is important and you might want some guidelines when starting the diagramming process. Most elements require a short name and a full name, both of which are displayed on the diagram. The short names are converted to uppercase as are the names of datastores. Function names, by convention, start with a verb (something other than "process") and are mixed-case phrases that indicate an activity. Flow names can be lowercase words or short phrases that indicate the type of data flowing. Store names are usually one word nouns that correspond, roughly, to entity names.

Assigning Data Usages to Functions One strength of the Dataflow Diagrammer is that you can identify the data source of processes, flows, and stores. You assign the entity and attributes to a function in the Properties window, as Figures 5-5 and 5-6 show.

Note that you need to specify an entity that already exists in the repository. This means that you need to use the ER Diagrammer to create the entities and attributes before or at the same time as you create the DFD. You choose entities and attributes from drop-down poplists in the Properties window and then fill in the usages for the entities—Create, Retrieve, Update, Delete, Archive, Other (which refers to a user-defined usage)—and for the attributes—Insert, Retrieve, Update, Nullify, Archive, Other.

When assigning data usages, you will save a step if you enter the entities you will use for functions on the Attributes tab. Select the entity at the top of the window and then select the attributes one at a time. When you move back to the Entity tab, that entity will appear as if you had entered it there first. Of course, you will still have to assign usages (Create, Retrieve, Update, Delete) on the Entity and Attribute tabs. You can also use the Function/Attribute Matrix utility on the Utilities menu to assign attributes to functions, as described later in this chapter. You can also use the Matrix Diagrammer to assign the create-retreive-update-delete usages as Chapter 6 discusses.

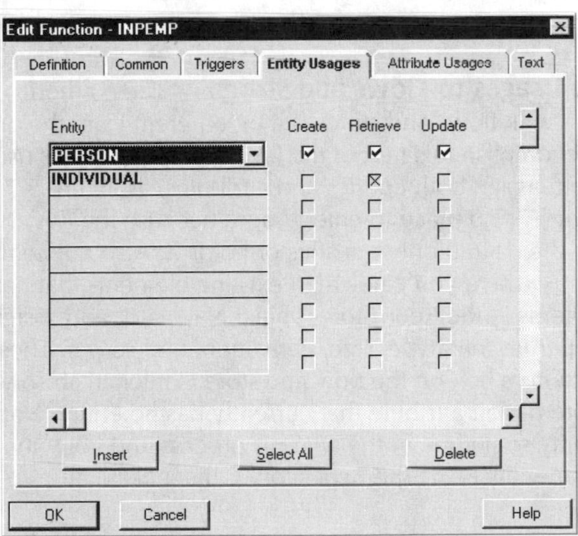

FIGURE 5-5. *Entity usage assignment for a function*

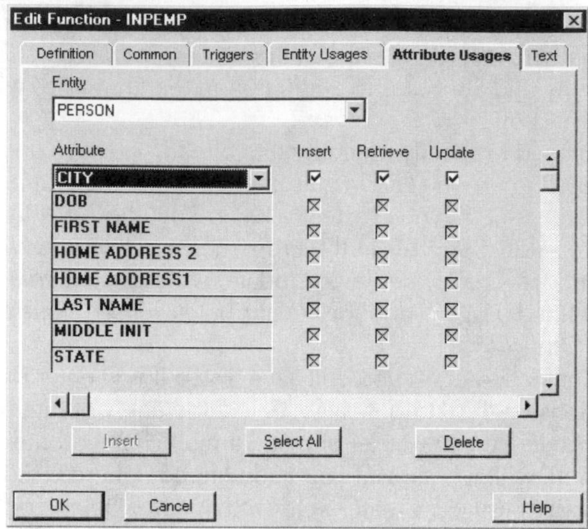

FIGURE 5-6. *Attribute entity usage assignment for a function*

TIP
To move up and down in the list of attributes or entities in this Properties window, use the CTRL-UP and CTRL-DOWN keys. The UP ARROW and DOWN ARROW keys do not work as you would expect.

Assigning Data Usages to Flows and Stores The method you use to associate the data with flows and stores is a bit different from the one you use for functions. You accomplish this task in the Properties window as usual, but you use the Contents tab to assign both entities and attributes, as Figure 5-7 shows.

Notice that there is no place to enter usages because the flow or store does not make changes to the data; it only transfers or holds it. Also notice that this window has a *data item* box where you can assign existing elements that have no entity. You create data items in the Repository Object Navigator and assign them attribute-like properties (datatype, size, derivation, and so on). These will then appear in the data item box on the flow and store Contents tab so you can specify that a flow or store has an attribute that currently has no entity. Naturally, you will assign it to an entity sometime in the analysis process and copy the properties into an attribute in that entity using the Repository Object Navigator.

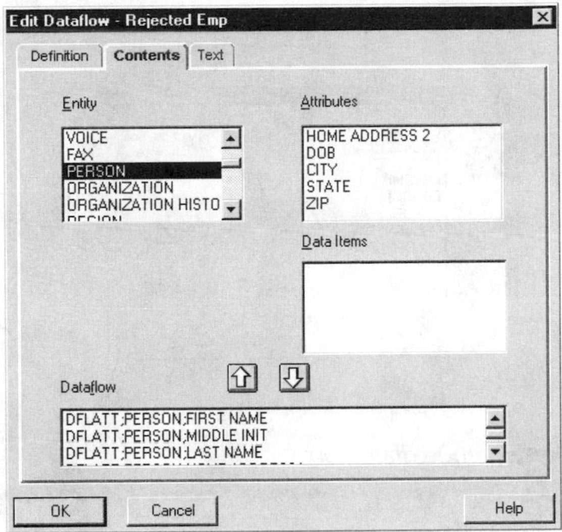

FIGURE 5-7. *Data usage assignment for a flow or store*

Other Techniques

The Dataflow Diagrammer also lets you resequence the function numbers. Normally the DFD numbers function in the order you create them. To change this order, you click the Resequence button on the standard toolbar (or choose **Utilities→Resequence** from the menu) and move the function names around in the box that appears using the arrow buttons, as in Figure 5-8. When you click the OK button, the function numbers will have the new order that you specified in the dialog box. Note that you must select a function before you click the Resequence button.

TIP

In all Designer/2000 diagrammers, if the button or menu choice you wish to use is disabled (dimmed) at any time, you have not performed the prerequisites for that task. Usually all the diagrammer requires is for you to select an object on the drawing, but you may have to do something else as well. The quickest way to find out what to do is to press the What's This help button (or Help) and then click the help cursor on the button (or select the menu item) in question. A help screen with information on that particular activity will appear.

Decomposing functions is another common activity in the Dataflow Diagrammer. This process is as simple as selecting the function you wish to further describe with other functions and selecting **File→Open Down** from the menu. To move to the

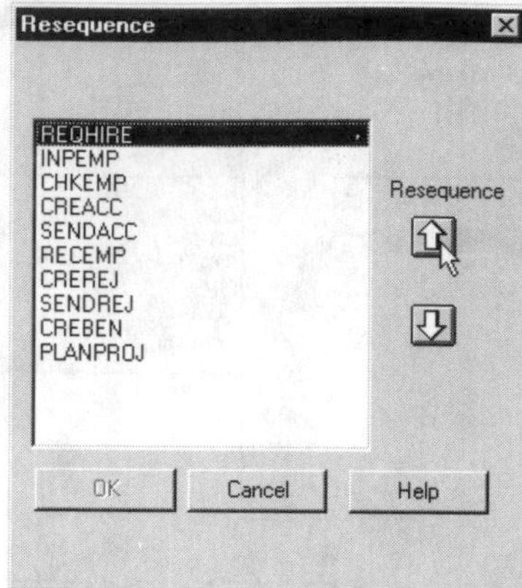

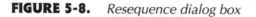

FIGURE 5-8. *Resequence dialog box*

diagram at the next level up from the one you are at, select **File→Open Up**. If that menu item is disabled, you are at the top level.

Dog-legs are angled flow lines and are useful when you are moving functions around and do not want a flow to intersect another function or store. You can have as many dog-legs on a particular flow as you want, but the fewer dog-legs you have, the easier your drawing will be to read. You have to weigh this guideline against the one that no flow lines should intersect a function or store. You can create a drawing point for the dog-leg by selecting the flow, holding down the SHIFT key, and clicking the mouse button in the middle of the flow. Figure 5-9 shows a dog-legged flow. To eliminate a dog-leg point, hold down the SHIFT key and click the mouse cursor on that point.

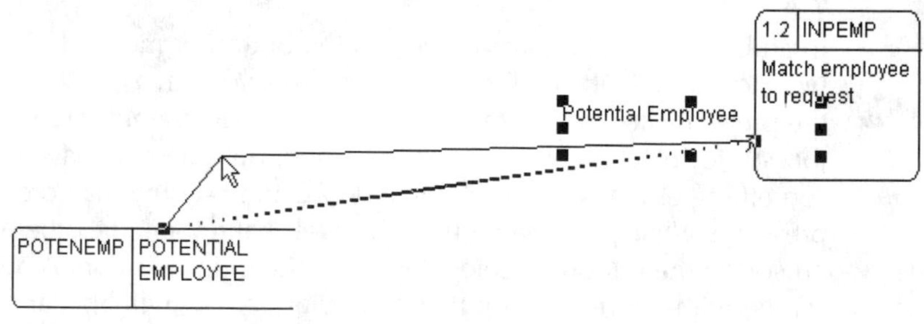

FIGURE 5-9. *Dog-legged dataflow*

You can specify triggered functions for each function in the Triggers tab of the function's Properties window. A triggered function is one that occurs as a result of this function's completion. For example, if Function2 starts as a result of the completion of Function1, Function2 is a triggered function. To specify this relationship, you open the Properties window for Function2 and specify Function1 as a trigger function. You can also specify trigger information in the Process Modeller, and it will appear in the Functions/Events—Triggering node under the Business Function node in the Repository Object Navigator. This information will appear on reports for the function model.

Other Menu and Toolbar Functions

The Dataflow Diagrammer features conform closely to the features common to all Designer/2000 tools discussed in Chapter 2. The Window and Help menus and toolbars contain the normal choices, and the Tools menu has selections for standard repository utilities and other tools you might want in the Systems Modeller component. In addition, it offers access to the Module Structure Diagrammer where you diagram the hierarchy of Design phase modules.

The File menu also contains all standard diagrammer features, including Open Up and Open Down to allow you to easily create or move to a lower- or higher-level diagram. The Edit menu, too, is standard, except that the Preferences choice has appropriate settings for viewing Dataflow Diagrammer elements. The View menu contains the same zoom, grid, toolbar, and status bar choices as the other diagrammers. Remember that you can delete an existing diagram from the File menu.

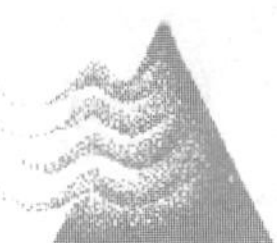

TIP

When you choose Open Up or Open Down to go to another diagram in the hierarchy, Designer/2000 keeps the original diagram open. A list of open diagrams will appear on the Window menu, and you can navigate back and forth by selecting the diagram names from that list rather than worrying about which function is the parent for which other function.

The Utilities menu has items similar to those in all Designer/2000 diagrammers: for using AutoLayout; applying Rescale Diagram to fit it on a certain number of pages; using the Resequence, Split Dataflow, and Divide Dataflow functions mentioned in the preceding discussion; and loading the Application Design Wizard. In addition, it provides a utility to convert dataflow diagrams from a repository migrated from version 5.0 or 5.1 of Oracle*CASE to Designer/2000.

Function/Attribute Matrix Utility

The Utilities menu also provides the Function/Attribute Matrix utility, which presents a dialog box where you can select the function or functions you wish to act on. When you click the OK button, Designer/2000 adds attribute usages for all entities used by the selected functions.

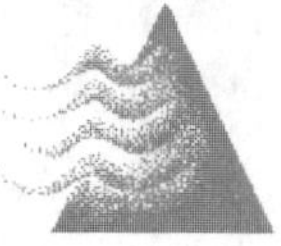

TIP

You can also use the Matrix Diagrammer, discussed in Chapter 6, to attach attributes. This diagrammer helps you assign CRUD (create-retrieve-update-delete) data usages to functions for which you have already assigned data. The Matrix Diagrammer also helps in the initial assignment of entities and attributes. However, if you will be using most or all of the attributes for an entity, the Function/Attribute Matrix is the fastest tool to use.

Where Does This Information Go?

The element definitions you create or diagram in the Dataflow Diagrammer show up in other phases as well as later in the Analysis phase when you create different diagrams such as the Function Hierarchy diagram or even the Process Modeller. They also appear in the Repository Object Navigator with the names listed in Table 5-3. Notice that Table 5-3 is similar to the one for the Process Modeller, discussed in Chapter 3, as it diagrams essentially the same objects but in a different way. In addition to these elements, the Application Design Wizard converts function data usages and flow data usages to module usages and module parameters, respectively.

Dataflow Diagrammer Element	**Repository Element and Future Use**
Datastores	Datastores; used to cross-check data usage in functions
Externals	Externals; assigned to a business unit or entity and used on reports
Functions	Business Functions; used by the Application Design Wizard to create modules
Dataflows	Dataflows subnode under Business Functions and under Datastores; used to cross-check data usage in functions

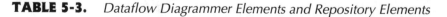

TABLE 5-3. *Dataflow Diagrammer Elements and Repository Elements*

Legacy System ERD

The legacy system ERD consists of entities that represent tables in the current (legacy) system. You create the legacy system ERD in three basic steps that each use a different Designer/2000 tool:

1. *The Reverse Engineer Database utility* automatically inserts information on current tables and views into the repository so you do not have to manually add the definitions—normally a time-consuming and error-prone activity.
2. *The Table to Entity Retrofit utility* automatically creates entity definitions from the table definitions created in the preceding step.
3. *The Entity Relationship Diagrammer* creates one or more diagrams to represent the entities the utility created.

This section discusses these steps and the utilities you use to perform them. As you create the legacy system ERD, notice how most of the work is automated when you use Designer/2000. Instead of performing what is typically a time-consuming manual process, with Designer/2000 virtually all you need to do is check that the objects were created successfully.

Reverse Engineer Database Objects Utility

Reverse engineering (also called design recovery) in Designer/2000 means loading the repository with objects that exist in the database or file system. There are two types of reverse engineering utilities: database objects and front end program files (specifically, Forms and Reports). This section describes the database reverse engineering facility that is actually grouped with the Reconcile and Server Generator utilities and has an interface similar to that of those tools.

The task is quite simple from the Designer/2000 point of view: start the utility, specify the database objects you wish to bring into the repository, and click OK.

Start the Utility The Reverse Engineer Database Objects utility does not have a separate button in the Designer/2000 window, but you can get to it from the Utilities menu of the Repository Object Navigator, Data Diagrammer, Module Structure Diagrammer, and Module Logic Navigator. You will see the screen shown in Figure 5-10 no matter where you start the utility from.

The Reverse Engineer From box allows you to choose a source for the session. If you choose File, you will be able to enter (or find) the name of an existing file that contains SQL data definition language (DDL) commands. The utility will read that file and create repository definitions for CREATE TABLE, CREATE VIEW, and ALTER TABLE statements in Oracle7, Oracle V6, or ANSI standard SQL.

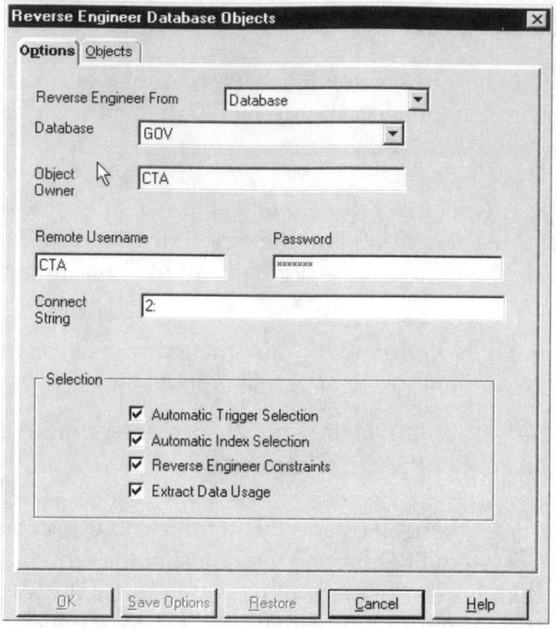

FIGURE 5-10. *Reverse Engineer Database Objects Options tab*

If you choose Database as the source, you fill in the connection information: the name of the owner of the objects, the login name, password, and database connect string. The login name can be any user who has select access to the objects, but if you are reverse engineering triggers, you have to log in as the owner of the tables for which those triggers are created. You also have to choose the name of a database repository definition to associate with the new objects. For example, your repository might store objects from three databases, each of which has a separate definition in the Databases node in the Repository Object Navigator. You would pick one of those as the database for the new objects, and the new objects will have a property that specifies that database.

You can also specify objects for Designer/2000 to automatically reverse engineer at the same time as the objects you select. For example, you can specify Automatic Index Selection to reverse engineer all indexes defined for a table when you reverse engineer that table. Extract Data Usage creates definitions in the procedural code modules for tables and columns that are referenced in those modules. This definition helps track which modules use what tables.

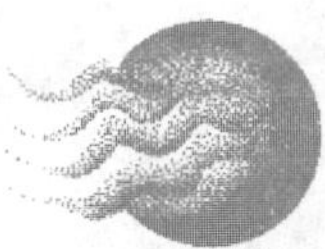

NOTE
You must have at least one database definition in the open application system or the utility will not produce any output.

Specify the Database Objects After you specify the connection and automatic generation information, you click the Objects tab, and Designer/2000 will log you in to the user account and database. You then select the objects to be reverse engineered. You can reverse engineer the following object types in the database:

Clusters
Functions
Indexes
Packages
Procedures
Sequences
Snapshots
Tables
Tablespaces
Triggers
Views

For each of these types, you select the object names you want to reverse engineer and move them down to the working area, as Figure 5-11 shows.

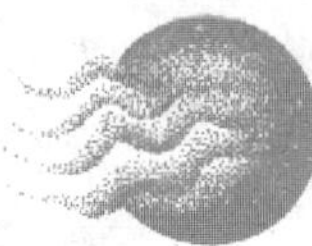

NOTE
You cannot reverse engineer an object that already exists in the repository. If you need to do so, temporarily rename the existing object and run the reverse engineering utility on that object. If there are references to the old object (for example, a foreign key in another table that refers to the old table), you will need to reattach them to the new object. Alternatively, you can run the Reconcile utility and determine what the differences are in the database and repository object and make the changes by hand or using the API. Note that the reverse engineering utility can add columns or constraints to an existing table definition if the columns are in the database but not in the repository, but cannot delete column definitions if they do not exist in the database.

Click OK When you are done selecting objects, click OK to run the utility. When the utility is done, it issues a report of the results, which you can read and save if you wish.

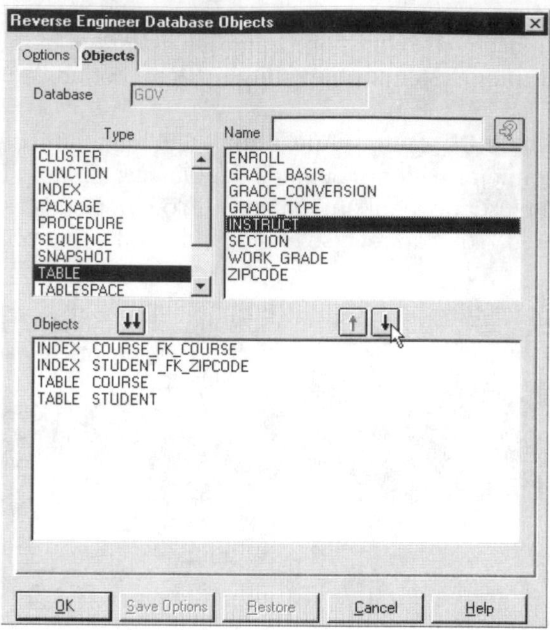

FIGURE 5-11. *Selecting objects to reverse engineer*

To create the legacy system ERD, you will want to reverse engineer just those tables needed in the system with views, snapshots, triggers, and indexes. If you will be using other database elements in the system design or your objective is to create a complete set of repository objects that you can build from, you should choose all these objects and reverse engineer them.

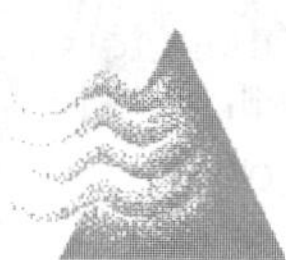

TIP
If the number of objects to reverse engineer is large, you may find it easier to run this utility more than once with subsets of objects.

NOTE
If you run this utility from the Repository Object Navigator, you may not see the new objects in the hierarchy window until you requery the node in which they appear. Select the object type node (for example, Tables) and click the Requery button.

Table to Entity Retrofit Utility

The preceding step created table and other definitions in the repository for the existing legacy objects. If you want to use these objects for analysis tasks, you need to create entity definitions to match the table definitions you just reverse engineered. The Table to Entity Retrofit utility performs just this task. You follow three steps to run it: start the utility, select the object names, and click the Reverse Engineer button.

Start the Utility You can start this utility from the Utilities menus of the Repository Object Navigator, Entity Relationship Diagrammer, and Data Diagrammer. When you choose this menu option, you will see the screen shown in Figure 5-12.

Select the Object Names Click the Candidate Tables button to display a list of available tables that do not have entities associated with them. Designer/2000 gets this information from the table association called Table Entity Usage. If a table does not have any objects in that node, it will appear as a candidate table. Note that views and snapshots cannot be retrofitted. Note also that you can name the entities differently than the tables if you wish in this dialog box.

Click the Reverse Engineer Button After you select the tables, you click the Reverse Engineer button. Designer/2000 will create the definitions for entities from tables, attributes from columns, relationships from foreign key constraints, and unique identifiers from primary keys constraints. These are the elements you need for the next step in the process of creating the legacy system ERD.

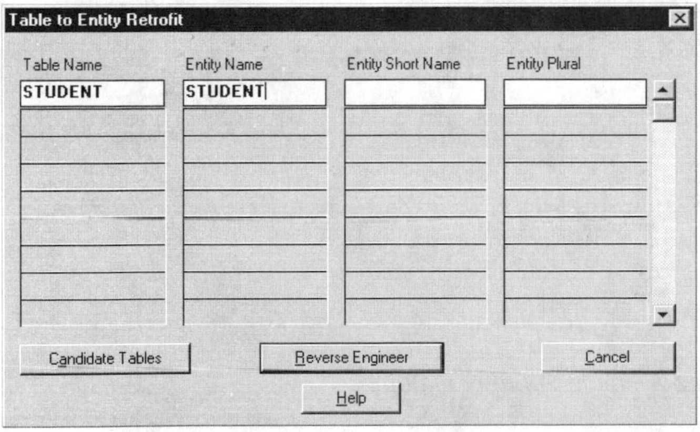

FIGURE 5-12. *Table to Entity Retrofit utility*

Entity Relationship Diagrammer and the Legacy System ERD

This section continues the discussion of the Entity Relationship Diagrammer begun in Chapter 3, and this tool is discussed further in Chapter 6, as you will use it frequently in the requirements analysis step of the Analysis phase. Here, you will learn how to automatically create the legacy system ERD from the retrofitted tables created with the Table to Entity Retrofit utility. The real objective of the ERD in this part of the Analysis phase is to represent diagrammatically the data elements from the legacy system in an analysis format. However, the simple technique discussed here is useful even if you do not want to produce a legacy system ERD.

Create an Automatic Layout of Existing Entities Since you have all the entity definitions, all you need to do is open the ER Diagrammer, create a new diagram, and choose **Edit→Include** for all the entities you reverse engineered and retrofitted. Figure 5-13 shows the Include Entity dialog box. Note that you can select all entities with or without relationships (in this case, you want entities with relationships), and you can choose where the layout will appear. Choose Whole Diagram to put the new objects anywhere in the drawing area, New Area to have the utility pause and wait for you to draw an area for the new objects, or Same Area if you have created a new area before and want to use this same area. If you want to see the layout area you are using, select **Edit→Preferences** from the menu and check the Show Layout Area check box.

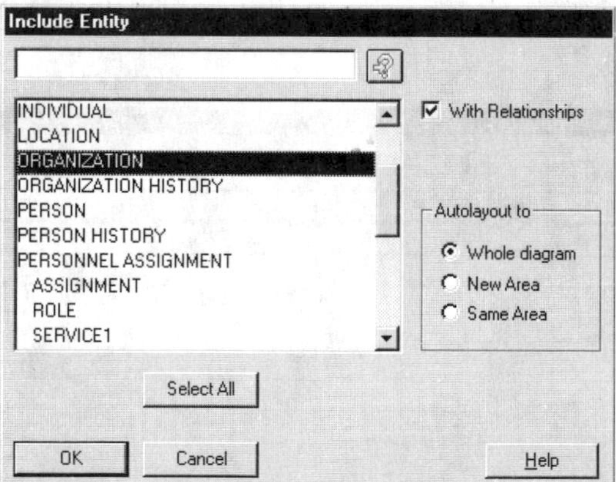

FIGURE 5-13. *Include Entity dialog box*

TIP
Examine the preferences by choosing **Edit→Preferences** and decide if you really need to see all the labels and elements. Depending on your audience, there may be some items you wish to omit from the diagram to make it look simpler. For example Hidden Arcs—arcs that have only one relationship on the diagram—are normally displayed, but this symbol may be confusing to some viewers. You can turn off this symbol by unchecking its check box.

A good thing to do the first time you display objects in the drawing is to try some of the Autolayout combinations. Just click the Autolayout button (or choose **Utilities→Autolayout** from the menu) and the diagram will be redrawn in a new layout. You can always go back to the old layouts (except the first one) by using the Previous Layout button (or choosing **Utilities→Previous Layout**). Autolayout provides New Area and Same Area menu options for placing the new layout; these act the same way as the similar options in the Include dialog box. Also, you can choose the objects to which Autolayout applies by selecting them and then clicking the Autolayout button.

At this point, you should spend some time with the layout and arrange it to your satisfaction. At the end of this process, you will have a legacy system ERD.

Tracking Report Audits with User Extensions

Another Designer/2000 deliverable in the information gathering step of the Analysis phase is a method for tracking existing (legacy) reports using the repository. The creation of this deliverable consists of two steps:

1. Add a user extension to the module element type.
2. Create modules for each report.

Add a User Extension

In the Analysis phase you need a way to store definitions for and assign priorities to the legacy reports. You can store the report definitions in the Designer/2000 repository module element. A module is a finished application, usually a form or report, that acts as a distinct part of the system. Modules can also be menus, background, triggers, procedures, functions, packages, and so on. In this case, the module will be a report type with a property called Legacy Status and will be used to assign a priority level for the legacy report auditing process.

The problem is that Designer/2000 does not have a property for a module called Legacy Status. The Designer/2000 User Extensibility feature can solve this problem. You can define a new property for the module element type called

Legacy Status and, as you create the definition for each report in the repository, assign a value of Keep, Discard, or Modify. Then when you list the legacy reports, each can include one of these values as its Legacy Status designation, and reports can even be grouped according to their Legacy Status designations. This process of entering and making choices regarding the status of the legacy reports is really part of the audit process itself.

The User Extensibility feature is provided by the Repository Administration Utility and is covered in Chapter 4. You should refer to that chapter for more information on the concepts and mechanics of user extensions. Briefly, you need to name a single unused user-defined property as Legacy Status. When you publish this extension, you will see it in the repository module's Properties window, which you use to assign a status to each legacy report.

Create Modules Definitions for the Legacy Reports

Creating module definitions in the Repository Object Navigator is largely a manual process consisting of clicking the Create button after selecting the Modules node. You then fill in the name, purpose, and language of the report. If the language used is not on the list, you can add the appropriate language under the Languages node. You should also fill in the Legacy Status property that will appear in the module's Properties window. If your legacy reports are written in Developer/2000 Reports, you could also use the Reverse Engineer Report utility to create the module definitions from existing Reports (.RDF) files.

If you have a large number of reports (a hundred or more) you might consider another way to insert the modules—using the Designer/2000 Application Programmatic Interface (API). Assume you have a table that stores the names of all the reports in your system. You could write an API procedure to read that table and create repository definitions for each module there. Chapter 14 describes how to use the API and provides some sample code to get you started. You should probably not consider this approach if you have only a small number of tables because the coding work involved may take longer than manually entering the module definitions. Then again, if you did create an API routine, you could reuse it for the same purpose in other projects.

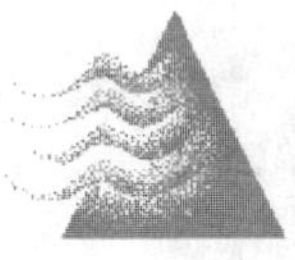

TIP

If you need to create multiple elements of the same type in the Repository Object Navigator, start the process by selecting the element type node and clicking the Create button. You will see a new Properties window and a blank line in the hierarchy for the new element. Immediately start typing the name of the element you are creating, and Designer/2000 will enter the name on the blank line in the hierarchy. Then shift your focus to the Properties window, fill in the other required properties, and shift your focus back to the Repository Object Navigator window by clicking the name (not the icon) of the new element. If there are no required properties other than the name, do not shift the focus back and forth. Then press the ENTER key, and Designer/2000 will save the new element and create another new element with a blank name. After creating the elements in this way, you can go back and fill in other properties that are not required but are needed to make the definition complete.

Conclusion

You now have an idea of the scope of the methodology and Designer/2000 work in the first part of the Analysis phase: information gathering. The main goal in this step is to obtain a set of interview documents, system requirements, legacy documents, and even rough diagrams that are as complete as possible so you will have a good starting point for the analysis in the next step. Designer/2000 can assist in creating the diagrams and storing and organizing the key information in the information gathering step. Its repository can serve as a central storage place for the many details that you collect regarding the project and its needs.

The next chapter continues the discussion of the Analysis phase. In particular, it discusses how to use the information you have gathered to fully analyze the requirements, using the Designer/2000 tools to create key deliverables and manipulate and understand the information in the repository.

CHAPTER 6

Analysis: Part II—Requirements Analysis

I've been in analysis for 15 years and it hasn't done me a bit of good.

In the first stage of the Analysis phase, requirements are collected from the users. In the second stage of Analysis, these requirements must be organized in a meaningful way before the system can be designed.

Overview of Requirements Analysis

At this point in the CADM process, unit-level analysis has been completed. The development team has amassed a large amount of data, including interview notes, preliminary ERDs and function hierarchies, report audits, and legacy system documentation. Now all of this information has to be logically packaged into a requirements document.

The traditional CASE method does not explicitly provide for a requirements document. This deficiency can cause user dissatisfaction and, ultimately, system failure. One resolution to the problem of how to deliver exactly what the user wants and needs is to team up with the users to produce a requirements document that includes process flows, analysis ERDs, and function hierarchies. This document is the main deliverable in the Analysis phase.

The need for a requirements document is based upon a simple idea: a system designer must first have a clear and precise description of the business area's requirements before beginning to develop a solution. Then the designer can create a system that truly meets the user's needs. To successfully complete the Analysis phase, all the business requirements must be documented. Only after this is done can decisions about the design of the actual system be made.

The primary deliverable of the Analysis phase is the requirements document. This is usually a very long, detailed document that includes all of the information gathered from various sources. Without a requirements document, analysts can only take their ERDs, functional models, and screen dumps and ask the user, "Does this work?" The ERDs, function hierarchy, and prototypes can be used to help validate the system with the user; but the knowledge transfer must also be verified in order for the system to be implemented successfully.

During Analysis, the focus continues to be on the user, coupled with both the new and old systems. The users have invaluable knowledge of the legacy system as well as information on how the new system should work. This information is elicited from the user; and then the focus shifts to analysis. The information is rearchitected in the form of ERDs and function hierarchies, but a direct reference still is needed to the information the users provided regarding what they want in the new system. You will not be certain that the system will be built correctly unless there is a cross-check. The requirements document provides this cross-check.

The current system development process usually moves directly from knowledge acquisition to the placement of information into the Designer/2000 repository. Creating a requirements document provides a crucial control point in the CADM process when moving from knowledge acquisition to the generation of function hierarchies and ERDs. It also provides the client with a deliverable to verify that the knowledge acquisition occurred. Therefore, the requirements document must be designed to provide this verification.

The information elicited from the users should be structured to avoid simply listing one unrelated concept after another. First, information should be broken into categories based on business functions. Second, the document should be in a form that can be cross-checked against the models. The analyst must be able to say, "What we designed is something that makes sense." Verification of the models is the last part of the Analysis phase.

The existence of a requirements document does not mean that the user is not involved in the development and validation of the ERDs and function hierarchy. Indeed, users should be directly involved in all parts of the system development process. This will add significant time to the Analysis phase, but the alternative is running the risk of not meeting user needs. Without user involvement, you risk not getting user buy-in to whatever is being analyzed, designed or built. Users look at the proposed system as "yours" not "theirs" and will be more inclined to distance themselves from it.

The requirements document should be broken into several sections: one section at the global project level and one for each *subsystem*. A subsystem consists of the modules that projects are traditionally divided into so that work can be allocated. The difference between project-level and subsystem-level requirements is that a project-level requirement applies to the entire project. Examples of project-level requirements include project-level hardware requirements, overall business needs, and notes on the user interface. However, most requirements will be found in the subsystem-level requirement lists. These lists contain specific requirements for such subsystems as sales and manufacturing. Many requirements will be included in more than one subsystem area.

The requirements portion of the Analysis phase is where the analysts bring together all of the collected material from users and extract the relevant system requirements. This process includes determining the appropriate ERDs to create, and finalizing process flows that describe both the legacy system and potential changes to it as well as new process flows that may be relevant to the system being created. The goal is to create a coherent statement of all the system requirements for the proposed system. This requirements portion of the Analysis phase is discussed in detail in Chapter 6. In this chapter, you learn about the various methods of information gathering and how Designer/2000 supports these activities.

Structure of the Requirements Document

For a very large project, the requirements document could consist of hundreds of pages. A requirements document outlines the needs of the users for the entire system. A carefully defined and prioritized list of requirements coupled with the business models and matrices result in a requirements document that gives the development team considerable insight into the business.

Ideally, the users should participate in all efforts during the Analysis phase, identifying, verifying, and mapping requirements and developing and validating the process flows, ERDs, and function hierarchy. Indeed, the users should be directly involved in all parts of the system development process. This may add significant time to the Analysis phase. However, failure to involve the users increases the possibility that requirements are incomplete and inaccurate and that the users will not take ownership of the system. In other words, the developer should not complete the jobs in this phase alone.

This section discusses each part of the requirements document. The sections of the requirements document are as follows:

- Function hierarchy with system requirements: that is, a structured list of all requirements elicited from users, including the requirements for the legacy system
- Full documentation of the legacy system (as discussed in Chapter 5)
- Report audit (as discussed in Chapter 5)
- Business objectives and critical success factors for each business area that the system will support
- Analysis ERD
- Process flows for all business functions

After all of the necessary requirements have been collected, the information must be analyzed, organized, and documented for ease of reference. The information elicited should be structured to avoid lists of one unrelated concept after another. You do this by first dividing the information into categories based on business functions. You then organize these functions into a top-level function hierarchy.

Function Hierarchy

After conducting all the user interviews, JAD sessions, and legacy system walkthroughs, the analyst is left with a large binder of notes. These notes may be structured by functional area, but often requirements may span several areas, and there is no clear outline showing what requirements go where. The analyst should attempt to expand the function hierarchy from the Strategy phase. The goal is to end up with an Analysis phase function hierarchy.

Massaging the data will require you to add the next layer down on the function hierarchy. These additions are based on the requirements, tasks, and decisions of the users and the requirements retrieved from other sources. When addressing requirements from users, the users may be categorized by class. For example, all users involved in data entry of sales information might be in one functional group. Another group might be those who work with math functions—users from this functional group might want online screen calculators, for instance. An individual user may be a part of one or many functional groups.

Traditionally, Designer/2000 has been used to identify the navigation menu and modules used to build the hierarchy. Although this is not a basic capability, it also is possible to extend Designer/2000 to organize user requirements. At this point, the analyst can build the function hierarchy. Each person on the development team can read a few pages and try to sort the requirements into modules. As the process moves closer to the Design phase, it becomes increasingly important to be precise regarding which requirements go with which function or module. However, at this point the goal is simply to place each user requirement somewhere in the function hierarchy. General requirements go high up in the tree, with details attached to specific functions at the leaf level.

Once the user requirements are sorted and organized in the function hierarchy, the analyst needs to look at each function. Redundancies need to be eliminated. Sources of conflict should be identified and harmonized. If the requirements for a function are inadequate to build that function, the analyst needs to collect more information before proceeding. All of the collected requirements need to be detailed enough for the analyst to build a function that meets user needs.

Once it is completed, the function hierarchy needs to be summarized and organized into a more coherent diagram. Within each function, requirements can be broken down into specific requirements types:

- Performance specifications, such as response time
- Functional requirements: that is, what the function accomplishes

For each subject area, create a function hierarchy, sorting the users, user classes, and sources into topics. Keep in mind that some users will appear in more than one category. Boundary spanners cross more than one technical area. All other users should fall into specific areas. Each task that the user identified should become a function in the next layer of the function hierarchy. Everything else should become a requirement that pertains to one or more tasks in that area. Try to fit the rest of the requirements into the function hierarchy and into categories. When it is unclear where to put a particular requirement in the function hierarchy, put it higher on the tree.

Ideally, all requirements should reside in the CASE repository. Unfortunately, CASE does not easily support this. You can use user extensibility in Designer/2000, as mentioned in Chapter 4, to store the requirements and map them to the function hierarchy.

Functions should be mapped to entities to ensure that the function hierarchy is complete and to identify redundancies. For example, if you find that there is no CREATE usage for a particular entity, then you obviously are missing a function. If an entity can have information deleted by several different functions, there may be a problem in the design.

You can then use this information to map the main functionality of the old system to the new system. You can also use it to make sure that no legacy-supported business function was missed in the design of the new system and to map legacy fields to the new system attributes.

Note that functions should not be mapped to attributes. The cost to determine that level of detail outweighs the added benefit.

Business Objectives and Critical Success Factors

The purpose of the next section of the requirements document is to document the goals, objectives, and critical success factors of the business area. Goals are the broad themes, directions, and aspirations of the business area. Objectives are the measurable targets that are set to determine whether a goal is met. Critical success factors are those things that have to go right in order for the business to achieve its goals. These objectives and factors are usually identified during management interviews. It is important to include this strategy-type information in the requirements document since everything that follows in the life cycle should support this section.

This section should also verify that the business importance of the system has been communicated to the design team. Without this high-level perspective, it is impossible to make intelligent design decisions on such basic features as fault tolerance and design flexibility.

The objectives and critical success factors can be directly obtained from user managers. If the users have not thought through their business objectives and critical success factors, the analysis team should guide the users through these important first steps in the development process.

Most of this work should have been done in the preparation of the strategy document. However, in Analysis, these objectives should be expanded and reconfirmed to include the perspective of rank-and-file users. In addition, success factors critical to the development of the system should be identified.

Analysis ERD

A picture is worth a thousand words; and one ERD is worth a thousand requirements. The analysis ERD stores many of the business requirements in one place. The ERD can then be used to communicate between the users and developers a common understanding of the data requirements and rules.

What is the analysis ERD? It is a compact representation of most (often hundreds) of the data-related business requirements. The analysis ERD should not be concerned with speed or performance. Its only goal is to capture as many business rules as possible. The more rules captured, the better. The analysis ERD is the core of the requirements document.

Ideally, the ERD should reflect *all* of the data business rules. However, some rules may need to be expressed in text form. Therefore, the analysis ERD is not complete unless it also contains written, explicit business rules not contained in the diagram. There must be clear and precise descriptions of each entity in the ERD.

The process of creating the ERD is as follows:

1. Bring together the unit-level analysis ERDs from the first stage of the Analysis phase. Build the ERD at the entity level. Include some attribution information, but only to illustrate the entity. For example, a university database may contain an intersection table called "enrollment." In this case, show the class grade in the enrollment entity to illustrate what kind of information should be stored in that entity.

2. Audit the diagram against the user requirements with a senior modeller who has not yet seen the diagram. Defending a model to someone else is one of the best ways to find flaws and problems. Even skilled modellers can make mistakes.

3. Fully attribute the model by scrutinizing all user requirements and reports to be supported. Important sources for attributes are screen shots of the

new system, legacy system screen shots, old reports, and new reports. Users can also be asked to identify attributes. If the ERD cannot support the generation of a report, more work needs to be done.

4. Audit the logical ERD with the developer using real business transactions. Even though tables do not exist yet, transaction information can be stored in the entities as if they were tables. Again, don't worry about performance. The purpose of this auditing process is simply to see whether all requirements are included and can be stored, or whether more work needs to be done.

5. Map the data related requirements to the analysis ERD entities or relationships.

During the creation of the analysis ERD (just as with the strategy ERD), the analyst needs to spend time creating good entity names and descriptions. However, without worrying about entity names, the diagram should be audited solely for entities, relations, and descriptions to make sure it encompasses all the input. This is not to diminish the importance of entity names. These are crucial. However, the question is when to come up with these names. Initially, it is more important to agree on the descriptions of what the entities represent. Then the entity names themselves can be determined.

After the ERD presentation, it must be clear to everyone what the ERD represents. The diagram serves as a logical model of the business area data requirements. Since it is still just a logical model, it cannot be critiqued for performance considerations at this stage.

Process Flows

The flow of work tasks within an organization is frequently not optimal. Duplication of effort is common. After someone spends the afternoon typing, printing, and submitting reports to other departments, the people that receive the information may reenter the same data so it can be printed in a different format or used for calculations. A process flow makes the duplication of effort apparent.

For example, the steps that a company takes in processing an application for membership can be tracked. Instead of viewing the process from the point of view of one user, you want to examine it from the perspective of the company. You may discover that after an application arrives, it is entered into the legacy system by the application processing group (the people who receive applications and retrieve the necessary information on the applicant, such as name and address). Then the application is entered again by the people who approve applications and again by the people who issue and track new members. By modeling the process flow, opportunities to re-engineer business efforts can be identified.

Process flow modeling illustrates what an enterprise does and how it does it, and when information systems are used to support business processes. User involvement in process flow modeling is essential. Users are the primary sources of information, and like other models, the process flow model will go through several revisions with the user before it is finalized at the end of the Analysis phase.

Processes are not usually neatly organized hierarchies. Some processes must precede other processes. Some processes may follow other processes. Still other processes spawn processes of their own. Some process flows are linear. Others loop back on themselves or support various degrees of parallelism. These process flows are integral system requirements that cannot easily be placed within the function hierarchy.

One of the main uses of process flow modeling is to determine the appropriate use of task queues or other workflow-related system modifications. To achieve this objective, every function that can be separated from another function either by time or by its users must be individually modeled. For example, answering a customer's phone call and entering a diary event on the system noting the phone call would not be two functions because those two events always take place right after each other and are always done by the same person. However, taking a customer order and approving the order would be two tasks because they are done by two people. Similarly, taking an order and shipping goods would probably best be modeled by two processes, even if these tasks are done by the same person because the two processes might be separated by time.

Here is the technique for creating process flows:

1. Identify primary business processes. These are probably the top-level functions from the function hierarchy.

2. Identify subprocesses within each primary process. Each subprocess may be repeated in more than one primary process. Subprocesses are a collection of tasks or activities that support a primary process.

3. For each subprocess, identify the title of the person who performs it, the department in which the subprocess is performed, and whether the subprocess is manual or automated. If the subprocess is automated, identify the functional area (for example, sales, manufacturing, or shipping) that does the task.

Identify how the tasks relate to each other. Recognize that tasks can be ordered in more ways than by time. Note that a manual task usually *spawns* a computer task, and a computer task usually *precedes* a manual task. There may be other verbs required to reflect your process flows. You will probably need to use decision boxes to reflect the flow of tasks. Create dataflows among and between subprocesses to identify their sequences.

Assigning Requirements to Functions

Assigning system requirements to functions takes place during requirements analysis. Much of the checking has already been built directly into the process because you are building the functional model directly from the requirements list. However, as a safety measure, you should map the system requirements from the requirements document to the ERD and process flow models to determine where each requirement is met, why it is met, who meets the requirement, and how the requirement is met. A report should be created in this phase listing all of the requirements with the areas and nodes to which they pertain and where they are met in the models. You can conclude that your analysis is complete if your ERDs and function hierarchies successfully capture all of your requirements.

Analysis allows you to span the boundary between discussions with the user and the design of the system. Adding a requirements document to the process gives the users and the development team more confidence in the process and a shared understanding of the business requirements that will be leveraged during the Design phase.

Table 6-1 shows the results of a requirements document after cross-checking.

Summary of Requirements Document Creation

In summary, take the following steps to complete the requirements document:

1. Create a detailed function hierarchy that is decomposed to the elemental level.
2. List all system requirements and map each requirement to zero or more functions.
3. Create the ERD.
4. Map each requirement to zero or more entities.

Note that a single requirement may be mapped to one or more functions, one or more entities or, if out of scope, to no functions. Table 6-1 shows a report that maps requirements to functions. A similar report should be built to show the mapping of requirements to entities. Appropriate exception reports would include requirements that are not mapped to either functions or entities, as well as functions or entities that have no system requirements associated with them.

On one project the authors worked on, no requirements document was originally planned. The user strongly pushed for documentation of user requirements. Unfortunately, the senior development staff was not responsive to the user's requests and resisted the full documentation of all the business

#	Pg	Source	Requirement	Area	Function Reference	Level of Importance	Completion Comments
1	88	Maggie Brown's interview	Report the number of sales per salesperson.	Sales	SAL1000 SAL2000 SAL3000	Done	Implemented in function hierarchy. Also, references SALES FORCE and UNITS SOLD entities.
2	3	Legacy system	No salesperson can sell to a customer outside his or her territory.	Pricing	PRI0090 PRI0100 PRI0110	Done	Implemented in function hierarchy. Also, references SALES FORCE, CUSTOMER, and REGION entities.
3	15	Legacy system	Create and update a list of the current sales force.	Sales	SAL1050	Done	Implemented in function hierarchy. Also, references SALES FORCE entity.
4	10	Dan Fleece's interview	Provide online access to the customer database to help customers plan their orders.	Sales	None	Out of scope	This will be implemented at some future point.

TABLE 6-1. *Sample Results of a Requirements Document (after Cross-Checking)*

requirements. The development staff felt that such documentation would be a duplication of effort, because the CASE tool provides for descriptions of each function. However, this was not enough for the user. The user wanted a list of everything that has been discussed in this chapter for the requirements document, from detailed requirements to process flows.

The user got tired of consultants coming on site, taking information, and putting it directly into the functional models and ERDs. This approach made it impossible to cross-check the information. The project manager could not track who performed or authorized what functions (especially when information such as sources and topics was not noted in the CASE tool). Development funds were spent on complex ERD modeling when some of the data being modeled was not even required for the system. Furthermore, duplicated functions were hard to find, and it could only be inferred from the description of a function exactly who needed that function.

Using a requirements document, the authors were able to cross-reference requirements by entity model, function model, and source. A tool was created for the users and developers that validated the information transfer. By mapping system requirements to the CASE tool deliverables, the ERDs and function hierarchies were validated.

Without a requirements document, it can only be hoped that someone can remember all of the requirements while validating the ERDs and functional hierarchies. A better approach is for developers to obtain the user's approval of the requirements and then model them in a way that achieves the appropriate goal.

Often, there is a lack of consistent quality in CASE development efforts. Frequently, project leaders put the emphasis on generating a product rather than on satisfying the user's needs. The pressure to produce a project quickly encourages an informal approach to methodology and documentation. Perhaps the fault lies in not having a formal development strategy that would improve the chances of success. It is a key point of this chapter that, except for very small projects, every project team should create a requirements document. This document is the main deliverable from the Analysis phase of the project.

Security

At this stage of the SDLC, you have noted and collected diagrams of different individual's opinions regarding security. For analysis of this information, you need to determine the level of security requirements associated with each attribute in the logical database and each function in the function hierarchy. You will need a basic level of security for the whole application using roles, passwords, and user profiles. In addition, using the security requirements gathered from the users, you will need to identify a security level for each of the elements in the repository and assign each a security level on a scale of 0 to 3, as follows:

- 0 = Information for which no additional level of security is needed. Examples include mail-stop information and office locations.

- 1 = Information which would not cause a huge hardship to the organization if released but which, as a matter of policy, should be kept reasonably secure. Examples include home addresses and telephone numbers of employees.
- 2 = Information which could potentially be damaging either economically or to the reputation of the organization. Examples include payroll information and personnel files.
- 3 = Competitive or strategic information whose unauthorized use or manipulation could seriously affect the organization. Examples include customer lists and contracts.

The deliverable of the security information requirements is the assignment of a security rating of 0 to 3 to each relevant repository element. You can assign these security ratings in two steps. First, define a user extended property called Security Rating for each relevant element type. Then assign the appropriate security rating to each element instance.

Executive Information System (EIS) and Ad Hoc Query Needs

EIS and ad hoc query needs must considered separately since they are different from other requirements. In the Analysis phase, it is not necessary to go into much depth, but the developer should have a reasonable understanding of these needs and where they will fit into the finished system. Any of these needs that can be met by the core production system should be included. Regardless of whether the project is a warehouse system, production system, or even a redesign of a legacy system, these requirements should be gathered.

How should the analyst gather the EIS and ad hoc query requirements? With ad hoc query requirements, the goal is the same as in requirements analysis: namely, to get a good set of requirements. Again, the analyst cannot rely on a single source for this information. Using multiple sources is even more important in this instance. There are four good ways to gather ad hoc query information:

- Interview the users. Asking the users what they do in a general way is the least effective way to gather ad hoc query information, and asking what users would do with a tool they have never seen and perhaps can't imagine isn't likely to yield much useful information either. However, some information will be collected.

- Every IS department receives ad hoc reports. Many of these actually wend their way into the production reporting cycle. The developer should find all of the one-time special reports requested for the past six months to one year and analyze them.
- Many systems have a utility report that runs to a file. Users take information from this report and generate their own report forms. The developer should find the actual reports generated and analyze them.
- The most effective way to gather information on ad hoc user requirements is by using a query log. Ask users to imagine that they have their own perfect in-house systems person. Any time they want a particular (imaginary) report, the systems person can produce the report in 10 to 20 minutes. Users can be asked to write down what they would ask such a person to do. They can write down all of their questions for a specified period of time, such as one week. This will help ensure that the new system has all the information needed to respond to the users' questions. Unlike user interviews, this query log is not created during an interview but during actual work. This type of information gathering technique usually has a high compliance rate. It also gives the developer a good idea of who the high-end ad hoc query users are. Some may enter ten or more queries per day.

When all this information is gathered, the analyst should have a good idea of what the user ad hoc query requirements are.

For EIS requirements, the same techniques can be used. The executive group may or may not use the utility reports. However, the query log is even more important for executives. Because the number of information requests may be lower for executives than for other users, the executives may need to keep query logs for a longer period of time for you to gather enough questions.

Business Process Re-engineering

The current method of doing business may be grossly inefficient. The time when a system is being designed provides an excellent opportunity to rethink the way that business is done. Successful business process re-engineering efforts purport to achieve a dramatic increase in productivity by radically changing business processes and their supporting information technology infrastructure.

A common measure of return on investment is productivity. Information technology (IT) in general has often been deployed with the intent of increasing productivity. This claim, however, has been disputed. Stephen Roach, a principal and economist at Morgan Stanley, has found that investing in IT has not increased productivity and coined the term "productivity paradox" to describe this effect. It is noteworthy that Roach is changing his position. He now believes that IT is finally increasing productivity, but it is not technology alone: it is IT *and* process re-engineering that increase productivity.

Not only does re-engineering have the potential to add value through increasing productivity, but it adds value in other ways as well. For example, re-engineering can add value to the firm by increasing revenues through higher contribution margins, by increasing the output price through superior quality, or by increasing technological flexibility to provide the basis for achieving higher margins in the future. These benefits are known as price recovery, which is defined as the ratio of the prices of outputs to inputs. Figure 6-1, the American Productivity Center (APC) profit variance matrix, shows the effects of input quantities, output quantities, input prices, and output prices on profitability. Re-engineering can achieve a dramatic increase in both productivity and price recovery. Value can accrue to the firm that invests in IT change efforts through increased scalability, flexibility, customer satisfaction, and quality, and reduced cost and cycle time. The profit variance matrix facilitates multi-criteria evaluation of technological change by relating these disparate sources of value to profits through productivity and price recovery.

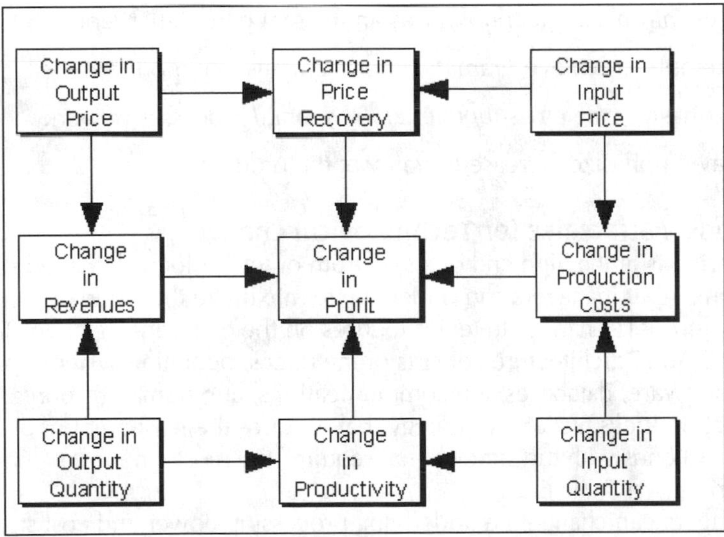

FIGURE 6-1. *American Productivity Center profit variance matrix*

A confluence of factors, including technical and managerial factors, is now leading organizations to change. This study found several reasons why firms decide to undertake re-engineering efforts. These factors will be reviewed after re-engineering is defined.

What Is Re-engineering?

Re-engineering was first touted by information technologists. In the 1991 and 1992 annual Computerworld surveys, technologists reported that re-engineering was the issue of main concern to them. Since then, a plethora of seminars, consulting houses, and senior managers have sprung up to meet the demand for re-engineering knowledge. Even so, business process re-engineering still continues to top the list of senior management concerns, according to CSC Consulting Group's 1994 survey on critical issues in IS management.

Re-engineering strives to achieve an order-of-magnitude increase in performance. It asserts that work should not be organized by vertical functions, such as purchasing, manufacturing, or sales, but that it should be organized by value-added, horizontal processes that cut across the traditional functional areas.

Re-engineering has the following key themes:

- Involves *radical* redesign and restructuring of work
- Uses *information technology* as an integral part of that redesign
- Attempts to achieve *dramatic* improvements in performance
- Emphasizes the *cross-functional, horizontal* processes of work
- May emphasize increased *quality* of the product

"Re-Actions": Strategies for Technological Change

Re-engineering is at the high end of a spectrum of technological change strategies, or "re-actions," that managers can undertake to maximize the value of their firm. This discussion of IT change strategies focuses on the components of an IT architecture. An IT architecture consists of interfaces, operating systems, hardware platforms, software, databases, telecommunications, and human resources.

This section looks first at the strategy that requires the least amount of change, rehosting, and ends with the strategy that requires the most amount of change, re-engineering (see Table 6-2).

IT managers can change the underlying processing power and cost structure of the IT platform through *rehosting*. Rehosting is the change effort that, from the user's perspective, involves the least amount of change. Rehosting typically involves migration from a mainframe platform to a minicomputer, workstation, or

	Process	Software	Hardware	Data	People
Rehosting			X		
Repackaging		X			
Rearchitecting		X	X	X	
Re-engineering	X	X	X	X	X

TABLE 6-2. *Targets of IT Change Strategies*

PC network platform. For example, General Electric moved its financial transaction processing from an IBM 3090 mainframe to a networked Intel 486 PC. The Intel platform uses the same data files and file formats that were used on the IBM mainframe. With rehosting, software applications retain their functionality. Indeed, the users may not even notice the change in hardware, because there is no change in the applications. Firms rehost to reduce cost and increase flexibility. Business value accrues directly from the reduction in the hardware cost, and indirectly from increased flexibility. It is much quicker and more cost effective to scale up a workstation-based platform than a mainframe platform.

IT managers can also change the interface, and thus part of the operating system, through *repackaging*. One common repackaging effort that many organizations are undertaking is moving from a text-based interface, such as DOS, to a graphical user interface, such as Windows.

There is more to the IT architecture than the interface and the hardware. The IT manager can change the way information is gathered and data is organized by *rearchitecting* the system. Rearchitecting makes some change in the functionality of the system, although the underlying business process remains the same. For example, changing a database from a network structure to a relational structure is a rearchitecting effort. The relational structure will allow the user to ask questions about the information that could not be asked under the network structure.

Data integration is a second type of rearchitecting effort. Organizations that want to make coordinated, enterprise-wide decisions find that they cannot do so because data fields that should be the same in two different databases are not the same, because different code is used in different parts of the database. Moving to a client/server architecture consists of two re-actions: rehosting and rearchitecting.

Re-engineering is the re-action that causes the most change. The primary goal of re-engineering is to change the business process. Because the business process will be changed, the IT platform will also most likely need to be changed. Re-engineering seeks to radically change business processes to achieve dramatic improvements in performance.

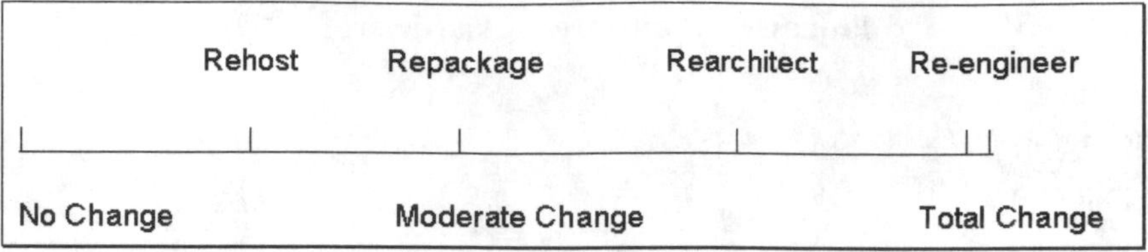

Change Drivers: Why Re-engineer?

A wide variety of factors are driving organizations, and financial services firms in particular, to re-engineer, including the following:

- Cost pressures
- Fragmentation
- Technological change

Cost Pressures

For a variety reasons, organizations may become highly motivated to cut costs. For example, in the late 1980s in the banking industry, defaults on loans and a recessionary economy motivated firms to cut costs, and in the early 1990s the pressure to reduce costs stemmed from the corporate culture. Although 1993 was a profitable year for the banking industry, particularly from trading operations, the corporate culture continued to emphasize the importance of cutting costs. Consequently, financial firms began re-engineering their operations to achieve cost savings.

Fragmentation

In the first half of the 1900s, managers designed organizations by dividing work into the smallest tasks possible and then coordinated those tasks in a hierarchy. Firms were organized by vertical functions. This structure was based on scientific management, which stipulates that an employee would be the most efficient and productive, and thus the entire workflow would be the most efficient and productive, if work were organized into as many small, different tasks as possible. The underlying idea was that specialization was good: the more one performs a task, the better one performs it.

This organization of work maximized the number of hand-offs from one individual or functional area to another. In today's business language, scientific management advocated the *fragmentation* of work.

Excessive fragmentation, together with a functional organization, can lead to a number of problems. First, the time required to produce a product or service in a fragmented and vertical environment may be too long. Each time a hand-off occurs, the work is passed to the next person. There, the work waits in the person's in-box, where it may spend a short time (several minutes) or a long time (several hours or even days). In some cases, the work may actually spend more time waiting in the in-box than actually being attended to. For example, IBM Credit Corporation found that the financing process took an average of two weeks, yet the actual work totaled only 90 minutes.

Today, it is no longer acceptable for work to sit idly in an in-box: customers take their business to organizations that do the job quickly. Fast cycle time is not simply an added benefit to products or services; it is a requirement to remain competitive.

Excessive fragmentation and a vertical structure may lead to a second difficulty: the lack of a strong customer orientation.

A third difficulty is that responsibility for the entire process is diffused across several managers and departments. Thus, any errors that occur in the process are difficult to account for because no one person is responsible for the process as a whole. There is a strong focus on increasing the quality of work in today's business environment.

Suboptimal performance on an enterprise-wide basis is another potential problem resulting from fragmentation. Different departments are responsible for different pieces. Each department may be evaluated on its own functional measures, but these measures may not lead to enterprise-wide optimization. Opportunities to improve performance occur when work goes from one department to another.

Technological Change

Information technology is continually advancing, providing almost continual opportunity to re-engineer work. For example, the increase in object-oriented technology has led many financial services firms start to rethink and re-engineer the way they build financial instruments.

To further understand the technology challenges motivating the demand for re-engineering, the following paragraphs briefly review the evolution of information systems over time in terms of three variables: change drivers, the current IT architecture platform, and IT platform redesign moderators.

Decision-Making Framework for Re-Action

The components of a decision making framework are shown in Figure 6-2. This framework integrates a number of ideas to help senior managers who want to make decisions about what their technology platform should be and what re-action strategy would be appropriate for them to undertake. *Re-actions* are the series of change mechanisms, such as rehosting or re-engineering, for moving from the

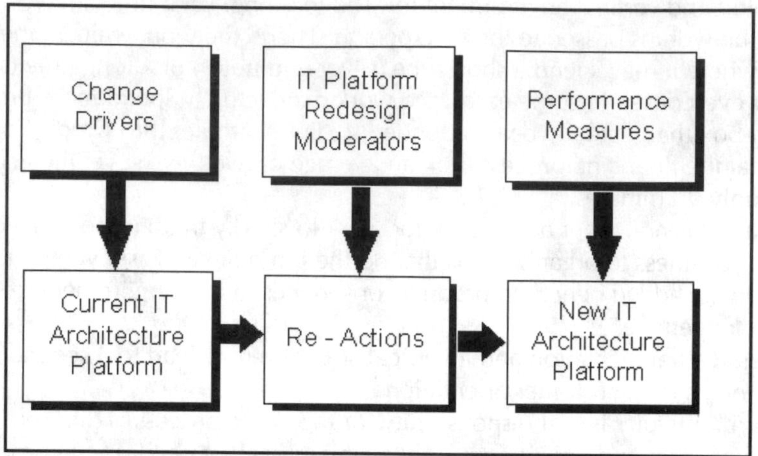

FIGURE 6-2. *Framework for re-action decision making*

current IT platform to a new IT platform, as discussed earlier. Three sets of variables influence the re-action strategy that the manager selects: change drivers, the current IT architecture platform, and IT platform redesign moderators.

Change drivers, such as cost pressures and fragmentation, were discussed in the section, "Change Drivers: Why Re-engineer?" For managers to change the IT architecture, there must be some description of the architecture itself. Changes in the IT architecture as discussed earlier in this chapter have been classified according to the scope and target of the change (such as re-engineering effects on hardware, software, data, people, and process). Senior managers also use the following *IT architecture platform* descriptors when describing their platforms:

- **Flexibility** The ability to easily add functionality or services or customers
- **Interoperability** The ability to easily add and remove modules, incorporating "plug and play" philosophy; also, the ability to communicate with all manner of databases and operating systems, incorporating open standards and portability
- **Scalability** The ability to easily increase the volume of transactions by 50 percent or 200 percent; expandability
- **Reliability** The ability to achieve fault tolerance and availability
- **Security** The ability to safeguard the information system resources

These characteristics are used to describe both the current IT architecture platform and the new IT architecture platform.

IT platform redesign moderators are the constraints that every organization faces. These constraints include the following:

- The budget constraints for the re-action effort
- The length of time within which the re-action effort must take place
- The skill set of the people involved (critical when the re-action effort uses new technologies, such as object-oriented development)

Performance measures are key in this model. It is no longer sufficient to invest only in re-actions; managers require some analysis of the worth of investing in the change.

Keys to Successful Re-engineering

The keys to successful re-engineering include the following:

- Senior management must be committed to the re-engineering effort. There is a lot tied to the status quo. To get people to accept changes, management needs to support the re-engineering effort and make this support visible. The management team must have the will to make the necessary changes and lead the process. This means that senior management needs to be committed to the future environment.
- The scope of the effort must be large. Because re-engineering occurs across multiple product lines, the opportunity to achieve the greatest gains from re-engineering occurs when re-engineering efforts are undertaken across broad functional areas.
- Re-engineering is a cross-functional activity and therefore support by many groups is essential. This support can be achieved through an interactive workshop. All the groups need to be integral parts of the re-engineering effort. The change in culture needs to be managed.

In conclusion, re-engineering has the potential to improve the productivity and price recovery of cross-functional processes. By reducing redundancy, it can reduce costs. By increasing flexibility, it can facilitate the inclusion of new products. Successful change requires senior management commitment, management of the change in the company culture, and a large scope that extends across functional areas or products.

Modifications for Smaller Systems

As mentioned in the discussion of the Pre-Analysis phase, in smaller projects Analysis is less important. For smaller systems, you can use an informal analysis technique. An ERD is still necessary, but you can directly create module definitions bypassing the function hierarchy. Designer/2000 is so sophisticated that analysts can begin building and tinkering right from the beginning. The software being built acts as its own requirements document. Designer/2000 provides a rapid application prototyping environment that enables small projects to be completed without taking many of the formal steps of CADM, the modified CASE methodology.

Medium-sized projects still require careful analysis. For these projects, no aspects of the Analysis phase should be eliminated.

When Is Requirements Analysis Complete?

To determine when requirements analysis is complete, you must look at each of the deliverables individually.

Auditing the Analysis ERD

To fully encapsulate the business requirements, you must make sure complex business transactions can be stored in the model. Does the model have the capabilities needed to store all the information associated with the most complex business transactions? Does the data structure support the most complex questions? Asking these questions is called trying to break the model.

The best way to try to break the model is to formally present the model to other developers and, if possible, an outside auditor. This auditor should be a senior modeller, preferably from outside the development team, whose role is to ask the tough questions that others may not think of. This audit of the logical model should be considered a formal step in the system development process. The person defending the model should arrive with some of the complex transactions tested and demonstrate how the model supports those transactions.

Business rules that cannot be captured within the model should be discussed. Places where the model fails should be identified. There are always interesting decisions made during the modeling process. Frequently, earlier in the process decisions are made to explicitly not include some business rules in the data model because of the extra complexity they would add to it. All such modeling decisions should be revisited and defended during this audit process.

The audit of the ERD is one of the key factors in the success of a project that too often is overlooked. The development team should not just build an ERD with 200 or more entities and assume that it is correct. This is the last opportunity for easily implementing user requirements into the data model. Thus, it is important to audit and validate the thought processes that went into the creation of the model. This model will be used as the foundation for the rest of the system.

Auditing the Analysis Level Function Hierarchy

The audit of the function hierarchy is far less critical than that of the ERD at this point in the system development process. There will be other opportunities to modify the function hierarchy in the Design phase. What is important at this point is to make sure that functions have not been generated excessively. Analysts must keep in mind what these functions will eventually be used for: that is, to generate modules. The function hierarchy should more or less correspond to application modules. For example, even though CREATE NEW EMPLOYEE, UPDATE NEW EMPLOYEE, and DELETE NEW EMPLOYEE are three separate functions, there is no reason not to combine these within the function hierarchy. To do otherwise causes the function hierarchy to expand to an unreasonable size. For example, the authors worked on one system where the individual in charge of the function hierarchy created almost 300 functions for one business area of a system. After a review of the function hierarchy, that number was reduced to about 50.

As mentioned earlier, the main purpose of the function hierarchy is to help organize system requirements. So long as you can neatly organize and distribute system requirements, you can be reasonably satisfied that the function hierarchy is correct. However, you still need to have some reasonable confidence that the function hierarchy with its associated requirements is adequate. To ensure this, you should again use the process of explaining and defending the function hierarchy in front of the development team and an outside auditor. This review should be much quicker and less traumatic than the ERD review.

One important validation that the function hierarchy and ERD are complete is accomplished by mapping the way each entity interacts with each function. For each function, you should specify the impact of that function on each affected entity. Then you should specify whether that function can create-retrieve-update-delete instances. This CRUD matrix will help you validate whether there are sufficient entities to support all business functions and whether each entity has adequate functions associated with it. Exception reports can be run to indicate which functions are not associated with any entities and which entities lack functionality. In general, every entity will require at least one function with CRUD capability.

Auditing the Mapping of Requirements to Functions

Mapping all of the requirements is a big job, and it is often done by less experienced members of the development team. Thus, the audit of the mapping process at this point is important. You should make sure that system requirements have been both correctly extracted from source notes and correctly mapped to the functions in the hierarchy. Sample checks of several source documents should be done for each developer. Even though monitoring should presumably occur during the information gathering process itself, a final audit still should be conducted at the end of the requirements analysis phase.

Auditing the Process Flows

The process flows represent the development team's understanding of how business transactions occur within the organization. If BPR is performed, the re-engineered process flows should also be audited.

The translation of a business process to a process flow diagram is straightforward, so process flows can be audited directly with users. Therefore, the defense of the process flows should involve users to a large extent. Again, you should present the process flows to a group of users and senior development team members for audit. For a complex system, it might be appropriate to have two defenses: one with the entire development team to iron out development issues, and a second with users and some development team members to handle user issues.

Auditing the Legacy System Review

You do not need to directly audit the legacy system review. Assuming that some of the existing system developers are still available within the organization, they can audit and sign off on the review. If more than one legacy system developer is available, have one help with the review itself and the second perform the audit.

Completing the Report Audit

The users can supply information on the report audit. Depending on how the information was gathered, results of interviews, questionnaires, and so on can be returned to the users for sign-off. When users agree that these items are correct, the report audit is finished.

Auditing Business Objectives and Critical Success Factors

As with the report audit, the records of the business objectives and critical success factors that have been collected can be distributed back to management at all appropriate levels for sign-off.

When this and all of the other parts of the requirements document are finished, then requirements analysis can be considered complete.

The Analysis Phase in Designer/2000: Requirements Analysis

Designer/2000 supports many of the activities you perform in the requirements analysis step of the Analysis phase. Its Systems Modeller diagrammers and some of the repository utilities will help you capture, analyze, manage, and process the information you have gathered about the business and represent it with repository definitions. Table 6-3 shows the diagrammers and utilities that you typically would use in the requirements analysis part of the Analysis phase.

This section discusses the functions of these diagrammers and utilities and the work you perform in the Analysis phase. This discussion relies on the basic information on the Designer/2000 tools introduced in Chapter 2. If you need extra assistance as you work in these tools at any point, the Designer/2000 help system and cue cards can answer specific questions and provide step-by-step instructions as you use the tools.

Here is one approach to the sequence of Designer/2000 work in the Analysis phase:

1. Use the *ER Diagrammer* to define the data side of the business.
2. Use the *Process Modeller* or *Dataflow Diagrammer* to refine the process flows.
3. Use the *Function Hierarchy Diagrammer* to refine the process hierarchy and attach entity usages to functions. You can also add attribute usages here, or use the Function/Attribute Matrix utility instead.
4. Use the *Matrix Diagrammer* to define CRUD for the entities only. Applying CRUD to attributes can wait until the module data usages are created in the Pre-Design phase or can be done here as well.
5. Use *Repository Reports* to show the details of the work you completed.

Activity or Deliverable	Designer/2000 Tool
Analysis ERD	Entity Relationship Diagrammer
Synchronize all attributes in a domain.	Update Attributes in a Domain utility
Insert attribute usages for functions.	Function/Attribute Matrix utility
Complete the process flow analysis.	Process Modeller or Dataflow Diagrammer
Perform function reorganization and decomposition.	Function Hierarchy Diagrammer
Perform CRUD to cross-check or assign entity usage.	Matrix Diagrammer
Document the analysis objects.	Repository Reports

TABLE 6-3. *Analysis Deliverables and Designer/2000 Tools: Requirements Analysis*

This approach gives you the choice of filling in attribute usages for functions manually (in the Function Hierarchy Diagrammer or Dataflow Diagrammer) or accepting the default values from the Function/Attribute Matrix utility. You need these in the Pre-Design phase when you run the Application Design Wizard to create candidate modules. However, you spend time in the Design phase refining the table and column usages for the modules anyway, so you can consider accepting the default attribute CRUD in the Analysis phase and refine them in the Design phase (where they are manifest as module column usages). At that point, the design will be more stable, and you can pay attention to not only the data column properties but the display column properties.

The following paragraphs discuss the requirements analysis tasks within the framework of these five steps.

More on the Entity Relationship Diagrammer

Chapter 3 covered the basics of the ER Diagrammer and its use in the Strategy phase. This chapter expands on that information and relates this diagrammer to the work you do in the requirements analysis part of the Analysis phase. In the Strategy phase, you create a strategy ERD that contains a rough idea of the basic entities and may or may not contain attributes. In the Analysis phase, it is important to create entities for all significant items in the system as well as to fill in these entities with attributes. Therefore, the level of detail in this stage is much greater than in the

Strategy stage, although you can use the strategy ERD as a starting point for this work. In fact, you should create a separate strategy ERD and analysis ERD because of the different levels of detail, though the second ERD builds on the first. In addition, if you are performing business process re-engineering, you should also create an ERD that diagrams the entities created or modified in the re-engineering process.

Remember that the ER Diagrammer handles the data-related elements only, and that you need these when you assign entities and attributes to functions. Therefore, your work on entities and attributes has to be at an advanced stage of completeness before you start defining function data usages. Of course, the process and data models are often developed and refined simultaneously and modified in an iterative way, so you probably should not create the final function entity usages until both models are as complete as possible.

The following sections describe tasks you perform to create domains and attributes in the ERD—elements that were not necessary in the Strategy phase. While you can determine and use some domains in Strategy, you will have a more complete picture of the system in Analysis and it will be easier to define the rest at this point. While you may find a use for some domains and attributes in the Strategy phase, you should not spend much time and effort on this there, as you will have to revisit this process in the Analysis phase.

Defining and Using Domains

A *domain* is a set of allowable values and format rules for an attribute (or column). The Designer/2000 implementation of the relational database concept of domains is quite powerful and well integrated into the repository. You can attach a domain definition to an attribute in the Attribute properties window in RON or on the Attribute tab in the Edit Entity properties window in the ER Diagrammer. The attribute will then take on all the characteristics of that domain. If you change any attribute property that the domain is in charge of, such as the length, the domain name will be removed to indicate that the attribute no longer reflects values from the domain.

A benefit of this approach is that you can manage the characteristics of a group of attributes that are assigned to the same domain by changing the underlying domain definition. Another benefit is that you can enforce standards on datatypes for particular uses. For example, suppose two different analysts create two different entities, both of which have an EMPID attribute. Without a domain for this attribute, one analyst could make the datatype for the EMPID attribute VARCHAR2(6), and the other could make it NUMBER(10). With a domain called EMPLOYEE ID, each analyst can attach it to the attributes and does not need to worry about the actual datatype and size.

Before attaching the domains, you have to create them by choosing **Edit→Domain** from the menu and filling in the Edit Domains window as Figure 6-3

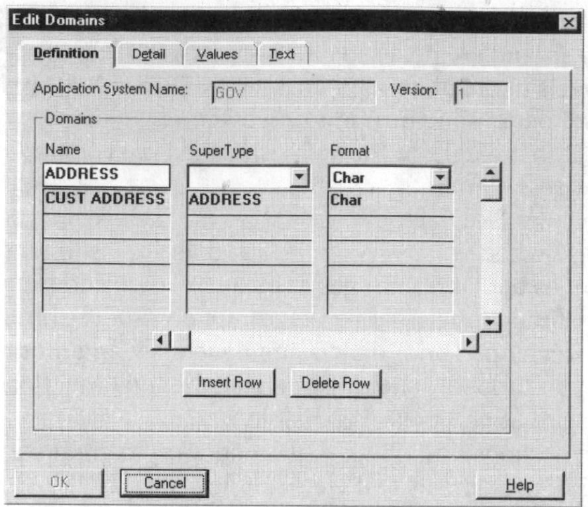

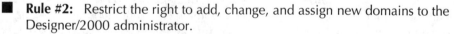

FIGURE 6-3. *Edit Domains window*

shows. Alternatively, you can create the definitions in the Repository Object Navigator, but the Edit Domains window is closer to your work when you are in the ER Diagrammer.

Before you add attributes to your entities, create as complete a set of domains as possible. Make two rules for the use of domains in your system development:

- **Rule #1:** Ultimately base all attributes on domains, regardless of whether only one attribute pertains to a particular domain. Analysts may, however, temporarily assign datatypes, sizes, and values if no existing domain fits a particular attribute they are creating.
- **Rule #2:** Restrict the right to add, change, and assign new domains to the Designer/2000 administrator.

When an analyst needs a new domain, the analyst can assign properties manually, without using a domain. The Designer/2000 administrator (or your data administrator if you have one) should periodically look at the repository to see if there are any attributes without domains. If so, the Designer/2000 administrator should create a domain using the sizes and types the analyst used for the attribute itself and attach the new domain to the attribute. This sounds like a lot of administrative work, but you can write Designer/2000 API routines to help automate it, and this procedure will help enforce standards and consistency in attributes.

The details you define for a domain include the datatype and size of the attribute and a separate datatype and size for the column. The same domain can describe both attributes and columns, and you can have different datatypes for each. This approach is useful when you have a data element that contains, for example, monetary data. The datatype for the attribute may be Money, but since there is no Money datatype for a table column, the column datatype would be Number. The Detail tab of the Edit Domains window has more information than the Definition tab if you want to describe the domain more fully, as Figure 6-4 shows.

The Values tab is where you enter the values used to validate data columns with this domain attached to them. For example, you may have a Yes/No attribute that has a domain YES NO attached to it. The YES NO domain, in turn, may have a set of valid values defined on the Values tab: one for Y and one for N. This information eventually ends up in reference tables for the finished application or in the application or database code to validate the value entered in the table.

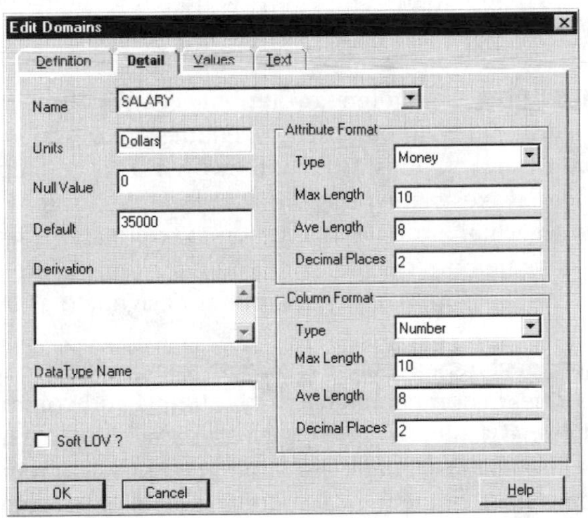

FIGURE 6-4. *Detail tab of Edit Domains window*

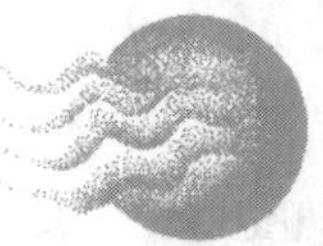

NOTE

Domains can be based on domains. The Edit Domains Definition tab has a Supertype property that allows you to specify an existing domain name that is the parent of the one you are defining. This documents that the domain is a subset of another domain and has characteristics in common with it. Although there is no automatic property sharing, you can set up a hierarchy of domains in this way if you need to.

Adding Attributes

An attribute is an atomic piece of information that describes an entity. Entities have two or more attributes that give details and further identify the meaning of the entity. Designer/2000 uses three symbols to show different types of attributes:

#	Indicates a unique identifier that consists of one or more attributes that identify one instance of this entity
*	Indicates mandatory attributes that must contain values
o	Indicates an optional attribute that can be null or unknown

After you create the entity, you double-click the entity's symbol in the ER Diagrammer to pop up the Edit Entity window and then click the Attributes tab to display the area shown in Figure 6-5. Here you fill in the name and domain of each attribute you have determined in the analysis process that describes this entity.

Foreign Key Attributes Foreign key attributes exist only as the relationship lines shown between entities. In other words, entities are described by the attributes and foreign key relationships that they own. This concept, while simple and flawless in logic, makes some people uncomfortable because they prefer to see the foreign key as an actual attribute in addition to the relationship line. In addition, entities have unique identifiers, not primary keys. There may be more than one unique identifier for an entity, but one is designated as the primary unique identifier.

Primary unique identifiers in entities become primary keys in tables, and relationships in entities become foreign key constraints and columns in tables. A key is really a relational database concept, and although you eventually convert this set of entities into relational database tables, that physical representation is a detail that is inappropriate at the logical modeling level of the Analysis phase. Regardless of your views on this potentially controversial subject, while working with Designer/2000, you will get used to creating entities that do not have keys.

The Attributes tab lets you quickly enter the names and domains of all attributes. Remember that CTRL-DOWN ARROW moves the cursor to the next line,

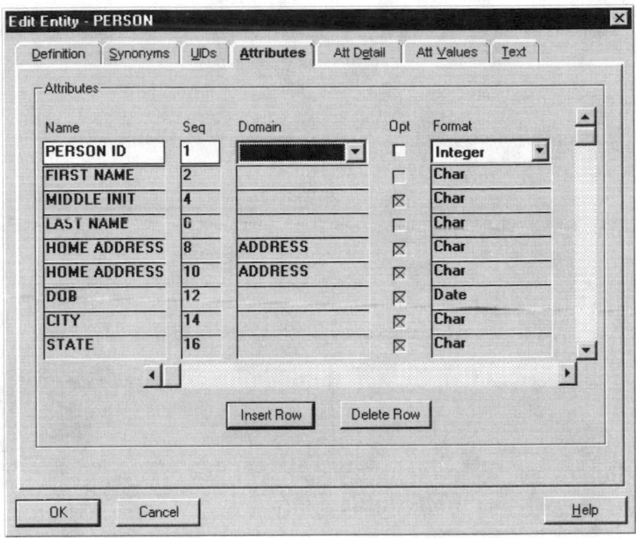

FIGURE 6-5. *Edit Entity window with the Attributes tab*

and CTRL-UP ARROW moves the cursor to the previous line. You can also look at a detailed view of each attribute in the Att Detail tab, as Figure 6-6 shows.

Unique Identifier Attributes After defining the attributes, you can select the attributes that are the unique identifiers (UIDs) for that entity. The UIDs tab in the Edit Entity window allows you to assign attributes as UIDs. Note that you can specify attributes for more than one UID for each entity by adding a row at the top of the dialog. Also, a single UID may consist of one or more columns and relationships. You have to specify one of the UIDs as primary to create the primary key of the table based on this entity. The Attributes tab lets you specify which attributes participate in the primary UID.

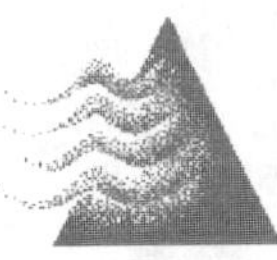

TIP
Be sure to give the unique identifier a sequence number as the repository will not accept the entry without it.

Attribute Text The Edit Entity window contains a Text tab where you can enter text on either entities or attributes for that entity. As Figure 6-7 shows, if you choose to attach text to attributes, a field appears where you can choose the attribute. You can then assign different types of text for the attribute—such as Derivation Expression, a SQL-like statement that calculates a value for the attribute

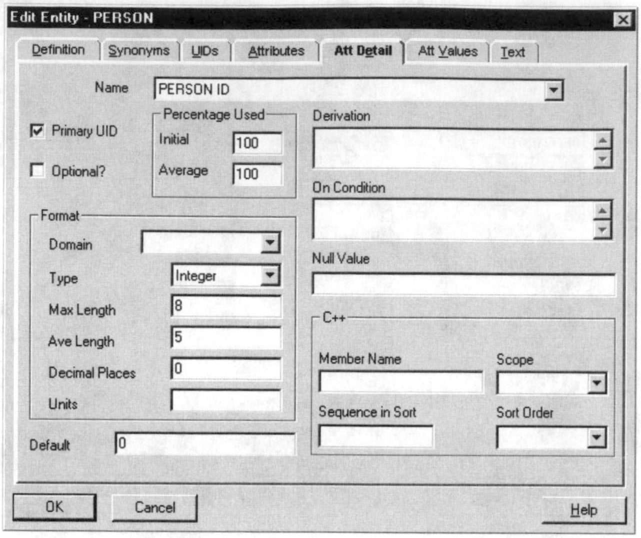

FIGURE 6-6. *Att Detail tab of the Edit Entity window*

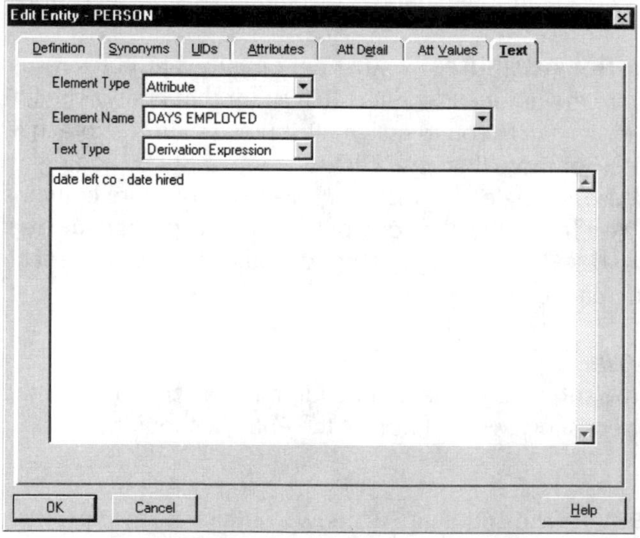

FIGURE 6-7. *Edit Entity Text tab with Attribute text definition*

based on other attributes in the entity. This expression is transferred to the column when the table is created from this entity.

Detailing Relationships

Relationships have a properties window called Edit Relationship that you display by double-clicking the relationship line. This window contains places to change cardinality and optionality as well as the name of the relationship you specified when you first defined it. Another property in this window is the C++ set or pointer name that the C++ Object Layer Generator uses to create a class member from this relationship.

Primary UID Relationships If a relationship is part of the primary UID, you can also specify the primary UID in the Edit Relationship window. You can also specify a primary UID only for the many side of a relationship, and when you do, a crossbar will appear by the many (crow's foot) symbol to indicate that the relationship is part of the primary UID, as in the following illustration.

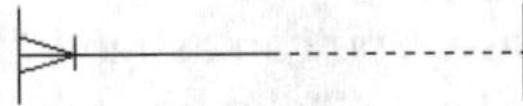

Transferable Relationships Designer/2000 uses another special symbol for relationships that are not *transferable*—that is, for a relationship in which you may not move the end specified as nontransferable from one entity to another. You define a nontransferable relationship in the Edit Relationship window by unchecking the Transferable check box. A diamond will appear by the end of the relationship you specified, as in the next illustration.

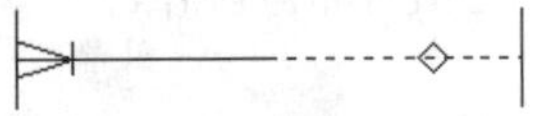

Other Relationships All combinations of optionality and one-to-many relationships are available in the ER Diagrammer. You might consider not resolving many-to-many relationships at this stage of the SDLC; these cannot be implemented in tables of a relational database system, so you must resolve each such relationship into two one-to-many relationships attached to an entity called an intersection or associative table created just for that purpose. This is the classic technique for resolving many-to-many relationships; nevertheless, many-to-many relationships are valid logical concepts, and you can leave them in at this stage. When the entities become tables in the next phase of the SDLC, you can resolve the many-to-many relationship into an intersection table and two one-to-many relationships so you can implement them in the relational database. If, however, you find in the Analysis phase that there are attributes associated with the many-to-many relationship, you can create an entity in the ER Diagrammer for the intersection and put those attributes in it.

The same considerations apply to arc and subtype-supertype relationships. You cannot implement these directly in a relational database system (though you can diagram them on the Data Diagrammer and create check constraints to enforce them); but you can resolve them when you move to the Design phase. The decision regarding whether to resolve these relationships in the Analysis or Design phase is based on concerns similar to those relevant to many-to-many relationships. If there are additional attributes that the relationship implies, or if the relationships are confusing to those who need to understand them, you should consider resolving these relationships in the Analysis phase by creating extra entities.

Completing Entity Details

In this part of the Analysis phase, you need to fill in some information on the entities that you have not needed before. Volume information will help you in future phases to size the database. You can assign Initial, Maximum, Average, and Growth Rate values on the Edit Entity Definition tab. This tab also shows the names you gave the entity when you originally defined it, and you can change these if you want to. Another property indicates whether this application system owns this entity. If the entity is shared from another application system, you cannot change its properties.

Another property in the Edit Entity window that you should pay attention to at this stage is C++ Class Name, which is the name used for the C++ class you will generate from this entity. Also, you should review the Synonyms tab where you list the alternative names that the system uses for this entity. Since these names identify the entity, they must be unique in the system. These names will be used as synonyms for the table generated from the entity.

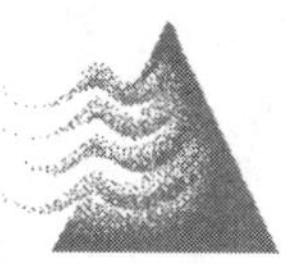

TIP

When providing a short name for an entity, remember that ten characters are maximum and seven or fewer are recommended.

Using the Update Attributes in a Domain Utility

The ER Diagrammer has a menu choice for loading the Update Attributes in a Domain utility. This utility is also available in the Repository Object Navigator (**Utilities→Update Attributes in a Domain**). It does what the name implies: for selected domains, it updates the attributes attached to them. For example, suppose you created three attributes and based them all on a domain called ADDRESS that you defined as VARCHAR2(25). You found out later that addresses can contain up to 35 characters, so you change the domain definition to accommodate the increased size. The attributes that have this domain attached to them are not automatically updated to the new size, so you run this utility to accomplish the update.

When you choose **Utilities→Update All Attributes within Domains** from the menu, a dialog box with a list of existing domains appears, as in the following illustration.

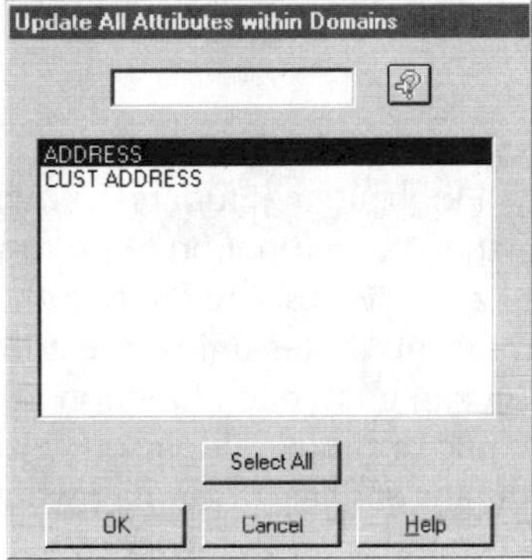

You select the domains and click the OK button. The utility will scan the repository for all attributes that have the domains you selected and update their definitions to reflect the current state of those domains.

Filling in Attribute Usages with the Function/Attribute Matrix Utility

Filling in the attribute usage for functions at some level is important at this point in the development life cycle. Although you will need to revisit the assignments in the Design phase when you tune the module data usages, you need to at least assign attributes to functions, even if you do not refine their CRUD properties. You first need to assign entities to functions in the Function Property window for each function in the Dataflow Diagrammer or Function Hierarchy Diagrammer. Alternatively, you can use the Matrix Diagrammer described in this chapter to perform this task. Once this task is complete, you can run the Function/Attribute Matrix utility to obtain a rough-cut set of attribute usages.

This utility is available on the Utilities menus of the Entity Relationship Diagrammer, Repository Object Navigator, Dataflow Diagrammer, and Function Hierarchy Diagrammer. When you choose this item from the menu, the Create Function/Attribute Matrix dialog box shown in the following illustration appears.

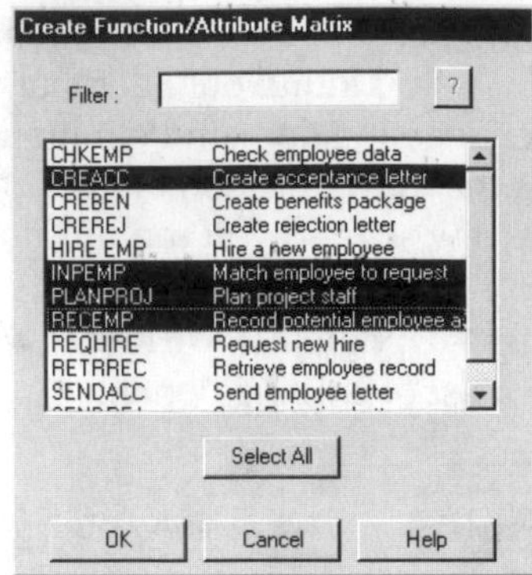

Select the functions for which you wish to generate attribute usages and click the OK button. The utility will look at each function you selected and add attribute usages for the entities attached to each function (with function-entity usages). Note that this process will load all attributes for the entity if they are not already defined as usages, but it will not remove attributes unless the attribute no longer exists. When this utility is done, you can go to each function definition and remove attributes that are not applicable or modify the insert-retrieve-update-nullify characteristics (as with CRUD for entities). You may want to perform this task in the Matrix Diagrammer, but you can also do the work in the function diagrammers. As mentioned, you may consider not spending time on refining the attribute CRUD and instead spend time in the Design phase working on the column CRUD.

Where Does This Information Go?

The information you model in this diagrammer, as with the information you model in all diagrammers, is available in the repository for other phases of the development process. You use the entity and attribute definitions when you attach entity and attribute usages to functions. Also, in the next phase, Pre-Design, you will create physical design data objects from these elements as shown in Table 6-4.

The Process Modeller and Dataflow Diagrammer in Requirements Analysis

Chapter 3 explains the Strategy phase and how to use the Process Modeller in detail. The process diagramming activities you perform in the requirements analysis stage of the Analysis phase are no different from those you perform in the Strategy phase. However, at this stage you need to add and confirm more detail in this tool (or in the Dataflow Diagrammer) to ensure that you have represented all major flows and processes in the system that are driven by system requirements. Also, you need to decompose functions and processes down to *atomic* levels. That is, you

Strategy and Analysis Data Element	Design Data Element
Entity	Table
Attribute	Column
Primary unique identifier	Primary key constraint
Nonprimary unique identifier	Unique constraint
One-to-many relationship	Foreign key constraint and foreign key column
Many-to-many relationship	Intersection table and foreign key constraints
Arc and subtype/supertype relationships	Single tables or multiple tables with special columns to link them

TABLE 6-4. *Analysis Data Elements and Their Design Data Element Counterparts*

need to reduce or decompose the function to a point where it can no longer be broken into subfunctions. If you can break a function down to a lower level, you need to create another level diagram in the function hierarchy to represent the subfunctions.

To create this lower level, select the function and choose **Open Down** on the File menu. This procedure opens a new diagram with the base process of the selected process. You place functions, flows, and stores on this diagram to describe the upper-level function. This is the essence of how you perform functional decomposition in the diagrammers. You will also use the function diagrammers when performing business process re-engineering to show the new or modified flows resulting from the re-engineering process. There may also be re-engineered data elements that you represent in the ER Diagrammer to go along with the new flows.

You should exercise moderation in decomposing functions, since this is an area where "analysis paralysis" can set in—that is, where you can get stuck in the Analysis phase, spending more and effort than you originally budgeted and finding that the functions you analyzed first are no longer applicable because so much time has elapsed and the business has changed its policies since you began.

Another point to remember is that the functions and flows you created in the Strategy phase may not be fully applicable to the Analysis phase diagram. You may have to split or combine processes to more accurately reflect what the final system will accomplish. These are all activities you perform in the Analysis phase in either the Process Modeller or Dataflow Diagrammer. You can also accomplish the task of reorganizing functions in the Function Hierarchy Diagrammer. One approach is to partition the business area and focus first on decomposing and detailing the area you will implement first.

Process Modeller

In addition to constructing the function hierarchy in the Analysis phase, you also should pay attention to some of the detailed characteristics of the diagrammed elements. The Process Modeller lets you assign detailed time, cost, and resource amounts for each process step, flow, and store. This procedure is useful if you are analyzing the time characteristics of the processes and flows, particularly in a business process re-engineering effort. The time and cost information you enter appears on reports such as the Activity Based Costing report. It is also the basis for determining the time it takes each element to become active when you animate the diagram.

All the cost, time, and resource assignments you make will appear later on reports. This feature allows you to specify a large number of critical details about each process and then summarize them later in various reports. It also helps you think about the processes and the kind of information you need for each one, which helps you make your model complete. The time and resource information you enter here is not reused by Designer/2000 in the Design phase, but it can be quite helpful during the Analysis phase to give you insight into the business functions and extract requirements.

You assign time and cost amounts on the Main tab of the Edit Process Step window for each element as in Figure 6-8.

Time You can track the times of various types for processes, flows, and stores. You fill in for each type a unit of time (minute, hour, day, week) as well as an amount. You can track the following times:

- *Prior Delay* identifies the time that elapses between the time control passes to this element and the actual work starts. You should not specify both Prior Delay and Post Delay for the same element, so if one of these items is specified, the other should be zero.
- *Work* indicates how long a process or flow (or even a store) takes to perform its action.
- *Quality Check* designates how long a cross-check of the completed work takes (if one is performed).
- *Post Delay* is the amount of time that elapses after the completion of the work and quality checks before control passes to the next element. If you need both Prior & Post, define Prior on one element and Post on the next element in the flow.

- *Total* sums the previous time fields automatically. You can override this summing by typing an amount, but if you change any of the fields above, this item will recalculate the total. This number and its units will appear on the drawing for processes when the view is in Symbol mode.
- *Measured Times* gives you a way to show a minimum and maximum amount of time for this element or to assign times that you define. In other words, the definitions of these two time fields are up to you.
- *Critical Path Times* indicates if this element is in the critical path. If so, a delay here affects the completion of the entire set of processes. These times cannot be updated and are calculated when you choose **Utilities→ Calculate Critical Path** from the menu.

NOTE

The breakdown of times is really only a suggestion. If you have other needs for the fields, you can assign times for actions other than prior delay, work, quality check, post delay, and so on.

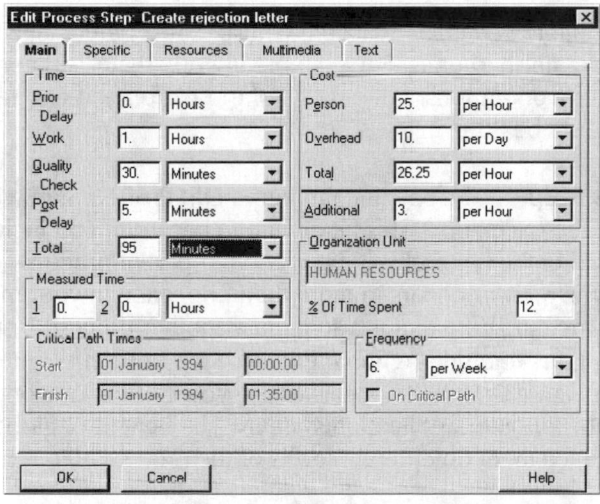

FIGURE 6-8. *Main tab of the Edit Process Step window*

The other time fields on the Main tab are % of Time Spent, for designating the percentage of the total time that the organization unit this element belongs to spends on this activity, and Frequency, for designating the number of times this process or flow occurs in the base process you are diagramming.

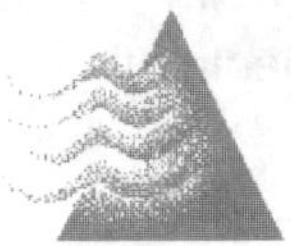

TIP
If you want to use the time capabilities of the Process Modeller but do not want to get bogged down in determining the times for various types of tasks, you can enter just the total time. Although you will lose some details, you will still be able to run the animation and watch for slow elements.

Cost You can assign costs for Person (personnel) and Overhead (costs such as rent and utilities). These are actual monetary designations, and Designer/2000 adds them together into the Total field (which you can override by typing an amount). As with time, you designate the unit of time to which the cost applies. You can also specify Additional for costs not specified by the other two categories. This cost has a per unit designation for costs of raw materials using a unit measurement.

Resources The Resources tab, shown in Figure 6-9, has two main areas:

- *Resources,* where you indicate the amount and type of materials you need for this process (or flow): for example, 1 typewriter.
- *Yield (Quality Percentage),* where you specify a percentage to indicate the amount of finished units. For example, if you create 100 complete computer workstations, but only 95 of these are good enough for use, the yield would be 95.

Global Process Step The Specific tab in the Edit Process Step window has a Global Process Step check box. This box will be checked if you include a process from another level of the hierarchy or from another parent process—which you may do if the same activity occurs in more than one place in your model and you need to show something here that is also part of another process. You accomplish this by choosing **Edit→Include→Global Process Step** from the menu. The selection screen shown in Figure 6-10 will appear, where you can include one or more processes from this or other application systems. The benefit of global process steps is that you can place them on different levels of the process hierarchy.

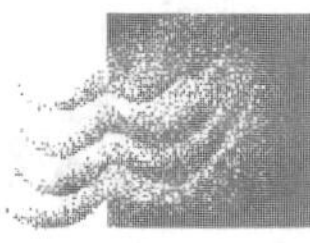

CAUTION
Including global processes from other application systems can be time consuming.

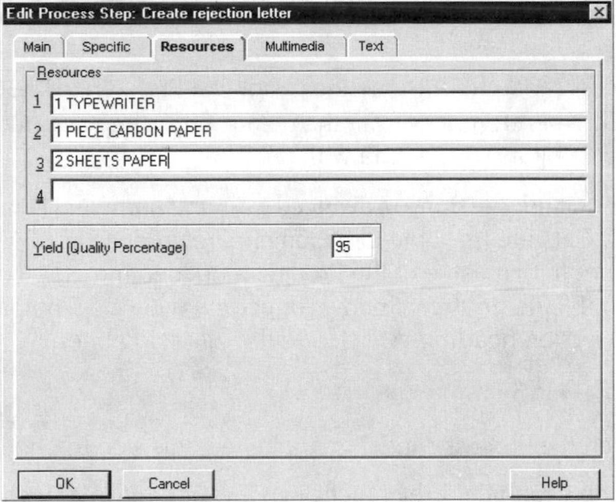

FIGURE 6-9. *Resources tab of the Edit Process Step window*

Once a global process is in your diagram, you can position it and view its properties, but you will not be able to change it unless you go back to the source process. Designer/2000 determines automatically whether or not this process is a global process step and places a check mark in the check box on the Specific tab.

Saving Graphical Preferences in the Process Modeller

You can save the graphical preferences you set for a particular diagram in a file so you can use them in other diagrams or change them temporarily and then restore them. The files you create are available to any Process Modeller diagram in any application system. Follow these steps to create and save the graphical preferences:

1. Check that the Windows directory contains a file called BPMOD10.CFG (the actual name of your Windows directory is specific to your installation). If this file is in the root directory, move it to the Windows directory. If there is no file, subsequent steps will create one.

2. In the Process Modeller, display the Graphical Preferences window by selecting **Edit→Preferences** from the menu. Click the Save button to register the BPMOD10.CFG file with the tool.

3. Select **File→Configuration→Advanced** from the menu and choose the BPMOD10.CFG file from the Use Element Preference Set pop-up list. If this file is not in that list, exit the Process Modeller and edit the BPMOD10.INI file (in the Windows directory) with the Notepad editor. Under the section heading [Misc], add the following line:

```
ElementPreferenceSet=bpmod10.cfg
```

Then reopen the Process Modeller and repeat this step to choose the file.

4. Return to the Graphical Preferences window and make any changes you want. When you click Save now you will see the Named Element Preference Set window, where you can choose an existing preference file (with a .CFG extension) or type a new name.

When you want to apply a saved preference set, all you need to do is choose it in the Advanced Configuration (**File→Configuration→Advanced**) dialog box. You save the new sets in the Graphical Preferences dialog box (**Edit→Preferences**).

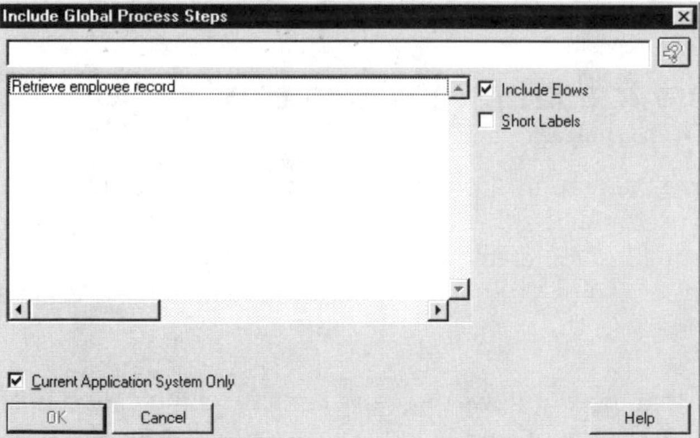

FIGURE 6-10. *Include Global Process Steps Dialog box*

Dataflow Diagrammer

The Dataflow Diagrammer is also available and applicable to the tasks in the Analysis phase. Some analysts use this diagrammer instead of the Process Modeller to complete the process flows, and some use only the Process Modeller; each has a slightly different focus, as Chapter 5 discusses, and you can use either one or both.

All preceding cautions about analysis paralysis also apply to this diagrammer. You should temper your urge to be complete in modeling the processes and flows that make up the Analysis phase model of the business.

Techniques and Properties There are a few techniques and properties you should pay more attention to in this phase than in the Strategy phase. One of these is *reparenting*: moving a subfunction from one parent to another at the same or a higher level. For example, suppose that functions 1.1.1 and 1.1.2 describe function 1.1. You decide that function 1.1.2 really belongs under 1.2, so you perform reparenting: you drag the function out of the frame function and drop it outside the border. The New Parent dialog box will appear as shown in Figure 6-11.

After you select a parent function in this dialog box and click OK, the Dataflow Diagrammer draws the function where you dropped it and renumbers it to reflect its parent; in this case, the function becomes 1.2.1.

You can make a frame function the parent of a global function (one outside the frame function) simply by dropping the global function inside the frame. You will be asked to confirm this operation, but the New Parent dialog box will not appear because the new parent is the frame function.

Properties you should pay attention to here more than in other phases appear in the Edit Function window. The Definition tab, shown in Figure 6-12, contains the

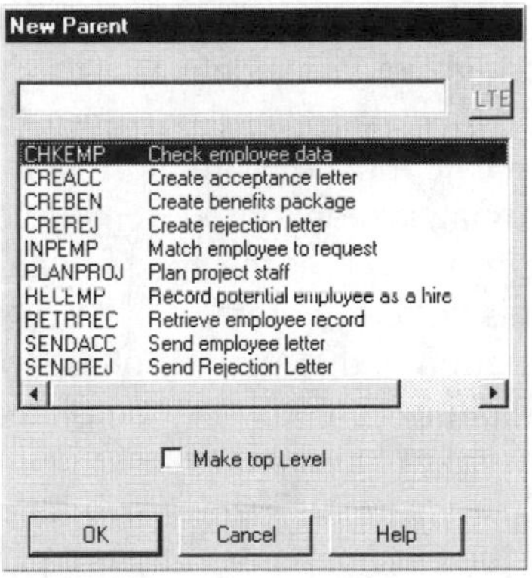

New Parent
LTE
CHKEMP Check employee data
CREACC Create acceptance letter
CREBEN Create benefits package
CREREJ Create rejection letter
INPEMP Match employee to request
PLANPROJ Plan project staff
RECEMP Record potential employee as a hire
RETRREC Retrieve employee record
SENDACC Send employee letter
SENDREJ Send Rejection Letter
Make top Level
OK Cancel Help

FIGURE 6-11. *New Parent dialog box*

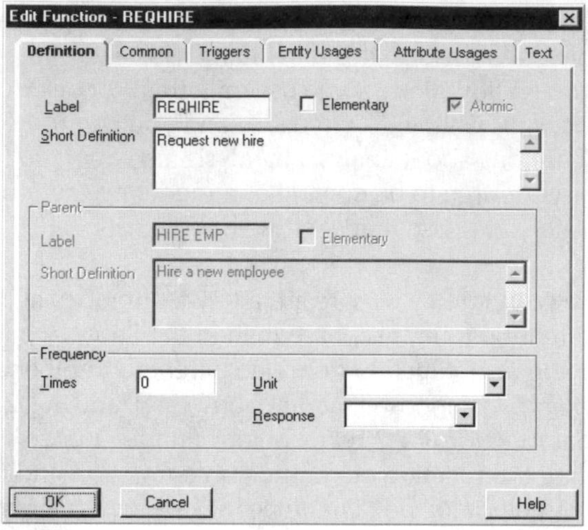

FIGURE 6-12. *Definition tab of the Edit Function window*

Label and Short Definition specifications, both of which appear on the diagram as well. The Parent section of this tab shows the label, short definition, and elemental characteristics of the function that is at the level just above this one.

The Frequency area is the same as for the Process Modeller. Here you can assign the number of times and the time period in which this function occurs within the frame function. The Frequency area also has a key field called Response where you can specify Overnight or Immediate. Overnight functions are those that do not happen immediately when started and become utility modules later in the development process. Immediate functions are those that happen right away when started and will become manual, screen, or report modules later in the life cycle. The Application Design Wizard also uses this field to determine which functions it can group together. Thus, this field is important.

You should also pay attention in the Analysis phase to the Elementary check box. You check this box if the function must be completed successfully or else the data or system must be reversed to the state it was in before the function started. The Application Design Wizard uses this value when it determines which functions it converts into modules for the Design phase. Therefore, be sure to be accurate here if you will be using that utility later.

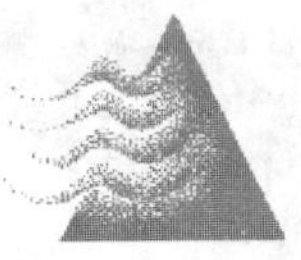

TIP

Fill in the Elementary and Response fields in the Edit Function window's Definition tab if you plan to use the Application Design Wizard later in the life cycle to generate candidate modules for the final application. In addition, be sure you enter entity usages for the function; otherwise, Designer/2000 will treat the function as a manual function that will have a manual module created for it (one with no code generator and therefore no program code).

The last area to note in the Edit Function window for the Dataflow Diagrammer elements is the Text tab. This area appears in one form or another in all diagrammers, and many of the text types are the same for elements that may not even have diagrammers. The Text tab allows you to store information about the element in a free-form text area. Figure 6-13 shows the types of text you can store for the function element.

You can select these types one at a time and fill in the text area that appears below. The text types are the standard ones that Designer/2000 defines for each element, and certain types appear only for certain elements. For example, Value Chain Analysis, where you store text about the added value that this process adds

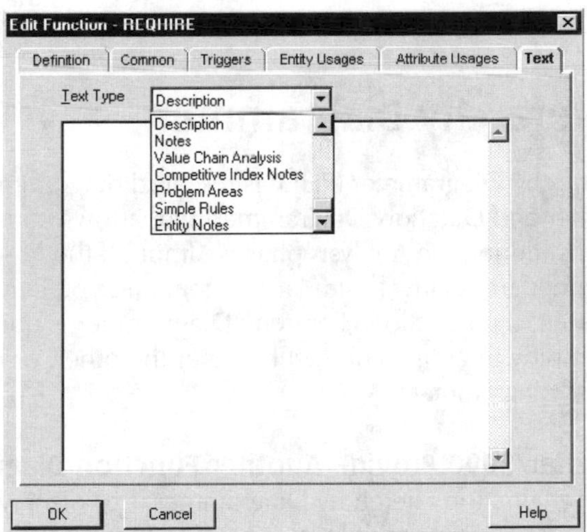

FIGURE 6-13. *Text tab and types of text you can store for a function*

to the system, describes only functions, stores, and flows. Other elements may have fewer or more types of text, but Notes and Description are available for all. If you need more or different text types for any element (and not just those provided for the Dataflow Diagrammer), you can define them with user extensions to the repository.

The text here is only for your use in documenting the system, and although you can list the information in reports, the text itself does not have any additional effects in the Design phase.

The Context Diagram You can include a context diagram in your dataflow diagram set. This diagram contains only one function and one or more externals with flows to and from the function. Although you will decompose this function in later steps, you do not show subfunctions, internal flows, and data stores in the context diagram itself. This diagram is useful for showing the scope or boundaries of the system as a whole and the entities outside the system with which it interfaces. You do not show dataflows between externals as those are outside the scope of the system.

The Dataflow Diagrammer allows you to construct a context diagram by using the top-level function (1.0) and drawing it by itself on a diagram. There are no other functions at that level, so the function numbers will start with 1.1 for the next level down from the context diagram. This diagram is useful in the Strategy phase as well, but as with the other dataflow diagrams, you expand and refine it in the Analysis phase.

Function Hierarchy Diagrammer

The Function Hierarchy Diagrammer (FHD) is the third diagrammer (along with the Process Modeller and Dataflow Diagrammer) that allows you to model processes (functions) during the Analysis phase. Although the Process Modeller and Dataflow Diagrammer are relatively similar in intent and you can use one in exclusion of the other, the Function Hierarchy Diagrammer is quite a different tool that you usually employ in conjunction with one or the other, or both, of its companion process diagrammers.

Why Does Designer/2000 Provide Another Function Diagrammer?

The objective of the Function Hierarchy Diagrammer is to display the functions in your system in a hierarchical or multilevel view. The functions themselves are the same as the Process Modeller process steps and the Dataflow Diagrammer functions, but the diagram itself (in one of its views) looks more like a typical organizational chart, as Figure 6-14 shows.

The activities you perform in the Function Hierarchy Diagrammer are similar to those in the other two diagrammers, but this diagrammer offers a view of the

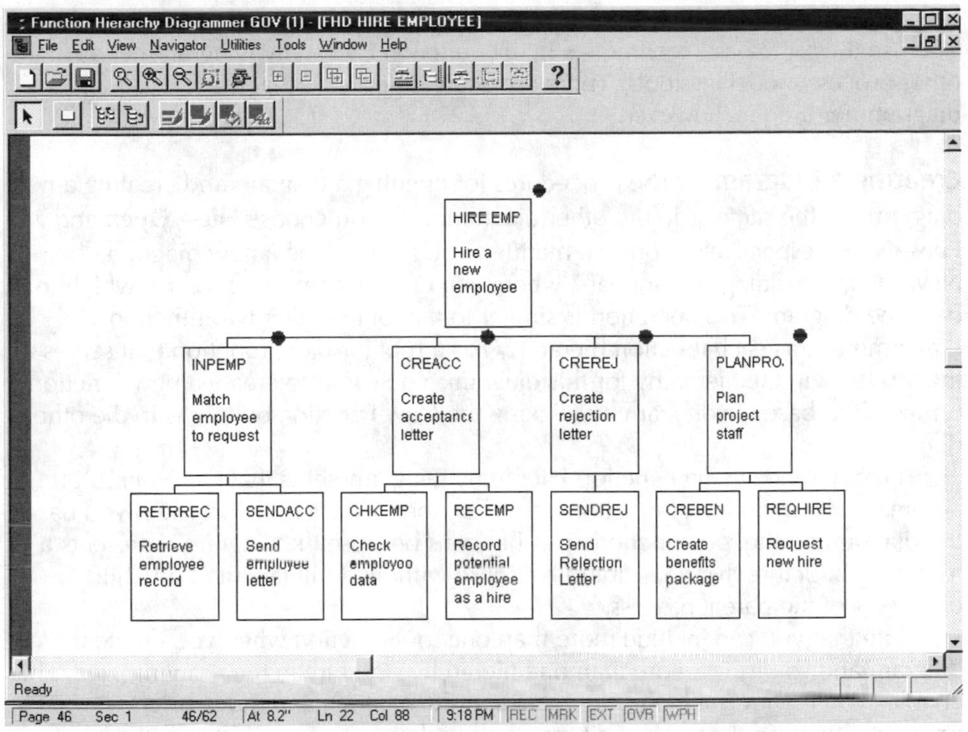

FIGURE 6-14. *Function Hierarchy Diagrammer*

business based primarily on logic, without any indication of user group, department, or data store, and allows you to manipulate the hierarchy itself. The lines between functions do not represent flows, but parent-child relationships. The function at the top of the diagram represents the highest-level function that you are representing in this diagram. The next row of functions represents the decomposition of, or subfunctions within, that function. Each of those functions could, in turn, be decomposed into other subfunctions, which would appear in the next row of the hierarchy.

This diagrammer is like the Dataflow Diagrammer in that you can attach entity and attribute usages to each function. Despite the differences between the Function Hierarchy Diagrammer and other diagrammers, the FHD gives you another tool for handling functions, which are among the most important elements in the repository since they affect the finished application programs.

Basic Techniques

You use the same basic techniques in the Function Hierarchy Diagrammer as in the other process modelling tools. There are a few differences that make this diagrammer unique, however.

Creating a Diagram The procedures for opening a diagram and creating a new diagram are the same as in the other diagrammers: you choose **File→Open** and **File→New**, respectively, from the menu. If you are creating a new diagram, the New Diagram dialog box appears, where you can choose a function on which to base the diagram. This operation is similar to that of the other two function diagrammers, as each function hierarchy has a root (or base) function that serves as the top level in the hierarchy for this diagram. You can also create a new function on which to base the diagram by clicking the New Function button as in the other diagrammers.

The difference in the Function Hierarchy Diagrammer is that Designer/2000 automatically includes all functions that describe the root function when you base the diagram on the root function. This happens because the diagram represents a hierarchy structure that does not make sense without a full layout of all child processes of the parent process.

Note that you can include more than one root function when you create the diagram and so display more than one hierarchy structure in the drawing area. This enables you to view multiple structures at the same time and move or copy functions between them. The Edit menu also allows you to include another root function (**Edit→Include Root**) or remove one or more root functions from the diagram (**Edit→Exclude Root**).

Setting the View The FHD is unique in the way it lets you view multiple levels of the function hierarchy at the same time. This feature enables you to see the functions that make up a particular function. The parent functions and all *branches* (its children and their children) will appear on the diagram. There is no practical limit to the number of levels displayed, although displaying too many levels on the same diagram may make the diagram difficult to read.

Once you have opened or started a new diagram, you can change the view of the hierarchy to any of three styles using the Utilities menu, as shown in Figure 6-15:

- *Horizontal* is the default layout. This view shows each level of the hierarchy in a horizontal row.
- *Vertical* displays each level of the hierarchy in a vertical line, with each level indented slightly to the right of the one above it.

- *Hybrid* is a combination of vertical and horizontal views that shows parent functions in a horizontal layout and childless functions in a vertical layout. This view is the best of the three for reading multilevel hierarchies.

You can select one or more functions and cause the functions under them to conform to either a horizontal or vertical layout, no matter what the rest of the diagram is set to, by selecting Horizontal Layout Selection or Vertical Layout Selection, respectively, from the Utilities menu. Thus, you can place functions on the diagram using a mixture of layout styles. The standard toolbar also provides buttons for these options.

You can also manipulate the function hierarchy views within these basic layouts in other ways. In the diagram, a red circle with a + sign appears next to a function if there are levels under it that are not shown. If you double-click the + sign, the diagrammer will show the child functions, and the red circle will contain

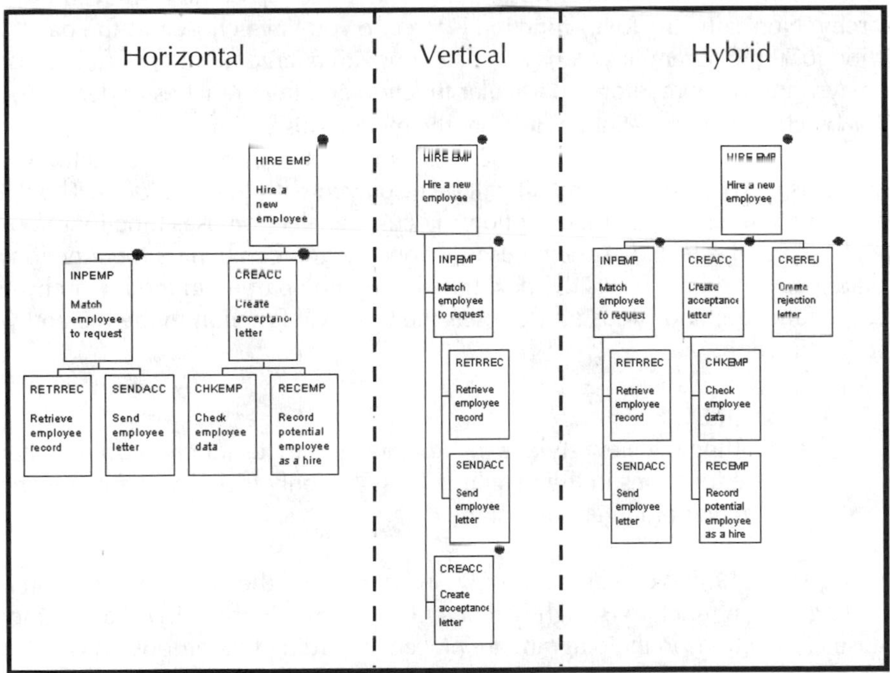

FIGURE 6-15. *Horizontal, vertical, and hybrid views*

a – sign, which you can double-click at any time to hide the child functions. This procedure is similar to the one you use to expand and collapse element nodes in the Repository Object Navigator. The Navigator menu contains selections that match these actions:

- *Expand* and *Collapse* displays or hides, respectively, child functions of the parent functions you have selected (by clicking or drawing a selection box around them).
- *Expand All* and *Collapse All* displays or hides, respectively, all child functions of the selected parent functions and their children.
- *Expand Tree* displays all child functions of all parents in the entire diagram no matter how many root functions are displayed and no matter which functions are selected.

Another way to manipulate the functions you see on the drawing is to set the *focus function.* The focus function is the function at the top of the displayed hierarchy. Normally, the focus function is the one you have chosen as the base function for the diagram. If you have a diagram with a large number of functions, you may want to zoom in on a particular function and the branches under it. You do this by choosing **File→Set Focus** from the menu. This will display a list of functions you can use as the focus functions. Note that you can select multiple functions as focus functions, and all will be displayed with their children. The File menu also provides several focus options: Focus on Selection uses functions you have clicked and selected as the focus functions (so you can bypass the function list dialog box), Focus Up sets the next function up (the parent) in the hierarchy as the focus function, and Focus on Root sets the top-level function in the hierarchy as the focus function.

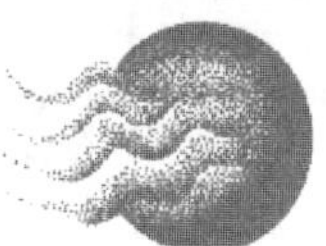

NOTE
Setting the view style, expand view, and focus function do not alter the functions in the diagram. These are only techniques for viewing smaller or larger parts of the diagram.

Drawing Objects You can draw only one symbol on the FHD: the function symbol. Placing a function is slightly different from work in the other diagrammers because all functions in the diagram are placed according to their positions in the hierarchy and are sized the same. Thus, you do not have a choice as to placement or size; you can only specify which function is the parent of the function you want to create. You create a function on the diagram by clicking the function drawing button in the toolbar and clicking the function that will be its parent. The prospective parent function will be selected as you fill in the Create Function dialog box as shown in Figure 6-16. If you want to create a new root function, click

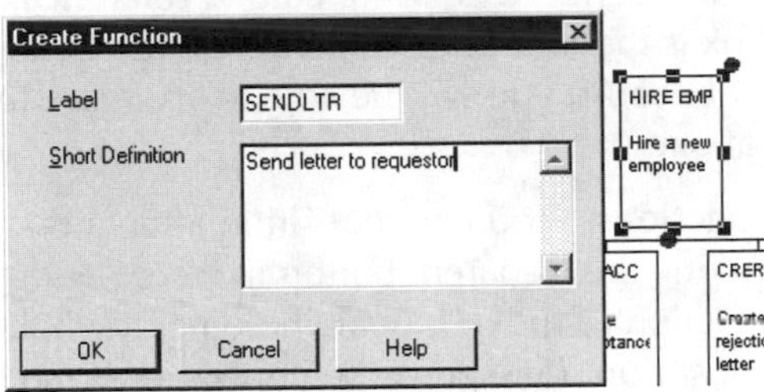

FIGURE 6-16. *Create Function dialog box*

an empty space on the drawing area (not on a function), and after you fill in the Create Function dialog box, the diagrammer will place the new function in a free area (not necessarily where you clicked).

You can include functions already in the repository with the **Edit→Include Root** menu selection. Since this is a hierarchy diagrammer, when you include the function, you will also include its children automatically. If you do not want to see the children, you can set the focus function or collapse the function branch as previously mentioned.

TIP

All diagrammers in the Designer/2000 set allow you to pin a drawing button so you do not have to reselect it if you are drawing objects of the same type. If you want to draw three functions, for example, you can hold down SHIFT when you click the function button. This pins the button so you can draw as many functions as you want without having to press the function button before drawing each one. If you want to stop placing functions at any time, you click the Select toolbar button.

Using the Symbol Set The symbol set consists only of one symbol—the function—and the connector lines that are drawn automatically when you place a function. There are a few more techniques you can use other than those already mentioned to manipulate these symbols. These techniques consist of the following:

- **Resizing functions** Although all function boxes are the same size, if you resize one function, all others will automatically match that size. Alternatively, you can set the size and spacing with the **Edit→Preferences** dialog box. This approach is particularly useful when you turn off the display of function definitions (using **Edit→Preferences**) so the only text in the function box is the label. Then small function boxes will reveal the structure better because you will be able to see more functions and their relationships at once.

- **Reparenting functions** You can reposition a function from one parent to another by clicking the Reparent button in the drawing toolbar, clicking once on the function to move it while holding down the mouse button, dragging the cursor until it is over the new parent, and then releasing the mouse button.

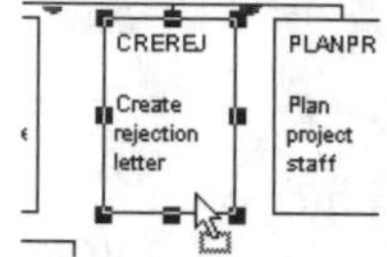

- **Resequencing functions** Reparenting moves functions across hierarchical levels or from one parent to another, but sometimes you may want to move functions around within the same level. You accomplish this by pressing the Resequence button, clicking the function you want to move while holding down the mouse button, dragging the cursor until it is over the function that will directly follow the one you are moving, and releasing the mouse button.
- **Setting preferences and colors** If you select one or more functions and choose **Edit→Preferences**, you can apply color, fonts, and line widths to the selections. You can also press the corresponding buttons on the drawing toolbar for Line Width, Line Color, Fill, and Font (as you can with any Designer/2000 diagrammer). Note that the **Edit→Preferences** dialog box also contains other preferences that you can change, as Figure 6-17 shows.

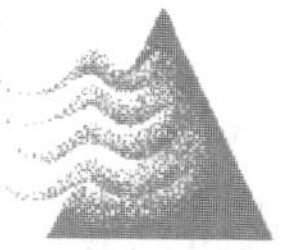

TIP

Sometimes your drawing will contain a stray pixel or two of a line that remained when something was moved or you scrolled the window. Since there is no redraw action in any of Designer/2000's diagrammers, you have to force the tool to perform a redraw operation. The easiest way to do this is to use the window icons in the top-right part of the window to minimize the drawing window (not the MDI window) and then maximize it again.

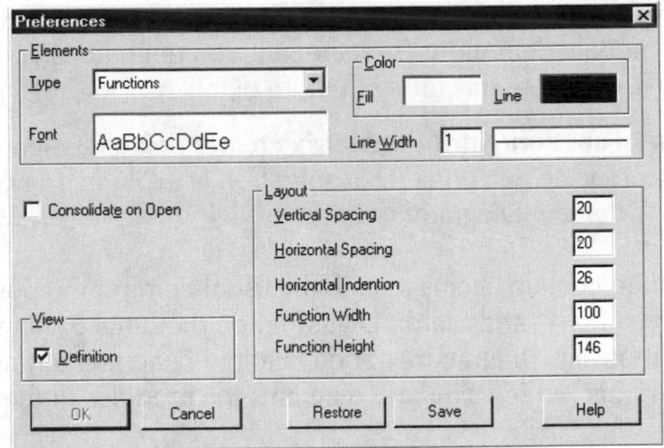

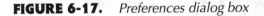

FIGURE 6-17. *Preferences dialog box*

Naming Objects The naming conventions you use for function properties in this diagrammer are the same as in the other function diagrammers. The Label property is a one-word abbreviation for the action, and the Short Definition property is a phrase starting with a verb that describes the action. The functions you place in this diagram are the same functions you draw in the Dataflow Diagrammer and Process Modeller, and you use the same naming conventions for these tools.

Defining Function Properties The Function Hierarchy Diagrammer presents exactly the same properties window as the Dataflow Diagrammer. You can double-click the function or select the function and choose **Edit→Properties** from the menu to display this window. Chapter 5 and the preceding explanation of the Dataflow Diagrammer in the Analysis phase describe these properties in detail.

Other Menu and Toolbar Functions

In addition to the menu and toolbar activities just discussed and those that are common to all Designer/2000 diagrammers, there are a few additional functions specific to this diagrammer:

- **Navigator→Navigate** displays a list of functions on the diagram. If you choose a function from this list, the diagram will center on that function, although the selection and focus will remain unchanged.

- **Utilities→Application Design Wizard** loads the repository utility that creates module definitions from the function definitions you created. Chapter 7 discusses this utility in more detail.
- **Utilities→Function/Attribute Matrix** creates default assignments of attributes to your functions. This operation is explained in Chapter 5 in the section "Dataflow Diagrammer."

The Tools menu contains items to call: the usual common Repository utilities, Repository Reports, RON, and Matrix Diagrammer; the other Systems Modeller tools, Entity Relationship Diagrammer and Dataflow Diagrammer; and the Module Structure Diagrammer, which similarly diagrams the modules in the physical model.

Typical Function Hierarchy Diagrammer Tasks in the Analysis Phase

The features of the FHD enable you to identify a set of functions from the information gathering part of the Analysis phase and develop them into a complete function model in the requirements analysis part. The Function Hierarchy Diagrammer allows you to concentrate on the various levels and the structure of the functions of the business without being distracted by representations of dataflows or stores. You perform functional decomposition here as you do in the other function modellers, but the difference here is that you can actually see multiple levels of decomposition at one time so you can easily reposition and reparent functions. The ease with which you can move and reparent functions is one of the strengths of this diagrammer.

Since visual representations of the dataflows and stores are also important, you will normally use this diagrammer in conjunction with either the Dataflow Diagrammer or Process Modeller. Those other diagrammers show you how information flows from one process and store to another, and this diagrammer shows you the big picture of how these functions relate to one another hierarchically.

CAUTION

Consider function hierarchy diagramming complete when you have decomposed functions down to the level where all requirements can be mapped. There is no sense, although there may be a temptation, to model functions that will not fulfill a business need. You should, of course, model functions that are manual if they fulfill a requirement. The driving force behind all you do in the life cycle should be the business requirements.

Where Does This Information Go?

The function elements in the Function Hierarchy Diagrammer are the same as those in the other process diagrammers. Table 6-5 summarizes their use as elements in the Repository Object Navigator as well as what happens to them later in the life cycle.

Matrix Diagrammer

In the Analysis phase, you create CRUD (or at least CUD) usages for functions at the entity level. This means you have to define the entity data usages for each of the functions in your system. You also need to examine each function to make sure there is a way to enter all the data in entities through existing functions or through functions or processes outside your system that you can explain. You must also ensure that there are create, update, and delete characteristics for each of the entities, or that you have a valid explanation of why there is not. For example, you may not have a create characteristic associated with an entity that represents data in an entity in another system if you do not insert data into that entity but only

Function Hierarchy Diagrammer Element	Repository Element and Future Use
Functions	Business Functions. These are used by the Application Design Wizard to create modules
Hierarchy connector lines	Parent Function property of the function element. These determine the atomic functions which are the functions without children.
Data usages: entity	Function Entity Usages under the Business Functions node. These are the basis for choices the Application Design Wizard makes regarding the grouping of functions into modules, and they become table usages for the module.
Data usages: attribute	Attribute Data Usages under a particular entity's Function Entity Usages. These are used the same way as the entity usages but become column usages for the module.
No data usages	If a function has no data usages, the Application Design Wizard will create a manual module that will not have code generated for it.

TABLE 6-5. *Function Hierarchy Diagrammer Elements and Repository Elements*

retrieve data from it. In this case, the entity should have only a retrieve (R) characteristic associated with it, not CRUD.

The Matrix Diagrammer (MXD) is the easiest tool you can use to create, check, and modify data usages (CRUD) for functions. If you define a diagrammer in Designer/2000 as a tool that lets you choose symbols and draw them on the drawing surface, the Matrix Diagrammer is really more of a repository utility than a diagrammer. As with the diagrammers, though, you can save a particular matrix and open it later.

However you classify it, the Matrix Diagrammer is an essential tool in the SDLC as it lets you quickly cross-check and modify the work completed in other tools using associations between elements. Figure 6-18 shows a sample MXD session with the Matrix window on the left and the Properties window on the right.

How to Create a Matrix

The best way to see how the Matrix Diagrammer works is to create a sample matrix. Assume that you need to check the function data usage of entities during the Analysis stage. The Matrix Diagrammer lets you view a grid with the functions as the rows and the entities as the columns. The intersection, or *matrix cells*, of the rows and columns consists of the entity usages—CRUD. These matrix cells represent the association between one element and another (for example, functions

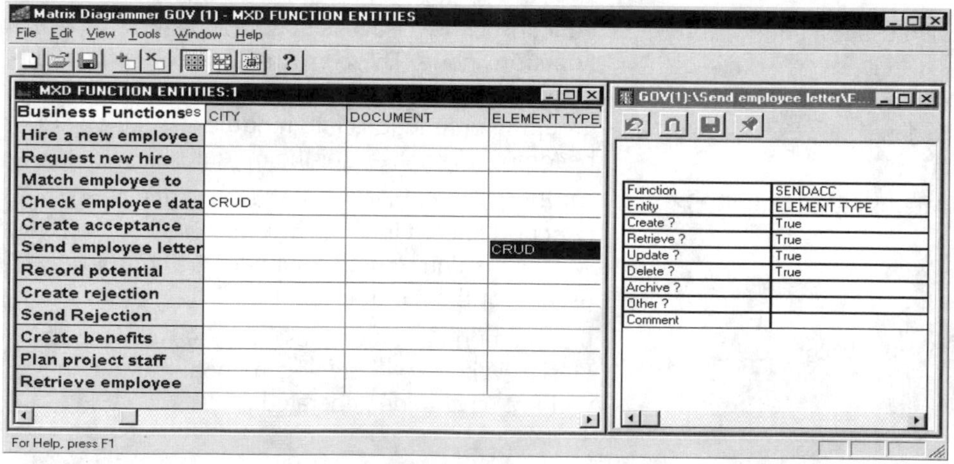

FIGURE 6-18. *Sample Matrix Diagrammer session*

and entities). There are three basic steps in creating this grid, or matrix, after you open the Matrix Diagrammer:

1. Select **File→New** from the menu. This step displays the New Matrix window as the following illustration shows.

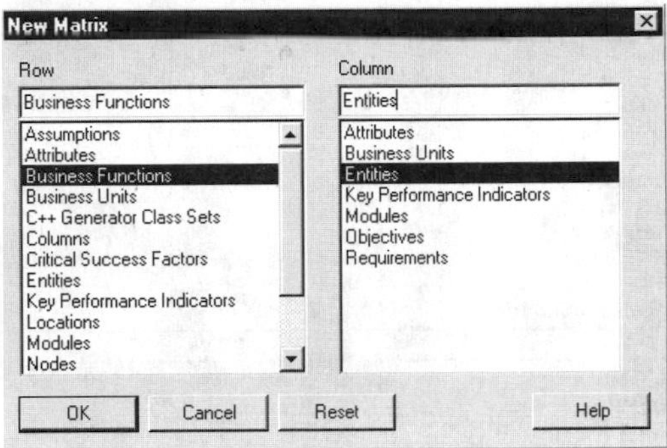

2. Choose the row and column elements and click the OK button. In this example, you select Business Functions for the rows and Entities for the columns as in the preceding illustration.

3. Create the row, column, and intersection properties in the Settings window as shown in Figure 6-19. This step is further explained in the following discussion.

When you define a new matrix, the last dialog box you fill in is in the Settings window. The row and column properties specify the information used for the headings. The intersection properties designate which properties of the association are displayed. Each of the tabs (Row, Column, and Intersection) has a Font button you can click to choose the font for each of these parts of the matrix.

For example, the functions appear on the row axis, so you would enter something to identify each row. A good choice here would be the Short Definition property as this is the name shown in all the function diagrammers, but you can also include any other property that describes the function.

All properties you choose will appear on the left side of the matrix as the heading (label) for each row. You can specify the format of rows by filling in the number of characters you will see of each property (the Columns field) and the number of lines used for that value and the justification format (left, right, or centered). There is also a setting for the ordering of the rows within the property values (ascending or descending). You can filter using a limited set of conditions to view only a subset of values by filling in the Filter item. There are buttons on the

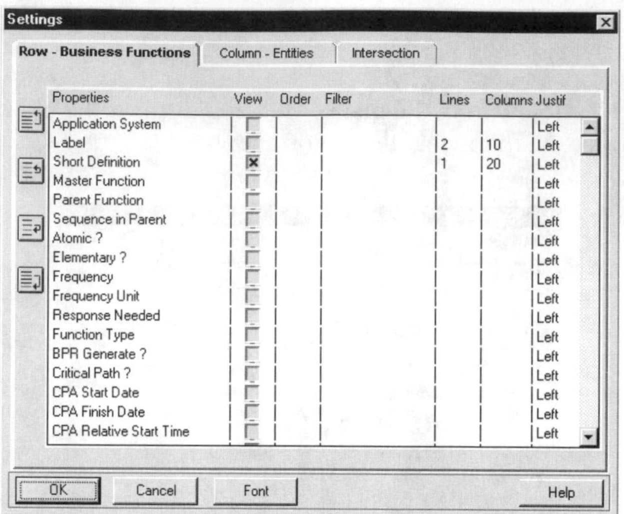

FIGURE 6-19. *Settings window for the new matrix diagram*

left side of the window to reposition the properties so you can see them in a certain order within the matrix.

After you have completed the row information, select the Column tab and fill in the same type of information for the column headings, which will appear at the top of each column. The Name property is the best choice for the entity labels, and you may want to specify a value less than the default of 20 as the number of characters (Columns).

Click the Intersection tab to choose the properties of the association between functions and entities that you want to see. A Displayed As area lets you indicate the letter that will identify the particular property in the matrix. In this example, you can select Create, Retrieve, Update, and Delete for the properties and leave the default Displayed As area as is. You can also specify a separator character (the | symbol) to separate the letters, so you might see something like C|R|U|D in a matrix cell for an entity that has all four usages for a particular function.

When you click OK on the Settings window, the diagrammer will build a grid with functions as rows and entities as columns. As with the other navigator-style utilities, you select **Window→Tile Vertically** from the menu to arrange the windows in the utility.

Matrix View Modes

The intersection of the rows and columns shows the CRUD for the entities. You can display the matrix itself in several view modes. Each view mode can be selected using either an option on the View menu or a toolbar button. The view modes are as follows:

- *Standard view mode* (the default) displays the letters that you specify on the Intersection properties tab in cells with a data usage.
- *Iconic view mode* displays only check marks where any properties (usages) exist for the intersection. This view is good for seeing where usages are missing as you can see more columns and rows than in Standard view mode.
- *Micro view mode* (or Micromap mode) displays only a black box where usages exist. In this view, the diagram is collapsed into a smaller view, so you can navigate to an area quickly by dragging a selection box to the desired area and switching to one of the other view modes.

How to Modify the Values

If you select one of the intersection cells, the Properties window on the right allows you to view and edit the properties of that intersection (the actual CRUD). You can group intersection cells together and apply the properties to the group from one Properties window. You can also insert or delete existing repository elements by selecting the header label for the row or column and clicking the Create or Delete toolbar buttons or selecting **Edit→Create** or **Edit→Delete**, respectively, from the menu.

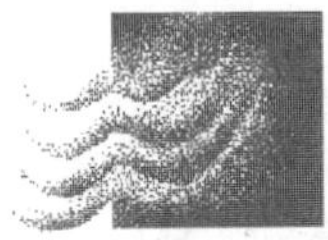

CAUTION

Remember that this is a live view of the repository, where you can modify element definitions directly. Anything you do to change the usages will change the repository data, and if you delete an object, there is no procedure for undoing the change.

You can also change a property of a row or column element by clicking the label. The Properties window will show all properties of that element just as they are shown in RON, and you can edit them directly in this window. In the Matrix Diagrammer, however, you cannot see the subnodes and elements under this element as you can in RON.

Other Techniques

If the matrix is in Standard view mode, you can resize columns and rows by dragging the separator lines between them out or in. Resizing one column or row will resize them all at the same time. You cannot resize columns or rows in the other two view modes.

The Properties window acts much like the one in RON, and you can pin it in the same way. Note that only one Properties window is available for each Matrix window. You can, however, open more than one Matrix window at a time for the same matrix (using **Window→New Window**). This lets you see different parts of that matrix at the same time if you want to compare properties or usages.

Other Menu and Toolbar Functions

The Matrix Diagrammer uses the same File functions as the other Designer/2000 tools. The Edit menu has a selection for Properties that opens the Properties window if it is not already open. A Settings selection opens up the Settings window you used to define the matrix when you created it. This selection is quite handy for making changes to a diagram's setup after you have worked with it.

The Tools menu contains items for all the diagrammers as well as the major utilities (RON and Repository Reports).

Other Possible Matrices

You can create matrices to represent numerous combinations of repository elements. Business Units to Business Functions shows you which business functions are performed by which organization units. This information was entered in the Process Modeller when you created process steps (functions) in organization units (business units). You can then add other business unit assignments to that function in RON (the Function Business Unit Usages node under a particular business function).

A matrix of Tables (called Relations in the New Matrix window) and Modules shows which tables, views, and snapshots are used by which modules. You can also create a matrix of the new Requirements element you added to Functions in the Pre-Analysis stage to quickly view and enter the mapping of system requirements to functions. A Relations to Entities matrix shows which tables were created from which entities. If you decide to define function attribute usages, a Business Functions to Attributes matrix may be useful. Generally, any two elements that have an association type linking them may be matrixed.

Where Does This Information Go?

As mentioned, the information in the Matrix Diagrammer is basic repository data that you are manipulating and displaying for the particular elements in a format different than that used by RON.

Repository Reports in the Analysis Phase

As in all phases, Repository Reports are available to give you organized lists of elements and quality-check reports. At this point, you should concentrate on reports in the following groups:

- **Data Model** For example, the Quality Checking of Relationships report shows relationships with potential problems. The Entities with No Relationships report may help you determine whether you really want this condition in your model.
- **Function Model** Reports include the Function to Entity Matrix report from the Matrix Diagrammer and function modellers.
- **Dataflow Model** Reports include Functions Not Included on a Dataflow Diagram, Functions without Input or Output Dataflows, and Dataflows between a Function and an Ancestor, which can aid quality checking.
- **BPR Model** Activity Based Costing is a key report to run to see which processes and flows take the most time, are most costly, and are therefore candidates for re-engineering.
- **Quality** Some of these reports appear in other groups, but one you might want to run is Entities with no Attributes to see what is missing in your attribute list.
- **User Extensibility** You can run a flexible report called Element to Element and specify the X-axis element as Requirement and the Y-axis element as Business Function to get a summary of your requirements mapping. You can also run a report called <Element> Definition on the Module properties to see not only the module definitions but the user-extended property you added for Legacy Status for use in auditing legacy reports.

Remember that if you look at the Repository Reports hierarchy using View by Group, the same reports may appear in more than one group. Also recall that a fuller description of each report is available by invoking the help system while in Repository Reports. This will open a help listing of all reports, and you can choose from this list to display a full description of an individual report. Also, you may want to review the explanation of Repository Reports in Chapter 4.

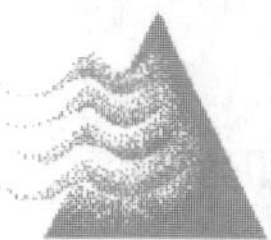

TIP

Another way to quickly get information on what a report does is to click the Context-Sensitive Help button in the toolbar. The cursor changes to the arrow-help icon. When you click with this cursor on the report you are interested in from the hierarchy, the help system opens up to the topic that describes that report. The F1 help keypress only shows an alphabetical list from which you choose, but this jumps right to the correct topic.

Conclusion

This chapter discussed the most salient aspects of requirements analysis. It described how you should leverage the data collected during the information gathering stage to build a requirements document. The quality of the requirements document depends on the validity of the data, the participation and support of the users, and the skills of the development team in documenting formal requirements both in a narrative form and through the models. This chapter also discussed a hybrid approach to Analysis using business process re-engineering.

The data and process models and the information that underlies them reside in the Designer/2000 repository and enable you to coordinate the vast amount of knowledge that must be collected and updated during the System Development Life Cycle. In the next chapter on the Pre-Design phase, you will see what is needed to further exploit this repository of information and prepare for the Design phase and how careful planning and completing some utility procedures can lead to success in the Design phase.

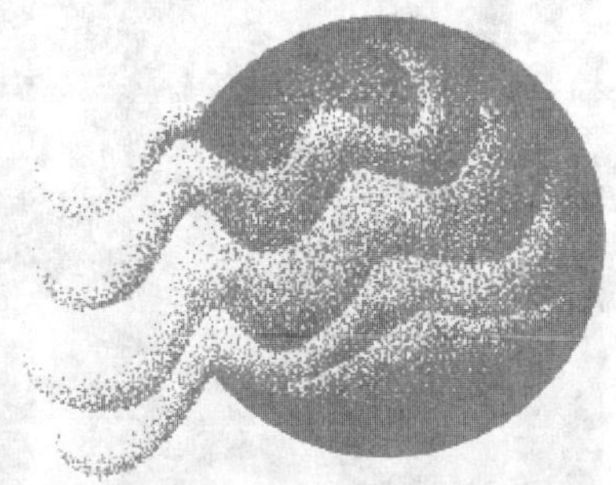

CHAPTER 7

Pre-Design

His designs were strictly honorable, as the phrase is; that is, to rob a lady of her fortune by way of marriage.

—*Henry Fielding*, Tom Jones

The Pre-Design phase could be called the "speak now or forever hold your peace" phase. It is the last opportunity for users to add input to the project that will be reflected in the system design. System requirements are frozen at the end of Pre-Design. Thus, it is very important to think through both the application and database aspects of the system before the actual Design phase begins.

Overview of the Pre-Design Phase

In the Pre-Design phase, the various design standards, including GUI standards, coding standards, and design naming conventions, are determined along with the ways in which Designer/2000 will support these standards. Next, a conceptual design of the applications is generated; this design should include detailed storyboards and a list of the modules to be developed, with the system requirements mapped to those modules. Finally, the remainder of the Design phase is planned, including procedures for resolving design conflicts and criteria for determining when the design is complete.

The Design phase itself includes two broad subphases:

- **Physical design of the database** Notice that you will already have a complete ERD from the Analysis phase and a conceptual design of the applications from the Pre-Design phase.
- **Physical design of applications** Here you specify in detail exactly how the applications will interface with every field of the database.

At the end of the design process, you should have a fully specified database and associated applications. The design plan generated in the Pre-Design phase must keep this goal in mind.

Deliverables

There are several sets of deliverables in the Pre-Design phase:

- **Design standards**
  - GUI design standards
  - Coding standards

- Design naming conventions
- **Conceptual design of applications**
  - Storyboards for applications
  - Module structure for applications
  - Map of requirements to modules
  - Functional descriptions for each module
- **Design plan**
  - Database design plan
  - Application design plan

A high-level testing plan must be in place to determine, in principle, how design testing will be accomplished.

Design Standards

Three types of standards must be considered in the Pre-Design phase: GUI design standards, coding standards, and design naming conventions.

Setting GUI Design Standards

Before setting GUI design standards, you need to decide how much work you want the generator to do in building applications. Compared to what is possible with a sophisticated application development tool such as Developer/2000, the capabilities of the Designer/2000 generator are very limited. Therefore, you have two choices:

- Be satisfied with relatively basic, unsophisticated GUI applications.
- Recognize that after Designer/2000 generates applications, there will be some amount of work required to complete development of screen modules.

Realistically, the Designer/2000 tool generation capabilities are not adequate to generate a robust suite of screen modules, and the GUI standards designer must be aware of what Designer/2000 is capable of generating. The GUI standards designer must accept a less than ideal GUI standard in order to take advantage of the productivity-enhancing capabilities that the Designer/2000 generators provide.

The alternative is to set GUI standards independent of Designer/2000 and the screen module development platform, thereby greatly increasing the cost of building the applications.

GUI features fall into three categories:

- **Features built automatically using Designer/2000 generators** These include applications that require a basic layout of database fields, buttons, poplists, and other standard GUI items.
- **Features easily supported by the screen module tool but which cannot be generated directly by Designer/2000** In the Forms component of Developer/2000, these include stacked canvases, multiwindow applications, and tab controls.
- **Features that cannot be easily built using a screen module design tool** For Forms, for example, these include heavily graphics-oriented programming of the type required to create an organization chart or dynamically create a PERT/CPM diagram, and complex manipulation of rich text objects.

As much as possible, you should try to restrict GUI features to the first type, using the other two types of features only when the benefits outweigh the costs. It is possible to achieve near-100 percent generation if you are willing to make some compromises in your design standards.

How much generation should be achieved? First, you need to determine a strategy for building screen modules. There are two choices:

- Generate the screen module as best as possible and then modify it and keep track of the modifications. This procedure entails breaking the link between CASE and the generated module. Therefore, the designer will be making modifications that cannot be completely reverse engineered.
- Store everything possible in the Designer/2000 repository. Some companies (such as Bristol Meyers Squibb in New Jersey) have been quite successful in placing complex screen module triggers in the Designer/2000 repository.

One way to keep the link to CASE reasonably intact is to use a different template, containing all module-specific information, for every screen module. Then if you need to regenerate the module, all information, including triggers, will be available in the template. This approach can greatly reduce the time spent after regeneration to finish the creation of the screen module.

The question that needs to be answered is what type of screen modules are being created? If you can settle for basic applications, 100 percent generation is possible for a reasonable subset of screen modules. However, this means that the GUI standards for those modules must be dictated by what Designer/2000 is able to generate. Only when new versions of Designer/2000 are developed that allow all modifications to the modules to propagate to the repository will developers really be able to plan the exact screen modules at this stage. A common repository for Designer/2000 and Developer/2000 and 100 percent reverse engineering may not be a reality for quite some time.

The best solution may be to strive for 100 percent generation for simple screen modules, modifying GUI standards to accept screen module generation limitations. For key modules, use Designer/2000 for initial screen module creation and then make modifications from there. Whether it is possible to get all the module information into the template will depend upon the module itself. You may be able to perform regeneration in a short time; some modules may require regeneration by hand.

What is the impact of accepting 100 percent generation?

- A greater number of modules and screens than is desirable
- Screens that are not as attractive and well laid out as they might be
- Less information on each screen
- Screens not as professional looking as those built from scratch by a skilled GUI designer

A complete discussion of GUI standards would fill a book. There is no way to thoroughly cover the topic here. However, the following paragraphs present some basic principles and strategies to keep in mind.

There is no industry standard for GUI development. Different companies have radically different standards of how screens should look. Thinking through how screens should be created helps avoid fundamental differences in the way screens look within the same application. In the old character-based environment, screens within the same company usually had a reasonably consistent look and feel. With GUI applications, organizations often have many applications that are grossly dissimilar. Look and feel standards should be determined for each type of application.

Applications fall into five basic categories:

- **Navigation applications** These include full-screen (menu) applications with many buttons. The user clicks the buttons to move to different parts of the screen. Typically, the first screen that the user sees in the application allows direct navigation to the appropriate place in the application.

- **Administration applications** There are several choices for handling the administration of code description tables. The table structure for these must be decided upon first. For some developers a clean approach works best, with a different table for each code description. However, this approach leads to a great number of tables. Other developers prefer to combine all descriptions in a single table. Choices can then be made about the look of the screen. A good strategy is to have one single administration module (or form) that supports the maintenance of all administration applications. Tables that don't fit on one screen can be grouped on tabs within the same application.
- **Master-detail applications** A master-detail application is a standard application in which there is a parent-child relationship between two sets of records. For the current record in the master block, associated detail records are shown in the detail block: for example, departments and their associated employees or purchase orders (POs) and their associated PO details. The master record information can be displayed in several ways: in a single-record block, multirecord block, or poplist. The detail records can be displayed in single-record or multirecord blocks. The appropriate standards for each type of master-detail application must be considered.
- **Locator applications** This common type of application allows you to quickly and easily locate a specific record. For example, in a PO system, you can easily find a particular PO if you know the PO number. However, if all that you know is which department initiated the PO and that the PO was issued in the past two months, you will have problems finding the correct information. Therefore, to make it easy for users to locate particular records, it is customary to build a separate application that helps users locate specific records. Such an application has an area at the top of the screen to set criteria and an area at the bottom of the screen to display query results. Double-clicking a retrieved record in the locator automatically opens the primary application associated with that record and retrieves the record into the application.
- **Complex applications** These include applications with a lot of information and calculated fields. Because of the emerging Windows 95 interface standard, the best way to handle these complex forms is with tabs. According to the tab selected, the user can display different stacked canvases. In Forms 5.0, the native tab object allows editing access to all tabs, even in design mode. This feature is very useful since the developer won't have to worry about stacked canvases. The one problem with tabs is

that they take up a full line that is the height of the tab, which can be a waste of screen real estate. A big canvas that scrolls and multiple pages accessed by Next Page/Previous Page buttons are alternative ways of handling a large amount of information; however, these are now considered outdated approaches and should not be used.

For each form, no matter what the type, certain decisions need to be made. The tool bar functions need to be determined. Insertion, modification, and deletion functions need to be made available to the user. Features should be obvious to the user and consistent on every form. The designer can assume that users have some training. Nevertheless, actions should be natural and designed from the user's point of view. An example of a user-unfriendly action is a procedure that requires the user to choose a button or item called "Clear Screen" to create a new record, before inserting information in a new record and saving it. This selection is not logical from a user standpoint. Instead there should be an Insert button. The user can then click the Insert button, which should display a prompt asking the user to "insert record and save" and then clear the screen.

Screen Resolution and Color

Developers should design the system on a machine with higher resolution than that of the client or user. The designer needs at least a 1024 x 768 monitor when designing for an 800 x 600 monitor. A good monitor for a designer is 1200 x 1024 on a 21-inch screen. Newer monitors will support 1600 x 1200. In this format, the items are very small, but the layout takes up only a quarter of the screen required by 800 x 600 development. This benefit may be worth the eye strain.

There are numerous books on GUI design standards. All recommend keeping the number of colors and fonts to a minimum. Many hours can be wasted thinking about appropriate fonts and colors. The best the developer can hope for is that no one hates the choices. It often pays off to make boring selections since different machines with different video boards display things differently. The monitor used also affects the display. The developer should create samples and test them on the client machines with the users.

Screen Real Estate

Conservation of screen real estate is extremely important. Screen real estate is the designer's most precious commodity. It is very easy to waste screen space by not thinking about the layout of the application. The best way to minimize wasted screen space is to think carefully about every pixel.

For example, in a multirecord block, don't put any pixels between fields. Start at the top and fill the screen one layer at a time. Each block or area should be laid out horizontally to maximize the use of screen space.

Here are some suggestions for making the most of screen space:

- Do not put titles on screens. Put titles on the windows.
- Designer/2000 generators automatically place a frame around an area, with the label on the top-left area of the frame. Putting the label inside the box wastes less space. Instead of using the default block frame, use the Vertically Stack option of the Align Objects choice in the Arrange menu to ensure that no space is wasted between fields.
- Stack the labels horizontally next to the fields laid out horizontally and move them two pixels away. The recommended space between horizontal fields is ten pixels.
- It is important to decide how many rows are realistically needed for multirecord frames. If the user will be looking at a large table, you should try to place as many records on the screen as possible. A form that displays the names of as many employees as possible, for example, may be easier to use. However, for something like a list of the disk drives attached to PCs, where 90 percent of the users will have only one choice, 5 percent will have only two choices, and 5 percent will have three or four choices, it doesn't make any sense to display lots of records on the screen.
- If there is a lot of information, try to let the user see as much as possible on one screen. Using a crowded screen is often better than using more than one screen or a simpler but less useful screen. This is a stylistic decision that should be driven by the user. Through re-engineering, you may be able to fit information from several screens on one screen without the use of tabs.
- An efficient way to handle records with long text fields (such as fields for notes, comments, and descriptions) is to divide the screen into two parts. The top part can show the important fields (all records). The bottom part can show the note, comment, or description associated with the selected field. You can accomplish this in Developer/2000 by setting the Items Displayed option on the Property sheet to 1.

Buttons Buttons shouldn't be any bigger than necessary. They need to display the button label with a few extra pixels on each side. All buttons in a row don't need to be the same size. For example, an Exit button doesn't need to be as large as an Execute Query button.

Putting buttons across the bottom of the screen wastes less vertical space than stacking them vertically. Standard buttons take up 17 pixels. If buttons need to be placed vertically on the left side of the screen, a good strategy is to stack them next to their associated fields.

Buttons are most often placed at the top or bottom of a screen. Other, creative solutions are possible, such as placing buttons in a horizontal row in the middle of the screen. This placement enables easy use, and the row of buttons makes a natural divider for the screen.

Poplists Poplists are a major space-saving device. The space of only one record is needed for a poplist, but the poplist can display as many records as needed when it is selected. Two hundred records is a practical limit for poplists. A user will not want to have to scroll through a list longer than this. However, if you need to include more records in a poplist, you can use an LOV (list of values) as a search facility. You can use a button to bring up the LOV.

Logos In general, logos and fancy graphics are unnecessary. They take up a lot of space and have little use. Logos are not needed for internal forms within organizations. Employees don't need to see the company logo on every form. For forms going to those outside the company, place graphics and logos on a welcome screen rather than letting them consume memory, functionality, and space on the working forms.

Setting Coding Standards

Coding standards are essential to the readability and maintainability of your code. As with GUI standards, a complete discussion is well beyond the scope of this book. One of the best discussions of PL/SQL standards is contained in Steven Feuerstein's book *Oracle PL/SQL Programming* (Sebastopol, CA: O'Reilly, 1995). However, here is a "top-ten list" of important coding standards to follow:

1. *Use lowercase almost everywhere.* There may be some readability gained by using uppercase and lowercase; however, seldom are the two cases implemented consistently. Use uppercase for data values, e.g. "TRUE."
2. *Use % type for all local variable declarations that correspond to database objects.* This will minimize the amount of changes to your code when changes occur in the data structure.
3. *Use two spaces (not the TAB key) for indention in PL/SQL triggers.* By default, Oracle uses an eight-character indent for tabs. With this indent, after three or four levels of indenting, you won't be able to see the code on the right side of the screen.

4. *Use explicit cursors.* Explicit cursors decrease the number of database accesses.
5. *Generate functions and procedures and store them in libraries wherever possible.* Reusable code is one of the great benefits of PL/SQL. You should take advantage of this feature wherever possible.
6. *Within modules, implement global variables as local package variables.* Use database globals only for global variables that span modules.
7. *Create a standard list of abbreviations for variable names.* This list can be as extensive as you want. However, the use of only these abbreviations and no others is crucial to the maintainability of the code, so the list should be as short as possible, including no more than 500 abbreviations. Just as in the Analysis phase naming conventions, any words not on the list should be spelled out.
8. *Use CURSOR FOR loops to scan a set of records in a block.* This syntax makes the code tidy and more readable.
9. *Store functions and procedures that require heavy database traffic in the database.* This will minimize the amount of network traffic when these programs execute.
10. *Use very robust exception handling.* One of the best features of PL/SQL is its exception handling capability. One of the greatly underutilized features of PL/SQL is its ability to handle almost every abnormal condition and return to the user a meaningful alert informing them about what has occurred in the application.

A coding manual should be long enough to ensure consistency, but not so long that no one will read or follow it. Realistically, a few pages of tips are all one can expect the developer to comply with.

Establishing Design Naming Conventions

Naming conventions in the Design phase need not be significantly different from the standards used in the Analysis phase. Oracle provides relatively generous lengths for table, column, and PL/SQL variable names. However, particularly long table and column names can cause code readability problems. A better policy is to implement a slightly more aggressive naming convention in Design than was used in Analysis.

One approach is to develop a relatively extensive list of five-character abbreviations for all words in the database. Consistent use of naming conventions is important to make development as straightforward as possible. If you use a formal, rigorous abbreviation technique where only approved words are abbreviated, you can automate the process of moving from Analysis entity and attribute names, and other names, to physical table and column names, for example, by writing a simple procedure using the API. This is done by first running the Database Design Wizard utility, which automatically generates tables and columns from entities and attributes, then writing a utility using the API. This utility should replace words in the table and column names with approved abbreviations from the abbreviation list, which will ensure that abbreviations are consistently applied through all table and column names. Because much of the code will be automatically generated, there is less of a need than you might think to aggressively abbreviate.

Designer/2000 lets you preface all column names with a table abbreviation. This is not recommended, however; it unnecessarily lengthens column names and makes generic procedures written for similar columns more difficult to use. It is easy enough to preface column names with the actual table names where appropriate.

Both table and column names should be descriptive. Under no circumstances should tables be named with obscure codes. Module definitions should also be named with easy-to-recognize descriptive names using the same abbreviation list as the tables and columns.

Conceptual Design of Applications

The conceptual design of applications must be created before the database can be designed. Tool selection, storyboarding, modularization, requirements mapping, and the creation of functional descriptions are all part of this conceptual design process and will be discussed in this section. The conceptual design of the applications was moved to the Pre-Design phase because database design cannot take place without a very clear picture of what the application will look like.

Selecting Development Tools

There are several choices for Oracle application design. Systems designers need to decide which tool to use for building applications, choosing from among the following: Developer/2000, Visual Basic, C++ applications, WebServer, and Power Objects. This section discusses how to make this decision and the pros and cons of each tool.

Developer/2000 is Oracle's flagship product. It provides tight integration with the database and is a great development environment regardless of whether you are using an Oracle database or some other database. The Forms component of

Developer/2000 now supports (or soon will) both Web-based and client/server applications. The only reason not to choose Developer/2000 over other platforms is the availability of development talent within your own organization. If you have very strong Visual Basic, C++, HTML, or Power Objects talent, it might be sensible to choose one of these platforms instead.

Developer/2000 is the tool of choice for building applications. Because it is an Oracle product, Designer/2000 support is strong. An additional advantage to this choice is that it enables you to move between different hardware platforms, such as Macintosh and IBM, with few modifications.

Visual Basic is a full-featured language with thousands of libraries of extensions available. However, it is limited to the Microsoft Windows platform. If this limitation is acceptable and your organization has strong Visual Basic resources, this may be a good choice. Also, if the standard for application development throughout your organization is Visual Basic, it makes sense to be consistent. It is possible to use Oracle Designer/2000 to generate Visual Basic applications to run with an Oracle database or, with minor modifications, with any other relational database.

C++ is the flagship of third-generation languages. In the past few years, extensive libraries have become available to support C++ in a GUI environment. However, writing C++ code when modifications are needed is time consuming. Two to ten times as much C++ code must be written as what would be necessary in Forms. This can make developing applications costly. However, Forms is a fourth-generation language with limitations. In comparison to Forms, C++ gives the developer much more control over the application. Therefore, with C++ you can theoretically create applications that run much faster than those created with Forms.

Another advantage to C++ is that you can find good C++ programming talent relatively cheaply, whereas expert Forms talent is rare and expensive. C++ may not be a good choice, however, if you need to cross platforms because C++ requires significant rewriting of applications to move from platform to platform.

HTML is one of the Web languages. Applications written in HTML reside on the server and are brought to the client machine only when invoked. The big advantage of HTML is in distribution since there are no run-time worries. Applications are accessible to anyone with access to the World Wide Web.

A major disadvantage to HTML is that applications in this environment will run much more slowly than almost all client/server applications since all communication with the application requires network traffic back to the server. HTML is best for small, very light applications or those specifically designed for Web access. Also, HTML is not full featured. It cannot be used to build robust production-level applications because of its internal limitations.

Power Objects is Oracle's competitor to Microsoft's Access or Borland's Delphi. It is somewhat easier to use than Forms; but it is not as flexible. Complex applications cannot be built easily and, sometimes not at all. Many things that are possible to do in Forms are not possible in Power Objects. This product is so new that finding experienced Power Objects developers is difficult.

Creating Storyboards for Applications

A storyboard is a non-functioning prototype that allows users and developers to assess the quality of the application design.

Once the GUI standards are implemented within Designer/2000 as preferences and templates, the quickest way to create a storyboards application is by following this procedure:

1. Generate a default database directly from the logical ERD.
2. Generate default modules based on the crude function definitions from the Analysis phase.
3. Use those default modules to quickly generate sample data to populate the database tables.
4. Begin the process of refining the default modules to conform to the physical process flows already designed.
5. Continue to manually modify those sample modules until they conform to the basic look and feel of the final application.

Physical Process Flows

During Pre-Design, you must lay out the physical process flows in the new system. These physical process flows look like those at the logical level drilled down to another level of detail. The processes should be detailed enough to represent the elemental processes in the functional hierarchy. Each process will translate into a form.

Making the Application User Friendly

You need to consider a number of factors that affect the user friendliness of the application. In particular, the help system will play an important role in the way the user interfaces with the application.

Consider these factors:

- **Number of users** The more users there are, the more carefully the help system must be designed.
- **Level of users** A higher level of support must be designed for nontechnical employees than for systems people.

- **Complexity and flexibility of the application** The greater the complexity of the system, the greater attention that should be paid to software usability. For example, if the reporting system allows only the generation of simple, canned reports using default parameters, then little attention needs to be paid to the user interface. If, however, the reporting system allows dynamic selection of breaks, sorts, and filters, then much greater attention will need to be paid to the user interface.
- **Training** The more training that is provided, the more corners that can be cut on the user interface. Building a computer-based training system can also be cost effective if the user population is very large.
- **Documentation** Good manuals, tutorials, courses, and so on reduce the need for more sophisticated help systems. People don't usually like to look things up in a manual. With the availability of authoring tools, manuals and tutorials can easily be converted into online documentation.
- **Online help system** Help can be made available all the way down to the item level in applications. Using Designer/2000, this can be done relatively easily and cheaply.
- **Actual design of the application itself** It's possible, although rarely desirable, to put the instructions for the application right on the screen as text. Web applications frequently use this strategy.

You must consider all of these seven factors together to make applications user friendly. You cannot decide what to do in regard to one factor in isolation from the other six. In addition, the strategy you use to achieve user friendliness will be influenced by the tools you select and how easy it is to implement each of these. For example, in Designer/2000 it is very easy to implement item-level help when the application is being designed. As of this writing, there are no tools to cheaply create high-quality computer-based training. Your user-friendliness strategy will obviously influence the design of your applications—that is why the strategy must be chosen in the Pre-Design phase.

Of course, the cost of whatever user-friendliness strategy is used must also be considered; your goal is to minimize the cost of the overall system for its entire life cycle. You also need to consider the rate of user turnover and user expectations for user friendliness.

User expectations can be a big problem. As soon as the users sees a toolbar or menu on a GUI screen, they are going to expect an application that is as sophisticated as Microsoft Word for Windows, with every bell and whistle imaginable. These products have been through thousands of hours of user testing and refining and are mature versions. The best applications that you build are going to seem crude by comparison. However, your applications are not used by thousands or millions of different users. Most business software is built within a specific context. Also, although it can often cost the organization millions of dollars, your application will end up looking nowhere near as elegant as a commercially available word processing package available at the local computer store for a few hundred dollars or less. Unfortunately, there is no way for you to develop applications that are as sophisticated as commercially available software that still are cost effective.

In your designs, use the default behavior of the tools whenever possible. Avoid the temptation of trying to meet every user whim when designing the interface. Think very carefully about how to get the greatest user friendliness for the least cost, and at the same time educate users as to what is reasonable to expect from the applications being built.

Determining the Module Structure for Applications

You must determine which storyboard modules will be used in the final application. You may combine some of the current screen modules into one module and decompose others into several modules. Finally, it may be necessary to manually build whole new modules. These modules can be implemented within Designer/2000 by reverse engineering the modules to generate base modules within Designer/2000.

At this point in the CADM process, logical functions generated in Analysis exist in the function hierarchy. These were brought into the physical world as module definitions, and from these module definitions functioning module programs were generated. Using these functioning module programs, storyboards were created. Now you have determined the appropriate modules to use. In the context of Developer/2000 Forms, these modules correspond to .FMB files.

Your next step is to assess the correspondence between the set of appropriate modules and the information currently in the Designer/2000 repository. There is a three-step process to do this:

1. If a module in the repository is relatively close to one of the final modules, you can declare that this is the module that corresponds to the storyboard module.
2. If the storyboard module has no corresponding repository module, you should reverse engineer the storyboard module to create a repository module.
3. Repository modules that have no analog as storyboard modules should be discarded.

Mapping Requirements to Modules

At this point, the requirements from the original function hierarchy must be remapped to the new modules. The modules should be closely related to the functions from the original function hierarchy so this mapping should not be difficult.

Writing Functional Descriptions of Each Module: Creating the Design Book

Each module needs design notes that describe in detail how that module will function. These notes will guide the developer in the design of the application and will form the basis of the design book. The design book (which will be fully described in Chapter 9) is a complete, self-contained specification of each module. It should include everything from screen shots and system requirements to column-level usages and pseudocode for the triggers. It is the document from which the developer builds the module, and the tester uses the same document to make sure that the module meets design specifications. The conceptual design of the applications generates the first draft of the design book. The design book is completed in the Application Design phase.

Design Plan

The overall design plan addresses strategy, activities, and tasks necessary to design the two largest components of the new system: the database and applications.

Creating the Database Design Plan

Up until this point, it has not been possible to consider a plan for the database design; the conceptual design of the application must be complete before you can start thinking about building the database. The design plan for the database should include provisions for security, history keeping, denormalization, database instances, and capacity planning.

Security

Security can be handled in many ways within Oracle, such as through roles, profiles, login, and operating system and network security features. You will need to assess how security will be handled at the database level according to the application. Some applications, such as those involving money or personally sensitive or competitive information, will require much higher levels of security than those that concern information on internal business operations of a nonsensitive nature.

History Keeping

In the Pre-Design phase, you do not need to decide how to physically implement the system history; you simply need to decide what system history to keep. There are two types of history you can track:

- **Data errors** If, for example, the incorrect middle initial is printed on a check, this error needs to be changed, but is it necessary to keep a record of it? This depends upon the context. If the organization making the error is a bank, it may be useful to keep track of the error, but other businesses may not need to do so. You need to decide whether all errors, some errors, or only substantive errors will be documented. In the Pre-Design phase, issues such as what constitutes a "substantive" error can be defined.
- **Real changes over time** These changes are actual alterations in a record. You need to decide whether to keep track of this history. Examples of changes that should be kept track of include changes to a woman's name because of marriage, an employee's history within a department, and sales credited to specific departments. How to document these changes does not need to be decided at the attribute level at this stage. However, it is appropriate at this point to define just what history will be tracked.

Denormalization

In a perfect world, you would not have to consider the applications when building the database. However, machines are not infinitely fast, and all but the smallest databases will require some level of denormalization to make the applications run at an acceptable speed.

As with other issues at this stage, it is useful to include a policy statement regarding how to denormalize data. Databases that have a clearly defined policy on this issue are rare; however, a good policy is to normalize the data completely and cleanly until performance considerations demand a halt. A clean third normal form database should be generated and then denormalization should only occur when necessary. The policy should be used in all cases.

Copies of the Oracle Database

In working on a system, you need to have more than one copy of the database since otherwise changes would have be made to the existing production system. In most cases, there should be one copy for developers to experiment with, a second copy for testing, and a third copy for production. These three copies constitute a minimum. A fourth copy can be used for additional testing. In this case, one copy would be used for small-scale testing and another copy would be used for full production testing.

Capacity Planning

A big mistake often made in database design is not allowing for indexes. Indexes can be counted on without any careful analysis to add 50 percent to estimated data size. In a warehouse, it should be assumed that adding indexes will double the size of the database. How much space is really needed? For example, if you have 10 gigabytes of data in a legacy system, in the development instance, you first need to bring the legacy system into Oracle as is. This will require roughly 15 gigabytes of space, since Oracle doesn't store data as efficiently as most legacy systems do. In addition, you will need 5-10 gigabytes for indexing. In the test instance, you will need 5 gigabytes for the small test instance and 20-25 gigabytes for the large test instance. Similarly, you will need an additional 20-25 gigabytes in the production instance. Therefore, the 10 gigabytes of legacy data requires 81-95 gigabytes of disk storage.

The final aspect of database design planning is to have an auditor review the final physical database design and ensure that the choices made by the design team are appropriate.

Creating the Application Design Plan

The application design plan is relatively straightforward to create. Application design involves identifying the detailed column usage for each module and fully specifying the modules. Much of the final application design work is done in the Build phase.

Application design is among the most tedious, time-consuming, and unglamorous tasks of the entire design process. Therefore, it is very important to plan to review the accuracy of the application design. This review is discussed in Chapter 9.

Modifications for Smaller Systems

For small systems, the Pre-Design phase is unnecessary if standards are in place. Usually, the analyst can keep the small number of system requirements in his or her head and use sophisticated tools such as Designer/2000 to begin building almost immediately.

For medium-sized systems, you can cut some corners at this stage. Since the set of system requirements is relatively small, the designer does not need to map each requirement to the design book. It might be wise to perform a more global mapping: that is, to show which requirements map to which subsystem rather than to which elementary function. When in doubt, it is better to err on the side of more structure rather than less. No project ever failed because too much structure was imposed. For a medium-sized project, it shouldn't take you too much time to map requirements to functions.

Physical process flows may or may not be necessary for a medium-sized system, but it is usually a good idea to include them. Also, design standards and storyboards still should be completed for medium-sized systems. One big decision that needs to be made for these projects involves the use of templates and GUI design standards. The designer must ask these questions: Will this be a standalone project? Is it likely to be modified in the future? Should the system be built quickly and GUI design standards imposed afterward? For large projects, these decisions must be made before this point in the process. With medium-sized projects, designers may be using the software tools for the first time, and they may not know enough to design the GUI at this point. The project can then be used as a learning experience.

When Is the Pre-Design Phase Complete?

There are many parts to the Pre-Design phase for which to assess completion. Deciding when GUI standards are complete is a judgment call on the part of one or more senior developers. The question must be posed: Are GUI standards detailed enough to enforce consistency across screen modules? The answer will be apparent soon enough if GUI standards are inadequate since completed screen modules will be grossly dissimilar.

Any problems will also be evident during conceptual design of applications and coding standards. You also need to come up with as many guidelines as deemed appropriate to enforce consistency in PL/SQL routines; the fewer the standards, the greater the variability you will see in PL/SQL coding. However, if standards are too complex, you run the risk of overwhelming the developers so that they either do not comply with the standards or waste time adhering to standards that are not relevant.

Storyboards are complete when the users sign off on the designs. The users must spend sufficient time entering real transactions into the storyboard applications to make sure their needs are met. It must be made very clear to users that this is the final functionality they will see in the completed application; after this, no nonessential modification to the system will be allowed until after version 1 of the application is delivered.

Knowing whether applications have been correctly modularized is a judgment call on the part of the design team. If the individuals performing modularization are inexperienced, it is appropriate to temporarily bring in an individual capable of reviewing the decisions made during the modularization process.

The assignment of requirements and functional descriptions to modules is a straightforward process that can be reviewed by virtually any member of the design team. At this point, the designer needs to look at the design plan and ask the question: Will it be complete enough to keep testers happy? There must be sufficient detail in the design book so that the completed module can be tested. Without a detailed design book, a tester can only guess at the functionality of the module, and testing of the module will therefore be inadequate. It must be possible to ensure that the design meets the requirements. This can be done by mapping the requirements to individual modules.

What happens to this requirements document? Every requirement paragraph contains a separate and unique object to attach to tables, or a relationship, collection of tables, module, set of modules, or module connection. The only way to prove that the requirements have been met is to note where each and every requirement went, including the identity of the specific module and how the requirement was implemented. The whole point of a good design is that it meets the specifications laid out for it.

From this point forward in the CADM process, tasks are largely performed within the design team with little input required from outside sources. There is a serious temptation to turn over the remainder of the project to the development team with little outside review until the system is complete. However, the result of such a strategy will almost assuredly be the failure of the project.

The design plan *must* be reviewed throughout the remainder of the CADM process. This quality-control effort, involving people outside the design team, should continue to be an important part of the overall system development process.

The Pre-Design Phase in Designer/2000

Designer/2000 assists your work in the Pre-Design phase by providing a foundation for the steps you perform to prepare for the Design phase. Table 7-1 shows the Pre-Design activities or deliverables that Designer/2000 supports and the Designer/2000 tools that handle them.

Other than the GUI design standards, the main deliverable in the Pre-Design phase that Designer/2000 supports is the storyboard or conceptual application design. The storyboard is really a prototype of the complete system that you can use to communicate your ideas to users or clients. The main steps in creating and processing this storyboard in Designer/2000 are as follows:

1. Map attributes to functions (if you did not do so in the Analysis phase) using the Function/Attribute Matrix Utility.
2. Create a first-cut set of table definitions with the Database Design Wizard.

3. Create a first-cut set of modules and a module network with the Application Design Wizard.
4. Run the Server Generator to create scripts for the tables. Then run these scripts in SQL*Plus to create the tables.
5. Accept all non-manual candidate modules and generate screens, menus, and reports using the Forms Generator and Reports Generator.
6. Refine the forms and reports using Developer/2000 and rearrange the module network on paper—a non-Designer/2000 step.
7. Integrate changes in table design from the storyboard process into the repository.
8. Integrate modified modules and the module network structure into the repository using the Reverse Engineer Form and Reverse Engineer Report utilities and the Module Structure Diagrammer.
9. Map requirements to modules using the API or RON.

The following section discusses how to use the Designer/2000 tools that support these steps in the storyboard process as well as the work you do to create GUI standards. Note that the discussion of the Function/Attribute Matrix in the Entity Relationship Diagrammer in Chapter 6 applies to this phase as well, so you

Activity or Deliverable	Designer/2000 Tool
GUI design standards	Preferences Navigator and module templates
Insert attribute usages for functions	Function/Attribute Matrix
Storyboard	Database Design Wizard, Application Design Wizard, and generators
Integrate changes in tables from the storyboard	Reverse Engineer Database utility
Integrate changes in modules from the storyboard	Reverse Engineer Form utility and Reverse Engineer Report utility
Restructure the module network	Module Structure Diagrammer
Map requirements to modules	Repository Object Navigator or API

TABLE 7-1. *Pre-Design Activities and Designer/2000 Tools*

can refer to that chapter for the information on how to use that utility. Also note that this chapter does not discuss the generators as they are fully explored in Chapter 10 or the Module Structure Diagrammer as it is discussed in Chapter 9. The work you do in the generators in this phase is similar to the work you do in the Build phase and differs mainly in that in this phase you accept all the default preferences for each module when you perform generation.

Preferences Navigator

One important process you go through in the Pre-Design phase is the examination or creation of the graphical user interface (GUI) standards for the application modules. Code you generate from Designer/2000 automatically has a common look and feel and adheres to many recognized standards; however, you can also make some decisions to implement standards particular to your organization's environment. In addition, you can modify the way Designer/2000 handles many GUI issues. For example, you can set forms generation standards so all radio groups in the form have a raised border with a line width of two points around them with a title for the radio group inside the box.

Settings such as these are called *preferences* in Designer/2000, and there are preferences specifically for the type of generator you will be using: Forms, Reports, Visual Basic, MS Help, and WebServer. Each of these products has different considerations, so you will set different kinds of preferences for each, but you can edit and view all of them in the Preferences Navigator utility. There are more than 450 preferences, each with multiple levels of settings. Therefore, you can actually have a virtually unlimited number of combinations, and to effectively manage the preferences you need the help of the Preferences Navigator.

Starting the Preferences Navigator

When you start the Preferences Navigator, the following dialog box appears:

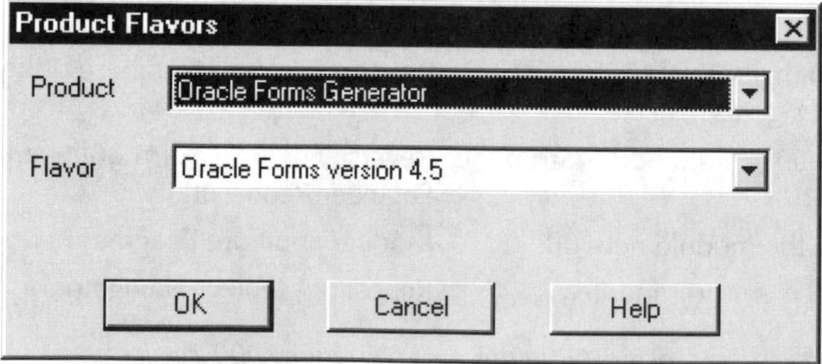

You select the generator for which you wish to view preferences using the Product field. You also select its *flavor*, or its version or style. For example, the Reports Generator product has two flavors: Oracle Reports and SQL*Plus. Next, click OK, and the Preferences Navigator window will appear. You can change the product and flavor at any time in the session by selecting **File→Change Product Flavor**.

The Preferences Navigator is a full-screen utility that has two windows—Preference Hierarchy and Properties Window—as Figure 7-1 shows.

Preference Hierarchy Window

The Preference Hierarchy window displays the preferences in a familiar navigator-style window. You work with the hierarchy the same way you do in the other navigator windows—expanding and collapsing nodes with the Navigator menu items, the toolbar buttons, or mouse clicks on the + and – icons next to the nodes. This window shows all preferences for one application system in a certain hierarchy consisting of preference nodes. These nodes are divided into five categories that explain the organization of the work you do in the preferences hierarchy: Levels, Instances, Items, Types, and Groups. The following section describes some of these categories. If you are interested in more detail, the online

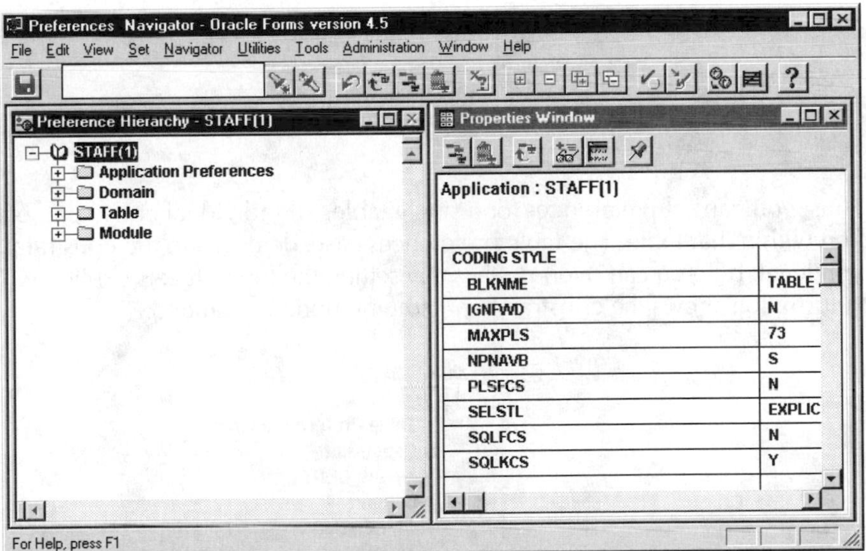

FIGURE 7-1. *Preferences Navigator windows*

help system contains explanations that you can reach by selecting the Index in the Preferences Navigator help window and searching for the topic "Preferences Nodes."

Preference Levels and Types You can set preferences at different levels, and these correspond roughly to the Preferences Hierarchy nodes. Lower levels inherit preference values from higher levels, but you can always override a particular preference by setting it at the lower level. The first nodes you see in the hierarchy are Application, Table, Domain, and Module. The first one is the highest-level node, and settings here cascade to all levels. The other three nodes have individual instances that you can set for all tables, domains, or modules or for specific tables, domains, or modules. Figure 7-2 shows these nodes expanded one level down to show the instances.

You set the application-level properties for system-wide standards that you want across all generated applications no matter what the source. You must have administrator privileges for the application system to set application-level preferences. Then you set individual domain-, table-, or module-level preferences for specialized needs.

The table-level instances are divided into Table Preferences, Constraint, and Column categories, as the following illustration shows.

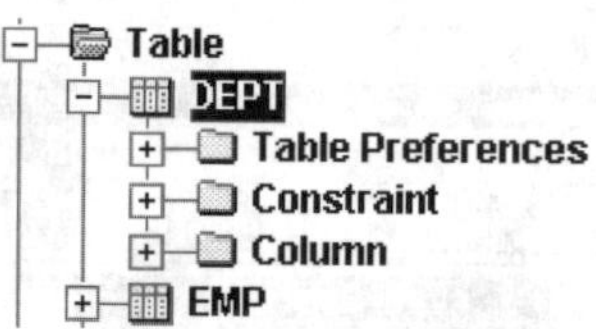

Thus, you can set preferences for a single table, an individual constraint, or a column within that table. The table preferences cascade down to the constraint and column level, but you can override them by setting the lower levels explicitly. The next illustration shows the constraint and column nodes expanded.

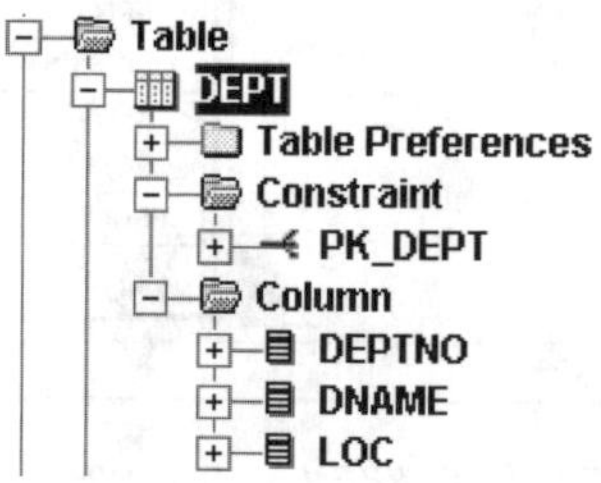

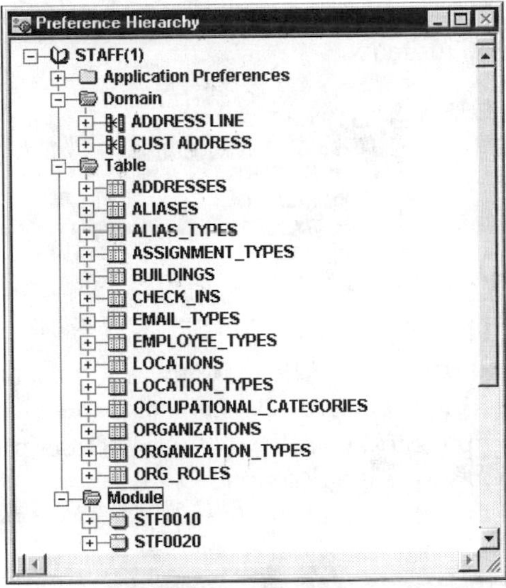

FIGURE 7-2. *Nodes expanded to show instances*

The same principle applies to the Module node, which provides Module Preferences and Detailed Table Usage preferences, as the next illustration shows.

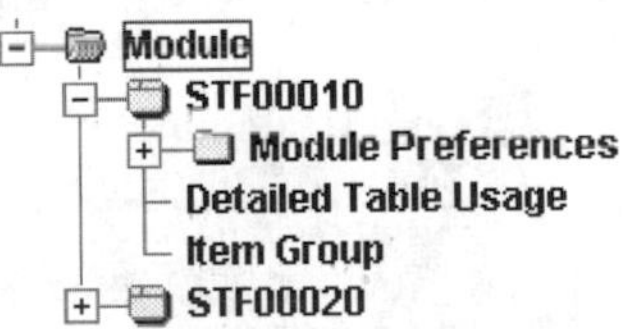

The next level after instances appears as the preference type nodes. These are the actual groups of preferences. The next illustration shows preference types such as DESCRIPTIVE FLEX and GENERATE OPTIONS for the DEPT table.

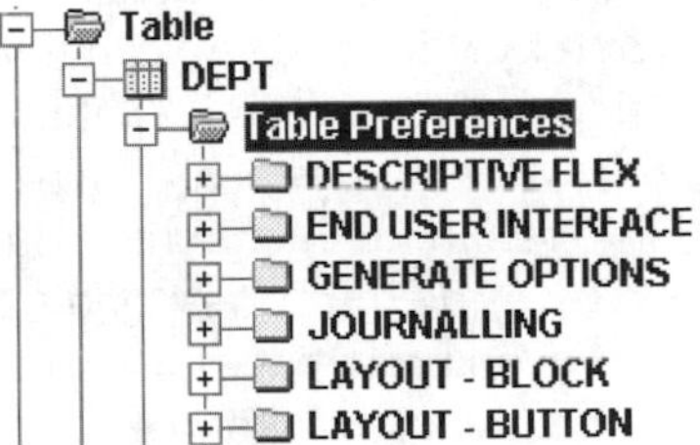

The last level shows the preferences themselves, such as RADBWD and RADDEC, as in the next illustration.

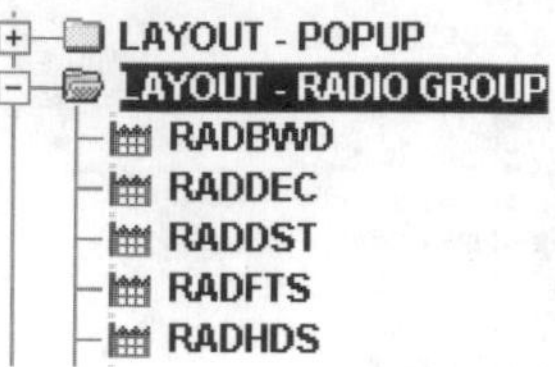

Other Views of the Hierarchy The default way to look at preferences is with their traditional, sometimes mnemonic, six-character names. You can also show the preferences as descriptive text by selecting **View→Description** from the menu. The following illustration shows the description view.

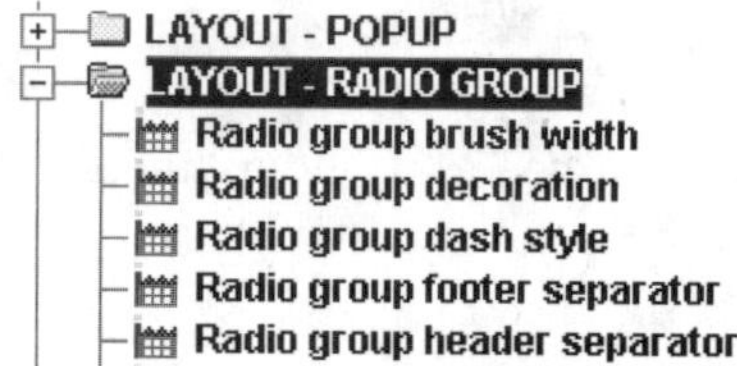

Another View menu choice displays the value at the same time as either the name or description. The next illustration shows the name and value view.

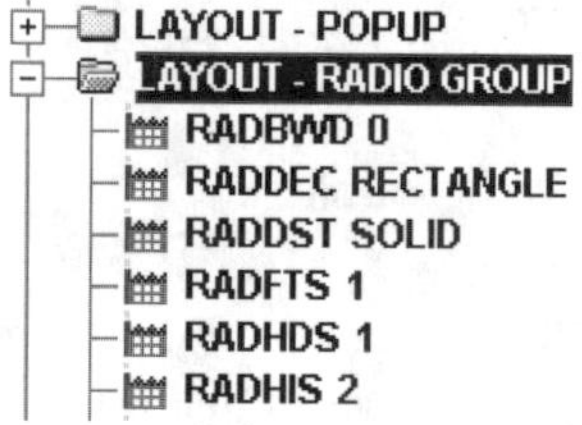

In addition to expanding and collapsing the hierarchy nodes to modify what you see in the Preference Hierarchy window, you can filter out some nodes to make the list easier to read using the View menu. That menu includes the Module Types option that lets you select which types of modules—Screen and Menu, Report, or All—that you want to see in the hierarchy. You can also select a list of preferences or types displayed by using the corresponding View menu items. Once you have filtered the list of displayed preferences or types with these menu items, you can remove the filter with the Remove Filter menu option.

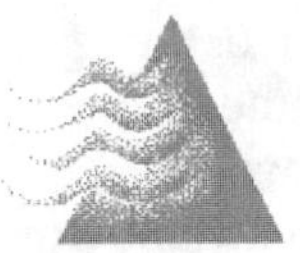

TIP
In this and other navigator-type windows in Designer/2000, you can press the HOME key to move to the top of the hierarchy and the END key to move to the bottom of the same level.

The next set of options in the View menu—Show All, Hide Defaults, Hide Application Level, and Show Modified—display both modified and default preferences, remove the preferences preset by Designer/2000, remove the preferences set at the application level, or show only the modified preferences. You can show whether preferences are set at a certain level below the node by selecting Indicate Preference Location from the View menu. This selection will make the **+** or – in the node icon red if a preference is set under it. The Hide Empty Branches menu item removes node contents for nodes that have nothing in them. Instances (another View menu item) expands the node you have selected to show the instances or occurrences of the lower levels (such as the EMP table under the Table node). When you select a module, you can choose Associations on the View menu to expand the nodes to show all preferences that could apply to that module. Remove Association Filter under that menu item resets the hierarchy as it was before the Associations item was chosen.

Properties Window

The Properties window displays either the value for a particular preference you select or a list of preferences for a node you select. Depending on what you select in the hierarchy, this window will show one or many preferences. For example, if you select the Application Preferences node, all preferences will appear in the Properties window. If you select the domain node, no preferences will appear until you select a specific domain in the subnode.

This window is like other properties windows in the navigator-style tools in that it allows you to select multiple nodes and apply properties (preference values) to the selected group. It has buttons for copying and pasting properties (for all settings other than the default), restoring default settings (the Unset function), filtering out all default properties or showing default and modified properties (the same functions as Show Modified and Show All on the View menu), showing or hiding the level icons next to each property, and pinning the display. This last button is handy if you want one Properties window to display values in one node and, at the same time, open another Properties window (through the Windows menu) to compare another node's properties.

Working with Preference Settings The Properties window is where you set values for the preferences. Designer/2000 ships with a set of default values called the *factory settings*. You can tell which properties have not been changed by looking at the icon; an icon that looks like a factory building appears next to a preference that has not been changed. Whenever you change a preference, the icon will change to reflect the level where the setting was made. This same icon will appear for that preference in lower nodes so you can always tell at what level you set a particular preference. The icons that indicate these levels are shown in Figure 7-3.

Named Sets

You can create a set of preferences you can use as a group. This is called a *named preference set* because you select and manage it by name. These named sets are useful when you generate modules as you can attach a specific set of preferences to a module temporarily for that one session without changing the module preferences. Another use of named preference sets is that they allow you to attach the same set of preferences to different parts of the hierarchy.

You create a named set by selecting **Set→Create** from the menu. You fill in the name of the new set and click OK. If the Named Sets window is not displayed at that point, you select **View→Named Sets Window** from the menu. If that menu item is disabled, check the Window menu to see if the window is open but minimized. This window shows all named sets in the application system, and you can expand it to view the preference types, as Figure 7-4 shows.

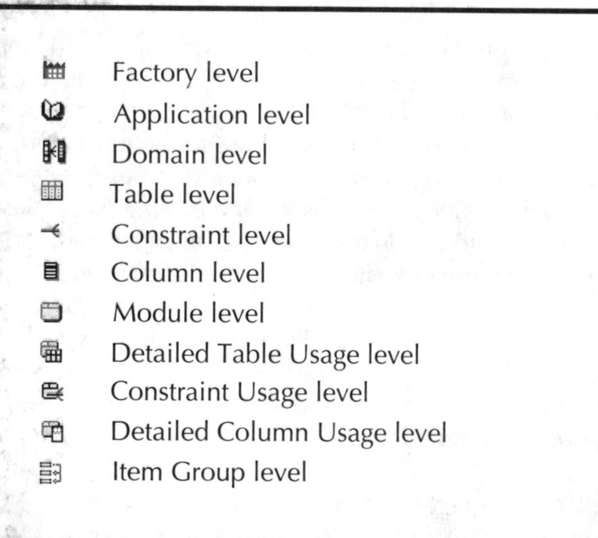

FIGURE 7-3. *Preference level icons*

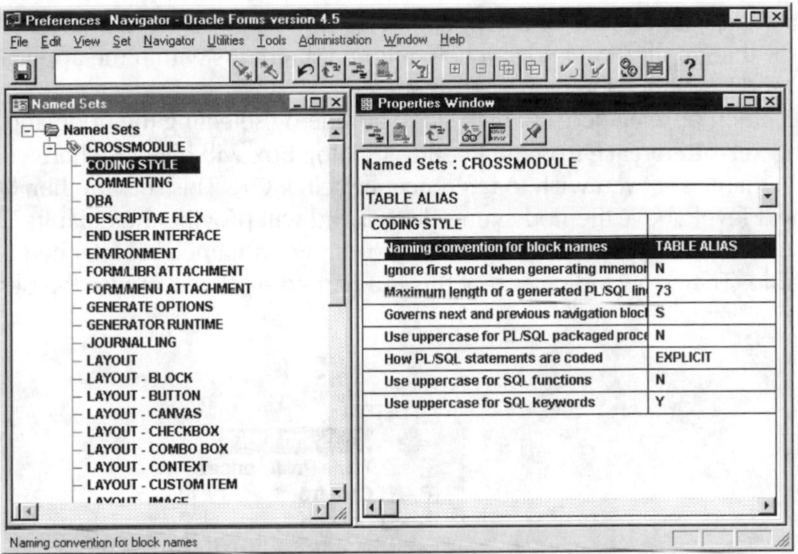

FIGURE 7-4. *Named Sets window with Properties window*

You can then set the preferences to the values you want and save them as a named set. Another way to create a named set is to select an instance node and select **Set→Create As** from the menu. This will copy all preferences from that node, with their settings, to the set you name.

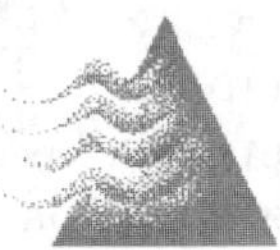

TIP

An alternative to named sets when you want to quickly copy the settings from one node to another is to use drag and drop. Select the node you wish to copy from and hold down the mouse button as you drag to the target node and release the button. The rule is that you must drop the node on another node at the same level. For example, you can drop one table node on another because they are at the same level in the hierarchy.

The Copy From item in the Set menu copies a preference set from one application system to another. Note that you can also share named preference sets with or from other application systems using RON (as you share other objects). If you do so, you can put all cross-system preferences in one set and have all developers in charge of application systems attach the named set. This procedure will help enforce corporate standards across all applications as all default preferences will be the ones set in the named set instead of the factory settings. If you attach the named set to the application level, it will also serve as a standard setting for that application and can help enforce standards within the application system (and beyond, if the named set is shared).

You attach or reference a named set to a node by selecting the node and choosing **Set→Reference** from the menu. A dialog box will appear where you select the named set you wish to reference and click OK. This set will then be at the next level above the node you selected and will provide the defaults for all subordinate nodes. The next illustration shows a named set attached to the DEPT table. The arrow indicates that this is a named set that provides the default settings.

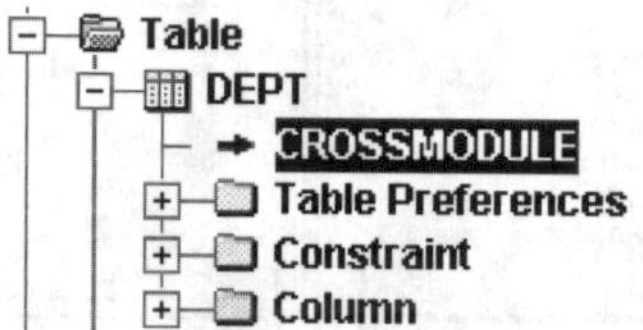

The last item on the Set menu, Dereference, allows you to remove the reference or detach the named set from this node.

Protecting and Freezing Preferences

After spending some time examining and modifying the preferences, you might want to prevent others from changing them. Since preferences are so powerful and can radically modify the appearance and actions of a generated module, you may want to put one person in charge of maintaining preferences on the higher levels (perhaps the data administrator or Designer/2000 administrator). Sometimes a developer may need to modify module-level preferences for a specific purpose, which could be allowed if the preferences do not violate higher-level standards. In any case, the issue of who sets the high-level preferences is worthy of consideration and a policy decision.

Designer/2000 provides two options to lock preferences: Protect and Freeze. Protect lets you select an instance node or nodes and specify that no additional modifications can be made. The Utilities menu contains Protect from Update, Allow Update, and Remove User Preferences options. The first allows you to prevent others from modifying a node you select. All preferences in all levels below that node will be protected when you select this option, and a special icon (a fence gate) will appear to show that the node is protected. Others may remove your protections, though, if they have administrator privileges on the application system. Allow Update removes the protection for the nodes you select. Remove User Protections eliminates the protections placed by the current user at all levels. In addition to the Utilities menu items, the Administration menu contains an item for Remove All Protections that lets the application owner or anyone with administrator privileges remove all explicit protections placed by anyone on this application system's preferences.

The Administration menu contains selections for Freeze and Unfreeze that act on a selected instance node. The menu also includes an Unfreeze All option to unfreeze all nodes whether selected or not. A node can be frozen only by users with administrator privileges for the application system (granted in RON). Freezing prevents other users from modifying any subnode preference. If you freeze the application level, no preferences can be changed, but you can also select one or more lower-level nodes to freeze. A pin icon will appear next to the frozen node to indicate the node status.

Other Menu and Toolbar Functions

In addition to the normal items, the File menu contains Save, Save and Requery, Requery, and Revert options. You use Save to commit the changes you make to the repository, and you can undo changes with Revert. The Preference Hierarchy window reflects the state of the repository since you last expanded a node. Since you may make changes in the Properties window after you expand a node, you need a way to requery the repository so that the hierarchy reflects those changes. The Requery menu item and the Save and Requery menu item allow you to do that.

The Edit menu has the normal Undo option as well as Unset, which restores the selected preference or node to the default setting, and Unset Cascade, which applies to all subnodes. The Edit menu also includes the Select Instances, Select Preferences, and Select Types options. These work like the View menu items, already discussed, to reduce the number of preferences that the Preference Hierarchy window displays. As usual, a Preferences menu item displays the window where you set preferences for the Preferences Navigator itself.

The Navigator menu contains the same type of items as the other navigator tools: Expand, Collapse, Expand All, Collapse All, Set Mark, Goto Mark, and Find.

The Utilities menu provides options you can use to go directly to the generators or to generate a module as a different type—Generate and Generate As, respectively.

The Administration menu contains freezing and protection options. If you are not the owner of the application system or do not have administrator privileges for the application system, these items will be disabled.

Where Does This Information Go?

The preferences you set here affect the way the generators run. Therefore, when you set an application-level preference, it will affect all modules for that product which you generate in this application system. If you set a module-level preference, it will affect the generation of only that module. The Designer/2000 generators use the preferences you set for a specific product and flavor to guide the generation process. In addition, you use a named preference set when running the generator for a particular module. Since you can have more than one named set, you could attach sets one at a time to the same module and see how they affect the output. This is a powerful tool for seeing how preferences affect generation and will assist you in using preferences productively. The discussion of generators in Chapter 10 provides some examples of preferences you might experiment with.

Database Design Wizard

One of the objectives of the Pre-Design phase is to create a working storyboard or prototype to show what the system will consist of. The first requirement of the storyboard is a rough-cut table structure. The Database Design Wizard (DDW) Repository utility allows you to create tables for the Design phase from entities in the Analysis phase. At this point, you are concerned less with completeness and accuracy in the table designs than with the creation of a data repository you can use as a basis for storyboard modules. You will spend the Design phase refining the rough-cut table and columns according to user feedback from prototype sessions and denormalization considerations that you, as the database designer, impose.

The Database Design Wizard is available from the Designer/2000 window launchpad application as well as from the Utilities menus of several other tools, such as the Repository Object Navigator. It is highly customizable but also has a good set of defaults and can be run with minimal intervention on your part. Although you can run this utility more than once to create column and table definitions, you should wait until the Analysis work is as complete as possible before you run it for the first time. The reason for this is that the DDW cannot delete definitions, and if your entities are not fully formed when you run the utility the first time, table or column definitions may not be correctly based on the entities and attributes.

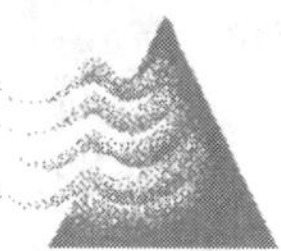

TIP

Start the Database Design Wizard from RON or another tool instead of the Designer/2000 window launchpad application. If you start the DDW from the Designer/2000 window, it will run in the same session, and you will not be able to return to the Designer/2000 window to start another tool while the DDW is running. In addition, if you select entities in RON before starting DDW, those entities will automatically have the In Set? setting checked when DDW starts.

What the DDW Does

Table 7-2 shows the Analysis elements and the Design elements that DDW creates from them. Notice that the DDW translates some relationships into objects that a relational database can support.

Analysis Data Element	Design Data Element
Entity	Table
Attribute	Column
Primary unique identifier	Primary key constraint
Nonprimary unique identifier	Unique constraint
One-to-many relationship	Foreign key constraint and foreign key column
Many-to-many relationship	Intersection table with foreign key constraints and foreign key columns
Arc and subtype/supertype relationships	Single tables or multiple tables with special columns to link them

TABLE 7-2. *Analysis Elements and Corresponding Design Elements Created by the DDW*

Generally, the DDW creates tables and columns in a one-to-one mapping from entities and attributes, respectively. The tables and columns the DDW creates will have properties copied from the corresponding entities and attributes, respectively. Entity plural names become table short names with spaces converted to underscores. For example, a column will have the same datatype, size, mandatory characteristic, and so on as the attribute it is derived from. The utility will create a foreign key column on the many side of a one-to-many relationship and also create a foreign key constraint from that relationship. It will create a primary key (a *surrogate key*) for the table if the entity does not have a primary unique key defined.

If there is a many-to-many relationship, the utility will create a separate table called an *intersection table* (also known as an associative table in other disciplines). This table contains the primary keys from both tables generated from the entities in the many-to-many relationship. The many-to-many relationship becomes two one-to-many relationships between the original two tables and the new intersection table. This action agrees with the generally recognized method for handling many-to-many relationships in the Design phase. Another situation that must be resolved in the relational database implementation is the subtype-supertype relationship, and the DDW provides four ways to handle it, as Table 7-3 shows.

In all cases you specify that you want to generate tables. The discriminator column mentioned for the supertype implementation identifies to which of the subtypes a particular record belongs.

Table Mappings Tab

When you are satisfied with the entity and attribute definitions and are ready to move into the Pre-Design phase, you start the DDW and fill out the items on its

Mapping Approach	Result	Implementation Method in DDW
Supertype implementation (single table)	Single table for subtype and supertype with discriminator column	Include the supertype only for the run set. Subtypes should have the Map Type set to Included.
Explicit subtype implementation (separate tables)	Separate tables for each subtype with supertype columns in each	Specify the subtypes but not the supertype in the run set.
Implicit subtype implementation	Separate tables for subtype and supertype; subtypes have supertype columns, but the supertype does not have subtype columns	Specify the supertype and subtypes for the run set.
Arc implementation	Separate tables for subtypes and supertype; subtypes do not have supertype columns, and the supertype has a separate foreign key column for each subtype	The first time you run the utility, specify the supertype and subtypes for the run set but no columns or keys. The second time you run the utility, check the Arc check box for each subtype and specify the modification of tables, columns, and keys.

TABLE 7-3. *Approaches to Mapping Subtype-Supertype Relationships*

various tabs. The first tab you see when you open this utility is Table Mappings, as shown in Figure 7-5.

This tab is where you specify which entities you want to use as the bases for tables. It shows the current set of entities and any tables already created from them. You click the In set? check box if you want to create a table definition for this entity or if a table definition already exists and you want to add extra columns from new attributes of the entity. If you manually fill in the table name by selecting an existing table from the poplist in the Table item, DDW will immediately create a table entity usage.

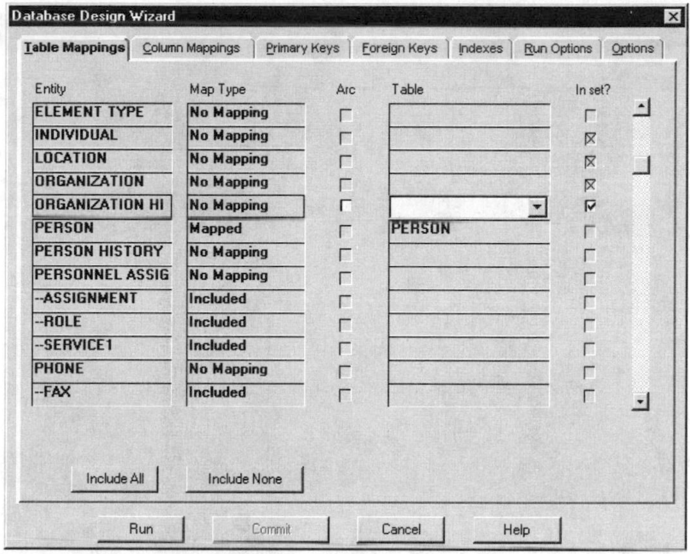

FIGURE 7-5. *Database Design Wizard Table Mappings tab*

You can choose all entities or no entities with the Include All and Include None buttons. If you choose to include an entity, the DDW will automatically include all its attributes in the run set. The Arc check box is where you specify arc relationships when implementing a subtype/supertype relationship or arc relationship, as mentioned in the preceding table.

Run Options Tab

The next step you take when you run the DDW for the first time is to fill in the Run Options tab shown in Figure 7-6. This tab presents a list of the elements you are implementing and allows you to customize the Create and Modify actions for tables, columns, keys, and indexes. Generally, you leave these set to the default choice, Create, when first running the utility so you can create all elements. Then, on subsequent runs, you might choose to update certain element types. Note that you can both create and modify a type of element in the same run.

This tab also has an area in the top-right corner for specifying which properties this run will modify. At the bottom right, you can state when you want the commit to occur. Committing after each phase is the most efficient procedure and, if an unrecoverable error occurs in the middle of the run, you will still have definitions for everything the DDW did before the last commit operation. Committing at end of the run will roll back operations to the state before the run if an error occurs.

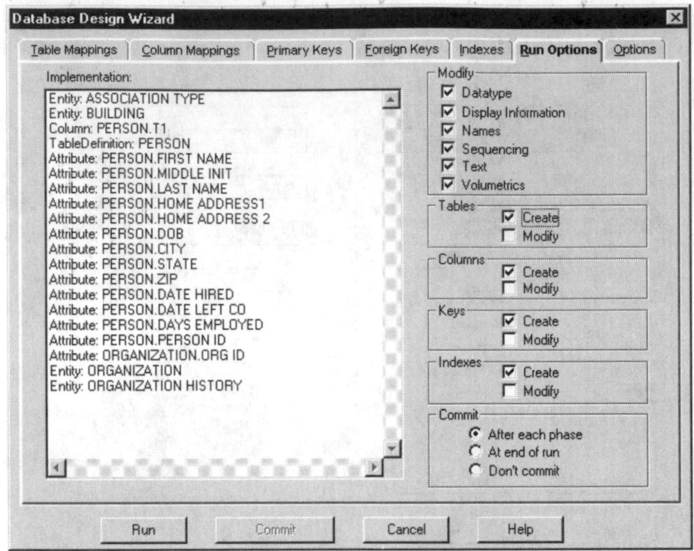

FIGURE 7-6. *Run Options tab*

This procedure is useful if you want to ensure that if the run completes fully it is written all at once, or if it fails at some point all changes are reversed. If you choose Don't commit, the DDW will run and validate the design but not insert the elements in the repository. This option is useful if you want to do a dry run to see what the utility will create.

Options Tab

The DDW utility will run correctly with other defaults after you fill in the Table Mappings and Run Options tabs. However, you may want to specify some of the properties for the run on the Options tab, shown in Figure 7-7. Some of the properties you can set here are the database type, database name, tablespace, and storage space for tables and the tablespace and storage space for indexes. These all refer to element definitions that are in the repository and that you can have the DDW attach automatically to new tables in this run. This tab provides an alternative to running the utility and manually changing these properties in the RON, which is a more time-consuming process. You can also specify naming conventions such as column prefixes, foreign key names, surrogate key names, unique identifier length, and table prefix.

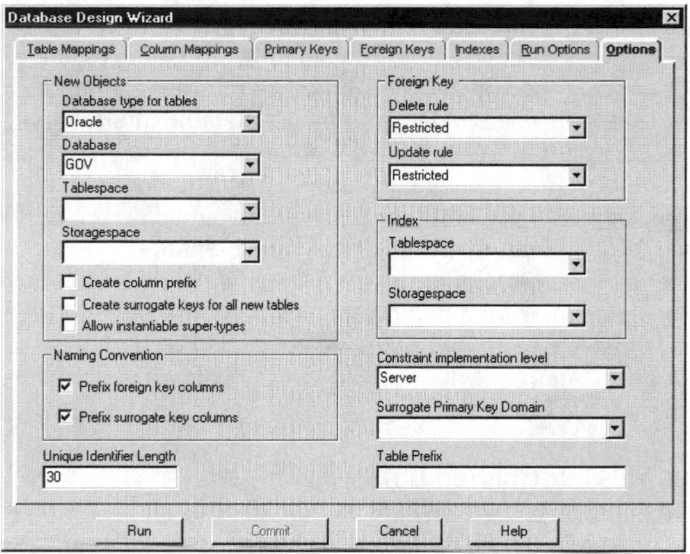

FIGURE 7-7. *Options tab*

Here are some other properties you can set on this tab:

- *Delete rule and Update rule* for the foreign key columns.
- *Create surrogate keys for all new tables* to provide a primary key if a table does not have one.
- *Surrogate Primary Key Domain* to specify the datatype and size of the surrogate key.
- *Constraint implementation level* to specify where the constraints are validated—on the client side, server side, or both.
- *Allow instantiable supertypes* to give the supertype a value in the discriminator column if a row represents the supertype. This property handles the single-table implementation of subtype/supertype relationships, which creates a discriminator column to store a value indicating to which subtype a particular record pertains.

If you want some tables to have certain settings and other tables to have different settings on these DDW tabs, you need to run the DDW utility more than once and specify different settings for each run.

Column Mappings, Primary Keys, Foreign Keys, and Indexes Tabs

The Column Mappings, Primary Keys, Foreign Keys, and Indexes tabs allow individual control over the way DDW handles the relevant elements. Basically, each tab shows the mapping of entity information to table information (such as attributes to columns and primary unique identifiers to primary keys) and lets you specify which of these individual elements the DDW should include in the next run. The information on these tabs makes sense only after you run the utility for the first time since the tables are mapped at that point to entities.

These other tabs are useful if, after you run the DDW for the first time, you create additional attributes for a particular entity. On the Column Mappings tab you can specify that these new attributes are associated with existing columns in the table definitions. Alternatively, you can specify that you want to create new columns from these attributes.

Where Does This Information Go?

The element definitions you create here are stored, as usual, in the repository. Each element you create with the DDW also has a link or association to the logical analysis element that was its source. Table 7-4 summarizes the elements produced by the DDW and their future use in the system life cycle.

Application Design Wizard

The work you do in the DDW provides the basis for the work you need to do in the Application Design Wizard (ADW). The ADW is a repository utility that works

Element	Future Use
Table definition	Detailed table usage in a module for finished application code. Incorporated into the DDL script produced by the Server Generator.
Table entity usage	Mapping of the table to an entity occurs in the DDW. RON displays this as a subnode of the table.
Column definition	Detailed column usage in a module for the finished application code. Incorporated into the DDL script produced by the Server Generator.
Column source	Mapping of the column to an attribute occurs in the DDW. RON displays this as the Source Attribute property for the column.

TABLE 7-4. *Elements Created by the DDW and Their Future Use*

similarly to the DDW: it creates Design elements from Analysis elements—in this case, modules from functions. Your system analysis consists largely of the data model and function model, so after you finish translating the entity definitions to table definitions and the function definitions to module definitions, you can build a complete set of application files that you can use for the storyboard process.

A *module* is a repository element that basically represents a program or part of a program in your final application. It can be a menu, screen, report, utility, or script that performs some task or provides a user interface to the database. There are different *languages* for modules that designate the tool used for the finished code.

The ADW, like the DDW, is available from the Designer/2000 window and the Utilities menus of various tools such as RON. The interface is essentially simple but has an intricate set of rules for creating module definitions from function definitions and module structure networks (hierarchies) from business unit usages. Table 7-5 shows the elements this utility creates in Design from elements in Analysis.

Your function model should be as complete as possible before you run the ADW so it will give you a set of modules that closely matches your needs. You need to run the ADW with two different settings for each function branch: first to create *candidate modules* (generated modules you need to explicitly accept) from functions and again to create a module structure from the function business unit usages. You cannot create a module structure without modules, so you must follow this sequence of first specifying creation of modules and then specifying creation of menus. Other than the initial runs to create modules and menus, the ADW is not intended to be run iteratively on the same elements as the DDW is.

The ADW Window

When you start the ADW, the window shown in Figure 7-8 appears. There are fewer entry fields to fill out for the ADW than for the DDW, and they are grouped

Analysis Data Element	**Design Data Element**	**Finished Product**
Function	Module	Form, Report, PL/SQL script
Function business unit usages	Module network structure	Menu
Function entity usages	Module data usages (detailed and summary)	Table usages in finished code
Dataflow data usages	Module arguments	Parameters passed between modules

TABLE 7-5. *Analysis Elements and Corresponding Design Elements Created by the ADW*

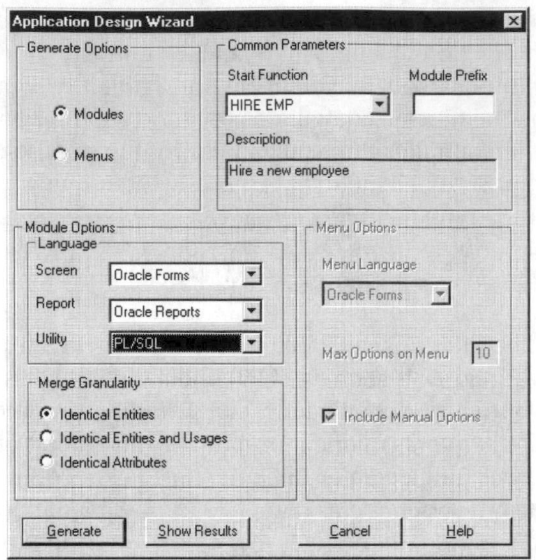

FIGURE 7-8. *Application Design Wizard window*

into different categories: Generate Options, Common Parameters, Module Options, Menu Options, and Merge Granularity. Most of the defaults suffice, but you should pay particular attention to Generate Options and Start Function (in the Common Parameters group).

Generate Options The Generate Options area is where you specify whether you are generating modules or menus. Remember that you cannot generate menus unless you already have modules that you have accepted (Candidate property is null, not True).

Common Parameters The Common Parameters area is where you designate the Start Function. The ADW generates a module for this and all other applicable functions under it in the function hierarchy. If you want to generate modules for all functions, leave this field blank. The Module Prefix field lets you specify a short prefix that ADW uses to name the modules. All modules will have a short name of this prefix followed by a number. The default prefix is the first six characters of the application system name for modules and the application system description for menus. Also, the ADW inserts a value for the Description property of each generated module definition. The default for this field is the Short Definition property of the function, but you can modify the default by editing the value.

Module Options If you are running ADW for modules, the Module Options area is enabled so you can indicate the language for screen, report, and utility modules that the ADW generates. Part of the process ADW goes through when creating the candidate modules is assigning a module type. This is assigned as a module property along with the language for the type that you specify here. Notice that the default settings—Forms, Reports, and PL/SQL—will work at this stage, and that you can change individual modules in RON or the module diagrammers at a later time. The Language property corresponds to the generator you use to create the finished code. The Language poplist includes other options besides the supported generators, so be careful to specify Forms, Reports, Graphics, Visual Basic, WebServer, or C++ if you will be using one of these generators.

Menu Options If you generate menus in this ADW run, this area is enabled. Here you choose the menu language (Oracle Forms is the default) assigned to the menu. Max Options on Menu defines the maximum number of items you can have in each menu. If there are more, ADW creates another menu to hold them. The items that ADW groups on a particular menu are governed by the menu rules discussed in the section "ADW Rules." The last field in this area is Include Manual Options. If you check this, ADW will add the modules it determined to be manual to the menu structure. You can use these for information screens that tell the user what to do manually, but if this does not apply to your system, uncheck this box.

Merge Granularity When creating modules, you can determine the rule ADW uses to group functions into modules. You choose one of three options for Merge Granularity:

- *Identical Entities* merges functions into one module if they have the same entities mapped to them.
- *Identical Entities and Usages* combines functions into one module if the functions have the same entities and same CRUD for those entities.
- *Identical Attributes* joins functions into one module if those functions have the same attributes mapped to them.

Running the ADW for Modules

After choosing Modules under Generate Options and completing the other fields in the ADW window, you click the Generate button. The ADW will run and display a log screen as it runs. When it is finished, you can click the Show Results button to see a report of the modules that were generated. You can also run a repository report called Candidate Module Definition to get more details. If you want to start over, you need first to delete the candidate modules using RON.

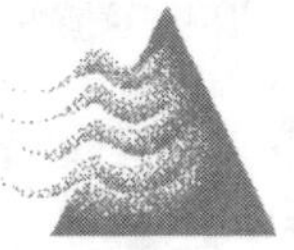

TIP
If the ADW seems to freeze when running but the Close button is enabled, move the log message window down and look for a message dialog box. After you dismiss that dialog box, you will be able to proceed.

Running the ADW for Menus

After generating candidate modules, you need to accept the candidates. Then you can run the ADW again to generate the module hierarchy for menus. Fill out the same screen as you did for modules, but this time specify Menus under Generate Options and fill in the Menu Options area. Again, you want to specify an upper-level function in the Start Function field. The menu name is derived from the application system Description property.

When you have filled out the fields for menu generation, press the Generate button and, after the ADW finishes, examine the results using the Show Results button.

CAUTION
Modules have dependencies that mandate a certain sequence for the tasks you perform in the design wizards. Be sure to run the Database Design Wizard or in some other way create table definitions before running the Application Design Wizard. Also be sure to run the ADW to create module definitions before running it to create menu modules.

ADW Rules

The ADW follows five types of rules in creating the module definitions:

- Function mapping
- Module categorization
- Module grouping for menus
- Module data usage
- Module arguments

If you understand the decisions that the ADW makes to create modules, you can more easily interpret the results and get more out of the utility. Note that there is additional information on these rules in the online help system under the topic "Candidate Modules in the Application Design Wizard." Follow the link from the topic on the contents page titled "How the Application Design Wizard Works" to reach this information

Function Mapping Rules In general, one module is created for each function in the hierarchy under the one you specify as the Start Function when you run the utility. A function must be one of three types: a leaf (atomic) function with no elementary or common function parents, a common function, or an elementary function. A *leaf function* is one at the end of the hierarchy tree (it has no children). A *common function* appears more than once in the function hierarchy. An *elementary function* must be completed successfully or its work will be rolled back.

Modules are merged if they are not manual (that is, they have entity usages) and are associated with functions that have the same Response Needed property, input parameters, business unit usages, and similar data usages (based on the granularity you set in the ADW window).

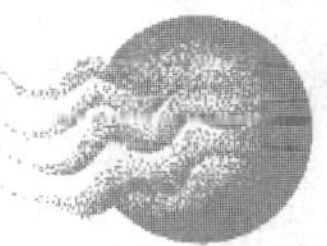

NOTE
If ADW merges functions into one module, it will also merge the text (descriptions and notes) from those functions.

ADW will duplicate a module if the function it is based on has more than one business unit usage. ADW will create one module for each business unit for that function.

Module Categorization Rules The next step ADW takes after creating modules is to categorize them into types. It categorizes a module as manual if no tables are implemented for entities of the functions. It creates a report module if the function has read-only data usages. It produces a utility module if the Response Needed property of the corresponding function is Overnight. It creates a screen if the Response Needed property of the corresponding function is Immediate. If none of those conditions apply, the module becomes a screen type.

Module Grouping Rules for Menus Just as there are rules for ADW to follow when it creates modules, there are also rules to follow when it creates menus. The application-level menu module is generated as the top level (main menu), and this module calls the first-level menu modules. ADW generates the first level of menu modules from the module business unit usages (derived from the function business unit usages). If the module is not associated with any business unit, ADW groups it in a Miscellaneous menu. The next level of menu hierarchy groups modules by module type: for example, reports or screens. The menu system therefore has the following structure:

Top level	Application system (main menu)
First level	Business unit grouping
Second level	Module type grouping
Third level	Individual modules under the specific types (menu items)

If you do not like this division of modules into menus, you can change it in the Module Structure Diagrammer after the ADW runs (as discussed in Chapter 9). Note that the menu modules you create in this ADW run are candidates as well, and you have to accept them before you perform any generator work.

Module Data Usage Rules ADW creates a module table usage (summary and detail) from the function entity usages of the function the module is based on. For example, assume that MODULE1 was created from FUNCTION1, which has ENTITY1 as a usage. If there is a TABLE1 with ENTITY1 mapped to it, the ADW creates a module table usage for MODULE1 of TABLE1.

Column usages are similar; they are mapped to the table if the function has the corresponding attributes mapped to it. If the DDW created a surrogate key for a table, that will be mapped to the module table usage even though there is no corresponding attribute. Another rule is that if a table has an INSERT usage on the module, ADW will add all mandatory columns as module column usages whether or not there are corresponding attribute usages. Note that this rule applies only to tables that have INSERT usages.

Module Argument Rules ADW creates module arguments based on the attributes and data items in the dataflows associated with the corresponding function. If the dataflow is an input, the source must not be a datastore; and if the dataflow is an output, the destination must not be a datastore. The type of the argument is IN if the dataflow flows into the function and OUT if the dataflow flows out of the function.

Where Does This Information Go?

The Application Design Wizard produces *candidate modules*—modules that are not ready for generation—that you can later accept as application modules in the Module Structure Diagrammer or Repository Object Navigator. After accepting a module, you can then generate working code from it with any of the Designer/2000 generators. The ADW creates modules with module data usages based on the functions and function entity usages. You diagram the module hierarchy or structure in the Module Structure Diagrammer to show and manipulate the menu system. Table 7-6 shows how these elements are used in future stages of CADM.

Data Element Created by the ADW	Future Use
Modules for screens, reports, and utilities	Used to generate code in Forms, Reports, Graphics, and WebServer
Module associations and menu modules	Application system menu structure and menu module
Detailed and summary module data usages	Module data usages that specify how tables and columns are used in modules
Module arguments	Parameters passed between a calling module and a called module

TABLE 7-6. *Future Use of Data Elements Created by the ADW*

The ADW can go a long way toward the creation of rough-cut modules, but before you generate prototypes for the storyboard, you need to accept the modules and then reorganize the hierarchy, define missing modules, and eliminate the extra modules the ADW produces. The Module Structure Diagrammer, described in Chapter 9, lets you accept candidate modules and further assists in this reorganization.

Integrating the Storyboarded Tables

The storyboard process produces the first, rough-cut set of tables that you can use as a starting point for the database design part of the Design phase. The next step is to integrate the changes you have made, or want to make, into the repository based on information you gained in the storyboard process. These changes may be the result of modifications you make to the table definitions in the database or notes you take when you work on the storyboard. Table 7-7 summarizes the possible status of a table after the storyboard process and how you use Designer/2000 to integrate these changes.

Note that you can use the Reconcile utility, described in Chapter 11, to determine the differences between the database tables and the repository definitions of those tables. This tool is quite useful and powerful, but it will not modify the tables for you. The main tools for that are the Repository Object Navigator for manual changes to table definitions and the Reverse Engineer Database utility for automated modification of table definitions.

Action on Table during Storyboard Process	Method for Integrating Table into Repository
Column information was changed, but the database table is similar to the repository table definition.	Delete extra repository columns manually in RON; add columns not in the repository with the Reverse Engineer Database utility
Database tables were combined or split.	Delete the repository definitions and use the Reverse Engineer Database utility.
New database tables were created.	Run the Reverse Engineer Database utility to add the repository definitions.
Table was intentionally deleted in the storyboard process.	Delete the table definition using RON or the Data Diagrammer.

TABLE 7-7. *How Tables from the Storyboard Process Are Handled*

Integrating the Storyboarded Modules

After you generate the default set of modules in the ADW and accept the candidate modules using the Module Structure Diagrammer (as discussed in Chapter 9), you use the Oracle Forms and Reports Generators to create the screen and report files (as discussed in Chapter 10). Then you work with the modules as program files in the storyboard process to refine and revise them using Developer/2000. When you are satisfied with the storyboard files, you need to restore them to the repository module definitions. During the storyboard process, you may have changed data usages, merged files, and eliminated unnecessary files. You need to integrate these changes into the repository module definitions so you can further refine the definitions and create finished code. If you change the interface standards during the storyboard process, you can incorporate those changes into the templates or preferences.

The method you use to integrate files into the repository module definitions depends on the file status, as Table 7-8 shows. You should keep track of changes as you go through the storyboard process so you can determine the file status. When you are done with the storyboard integration, the repository should have one module for each module in the storyboard.

Note from the references to Developer/2000 that it is assumed that you perform the storyboard operation using Oracle Forms and Reports. You can use Oracle products for this work even if the finished modules will be in other languages as all you need to do is change the language from Forms or Reports to the appropriate one before you perform generation.

Status of File after Storyboard Process	Method for Integrating Module into Repository
File is similar to the module in the repository (its tables did not change significantly).	Make changes to the existing module manually in RON or the Module Data Diagrammer.
File is a combination of modules in the repository.	Delete the module in RON after moving the table and function usages to the other module.
File was created after generation and has no repository module definition.	Run the Reverse Engineer Forms (or Reports) utility to add the module definition based on the file you created in Developer/2000.
File was intentionally deleted in the storyboard process.	Delete the module definition using RON or the Module Structure Diagrammer.
File navigation (calls) was changed.	Manipulate the module structure using the Module Structure Diagrammer.

TABLE 7-8. *Handling of Modules from the Storyboard Process*

The Designer/2000 tools (Module Data Diagrammer, Module Structure Diagrammer, and RON) you use to integrate the modules into the repository are discussed in Chapter 9. The following section discusses how you reverse engineer Forms and Reports when you develop modules outside Designer/2000 and need to create module definitions for them.

Reverse Engineer Form and Report Utilities

The Reverse Engineer Form and Reverse Engineer Report utilities are available from the Repository Object Navigator and Module Data Diagrammer. They are actually part of the generator utility set and are used to create module definitions with related table and column usages for existing Oracle Forms or Reports stored in the file system or database. The following discussion concentrates mostly on the Reverse Engineer Form utility, but the Reverse Engineer Report utility has similar features and methods.

If you are reverse engineering a file, you need to fill in fields only on the File tab (or the Source tab for Reports), shown in Figure 7-9. You use the Database and Form Option tabs (or Report Option tab for Reports) only if you reverse

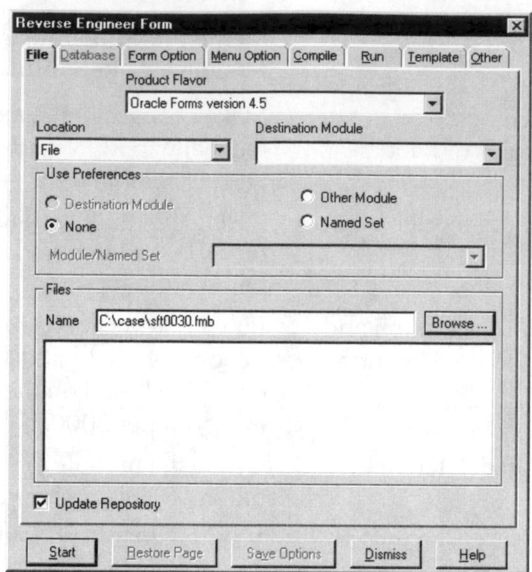

FIGURE 7-9. *Reverse Engineer Form File tab*

engineer a form stored in the database. There are no database options for Reports reverse engineering.

Note that the table and column definitions must already exist in the repository if they are used in the module. For your purposes in the storyboard process, this will not be a problem unless you added columns or tables manually to the database. If you did that, you need to run the Reverse Engineer Database utility to add these definitions to the repository. This utility is explained in Chapter 5 in the discussion of the legacy ERD. Of course, you can always manually add the columns or tables using RON.

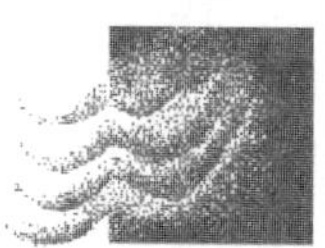

CAUTION
Be sure the definitions exist in the repository for the tables and columns used by the form or report you are reverse engineering. Otherwise the utility will fail.

You fill in the Product Flavor, Location (File or Database), and Destination Module (if you want to overwrite an existing module) fields. If you do not specify the module name, the utility will create a module with the same name as the file (without its extension). You can either type in the filename or use the Browse button to search the file system for the file. If you want to reverse engineer more than one form at a time, you can select more than one file from the Files dialog box. You do not need to fill in the Use Preferences area. You can also ignore the tabs for Menu Option, Compile, Run, Template, and Other as these are used only for forms generation.

After completing the fields in this window, you click the Start button, and the utility creates (or overwrites) the module and both summary module table usages (used for impact analysis reports) and detailed module table usages (used for module generation).

The Reverse Engineer Forms utility creates the module, module table usages, and links (if there are links). It also sets the display datatype property of columns based on the item type in the form; although it does not generate values for list items or check box items. While it does not create definitions for boilerplate decoration or prompts, it does load the column name into the prompt property of the detail column usage for the module.

The Reverse Engineer Reports utility creates module table usages, but not links, if there are links in the report data model. Also, it will not create any layout items like boilerplate or prompts nor will it create trigger code definitions for report triggers. The Reverse Engineer Reports utility will, however, create argument definitions for user parameters in the data model of the report.

Module Structure Diagrammer in Pre-Design

After you restore all modules to the repository so there is a complete and accurate set reflecting the results of your storyboard process, you need to modify the module structure to match the one you storyboarded. The module structure or network is a linking of modules in a hierarchical manner to show which module calls which other module. The module structure diagram represents the menu structure of the finished application modules. It looks much like the function hierarchy diagram you produced in the Analysis phase but has a different focus.

NOTE
The function hierarchy diagram shows a hierarchy of detail levels whereas a module structure diagram shows a hierarchy of module calling.

The Module Structure Diagrammer (MSD) is the tool you use to view and modify the module structure. It is explained fully in Chapter 9 and it is integral to the iterative Build phase as well as the Design phase. The tasks you accomplish in this diagrammer for Pre-Design include the following:

- **Accepting candidate modules** The Application Design Wizard only creates candidate modules. You need to accept these before you can generate the files for the storyboard. The Utilities menu choice Accept Candidate accomplishes that task.

- **Creating new modules** You can create new modules in the MSD for the files you added in the storyboard process that were not in the original set produced by the Application Design Wizard. This tool allows you to draw a module in the correct place in the hierarchy and fill in details regarding the type and language as well as the parameters and grants.
- **Modifying module definitions** Just as you can specify properties for new modules in the Module Structure Diagrammer, you can modify existing modules and create duplicate usages of the same module directly in this diagrammer. This refinement is easier to perform in this diagrammer than anywhere else because you can see which modules call which modules and modify properties with these relationships in mind.
- **Rearranging module calls** The strength of the MSD is that it enables you to quickly rearrange the structure of the module calls and menu system by dragging and dropping modules from one part of the diagram to another. You need to perform this activity after completing the storyboard process, where you determine the order for the modules.

Repository Object Navigator and API in the Pre-Design Phase

As you work in the Pre-Design phase, you may want to check various features of the rough modules or tables. The Repository Object Navigator provides the fastest way, in most cases, to see properties and related information on elements. You can navigate through the hierarchy and find the element you want to view and inspect and change its properties. In addition, you can group elements together and change properties of the group in one action.

One of the last steps in Pre-Design is to synchronize the mapping of system requirements to modules. Although the Application Design Wizard creates modules from functions and copies the data usages, there is no utility to copy requirements from functions to modules. You need to associate these two elements because one of the checks you perform in the Pre-Design phase examines whether all requirements have been addressed by modules in the system. If they have not, your system is not fulfilling some need, and you will need another module. Therefore, you should be sure to copy the requirements from the functions to the modules derived from those functions.

You create new repository elements in the Pre-Analysis phase with the User Extensibility feature as Chapter 4 describes. In Analysis, you fill in instances of these new elements to provide the link between requirements and functions using the Repository Object Navigator, the Matrix Diagrammer, or a utility you write using another tool such as Developer/2000.

In the Pre-Design phase, the requirements are already assigned to functions, so all you need to do is copy these assignments to the modules. Since each module definition also has a module function usage—the function or functions from which the module was derived—you can look at the corresponding function and copy the requirements assignment.

First you need to use the User Extensibility feature to create an association element to link requirements to modules as you did to link requirements to functions in the Pre-Analysis phase. Then you need to assign each requirement to one or more modules in RON or the Matrix Diagrammer. Alternatively, you can write an API procedure that looks at each function one at a time and determines the requirements associated with it. Then it finds the module or modules based on that function (using the Module Function Usage element) and assigns those modules the same requirements. This relatively simple API routine can save a lot of manual work in RON.

Conclusion

The design plan lays out how both the database and the application will move through the Design phase. It also specifies how conflicts will be resolved and how any changes in system requirements that arise during Design will be handled. In the Pre-Design phase you develop GUI standards that will guide your work in the Design and Build phases. You also create a complete prototype of the conceptual application design plan—the storyboard—containing sample tables and mockups of screen and report modules. This may sound a bit like the actual Design phase as you are making decisions about the finished application, but it is really more like a rehearsal for the Design phase. Designer/2000 allows you to quickly create design objects (tables and modules) from the work you do in Analysis and supports the rapid prototyping needed to create the storyboard that you show users.

The next phase in the life cycle is Design, where you further refine the rough-cut elements developed during Pre-Design. The next two chapters discuss the data and functional areas you work in during Design—database design and application design, respectively.

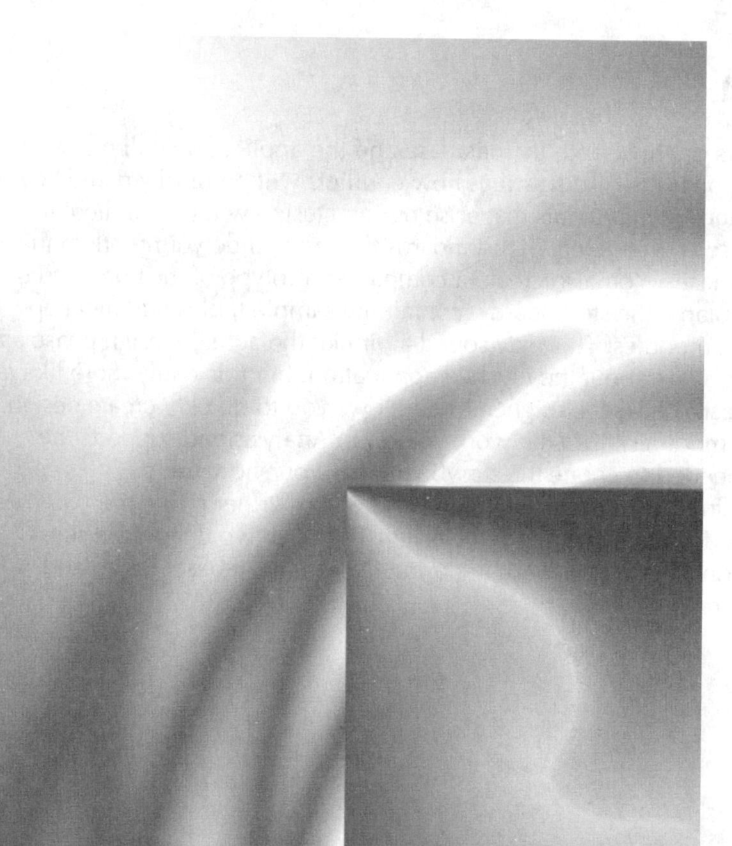

CHAPTER 8

Design: Part I–Database Design

Definition of reverse engineering: Rev Eng of the ERDs.

Physical database design is a huge topic that can easily fill a book. Thus, this chapter only briefly outlines the decisions that need to be made when designing a physical database but does not go into the details regarding how these decisions are made or the pros and cons of the various choices.

Overview of Database Design

Modifications to the underlying data structure needed to provide adequate application performance have a major effect on the database design. However, at this point in the process, the applications do not yet exist. The conceptual design of the applications exists, but the quality of the design of the database can't be tested until the actual applications are created.

You need recognize, however, that you cannot consider physical database design independent of the applications associated with it. If denormalization is taken too far, you run the risk of making your applications difficult to maintain. Conversely, if not enough denormalization is performed, applications may be difficult to write and will run very slowly. Thus, you must perform a balancing act between performance and conceptual cleanliness.

The goal of good physical database design is a product with low long-term costs of development and maintenance that delivers acceptable performance. This goal requires that standards be set for performance. The designer's job then becomes to do what is necessary to achieve desired performance while staying as close as possible to a third normal form database.

What you need to do in this phase is to make the best educated guess at the appropriate database design. Only when the database has been built and populated, and applications that operate on the database have been created, can the quality of both the database and application design be tested.

The basic strategy of database design is to map entities to tables, making adjustments for subtypes, denormalization, aggregation, and summary tables. Other considerations are the data-level system requirements. You need to ensure that these requirements are all taken into account during the design of the database. As you map entities to tables, you will also copy references to the associated data-level requirements. This procedure will maintain the link between the database and the data requirements.

This chapter emphasizes topics that frequently cause problems for novice database designers. It makes no claim to completely describe all of the issues surrounding physical database design. This chapter, then, discusses how to use Designer/2000 to design the database.

In general, you should start with a more or less clean third normal form database, add columns redundantly throughout the database, and use triggers to update the information. You may also need to build aggregation tables from the database in batch mode to make applications run in acceptable time frames.

Several steps can be taken at this point in the CADM process:

- Specify tables.
- Determine the primary keys for the tables.
- Implement dependencies.
- Assign attributes to tables.
- Implement complex business rules.
- Create redundant columns.
- Create summary and aggregation tables and views.
- Create code description tables.
- Track history.

Specifying Tables

When specifying tables for a database, you should not simply take the ERD and, with very little thought, generate a table for each entity, nor should you ignore the logical ERD as a major influence on the physical design. Either of these approaches will generate a poor database. In the first case, not only will applications probably run unacceptably slowly, but they will be difficult to maintain. In the second case, you may find it easy to build version 1 of the system, but this system will be completely inflexible and will be difficult for developers who did not work on the original system to understand. Therefore, you should try to stay as close as possible to the logical ERD in building the physical tables.

This rule does not apply, however, to the following elements:

Entity Subtypes

Subtypes, such as hourly employees and salaried employees, cannot be mapped directly to tables. The designer can physically implement the subtypes in one of the following ways:

- Using a single table with a single entity and all subtypes
- Using one table for each subtype

- Using one table for each subtype and one table for the supertype
- Generically, accommodating any number of supertypes and subtypes

Very Large Tables

Tables can become very large. It is not unusual for a main transaction detail table for an organization to contain 20 million rows. When you have tables with millions of rows, you should set up a test to see if applications will able to run at all. You may need to decrease the size of the table by partitioning it. Tables can be partitioned in several ways:

- **By date** Each year's transactions are in a separate table. The difficulty with this approach is that any applications spanning more than one year will have to access multiple tables.
- **By subject area** A company may have multiple lines of business. Transactions associated with different kinds of business can be separated into different tables. However, again, applications spanning more than one business area will need to access multiple tables.

Partitioning increases the complexity of the application and, if not done correctly, can actually hurt performance. Partitioning should be done only if all other strategies fail to generate adequate performance.

Pre-Joined Tables

Joining master-detail tables together, thus violating first or second normal form (depending upon how the join is done) was a common strategy throughout the 1980s. Experience has shown that storing pre-joined tables, in the long run, costs more than it saves. Making any modifications to the system becomes a very complex procedure. This strategy should not be used unless absolutely necessary. A preferable approach that is very similar is to use redundant columns within tables. This strategy is discussed later in this chapter.

Determining Primary Keys for the Tables

This book assumes that you know enough about design to determine appropriate unique identifiers (UIDs). However, you need to decide whether to use soft-key system-generated UIDs or logical UIDs. Under what circumstances should you use system-generated UIDs instead of logical UIDs?

Using a system-generated UID for every table can be efficient. When writing code and procedures, the foreign key constraints are always known. Columns are neat and tidy. You need not worry about foreign key constraints becoming particularly large. The best reason for using system-generated UIDs is that, otherwise, logical UIDs can be cumbersome. For example, the logical UID for a telephone call consists of the originating number, date, and time. This sequence makes sense logically but does not provide an intuitively attractive UID. The allocation of that call to one or more accounts for billing purposes requires logistical work. If you use only system-generated UIDs, these problems disappear.

There are other benefits as well. If structural modifications are made to the database that affect the UID and system-generated UIDs are not used, the changes will propagate to other tables and constraint names, possibly affecting triggers, applications, and other work occurring after the UID is generated. When you use a system-generated UID, modifications can be made that do not propagate through the system. In addition, system-generated UIDs don't require as skilled a modeller.

Under what circumstances should system-generated UIDs not be used? In code description tables (lookup tables), it doesn't make sense to use system-generated UIDs. These tables typically don't change or change infrequently (unless, for example, a new phone system is installed). The UID in this case is the code.

System-generated UIDs waste space and add unnecessary columns. You will need to put a uniqueness constraint on logical candidate keys anyway. When an insert operation is performed, the sequence generator must be called. In addition to a column, a whole additional index must be stored.

Using system-generated UIDs, it is much easier to be lazy and create a bad database design. When you use logical UIDs for tables and they propagate, you can more easily spot logical inconsistencies in the database.

Implementing Dependencies

In a logical ERD, the horizontal bar crossing a relationship line connecting entities connotes *logical dependency*. This means that the child entity has no meaning outside of the context of the parent entity. Even at the physical design level, it is important to keep in mind that entities are dependent. For example, a PO detail makes no sense outside the context of a PO; it is a part of the parent entity.

Under what circumstances should a relationship between two physical tables be made dependent? The two associated entities don't have to be logically dependent. All that is of concern is what happens with UIDs: UIDs cannot change. The child entity can never move to another entity over time. It must always be associated with the parent entity. The primary access method for the entity should be consistent with the primary key index. Dependent relationships are troublesome to use in the Design phase: the criteria for their use varies between Design and Analysis, so relationships that are not dependent in Analysis may become so in Design and vice versa.

Assigning Attributes to Tables

At the end of the application design process, you will refine the database. At this point, you should err on the side of including attributes that may later be deemed unnecessary. The first step in assigning attributes is to map all attributes from the logical model. Then look at the conceptual design of the application and add any columns used in the conceptual model that are missing in the data model. Such columns may reveal omissions in the Analysis phase. These columns may also have to be added to the logical model. Add redundant columns in a separate step, discussed later in this chapter.

At this point in the system development process, it is important to be careful about the physical characteristics of the data. A lot of work involved in attribution is easily overlooked. Addresses are a common example. In Analysis, a field simply called "address" may be specified for an entity. However, as you move into physical design, you need to worry about how addresses work in the real world and how you can search and report on them. If you want to print mailing labels easily, you should probably store each line in the address label as a separate field. For ZIP codes or postal codes, you need to consider different postal code conventions for different countries. Will you have a separate postal code column for each country with appropriate validation or will you store the postal code in a single column and then write a complex validation trigger? Some countries write addresses in an order different than that used in the U.S. Will you have an address and then an address label in a redundant column or will the application handle this situation?

Sometimes, it is important to be able to search on a geographic unit that is not normally part of the address. For example, in the U.S., the ability to display reports by county may be important in some applications. Will this be handled by storing county names with each customer or with a separate table showing which cities are in which county? For marketing purposes, do you need to be able to detect whether an address is for a single family dwelling, apartment, or office building? If you are interfacing address data with census data, such a question becomes very important.

These are some of the many questions that may arise during attribution. For each table, each column must be carefully considered to determine its physical representation in the database. Pay particular attention to addresses and phone numbers. They are some of the most frequently stored datatypes. They appear simple in the logical model but can be quite complex in the physical design.

Implementing Complex Business Rules

There are always data-related business rules that cannot be supported through the table structure and referential integrity constraints. You have to decide how to enforce such business rules. Some examples of such business rules are recursive rules. If you are implementing a hierarchical structure through a recursive relationship, you probably have a business rule that states that an individual cannot be his or her own grandfather. In other words, it is not possible for person A to manage person B, person B to manage person C, and person C to manage person A. Similarly, if you have a budget allocated to various accounts, you probably do not want the allocated amount to exceed the budget.

How can these rules be enforced? Here are five approaches:

- Rules can be enforced with a trigger on the database side by using BEFORE INSERT, BEFORE UPDATE, and BEFORE DELETE triggers.
- Rules can be enforced on the client side in the application.
- Rules can be enforced on both database and client sides.
- Rules can be enforced in batch mode by running a periodic check of the database to identify violations.
- Rules may not be enforced at all.

Of course, enforcing business rules does decrease performance. The best way to handle rules is to enforce them on both the database and client sides. That way, the database is protected against applications with errors and updates through SQL*Plus. Enforcement on the client side allows you to alert the user to violations in business rules without accessing the database. If enforcement on both sides makes performance unacceptable, use one of the other approaches.

Creating Redundant Columns

The ease of writing database triggers enables you to create redundant columns that are automatically updated by operations on the database and do not require the application to update the redundant data. There are a two different types of redundant columns worth considering:

- **Calculation columns** For example, the total of a purchase order (PO) column should be a redundant column so that calculating the total does not require summing PO details each time. You just need appropriate triggers on the PO detail column to keep the total current.

- **Key fields** These are best explained using an example. Our database has four tables: department, employee, sales, and employment history (which is an intersection table between employee and department). There is a one-to-many link between employee and sales. The only way you can find out total sales for the department for a period of time is to first determine the appropriate employees for that department for that period of time. Then you must use a correlated subquery to determine the appropriate sales for each employee. Such a query would not execute particularly quickly. If, however, you redundantly store the department UID in the sales table as the key field, then you can calculate department sales for a period of time directly.

Creating Summary and Aggregation Tables and Views

Instead of using complex joins for a specific application, another approach is to create a redundant table. Just as with redundant columns, you can use database triggers to keep the redundant table correct and consistent with the rest of the database.

Redundant aggregation tables are also useful, particularly for reporting. An example of a useful aggregation table is "Monthly Sales by Customer." For most reports, you are not interested in individual sales. You can have an aggregation table for monthly sales by customer. A handy trick when using aggregation tables is to store cumulative amounts rather than monthly amounts. That way, if you want to determine the total for a time period, rather than aggregating all records for a particular time period you need only to retrieve the first and last records for that period and subtract.

Summary and aggregation tables can be implemented as views. The advantage to a view is that it takes very little storage space in the database. Another advantage is that no increase in the overhead of transactions is required to maintain the table. A disadvantage is that performance when retrieving information from a view is much worse than when retrieving the information from an aggregated table.

Creating Code Description Tables

Some columns in a database will be associated with specific and reasonably constant lists of values: for example, male/female. Other lists of values are less stable. How can these two types of lists be handled within the database? One way is to place a check constraint on the field. This is appropriate for very small lists of values such as gender, Boolean variables (yes/no, true/false), and marital status (single/married/separated/divorced/widowed). However, check constraints are inappropriate for lists of values that change over time, such as the valid car colors for Ford Motor Corporation. There may be dozens, or even hundreds, of colors over time.

For these less-stable lists of values, you need to store the information in code description tables. You can store all code description information in one big table or store each validation list in its own table. Which of these methods is better depends upon a number of factors. Having code lookup tables in memory is ideal. The best solution is to have all code descriptions in one table if all of this data will reside in memory. If you have many code description tables or lists with many values, however, all of the data will not reside in memory. Probably the best approach is to put all code description lookups in a single table but build views on top of the table so that the physical implementation is transparent to the application. That way, the underlying architecture can be changed if necessary without affecting the application.

Tracking History

All things change over time. Sometimes it is necessary to restore a piece of information to its status at an earlier time. For example, an insurance policy (such as a house or automobile insurance policy) might be based on an address. A claim may require the company to re-create the policyholder's earlier address to validate that the policy was written correctly, and various factors associated with the policyholder may have changed. If only current data were stored, the insurance company might not be able to substantiate some claims. This issue may also apply to payroll information and any other data where there is a need to look at information at specific points in time.

Sometimes, depending upon the application, history is not important to track. For example, when an employee joins a company, the company may want to keep track of the schools he or she attended. If, after six months, it is discovered that one of the school names was misspelled, is it necessary to keep track of the correction of the misspelled name? This history is probably not important unless you are interested in keeping track of the coding accuracy of the data entry personnel. There is no general rule for determining whether history should be tracked or not. This decision needs to be made on an application-by-application basis.

There are four methods of keeping track of system history:

- **History table** This is a separate table that mirrors the actual database table except that each record has a time stamp. Each time a record is changed, the old record is copied into the history database so that it is possible to go back to a specific point and re-create the data at that point. The advantage of this method is that if history needs to be tracked on only a subset of items, the history table need contain only the columns of interest. The disadvantage is that this history table needs to be joined to the original table, so if the history table is used frequently, it will slow down performance.

- **Transaction log table** Anything that occurs that is worth keeping track of is put into a transaction log table or tables. The advantage of this method is that if you are interested only in current data, it is an easy way to keep track of all historical data without slowing down performance. However, since this table is not connected to anything, it is much more difficult to go back and re-create the earlier data. This method is appropriate only for systems with a very infrequent need to access historical data.
- **Periodic backup of the database** This approach is one sure way of keeping track of historical data. However, it requires restoring the backup copy every time historical data is queried. It is a simple but very inefficient method.
- **Combined history and current status table** Historical and current data can both be stored in the same table. Any time a change is made to a relevant field, a snapshot is made of the whole record, and it is stored in the same table. A start date and end date are added to the underlying table, and all data is stored in the same place. This method is simple to use. It is easy to put a single table view on top of that table to show only records that are current. The disadvantage is that if the combined table is large or particularly volatile, it can cause system performance to degrade.

DBA Issues: Capacity Planning, Snapshots, and Replication

You won't know exactly how large the tables are going to be until legacy system data migration is complete. However, you can at least come up with a relatively good estimate of table size to determine whether you need to partition tables. You should be able to estimate the approximate number of rows in each table and how fast the table will grow. For each column in the table, you can make an educated guess regarding its size by looking at the legacy data and at how often a specific field is used. For VARCHAR2 fields, you can estimate the average length. This information will give DBAs the information necessary to determine tablespaces and physical locations.

Oracle can support very complex application environments. Using a distributed database environment implemented through Snapshots and Replication, it can support worldwide applications which would otherwise be impossible.

Modifications for Smaller Systems

Modifications to the database design process must be made for smaller systems. However, there are different criteria for determining just what constitutes a smaller system in database design than in earlier phases. A large system in earlier phases was one with a large number of entities and applications. What makes database design complex is the size of the tables and, to some extent, the number of users. Database design becomes more complex when the overall amount of data increases and when individual tables are very large. Also, database design is complicated by volatile data (that is, hundreds of transactions happening every second). If none of the tables have more than 100,000 records, then you can probably use a third normal form database.

For these smaller systems, you will not need summary and aggregation tables and views. These items are generated to facilitate performance and are relatively unimportant in a small system. The bigger the tables, the higher their transaction load and the greater the extent of denormalization required to achieve adequate application performance.

When Is Database Design Complete?

Database design will not really be complete at the end of this phase. As you design applications, you will make modifications and refinements to the database. Therefore, you do not need to be particularly concerned about making the database design perfect at this point. You do need to be sure that every field on every screen in the conceptual application design created in the Pre-Design phase is in the database. Similarly, you need to be sure that all attributes in the logical model correspond to columns in the physical tables. You will, of course, add views and summary and aggregation tables where appropriate; but these decisions can be modified during application design. It is sufficient that the senior development team members approve the database design.

The Design Phase in Designer/2000: Database Design

The main objective of the database design part of the Design phase is to refine the definitions for all database objects needed in the system. The Design phase consists of two main tasks: database design and application design. You need to have a good start on the database design before you can begin the application design because the modules you work on in the application design part rely on the tables you defined in the database design part. This is an iterative process, though, so you will be defining some tables as you define modules. Your goal should be to have as complete a set of table definitions as possible before you start the application design part of this phase. Designer/2000 provides support for this work in its diagrammers and utilities, as Table 8-1 shows.

Note that this section makes no mention of the Database Design Wizard, although its name implies that it might be useful in this phase. The Pre-Design phase uses it extensively to create the tables needed for the storyboard process. However, you may find it useful to refine entities and rerun this utility for a certain subset of tables after you gain more information on the database in the Design phase.

As mentioned for other phases, the following discussion of Designer/2000 tools assumes that you have reviewed the notes on the common interface for Designer/2000 in Chapter 2. In addition, be sure you are comfortable with the organization and access methods for information in the online help system as this is the best facility to use when you have a question about an operation while using the tools.

Activity or Deliverable	Designer/2000 Tool
Refined table design (with views and snapshots)	Data Diagrammer or RON
Denormalization of data structures	Data Diagrammer or RON
Summary, journal, and code tables	Data Diagrammer or RON
Integrate existing tables not incorporated during Pre-Design	Reverse Engineer Database utility
Synchronize columns belonging to domains	Update Columns in Domains utility
Code for denormalization (aggregates and summary columns or tables)	Module Logic Navigator
Document the database design	Repository Reports

TABLE 8-1. *Deliverables and Designer/2000 Tools in the Design Phase: Database Design*

Data Diagrammer

In the database design part of the Design phase, you refine, revise, and replace the tables you created for the storyboard process. The process of integrating the storyboarded tables into the repository occurs in Pre-Design, so in the Design phase you start with a rough draft of the table definitions already in the repository. The activities you perform on these definitions include checking the primary and foreign key relationships, denormalizing the tables for performance or other reasons, and creating definitions for as many views and snapshots as you know about. The Build phase may also include creation of more views and snapshots as needs arise in the application.

This is an appropriate phase in which to specify the database triggers you know about. These triggers consist of PL/SQL code that runs automatically when the table is accessed with INSERT, UPDATE, or DELETE. They are a potential place to locate the code that supplies derivation or summarization values which may result from your denormalization process. For example, you might want an AFTER INSERT, UPDATE, or DELETE statement-level trigger on an ORDER_ITEM table that sums the line totals and updates the GRAND_TOTAL column in the ORDER table. Although you write and debug program code in the Build phase, you can define triggers as well as some of their functionality in the Design phase.

In addition, you should examine each table and column definition and fill in as many details as possible about how each will be displayed in the application modules. The more complete you are in this phase, the less frequently you will have to pause during the application design part of the Design phase or the Build phase to fill in missing details. Also, if you fill in the table and column definitions as completely as possible in the Design phase, whenever the tables are used in modules, the table usage will inherit some characteristics of the table definition. Therefore, you can make choices at this point about the common way the tables will be viewed or used. For example, suppose you have a table definition that is used in four modules. If you complete the display properties of the table definition, all four modules will use those same properties. Of course, you can override the table settings and provide more details on the module level, but the table-level properties will give you a good set of defaults and reduce the amount of customization needed for the modules.

The Data Diagrammer (DD), also called the Data Schema Diagrammer, allows you to diagram *relations*—tables, views, and snapshots—with their relationships. You can show the columns, keys, and databases to which the relations belong. This tool has functionality that parallels that of the ER Diagrammer, which is used in the Analysis phase. Although the symbol set is slightly different, both tools model data (logical or physical), show overall containers for details (entities or tables), display the details of those containers (attributes or columns), and diagram the relationships between containers (relationships or foreign keys). In fact, an entity relationship diagram and a data schema diagram may display the exact same data elements but at different stages of CADM. The logical and physical models are often different, and Designer/2000 provides the DD so you can represent the physical design model and still keep the logical analysis model intact. Figure 8-1 shows a DD session.

Basic Techniques

The Data Diagrammer closely parallels the ER Diagrammer, so that many of the techniques are the same. Opening a diagram and creating a new diagram are accomplished the same way as in the other diagrammers, through the File menu or toolbar buttons. As in the ER Diagrammer, when you start a new diagram, a blank drawing area opens up. You can place any existing tables or draw new tables in this area. Drawing a new table creates a table definition in the repository. Any subset of tables can appear in any given drawing, and you can diagram a particular table in more than one drawing.

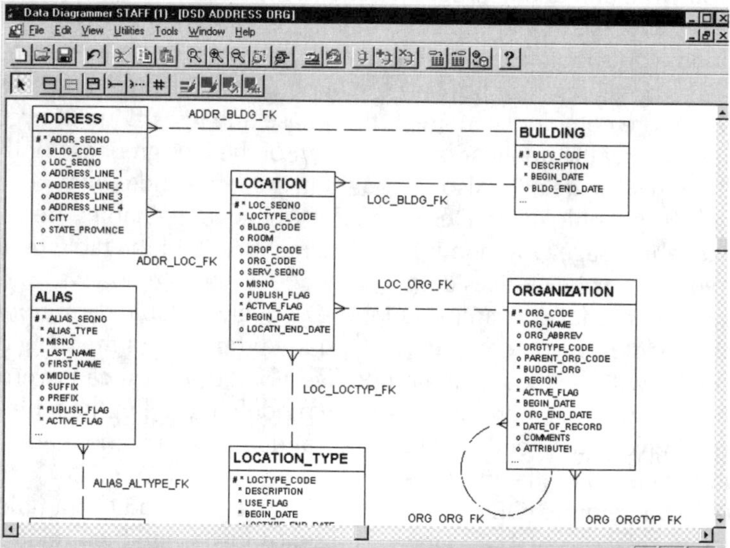

FIGURE 8-1. *Data Diagrammer session*

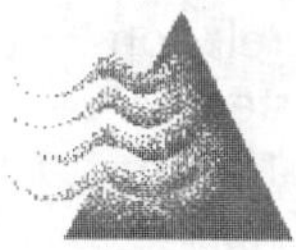

TIP
In this and any other Designer/2000 diagrammer, you usually should maximize both the MDI (outer) window and the drawing window as soon as you open a diagram or create a new diagram. This gives you the most drawing surface, and you will not need to scroll up and down or left and right as often. Also, reducing the view with **View→Zoom Out** will give you a larger view of the diagram. You can always zoom in when you need to, but you can perform most operations more efficiently when you can see more of the drawing area.

Including Existing Tables You place existing tables on the drawing by selecting **Edit→Include** from the menu. The Include Tables/Views/Snapshots window has a few more fields than the corresponding one in the ER Diagrammer, as Figure 8-2 shows.

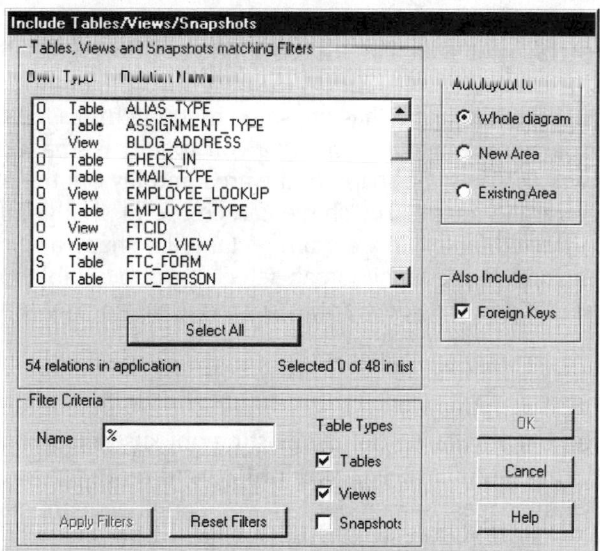

FIGURE 8-2. *Include Tables/Views/Snapshots window*

The list that appears in the top-left portion of this window shows the relation name and type (table, view, or snapshot) and whether the application system owns or shares it. The Filter Criteria area lets you change the contents of the list. After choosing the types and entering name criteria in this area, you press the Apply Filters button, and the list changes to reflect these filter entries. As with the ER Diagrammer, you can also specify whether or not you want to include the relationships and which area you want the diagrammer to use to lay out the new objects (Whole diagram, New Area, or Existing Area).

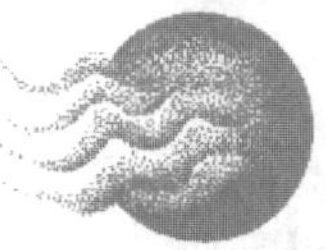

NOTE
The Data Diagrammer is an ER Diagrammer for tables. It represents the physical (design) data model, which may differ from the logical data model you diagram with the ER Diagrammer.

The **Edit→Preferences** menu item lets you modify the minimum table box size in cells and specify the size of each cell. Nevertheless, when you include an existing table, Designer/2000 will ignore these settings and make the boxes for each table large enough to hold the column names (whether or not they are shown). You can resize these, of course, when they are placed on the screen.

Using Autolayouts As with the ER Diagrammer, you can use the Autolayout feature after Designer/2000 places objects to see if one of the random arrangements is closer to your needs. Autolayout has the same menu items as the ER Diagrammer for a new area or same area layout. If the area you specify is smaller than the objects, the DD will use only the shape of the area and lay out the objects in an area large enough for them to fit. The shape can be useful, though, if you want all the tables, or selected tables, in a certain rectangular shape and in a particular part of the drawing area. Note that you can select a group of tables and apply Autolayout to just that group if you want. Also, the Preferences window (CTRL-F) lets you display the area you are using for the autolayout.

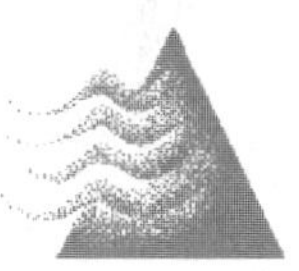

TIP
After initially laying out the existing objects, select **Utilities→Minimise Number of Pages** to reduce the number of blank pages. Remember that you can change the page orientation in the **File→Print Setup** dialog box at any time if you prefer to use landscape mode.

When you move objects around on the diagram, particularly relationship lines, it is helpful to turn on grid snap in the Preferences window, shown in Figure 8-3. This will help you line up objects more easily.

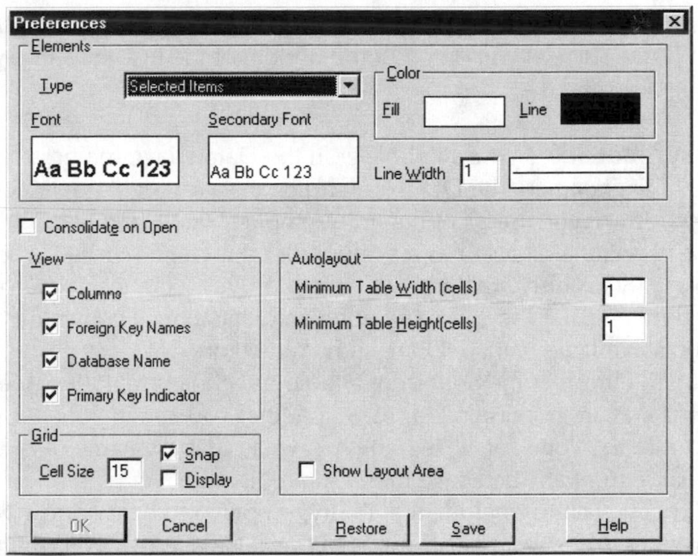

FIGURE 8-3. *Preferences window*

Drawing Objects You draw objects in the Data Diagrammer the same way as in other diagrammers: click the appropriate button and draw the element in the drawing area. The choice of what tables to put in what drawings is up to you; however, for one diagram, you might want to select a subset of tables that represent a single functional area. You can expand the drawing to cover more pages by dragging a table outside the page boundaries, thus creating a new page. In this way, you can represent your entire system in one diagram with as many pages as needed. Changing the layout of a large diagram is not a trivial matter, however, so the subset approach may be necessary.

You can change the font of particular objects, which may be helpful if you want to reduce the size of the table boxes. Select the tables you want to change and press CTRL-F or select **Edit→Preferences** from the menu. You can also change the font and color of the elements selected in this window, or you can change them by clicking the visual attribute buttons on the toolbar.

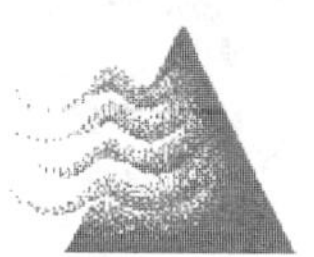

TIP
To move a pig's ear (self-referencing) relationship, click it to select it and move the whole line by clicking the middle of the arc (not the end). You can drop it close to a corner, and the relationship line will span the two adjacent sides.

You can draw a dog-leg (angled) relationship line by clicking the relationship and holding down SHIFT as you drag out the middle of the line the same way as in the other diagrammers.

Using the Symbol Set The symbol set in the Data Diagrammer is similar to that of the ER Diagrammer. The DD uses hard boxes (with right-angle corners) instead of soft boxes, and it uses only two types of foreign key relationships: mandatory and optional. It also has a symbol for an arc relationship, which indicates mutually exclusive columns in the table. This relationship is not implemented in the database code, but you can create check constraints to enforce it. The symbols available in the DD are shown in Figure 8-4.

Note that an ellipsis at the bottom of a table box means that the table contains more columns that are not displayed. Also note that you can include tables that are assigned to more than one database (which have a database name of ALL) and display any table from any database in the same diagram.

Other drawing features include the ability to open another window that contains the same diagram by choosing **Window→New Window** from the menu.

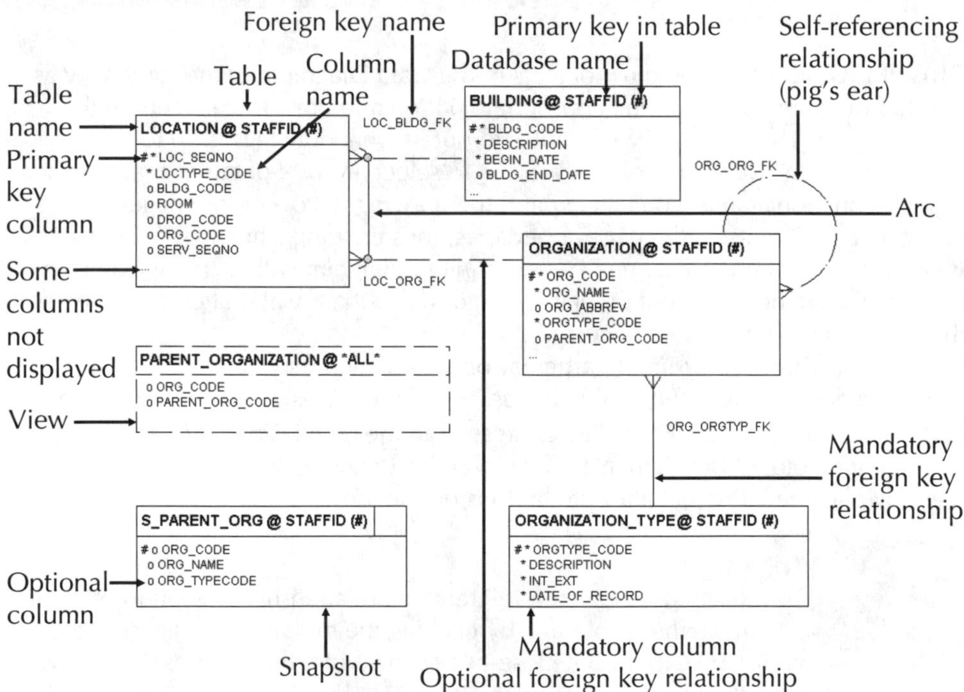

FIGURE 8-4. *Data Diagrammer symbols*

You can open many diagrams at the same time and shift between them by using the Window menu or pressing CTRL-F6. To close extra windows, you choose Close from the drawing window menu in the top-left corner of the window frame.

Naming Elements One refinement step you perform in the Design phase is to check the names of all data elements to be sure they match your naming conventions. One decision you made early in the life cycle was whether or not to use plurals for table names. The table name derives from the entity plural name, so you can force a table name to be singular in the Analysis phase by defining the Plural Name property for the entity with a singular word. The Database Design Wizard (DDW) uses the entity plural name as the table name. If you decide to use plural names for tables, you can accept the default entity plural name, and the table name will be plural when DDW creates its definition.

Whatever system you use, it is important to be consistent, so if you add a new table after the DDW is done, use your naming standard. One of the most common standards is to use descriptive but short names for columns. This name may or may not be the same as the attribute name, but there will be less confusion if the names of attributes and columns are similar. Remember that rules apply to column names that do not apply to attributes. For example, column names may not start with a number and must consist of one word of 30 characters or less (in an Oracle database).

Another decision you make when running the DDW is whether or not you want a column name prefix. The DDW can create column names with the entity short name as a prefix. The benefit of this approach is that each column in the final database will have a unique name that indicates the table it is in. The drawback is that foreign key and primary key names will be different, and the means for joining tables will not be as obvious. As with the plural table names, if you decide to use the column prefix, be consistent when you add columns to tables after the DDW runs. Therefore, if you use the column prefix, use it everywhere.

NOTE
You can create table names using reserved Oracle words, but the TABLE CREATE script will fail when you run it. You can check for these names by using the Invalid Database Objects Quality Control report in the Database Design group of Repository Reports.

The DDW creates foreign key columns and foreign key constraints for relationships, and it names the column and key based on the short name of the entity. For example, suppose there is a relationship between the EMPLOYEE entity (short name: EMP) and the DEPARTMENT entity (short name: DEPT) that states that an employee must belong to one and only one department and a department may be composed of one or more employees. The DDW will create a foreign key column from the relationship and name it either DEPTNO or DEPT_DEPTNO, depending on whether the setting of the Prefix Foreign Key Columns option on the Option tab is unchecked or checked, respectively. The foreign key constraint will have a name of EMP_DEPT_FK to show that it is in the EMPLOYEE table and references the DEPARTMENT table.

The other task that the DDW performs is to create foreign key indexes that are named by adding the suffix _I to the foreign key name. The primary key constraints are named with the table alias (entity short name) with a _PK suffix. If you use different naming standards or need additional keys or indexes, you can change the names in the table properties window as described next. If you can adjust to the Designer/2000 naming convention, though, you will not need to rename these elements.

Modifying Properties All properties for the diagrammed objects in the Data Diagrammer are available in the Edit Table properties window, shown in Figure 8-5.

You can display this window by double-clicking the table in the diagram, choosing **Edit→Element→Table/View/Snapshot** from the menu, or selecting the table and choosing **Edit→Properties**. Through the **Edit→Element** menu choice, you can also view and modify triggers, foreign keys, and domains, but there is no diagrammatic symbol for triggers and domains.

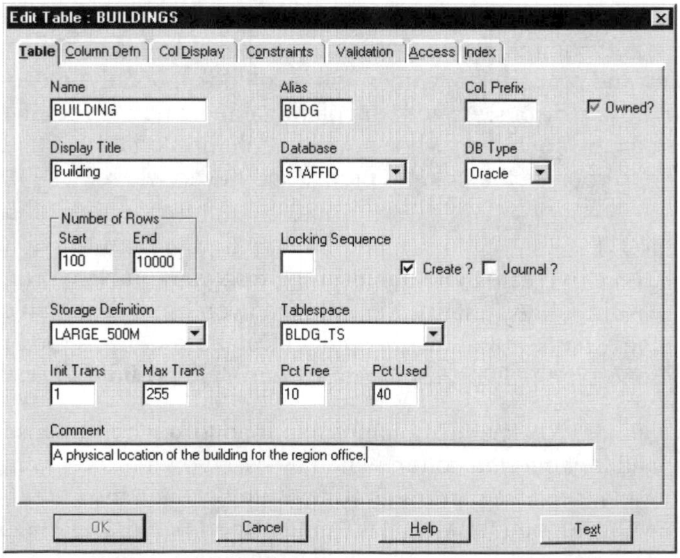

FIGURE 8-5. *Edit Table properties window*

A separate properties window, Edit Foreign Key, is available for foreign keys by choosing **Edit→Element→Foreign Key** from the menu, by double-clicking the foreign key symbol, or by choosing **Edit→Properties** after selecting the foreign key symbol. However, the foreign key definitions also appear in the Edit Table properties window. Therefore, all foreign keys, indexes, columns, and table access rights, as well as the primary key information, appear in the Edit Table properties window. The window itself has a number of tabs to organize the properties. Note that a Text button is visible on all tabs. This button opens a dialog window for entering text (notes, descriptions, and derivation expressions) for the active object.

The Edit Table window includes the following tabs:

- **Table** This tab contains settings that apply generally to the table such as the storage definitions and volume information, as Figure 8-5 shows. Note that storage definitions and tablespaces are separate repository elements that you need to define using RON before you can assign them to the table. These definitions will be used when you generate the server code with the Server Generator. The Comment field designates the text for the COMMENT ON statement that the Server Generator creates when it produces a TABLE CREATE statement.

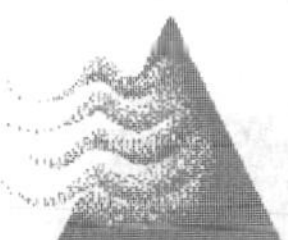

TIP

If you check the Journal property on the Table Edit window, running the Server Generator for this table creates a TABLE CREATE statement for an additional table, called a *journal table,* that holds all historical information regarding who changed a row in the table and what values changed. Basically, the journal table is a duplicate of the main table that has no repository definition but stores the values that all columns contained before a DML operation occurred. This table provides an easy way to perform table-level auditing. The Forms Generator creates the code to support this table based on the generator preferences: JNNTMD, JNNTRQ JNSSID, and WHTIME.

- **Column Defn** You can assign properties to columns and define extra columns on this tab. An expanded view of this tab is shown in the following illustration. The specific properties are discussed in the section "Column Properties" later in this chapter.

Table | Column Defn | Col Display | Constraints | Validation | Access | Index

Column Name	Seq	Domain	Datatype	Avg Len	Max Len	Dec P	Opt	Init Vol	Final Vol	Uppercase	Create?	Default Value	Oracle Sequence
BLDG_CODE	1	BLDG CODE	Char	6	6		☐	100	100	☐	☑		BLDG_CODE_S
DESCRIPTION	2	DESC60	Varchar2		60		☐	100	100	☐	☒		

- **Col Display** Part of the column definition includes details regarding how the column is used in modules. This tab contains information on the display characteristics: display length and height, column ordering sequence (which could be different than the column order for the DDL statement), format, prompt, hint, and other properties. These are discussed in more detail in the section "Display Properties."
- **Constraints** The table definition includes details on all constraints, as the Server Generator will create them along with the table DDL statements. Figure 8-6 shows the Constraints tab, which has subtabs for different types of constraints: Primary, Foreign, Unique, and Check. The specific properties are discussed in the section "Constraint Properties."
- **Validation** Each column in the table can have a set of valid values associated with it on this tab or on the domain attached to this. The Server Generator will create column check constraints to enforce the values when it creates the DDL script for the table. You cannot specify the names of these constraints, however, so you may want use the Check subtab of the Constraints tab to define table check constraints instead. Another set of properties on this tab relates to denormalization and allows you to specify the table and column from which this column is derived. This allows you to document your normalization decisions.
- **Access** Table definitions can have access privileges associated with them. The Access tab is where you make these assignments to existing database user and group (database role) definitions that you create in RON. The Server Generator will create the user and role statements to set up the users and roles (called User Grants and Role Grants in the Server Generator). If you assign access rights on this tab, the Server Generator can also create the grant statements for the roles and users you specify who have rights to this table.
- **Index** In Oracle7 databases, creating the primary key constraint automatically creates a unique index. If you used the Database Design Wizard to create a table from an entity, indexes will be created automatically for all foreign keys which is recommended for Oracle databases. These indexes will appear on this tab, though the primary key indexes will not because specifications for such items as the tablespace and storage definition are on the Primary subtab of the Constraints tab.

Creating Triggers The database trigger is another type of object you can define in the DD. The **Edit→Create→Trigger** menu choice displays the Create Trigger window shown in Figure 8-7. You can modify an existing trigger by choosing

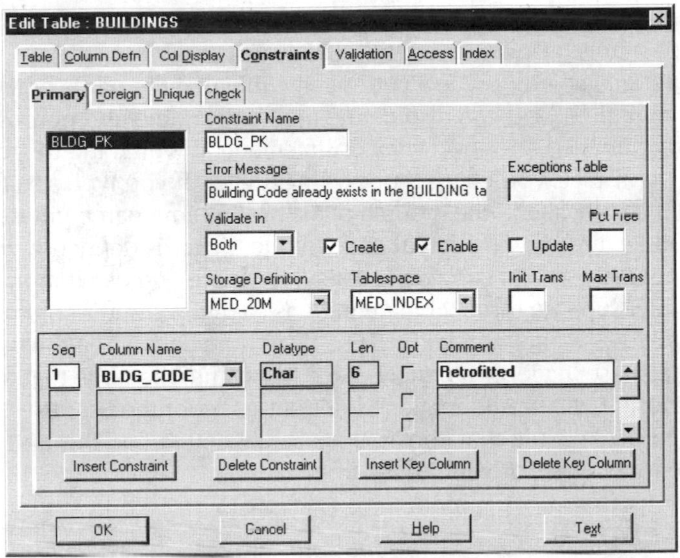

FIGURE 8-6. *Constraints tab of the Edit Table window*

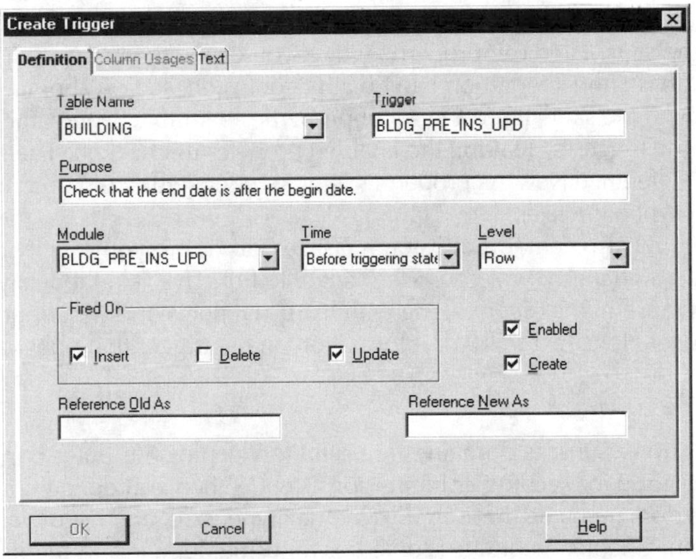

Create Trigger
Definition
Column Usages
Text
Table Name
BUILDING
Trigger
BLDG_PRE_INS_UPD
Purpose
Check that the end date is after the begin date.
Module
BLDG_PRE_INS_UPD
Time
Before triggering state
Level
Row
Fired On
Insert
Delete
Update
Enabled
Create
Reference Old As
Reference New As
OK
Cancel
Help

FIGURE 8-7. *Create Trigger window*

Edit→Element→Trigger from the menu, and the same window will appear with a disabled Table Name property and a title of Edit Trigger.

The Create Trigger window lets you specify (initially) the name of the table for which this trigger fires. You can also define the trigger name and purpose as well as the time (before or after) and level (row or statement) at which the trigger occurs. The Module poplist lets you choose an existing trigger. If you type a trigger name, the DD automatically fills in the module name as the same name unless you have defined a module already. The actual code for the trigger is defined in the module definition properties, so you can create a single module and use it in many triggers.

For example, suppose three table definitions each have audit columns such as UPDATED_BY (user name) and UPDATED_DATE (the date when the user updated the row). A database trigger is a perfect place to execute the code that fills these columns because it will fire no matter what front-end tool the user uses. Therefore, you can create one module that contains the actual code to do this and attach this same module to a trigger for each of the three tables.

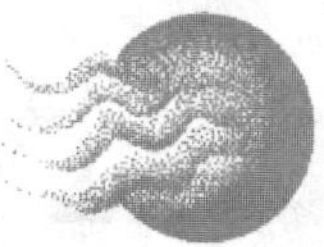

NOTE

When you press the OK button, the Create Trigger window will keep prompting you to create another trigger definition until you click the Cancel button.

The other fields in this window let you specify when the trigger fires. Note that you can have more than one trigger per table. If multiple triggers for the same table have the same Fired On property, which you can actually create in an Oracle7 database, the interaction can be a bit confusing, so you should use only one trigger with the same Fired On set of properties per table. You can delay the enabling of the trigger by leaving the Enabled property unchecked. The Reference Old As and Reference New As properties let you redefine the :old and :new default bind syntax prefixes.

This window also contains a Column Usages tab where you specify the columns that, if changed, will cause the trigger to fire. The Text tab lets you define the WHEN clause of the trigger along with the usual notes and description. It also contains a User Help Text field for information on the trigger that you want to store online.

Using Domains Just as domains are useful for keeping attributes consistent, they are also good for keeping columns consistent. When you define columns, you can attach a domain name that supplies the datatype, size, and list of valid values to the column. Chapter 6 contains some tips for using domains, in the discussion of the ER Diagrammer. One tip is to use domains to set the properties for all columns. This approach will make changing the column definitions easier because you can change a domain and then run the utility as described here to synchronize all columns that have that domain attached to the new property values.

You can create and edit domains in RON or the DD by choosing **Edit→Element→Domain** from the menu. The following illustration shows an expanded view of the Definition tab of the Edit Domains window. The DataType Name field is for a C++ datatype that corresponds to this domain, if any.

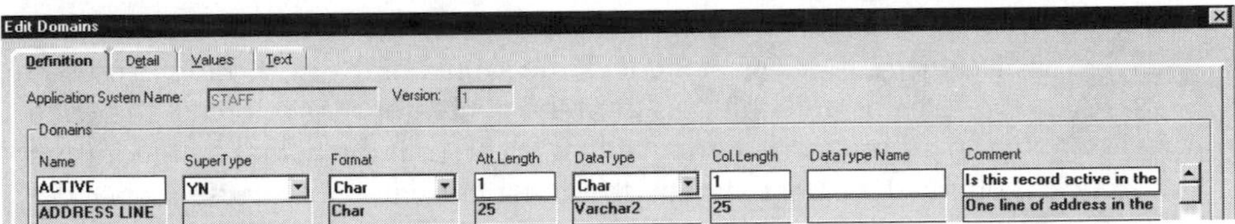

Notice that this window also has a Detail tab, where you can specify more properties for one domain at a time; a Values tab, which provides a list of valid values for each domain; and a Text tab, where you can specify the standard description and notes.

Adding Derivation Expressions The text area of the Edit Domains window (and of the Column Defn tab in the Edit Table window) allows you to add a derivation expression that provides a source value to the columns based on it. Domain derivation expressions cascade into all columns based on the domains unless those columns have their own derivation expressions. For example, in the BUILDINGS table, if you want to calculate the first day of the next month from BEGIN_DATE and place that value in BLDG_END_DATE, you define a derivation expression for BLDG_END_DATE (or for the domain on which it is based) as follows:

```
LAST_DAY(BEGIN_DATE) + 1
```

If you use this table in a form, the Forms Generator will generate the procedure shown in the following illustration called from a WHEN-VALIDATE-ITEM trigger on the BEGIN_DATE item.

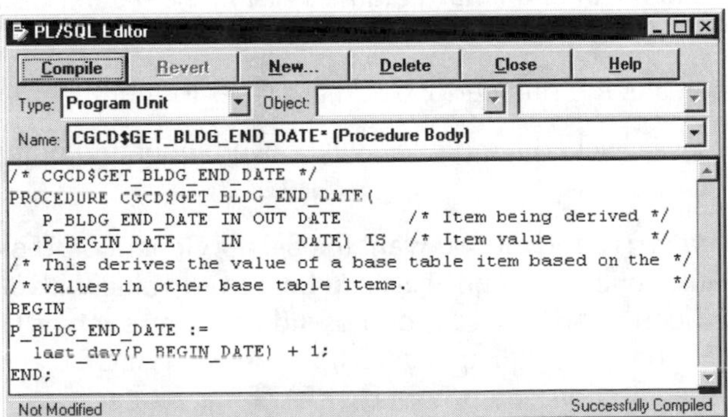

If the derivation expression is a reference to a stored function or forms built-in procedure, you can precede the function call with the word "COMPLEX:". Refer to the help system topic "COMPLEX: Expressions" in the Forms Generator help system for more information on this feature.

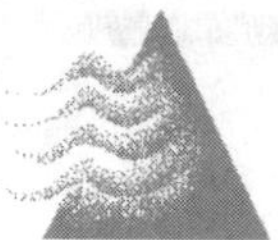

TIP

Designer/2000 does not check the syntax of the derivation expression for domains and columns until the generator runs to create the code. If the expression is wrong at that point, or if the actual table for the column does not exist yet, the generator will fail because it checks the expression as a valid column expression in a SELECT statement. In the BLDG_END_DATE example, the generator creates the statement `SELECT LAST_DAY(END_DATE) + 1 FROM BUILDINGS`. If the database rejects this as a valid statement, the generator deems it to be invalid.

Column Properties

It is important to examine and correct the detailed column properties in the Edit Table window because module data usages are based on the table and column definitions by default. Therefore, if you complete the column definitions as much as possible in this area, you will have less to do when you define data usages for the module. Also, some properties on the table and column definition do not appear in the module table and column usage definition. The major properties are as follows:

- *Data Type* is the database datatype that the Server Generator uses.
- *Max Len* is the width of the column in the database.
- *Opt* designates whether the column is optional or not. A check mark means it may contain a null value.
- *Domain* assigns the domain name to the column.
- *Avg Len* and *Initial* and *Final Volume* assist in the database sizing procedure later in the Build phase.
- *Dec P* indicates the number of decimal places for numbers.
- *Uppercase* is checked if modules will convert input and output to be uppercase.
- *Default Value* is handy if you want the Server Generator to create a default value clause for the column. This can be a fixed value with a matching datatype, such as ABC or 123, or a pseudo-column such as USER or SYSDATE. The value will appear as a DEFAULT VALUE clause in the column specification of the TABLE CREATE statement.

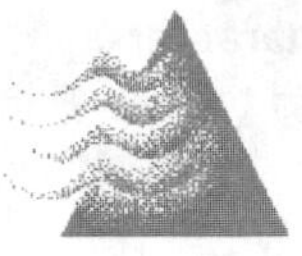

TIP
Although you can use a default value of USER in a character column (to automatically enter the name of the user who created the record), the DDL generated will contain quotation marks around the word USER: for example, `CREATED_BY VARCHAR2(30) DEFAULT 'USER'`. You will need to remove the quotation marks before running the DDL against the database. Another way to specify the default value of USER is to use the value: `''||USER||''` which will use the actual pseudo-column USER concatenated with null strings. This is an extra bit of typing but will have the correct result.

- *Oracle Sequence* will create code in the modules to assign a number from a sequence database object. You need to define the sequence first in RON before you can use it here.
- *Create* is checked if you want to include this column in the DDL TABLE CREATE script.
- *Seq* is the sequence in which the columns will be created in the TABLE CREATE script.

Note that this order is important for efficient use of Oracle database blocks. A common practice is to put the primary key columns first in the list, then the unique key columns, then other mandatory (NOT NULL) columns, and last, optional columns. You can determine your own ordering system, but try to keep optional columns at the end. You can specify a different order for the display of the columns on the Col Display tab.

Display Properties In addition to the column properties, which apply mostly to the table itself, you also define properties that the module uses by default to specify how the column is displayed. Here are brief descriptions of each of the display properties as they appear on the Col Display tab of the Edit Table window:

- *Display* specifies whether or not this column is displayed in the module. The table may generate key or column values that the user does not need to see, and you can turn this property off for those or other columns. Surrogate primary keys that the ADW creates for tables with no primary keys are not displayed by default.
- *Disp Datatype* lets you determine the GUI control or datatype used to show the column value. For example, you can specify an item as a combo box, check box, button, radio group, VBX control, OLE container, and so on.

- *Disp Len* specifies the length (width) of the generated item in characters. The generator determines the actual width based on the font and the average width of a character in that font.
- *Disp Ht* specifies the height of the generated item in characters. The generator determines the actual height the same way it does the length.
- *Disp Seq* specifies the order in which the items will appear in the module. Note that this order may be different from the order in which the columns are arranged in the table. There is no need to assign a display sequence number to a nondisplayed column.
- *Format* lets you enter a format mask for number or date columns to modify the way the value appears.
- *Highlighting* contains a value indicating the type of highlighting used in this column in a report. Note that this must be a valid Reports highlighting attribute.
- *Prompt* specifies the item prompt in a form or the column label in a report.
- *Hint* specifies the text that appears in the hint line in a form. By default, the DDW assigns the comment on the attribute from which this column is derived.
- *Order Seq* is used only if this column contributes to the sort order or default ORDER BY clause for the table used in the module. For example, if the table is ordered by LastName as the first sort key and then FirstName as the second sort key, the LastName column will have 1 as its Order Seq property, and the FirstName will have 2 as its property.
- *Sort Order* is either Ascending or Descending if Order Seq is specified for this column. If Order Seq is not specified for the column, this property is meaningless.
- *Descriptor Seq* specifies the order in which columns are used for this table's *descriptor.* A descriptor describes a row in the table to the user. This feature is handy if you use a number or code as the primary key to identify the row. Instead of showing this number, you can define another column or set of columns as the descriptor. Descriptors are used by the module to form table lookup usages. Placing a number in this column signifies not only the order of the column in the descriptor, but that the column is actually used in the descriptor.

- *Autogen Type* facilitates table-level auditing. For example, you can define a column called USER_CREATED and give it an Autogen property value of Created By. The generators will create the code to load the values into columns at the proper time. Other Autogen property values are Date Created, Date Modified, and Modified By.

  Another Autogen Type value is Seq in Parent, which assigns the next unique sequence number within the same primary key (parent). For example, suppose you have an ORDER table that has a primary key of ORDERNO. You also have an ORDER_ITEM table that has a primary key of ORDERNO and LINENO. If you define LINENO with an Autogen Type property of Seq in Parent, the generator will create the code needed to create a unique number for this column within the same ORDERNO value (parent). Thus, order number 1 might have line number 1, 2, and 3, while order number 2 might have line number 1 and 2. Designer/2000 will produce the code to create a new sequential line number for each new line item record.

Many of these properties also appear on the detailed column usage for the module. You define them for the table so the module will take its defaults from these settings. Therefore, if you set properties in a certain way for a certain column in all (or most modules), you can set these in the table usage definition so you will not need to set them for each module that uses this column. This procedure can save much time and effort and allow you to implement standards on the column level.

NOTE
Many of these properties have a dramatic affect on the generated code. For example, if you forget to define prompts for the column display property and generate a form module from the definition, the form will appear with field items but no labels for the items.

Constraint Properties

The properties for each type of constraint—primary, foreign, unique, and check—differ slightly from one another, but all require that you specify the name of the constraint in the database; Create if you want to include this constraint with the table DDL statement, and Validate In to indicate where you want the constraint enforced. You also define the error message that appears if the constraint rules are violated; Server validation places the DDL code in the database, Client validation places the code in each module, and Both places the validation code in both places. Another common property is Enable, which specifies whether the constraint is active when you first create it.

When you define a check constraint, use the text area's When/Validation Condition to hold the constraint text. For example, When/Validation Condition text on the BLDG_TYPE column might be as follows:

```
BLDG_TYPE IN ('HRISE', 'RANCH', 'CABIN')
```

Any statement that you would place in an ALTER TABLE ADD CONSTRAINT statement is valid for this type of text when you define check constraints.

Primary key constraints have properties for specifying storage parameters and the tablespace. Foreign keys can be defined as mandatory (a value is required in the foreign key column) or transferable (you can update the foreign key value when running an application module; this will not translate to server code, but to client code).

Other constraint properties are well documented in the help system and easily understood if you know the possible variations and capabilities of the different types of constraints.

Update Columns in a Domain Utility

Just as you used a utility in the Analysis phase to update attribute properties from domains that had changed, you can update columns in domains. This utility is available on the RON Utilities menu and is called Update Columns in a Domain. If you change properties for a domain, you can run this utility to synchronize column properties for columns based on that domain. This utility works the same way as its counterpart does for attributes. You select the domain or domains whose columns you want to update in RON. Then you choose the utility from the Utilities menu, and the utility will run without displaying any other dialog windows. You can then requery the Tables node to synchronize the Object Navigator window with the repository.

You should perform this operation before running the Server Generator and also before assigning tables and columns to modules. This operation will ensure that the definitions you use conform to the latest version of the domains.

Soft LOVs

The column and domain windows have a property called Soft LOV. If you check this box, Designer/2000 will create code in the module where this table is used to validate and provide a list of values from a reference table. You need to run a utility from the RON menu to create this table by choosing **Utilities→Generate Reference Tables→Update reference code tables**. This will create and load the table (called CG_REF_CODES by default) with the values from column and domain valid value definitions. The Module Data Diagrammer also includes this utility on its Utilities menu.

View and Snapshot Definitions

The discussion thus far has focused on table definitions. Snapshots and views have similar properties, and the DD treats them similarly. You can even define foreign key constraints between views (or between views and tables) that will not be implemented in the database but will document a relationship between the definitions. You can specify the enforcement of this type of foreign key constraint on the client side, and Designer/2000 will create validation code in the module it generates. You can also create a foreign key between relations in different databases, but again, the database will not support that code, and you will need to specify client-side validation or enforcement of the foreign key.

The main differences among views, snapshots, and tables are on the first tab of the Edit window. Figure 8-8 shows the first tab of the Edit View window.

Since a view is based on another table or tables, you also need to define the relation (table or view or snapshot) this view is based on. The Base Relations tab lets you enter the objects that this view is based on. The Base Cols tab allows you to specify, for each column in the view, the source column in the base table for each view column. Note that you have to define the base tables first so that there are base columns to choose from. If the column is based on an expression

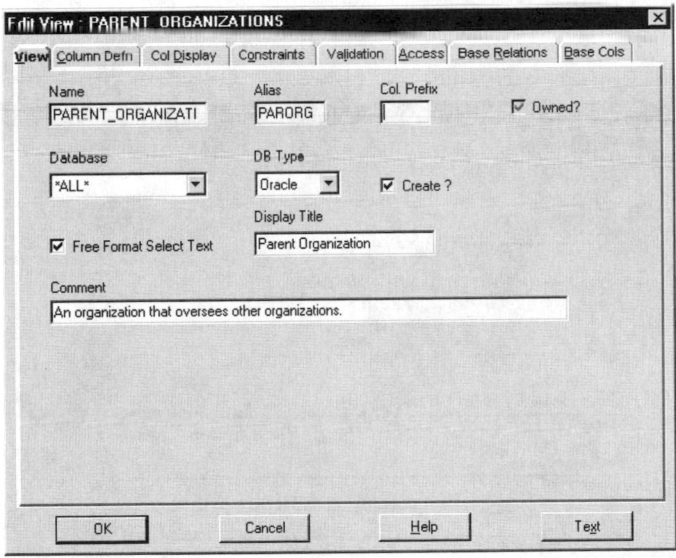

FIGURE 8-8. *Edit View window*

(calculation or decode, for example), you leave the Base Column field blank and fill in the Expression field with the actual calculation or expression (such as UPPER(LNAME)). The WHERE clause for the view statement is defined in the Where/Validation Condition text area. When you define the base relations and columns in this way, Designer/2000 automatically constructs the text for the Select Text area from the base column names.

You may be basing the view on a SELECT statement that includes tables from other databases or application systems. However, since the only tables available to the Base Relations Table/View field are those that are either shared or owned by the current application system, you cannot use that method to document the source of the columns. The first tab of the Edit View window contains a property called Free Format Select Text. If this is checked, you enter the actual FROM clause as well as the WHERE clause for the view in the Where/Validation Condition text area instead of defining base relations. Also, if Free Format Select Text is checked, you need to specify the column list in the Select Text property. This option gives you the flexibility to include tables from any source, although you will not be able to determine the source of the columns as precisely.

Snapshot definitions are nearly identical to view definitions, and Designer/2000 treats them similarly. The main difference is on the first tab, shown in Figure 8-9, which contains snapshot-specific fields for refresh times and storage parameters.

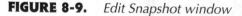

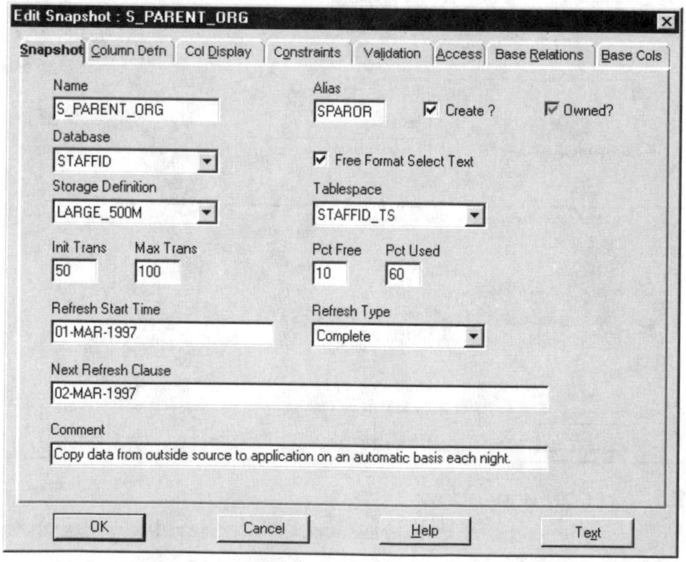

FIGURE 8-9. *Edit Snapshot window*

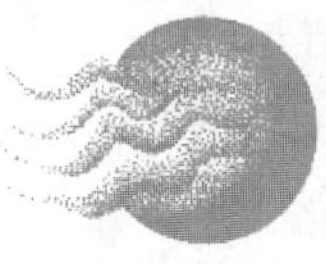

NOTE
Consult the SQL language reference manuals or ask for help from your DBA if you need an explanation of the effect of a particular value in the data definition areas. Alternatively, have the DBA review the DDL scripts that Designer/2000 produces to check for omissions or errors in your definitions.

Other Menu and Toolbar Functions

As in all Designer/2000 tools, the toolbar buttons provide a quick way to call the most common functions from the menu. The File menu has no unfamiliar items, and the Edit menu closely mirrors the functions in the ER Diagrammer Edit menu. The View menu offers the common diagram view manipulation functions.

The Utilities menu contains the usual set of Autolayout, page minimization, and arc drawing functions. It also includes the Database Design Wizard, Table to Entity Retrofit, Generate SQL DDL, Reverse Engineer Database, and Reconcile utilities.

The Tools menu has the usual Repository utilities: Repository Reports, RON, and the Matrix Diagrammer. It also contains items to call the ER Diagrammer and Module Data Diagrammer. The Window and Help menus include the usual items.

Using RON Instead of the DD

You may find it easier to define a table in the Repository Object Navigator than in the Data Diagrammer. One reason to use RON is that you can easily create a number of definitions and apply common properties to a group of tables. Another is that all related properties for each element are in one properties window and not spread across a number of tabs and text areas.

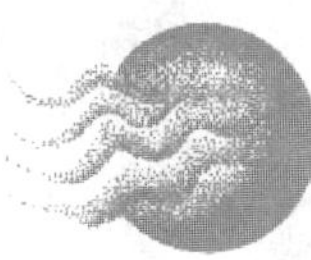

NOTE
RON also lets you define synonyms for tables which are used by the Server Generator to create CREATE SYNONYM scripts. The DDW creates these synonyms from the synonyms of entities, but you can also add to them in RON. Synonyms serve as aliases for tables and to simplify cross-database table access.

On the other hand, RON is not as efficient if you do not know where to find particular elements. For example, the Edit Table properties window in the DD contains all column, index, and constraint definitions related to a particular table, in addition to the table information itself. RON spreads these properties across a number of different element types, such as tables, columns, primary key constraints, foreign key constraints, indexes, and check constraints. Therefore, it may take a bit more time to find a particular element in RON than in the DD. One suggestion is to use the DD until you become familiar with the element types it uses. Then use RON as it may be more efficient to not have the overhead of a drawing tool.

Quickly Creating Multiple Objects in RON

As mentioned in Chapter 5, you can easily create multiple elements of the same type, such as tables, in the Repository Object Navigator. Start the process by selecting the element type node and clicking the Create button. You will see a new Properties window and a blank line in the hierarchy for the new element. Immediately start typing the name of the element you are creating, and Designer/2000 will enter the name on the blank line in the hierarchy. Then shift your focus to the Properties window (by clicking the mouse in it), fill in the other required properties, and shift your focus back to the Repository Object Navigator window by clicking the name (not the icon) of the new element. If there are no required properties other than the name, do not shift the focus back and forth. Then press the ENTER key, and Designer/2000 will save the new element and start creating another new element with a blank name. After creating the elements in this way, you can go back and fill in other properties that are not required but are needed to make the definition complete.

Other Database Objects Whether or not you use RON to create table, view, and snapshot definitions, you need to use it to create the database objects listed in Table 8-2, because there are no other definition windows available in any other tool (except the Matrix Diagrammer).

Where Does This Information Go?

In general, all information in the DD is destined to become server code. Therefore, although this diagrammer includes various element types, all are the basis for DDL scripts that the Server Generator produces. You run these scripts in the database to create the database objects for the final application. The other Designer/2000 tool that uses the definitions in the database design area is the Module Data

Repository Element	Can Reverse Engineer	Can Generate Creation Code	Notes
Cluster: hash and index	Yes	Yes	Clusters physically locate table columns next to one another in the database files to increase performance.
Communities	No	No	A community is a group of database servers that use SQL*Net to communicate and share a common protocol.
Databases (Oracle and ANSI)	No	Yes	The DATABASE CREATE statement can be generated by checking the Database Creation command on the Options tab of the Server Generator.
Database files	No	No	This element gives you a place to store information on the database files and redo files that make up the database.
Groups	No	Yes	Groups correspond to database roles and grants to those roles.
Nodes	No	No	Nodes are storage devices such as one or more machines or a part of one machine.
Oracle database user	No	Yes	This element corresponds to database users and grants to those users of system and object privileges.
Record files	No	No	This element documents flat files with records in them.

TABLE 8-2. *Designer/2000 Support for Other Design Phase Objects*

Repository Element	Can Reverse Engineer	Can Generate Creation Code	Notes
Rollback segment	No	Yes	This element defines the database rollback segment.
Sequence	Yes	Yes	The sequence is used to create unique number values for columns. You can attach these to columns in the DD and in the Module Data Diagrammer.
Source file	No	No	This element defines a C++ source code file you will want to document in the repository.
Storage definition	No	No	Storage definitions attach to tables and other objects that require database space; they become part of the actual database objects rather than separate objects themselves. They are handy for managing the storage clause of a number of tables that have those properties in common.
Tablespace	Yes	Yes	Tablespaces attach to table, snapshot, index, and primary key definitions.

TABLE 8-2. *Designer/2000 Support for Other Design Phase Objects* (continued)

Diagrammer. Modules that are not manual have data usages associated with them. These usages consist of the tables and columns the module uses as well as the way these are used (create, retrieve, update, and delete). The details of a table in the module usage default to those set in the table definition itself. Although you can override the defaults on a module-by-module basis, the foundation comes from the table definition itself. Table 8-3 shows the major element types represented in the DD and the use for these elements later in Designer/2000 work.

TIP
The key to success in the DD (indeed, in all of Designer/2000) is knowing what the result will be when you set or ignore a particular property. When in doubt regarding what clause a particular property will generate to in this diagrammer, create a test table or element and run the generator before and after specifying the setting to note the differences in the script that the Server Generator creates. The extra time it takes to learn the properties will benefit you in the long run.

Data Diagrammer Element Definition	Future Use for Element
Table	Server Generator CREATE TABLE statement. Module Data Diagrammer (MDD) module data usage.
View	Server Generator CREATE VIEW statement. MDD module data usage.
Snapshot	Server Generator CREATE SNAPSHOT statement. MDD module data usage.
Column for table, view, or snapshot	Column definition in respective Server Generator CREATE TABLE statement. MDD module data usage.
Foreign key constraint	Server Generator ALTER TABLE constraint statement. Table links in MDD.
Primary key and unique key constraint	Server Generator ALTER TABLE constraint statement.
Check constraint	Server Generator check constraint clause for column definition in CREATE TABLE statement.
Index	Server Generator CREATE INDEX statement.
Trigger definition	The Server Generator combines this with the related module code to build a CREATE TRIGGER statement.
Domain or column values list	Specific module generator (such as Forms or Reports) creates a list of values for, and code to validate against, a reference code table.

TABLE 8-3. *Data Design Element and Future Use in Designer/2000*

Reverse Engineer Database Objects Utility in the Design Phase: Database Design

Even at this stage of the process, you need to create repository definitions for tables that exist in a database somewhere but have no repository definition. The Reverse Engineer Database Objects utility described in Chapter 5 and available in the RON and DD assists you by adding table definitions for tables or views in the database or in a CREATE TABLE script in the file system. You can also reverse engineer a snapshot from the database though not from a script file.

When you reverse engineer tables, you can choose to reverse engineer other objects automatically as well. This option appears on the Options tab of this utility as shown in the following illustration.

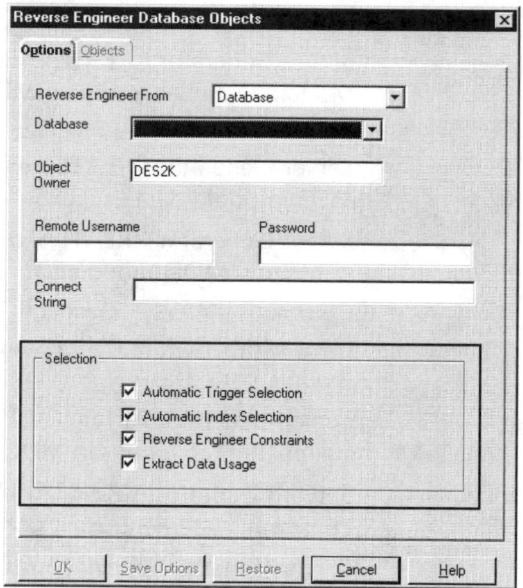

The first three choices, if checked, automatically reverse engineer the triggers, indexes, and constraints for the tables you select on the Objects tab. You can also select these manually if you do not want to have the utility automatically reverse engineer them. The last check box, if checked, will cause the utility to create column usages on the PL/SQL code (packages, functions, procedures, and triggers) you are reverse engineering. The table and column definitions for those columns must already exist for this to work, so you would reverse engineer the tables first and then the PL/SQL code.

Module Logic Navigator

Part of the denormalization process you perform in the database design part of the Design phase includes creating summary and derived columns and tables. You can express your design thoughts on these elements as PL/SQL code using the Module Logic Navigator (MLN). While you will spend more time using this utility in the application design part of Design, it is appropriate to mention it here for the denormalization process. The mechanism that performs the summarization or derivation consists of some PL/SQL code in the server (a trigger perhaps) or application module that calculates or sums values from one table or column to another. This PL/SQL code is considered a module just as the reports, forms, and triggers that call it are considered modules. This tool allows you to create the PL/SQL modules that pertain to the Design phase and to fill them in more fully with code during the Build phase.

CAUTION
The Module Logic Navigator makes creating PL/SQL code as easy as dragging and dropping constructs from one window into another. However, unstated prerequisites for effective use of this tool are an understanding of programming logic and knowledge of how to build PL/SQL programs. The more experience you have with these prerequisites, the more effective you will be in defining PL/SQL modules with the MLN. If these subjects are new to you, before beginning work in the tool you should get help with both logic and PL/SQL programming by consulting a knowledgeable person, studying these topics on your own, or pursuing formal training.

The Module Logic Navigator (MLN) assists you in creating and editing modules that use PL/SQL. You can easily define new modules or edit existing ones with the properties windows. The tool helps you enter correct PL/SQL syntax and gives you an outline menu of PL/SQL constructs and tools. It provides a built-in syntax checker that you can start with a button or menu choice. You can also run a utility that creates Summary Usage elements that track which tables and columns you use in which modules. Figure 8-10 shows the Module Logic Navigator and its main work areas.

The preceding section discussed how to create trigger definitions using the Data Diagrammer. Those triggers are linked to modules for which you define code in the Module Logic Navigator. The Server Generator combines the trigger linked to the module and the module that contains the code to produce a CREATE TRIGGER script. There are other types of PL/SQL modules you can create with the MLN, and there are several methods you can use to define the code for the module.

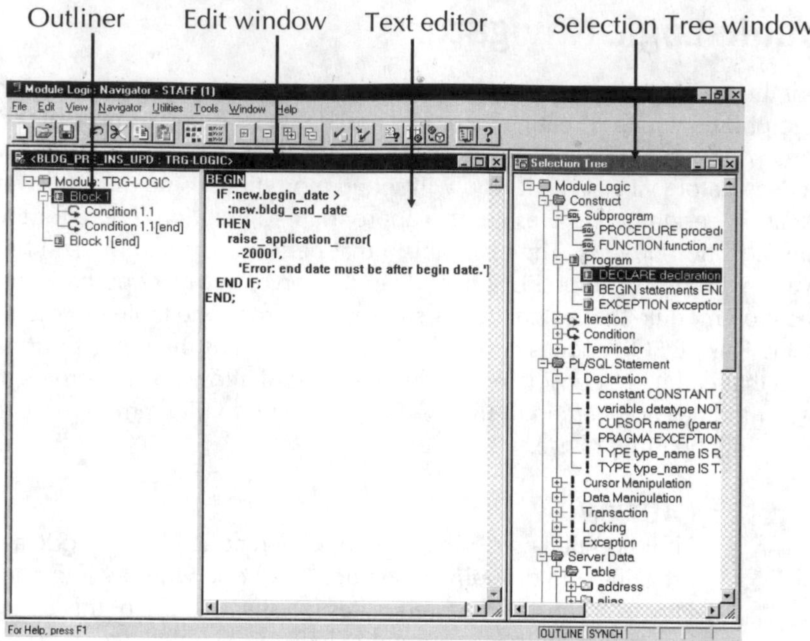

FIGURE 8-10. *Module Logic Navigator work areas*

Types of PL/SQL Modules

When you create a new PL/SQL code module using this utility, you specify the type of module. There are five types of PL/SQL modules that determine what type of server code the Server Generator will create:

- **Cursor** This is not a server object by itself but can be contained in the other types. The benefit of the cursor type is that many other PL/SQL types can share the same cursor definition.
- **Function** The Server Generator creates a CREATE OR REPLACE FUNCTION statement from this definition.
- **Package** The Server Generator creates CREATE OR REPLACE PACKAGE (and PACKAGE BODY) statements from this definition.

- **Procedure** The Server Generator creates a CREATE OR REPLACE PROCEDURE statement from this definition.
- **Trigger logic** The Server Generator creates a CREATE OR REPLACE TRIGGER statement from this definition.

Methods of Defining PL/SQL

There are different ways of defining these types of PL/SQL modules. Since the Server Generator processes all of them to produce code with the same results, the choice of which one to use is up to you. In all of the methods, you set properties on the Edit Module window, which you load by selecting **Edit→Properties** from the menu when the cursor is in the Edit window of the MLN.

Free Format With the free format method, you define the PL/SQL text with the declaration, executable body, and exception sections, but no header (CREATE xxxx AS). Select the Free Format radio button in the Edit Module window (on the Server Details subtab of the Definition tab). Then fill in the PL/SQL text in the text edit area by typing it, pasting it from another editor, or dragging and dropping constructs from the Selection Tree window. The PL/SQL text is also available in the text area of the Edit Module window (PL/SQL Block text type). The Server Generator constructs the header from the module short name (or implementation name if there is one) and the PL/SQL module type. It uses the PL/SQL block text to generate the body of the module code. All PL/SQL modules are set by default to free format text except packages, which are set to declarative.

Declarative The declarative method of defining PL/SQL text consists of explicitly writing only the executable body and exception sections of the code. The variable declaration, data structures (record and table datatypes), parameters, and return datatypes are all stored as separate elements in the repository. This type of detail is handy if you want to control the use of the various elements in your PL/SQL code and list them on repository reports. Click the Declarative radio button on the Server Details subtab of the Definition tab to define this module as declarative. The declarative method is well documented in the help system and cue cards, so this chapter does not detail the operations needed for this method.

O/S File The O/S file method uses existing code you have created with one file per module. You fill in the Source File field in the Edit Modules window with the full path and name of the file that contains the complete CREATE statement. This disables the Free Format and Declarative buttons and declares that you are using the O/S file method. The Server Generator creates a script that consists of comment lines and one line that executes the file:

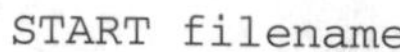

```
START filename
```

The *filename* is the name you typed in the Source File field. While the MLN can perform syntax checking with the other two methods, no checking is performed with this method as whatever is in the file is what you get for server code. You can define the text and check it in the Module Logic Navigator. If you then save it by exporting it to a text file, you can define that text file as the source for your module.

The method you use is determined by your comfort with PL/SQL. If you are comfortable with the language, you will find the free format method faster and easier. If you need some help with PL/SQL or want as much of the structures and components of your code as possible as elements in the repository (for reporting purposes, for example), the declarative method may be more appropriate. If you have an extensive library of files that you do not wish to move into the repository, the O/S file method is best. You can also use a combination of all three. Be careful when using the O/S file method as you need the external file in the file system. If you move the file, you have to be sure to redefine the Source File name property in the module properties.

Basic Techniques

Although the Module Logic Navigator provides complete online help and cue card systems to assist you in performing basic activities, you should know a few techniques before you start using the tool. The unit of work in this utility is the module, instead of the diagram as in the diagrammers. Creating a new module is the same as creating a new diagram in the diagrammers: choose **File→New** from the menu or click the New button. The following dialog box appears.

Create Module
Short Name: BLDG_PRE_INS_UPD
Module Name: BLDG_PRE_INS_UPD
Purpose: Check that the begin date is before the end date
Language: PL/SQL
Type: TRG-LOGIC
Copy Module
OK Cancel Help

If you want to edit an existing module, you can choose **File→Open** from the menu. Note that only modules that have a Language property of PL/SQL are available in this tool. You can examine or change module properties by selecting **Edit→Properties** from the menu when the cursor is in the Edit window.

CAUTION
If you change the module Language property to something other than PL/SQL, you will not be able to open the module in the Module Logic Navigator. If you do this by mistake, open RON and change the Language property of the module back to PL/SQL. After you commit the changes, you will be able to again open the module in the MLN.

You can select **Window→Tile Vertically** to arrange the two windows side by side and then drag the side of the Selection Tree in and expand the Edit window as shown earlier in Figure 8-10. This will give you the maximum amount of space in the edit area, which is the main work area. Your next steps in the Module Logic Navigator are concerned with defining the code for the module and changing the properties of the module.

Defining Code

When you work with the declarative or free format methods, you place PL/SQL block (BEGIN...END) code in the edit area either by typing it directly or dragging and dropping words and phrases from the Selection Tree area. The Edit window contains the Outliner area where the MLN shows the basic structure of the program you write in the text editor. This outline is arranged in a standard navigator format with nodes you can expand and collapse so you can quickly review the logic. It also allows you to jump to a particular spot by clicking the structure name to move the selection in the text editor to that structure. This feature is implemented by a preference called Tracking that you can disable in the Preferences window (**Edit→Preferences**). Click the Synchronize button (or choose **Utilities→Synchronize** from the menu) to coordinate the outline display after you make changes in the text area.

Typing directly in the text editor is the same as typing in any other editor. The text editor tries to determine what you are typing and automatically indents each line based on the line above it. The editor also recognizes keywords that you type and automatically converts them to uppercase. The automatic indention and keyword recognition are also preferences you can modify in the Preferences window. The text editor enables the Edit menu items (or standard key presses) for accessing the cut, copy, and paste functions. Since you can open more than one module at a time in the Module Logic Navigator, these functions allow you to transfer or copy code from one module to another.

The Selection Tree window provides a drag and drop capability for keywords. It too has a navigator-style arrangement, so you click a node to expand or collapse it. There is only one Selection Tree window no matter how many modules you have opened in different edit areas. The Selection Tree provides a complete summary of all PL/SQL language elements, including the tables, columns, and other database objects you have defined in the repository. The main nodes are Construct, for PL/SQL structure words such as BEGIN...END and IF...THEN...ELSE...END IF; PL/SQL Statement, for variable, constant, and cursor words; Server Data, for database objects you have defined in the repository such as tables, views, and snapshots; and Static Data, for PL/SQL functions such as TO_CHAR and TO_DATE as well as exceptions and datatypes.

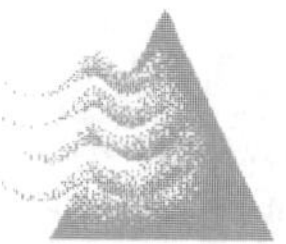

TIP

Turn on the icons for the Selection Tree nodes by making that window active and choosing **View→Iconic** from the menu. You can show icons for the Outliner area separately using the same method. The icons give you an idea of the type of word or structure you are manipulating and can give you a quick picture of the logic in your module.

Performing the drag and drop operation is as easy as finding the words you want in the Selection Tree hierarchy, clicking them, holding down the mouse button as you drag them into the edit area, and releasing the button when the cursor is at the right line of code. This method gives you perfect spelling and structures (IF...THEN...ELSE...END IF) every time, but it may be faster in some cases to just type the words directly if you are used to the syntax.

If you drop a word or construct into the edit area, it will contain a note on what you need to fill in. This note will have the SQL comment symbols /* */ around it so it will not hinder the syntax check. If you check the **View→To Do Statements** menu option, the Outliner will display a node indicating what you have to fill in, as in the following illustration.

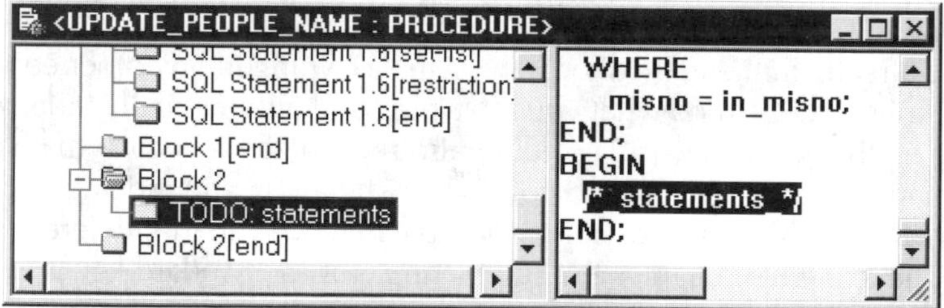

This feature highlights areas that you still need to work on; the TODO notes will vanish when you fill in code for those areas.

There are a few more operations you can perform once you have typed text into the text area. One of these operations, as mentioned before, is clicking the Synchronize button (**Utilities→Synchronize**). You know the Outliner display is out of synch if the Outliner lines are highlighted in gray as shown here (you can change the highlight color in the Preferences window).

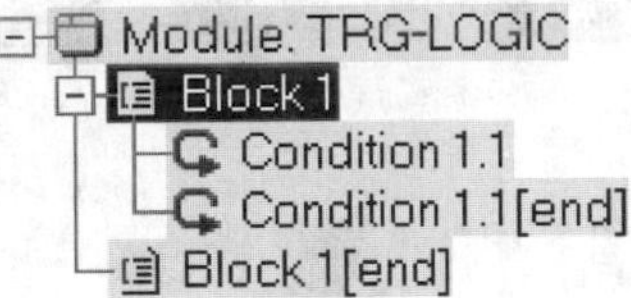

This sort of display means that it is time to synchronize the display of structures in the Outliner with the structures you have typed or dragged into the edit area. You can also perform a syntax check to verify that you have typed keywords correctly. Click the Check Syntax button or choose **Utilities→Check Syntax** from the menu. If you did not save the module before doing this, the utility will ask if you want to save. Then the syntax checker will review the code and report on errors in a window like the one shown here:

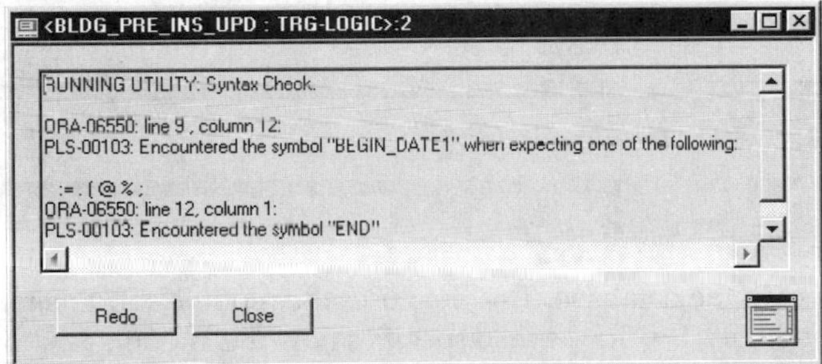

If there are errors, you can leave this window open as you fix them in the edit area. Then click the Redo button to check the revised code.

Changing Module Properties

The Edit Module properties window appears as in Figure 8-11 if you select **Edit→Properties** from the menu when the cursor is in the edit area. This window contains all module properties on various tabs.

The Definition tab includes four subtabs: Module, Client Details, Client Help Details, and Server Details. The Client Details and Client Help Details subtabs are not available for PL/SQL type modules, so you should concentrate on the other two in the MLN.

The Module tab contains basic name and type definition fields. It also contains entry areas for complexity and size, which you can report on later. If you have completed the module generation, you can mark the module as complete by checking the Complete? box. Any subsequent attempts to generate it will then fail. The Server Details tab lets you specify the method, as mentioned before, as well as the implementation name, where you can specify the name you want to use to

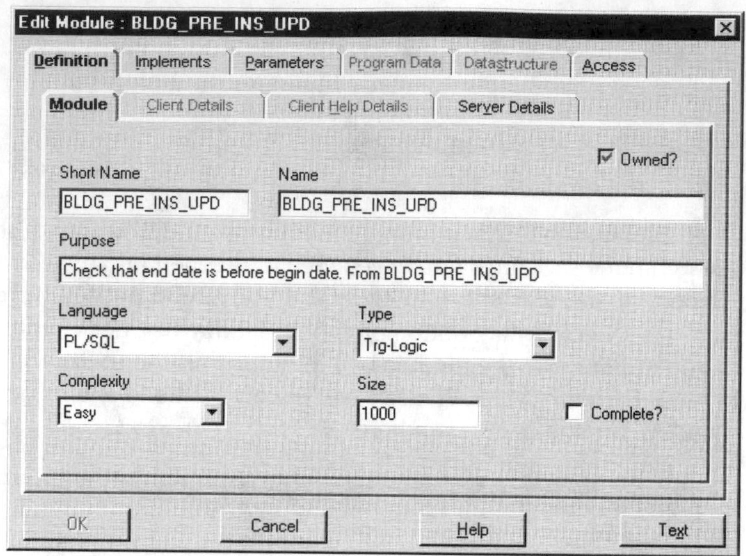

FIGURE 8-11. *Edit Module window*

create the object in the database. This field uses the module short name, in lowercase, by default. The Scope field specifies how this module is known if it is in a PL/SQL package. Procedures and functions in packages can have private scope (known only to the other package functions and procedures) or public scope (known to any user who is granted access to the package). A third scope choice, Protected, is not currently used. The Function Return Type field lets you define the datatype this module returns if it is a function. If you check the Create box, you indicate that this module is ready to be generated.

Another tab in the Edit Module properties window is the Implements tab, where you specify or view the functions from which this module is derived and the business units for which this module performs work. The Application Design Wizard uses the business unit implementation information when it generates menus from the existing modules.

The Parameters tab gives you a place to specify the input and output parameters for PL/SQL modules (and the input parameters for forms and reports). You fill in details such as the name, domain, datatype, and length. The Server Generator uses these details when producing the DDL code for this module. You can fill in parameters for both the free format and declarative methods.

The Program Data tab holds information on the data elements you define in the DECLARE section. This is applicable only to the declarative method and will be used by the Server Generator to create the constant, variable, or exception code in the declaration section of the PL/SQL block.

You can define composite (combined) datatypes on the Datastructure tab, including cursors, tables, and records. You give each data structure a name and type and indicate which items it contains. You can use the handy poplist in the bottom-right corner of this window to copy columns from existing tables into the items list.

The Access tab contains information on the execution privileges you grant for this module to users and roles. Note that these user and role (group) definitions must already exist as repository elements. You can enter them in the Repository Object Navigator.

In addition to the Edit Module properties window, which concerns the module you have open in the utility, you can use the **Edit→Elements** menu item to view and modify Module (other modules), Trigger, Table/View/Snapshot, and Summary Usages (how the module uses a particular table for create, retrieve, update, and delete) properties.

Defining Packages

PL/SQL package definitions require some different considerations as they are potentially made up of many modules. There is a calling hierarchy that you define and view in the Module Structure Diagrammer. The important point to remember is that the package specification is one module by itself, and all the subprograms (cursors, procedures, and functions) are also individual modules linked to the specification with an invoked (link) value of Include. This joins the subunits to the specification so the Server Generator can construct one DDL statement from a number of modules. The work you do in the MLN is modularized automatically because, even though you may be working on a large package of PL/SQL units, you have to think of them as individual modules. Another important point about packages is that you can declare the subunits as private—without a calling interface from any outside code—or public—where everyone who has access to the package also has access to the subprogram.

Changing Preferences

The Preferences window gives you control over some of the ways the Module Logic Navigator works or looks. Choose **Edit→Preferences** from the menu (or press the F2 key) to display the Preferences window shown next.

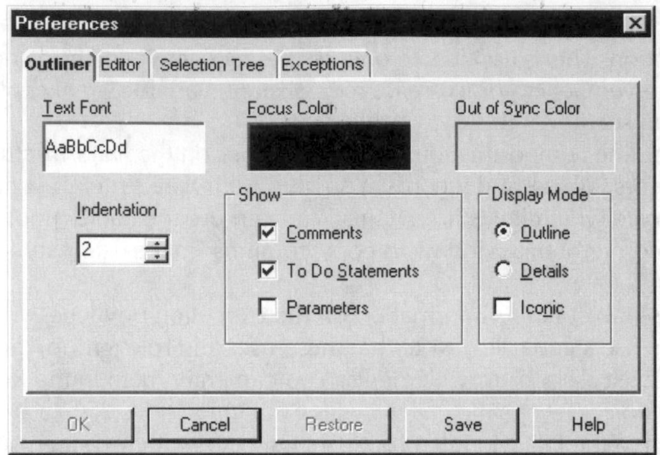

The Outliner tab lets you specify color, font, and indentation for the Outliner as well as whether to show comments in the code as a special node. On the Editor tab you can specify the indentation, number of characters before the text wraps, and automatic features such as tracking and keyword recognition, as mentioned before. However, you cannot select the font for the editor. The Selection Tree tab lets you customize the font and color for this window and specify indentation. On the Exceptions tab you can choose the exceptions that are copied as a set when you drag the Exception node from the Selection Tree into the editor area. This lets you pick a set of exceptions that you commonly include in PL/SQL blocks.

Other Menu and Toolbar Functions

Some other features of this utility are available from the menu or toolbar buttons. The toolbar buttons, as usual, repeat the functionality of some of the menu items. Some menu items are disabled until the cursor is in the window or area they apply to. Therefore, if a menu item you want to use is disabled, check the position of the cursor. The File, Window, and Help menus contain the normal items you find in all Designer/2000 tools.

In addition to the functions mentioned in the preceding discussion, the Edit menu allows you to create PL/SQL modules with the standard create dialog window (**Edit→Create→PL/SQL Module**) so you do not have to display the module in the utility to create it. It also lets you create a trigger through the **Edit→Create→Trigger** menu item. It provides Import Text and Export Text menu items to paste text from an external file and save it in an external file from the editor area, respectively.

The View menu allows you to tailor the look of this utility with check items that turn on and off displays of Outline, Details, Comments, ToDo Statements,

Parameters, and Iconic items. The items that are enabled at any particular time depend on whether the cursor is in the Outliner, text, edit, or Selection Tree area.

Items on the Navigator pull-down menu handle the normal expand, collapse, and mark functions in the Outliner and Selection Tree hierarchy windows. The Find menu item allows you to search for a particular string of text in the edit area.

The Utilities menu contains, along with the items already discussed, the Generate SQL DDL (Server Generator), Reverse Engineer Database, and Reconcile utilities. It also includes a selection to copy from one module to another in case you need to use the code from one package in another package. The Generate Summary Usages option is discussed in the next section.

The Tools menu includes options to run other Repository utilities: Repository Reports, Repository Object Navigator, and Matrix Diagrammer. You can also run the Module Structure Diagrammer from this menu to display the module calling hierarchy.

Generate Summary Usages Utility

The Generate Summary Usages utility, available from the toolbar and the Utilities menu, gives you a fast and easy way to attach data usages to the module definitions. While these usages are not required for PL/SQL modules like they are for reports and forms modules, they are useful for ensuring that the objects you use in the PL/SQL code are defined in the repository. For example, you can create a module which includes this code:

```
SELECT begin_date1 INTO v_date FROM buildings; [s & semi-colon]
```

If you run a syntax check on this code, it will pass because there is nothing wrong other than that the BUILDINGS table does not have a BEGIN_DATE1 column. When you run the Generate Summary Usages utility, Designer/2000 tries to include usages for all table and column information referenced in the code. Since it cannot find a repository column called BEGIN_DATE1 in the BUILDINGS table, it displays the following error message:

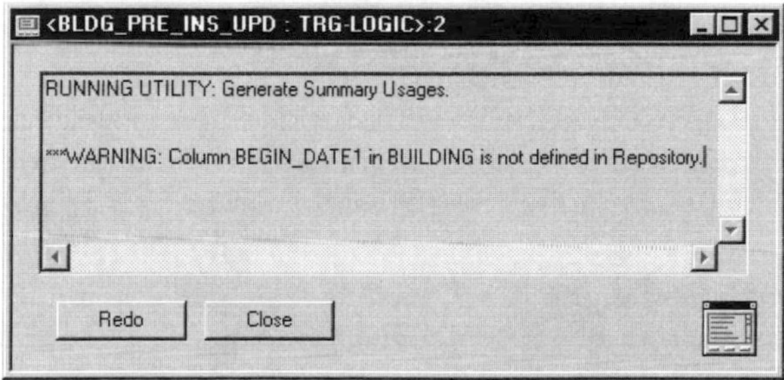

Another benefit of creating data usages for modules is that they document the data in each module so you can run repository reports that show the use of particular tables or columns. This type of report is essential if you are interested in impact analysis or the dependencies for a module.

Using RON to Create Modules

An alternative to using the MLN to define PL/SQL modules is the Repository Object Navigator. If you are comfortable with PL/SQL programming, you may find it easier to define a module as free format text and use your own text editor to create the code. Then you can copy and paste from your editor to the PL/SQL Text property in the module in RON. This bypasses one of the more powerful parts of this tool—the ability to drag and drop PL/SQL structures into the editor—but the process may be more efficient if you do not need that kind of assistance. Using RON to edit the text gives you a more fully featured text editor (TextPad or another of your choosing that you set in the RON preferences). It also lets you move quickly from one module definition to another without having to open new "files" as in the MLN. In addition, you can group modules together and apply properties as a group in RON but not in the Module Logic Navigator.

Using the Reverse Engineer Database Objects Utility to Create Modules

You can also create PL/SQL modules the hard way. That is, you can create the code with a text editor and run it in the database to create the object. You can then run the Reverse Engineer Database Objects utility to create repository definitions for the code using the free format text method. The benefit of this approach is that, if you have a good working knowledge of PL/SQL and are accustomed to the manual coding method, it will put the code you write in the correct place in the repository. You will want to examine the definitions, change names, and possibly convert to the declarative method after the utility runs, but this method gives you a start. The biggest drawback to this method is that you have to create the code and all data objects it uses in the database. This procedure takes up additional storage space in the database. There is no way currently to reverse engineer from a script file to create PL/SQL modules as you can with tables.

Where Does This Information Go?

PL/SQL modules are all used by the Server Generator to construct scripts of DDL code that you use to create the database objects. While you cannot create server code from a cursor type of module, the Server Generator can create DDL scripts for package, procedure, function, and trigger modules. The module definitions appear in the Module node in the Repository Object Navigator, and you can diagram their calling hierarchy in the Module Schema Diagrammer.

Repository Reports in the Design Phase: Database Design

You may want to run Repository Reports in this part of the Design phase to see the detailed table and column definitions. The System Design group of reports contains most of the reports you will want to run at this point in the life cycle. The Table Definition and Column Definition reports are handy for getting a quick list of the definitions in the repository. There are corresponding reports for views, snapshots, and constraints as well.

The Database Design group also contains reports that apply to the objects you define in this phase. An interesting report (if you have filled in table volume information) is the Database Table and Index Sizing Report, which provides sizing estimates for tables and indexes as well as a total size for these tables and indexes. If you set the value of the Include Help parameter to True, the report will also include the formula for calculating the sizes. Other Database Design group reports handle some of the other elements not shown in the Data Diagrammer, such as files, rollback segments, sequences, tablespaces, and clusters.

You can run the quality control reports to check the database design elements. The Table Quality Control report (in the System Design group) provides table definition details and lists possible problem areas such as tables without columns, tables and tablespaces that span more than one database, and other constraint, trigger, and table issues.

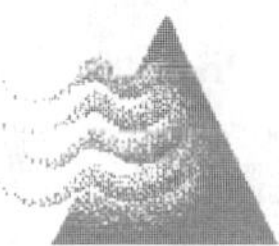

TIP

Explore the quality control reports in each appropriate group as you progress through the development life cycle. They point out omissions or unusual definitions that you may need to fix and are a good way to start a thorough cross-check of the work you do in the repository.

Conclusion

During database design, you design the physical database that will support your application. You make an educated guess regarding summary and aggregation tables, recognizing that changes will probably have to be made as the application is designed.

Even though you must think of a system as a whole including both database and application, in this part of the Design phase you focus on the building of the database while taking into consideration the application design. It is not possible to design the database directly from the ERD without considering the application that will run on top of that database.

Designer/2000 supports the database design part of the Design phase in quite a detailed way. You can define the tables, views, and snapshots that make up your physical design, as well as the code modules, such as triggers that relate to those tables. Once you have the data side under control, you can move on to the remainder of the Design phase and handle the application side. The next chapter explores the application design process and the Designer/2000 tools that assist in creating and defining modules that are ready to be generated.

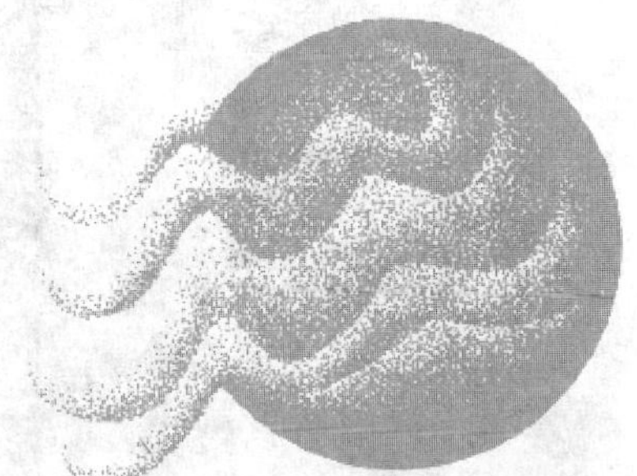

CHAPTER 9

Design: Part II—Application Design

Fill in both sides of the application completely. Make no marks in the area labeled "For Office Use Only." Be sure to enclose your check with the application.

At this point in the system development life cycle, you have developed the basic database design and application storyboards. Upon completion of the application design part of the Design phase, you will have finalized the database design and will be prepared to build the database and the applications.

Overview of Application Design

At the simplest level, application design is the design of software, including the creation of structures that address modules, programs, procedures, navigation, internal controls, and security.

Application design is where you specify column level usages for each module. The main reason for doing this is to validate that the database design was completed correctly. The conceptual application design was created in the Pre-Design phase. Then in the database design part of the Design phase, you built the best database possible using the logical ERD and the conceptual application design. Now in the application design part of the Design phase, you will map the modules to the database. This will allow you to validate the database. You will be able to identify missed columns as well as extraneous columns not needed by the modules.

The reason for performing this mapping step in the CADM process before building the database is not just for the conceptual clarity of designing the system before building it. You cannot be sure that the database design is correct until you have mapped the columns to the modules. Therefore, not only does this mapping play a major role in the design of the applications, but it also validates the accuracy of the database design.

Complete the specifications for the modules using the following steps:

- Completely map each module to the database at the column level.
- Tune and complete the database design. At this point in the process, the database moves into the Build phase while the application design is being completed.
- Refine and finalize the design book.

Each of these steps will be discussed in detail.

Performing Column-Level Mapping of Applications

At this point, you need to return to the CRUD matrix. Each column needs to be carefully mapped to the modules. Recall that, up to now, mapping has been performed only at the entity level. Now you must perform mapping at the finest level of detail to completely specify the interaction of the modules with the database. This is done by reviewing the conceptual design of the modules and determining how the modules will interact with each column in the database. This is a complex and tedious job, so quality control on this task is important. The mapping itself can be done by rank-and-file designers; but the work should be reviewed by senior team members.

View Definitions

The design of the modules cannot be created module by module. You need to look at the modules as a group, using views where appropriate. One of the limitations of views until recently was that insertions could not be made in views based on multiple tables or that contained embedded functions. In Oracle 7.3, this restriction has been relaxed; insertions and data modifications in a multi-table view are now possible so long as the changes modify only one table at a time.

Before, views were useful mainly for reports and were of limited use for screen modules (such as Oracle Forms), but now they are useful for screen modules as well. For example, you may want to create views that bring lookup values into the data tables. This technique greatly reduces the number of tables or views required by each module. However, view creation needs to be carefully controlled to make sure that the minimum number of necessary views are created. The ability to create views should be limited to senior members of the design team.

Building applications and reports is frequently much easier if you build some intelligence into views. One powerful feature not often used in application development is the ability to embed functions in views. For example, in a PO system, a view in the PO table can store the total amount for the purchase order. Code can be written so that any time users need to know the total amount of a PO, they can reference that column. This method is very efficient since the code is stored in a shared SQL area. One of the nice features of Oracle is that if the same SQL code is called multiple times, the SQL code goes into a shared SQL area. When a user executes a SQL query, the application looks for the SQL statement in the shared SQL area. If the application finds the SQL statement, it doesn't need to reparse it. This feature makes the overall system much more efficient.

Tuning and Completing the Database Design

New fields will undoubtedly be discovered during the application design phase. When this occurs, they must be added to the database design to support the application design. You need to continually revisit the database design to incorporate changes that result from the application column-level mapping process. You should produce a column-level report showing which columns are used in which modules. Pay particular attention to columns that are not referenced by any application. Such columns should be deleted where appropriate. When this is done, the database design is complete and you can enter the Build phase.

Defining and Finalizing the Design Book

The design book is the primary deliverable from the application design phase. It includes the full functional description of the application down to the detail level. It should also describe the overall structure of the system and the process for creating the desired structure. In other words, it should answer these questions: What should the system look like? How can the business requirements be satisfied? It should also include module-by-module design specifications. For each module, the following sections should be included:

- Mockups of screens or report facsimilies.
- Mapping of each field displayed on the screen or report to a database field.
- Relevant portions of the ERD showing tables and the relationships among these tables required to support the module.
- Detailed description of the functionality of the module. Some default functionality (such as insert and modify operations) will be built in.
- All relevant requirements with respect to that module.
- Encapsulation of all design-level analysis.

The design book should be a self-contained document that the designer can use to build the application. If a design book is not prepared, then your system cannot be tested because there is nothing to test against. Many automated tools are available to help testers perform testing. However, unless the tester is familiar with what the system is supposed to do at the detail level from both user interface and database standpoints, then the tester cannot audit the effectiveness of the application. The tester must look at the requirements and answer the questions: Does the application satisfy the requirements? Does the application work according to the design?

The design book should also present report specifications and describe navigation within applications.

Report Specifications

The design book should include an example of what each report looks like. The designer needs to know the underlying queries that will support the report. Any flexibility desired in the report (for example, filtering or sorting) needs to be declared at this point. Report distribution and security can be handled in the Implementation phase and need not be addressed here.

Navigation

Decisions must be made at this point regarding navigation within applications. The following options are available:

- Dedicated navigation application: that is, buttons on the screen
- Toolbar buttons
- Menu options
- Triggers on the form: for example, double-clicking the name of an employee in one application to display that employee's record in a second application

You need to establish the underlying functionality of navigation. You must decide for each application what other applications can be reached and determine how the user will move among and between these applications. Will the user be firing off database transactions or merely navigating to a different application?

There are two ways to document navigation:

- **Navigation flow chart** Each module is a box on the screen with lines connecting applications to show the navigation paths. The lines themselves can also describe how the application path works: for instance, by using menu options, toolbars, buttons, or some other trigger.
- **Matrix** All modules are listed on both axes of the matrix. Within the cells of the matrix, you can specify how navigation from one application to another is performed.

Although both methods work, the matrix is much more compact. The matrix enables the developer and tester to quickly and easily see which application maps to which other application, thus making it easy to verify whether or not applications meet the specifications. Matrices are less helpful to the designer, however. It is easier for a designer to use a navigation flow chart since this also shows how the navigation paths function. Thus, you should use both approaches since the system will require both development and design whether by the same or different people.

Internal Control and Security

The design of a high-quality internal control system requires the skills of two different groups. One group is the systems people who understand how roles, user profiles, passwords, grants, views, and other database techniques can be used to help make the application and the database secure. You also need the skills of the internal auditor to help design an effective security system.

Security is not limited to computer controls. It encompasses not only the protection of the physical and monetary assets of the organization, but also the data that resides in its computer systems. When certain business processes of the organization are computerized, they must be considered within the perspective of the company's internal control system. Backup and recovery are also important parts of internal control and security and should be carefully considered toward the end of the Design phase. Decisions need to be made regarding how to protect the system against catastrophic events such as fires, floods, and hardware failure.

Sometimes, computer controls can help prevent human errors and fraud, and sometimes manual controls can help detect programming errors. For example, using an approved vendor list and approved purchase order items can help decrease data entry errors just as periodically physically counting inventory can help detect a computer error in a purchasing system. All controls and all exposures (potential opportunities for harmful events) must be considered together.

It is important to remember that database controls, application-level controls, and accounting controls are not three separate topics. A coherent security strategy mandates integration of all three types of controls. Traditionally, this has not been done. Database people, in general, do not understand accounting controls, and internal auditors have little understanding of database technology. Even now, the most common way that external auditors evaluate an internal control system is by first sending in a team of computer specialists to evaluate the computer controls and then sending in traditional auditors to independently evaluate the accounting controls. Such a strategy is conceptually flawed.

This section describes how an internal control system should be designed. The first step is to establish all of the various exposures in the new system. Since both the application and database need to be designed to determine what all these exposures are, this step could not be taken until now. The key tools you will use to find exposures are the physical process flows.

After looking at all the exposures in the system and determining the appropriate controls for a particular application design, you may conclude that the design itself is flawed from a control standpoint and needs to be rethought. Such a situation, however, is rare. Usually, small module-level changes are sufficient to implement a control. It is not possible to determine the exposures in a system until that system is defined. Whereas some exposures are common to all systems, each system will have some unique exposures associated with it. You may want to identify general exposures and appropriate controls and add those to the system requirements prior to completing the detailed application design.

Exposures are of three types:

- **Hardware failure** You should consider the possibility of every kind of failure, from the breakdown of a PC to a fire that destroys the computer room. Hardware failures that are the result of normal breakdowns, sabotage, accidents, and natural disasters should all be taken into account.
- **Human error** This group includes errors ranging from data entry mistakes to the inadvertent reformatting of the hard drive by the night operator. Human errors can be quite serious. For protection, one mid-sized bank had all of its wire transfers entered twice, by two data entry people. By an unfortunate coincidence, however, both data entry people pressed the wrong button and mistakenly transferred $1,000,000, instead of $1,000, to the Philippines.
- **Fraud** This is the most frightening exposure, particularly with respect to financial data, where diversion of funds is possible. However, fraud may also involve the improper use of competitive information or malicious destruction of system resources by disgruntled employees. In addition, fraud may be perpetrated by one individual, or it may involve collusion among two or more employees. Fraud involving collusion can be difficult, if not impossible, to protect against.

Every system has a different set of exposures. The physical process flows are useful for seeing what exposures may exist. For example, in a simple PO system, the process flow can be described as follows:

- An employee in a functional area initiates a request for a purchase order by entering it in the system.
- A manager approves the request online.
- The Purchasing Department approves the request online.
- The system automatically generates and sends the purchase order to the vendor.
- The goods arrive at the Receiving Department, which notes that these goods have been received and maps the shipment to the appropriate PO.
- Goods are distributed to the employee.

Such a process flow reveals several exposures of each type.

Potential hardware failures for PO example:

- Because this is an Oracle system, most of the potential hardware failures would not result in the loss of data.
- The main hardware exposure occurs if the system is down for an extended period of time. In such a case, the needed goods might not be ordered.
- The scanner in the Receiving Department may incorrectly scan an item so that the correct item is not checked off, and the item may not get to the employee who ordered it.

Potential human errors for PO example:

- The employee can erroneously enter the request.
- The manager may inadvertently approve a request that should not have been approved.
- The Purchasing Department may make the wrong approval decision.
- Goods may be misdirected by the Receiving Department or applied to the wrong purchase order.
- A programmer may accidentally create a bug in a program that causes transactions to be lost, altered, or mistakenly created.

Potential fraud for PO example:

- A user may fraudulently create a pre-approved purchase order record.
- A systems person may fraudulently create a purchase order record for himself or herself.
- Receiving Department personnel may steal or misappropriate delivered goods.

Once exposures have been identified, controls must be developed to protect the organization from these exposures.

One of the hardest facts to accept about internal control systems is that it is not appropriate to protect against every exposure. In the bank example mentioned earlier, where two clerks both entered the same incorrect data, after the error that sent $1,000,000 to the Philippines, the bank changed its procedure so that every transaction is entered by three different people. This increased data entry costs by 50 percent. The rationale used by the company to justify this expense was that the single error had cost it $999,000, which would pay for a lot of data entry security.

The point is that controls cost money. For a control to be cost effective, it must cause at least a proportional decrease in the probability of an exposure.

The designers, working with the users, need to identify the appropriate controls to protect against the identified exposures. The best controls are those that protect against multiple exposures. For example, overnight backups of the data that are stored off-site limit exposure to any event that could cause destruction of information. A high-quality, periodic financial audit will uncover most blatant irregularities in the system.

Protecting against fraud, particularly fraud involving multiple individuals, usually involves very careful manual controls. For example, a managerial review and sign-off of all purchase orders above a specific amount limits the ability of any employee to defraud the company. Simple system controls can help detect employees with abnormally frequent purchase order requests.

Once the internal control system is designed, you will need to update the design book for the modules to reflect any changes in module design that occur as a result of internal control measures.

Specific Oracle Controls

Oracle provides specific tools that can assist in the building of system-level controls, including

- *User profiles,* which can restrict access to products and prevent the use of outside products
- *Passwords,* which restrict access to the system
- *Roles,* which help manage the rights of different classes of users

Security Deliverable

The deliverable for system security is a control/exposure matrix. Prepare a matrix where one axis lists all of the exposures that have been identified. Across the other axis, list all of the plausible controls. At the intersection of each control and exposure, rate how effectively that control decreases the risk of that exposure. If a control has no impact on the exposure, leave the cell blank. If the control decreases the risk of exposure, rate its effectiveness as low, medium, or high.

For the bank where the data entry error occurred, for instance, a control that restricts the amount that could be entered to a realistic range would decrease the risk of exposure by only a small amount and would thus be rated "low." A control that requires all wire transfers to be reviewed and approved would be rated "medium" because there is no way to guarantee how carefully the reviews are performed. The control that the bank eventually implemented, triple entry of all wire transactions, provides an exceptionally high degree of control and would be rated "high."

Once the matrix is complete, you can evaluate the quality of your internal control system by its ability to protect the system from each exposure. You may also find redundant controls that can be eliminated. In the banking example, once triple entry was implemented, no other control was necessary to prevent data entry errors for wire transfers.

After the design of the internal control system is complete, a report can be prepared and delivered to management on the level of security that is in place for the system. Management can then decide whether that level of protection is adequate. This formal approach to internal control system design is commonly used in many of the world's largest organizations but is almost unheard of in smaller companies.

Test Plan

One of the important aspects of the design book is that there is enough information in it to support system testing. Specifically, testers will check to make sure that applications conform to the system requirements associated with that application. At this point in the CADM process, we have sufficient information to develop our test plan. Indeed, one of the reasons for doing the test plan at this time is that it forces the designers to carefully consider whether the design book is adequate to support the Test phase. A complete discussion of Test will be postponed until Chapter 11; but it is at the end of the Design phase that the test plan should be developed.

Modifications for Smaller Systems

For large systems, application conceptual design completed in the Pre-Design phase is followed by database design and application design in the Design phase and then by the database Build phase.

For smaller systems, the entire Design phase can be simplified. After conceptual application design is complete, the process can proceed directly to the design and building of the database. Then the design and building of the application can be completed. This is a radical change in design methodology, but for small systems it is appropriate. For medium-sized systems, the team must assess which path to follow—the one for small systems or the one for large systems—using its best judgment. When in doubt, follow the same development path for both medium- and large-sized systems.

When Is Application Design Complete?

User acceptance of screen designs already occurred in the sign-off process in the Pre-Design phase. All that remains is for the system developers to perform an internal evaluation of the completeness of the design. Each application within the design book should be audited for completeness by a QA person. Similarly, a random sampling of applications from each developer should be selected for QA using Designer/2000. Specifically, several applications from each developer should be checked for accuracy and completeness. Of course, if any applications fail the audit, extra work will be required. The principle for determining completeness is an internal audit by another set of eyes. The design process should always include review by an internal auditor to ensure adherence to design standards in multiple places throughout the process.

Application design is complete when the users sign off on the design book and the development team completes its own internal sign-off based on the design book and validation of the information in Designer/2000. Another way to ensure that the design is acceptable is to perform a system walkthrough with users.

The Design Phase in Designer/2000: Application Design

In the application design part of the Design phase, you fully define the modules (screens, reports, menus) that make up the finished application. Designer/2000 helps you enter these definitions in an organized and methodical way so you can completely specify the details. The Designer/2000 definitions serve as the program specifications from which you generate the final application in the Build phase. Another important activity in this part of the Design phase is the cross-check of the database design. You want to be sure that the data elements you defined in the database design part of Design are fully utilized and included in the set of modules you produce. Designer/2000 facilitates this type of checking as well.

Table 9-1 shows the activities and the Designer/2000 tools you use for them in the application design part of the Design phase.

The work you do in this part of the Design phase with the Data Diagrammer is similar to the work you did in the database design part of Design, described in Chapter 8. The main reason to use this tool in the application design part of Design is to add to or modify database definitions you created earlier in the life cycle. You may need to do this as a result of something you learned or thought of when defining modules. You also may visit the properties windows for the database elements to more fully define the display characteristics of the columns. This

Activity or Deliverable	Designer/2000 Tool
PL/SQL module specifications	Module Structure Diagrammer or Module Logic Navigator
Supplement table definitions	Data Diagrammer
Rough-cut of module data usages from functions	Create Default Module Data Usages from Function Usages utility
Module layout and data usage specifications for screens, reports, and charts	Module Data Diagrammer
Restructure the module network (menu modules)	Module Structure Diagrammer
Create reference, code, and help tables	Generate Reference Tables utility
Exposure control matrix	User Extensibility feature and Matrix Diagrammer
Cross-check the module CRUD	Matrix Diagrammer
Document the module specifications	Repository Reports

TABLE 9-1. *Application Design Activities and Designer/2000 Tools*

activity is discussed in the section "Module Data Diagrammer" as the display characteristics in those property windows are similar to those in the table properties window.

The work you perform with the Module Logic Navigator in this phase consists of filling in properties for the PL/SQL module definitions, as Chapter 8 discusses. This activity can also be carried out in the Module Structure Diagrammer as the module definition window is the same in both these tools. You do not complete the PL/SQL code in the module definition until the Build phase.

The Generate Reference Table utility is available from the Module Data Diagrammer and so is described with that tool. The Create Module Data Usages from Function Usage utility is discussed in that same section as its output affects the associations to the module definitions you work with in that diagrammer.

This following discussion assumes you have read the introduction to the Designer/2000 interface in Chapter 2. In addition, you will, as always, find it useful to be familiar with the online help system and cue cards when you work with these tools. The help system can assist you in unfamiliar operations as well as reinforce concepts you already know.

Module Structure Diagrammer

The Module Structure Diagrammer (MSD) produces diagrams that look essentially like function hierarchy diagrams. There is an important difference, however; while a function hierarchy diagram represents a hierarchy of details (or decomposition) for functions, the module structure diagram displays the module calling hierarchy or network. Therefore, the MSD is responsible for showing and allowing you to manipulate which module calls which other module. Since the menu system itself is made of menu modules, you work with that structure in the MSD. The kinds of calls you see here are menu to form, form to form, form to report, report to report, PL/SQL module to cursor, and so forth.

In addition to enabling you to manipulate the calling hierarchy, the MSD allows you to define new modules and edit the definitions of existing modules. All properties for modules discussed in Chapter 8 are available in this diagrammer for modification or supplementation. Another important operation you perform in this diagrammer is the acceptance of candidate modules that the ADW creates. You need an accepted module to generate code, and this diagrammer lets you easily accept individual or sets of modules. You can also accept candidate modules in RON, but this diagrammer shows the calling structure, and you can more easily see the context of a module in it than in RON.

You first use the Module Structure Diagrammer in the CADM life cycle when you produce the modules in the Pre-Design storyboard process. At that time, you create candidate modules using the ADW and accept them with this diagrammer so you can generate them for the storyboard. When the storyboard process is done, you have notes on modifications that are needed to the calling structure. You incorporate these modifications using the MSD and synchronize the repository definitions with the application modules you manually modified while storyboarding.

In the application design part of the Design phase, you return to this diagrammer and work with the rough-cut module definitions. In the MSD, you can change the calling order, refine the definitions, specify the calling types, and copy modules to other parts of the structure. Figure 9-1 shows a sample Module Structure Diagrammer session.

Basic Techniques

The Module Structure Diagrammer uses a standard Designer/2000 interface similar to that of the Function Hierarchy Diagrammer. As with the other diagrammers, you can represent a set of modules on more than one diagram, although including a module also includes all modules under it in the hierarchy.

Working with diagrams is the same as in other Designer/2000 diagrammers. You use the File menu or toolbar buttons to open, close, or create new diagrams.

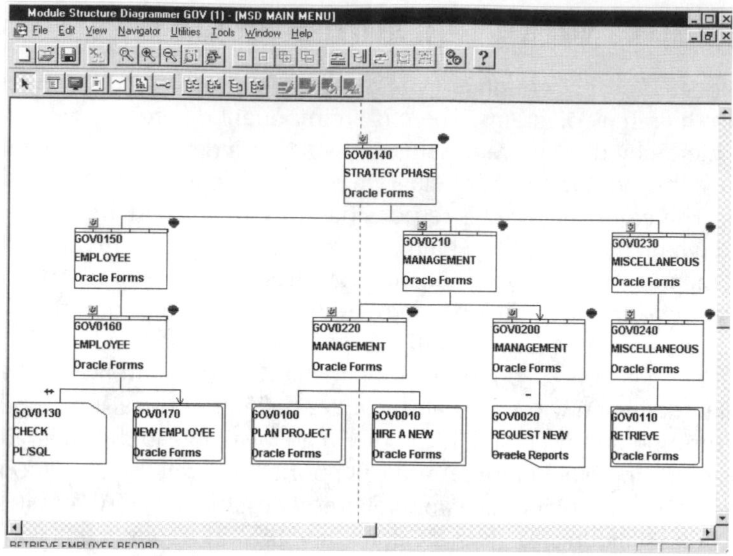

FIGURE 9-1. *Module Structure Diagrammer session*

When you create a new diagram, a blank drawing area appears in which you place existing modules through the **Edit→Include Network** menu item or by creating a new module using the toolbar buttons. You can only include networks, not individual modules, but if the network you want to include does not call other modules, **Edit→Include Network** will place that one module.

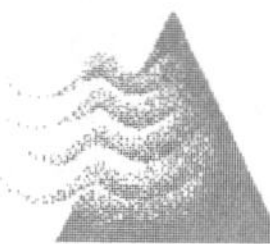

TIP

Generally, the Designer/2000 diagrammers do not save the view magnification setting when they save a diagram. Therefore, after opening a diagram you need to use the View menu or toolbar buttons to zoom in or out and restore your preferred zoom setting. Doing this right after the diagram opens and you have maximized the windows will save you time later in adjusting the view.

Drawing Objects You use only one main symbol in this diagrammer: the module. The diagrammer draws the connector lines between modules when you place or move modules. There are different buttons to create different module types, as the following illustration shows.

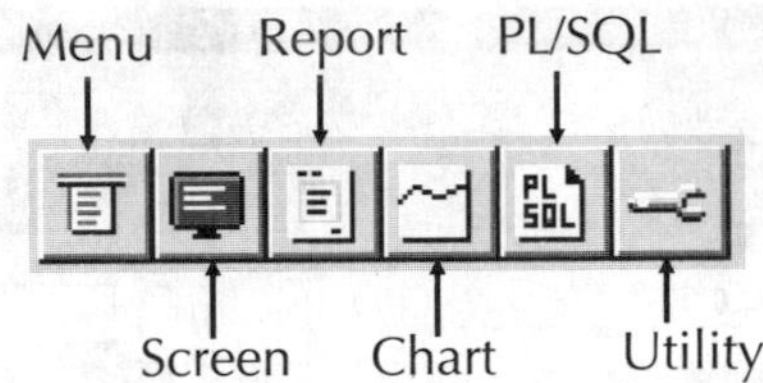

When you click on one of these module buttons, the cursor changes to a box that you can drop on the parent module. For example, suppose MODULE1 is on the diagram and you want to create MODULE2, which is called by MODULE1. You click the module button and then click MODULE1, which opens the Create Module window. After you fill in MODULE2's names and purpose, a new module will appear under MODULE1. If you want to create a module that has no calling (parent) module, you can drop the box on the drawing surface itself instead of an another module.

As with the Function Hierarchy Diagrammer, all modules have the same size boxes, and you can change the size of all of them by dragging in or out on the corner of one box. Alternatively, you can specify the new size in the Preferences window (**Edit→Preferences**). Other than being able to specify which module is the parent module, you cannot choose where a module is placed in the drawing area. There are, however, techniques for resequencing and reparenting, mentioned later.

MSD draws the *module association* connector lines automatically when you place the modules, and you cannot reposition them, although through the Preferences window, you can specify the vertical and horizontal separation and indentation between modules, which is basically what defines the lines. In addition, resequencing and reparenting operations will redraw the association lines.

The Preferences window contains fields for changing the sizes of the module boxes, as mentioned, as well as the fonts and colors used in the modules. You can also specify the line width and color for modules and association lines. There are also sets of check boxes for View, to specify which elements are shown on the diagram, and Details, to specify what information about each module is displayed. The default setting for both shows everything, but you can modify this if you wish and save that setup (with the Save button in that window). You access the Preferences window shown in Figure 9-2 by selecting Preferences in the Edit menu or pressing CTRL-F.

Like most Designer/2000 diagrammers, the Module Structure Diagrammer has toolbar buttons for changing the font, line size, and colors of elements on the drawing. You cannot change the association lines with these buttons, but they are handy for changing modules. Just select the elements you wish to change and click the appropriate visual attribute button (line width, line color, fill color, or font).

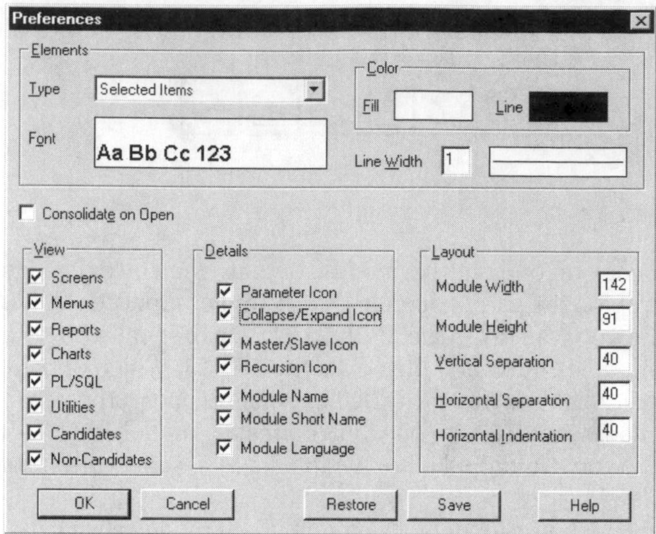

FIGURE 9-2. *Module Structure Diagrammer Preferences window*

You can delete a module from the diagram by choosing **Edit→Exclude Network** from the menu and choosing the module network to remove. This will remove that module and all of its children. The **Edit→Delete Module** menu item will delete the selected module or modules from the repository. The **Edit→Cut** menu item is permanently disabled for modules but works for text that you copy and paste from another source into the drawing area. You can remove a module association from the repository by selecting the child module and clicking the Delete Association button, by choosing the **Edit→Delete Module Association** menu item, or by pressing the DEL key.

CAUTION

Remember that the deletion of elements such as modules from the repository is not reversible. There is an implicit commit associated with a delete operation, so you cannot undo it. Fortunately, the Designer/2000 diagrammers usually ask for confirmation when you request a delete operation.

When you think about the module hierarchy, you can think in terms of parent and child modules. Parent modules call child modules and appear on top of the children or to the left of them, depending on your view mode. All modules you display in the Module Structure Diagrammer fall into four main categories based on where they are displayed in the network. A *solo* module has no network links, that is, no parent or children; a *root* module is the top of the hierarchy and has links only to child modules; a *full* module has links to both a parent and one or more child modules; a *leaf* module has links only to its parent—that is, it is the bottom of a particular branch of the hierarchy. These categories help you clarify how the location in the module structure network affects the behavior and use of the module in the finished application.

Using the Symbol Set The two main symbols include variations that let you indicate the module type and calling connector type. Figure 9-3 shows the symbol variations that the MSD displays.

Each of the six module types has a different default color. You can change these colors in the Preferences window before you draw the network, and the modules will use those new colors. Click the Save button in that window if you

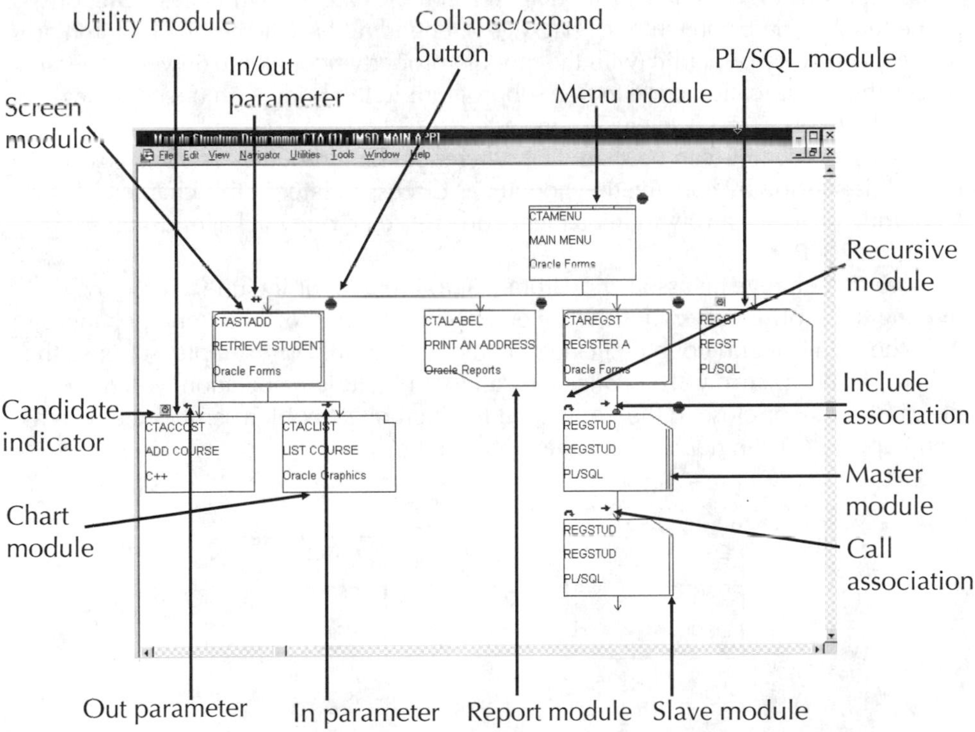

FIGURE 9-3. *Module Schema Diagrammer symbols*

want to save the color changes between sessions. There are actually more module types than symbols, and some symbols cover several types. The PL/SQL module symbol represents the procedure, function, package, cursor, and trigger logic module types. The Utility symbol represents the utility, background, manual, and general module types. All other symbols are only used for their own type.

Defining Association Types The associations have different types as well: either call or include. *Call associations* mean that the parent and child modules are separate, and the parent runs or calls the child. *Include associations* apply only to PL/SQL modules that use the free format or declarative method of definition and can accommodate cursors that need to be included in procedures, functions, or packages.

The include association is also good for creating packages as all subprograms—procedures, functions, and cursors—that are part of the package will have include associations with the package. These subprograms are separate modules themselves but do not make sense without the package specification. When the Server Generator runs on the package module, it assembles all child modules (functions, procedures, and cursors) into the package. Depending on whether the children are scoped as private or public (with the module property Scope), the Server Generator places the specification code for the subprogram in the body with the code or the package spec, respectively. The include association is a powerful tool because separate subprograms can be shared by different calling modules or packages. You effect this sharing by copying the module, as discussed later in this chapter. This technique provides a way to implement code reuse among packages using Designer/2000.

You can change an association from call to include, or include to call, by moving the mouse cursor close to the entry symbol into the child until it changes to the other symbol and double-clicking the mouse button. For example, suppose the call symbol is an arrow. To change the call to an include association, you move the mouse cursor close to the arrow until the include symbol (a semi-circle with a stem) appears. Then double-click the mouse button.

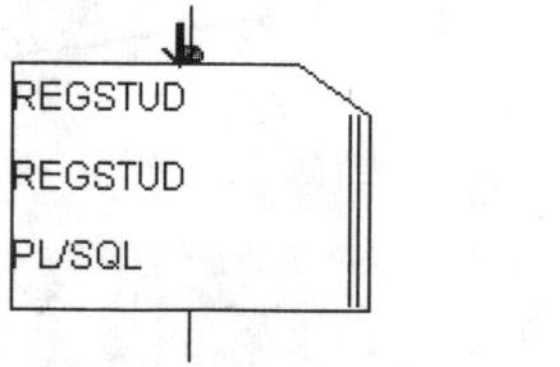

Changing an include association to a call association

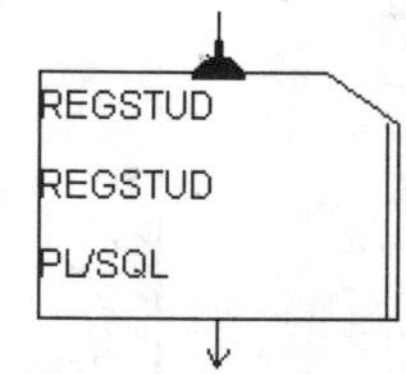

Changing a call association to an include association

Only certain include associations are valid: cursor to subprogram (function or procedure), cursor to trigger, cursor to package, subprogram to trigger, subprogram to subprogram, and subprogram to package. You can define other combinations, but they will not execute correctly in the database.

Defining Parameters When you call (or include) one module from another, you can pass parameter values to the other module. The parameter icon (a blue dash) appears above the called module as in the following illustration if a parameter or parameters is defined for it. The dash becomes an arrow when you define the in/out characteristics of the parameter in the property window.

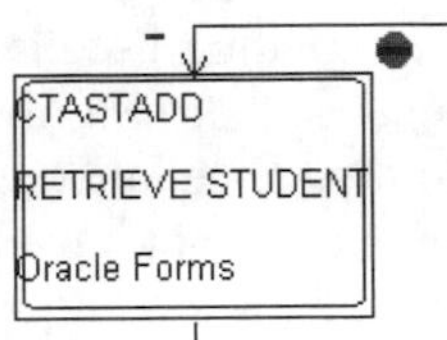

If you place the mouse cursor close to the association line, a horizontal arrow will appear. Then you can double-click, and the Edit Module window will appear, displaying its Parameters tab. On that tab, you can define, change, or delete parameters that are passed to the module. You can also create and modify parameters by displaying the Edit Module window (**Edit→Module** from the menu) and clicking the Parameters tab. An In/Out property defines whether the value of the parameter you list flows in from the caller (Input), is assigned in the module and passed back to the caller (Output), or is passed in and modified (Modify) by the module. This tab includes a horizontal scroll bar which you use to scroll from the Domain field on the left to the Desc field on the right. Other properties for parameters are well documented in the online help system.

Naming Elements The Application Design Wizard assigns names to modules based on the functions they represent. The name of the module is the same as the name of the function it is based on. The ADW forms a short name using the prefix you specify in the ADW window and a number suffix (such as 0040). These names have no special meaning, and you will want to change at least the suffix. File management will be easier if you give all modules from one application system the same prefix. Therefore, one of your naming conventions could be that modules start with two or three letters that indicate the application system and end with five characters that are abbreviations indicating the purpose or use of the module. This would create an eight-character filename, which would work in all operating systems. If you will be using the files only on operating systems that are capable of longer file names, you can expand the suffix.

Other Techniques You can perform a number of other operations in the Module Structure Diagrammer to further manipulate and refine the structure. For example, you can change default menu structure that the ADW creates. This structure consists of a main menu with submenus for each organization unit (business unit). Under each of those menus are submenus for the various module types, and those submenus contain the actual module items. For example, Figure 9-4 shows a module network produced by ADW.

This network includes submenus for Management—modules derived from functions performed by the Management organization unit—and Miscellaneous—modules derived from functions not owned by a business unit. Under each of these submenus are submenus for the module types and for the items under each of those. In the case of the Miscellaneous menu, however, there is no need for another submenu because there is only one module type, so you could reparent the items directly to the Miscellaneous menu and eliminate the GOV0240 Forms menu. In addition, you might have a totally different menu organization in mind. Among the following techniques are some that help you move items around in menus and customize menus to suit your needs.

Accepting Candidate Modules When the ADW creates modules, it assigns a property called Candidate a value of True. You need to accept these candidates if you want to use them for generating modules. You can do this in RON, as the property appears in the Properties window for each module, or in the MSD, where

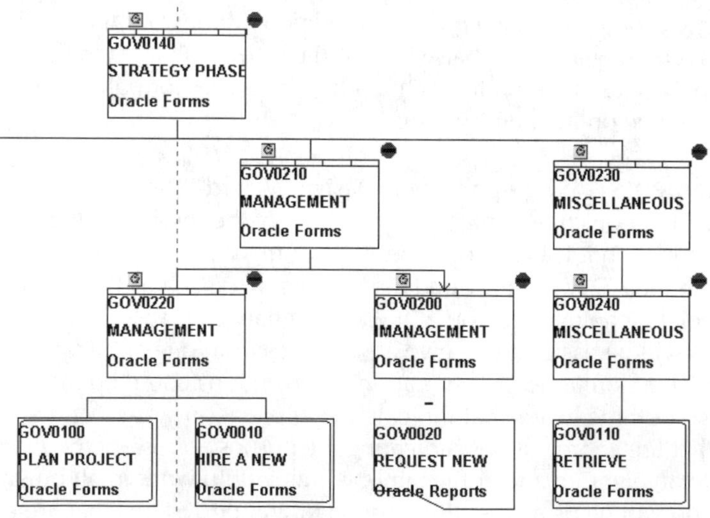

FIGURE 9-4. *Module network produced by ADW*

the property appears as a small button at the top of the module box. To accept candidate modules, you select the module or modules and choose **Utilities→Accept Candidate** from the menu. The button will disappear, and the Candidate property will change to null (which means not a candidate). You can also reject the candidate module by selecting it and choosing **Utilities→Reject Candidate** from the menu. This will display a warning and then delete the module from the repository.

Reparenting Modules If you want to move a module from one parent to another, use the Reparent toolbar button. Click the button; click the module to be moved and hold down the mouse button as you drag the cursor to the new parent; and release the mouse button when the cursor is over the new parent. The module and all its child modules will move to the new parent, and the association lines will be redrawn automatically to reflect the new network structure.

Resequencing Modules To change the order of modules under the same parent, you can use the Resequence button. Click on the button, click the module you want to move and hold down the mouse button as you drag the cursor to the module you want this one to be in front of (on top or to the left of), and release the mouse button. The module and all its children will move, and the association lines will be redrawn. Note that you can resequence modules only within the same parent. If you need to move a module to another parent or level, use the Reparent button.

Copying Modules You can make a copy of a module if you want the same module in different places or with different types in the network. For example, suppose you have a screen module from which you want to create a report. All you need to do is copy the module to a new module and change the module type to Report. The module data usages as well as all child modules will be copied to the new module. To copy a module, click the Copy Module button, click the module you want to copy and hold down the mouse button as you drag the cursor to the module you want to be the parent of the copy, and release the mouse button. This opens the new module window, where you fill in the name, short name, and module type (if you are changing it). If you release the mouse button on empty space in the drawing area, a new module network (root) will be created. When you copy a module, the child modules are copied as slaves (references to the original).

Creating a Slave Module An alternative to copying a module is to create a *slave* module, which is a referenced copy of the module. Unlike the copy module operation, this process does not create another module definition. A slave module is useful when you want to call the same module from more than one place in the network but do not want to create another module. It is also handy when you want an exact copy of the original that changes when the original changes. To create a slave module, click the Create Slave button; click the mouse button and hold it down on the module for which you want to create the slave; drag the mouse to the new parent (or an empty space on the drawing), and release the button. A slave copy will be created with one line on the right indicating that it is a slave. The original module—the *master*—will have two lines on the right indicating that it is the master.

If you want to change the assignment of which module is the master, select the slave module by clicking once to select the set (master and slave) and once again to double-select the slave (it will have thicker selection bars). Then choose **Utilities→Make Master** from the menu, and the selected module will become the master module of the set.

Creating a Recursive Call One use for the slave module is as a *recursive module* or *loop*. A recursive module calls itself, and a recursive loop consists of more than one module where the last module in the calling chain calls the first one. The MSD represents a recursive call with a circular arrow outside the top-left corner of the module box. To create a recursive call, click the Create Slave button, click and hold down the mouse button on the module that starts the loop, drag the cursor to the last module in the loop (which could be the same as the first if this is a recursive module), and release the mouse button. The last module will then call the first module in the set.

Modifying the View As in the Function Hierarchy Diagrammer, you can modify the Module Structure Diagrammer view in a number of ways. You can use toolbar buttons or Utilities menu choices to change the overall layout from vertical to horizontal to hybrid (a combination of vertical and horizontal). File menu selections for Focus up, Focus on Root, Focus on Selection, Set Focus reduce the number of modules you see on the diagram by setting the top-level module displayed. For example, 50 modules may be represented in a particular hierarchy, but you may want to zoom in on only seven of them in a certain branch of the network. You can select the module and choose **File→Focus** on Selection from the menu. This reduces the view on the drawing area and makes the module you selected the root module. Only that module and its children will be shown, although the diagram still consists of other modules, which are temporarily hidden.

You can modify the view of the network by collapsing or expanding the parent nodes. You can double-click the **+** button at the top-right corner of a parent module to expand the hierarchy under it. If a – button appears in that position, all hierarchy nodes are displayed, and you can double-click the button to collapse that branch of the hierarchy.

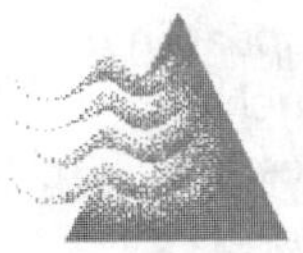

TIP
You can include text in the diagram by selecting and copying it into the clipboard from another application (like Notepad) with **Edit→Copy** and pasting it into the MSD with **Edit→Paste**. This lets you add notes and other text to the diagram, though you cannot change the font or color of this text. If you paste something onto the diagram by mistake, select it and choose **Edit→Cut** from the menu to remove it.

Other Module Properties You can refine or further specify the properties of the module in the Edit Module properties window as you do in the Module Logic Navigator, discussed in Chapter 8. You can display this window using four different methods in this diagrammer: by double-clicking the module symbol, by selecting the module with the mouse and choosing **Edit→Properties** from the menu, by pressing ALT-ENTER, or by selecting **Edit→Module** from the menu and choosing the module from the list that appears.

In addition to the properties discussed in the introduction to the Module Logic Navigator in Chapter 8, you can use the Edit Module tab to set Client Details and Client Help Details properties, though these are disabled for PL/SQL modules. The Client Details tab has fields for the following properties:

- **Format** This field specifies the layout of the form or report and contains choices such as Master Detail, LOV, Control Break, and Label. The format determines the style the generator uses to lay out the form or report, and most of these choices correspond to default layouts in the individual tool (for example, Oracle Reports has layout styles for Master Detail and Label).
- **Source Path** This field specifies the name and path of the file that contains the source code for this module.
- **Runtime Path** This field specifies the name and path of the file that contains the executable code for this module.
- **Command Line** This field contains the full command string that you would use to run the module from the calling module or environment command line. For example, the default command line for a form is

  ```
  CALL_FORM('<MODULE>', HIDE, DO_REPLACE);
  ```

  The generator will replace the '<MODULE>' string with the name of the file, so this line serves as a generic command for all forms.

- **Titles** This area supplies fields for Top and Bottom titles that appear in the margins for Reports modules. You can create generator items (such as CG$MB) in the template form to display these for Forms modules. The Short title field, which becomes the label of the menu item that calls this module, also appears in this area.
- **Implementation Name** This field specifies the name this module will have in the database or file system. If this will be a file, be sure to enter a valid file name.
- **Scope** This field specifies whether this module is private (not available outside the parent module), public (available outside the parent module), or protected (not used in this version of Designer/2000).

The Client Help Details tab contains fields for specifying information for your application's help system. These apply to the files produced by the MS Help Generator that will form an online file-based help system for your application.

- **Help File Name** This field specifies the name of the .HLP file in which help is generated. This is usually set only in the top-level root module, with all child modules using the same file name.
- **Graphic File Name** Generated help files can have embedded graphics, and this field lets you indicate the graphics file you want to use for the help contents topic on this module.
- **Context Id Prefix** This optional field specifies the prefix number the help system uses to reference the module help text in the HLP file. This number must be unique among all modules in your system so the Help Generator can create links for the design elements in the module. This is only useful if you are sharing or copying modules from other application systems.

A few text types (other than the usual Notes and Description types) are available on the Definition tab of the Edit Module properties window (click the Text button to display the text area).

- *PL/SQL Block* is the PL/SQL text for PL/SQL-type modules.
- *Module Generation History* lets you track changes made to the module (if the developer enters information when the change is made). The Forms Generator writes notes into this text area each time it generates the module.
- *Release Notes* holds information on version numbers and descriptions of those versions.

- *User Help Text* is text that appears in the online help system that you generate with the modules. If the module Language property value is of Oracle Forms, you can generate help in a table that is displayed in another help form. You can also specify the MS Help Generator for the help text to create a file you can compile into an .HLP file for file-based help in an Oracle Forms or Visual Basic module.

Other Menu and Toolbar Functions

The File, Edit, View, and Navigator menus consist of the items that this diagrammer has in common with other diagrammers (particularly the Function Hierarchy Diagrammer) or items already discussed in this section.

The Utilities menu includes the layout style selection items and master and candidate module utilities mentioned before. It also contains items to call the generators, Application Design Wizard, Generate SQL DDL, Reverse Engineer Database, and Reconcile utilities. All these are relevant to the elements you work with in this diagrammer.

The Tools menu lets you run other Designer/2000 diagrammers and utilities (such as RON and Repository Reports) as well as the Oracle Forms and Reports design and runtime programs so you can test or modify the modules generated by the applicable generator.

Using RON to Enter Module Definitions

The Repository Object Navigator offers another way to create new modules. You can create the module and assign its properties fully in the Properties window of RON, but the associations appear only in the Modules-Calling node of the module. It is much more difficult to determine the structure of the module network from this node than it is when you diagram with the MSD. However, it is easy to enter the module definitions in RON. In addition, if you need to enter many modules of the same type, it may be faster to use RON than the MSD as you can apply property values to more than one module at a time in RON. However, the aspects of the module that appear in the Edit Module window on tabs other than the Definition tab appear as subnodes of the module in RON. Therefore, you may find it easier to combine the two tools, using RON to create new modules (if there are many to create) and assign initial properties, and using the MSD to refine the definitions and calling information, as well as attach properties for parameters, data structures, and so on.

Where Does This Information Go?

The modules and module structures you work with in the Module Structure Diagrammer form the basis for the code you generate in the Build phase, as Table 9-2 shows.

Module Data Diagrammer Element Definition	Future Use for Element
Module definition	Basis for Forms, Reports, Graphics, Visual Basic, and WebServer Generators
Module structure	Basis for the menu system for the Forms Generator
Module association (both call and include)	Appears as Modules-Calling node in RON for the child module; used to create the menu
Call association	Module generator adds code to call one module from another (for example, from a menu to a form)
Include association	Server Generator creates a PL/SQL package with the included modules as subprograms in the package; used for PL/SQL modules only

TABLE 9-2. *Module Structure Diagrammer Elements and Future Use*

Module Data Diagrammer

The Module Data Diagrammer (MDD) is an important tool you use to refine modules in preparation for the generation process. You refine the module definitions and menu system with the Module Structure Diagrammer, and you refine the module data usages with the Module Data Diagrammer. Using the MDD, you can designate what data elements are used and how they appear in the layout. This diagrammer also acts as a front-end tool to call the generators. It offers a convenient way to work with the generators; you can start the generator from the MDD, generate the module and run it, make notes on changes you wish to make, exit the runtime module and return to the MDD, make the changes in the module definition, and start the process over. This iterative method for generating modules, represented in the following illustration, keeps the definitions updated as you make changes and gives you a quick way to test the effects of those changes.

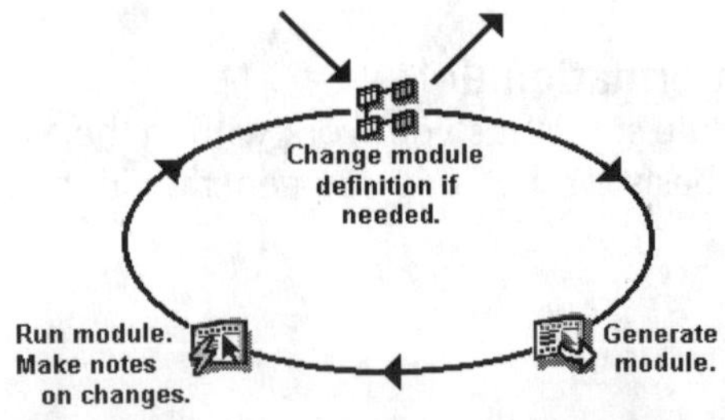

The module types you are concerned with in the MDD are screens, reports, and charts in various languages. Other types do not generate code other than server code and have no data usages or layout characteristics as screens, reports, and charts do. Each diagram in the MDD represents the data usages of one module. Although you can display the Edit Module property window if you need to change module properties, this is not the main activity in this diagrammer. If you want to display the module properties, select **Edit→Elements→Module** and choose the module from the list that appears. Property windows for other elements are also available from the same **Edit→Elements** menu item. These other elements are Table/View/Snapshot, Foreign Key (also available by double-clicking the link symbol), Detailed Usages, Summary Usages, and Item Groups. Figure 9-5 shows a sample MDD session.

Basic Techniques

Opening an existing diagram and creating a new diagram are accomplished as they are in the other diagrammers: through the File menu or toolbar buttons. If you create a new diagram, a dialog window appears where you can choose the module on which you want to base the diagram. You can create a new module from this window by clicking the New Module button. If you base a new diagram on an existing module and that module has data usages already defined, the tables, views, or snapshots (referred to generically as tables in this section) will automatically be drawn on the drawing surface.

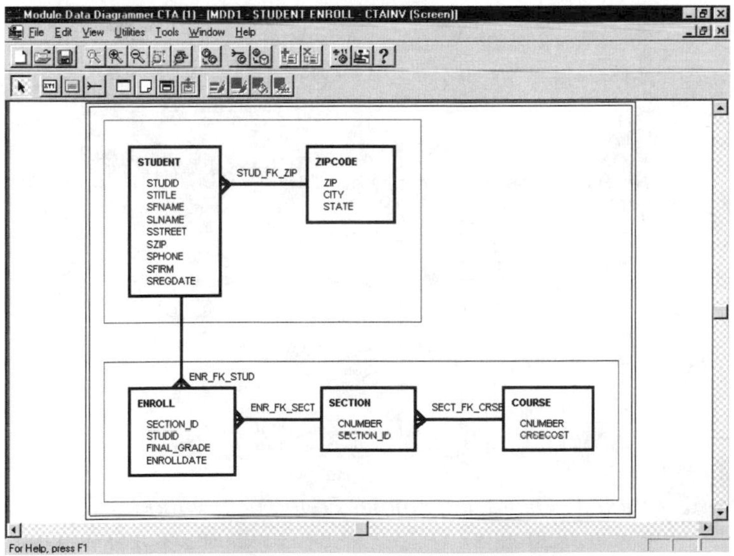

FIGURE 9-5. *Sample Module Data Diagrammer session*

As in most Designer/2000 tools, the Preferences window lets you specify element fonts and colors, the element types displayed, and other aspects of the diagram view. You can choose preferences by selecting **Edit→Preferences** from the menu or pressing CTRL-F. Figure 9-6 shows the Preferences window.

Drawing Objects To place a table in the diagram, select **Edit→Create→Detailed Table Usages** from the menu or click the Detailed Table Usage toolbar button. A list of tables will appear from which you can choose one or more to place in the diagram. This feature is similar to the Include function in some other diagrammers, such as the ER diagrammer, but you cannot specify the columns or foreign key links as you can in the other diagrammers. You can use the Link toolbar button to create the links from foreign key definitions, and you can use the Generate Default Links utility to place the links, as discussed later. To add column usages to the table usage, choose the **Edit→Create→Detailed Column Usages** menu choice (or toolbar button) after you select one—and only one—table.

Using the Symbol Set The MDD provides an easy way to visually specify the data in your module and the module layout. The placement of the tables in the diagram determines how they will be used in the module. *Base table usages* appear

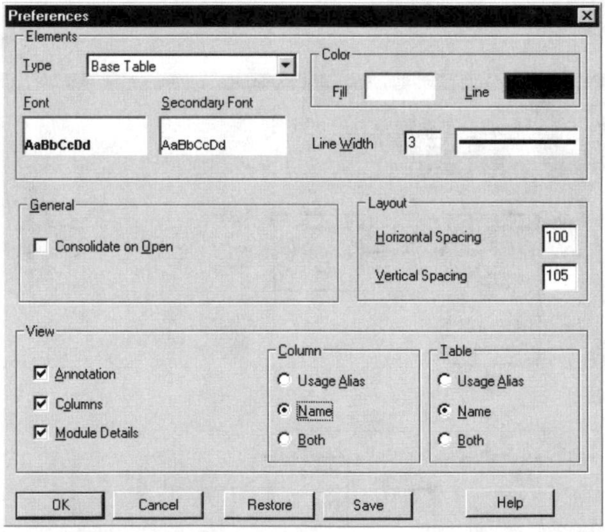

FIGURE 9-6. *Module Data Diagrammer Preferences window*

on the far left side of the diagram. *Lookup table usages* appear to the right of base table usages. A base table below another base table is in a *master-detail link*, and the detail of a master appears below the master in the diagram. Base tables and lookup tables have different default colors so you can easily distinguish them, but the positions also distinguish them.

Designer/2000 will not let you place a detail table above a master table if there is a link between them. The following illustration shows the proper layout for a master (ZIPCODE) and detail (STUDENT) table usage. Both are base table usages.

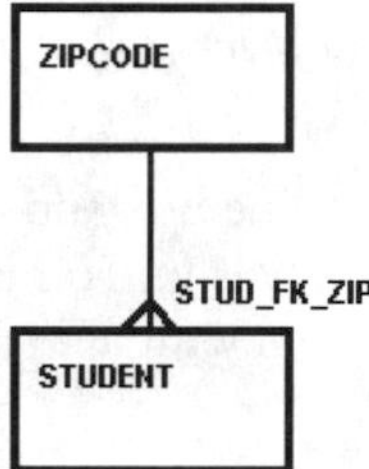

The following illustration shows a base table (STUDENT) and lookup table (ZIPCODE) in the proper layout.

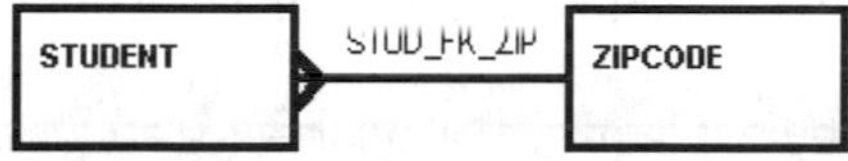

Lookup tables can be chained as in the following illustration.

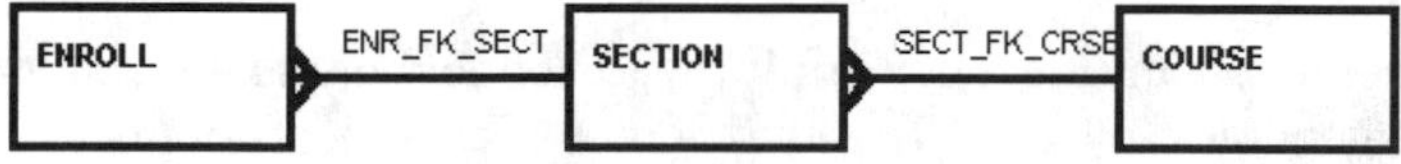

The last type of lookup table is a *treewalk link*, which represents a self-referencing table (like an EMP table that has a foreign key called MGRNO that points to the primary key EMPNO in the same table). This type is represented with a pig's ear symbol as it is in the ER Diagrammer and Data Diagrammer.

A base table represents a block on a Forms form, a group on a Reports report, a zone on a VB form, a record list in a WebServer application, or a chart in a Graphics display. The base table data usage must be appropriate to the module type. For example, a base table on a form may allow insert, update, delete, and select operations, but only select makes sense on a report. Lookup tables in the MDD are always select only. In fact, for a form module they do not represent blocks but nonbase table items in the base table block. The generated module will have code to implement the link.

The two main element symbols are the table and the link, as mentioned before. Variations on these symbols denote base and lookup usages. In addition to these elements, the diagrammer uses *placement items* to denote the location of the tables in the generated module. There are four types of placement items:

- **Window** This is a double-line box that specifies that all tables inside it will appear in the same window for Forms, on the same VB form for Visual Basic, on the same display layer for Graphics, or on the same Web page for WebServer.
- **Page** This item is a single-line box and exists within the window border. It indicates a new content canvas for Forms, a drill-down or report within a report for Reports, or a new layout area in Graphics.
- **Popup** This is another single-line box that you can distinguish from the page because it is contained within a page box. It specifies to the generator a new stacked canvas for Forms or a stacked zone for Visual Basic.
- **Same Page Popup** This looks the same as the popup box but is used only for the Forms Generator to specify that the enclosed tables appear on the same stacked canvas as another popup placement item.

Note that not all placement items are available for all types of modules. However, all are boxes that define the way a module will use the tables and where they will be placed. You can draw these placement items by clicking the corresponding toolbar button and dragging a box around the items that you want to enclose. One rule is that a lookup table usage must inhabit the same placement item as its base table usage.

The placement items are a powerful way to define the visual layout of the tables in the generated module. Try out different arrangements of placement items and generate each one to test the effect; your time will be well spent. This process will increase your understanding of the way the generators interpret the symbols on the diagrammer and speed up your work later.

Defining Item Groups A feature you can use in defining the column data usages is the *item group*. This is a set of items that have a name you define. The generators treat an item group as a unit, and all columns in it are displayed together in the generated module. For example, you can define an item group called Customer Profile that contains the name, address, and phone number of a customer. All these columns will be treated as a group, and when the generator decides to place items in different windows or different parts of the screen, it will keep the set of items close together. You can even specify a prompt for the whole group.

You create an item group by selecting the columns you want to include in the group and choosing the **Utility→Group Detailed Column Usages** menu item or toolbar button. A list of existing item groups will appear. If the item group does not exist yet, you can type the name in the filter field at the top of the window. The name of the item group will appear in parentheses after the column name so you know that the column is part of a group. You can remove a column from an item group by selecting it and choosing **Utility→Remove From Group**. You can remove the item group itself only from RON. (Look under the specific module for the Item group node.)

Other Techniques

The only way to move table symbols around on the diagram is to change their order. For example, you can change a lookup table link to a master-detail link by dragging the lookup table from the right side of the base table to the top of the base table. This will change the lookup table to a base table and the link to a master-detail link. The rules for links are listed here. If the move you want to make meets the criteria in one of these sets of rules, it will be allowed. Otherwise, you will not be able to perform the operation.

Rules for lookup links:

- A lookup table appears to the right of the base (or another lookup) table.
- The table directly to the left must have a foreign key to the lookup.
- The lookup table must have a base table at the far left side even if there are chained lookups.

Rules for master-detail links:

- A detail base table appears under a master base table.
- The foreign key for a link is always in the detail table.
- If the detail table appears under a lookup table, it too will be a lookup table.

To eliminate window or popup boxes, select the box and drag it around other tables in another window or popup screen. This combines the tables in the old window with tables in the new window.

Table and Column Display Properties

The table properties window, called Detailed Usages for Screen (or Report or Graphics) Module, contains a wealth of information that the generator uses to create the final code. While there are some different table display properties in the table definition and table usage definition, there are also some common properties. Most properties are carried over from the table definition to the module, so if you do not specify otherwise in this window, the generator will use the defaults set at the table level. This may be beneficial if you have a standard way you want a table to appear. This would be defined for the table and not changed for the module, so the generator would look at the table settings. The usage definition in the module overrides the table-level properties, so you could view the same table in different ways in different modules.

You will see a slightly different property window depending on whether the module is a screen or report. Most tabs that contain columns display a list of columns on the left. You select one of the columns, and the property values for that column appear on the right. Figure 9-7 shows the top parts of the Screen, Report, and Graphics Detailed Usages windows.

The following discussion highlights some of the more important properties on these Detailed Usages windows. Remember that more documentation is available in the online help system by pressing the Help button at any time when the window is displayed. The module type in parentheses after the tab name indicates the module types that use these tabs.

Table Details (All) The Table Details tab is different for each module type. For the Screen type it specifies the CRUD for the table as well as alias and title information. For the Report type it specifies the layout style (across, address, form, or tabular) and the maximum number of records per page. These are normally manual settings in the Developer/2000 Reports Designer tool. For the Graphics type it specifies properties similar to those for the Table type except that the CRUD properties are missing because they do not apply to graphics displays.

Chart (Graphics) The Chart tab holds information on the chart itself: chart layout style (pie, scatter, table, and so on) as well as placement of the graphic and maximum number of rows displayed.

Table Layout (Screen) The Table Layout tab contains fields for specifying the number of rows displayed, overflow style (which will create a scrolling stacked canvas if you set it to Spread Table), size of popup pages, size and position of windows, whether the windows are scrollable, and window title. The window title of the first base DTU in the module is used as the window title for the generated form.

Table Text (All) The Table Text tab specifies the standard Notes and Description text types. For all types, it also specifies text for a Where/Validation Condition that will act as the WHERE clause when data is retrieved from this table.

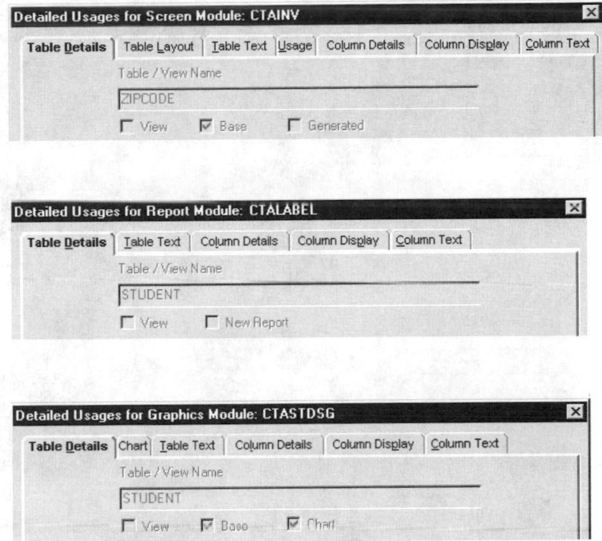

FIGURE 9-7. *Screen, Report, and Graphics Detailed Usages windows*

Usage (Screen) The Usage tab indicates the column usages in the generated form as shown in Figure 9-8. This tab includes settings for Display, Insert (enterable), Update, Select (queryable), and Optional (nullable). It also includes a Context setting that specifies whether this column is used to establish block context when the block continues to another page. If this property is checked and the block items spill over to another page, this column will repeat its value on the next page. The last property on this tab is Lov, which specifies whether the column appears in LOVs for foreign keys that reference this table.

Column Details (All) For the Graphics module type, the Column Details tab contains Order By so you can specify which columns are the sort columns. The Argument area lets you define a parameter that will be passed to the chart. You can also define the column as a summary column and specify the function used to calculate the value.

For the Report type, this tab has a Display option; if this option is unchecked, no field is created on the report. The Break option specifies that this column is used as a break in a report. The Summaries area contains the Source field, where you specify which column you are summarizing.

For the Screen type, this tab repeats the Usage properties from the preceding tab. It also contains options for specifying whether a column appears in the Order

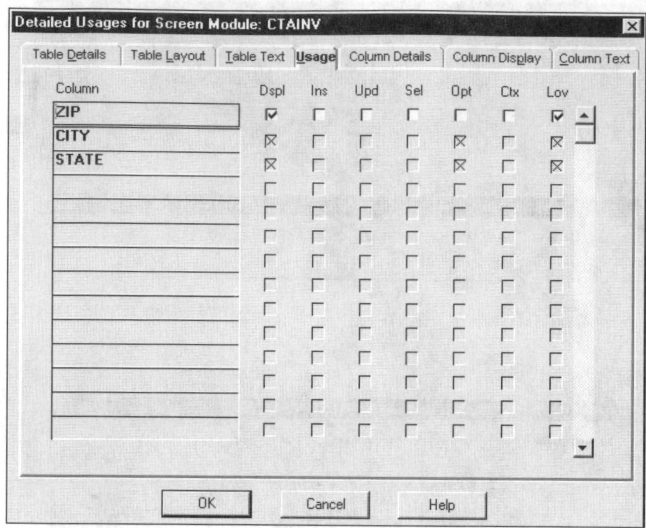

FIGURE 9-8. *Module Data Diagrammer Usage tab*

By clause and the sequence in that clause. It includes summary fields you can use if this column is a secondary (or repeated) nonbase table column and the computation function and type. In addition, there is a field for you to specify the hint line that appears at runtime in the bottom of the screen when the cursor is on the item generated from that column. There is also a default value that the generator places on the item properties for the item derived from that column.

For all types, there are buttons at the bottom-left corner which let you create, remove, or resequence the column list above them. Just highlight a column and press the appropriate button: Create, Delete, Move Up, or Move Down. You can also resequence a column by selecting it on the diagram, dragging it to the new location in that DTU, and dropping it there.

Column Display (All) On the Column Display tab, the Graphics type includes a Plot As Group to define the source of the plotted value. The Field area gives you a place to enter the display datatype, template, and axis origin. The Group Fields area manages the item groups that this chart defines. The last two fields, Label and Highlight, let you specify the field label and the formatting style.

For the Report type, this tab provides different Display and Item Group areas to reflect the nature of reports. It includes a Context specification so this column value can be carried from one page to the next if the page overflows.

For the Screen type, this tab provides a Display area for designating the field (item) prompt and justification of the value in the field. It also contains a display datatype field to specify the GUI control (check box, radio group, combo box, VBX control, and so on). This tab also has a field for specifying a format mask that the generator will write directly to the item properties in the form. The Implementation Item property is used to name an item in the template form on which this column is based for VBX and OLE controls. The Width and Height fields specify the size, in characters, of the item on the generated form. Since you will probably be using a proportionally spaced font, the generator calculates the actual size based on the average character size. The Item Group field supplies the prompt for the group and indicates whether the group is stacked on another group.

Column Text (All) For the Graphics and Screen types, the Column Text tab includes the usual Notes and Description text types as well as Derivation Expression, PL/SQL Block, Highlighting Condition, and User Help Text fields. The help text is the text written into the help table or help file to create the context-sensitive help system.

For the Report type, this tab is the same as for the Graphics and Screen types except it does not include the PL/SQL block text type.

Data Usages: Detailed and Summary

Whenever you attach a table (or view or snapshot) or column to a module, you are creating a *data usage* for that module that specifies which data you want this module to act on. If you create these usages in the Module Data Diagrammer, the association will be stored in elements called *Detailed Module Table Usage,* which you can view under the module node in RON, and *Detailed Module Column Usage,* which you can view under the specific table usage node in RON.

Summary data usages are created automatically when you create the detailed usages. Whereas the detailed usages can include the same table twice in one module, the summary usages record a table only once per module. The summary usages appear on impact analysis reports.

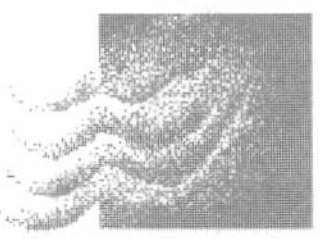

CAUTION

Although the summary column usages are created automatically from the detailed column usages, if you delete detailed column usages in preparation for deleting the column from the table, the summary column usage may not be deleted. You have to manually delete the summary usage or you will not be able to delete the column from the table.

Copy Function Usages Utility

The Utilities menu provides the Copy Function Usages option that lets you create table and column usages for a module from the functions on which the module is based. This utility examines the entity and attribute usages for the function or functions on which this module is based and creates corresponding table and column usages. Note that for this utility to work, all associations must be in place: module to function, table to entity, and column to function. This utility gives you a quick way to add the usages and provides a starting point for complex modules. This utility is the same as the RON menu item **Utilities→Create Default Module Data Usages→from Function Usages**.

Copy Summary Usages Utility

The Copy Summary Usages utility, available from the Utilities menu, is similar to the Copy Function Usages utility as it creates data usages for the module. The source of the usages, however, is the summary usages for that module. This utility is the same as the RON menu item **Utilities→Create Default Module Data Usages→from Summary Usages**.

Generate Default Links Utility

The Generate Default Links utility creates table usages links between tables in your diagram. It uses the foreign keys you have defined in the repository for the tables to link tables on the diagram and provide descriptors. To run the utility, select the **Utilities→Generate Default Links** menu option or click the toolbar button of the same name. The following dialog box appears:

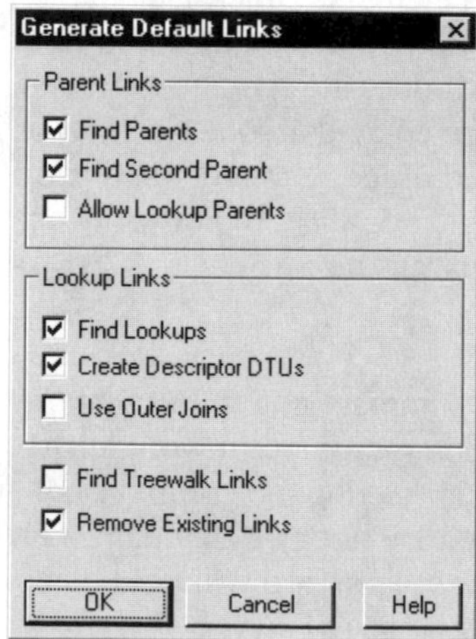

You can accept the defaults for the Parent Links, Lookup Links, and other link check boxes or, if you need more information on each check box, click the Help button in this window. Note that you can create the links manually using the Link toolbar button if the foreign key already exists.

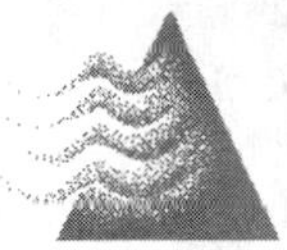

TIP
If you need a foreign key lookup link but you do not want to implement a foreign key constraint, create the constraint anyway and set its Create flag to False. The constraint will not be implemented in the DDL script, but you can still use it to create the links.

Generate Reference Tables Utilities

Code, reference, and help tables are automatically populated when you generate a module. Although the generators can create some of these tables when the first module that uses them is generated, it is best to explicitly create these tables so you know that the task is done. Use the **Utilities→Generate Reference Tables** menu item to create the following:

- **Help tables** If you decide to use the table-based help system, set the HLPTYP preference on the application or module level to HELPFORM. The generator will insert the help text into the table you create with the Generate Reference Tables utility as it generates the module. The help text will appear in a separate form when you run the module. Note that this procedure applies only to screens built with Oracle Forms. If you specify a HLPTYP as MSHELP, the form will use the help text from a help source file.

- **Reference code tables** These tables supply a list of allowable values to the Forms, Visual Basic, and Reports (for the parameters screen) modules. The generator loads the reference code when it generates the module from the Allowed Values node of the column or the domain on which the column is based. The generator also creates the program code to check the table and display lists of values of the reference codes.

- **Code control tables** Code control tables supply primary key columns with unique values from a table. This feature is useful for databases other than Oracle. If you use an Oracle database, the Oracle sequence object can supply the unique values. The Sequence Name column property allows you to designate the name of the repository sequence definition from which you will create a database sequence.

Other Menu and Toolbar Functions

The File menu contains the normal Designer/2000 items. Remember that you can include a title box in this and other diagrams with the window that appears when you choose **File→Summary Information** from the menu. In this diagrammer, you should also place a check mark next to the **View→Module Details** menu item if you want to see this title box.

The Edit menu contains the usual Edit features as well as the Select Same Group item, which selects all columns in an item group if you have selected one column already. It also contains the Include New item, which is like Consolidate because it synchronizes the existing elements on the diagram with those in the repository. However, this item functions specifically to add table and column usages and links that have been added to the repository (for example, in RON).

The View menu has the standard items as well as Annotation, Columns, and Module Details items. If you turn off Annotations, any text you have pasted from another application (such as Notepad) will not appear. Annotations are an easy way to add text to the diagram. Just select the text you want to paste from Notepad (or another source), copy it, and paste it into the MDD. Turning off Columns removes the display of columns in the diagram. The definitions are still associated with the module but not shown in the diagram. This feature is helpful if your tables have many columns or your module has many tables because it reduces the size of the diagram.

The Utilities menu contains items for generating and regenerating modules and server code in addition to the reverse engineering and reconcile utilities. You can also run the Application Design Wizard utility from this menu. The Copy Module item displays the Copy Module window so you can create another module by copying the diagrammed module.

The Tools menu contains the usual repository utilities as well as the other Design phase tools: MSD, Preferences Navigator, and DD. There are items for Oracle Forms and Reports runtime and design tools so you can test and modify the code you generate and define in the MDD.

Where Does This Information Go?

The main elements you use in the Module Data Diagrammer are the module definition data usages and the layout itself. These definitions are core components for code generation. To generate most code modules in Designer/2000, you need the module definition with its data usage definitions, the specific generator utility for that module type, preferences (either default or customized), and the module template (for Forms, Reports, Graphics, and Visual Basic modules). The particular generator combines the properties and associations of the module with the preferences and predesigned template to create the finished application module. As mentioned, this generation in the Build phase is an iterative process, and the Module Data Diagrammer is a perfect place to start the generator utilities.

Implementing the Control Exposure Matrix

One of the tasks in the Design phase is constructing an exposure control matrix. You can implement this system with user extensions in Designer/2000. This allows you to track the exposures and controls in the repository so you can run the Matrix Diagrammer to cross-check the assignments and include the control exposure plan in reports.

All you need to do is to create user extension elements for exposures and controls. These elements allow you to enter all details of those parts of the security system. You also need an association element with a property called Evaluation that relates the exposures and controls. You can then associate exposures to controls by placing a numeric Evaluation value in the association element.

Creating the user extensions is a job you complete in the Repository Administration Utility, discussed in Chapter 4. Filling in the association between exposures and controls is easiest in the Matrix Diagrammer, although you can also use the Repository Object Navigator. You can run reports on the new elements and associations using the User Extensibility group of repository reports or create your own reports with SQL*Plus or Oracle Reports.

Matrix Diagrammer in Application Design

Toward the end of the application design part of Design you should cross-check the design. One of the tools you use to perform this check is the Matrix Diagrammer, introduced in Chapter 6. Three main matrix diagrams are useful at this stage in the life cycle to ensure that the design is as sound as possible:

- Relations (Tables) and Modules
- Requirements and Modules
- Exposures and Controls

Relations and Modules

The first matrix you create in this phase cross-checks data and modules. You want to be certain that all data elements you defined are being used correctly and completely in the modules you designed. You can set up a matrix of Relations (tables, views, and snapshots) and Modules to check the create-retrieve-update-delete characteristics and determine whether any tables are missing from modules or some operation (create, retrieve, update, or delete) is not being performed anywhere in the system. If such exceptions exist, the matrix diagram will help you identify them so you can fix the usages.

This review may also point out a module that repeats the data usage of another module and, therefore, may not be essential to the application. It may also reveal that you need another module to handle some operation on a particular table or set of tables. Once you have a sense of where the trouble spots are, you can modify modules, add modules, and delete modules before running the matrix again to check the design.

Requirements and Modules

Another matrix you may want to run at this point shows requirements and the modules that fulfill them. In Pre-Design you created a user-extension element of Requirement and a user-extension association of Requirement to Module. The requirements linked to functions during the Analysis phase were passed on to their respective modules during Pre-Design so that each module has the same requirements as the functions from which it derives. The matrix you create at the end of Design shows these elements and associations and allows you to check that all requirements have a module. By carefully examining the matrix, you can determine whether there are any requirements without modules or modules without requirements. In the former case, you may need another module to fulfill the requirement. In the latter case, the module either was not assigned requirements or is unnecessary and should be deleted.

Exposures and Controls

You may want to develop user extensions and create an Exposure and Controls Matrix (Security Deliverable) using Designer/2000. This matrix enables you to check whether all exposures have at least one control. This matrix is one of the tools you used to enter the information in the first place, so you just need to open it again at the end of the Design phase and check whether there are controls for all exposures and exposures for all controls. If you find that you are missing controls, you have to add them. If you have controls without exposures, you can probably delete these extra controls.

Repository Reports in the Design Phase: Application Design

As usual at the end of a phase, you can run reports to show and check the work you have done in that phase. The appropriate repository reports you run at this point are in the Module Design, System Access, Quality, User Extensibility, and Impact Analysis groups.

Module Design The Module Definition and Module Network reports provide information on the menus and modules, respectively. The Module Data Summary report shows the data usages for a module, and the Functions Implemented by Modules report shows the functions from which your modules are derived.

System Access You need to check whether module security has been applied to implement part of the exposure control system. The Access to Modules by User Groups report lets you check the module access you have assigned to roles (groups) in the repository. Another check is user or group access to tables, but this report is one you need to write yourself as there is no such repository report available.

Quality In all phases of the CADM life cycle, it is important to run quality-control reports to cross-check the element definitions for completeness and validity. For example, the Invalid Database Objects Control report shows, among other things, any tables or objects whose names are Oracle reserved words. The Create Status Quality Control report lets you check whether the objects you want to create have the Create property set to True.

User Extensibility You can use reports in the User Extensibility group to display new associations or element types and their matrices. For example, you can report on the exposures and controls with the Element to Element Matrix report. You can also apply this report to the matrix of requirements and modules.

Impact Analysis Impact analysis reports show you what other elements will be affected if you change a module or table. For example, the Views and Their Table Derivations report shows which tables are used as the basis for the views in your system.

Conclusion

With the completion of the application design, the system is fully designed. Notice that there was very little explicit user involvement in this phase. There should continue to be user representation on the design team throughout the development process, but you are now no longer dealing exclusively with the collection and analysis of system requirements. These requirements are now being formatted in preparation for the building of the application.

Application design is one of the least-glamorous phases, requiring hours of tedious work but not generating a particularly interesting deliverable. Just as in the Strategy phase, there is an enormous temptation to cut corners in the Design phase. However, doing so would be a mistake. Application design helps you finalize the database design and prepare for the building of the rest of the system.

Although the Design phase requires extensive use of technical specialists, users also must remain involved. They assist by ensuring that:

- External design components such as screens, reports, and documentation meet their needs.
- Modules are mapped to the correct requirements.
- The security deliverable reflects their views of acceptable risks, priorities, and controls.
- The functional specifications for each module reflect the business.

The Designer/2000 tools thoroughly support the application design part of the Design phase. You refine the module structures and module definitions that you created in Pre-Design so they are ready for the Build phase. Another important activity in application design is the cross-checking of data elements against the modules you designed. This brings together the data and process parts of the application and ensures that the module definitions are as complete as possible.

The next chapter discusses the Build phase, where you produce the application code, and the Designer/2000 tools that assist you in that work.

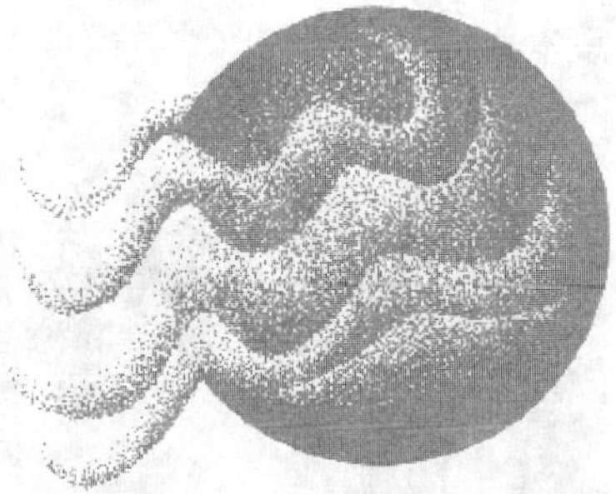

CHAPTER 10

Build

The youth gets together his materials to build a bridge to the moon, or, perchance, a palace or temple on the earth, and, at length, the middle-aged man concludes to build a woodshed with them.

—Henry David Thoreau

In the Build phase, we build both the database and the applications. If all the activities and deliverables identified in the previous phases have been completed carefully, building the proposed database should be a relatively straightforward process. However, building the modules to support the database still requires quite a lot of work, because you need to use the Designer/2000 module generators. The Designer/2000 generators are very powerful utilities that, when used correctly, can automatically generate nearly perfect production applications. Incorrectly used, however, generators can increase development time and provide little benefit to the project. The key to Build phase success is correct use of the generators.

Overview of the Build Phase

In the Build phase, you build the database and application; but there is also other work to be done. These are the steps in the Build phase:

1. First, you must build the database. This work includes physically configuring its location and creating instances.
2. Next, you must build a quantity of test data and perform data migration. Applications cannot be built with an empty database.
3. You must build applications and implement the internal control system. To build and validate the application, you will use the design book as a blueprint to ensure that all specifications are met. The developer should meticulously check off each system requirement in the design book as it is met during the building of the module.
4. As the application is built, you must perform tuning and unit-level testing to ensure functional and technical accuracy. This is a crucial step in the Build phase. This quality assurance process is perhaps the most critical part of the building process.

Each application must go through this build-test process to ensure that it is built correctly. In addition, you must consider the help system and user documentation.

Deliverables

The Build phase deliverables consist of the following:

- Unit tested application system
- Populated databases
- System documentation
- User documentation
- Help system and online documents

Building the Database

The actual building of the database is a relatively straightforward process. First, you have Designer/2000 generate the data definition language (DDL) script to create the tables. The generated table sizes will be too large for development, and they will not be placed in the correct tablespace for development. Make some manual modifications to the build script so you can create three copies of the database.

- **Version 1: Small tables populated with dummy test data** Dummy test data is unrealistic-looking test data that has been carefully constructed to validate the correctness of the applications and reports. You should use data that allows you to easily see whether the applications and reports are running correctly.
- **Version 2: Small tables populated with realistic-looking data** This version shows users what the application will actually look like. For this version, the developers and testers build the test data at the same time as the application. The creation of this sample data is then part of the testing process.
- **Version 3: Full-size database populated with real migrated data** This version is used for stress and performance testing.

Building Unrealistic Dummy Data

How much dummy data should you use in the first version of the database? Each core main table will require 200 to 300 records. For example, a sales database might be set up using 10 to 20 regions. Each region might have 0 to 20 customers, each customer might have 0 to 20 sales, and each sale might have 0 to 20 items. On the surface, it might seem like a lot of work to create dummy data for this many records. This process cries out for automation.

Even if it is not feasible to build a utility to automate this process, there is still an easy way to build thousands of rows of sample data quickly. By using a spreadsheet, you can easily build a data set that can be uploaded into the database using SQL*Loader. Let's generate a sample data set for the EMPNO, ENAME, and DEPTNO columns of the EMP table in Oracle's SCOTT/TIGER sample database as an example. In Table 10-1 we show an Excel spreadsheet that is set up to generate the sample data. Note that the actual SQL*Loader data is in column E. By simply typing in the first rows of the spreadsheet, the remaining rows can be quickly generated through Excel's Autofill command. The formula in cell E2 is

```
B2&A2&$C$2&B2&A2&$D$2&B2.
```

The remainder of the E column is populated by copying the formula down through the column.

This procedure saves a great deal of time in writing many rows of data and makes it very easy to tell if the modules are working correctly.

Notice that, when the ENAME field is displayed, you know that you are looking at the ENAME field. You know the value of EMPNO and the value of DEPTNO. The purpose of the dummy data is to support the application and report building process by providing an easy way to validate that the application and reports are performing correctly.

Dummy data should be published and not changed by the developers. After using the dummy data to check applications, a restore operation should be performed to bring the dummy data back to its original state. Otherwise, one developer's manipulation of the dummy data may cause another developer to think that the applications are not working.

Another reason for using dummy data rather than production data is that because the amount of data is relatively small, it enables applications and reports to run very fast.

Building Realistic Sample Data

Realistic sample data for the second version of the database can be built as part of the developer's testing process for the applications. Initially, the developer can use

	A	B	C	D	E
1	empno	deptno	string	string	empno,ename,deptno
2	1	10	,'ename	',	101,'ename101',10
3	2	10			102,'ename102',10
4	3	10			103,'ename103',10
5	4	20			204,'ename204',20
6	5	20			205,'ename205',20
7	6	20			206,'ename206',20

TABLE 10-1. *Excel Spreadsheet to Assist in Creating Dummy Data for EMP table*

the dummy test data version of the database to make sure that the basic functionality of the module is in place. Then the developer can shift the module to the second version of the database by logging in as a different user and use the module itself to generate sample data, using real business transactions supplied by the users. Additional realistic sample data can be generated by the module testers in a similar fashion.

Performing Data Migration

Data migration is the moving of legacy system data into newly created data structures. One of the most useful aspects of the legacy system data migration is that it also serves as an audit of the database design. It thus provides validation of the database structure, except for the new tables and columns not derived from historical data.

To perform the data migration, you follow these steps:

1. Upload legacy system extract files to Oracle temporary tables.
2. Correct inconsistencies in the legacy data.
3. Populate the database tables.
4. Populate the summary and aggregation tables.

Uploading Legacy System Files

Uploading the data is a relatively straightforward process. First, you create tables in Oracle that are exact images of the old system files. You create these tables in the develop instance. Then use SQL*Loader to perform a simple upload of the old system files to the Oracle temporary table.

The amount of disk space required will be much larger than the size of the old system files. First, enough DASD space will be needed to import the files for uploading into Oracle. Then more space will be needed for the temporary Oracle tables, which effectively doubles the amount of DASD space needed. In fact, the amount of DASD space required for such an operation usually is much more than double the size of the files to be uploaded. Databases have blank spaces in their files for data expansion. Space is also needed for indexing. However, in some cases, the amount of space required in Oracle will not be much different from the amount of space required in the old system files for the following reasons:

- In many legacy system files, all character fields are packed with spaces that use up potentially available space. On average, those fields are probably only half filled with information. As the VARCHAR2 fields are uploaded, the data will be compressed significantly.
- One of the filtering procedures performed by SQL*Loader is to selectively upload fields. Many existing old system fields will not be needed in the new system. These unnecessary fields do not need to be uploaded.

For estimation purposes, you can assume that 50 percent more disk space will be needed to upload the data into Oracle than was needed for the original legacy system files. DASD space used for the database can be minimal until the migration script is complete. Only enough space is needed to load a few thousand rows of data. All tables can be placed in the same tablespace, and no indexes need to be built. After a test migration is complete, DASD requirements can be estimated accurately.

Validate and Correct Legacy System Data

After the legacy system files have been uploaded, a staging area for the information will exist. Now you can determine how the data will migrate to the new system. You should check the quality of the information before beginning the migration. Even if legacy system tables that are exact replicas of the database tables are passed and loaded directly to the database tables, you should treat these logically as staging areas until they are validated. After the tables are validated, you can treat them as migrated tables.

It is important to ensure that no fields have logically inconsistent information. For example, the sum of the amount of claim and claim details should equal the claim total. You should validate this before migrating the data.

The old system may store certain information in multiple places. As a result, there may be inconsistent duplicate entries. These inconsistencies need to be found and eliminated.

The data validation should take place prior to the migration to the database. However, validation and error correction can also occur within the database tables. Scrubbing and validation routines should be saved as executable error correction scripts.

Populating the Tables

If the computer is fast enough, it is simplest to perform the migration to the database with the database constraints turned on. However, it may not be possible to get the migration script to run fast enough with the constraints enabled. In any case, the script can be written in such a way that it would work if the constraints were enabled. This requires careful ordering of the loading of the tables.

In general, the tables should be loaded in the following order:

- **Type 1: Peripheral tables** These tables are not based on changeable data. They include lookup tables and code descriptions. These tables will be populated first.
- **Type 2: Data tables** These tables don't change often, no matter how much data is being loaded. Some examples are client lists and employee lists.
- **Type 3: Volatile tables** These tables change over time.

Type 1 tables can be entered in (more or less) random order. Type 2 and 3 tables will require careful ordering, but the type 2 migration script should be run before the type 3 migration script.

The main portion of the script concerns the type 3 tables. Developers' time in testing the script can be optimized by limiting the amount of data to be migrated until the script is well tested. After testing, all of the information can be migrated, and then more extensive testing can be performed.

The script for each subject area should be created in three steps. After type 1 and 2 data tables have been stabilized, then the type 3 tables should be migrated and stabilized.

Preparing the Migration Script How much information should be extracted from the old system to test the migration? There are two options:

- You can initially use a very small extract from the old system, consisting of about one month's worth of data (or less). You will need enough information to create about 1,000 rows of data.
- You can use a full extract from the old system, adding a where clause to limit the amount of data migrated to the database. The advantage of this option is that you can more easily estimate how long the real script will take. For example, if 10 percent of the data is used in the extract, you can assume that the full migration will take ten times as long.

If the extract is limited to such a small amount of information, then the whole migration script will run in 10 to 20 minutes.

If you use the first option, you will not have a real sense of how long the script will take to run on the complete database since the information subset is so small. The first method uses a set of tables in the old system equal to perhaps 5 percent the size of the real tables. The second method uses the real tables; if 5 percent of the information is migrated, for example, then you can reasonably expect that the complete script will take about 20 times as long to run.

For this reason, if space is available, the second method is preferable. With only a subset of the information, you can validate only whether the script is logically correct; you cannot gauge whether the script is adequately tuned to run in a reasonable amount of time.

Coding the Script The actual script will be a series of SQL*Plus statements and procedure calls that handle data migration.

To begin each table's migration, you use a straight SQL*Plus statement to populate the table. This example uses the syntax from an insurance claim environment:

```
Insert into Claim (
                                  Claim_ID,
                                  Eff_Date)
            (select
            old system_claim_ID,                    - - Claim_ID
                                                    - - Eff_Date
from ...
where...);
```

This syntax is self-documenting and does not require modification if the structure of the underlying tables changes.

A major portion of the writing of this script can be automated. If you store legacy information in the Designer/2000 repository, then you can write a routine that will generate first cuts of the SQL*Plus portion of the routine. The table and column mappings are known, so you can automate the SQL*Plus statements. The script that is generated will not be accurate but will save a lot of time and typing.

In general, you will not be able to populate all columns with a simple SQL*Plus statement. Some columns can be populated using an Oracle-generated sequence number. Some columns require a special procedure to calculate them.

If a field that does not populate is mandatory (that is, not null), you have two alternatives:

- Disable the constraint, run the procedure, and then reenable the constraint.

- Populate the field with a dummy value, run the procedure, and then check to make sure that no dummy values remain.

The second alternative is preferable, although both methods are effective.

The problem of how to populate columns that don't map one to one still remains. Individual PL/SQL routines can be written to calculate each field. If multiple columns can be migrated in a single procedure, this will be done. Each subject area's procedures will be stored in a package, there will be one procedure for each table in the package body, and each procedure will handle all migration for the table that the simple SQL insert statement does not support.

Organizing the Script Each subject area should have its own script. Fields that require information from other subject areas should be left until later and placed in the area of the script known as overlapping fields.

There are three places to look to see where a particular field was populated. The procedure can be called

- With the table
- At the bottom of the script for that subject area
- In the overlapping fields section

Aggregation and summary tables have their own section.

The script structure is listed here. The script structure for type 2 and 3 tables is the same.

```
Type 1 tables
        table 1
                SQL
                fields that couldn't populate with simple SQL
        table 2
                SQL
                fields that couldn't populate with simple SQL
        table ...
                fields that required already migrated information
Type 2 tables
                (same structure as type 1 tables)
Type 3 tables
                (same structure as type 1 tables)
Overlapping fields
Aggregation and summary
```

Type 1 and 2 tables can be migrated completely because the tables are relatively small and stable. Type 3 tables, on the other hand, can be very large, so when you are developing the migration script, you should work with a small subset of the data. Then, once the script is debugged and tested, you can populate the tables completely.

Populating the Summary and Aggregation Tables

Summary and aggregation tables will not map back to tables in the database, so you must write the script for these populations by hand. The structure of the migration script for these tables is the same as that for the rest of the script.

Tuning Performance

You should build in code to monitor the progress of the script and identify the parts of the script that take the most time. This will help optimize the script. There is no point in optimizing a line of code that takes only a minute or so to run. Procedures requiring an hour or more need to be reexamined.

All indexes should be turned off for migration purposes. Indexes should be dropped and disabled at the start of the migration and rebuilt as the last step of the script. The rebuilding of indexes should be considered a part of the migration script and included in the time needed to set up the database.

Validating the Migration Script

The best indication that the migration script is valid is getting the modules to run. However, the script should be validated as fully as possible before the data is passed to the module developers. Developers should not be given obviously bad data. It is frustrating for a module developer to spend several hours debugging a module only to discover that the report is correct, but the underlying data is invalid. Several steps can be taken to validate the script:

- Before allowing migration, place extensive constraints on the database so that enabling the constraints provides a good reasonableness check of the data. The data must get through the constraints before it is passed to the tester.
- Use a tester to check the database. This tester should look at each of the columns of the migrated data and perform a SELECT DISTINCT operation on each one to check that all values are reasonable.
- Forms can be used to build very simple applications that support the one-to-many-to-many relationships throughout the database. These forms can be built quickly (in one or two days) for the whole database. Designer/2000 can be used to generate the Forms application.

- The final step in the validation process is the generation of the actual reports. At this point, a set of test modules should be generated based on whatever sample data extract is being used. The final test will be whether reports can be generated in the new system with the same numbers as in the old system. You should designate a QA person who will be responsible for performing tests and careful checks. The person doesn't need to be skilled; the person does need to meticulously examine the new reports field by field and compare them to the legacy reports.

As soon as all of the old system data has been migrated, the database will have to be retested. There are always a few errors in the process that do not show up until all of the data has been migrated.

Auditing the Database

It is important to know that the database has been built according to the data requirements. The module design and cross-checks helped to validate the database design, as did the legacy system migration. You must assume that during the building of the modules, further modifications will be made to the database. Therefore, you will need to audit the data structure during the Test phase.

The question then remains: what level of audit of the database design is appropriate prior to the building of the modules? If you performed a legacy system data migration, there is probably little need to fully audit the database. However, you do need to ensure that the Design and Build phase processes have been completed correctly. Therefore, as a minimum, you should randomly spot-check each developer's work in the Design and Build phases. If problems in the work of one or more developers become evident, or if there was no legacy system to migrate, a more thorough audit may be necessary.

Building the Modules

Module building is an iterative process. You generate the modules and then assess how different the generated modules are from the desired modules. Here, developers take different approaches. Some developers prefer to make changes to the Designer/2000 repository and then regenerate the module; others make all of their modifications within the screen module and perform reverse engineering where possible. The approach the developer uses depends in part on what tool the developer prefers. However, regardless of the approach, the resulting application should be the same.

You don't need to explicitly worry about internal control system implementation at this point because you have already made the necessary modifications to the design book required by internal control systems. The control requirements are simply another feature or function in the modules that you must build and test.

There are several basic steps in building the modules. First, you generate the module based upon the preferences you selected in Designer/2000. The following factors determine how closely your generated module matches the goal you are trying to achieve:

- How you specified the preferences
- How much of your code you already placed in the Designer/2000 repository
- The template you are using for the generation
- The complexity of the module

Next, you need to refine the module. You need to make the generated module conform to the system specifications. The easiest way to do this is probably by using the development tool—for example, Developer/2000—rather than making modifications within Designer/2000 and generating the module again. At this point, the link between Designer/2000 and the module is broken; if you generate the module, the refinement process will have to be redone, which is neither practical nor desirable.

The next step is to decide whether enough of the postgeneration work for this module can be embedded within Designer/2000 in such a way that future changes in the data structure will be reflected in the generated modules. If you decide you can achieve nearly 100 percent generation, including the modifications, then you should take the next step.

You need to implement all postgeneration work in such a way that changes automatically occur when the module is regenerated. There are three basic strategies for accomplishing this:

- Place the information in the Designer/2000 repository. This is the best approach. This way, all requirements are stored in the repository, and any changes are automatically applied to the regenerated modules.
- Embed the changes in a form-specific template.
- Make selective changes to modules and regenerate.

Using One or More Templates

You need to decide at this point whether to use one template or many. Forms generated by Designer/2000 include predefined features, triggers, code, and so on.

The developer can generate an underlying, base template (or template's template), which none of the forms will actually use as is. Assuming you want to stay close to Designer/2000, you should use a separate template for each form. To achieve this, you can modify the base template for each individual form. Thus, you will have two types of templates:

- A base template used for all forms within the system
- A form-specific template with the elements that don't fit into Designer/2000

To build the form, the developer can start with the base template and modify it to create the individual template for the form. In this way, the developer gets the best of all worlds since changes to the underlying template will propagate through referenced objects. Also, since the form is specific at the form level, regeneration will occur only in the form-specific template.

This base template should include the following:

- Property classes
- Help application
- Sample menu
- One or more attached libraries

Each form should be generated from the basic template and modified as necessary to support individual forms. The designer should try to put as many modifications as possible in the template so that when regeneration occurs, all modifications go along and reworking of the form is minimized.

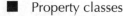

Tuning and Unit-Level Testing

The application and database cannot be tuned completely separately. You cannot simply tune one and then the other. Both components must be tuned together. This means that developing the tuning strategy requires both a skilled DBA and a skilled developer. Of course, some tasks, such as tablespace striping and RAID storage, will fall exclusively to the DBA. Some tasks, such as minimizing screen refresh operations that require access to the database, can only be addressed by the application developer.

Though some tuning problems can be solved exclusively by either database or application tuning, others require a combined approach. Each tuning problem must be considered individually to devise the best solution strategy. If the application is built according to standard development practices (that is, using explicit cursors and appropriate indexing in the database), tuning is an engineering issue. It involves establishing what is adequate performance for each process in the application. Once the application meets those standards, the development team can move on.

The initial unit testing procedure in the Build phase should proceed as follows:

1. Generate the application.
2. Develop the application using the dummy test data set.
3. Work with the application until you are satisfied that it runs properly.
4. Test applications and reports using a database populated with a small sample of realistic data. Make sure the layout makes sense for real data. It is easier to validate the system by running a test of business transactions with realistic data.
5. Run the application using a production-sized test database that will ensure adequate performance.

The next step is performance tuning. A complete discussion of performance tuning is beyond the scope of this book. However, the following is a list of standard classes of tuning problems and some possible techniques for solutions. (Note: Examples are specific to Oracle Forms, chosen here because of its wide use.)

1. The form takes too long to open.

- Technique A: Have the form DLLs load when Windows starts. This approach moves the delay from the form to Windows startup. Having the delay occur when Windows starts is not as noticeable to the users.
- Technique B: Have a very small welcome form that calls the first main form.
- Technique C: Delay initialization routines until necessary. For example, record groups that don't need to be populated until someone accesses a poplist do not need to be populated initially. Population can occur the first time the record group is selected.

2. The query takes too long.

- Technique A: Make sure there are appropriate indexes for the joined columns in the database.
- Technique B: Tune the SQL using standard SQL tuning techniques such as hints.

- Technique C: Don't perform the query very often. Bring the results of the query back locally if multiple accesses are required. One common problem with Forms is that post-query triggers are essentially correlated subqueries, which generate a query for each row fetched. One possible technique is to bring the results of the query back to the form in a record group and then, for post-query triggers, perform all accesses using the local record group.
- Technique D: Use views. Since it is now possible to update multiple-table views in a limited fashion, avoid using post-query triggers at all by using views.

3. Insert/modification/delete takes too long.

- Technique A: Reduce the number of indexes. There may be too many on the table.
- Technique B: Tune and rethink the database triggers.
- Technique C: Rather than directly inserting all data modifications, pass them to a transaction log and perform data modifications in batch mode.

4. A specific program unit is too slow.

- Technique A: Minimize database accesses. It is necessary to minimize the number of cursors; you may be able to combine information retrieved on one cursor. Don't perform any unnecessary fetches. Avoid the repeated use of system variables that require database access. For example, a call to SYSDATE in Forms actually executes SELECT SYSDATE FROM DUAL, even though you don't need to explicitly use that syntax. If a call to SYSDATE is in a loop, it can greatly slow the loop. Even if you need an up-to-the-second, accurate SYSDATE value, you can get this by executing one fetch to SYSDATE and then incrementing the SYSDATE value locally in the client.
- Technique B: The developer needs to intelligently decide whether the program unit should reside in the client or server. Program units that have little or no database access should reside in the client. However, program units that require extensive database access should, in general, reside on the server. For example, a program unit that performs complex string validation but requires no database access should certainly reside on the client. On the other hand, a complex function that calculates the amount owed by a client, possibly requiring hundreds of rows to be fetched into the procedure but

returning only one value, should reside on the server. By moving that function to the database, you can perform the function by simply passing the function call to the database and receiving the return value in the client. If that program unit resides in the client, however, it may require hundreds of network round trips. Judicious placement of functions and procedures on either the client or server side can greatly enhance performance.

These are just a few examples of common problems and their solutions. There are books written exclusively on the subject of database and application tuning.

After a form is tuned during the Build phase, it should immediately be passed to unit testing. This enables developers to get immediate feedback regarding whether the forms meet the design specifications. Such an approach allows you to catch problems in the Build phase before they propagate through all applications.

Once the developer is satisfied that the system is functioning properly, a crucial part of the Build phase is unit-level testing. Ongoing testing is very important in the Build phase. You cannot consider a module successfully built until it passes unit-level testing.

A tester should be designated to perform unit-level testing. This individual does not need to be highly skilled. The tester's goal is to find out when the program doesn't act as the user expects it to. Just because it works in the way the developer intended does not necessarily mean that it will perform as the user expects. The tester acts as a surrogate user. The tester should "click all the buttons" and log any problems with the system.

Unit-level testing consists of answering the following questions:

- Does the module meet design specifications as laid out in the design book?
- Does the module conform to GUI, coding, and reporting standards?
- Is performance in a realistic environment across all user machines and network configurations adequate? This question is a bit tricky to answer because it requires the simulation of multiple users; however, it is important to try to catch problems early, so put the module on a number of different machines and run minimal tests on the different configurations.

System problems should be logged in a systematic way. There should be a simple way for a user to log bugs and comments built right into the application. For instance, you could provide a toolbar icon that the user can click to open a dialog box for logging a comment or bug. This approach is ideal for testers and developers since the log can be linked to a bug-tracking system. In this way, bugs can be automatically passed back to the developer for modification or correction. If the developer disagrees with the tester's suggestions, the issue can be submitted for arbitration by a senior QA person.

Documentation

Both system and user documentation are important parts of the Build phase. Because of the way the system has been built using CADM, the system documentation is almost complete at this point. It should include all of the deliverables from the previous phases, reports generated by Designer/2000, and notes from designers and developers describing the decisions made throughout the process. All that is left to add are design notes made during the Build phase and testing results.

User documentation should include manuals, tutorials, possibly even computer-aided instructional programs (for large organizations), training materials, and courses. To some extent, abundant training can make up for any gaps in user documentation. Similarly, a good help desk system can make up for less comprehensive training materials. Users should be involved in the documentation process to ensure that its level is appropriate for successful knowledge transfer. A complete discussion of user documentation is beyond the scope of this book.

Modifications for Smaller Systems

For small systems, the Design and Build phases may occur simultaneously. For medium-sized systems, the Build phase process should be followed just as described in this chapter.

When Is the Build Phase Complete?

The Build phase is complete when all the applications pass unit testing, the user and system documentation both are nearly complete, the database is populated, and all elements have passed your company's initial quality review.

The Build Phase in Designer/2000

The Build phase is the point when everything comes together. All the careful analysis and design work you did before feeds into the Build phase and results in your final application. The exact activities you perform in Designer/2000 depend on your choice of products for the application modules. If you decide to use Oracle Developer/2000—Forms, Reports and Graphics—the Designer/2000 generators can give you a quite complete set of working modules, which may or may not need modification after generation. If you use the Visual Basic, WebServer, or C++ Object Layer Generator, you will have to use non-Designer/2000 products to perform some tasks, such as compilation after Designer/2000 generates code from the repository (although some of this work is automated in Designer/2000). Whichever front-end products you generate, Designer/2000 produces the Data Definition Language (DDL) scripts that create the database objects for Oracle or ANSI databases.

Table 10-2 lists the deliverables and activities that occur in the Build phase and the Designer/2000 tools that support them.

Chapter 8 introduced the Module Logic Navigator, which is used to complete the PL/SQL code definitions. Chapter 9 covers the Module Structure Diagrammer and the Module Data Diagrammer. Chapter 11 discusses how to perform unit testing to ensure that modules fulfill requirements. Chapter 11 also explores the

Activity or Deliverable	Designer/2000 Tool
Complete PL/SQL module code	Module Logic Navigator
Data Definition Language scripts	Server Generator
Refine Module Definitions	Module Data Diagrammer
Refine Module Network	Module Structure Diagrammer
Application-level standards	Preferences Navigator
Screens codes: Oracle Forms	Forms Generator
Module-level standards	Generator templates
Report code	Reports Generator
Chart code	Graphics Generator
Screens codes: VB and WebServer	Visual Basic and WebServer generators
Help system	MS Help Generator or help table system loaded with module generators
C++ class code	C++ Object Layer Generator
Journalling, code control, reference codes tables, and supporting code	Server Generator and module generators
Unit-test documentation	Repository Reports
Problem tracking	Repository Object Navigator or API
System documentation	Repository Reports

TABLE 10-2. *Build Activities and Designer/2000 Tools*

subject of problem tracking in the Build and Test phases. The section "Forms Generator Preferences" later in this chapter discusses some specific preferences you can change, but for a full explanation of the Preferences Navigator, see Chapter 7.

One of two primary objectives of the Build phase is to complete the database scripts and run them to create database objects and test data; the other is to build the application modules using the generator products. The creation of test data is outside the scope of the Designer/2000 tools, but the other main activities are fully supported.

Server Generator

You need to create database objects as the first step in the Build phase because the tables and other supporting objects must exist in the database before you can successfully generate code for a module. The Server Generator is a Repository utility that produces SQL*Plus text files you can run to create database objects. The code it produces contains the SQL DDL statements, as well as SQL*Plus comments to document the objects and provide messages as the script is run. It can produce code to create the following repository objects:

- Hash Clusters and Index Clusters
- Databases (Oracle) and Databases (ANSI)
- Groups, also called a *role grant,* which creates roles and grants
- Oracle Database Users, also called a *user grant,* which creates user accounts and grants
- PL/SQL modules for functions, procedures, and packages
- Rollback Segments
- Sequences
- Snapshots, with comments
- Tables, with synonyms, indexes, triggers, constraints, and comments
- Tablespaces
- Views, with comments

The definitions for each of these should be as complete as possible before you create the code for them. The properties for database objects and PL/SQL code definitions are best filled in using the Data Diagrammer and Module Logic Navigator, as Chapter 8 describes. You can also examine these definitions in RON using the Properties window.

Running the Server Generator

You can access the Server Generator from the Designer/2000 window application, as well as by choosing **Utilities→Generate SQL DDL** from the menus of several tools, such as the Data Diagrammer. The interface is similar to that of the Reverse Engineer Database utility. It uses three tabs: Selection, Objects, and Options.

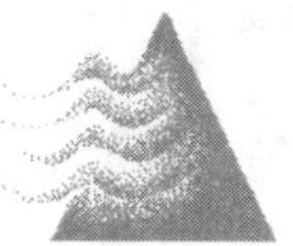

TIP

Select objects for which you want to generate code in RON and choose Server Generator from the Utilities menu. The selected objects will automatically appear as selections in the generator's Generate dialog box.

Selection Tab You use the Selection tab to choose the database definition that contains the objects you wish to generate. This is a required field, although it may appear initially as blank, and you can generate code for only one database at a time. You can also specify that the generator create triggers and indexes for the tables you select. This means you will not have to explicitly select the triggers and indexes on the next tab because the Server Generator will select those objects automatically. The last field lets you choose a database for object definitions that do not have a database property assigned. For example, if you are generating code for the CTA database and the definitions for TABLE1 and TABLE2 have no value in the Database property, you can select CTA as the default database so you can create the code for these tables. If you do not want the tables to appear, you can choose another database as the default.

You can use the Save Options button to save the settings of the check boxes for the next generator session. This button saves the Options tab items as well, but not the Objects tab items.

Objects Tab On the Objects tab, you can select the objects for which you wish to generate code. You select one object at a time from the list of objects at the top left (although you can actually highlight more than one at a time). Figure 10-1 shows this tab.

This dialog box is similar to the one for Reverse Engineer Database as it lets you select object types and choose object names to move to the Objects box (with the arrow buttons). Note that the primary key indexes do not appear in the list because they are generated automatically when you designate a primary key and create the table. Objects that do not have a Create property value of True will also not appear (unless you select the objects in the hierarchy window before starting the Server Generator).

Options Tab The Options tab, shown in Figure 10-2, specifies how to generate the PL/SQL package code, as well as the prefix of the filename you wish to

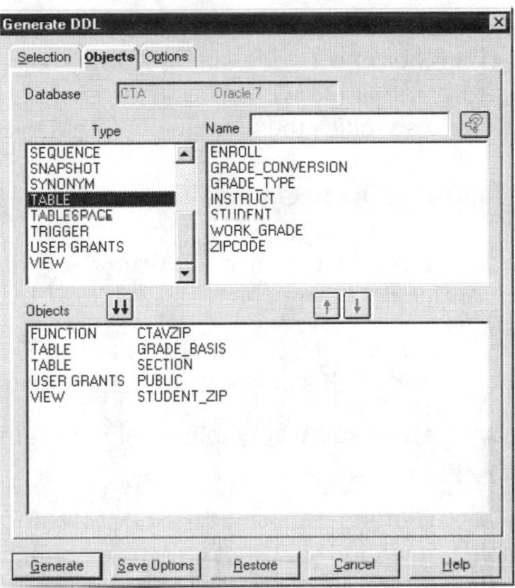

FIGURE 10-1. *Objects tab*

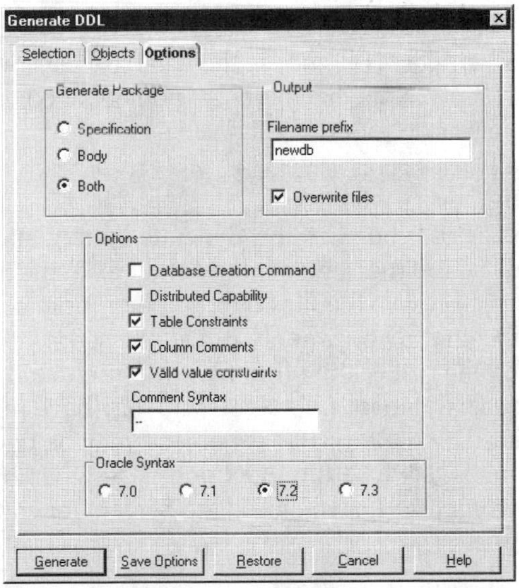

FIGURE 10-2. *Options tab*

produce. The Server Generator will create a file for each element type selected with file extensions based on the object (for example, table scripts have the extension .TAB). It will also create a file with an .SQL extension to run the other files. The Filename prefix field specifies the filename before the extension.

You can specify the following in the Options area:

- *Database creation command*: whether you want the CREATE DATABASE script generated for this database
- *Distributed capability*: whether you want to include CREATE SYNONYM and CREATE DATABASE LINK statements for remote database access
- *Table constraints*: whether you want table-level constraints such as foreign keys and primary keys
- *Column comments*: whether you want the COMMENT ON statements generated for table, view, and snapshot columns; comments for the tables, views, and snapshots themselves are always generated
- *Valid value constraints*: whether you want to create CHECK CONSTRAINT clauses from valid values assigned to the column and domain definitions
- *Comment syntax*: the style of single-line comments applicable to non-Oracle databases

The Oracle Syntax field lets you choose the database version number for which you want to create the scripts. Note that this and a number of other items are disabled if you choose to generate code for an ANSI database.

Generating the Code

After filling out the tab fields, you click the Generate button, and the Server Generator will display the log message window and create the SQL script files. When it is done, you can browse the files or run one or more of the scripts immediately. Remember that if you want to run all the scripts, the file with the .SQL extension will run the rest of the script files. It is useful to browse the code before running it to create database objects, as you may have missed some key property, and removing the created database objects may be complicated by table constraints. You can run SQL*Plus from RON or the Designer/2000 window at any point to start the scripts after you have closed the Server Generator.

Supporting Tables

In addition to the main application tables, Designer/2000 creates and maintains code for a number of support tables:

- **Help table** The table CG_FORM_HELP stores help text loaded from the definitions of tables, columns, modules, and module usages that have User Help Text defined. Generated Forms modules can access this text through a help form or help file.
- **Reference codes table** A table called CG_REF_CODES holds the valid values list and range for columns and domains. This table includes a low value, high value, description, and the domain name. Forms, Visual Basic, and Reports modules can use these to validate entries and provide lists of values for items derived from columns with valid value definitions.
- **Code control table** The CG_CODE_CONTROLS table is a source for unique numbers you can use as unique identifiers in tables. Forms and Visual Basic modules use this table to get the next available number rather than using a database sequence object (which is Oracle specific).
- **Journal tables** If you set the Journal? property to True for a table, the Server Generator will create the DDL for another table using that table's name plus a _JN suffix. This JN table will have the same set of columns in addition to columns for user name, date, and operation auditing. This table stores old records from the base table when a record is inserted, updated, or deleted, which allows you to audit changes made to the records. You can set preferences (in the JOURNALLING preference type) for the journalling actions.

The help, reference codes, and code control tables are considered reference tables as they are used by the code you produce in the modules in the forms. The module generators create the tables and load the text based on the module you are generating. You can also create and update these tables with information from all modules by using the Generate Reference Tables submenu of the Utilities menu of RON and MDD. Choosing an item in this submenu updates the particular reference table for all modules in the system. If the table does not exist when you choose to update it, the utility both creates the table and inserts or updates the rows.

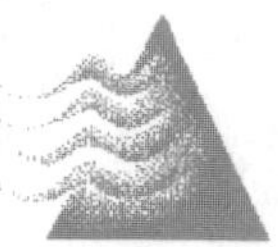

TIP
The Forms preference DVTABL lets you specify that the reference codes table name is based on the application name. You can specify the name of the code control table for a specific application or table according to the CCTABL preference.

The last support table mentioned, the journal table, is created separately for each table that has the Journalling property set to True. The Server Generator produces the TABLE CREATE script for that table when you create the script for the table you wish to journal. Although this journal table exists as a separate object in the database, there is no separate definition for it in the repository. The only indication that it exists is that the base table's Journal? property is set to True.

The module generators—Forms, Reports, Visual Basic—generate the code to support all these tables when the particular module is generated. For example, if you use help tables to supply the help system (instead of generating help files), the Forms Generator automatically generates code to process a request for help (via a menu selection, button click, or key press) and call another form. This help form queries the help table based on the cursor context and displays help text for that item.

Generating Modules

The general procedure for creating code from modules is to run the appropriate generator, specify generation options and preferences, examine the resulting application module by running it, make changes in the module definition, and then repeat the entire process. When you are done with this iterative procedure, you have both the refined definition in the repository and the finished code module (source and runtime or executable module).

After you create a module, you should test it to be sure it works as you expect. Then you give it to the QA group, where a unit test is performed to ensure that the module fulfills the requirements assigned to it. Chapter 11 discusses the techniques and Designer/2000 support for this unit test.

The next sections discuss in detail how to produce working Forms using the Forms Generator. The Forms Generator is the most complete of the generator products, so this book gives it more space than the other generators. The subject of code generation in Designer/2000 is material for an entire series of books, but the following will be enough to get you started. Subsequent sections also introduce the Reports Generator and briefly describe the other code generators that Designer/2000 provides: Graphics, Visual Basic, WebServer, MS Help, and C++ Object Layer. All generators are completely documented in the help system, which you can view quickly by clicking the Help button in the Designer/2000 window application and then clicking the button icon of the generator you are interested in.

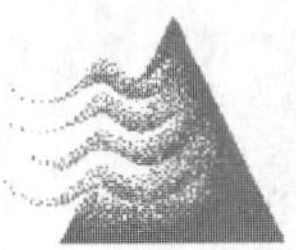

TIP
The best way to approach learning the generators is to budget some time to examine the preferences and templates. The help system provides a wealth of information on these and other aspects of the generators. Cue cards (from the MDD) provide a starting point. Also, be sure your module definitions are as complete and correct as possible before starting generation and be willing to change properties, generate and check output, and modify the definitions through many iterations.

Forms Generator

The Forms Generator creates screen and menu application files based on definitions in the repository. It creates blocks and items on the form based on table and column usages associated with the module. This section first details some of the requirements and then describes how to run the Forms Generator utility.

The result of a Forms Generator session is a standard Forms binary source (.FMB) file and, optionally, a runtime (.FMX) file as used in the Oracle Developer/2000 Forms product. You need the following components in addition to the generator itself, to successfully generate a Forms module:

- A *module definition* with the proper usages and links
- *Tables in the online database*
- A *template form* with default or customized generator items
- *Preferences* to support application standards

Using Module Definitions

All module properties are available in the Edit Module window of the Module Data Diagrammer and the Module Properties window of the Repository Object Navigator. The following are the minimum properties required for Forms generation:

- *Short Name,* which is a character string used as the name of the generated .FMB file. Be sure this name creates a file that can be stored in the operating system. For MS Windows operating environments, a name with eight characters or less will be the most portable.
- *Module Name,* which is used as the form title if there is no top title specified.

- *Type,* which identifies the type of finished module and must have a value of Screen.
- *Language,* which specifies the use of the Forms Generator and must have a value of Oracle Forms.

The other properties are optional but should be entered for completeness and for documentation purposes. Chapter 9 discusses the module properties in the section "Module Data Diagrammer."

In addition to the module properties, the module usage associations and their properties, listed here, affect the code generation:

- Detailed table usages (DTUs)
- DTU layout properties
- DTU link properties
- Detailed column usages (DCUs)
- DCU layout properties
- Secondary DCUs

Specific properties for the module usages and layout items are discussed in Chapter 9, in the section "Module Data Diagrammer."

Detailed Table Usages The DTU represents the overall structure of the form. It can be entered through the Repository Object Navigator or Module Data Diagrammer. The DTU links the module to the database objects by specifying the table operations allowed for the tables—create, retrieve, update, and delete (CRUD).

If a table is used more than once, it has multiple detailed table usages but only one summary table usage (which is automatically created when you create the detailed usages). The difference between the detailed and summary usages is that the tables appear only once in the summary usage but can appear more than once in the detailed usages. Additionally, the summary usages are not diagrammed in the MDD, whereas the detailed usages are diagrammed. The summary usages appear in reports to show which tables are used by the module. Both summary and detailed usages contain the CRUD, which is critical to the way the form is used. You need to ensure that the CRUD is correct before generating the form.

DTU Layout Properties In addition to placement items, discussed in Chapter 9, which let you tell the generator how to place the tables in the form (such as on a new page, on the same page, or in some other location), you can also specify layout properties for the module table usages for the following:

- *Overflow style,* such as wrap line, spread table, overflow area below, or overflow area right
- *Layout style,* such as tabular, form, list, and so on
- *Width and height* for the page and view
- *View X and Y position*
- *Window title*

The Window Title property of the first (topmost) base table in the diagram will be written into the Window properties of the generated module and will, therefore, appear as the form's window title when you run the form.

Base table DTUs become blocks in the generated form. Blocks are placed on canvases, which are placed in windows. In addition to the placement items and properties, you can specify preferences that affect the layout, such as the decoration of objects. These are discussed later in this chapter, in the section "Forms Generator Preferences."

DTU Link Properties For each DTU, you can define a link from one table usage to another. The links between tables are properties of the DTU and are based on foreign key constraints that exist between tables. The links can be lookup or base table links (master-detail relationships). The DTU Usage Type property indicates whether the table is a base table or lookup table. As discussed in Chapter 9, the Module Data Diagrammer automatically assigns the usage types when you place the table usage in a particular position on the diagram. It also assigns the link type automatically if you draw it on the diagram.

A lookup table usage is a detailed usage for a table that is used by another table (block) in a generated form to retrieve values into nonbase table display-only fields. Therefore, there will not be a separate block on the form for the lookup table usage, because the columns will become nonbase table fields in the base table block. Before you can create a valid lookup DTU, at least one base table DTU must already exist, and a foreign key constraint must exist between the base table and the lookup table. Remember that you can define a foreign key link for the purposes of the module table link and set the Create property to False so it is not implemented in database DDL code.

A base table (or master-detail) link defines the interaction between a parent (master) and child (detail) tables. The Forms Generator will create a block for each table with the code to synchronize the rows between the two blocks. Therefore, if you have a base table link between INVOICE and INV_ITEMS, with INV_ITEMS as the detail, you can query a particular master record, and the corresponding details will be shown automatically.

Detailed Column Usages A detailed column usage specifies that a particular column is used by the module and provides details regarding the operations allowed for that column—insert, select, update, and display. A detailed column usage is always part of a detailed table usage. Any given column may have many detailed column usages. A detailed table usage may contain more than one usage of the same column, as in the case of a secondary column usage or summary column usage as discussed in the following paragraphs. Also, if the table is used more than once in the module, the column may appear as a detailed usage more than once. The summary column usage is associated with a form only once for a particular column in the module no matter how many detailed usages it has.

DCU Layout Properties The properties for the detailed column usage are important to the Forms Generator when it makes decisions about how to create the finished module. The Display Sequence property overrides the column order of the columns in the table so you can specify any sequence you want for the items to appear on the form. The Column Prompt and Display Datatype properties show up on the form as well. If you include columns in an item group, the generator will keep the items created from those columns in the same area on the generated form.

Secondary DCUs You may want to create nonbase table items in the generated block for specific purposes, such as summaries, derived values, or even buttons. These nonbase table items are created using Designer/2000 objects called *secondary column usages*. A secondary column usage basically is a copy of an existing table column that has a display sequence number higher than that of the base table column usage. For example, suppose you have a table called TABLE1 that is used by MODULE1. This table has a column COL1 for which you want to create a secondary usage. You add a column to the detailed column usages with the name COL1 and designate a display sequence number higher than the original COL1 display sequence. This creates a secondary nonbase table usage that you can define as a summary, derived value, or button. The name of the new column usage must be the same as an existing column in the table usage, but the Forms Generator will name the item based on this usage in the form, using a different name.

You can generate secondary nonbase table usages for the following:

- *Summary or count items* that act on a group of detail block records but appear in a master block
- *Derived items* that take their values from other items in the block

- *Button items* that execute PL/SQL code
- *Current record indicator items* that mark where the cursor is in a multiple-row block
- *Empty items* for which you create code after generation

The following paragraphs briefly describe each type of secondary usage. In all cases, you start by creating another column usage in the Detailed Usages dialog box in the Module Data Diagrammer and giving it the name of an existing column in the column usage list.

- **Summary or count items** Create the secondary usage in the detail table for a master-detail link. In the Column Details tab, set the Summaries Type to Group, which associates the secondary usage with the parent, and change the Summaries Function to Sum or Count, depending on which function you want to perform. Sum will add the values of all records in the column on which you based this secondary column. Count will count the number of records. You also should specify the prompt, datatype, and size for the item. Forms Generator will create the item in the master block (although you define it in the detail table) with the necessary trigger code to populate the item with the summary or count from the detail table block.

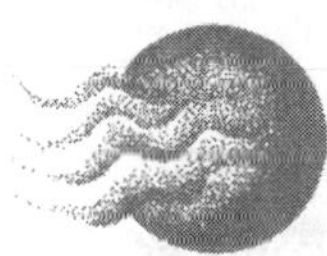

NOTE

You can control when the summary item is calculated by using the preference DSMOQM: Display Summary on Query of Master. The settings for this preference are Y, to calculate the summary whenever the master block changes, even if the detail block was not queried, and N, to calculate the summary only if the detail block is queried.

- **Derived items** Since a derived item acts on one row, you create the secondary column usage in the table usage that you want the item to describe. For example, to create a line-item total that is a calculation of PRICE * QTY in an ORDER_ITEM table, you add a secondary column usage called PRICE in the ORDER_ITEM table usage itself. Then you click the Column Text tab in the Detailed Usages dialog box and define a derivation expression text type. The text you enter in this area can be a SQL expression, such as PRICE * QTY. This text is validated with a SELECT *expression* FROM *table_name* statement, where *expression* is the text you place in the derivation expression, and *table_name* is the table usage table name. This type of text is validated when the generator checks the definitions. Therefore, the table must be created in the database if you want to generate the module.

Another type of text that you can enter is an expression of the form COMPLEX: *function_name*;—where *function_name* is the name of a PL/SQL function. For example, to load the inventory quantity of a product into a nonbase table item, you can enter `COMPLEX: in_stock(product_num);` as the derivation expression text. In this case, in_stock is a function you have defined to query the proper table and return the number of items in stock for that product number. The function can be defined in the template form, attached library, or database. This text is validated when the generator compiles the form.

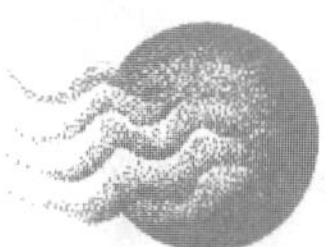

NOTE
Derivation expressions cannot use columns other than those in the same DTU.

- **Button items** A button item secondary usage is similar to a derived item usage except you use the display datatype Button for the item and the COMPLEX: derivation expression syntax. In this case, you can use Forms PL/SQL builtin procedures, as well as PL/SQL procedures. For example, `COMPLEX: highlight('ORDER_ITEM.QTY', QTY, '<', 50);` references a procedure you have written called highlight to change the visual attribute of a row if the quantity is less than 50. Another example is `COMPLEX: GO_BLOCK('DEPT');`, which uses a builtin Forms procedure to move the cursor to the DEPT block.
- **Current record indicator items** You can create a secondary column usage that visually indicates the row of a multirecord block that contains the cursor. The generator creates an item with the code needed to change the visual attribute of that item when the cursor moves into a new record. You need to perform a few steps in the template form as well, and these are documented in the Forms Generator help under the online help topic "Generating Current Record Indicator Items from Secondary Usages."
- **Empty items** You may sometimes want the generator to create an item but not attach code to it because you will do so after generation. This is considered an *empty* secondary usage, and you define it by specifying in the secondary column usage that this is not a button and has no summary function or derivation expression defined for it (otherwise it would be one of the other secondary usage types). The generator will take this item into consideration when it lays out the form, but will not create any code to load or maintain it.

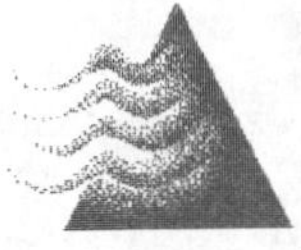

TIP

Designer/2000 ships with a calendar window form that you can attach to date items. This will appear when the user clicks the button or key to obtain a list of values when the cursor is on the date item and assists the user in choosing a date. To define this action, set the USECAL preference to Y, create a derived column usage for the date column, and specify `COMPLEX: display_calendar;` as the derivation expression. display_calendar is a procedure in the OFG4CALL.PLL library.

Using Tables in the Online Database

Definitions for tables used by the module must first exist in the Designer/2000 repository before you define the DTU. Also, the tables need to exist in the physical database if you want to run the generated forms while connected to the database. If you try to generate and run a form that uses a table that does not exist in the database, the Developer/2000 compile operation (also called *generation*) will fail, and you will not be able to run the form.

Using a Template Form

A template form is a form the Forms Generator uses during the generation process. Typically, you use a template form to define Forms objects that are standard in all your forms and that cannot be defined by preferences or the module definition. Although a template form is technically not required, it is highly recommended as it gives you more control over the finished form application. For more information on the template form, see the section "The Template Form," later in this chapter.

Using Preferences

Preferences are parameters that control the appearance and behavior of generated forms and reports. For example, the Block Decoration preference (BLKDEC) determines the style of line used to surround blocks on generated forms.The section "Forms Generator Preferences," later in this chapter, discusses preferences further.

Opening the Forms Generator Dialog Window

Once you have all the required components completely identified and defined, you can proceed to the generation process. The Forms Generator utility is available from the Designer/2000 window application as well as the Utilities menu in various tools such as the Repository Object Navigator.

As mentioned in Chapter 9, an easy way to work with the Forms Generator is from the Module Data Diagrammer. You can display the diagram for the module, run the generator and inspect the form at runtime, and go back to the MDD to

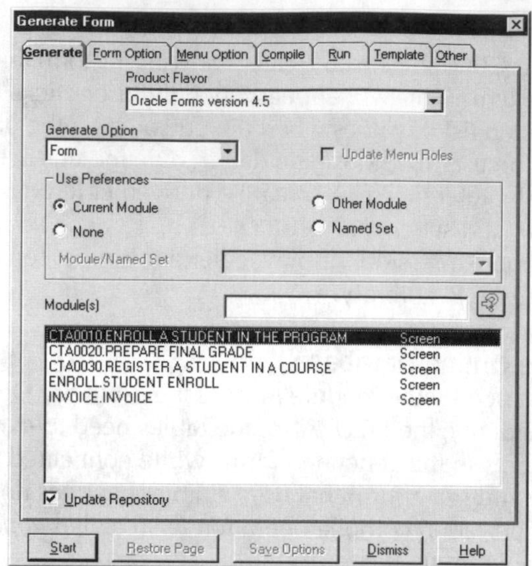

FIGURE 10-3. *Generate tab of the Forms Generator*

make changes you felt were needed when you saw the form run. You repeat this process until you have a satisfactory module. When the generator starts, it presents the window shown in Figure 10-3.

The settings and preferences in the tabs of this window are well documented in the help system, which is available by clicking the Help button. This dialog box has the following tabs.

- **Generate** The Generate tab lets you choose the type of module you want to generate in the session. You can also select which module to generate from a list that includes only modules with the language Forms. You can generate forms, menus, forms and menus, or menu roles. In addition, you can supply the name of a preference set to enable the generator to use preferences not attached to the module.

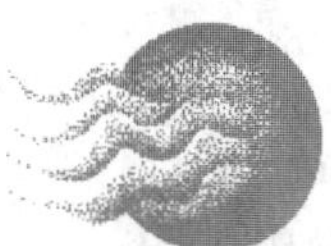

NOTE
The Update Repository check box appears in all generators and indicates that the generator will change the value of any column or table usage property that prevents generation. If you do not check this box, the generator will still change the property temporarily so it can perform generation, but it will not save that change in the repository.

- **Form Option** This tab contains fields where you specify the location of the forms files you will generate. You can store the forms created by the generator in the file system or in the database.
- **Menu Option** This tab has the same fields as the Form Option tab for menu generation. It allows you to specify locations and commands for menus that are different from those of forms.
- **Compile** This tab contains settings that indicate to the generator whether you want executable files and where those executables will be stored. You can also have the generator ask you as it is running whether it should create the executable files. Another option allows you to log in as a different user when the generation occurs. This option is handy if the tables that this form uses are owned by someone other than the repository user who is creating the form. An alternative is to have the table owner grant the repository user access to the tables and to also create private synonyms in the repository user's account for those tables. However, the fields on this tab provide a temporary solution that does not require you to delete extraneous synonyms later.
- **Run** This tab allows you to state what you want to happen when the form runs after it is generated and compiled. You can have the generator prompt you before running and, as with the compile options, log in with a different user account name when the form runs.
- **Template** This tab enables you to specify how the generator manages the template during the current run. Note that this tab specifies only the path of the file. The name of the file is specified by the STFFMB preference.
- **Other** This tab contains miscellaneous options you can enter for the generator session. You can specify a log filename, library path, and *regeneration report* (which contains details regarding code that the user modified or the generator created). The log file can be very useful in analyzing any inconsistencies in the generated form. This tab also has a setting for the maximum size of the generated name. If the short name of the module is longer than this value, the module will not generate. This option is handy if you think some modules may have names longer than those supported by the operating system.

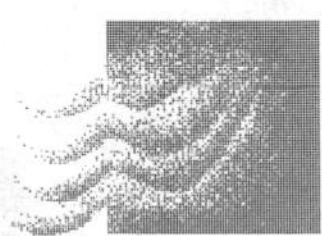

CAUTION

The path in all these dialog boxes must end with a path character. For MS Windows this is the \ character, so a path might be C:\DES2K\FORMS\. If you omit the \ character, the generator will fail at some point. The Browse button for these fields adds the path name correctly, so you can always use that button if you forget what format the generator needs.

Running the Generator

After you have completed all the information in the tabs, you click the Start button to begin the generation process. The generator runs and displays messages on the status of various settings and preferences as it progresses. It may stop to ask for input if something is unclear, and noncritical warnings may appear if a setting or preference is confusing or wrong. If an error occurs that stops the generation, you can examine the log window, shown in Figure 10-4, to see what the error was.

Generating Menus

Menu generation with the Forms Generator starts the same way as forms generation. That is, you start the Forms Generator from the Designer/2000 window application or from the Utilities menu of a tool such as RON. The first tab (shown in Figure 10-3) contains the Generate Option field. The Generate Option choices are Form (the menu is not generated), Form and Associated Menu (the menu is generated from the subnode of the selected form module), Specified Menu (for a particular menu module only), and Roles to create only the menu roles for Forms menu security. Choosing Form and Associated Menu or Specified Menu enables the Update Menu Roles check box, where you can specify whether you want to create menu roles for the menu (if you want to use the menu security feature of Forms). If you choose to generate the top-level menu in the hierarchy, the other menu modules under it become part of that menu file.

Template Menus The generator can merge an existing template menu with the module definitions to create the menu. You can store the existing template menu in

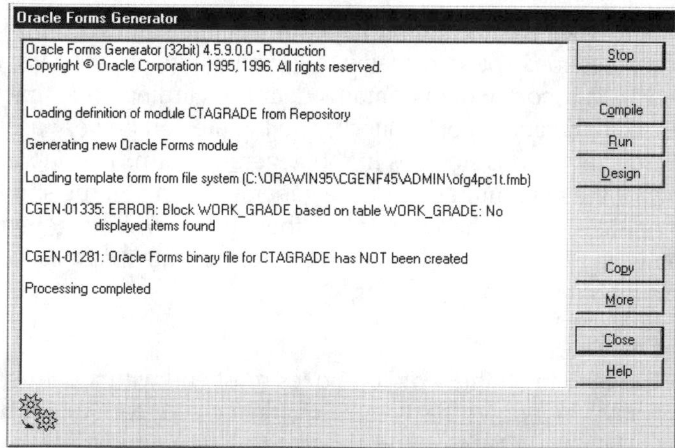

FIGURE 10-4. *Oracle Forms Generator log window*

a file or in the database. All the objects in the template menu (menus and menu items) are copied to the generated menu. If you have any referenced objects in the template, they become referenced in the generated menu. You can set preferences on the module level to specify the name of the menu template (the STMMMB preference).

Once you have identified the type of generation to perform, you click the Start button, and the Forms Generator creates the menu as you specified in the Generate Option. Remember that you can only run a menu module by attaching it to a form.

Generate Again and Regenerate

After you generate a Forms module the first time, you will likely want to change the definition, preferences, or even the template. After you make the changes, you have a choice of generating again or regenerating. Generating again overwrites the existing file with the new file you produce, and all post-generation modifications you made to that file will be lost. Regenerate uses the existing file as a starting point for the generation process, but does not incorporate changes you made to preferences or the template. Generating a module again is the same as generating it the first time, so you follow all the steps for generation to produce the code. There are no additional concerns as everything you create is new. The following discussion, therefore, concentrates on the regeneration process since it involves some steps that differ from those for normal generation. Whether you choose to generate again or regenerate depends on how much work you have done outside of Designer/2000, so it helps to know how the regeneration process works and how it modifies existing form objects and code.

Running a Regeneration Session You can choose Regenerate Form from the Utilities menu of the MDD or RON. After you choose this option from the menu, the Regenerate Form window appears. This window is the same as the Generate Form window except the Generate tab has only two options on the Regenerate Option poplist: Form, and Associated Form and Menu. The Other tab has a Regeneration Report field where you can fill in a filename for the report that shows the code that was kept unchanged and the code that would have been generated. The settings of the other fields are similar to those in the Forms Generator. When you have made the appropriate settings, you click the Start button, and the regeneration process will regenerate the report.

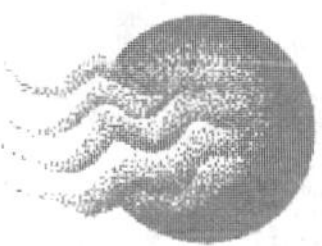

NOTE

You cannot cause the Form Generator to insert specific code in the generated triggers, but you can define database and forms library procedures and functions that are called by code the generator creates (for example, in the derivation expression of secondary column usages).

Regenerating with Existing Forms Objects Since new items not on the form are generated in the same way as they are using the Forms Generator, the main issue is how the regeneration process handles existing items in the form. The regeneration process merges the existing file with the definitions in the repository by first reverse engineering the form to obtain information from the existing form file. The process then updates the module definition in the repository. Then it regenerates the form to merge the existing file with the new definitions. It adds new blocks and items for new table and column usages that were added in the module definition after the form was created. It does not delete items for table or column usages that you removed after generation, however. The regeneration process does not change most item or block properties regardless of whether the usage definitions changed. For more information on the exact workings of the regeneration process, see the Forms Generator help topic "What Happens to the Form during Regeneration."

Regenerating with Existing Code The Forms Generator creates code that reflects the current repository definitions. It places comments such as `/* CGCD$DERIVE_ON_INSERT */` in the code before the BEGIN statement of the PL/SQL block. The regeneration process reads the comment and replaces the code under it with new code that reflects the current repository definitions. For example, the generated code might be the following:

```
/* CGCD$DERIVE_ON_INSERT */
BEGIN
   -- generator code
END;
```

If you make post-generation changes to the code and place your code outside the comment and END statement, the regeneration process will not modify or overwrite it. Otherwise, the regeneration process will overwrite the code within that block whether or not it created it.

If you want to retain the code within the block, you can change the comment heading so the regeneration process will not replace it. For example, you can change the aforementioned comment to `/* CGCD$DERIVE_ON_INSERT_changed */` to cause the regeneration process to ignore it. During regeneration, the Forms Generator produces a report that shows the code that was kept unchanged and the code that would have been generated.

CAUTION
The Forms Generator creates validation procedure code named with nine-character prefixes such as CGRI$CHK_ with the table name as a suffix. This means that your table names must be unique within the first 21 characters because procedure names may only be 30 characters long. You should consider this limitation when naming the tables if you will be using the Forms Generator.

Be careful of changing this comment in the generated code, because if you change something in the module definition that would result in new code, the existing code may not be correct, and the Forms Generator will not overwrite it with the new correct code.

Forms Generator Preferences

As mentioned in this chapter, one of the main components that the Forms Generator uses to construct the finished module is preferences that you set in the Preferences Navigator. Chapter 7 introduces the Preferences Navigator and discusses the various levels of preferences and how to set the values. This section builds on that information to explain how the Forms Generator uses preferences and provides some specific examples of preferences and their effects. This discussion can serve as an example, too, of how to work with the preferences of other generators.

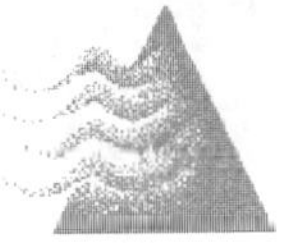

TIP
When first learning preferences, it is best to perform a quick test by changing a preference value or two and generating a form to see the effect of that change. This process takes a bit of time, but it will help you understand the effects of changing a particular preference. In addition, you can print a reference list of preferences to help you learn what they offer by expanding all preference type nodes under the Application node and selecting **File→Print**. Be sure to set the view to Description using the View menu before printing.

During module generation, preferences influence many aspects of the finished forms such as coding style and content, layout, generation settings, environment, and end user interface. Each preference is shipped with a realistic default value, referred to as the *factory value*. It is possible to generate forms using only factory values, but you can get more out of the generator by spending time carefully considering which preferences to change. You will save time you might otherwise spend in modifying the forms after generation. In addition, preferences allow you to establish and enforce code standards within a single application system, as well as for the entire enterprise.

CAUTION
Do not change the settings of too many preferences while you are still in the learning process. Create named sets and apply those instead of modifying all factory settings. This approach provides a more controlled and reversible way to test the effects of the settings.

Precedence of Preference Settings

The Forms Generator processes preferences in a strict sequence, starting at the lowest level. For example, the order of precedence for modules from lowest to highest is Detailed Column Usage, Constraint Usage, Item Group, Detailed Table Usage, Module, and Application. This is documented in the Preferences Navigator topic "Preference Levels." The generator uses the following rules for processing the different levels of preferences:

- If the generator finds that a preference is modified at a given level, it uses that value. It does not search for the same preference at a higher level.
- If the generator finds that a preference is not modified at a given level, it searches for the preference at the next higher level.
- If a preference is not set at any level, then the generator uses the default factory value.

For example, if a preference is set at both module and application system levels, the generator always uses the module-level preference because it is at a lower level.

Setting Preference Values

Each preference has a short name of up to six characters and a longer, descriptive name. You can display either the name or the description when using the Preferences Navigator to view the preference hierarchy. Preferences are grouped into preference types according to their functions. For example, all preferences that control the decoration of a block are members of the LAYOUT-BLOCK preference type. The BLKDEC preference, in this preference type, determines the style of line used to surround blocks on the generated forms. The poplist includes such choices as LOWER RECTANGLE, OUTSET LINES, and RECTANGLE for the line that will surround the block in the generated form.

The best strategy is to create a named preference set as a group of preferences that you attach to the application level. You can test this named set on the module level to see if it works before attaching it to the application level. Use the module-level preference only for special purposes, and use the application-level preference to set the standards. All modules will have the benefit of these standards if you do this. You can copy, transfer, and share the named set between application systems just like any other element, using the Repository Object Navigator. This will allow you to set the same standards among all applications that share or copy that named set. You can also use the Preferences Navigator menu item **Set→Copy From** to copy a named set.

A good strategy is to keep most preferences in named sets at the application level after testing them on the module level.

Sample Preferences

The list of preferences is so extensive that you might want to concentrate on a small subset while you are learning how they work. One of the most widely used categories of preferences is Layout because the layouts of generated forms with default preferences usually do not have the desired look and feel.

Sample Block Preferences Suppose you generated a multiple row block in a form such as that in Figure 10-5 using default preferences. You can change some of the default preferences that create this form with the preferences in Table 10-3. Open the module preferences node for the form and click the LAYOUT-BLOCK preference type node to display the preference names. Then change the values in the Properties Window as in Table 10-3.

The form generated with your new preference settings will look like the one in Figure 10-6. Notice that changing these few preference values produced a noticeable visual difference.

Sample Item Preferences You can continue this experiment to test some other preferences that modify the way items are displayed in a block by making the changes listed in Table 10-4.

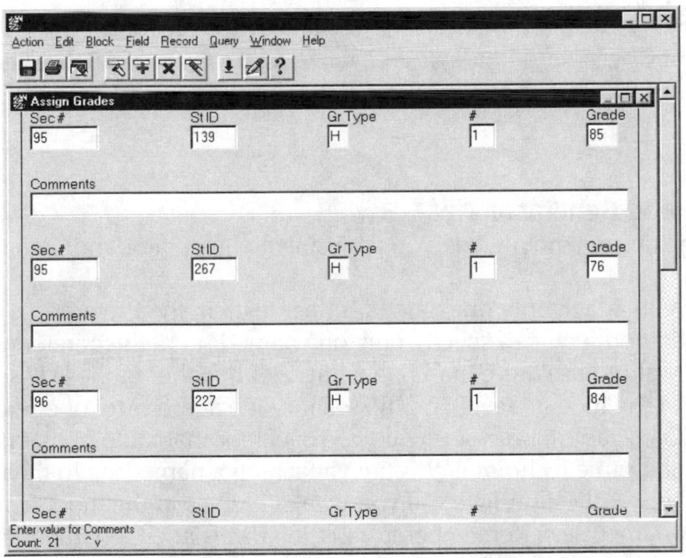

FIGURE 10-5. *Sample multiple-row block generated form*

Preference Name	Description	New Setting	Effect
BLKDEC	Block decoration	RAISED RECTANGLE	Border line around the block has lines with a raised look.
BLKVSB	Block vertical scrollbar	Y	Provides a vertical scrollbar for each block.
BLKSBP	Block scrollbar position	RIGHT	Indicates where the scrollbar will be positioned relative to the items in the block.
BLKOVF	Default block overflow action	SPREAD TABLE	The default value, WRAP LINE, causes the Forms Generator to wrap rows that are too wide to the next line. Spread table creates a scrolling canvas with one line per row.

TABLE 10-3. *Sample Block Preferences and Their Effects*

Preference and Generator Tips

The following tips will help when you are using the generator and preferences:

- You can attach only one named set per level in the Preferences Navigator. In addition, you can specify only one named set per generator session. If you want to use more than one named set in either of these cases, attach one at the module level and the second one at the level of one of the module's tables. Both sets will have effect for that table in that module. Use the same technique, this time attaching a named set to the module and the application levels, if you want all tables in the module to have both named sets. Remember to reset the levels after generation if this is not a permanent change.

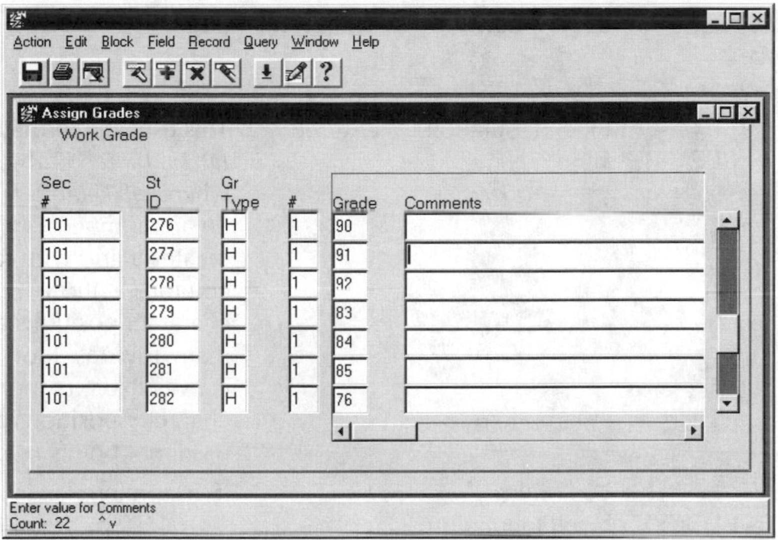

FIGURE 10-6. *Generated form with new preference settings*

- If you have two triggers of the same type (such as WHEN-NEW-ITEM-INSTANCE) at both the form and block levels and want to control their execution, set the ITMTRG or BLKTRG preferences to Before or After, depending on which one should fire first.
- If you want the same field displayed on pages 1 and 2, set the column Context property (in the Detailed Column Usage for the module).
- To display boilerplate on two lines in the generated form, separate the words with the | character: for example, CASE|Policy.
- To change the font and color of the generated boilerplate, set the CG$PROMPT visual attribute properties in the template using Forms Designer (available in the MDD Tools menu).
- Document your post-generation changes in the Notes text area of the module definition. Alternatively, you can use the Module Generation History text area that the generator writes to when generating the module.
- You can define an item group in the MDD that is used by columns in different tables. This allows you to tell the generator that items in different blocks should stay physically together.

Preference Name (Preference Type Node)	Description	New Setting	Effect
BLKTAB (LAYOUT - BLOCK)	Block tabulation table	5.25.45.65	This uses the format *tab1.tab2.tab3.tab4*, where *tab1*, *tab2*, and so on are numbers. This creates a grid with four columns at those character positions and as many rows as fit on the canvas. Note that only character positions are used, not points or pixels.
BLKUTT (LAYOUT - BLOCK)	Use of the block tabulation table	SD	If this preference is not set, tab stops are not used. SD means to use the tab stops to align the start of the items.
MODLIB (FORM/LIBR ATTACHMENT)	Module-specific library attachment	CUST	You can choose a library .PLL file, such as CUST.PLL, specific to your module. Do not include path or extension.
STFFMB (TEMPLATE)	The name of the template file	MAIN-FORM.FMB	You can change your default template, OFG4PC1T.FMB, to the template created specifically for your application: for example, MAINFORM.FMB without the path name.

TABLE 10-4. *Sample Item Preferences and Their Effects*

How to Proceed

The preceding discussion should get you started with preferences. When learning preferences, experimentation is a key task. You can start the Forms Generator from the Preferences Navigator, and you will find it easier to test new preferences by running the generator from Preferences Navigator. When you change a preference, you can generate the form by selecting a menu option and then return to the Preferences Navigator after examining the generated form. You should consider budgeting some research time into the Pre-Design phase and use this time to learn which preferences to use for which purposes. This research will greatly enhance the work you do in the Build phase as you will not have to stop in the heat of the coding and determine what effect a particular preference will have on the finished application. The earlier in the life cycle you can make changes to standards, the less expensive those changes will be.

The combination of preferences, the template, and module definitions is quite powerful. Add the PL/SQL libraries you can attach to the template, and you have an extremely flexible way to define the form. If you are accustomed to developing forms with Developer/2000, you may be frustrated initially because some tasks that are easy in Forms Designer may seem more difficult in Designer/2000. Most things are possible, however, and you will reap the benefits of keeping full definitions in the repository when you perform maintenance and add enhancements to the system. In addition, after you develop your first project with the Designer/2000 generators, you will know how the generators work and so be able to quickly and efficiently produce finished code.

The Template Form

Another important component of forms generation is the template form. This is a normal Oracle Forms .FMB file that serves as the foundation for the finished form. It contains standard objects, such as toolbars, that you want in your final application, as well as objects that the generator uses to influence the items, blocks, canvases, and windows it places in the form. Although the Forms Generator technically does not require a form template, you will find it is easier to control the generation process, and you will get better results, by using it. The Forms Generator uses the form template to do the following:

- Determine the coordinate system.
- Copy blocks, items, visual attributes, triggers, and library attachments to the generated form. These objects are called *user objects*.
- Take advantage of specially named objects called *generator objects* as the foundation for generated Forms objects (canvases, windows, buttons, control block items, and boilerplate).
- Apply specially named visual attributes, which are a form of generator object, to generated objects.

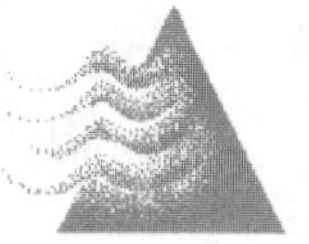

TIP
The more you know about the way Oracle Forms works, the more effectively you can use the Forms Generator. The Forms Generator does not substitute for knowledge about Forms unless you are willing to be satisfied with default behavior. You should find the best Forms developers you can and let them control the work performed with the Forms Generator. The skills of knowledgable Forms developers are important in all aspects of Forms Generation, but it is especially so when you start modifying the template form.

Typically, the template form is used to define objects that are standard requirements for the generated form but that have no place in the repository module definition. The generated form will copy a multitude of visual elements (boilerplate, toolbar buttons), properties, and code (procedures and triggers) from the template form. Using a template form can help you implement coding and GUI standards and ensure a consistent look and feel for the generated forms.

You can place two categories of objects in a template form—user objects and generator objects.

User Objects

User objects (or user items) are objects that the generator copies unchanged into the generated form. User objects can include the following:

- Windows and canvases
- Blocks and items
- Program units and triggers
- Referenced objects
- Library attachments

You can name user objects anything you want so long as the name does not begin with CG$, which identifies the generator objects. Place user objects in the CG$ header, footer, or toolbar or a user-named canvas. Also, be sure to keep user objects separated physically from any CG$ objects that may not be generated. The user objects can use the CG$ visual attributes in the template form as these are always copied into the generated form.

Generator Objects

Generator objects form the basis for certain types of generated objects in the generated form. The generator uses generator objects in the template form to set the attributes of generated objects and create special objects in the generated form. For example, the template form has a CG$AT generator object that creates an item with the application system title. You can place that item in any header or footer canvas, and the generator will create the item and the code to populate it with a value.

NOTE
If the generator does not recognize the name of a CG$ object in the template, it ignores the object.

When you place a new generator object in the template form, be sure it has a proper name (CG$*xx*, where *xx* is a special name) and is placed in the header or footer canvas. For generator objects that are items, only the first five characters of the name are significant: CG$ followed by a two-letter code. There are also generator objects for windows and canvases with names like CG$WINDOW_1 and CG$PAGE_1. If the canvas is a pop-up (stacked) canvas, it will have a name like CG$POPUP_2. You can define *implementation items,* which also have CG$ names plus suffixes you make up. Implementation items are used when you need to create OLE and VBX objects. Another example of an implementation item is CG$LB, which is used with the LOVBUT preference to create a list-of-values button of a certain size.

During generation, the Forms Generator creates different types of objects based on the settings of the generator item's Display property (in the Forms Designer item Properties window). If the Display property is set to True, the generator creates boilerplate text containing the value retrieved from the repository. If it is set to False, the generator creates a nondisplay item and sets the Hint Text property to the value retrieved from the repository. The advantage of using the Hint text property is that it can be used in triggers and program units by employing the GET_ITEM_PROPERTY builtin procedure. Check the Developer/2000 Forms documentation for more information on the GET_ITEM_PROPERTY builtin procedure.

There are also generator items for Forms functions, such as EXIT_FORM and PRINT. When the Forms Generator finds one of these in the form, it creates a button item with the proper WHEN-BUTTON-PRESSED trigger code to call the appropriate Forms function.

Table 10-5 summarizes some of the generator objects. A full list of the items is available in the online help system for Forms Generator under the topic "Accessing Property and Attribute Text." The topic "Objects That Call Standard Forms Functions" provides a list of the Forms function generator items.

Headers, Footers, and Toolbars

You can define specially named content and stacked canvases in the template as the foundation for headers and footers in the generated form. There are two types of header and footer objects: stacked headers and footers, which define information that is the same for all the pages in a window, and content headers and footers, which are merged with the regular canvases. These are named CG$STACKED_*xxx*

Name	Meaning
CG$AT	Application system title
CG$CN	Company name
CG$MN	Module name
CG$DT	Current date
CG$CM	Commit
CG$EQ	Enter query
CG$HP	Help

TABLE 10-5. *Some Generator Items and Descriptions*

and CG$CONTENT_*xxx*, respectively, where *xxx* is the type of canvas (header or footer).

Toolbars can be defined as a special type of stacked canvas designed to be used as a button bar. Toolbars become part of the window frame. You can also define graphics and a boilerplate in the toolbar. Toolbars are named CG$HORIZONTAL_TOOLBAR and CG$VERTICAL_TOOLBAR, for horizontal and vertical toolbars, respectively.

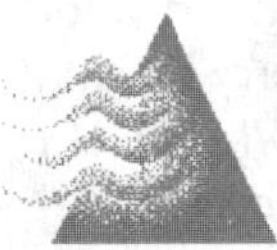

TIP
Whenever you need a button bar, use a toolbar (horizontal or vertical) instead of a header or footer because toolbars are always displayed. A header or footer, on the other hand, may become obscured when you scroll a window.

The Forms Generator uses the name of the canvas to determine whether the canvas is to be used in all windows or only in a specific window—for content canvases. Here are some examples of names:

- *CG$HEADER* is a content header for all generated pages except those with a specific content header.
- *CG$HEADER_1* is content header for the generated CG$PAGE_1 canvas.
- *CG$HORIZONTAL_TOOLBAR* is a toolbar for all generated windows except those with a specific toolbar.
- *CG$VERTICAL_TOOLBAR_0* is a toolbar for generated window 0.

Attached Libraries

Generator libraries of commonly called PL/SQL procedures are shipped with the Forms Generator. Whenever a form or menu module is generated, the library attachments are also generated. You can define additional library modules to be used by the generated form or menu module. If you attach these libraries to the template form, the generator will copy the attachments to all generated modules that are based on that template.

Referenced Objects

In the template form you can also include references to objects stored in other modules. If form-level triggers are referenced, the generator will not be able to add its own code to them, if it would normally do that. For example, the generator might have code that inserts the application title into the window title in a WHEN-NEW-FORM-INSTANCE trigger. If the template form references that trigger from another form, the generator will not be able to add any other code to it because referenced objects cannot be modified.

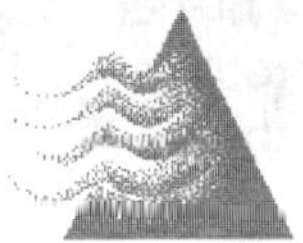

TIP

Whenever you generate a module using a template that contains references, make sure that the source module is accessible to the generator. The source module should be in an operating system file, a stored form in the same database as the repository, or a stored form in a different database as specified on the Compile tab of the Generate Form dialog box (in the Connect String field). Also, the source form of the referenced object must be available if you decide to open the generated form in Developer/2000 Forms.

Standard Templates

Designer/2000 includes two templates that support generation in Windows for deployment on Windows systems and a third template designed to be deployed with character coordinates on non-Windows platforms.

OFG4PC1T.FMB is one of the Windows template files. This template contains an iconic toolbar with bubble help, and it uses the application name as the application window title and the real coordinate system, in inches. The other Windows-platform template, OFG4PC2T.FMB, is the same except it contains navigation buttons or a poplist (from the CG$FF item) in a stacked footer for interform navigation. OFG4GUIT.FMB is the template for character-mode platforms.

Designer/2000 includes other templates as well. OFG4EXPT.FMB is a comprehensive source of generator items examples, but it is not suitable for generation. APPSGEN.FMB supports generation in Oracle Applications.

Customizing Templates

If you decide not to use one of the templates Designer/2000 provides, you can create a custom template and cause the Forms Generator to use it by changing the STFFMB preference to the name of your new template file. If you also change the template location, be sure to specify the new location on the Template tab in the Forms Generator window. The best way to create a custom template is to modify an existing template using Developer/2000 Forms Designer (available on the MDD Tools menu). Be sure to select **File→Save As** from the menu as soon as you open the template file and supply another name so you don't overwrite the base template file.

Strategies for 100 Percent Forms Generation

Information systems departments that use Designer/2000 measure how effectively they use the Forms Generator by the percentage of code that the generator produces that needs no change. Traditionally with Oracle CASE products, this percentage was relatively low, but Designer/2000 has the capability for a higher percentage. One hundred percent generation means that the code you produce from the generator needs no post-generation modification. That is, once the generator produces the .FMB file, you do not need to change it. The benefit of 100 percent generation is that it enables you to change your repository definitions, preferences, and template forms and generate the modules again to create a ready-to-use application.

This section provides a sketch of how you can approach the goal of 100 percent generation using the Forms Generator. The basic tactic is to create master forms and master code libraries that attach to the template form. You need to plan carefully before trying this approach, but the potential benefits are substantial. Figure 10-7 shows how the forms you generate copy and reference objects and code from module-specific files. As mentioned previously, you should employ a Forms expert to help with this work, as some advanced Forms concepts are involved in the creation of the forms and libraries. Unless stated, you perform all work in the Developer/2000 Forms Designer.

The Master Form

The master object library form, MASTER.FMB, is a standard Forms 4.5 .FMB file that provides objects that will appear in all forms in the application. Candidate objects for this form include the toolbar button block, toolbar canvas, visual attributes, and property classes. You copy these from the template form into the master form, delete them from the template, and create an object group to hold these objects in the master form. This object group is then referenced back into the template form using standard Forms 4.5 referencing techniques.

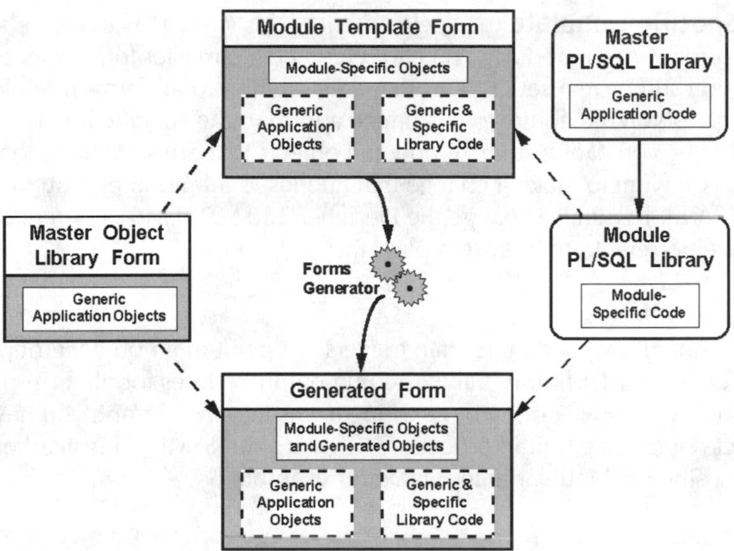

FIGURE 10-7. *Generated form sharing objects and code*

At the end of these steps you will have a template form with a referenced object group containing objects from the master form. Referenced objects are resolved when the generated form is opened in Forms 4.5 Designer, or when the form is generated via the executable file F45GEN32.EXE (or F45GEN.EXE in 16-bit operating systems). This referencing means that you can add or change the objects in the MASTER.FMB object group, and the changes will be reflected in all generated forms that reference the object group when the generated .FMB forms are compiled into .FMX (runtime) files.

NOTE

You can batch generate all of your .FMB files by calling F45GEN.EXE from a Windows 3.1 scripting program. If you use Windows 95 or NT, you can write a standard batch file to perform this task.

As a rule, the master object library form should not contain objects beginning with CG$, as these objects are usually modified by the Designer/2000 Forms Generator (and referenced objects cannot be modified). Thus, the CG$CTRL block and all CG$ canvases should remain in the template form. Visual attributes (for example, CG$ITEM) can be placed in the master form, however, because they are not modified by the generator.

Module-Specific Template A refinement of this strategy is to create a separate template form for each module. You can reference the master form object group from it so you still have a set of items that are common to all forms modules. This approach gives you the ability to customize a form to the specific needs of the module: that is, you can customize only the objects that are specific to that module. If you want to make a change that applies to all modules, you make it in the master form. Be sure to change the Designer/2000 STFFMB preference on the module level to refer to the new template file.

The Library

Forms does not allow code other than triggers to be put in an object group, so you need to create a master library that has common procedures for all forms in the application. If you move code from existing forms into this library, you have to use the indirect referencing builtin procedures COPY and NAME_IN instead of direct references using the bind variable syntax: for example,

```
student.studid := 100;  becomes   copy('100', 'STUDENT.STUDID');
```

and

```
x := :student.studid;    becomes    x := name_in('STUDENT.STUDID');
```

In the template you create all 121 possible form-level triggers, each of which has a call to a package called event_handler written in the library. For example, a WHEN-TIMER-EXPIRED trigger would have this code:

```
event_handler.when_timer_expired;
```

The package has a procedure for each of the triggers that call it. Initially, most of these have the code `NULL;` as a placeholder until code is written. However, the KEY- and ON- triggers, such as ON-MESSAGE, replace Forms default functionality, so you need to define code for those from the start. For example, the code for event_handler.key_exit would be the following:

```
exit_form;
```

Module-Specific Library Just as you can have a module-specific template, you can also have a module-specific library that is attached to the module-specific template. When you are determining which code goes in the master and which in the module-specific library, consider whether the code is useful outside the form you are developing. If it is, it is probably material for the master library. For example, standard security procedures or startup code that needs to be executed for each form should be in the master library.

This master library is attached to the module library directly, so you can attach the module library directly to the template form, and the master library will be automatically attached to the form as well.

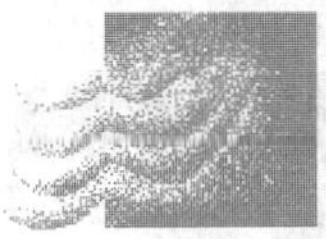

CAUTION
Be sure the block and item names in (or referenced by) the template do not conflict with table and column names you are using in the module.

Reports Generator

The Reports Generator and the Forms Generator have many similarities. The Reports Generator uses a combination of module definitions, preferences, and templates to create finished code. While you can create SQL*Plus reports that contain sophisticated use of the SQL*Plus command language, this discussion concentrates on the Reports 2.5 version of the generator. The preferences and templates used by the Reports Generator are Reports specific, but you can approach working with the Reports Generator components in the same way you do the Forms Generator components.

In the process of generating a report, the Reports Generator gathers input from several sources:

- *Repository definitions* for modules, table and column usages, and key constraints
- *Template reports* for two types of templates: *layout template,* for header page, trailer page, and margin information, and *parameter form template,* for the look and feel of the generated parameter form
- *Preferences* that influence the layout and the generation process

Report generation itself accomplishes three tasks:

- **Data model creation** The Reports Generator uses the module definition and preferences to create reports objects for queries, groups, columns, parameters, and links.
- **Report layout creation** The generator produces the layout using the data model itself, a template report, and preferences.
- **.RDF creation** The final product of the generation process is a report definition (an .RDF file in the operating system or a report definition stored in the database).

Differences Between Reports and Forms Generation

There are many similarities between the approaches you use to create forms and reports using the respective generators. There are also differences; for instance, the Reports Generator requires a layout template report whereas Forms Generator can work without a template (although one is strongly recommended). Reports Generator does not automatically produce an executable (.REP) file, whereas Forms Generator automatically produces the .FMX executable (if you have chosen the proper generator option). Although the Reports Generator can run from the .RDF file, you can click the Compile button in the generator's log message window to create the .REP file after the report is generated.

Another difference is that you do not need the COMPLEX keyword to execute PL/SQL code in the Reports Generator. You can reference a PL/SQL function or procedure directly in a column usage for the Report module. Also, unlike the Forms Generator, the Reports Generator does not have a Run tab; to run the generated report, you have to click the Run button in the generator log window. In addition, you cannot regenerate a Report as you can a Form, though the Reports Generator does provide the Generate As option (in RON and MDD) to create a Report from a Form definition.

Reports Generation Window

You can invoke the Reports Generator from the Designer/2000 Window application, as well as the Utilities menus of several other tools such as RON. When you start it, the Reports Generator opens a window, as Figure 10-8 shows. The window is similar to that of the Forms Generator and has Generate and Report Options tabs.

Generate Tab The Generate tab lets you choose between Oracle Reports 2.5 and SQL*Plus reports. You can also specify how you will use the preferences and whether you will use a named set of preferences. You also specify the module or modules you wish to generate.

Report Options Tab Figure 10-9 shows the Report Options tab, which contains the following fields:

- **Generated Report Location** Specify whether you will generate to a file system file or the database.
- **Directory** Specify the directory where the report definition (.RDF) will be generated. Be sure to end the directory name with a \ character.
- **Log File Name** Specify the name and location of the log file that contains information on the report generation session, including warnings and errors.

- **Template Directory** Specify where the Reports Generator looks for template reports.
- **Runtime User** Specify whether you want to run the report using a user account other than the repository user you are logged in as.
- **Maximum Module Name** Enter the maximum number of characters a module name can have. Zero means it can have an unlimited number.
- **Generate Default Summaries** Check this item to have the generator create summaries for numeric fields if they are not part of a key constraint.
- **Overwrite Existing Definition** Reports Generator prompts you before it overwrites an existing report file. Specify Yes to overwrite the file without a warning. Specify No to cancel the generation if the file exists. Specify Ask to have the generator prompt you for a decision during the generation process.
- **Convert from TABULAR to FORM layout** If the tabular layout style is too big to fit on one page, Reports Generator will prompt you to convert from Tabular to Form layout. Specify Yes to allow the conversion to happen automatically. Specify No to have the generator check the MINMSP (minimum space) preference and TABRAT (tabular ratio) preference to

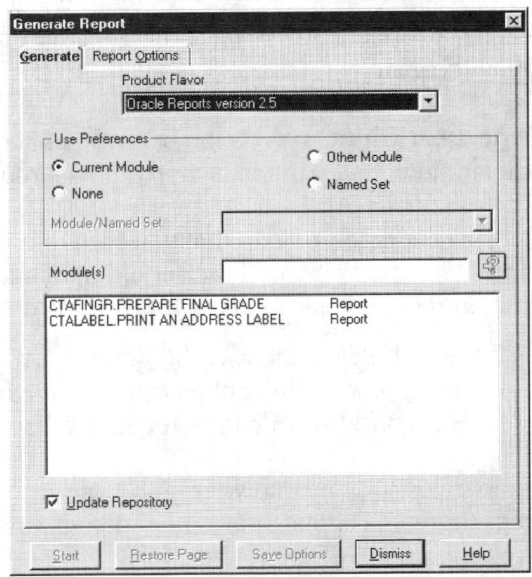

FIGURE 10-8. *Reports Generator window*

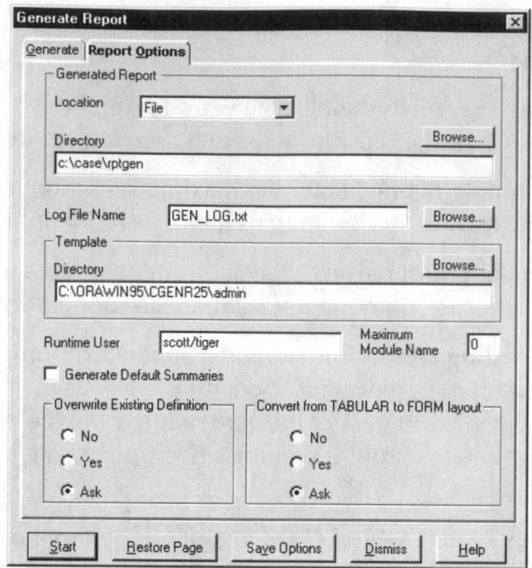

FIGURE 10-9. *Report Options tab*

determine what to do. Specify Ask to have the generator prompt you for a decision during the generation process.

Types of Reports Generator Objects As in Forms Generation, you can place two types of Reports Generation objects in the layout template report:

- *User objects,* which are report objects that you want the generator to copy unchanged to the generated report. These should not have names starting with CG$ and should not be placed in the body of the report template.
- *Generator objects,* which define the way the Reports Generator creates objects in the generated report. These objects must have names starting with CG$ and suffixes consisting of names recognized by the generator.

Generator objects allow you to bring into your report various pieces of information from the repository: the application system name, module name, module purpose, and so forth.

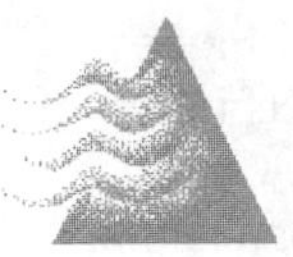

TIP

You can write the name of your company into your report using the CONAME preference for the value and the CG$CN generator item as the item on the report. This preference and item are also available in the Forms Generator.

Table 10-6 shows some of the template layout item objects you can use to generate a custom report. You place these objects as boilerplate into the report template, and the generator will lay out the items and create the necessary code to populate them with values.

Template Reports

Template reports are predefined reports that the Reports Generator uses to determine how to display the information in the generated report. Normally, the Reports Generator uses two template reports: the Layout Template report (required) and the Parameter Form Template report (optional).

Layout Template Report The Layout Template report contains objects that the generator creates exactly as they appear in the template and dictates the way the Reports Generator creates objects in the generated report. This report is responsible for the creation of header and trailer pages, as well as the margin layout. It also influences the layout of the report body. To use the layout template, you specify the filename in the LAYREP preference.

Parameter Form Template Report The Reports Generator uses the Parameter Form Template report to create the parameter form for your report. A parameter form template can contain both user and generator objects. You can

Layout Object	Description
CG$PROMPT	Field prompts
CG$FIELD	Field
CG$HEADER	Frame title
CG$PARAMETER	Parameter prompts
CG$SIZING	Font size for spacing

TABLE 10-6. *Layout Objects for the Report Template*

customize the parameter form to your specific needs using the same techniques as with the layout template. You have to ensure that the generator objects in the parameter form template are different from those in the layout template. One benefit of using a parameter form template is that you can define parameters that allow the user to reduce the size of the report by specifying which records will be retrieved at runtime. To use the parameter form template, you specify the filename in the PARREP preference.

Standard Template Reports Like the template Forms, the standard template reports can be used without modification. You can also modify them in Developer/2000 Reports Designer (available on the MDD Tools menu). Be sure to keep a copy of the original reports if you make changes. The standard templates are CGBMPT.RDF for Windows (bitmap) layout reports and CGBMPF.RDF for the parameter form of Windows reports.

NOTE

When you want to implement a drill-down report you can take advantage of a third template report, CGBMDT.RDF, which allows you to create a drill-down detail report. To specify this template, you use the DETREP preference. A drill-down report can be generated when you create two linked reports from one module. The help system contains more details on how to create this report.

Graphics Generator

The Graphics Generator creates different types of Oracle Graphics displays from chart module definitions in the repository. The module detailed table usage (available in the MDD) has a Chart tab. This is enabled if the module is a chart type and has detailed column usages defined. This tab allows you to select the layout style for the chart, placement, and size.

A graphics display consists of the chart (the visual display of data in the database), layers in the chart (multiple layout surfaces that can be hidden or displayed), and objects on the chart (graphical objects or imported objects and sounds).

Required Components

You do not need to specify any preferences for the Graphics Generator. Following are the required components for generating a chart display:

- **Module definition** You can use the MDD to specify a module with Oracle Graphics as the language and Chart as the type. The table and column usages become a SQL statement that provides the query for the chart display. You also define the fields that are displayed.

- **Chart template** The default chart template, CGDLFT.OGD, contains template displays and field templates that the generator uses to lay out the module. You can modify the template and add to or change the existing objects in this file.

Running the Graphics Generator

You can run the Graphics Generator from the Utilities menu of RON (using the Generate Module item), MDD (using the Generate item), or MSD (using the Generate item). Figure 10-10 shows the Graphics Options tab of the Graphics Generator.

The Generate tab contains a list of modules; from this list, you select a module to generate. If you start the generator from RON or MDD after selecting a module, the generator will open with the module preselected on the Generate tab.

You specify the generated chart location, template, database, and overwrite information. These fields are similar in intention to those in the other generators. You click the Start button to create the display, and the message log window will appear as the generator runs. This generates the .OGD source file that you can also run. When the generation process is done, you can choose to compile the file into an .OGR runtime file or to open the Developer/2000 Graphics Designer to modify or view the source file.

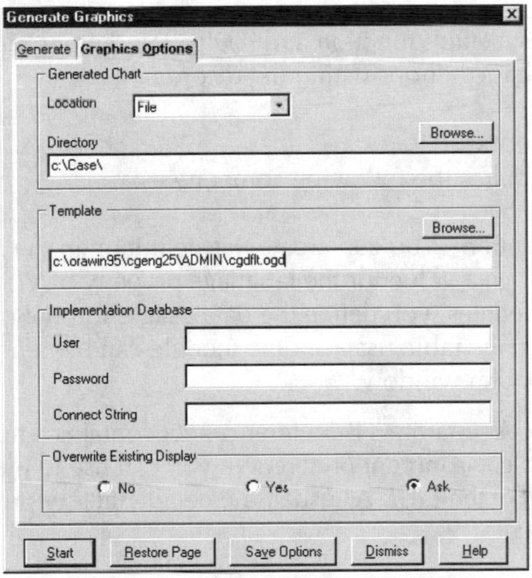

FIGURE 10-10. *Generate Graphics window with the Graphics Options tab*

Visual Basic Generator

The generator for Visual Basic (VB) creates the code for Visual Basic projects from module definitions. You then load the Designer/2000-generated code into the VB development tool so you can create a finished executable file. A VB project consists of one or more forms (windows) that contain zones for tables (similar to blocks in an Oracle Forms application). The generator creates controls (such as items) from the column usages and the correct VB code to access the data in the tables.

The VB Generator creates four different types of zones:

- *Context,* which is a query-only view of a single record displayed as a poplist of values. A separate property sheet window supplies insert, update, and delete functions.
- *Form,* which also displays a single record, but in this case the record can be updated.
- *List,* which displays a number of records in query-only mode. You can delete records in this type of window but not update them. The update and add functions for this type of window are supplied by a separate property sheet window.
- *List/Form,* which displays a record list box in the same window as the single-record view of the record selected in that list box.

For all zone types, default function and navigation buttons are automatically generated to enable basic actions within the record.

Required Components

The VB Generator requires the following components:

- **Module definition** You can create this definition in the MDD, MSD, or RON and assign a value for the language property of VISUAL BASIC. As with other modules, you define the data usages for that module and the links between the table usages. One module can be generated to more than one VB form window.
- **Preferences** A separate VB preferences set contains a number of interface and environment preferences you can use to modify the standard look and feel of the GUI. As usual, the default factory preferences will get you started.

- **Template project** Designer/2000 ships with standard VB template projects (.VBP files) that you can use to generate the code. You can also modify or replace these templates with your own.
- **Visual Basic 4.0 development tools** This is a separate non-Oracle product. You need this product to compile and create an executable file from the files that the VB Generator creates. You can also use this product to modify the files the generator creates or to customize the template projects.
- **Oracle Objects for OLE v2 Data Access Objects** This is another separate product that the generator relies on for access to database objects.

Running the Visual Basic Generator

You start the VB Generator from the Designer/2000 window application or any other tool that has a Utilities menu item for the generators (such as MDD or MSD). The window shown in Figure 10-11 appears.

You select the module you wish to generate and choose whether you want to generate to an existing project or a new project. VB projects consist of one or more forms that function as a unit; you can create as many or as few projects as you

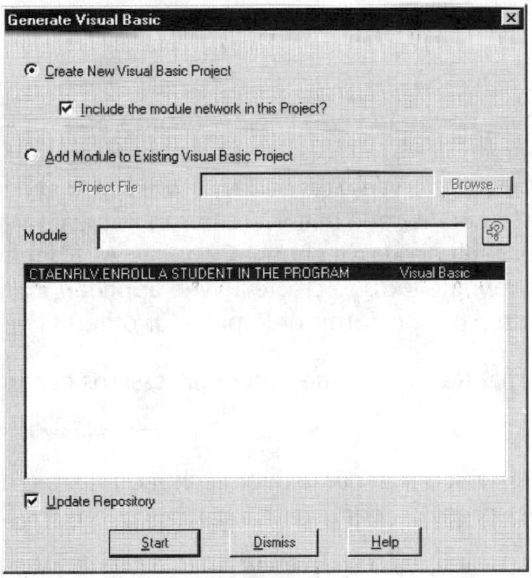

FIGURE 10-11. *Generate Visual Basic window*

want with the generator. Click Start when you are ready to generate. This will create the .FRM form files that contain the code and controls, as well as a .VBP project (make) file.

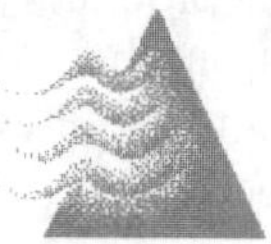

TIP
Be sure your module names are six characters or less because the VB Generator uses them as prefixes when creating filenames for the form files. Suffixes for these forms are two-digit numbers.

WebServer Generator

The WebServer Generator creates PL/SQL packages from modules that you define in the Module Data Diagrammer. You then run these PL/SQL scripts on an Oracle WebServer to create an application that you can run on the World Wide Web. The WebServer application creates the HTML code needed to present the page and queried data.

The WebServer Generator produces three files that have filenames consisting of the module name and an extension. The .PKS file contains the package specification, the .PKB file contains the package body, and the .SQL file runs the other two files to install the package in the database.

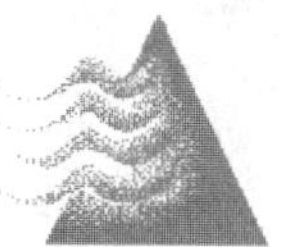

TIP
You can use the Reverse Engineer Forms and Reports utilities to create module definitions from existing forms and reports and change the language to WebServer. Then, when you generate these modules, you will obtain code that you can run to create Web applications. Alternatively, you can choose Generate As from the Utilities menus of appropriate tools to create a Web application from a module you have used for the Forms or Reports (or other) Generator.

The Web pages that result from the generator sessions can be categorized into four types:

- *Startup page,* which is generated for each module and displays a set of links to other pages or modules in the application
- *Query form,* which you use to enter query criteria for a database query
- *Record list,* which displays a list of queried records in a table or another type of list
- *View form,* which displays form-style details for a single record

Required Components

The WebServer Generator requires the following components:

- **Module definition** You create the module definition for this generator with WebServer as the language and Screen as the type. You must also define the module detailed table and column usages for the module. You can specify the HTML Formatting property for the column usage to designate how the column will appear on the Web page. Also, help text that you define for the module and its usages will appear as boilerplate text on the Web page. This text can include HTML WebServer commands such as htf.bold and htf.MailTo.
- **Preferences** The WebServer Generator provides separate preference types for the four types of pages mentioned earlier, as well as for DBA preferences. These give you individual control over the specific types of pages, as well as a way to enforce and create standards across all your WebServer pages.
- **WebServer database component** You must obtain and install a separate database server product, Oracle WebServer, which allows you to access an Oracle database from Web applications. The code this generator produces is run from the Oracle WebServer and calls commands specific to that product.
- **Web browser** You need to purchase a separate Web (HTML) browser product to test the application modules produced with this generator.

Running the WebServer Generator

You start the WebServer Generator from the Designer/2000 window application or from the Utilities menus of tools such as MDD and MSD. The window shown in Figure 10-12 appears.

The Generate tab allows you to select the module to generate and indicate whether you want to include the network of modules under that module. As usual, there is a check box where you can specify whether to update the module definition in the repository with changes made temporarily when the generator runs. If you are generating a WebServer module from a module with a different language using the Generate As menu item, the module definition will not be updated regardless of whether you check this box.

The Options tab has areas where you can specify where the PL/SQL code will be installed (database and user account), if you choose to install the code after generating it. You can also specify which Web browser you will use to run this application after it is generated and installed and the uniform resource locator (URL) of the Web agent serving this application.

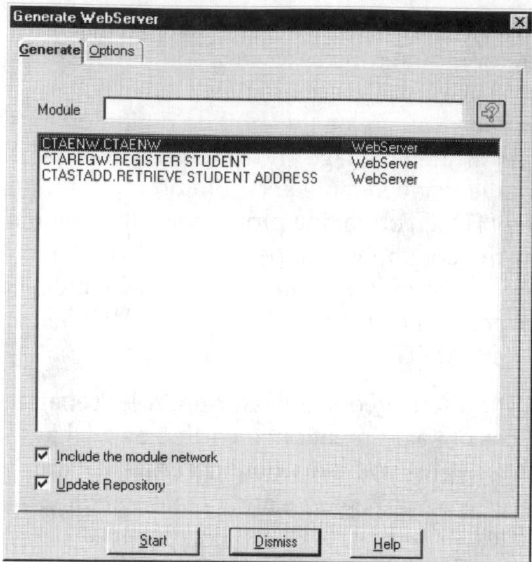

FIGURE 10-12. *Generate WebServer window*

After specifying the options and module information, you click the Start button, and the generator creates the script files for this Web application. If you filled in the Install and Run fields on the Options tab, you will be able to install the code and test it immediately. The URL of the starting page is

```
http://<web server address>/owa/module_name$.startup
```

where *<web server address>* identifies the machine, listener, and directory name of your Web server and *module_name* is the short name of the module.

MS Help Generator

The MS Help Generator creates help files in MS Help (WinHelp) format that attach to your Forms and Visual Basic applications. It provides support for the standard MS Windows help system with text links, embedded graphics, multiple topics, a glossary, and a contents topic. This system is an alternative to the help table system described in the section "Supporting Tables" earlier in this chapter. The user help text you define for table, module, and detailed module usages creates the text of the help topics in the help file.

The MS Help Generator requires the following components:

- **Forms preferences** The Forms Generator preference HLPTYP (under the END USER INTERFACE preference type) specifies how help is displayed for modules. Set this preference to MSHELP if you want the form module to use the help file system, and the Forms Generator will create the proper code to call the help file.
- **Help preferences** You can set additional Help Generator preferences in the Preferences Navigator to cause the generator to perform in a certain way. For example, the TUPLCT preference specifies whether you want a new help topic (page) for each table usage.
- **User help text** You can define user help text for all or some of the following definitions: table, column, module, detailed table usage, and detailed column usage.
- **Help compiler** You need to obtain a separate non-Designer/2000 program to create compiled .HLP files from help source files that this generator produces.

An optional component is the Business Terminology node in RON. If you create definitions of this element type, the MS Help Generator will create a glossary topic with a pop-up definition for each Business Terminology definition. It will also create a Glossary button that appears in the help file toolbar so the user can access the glossary more easily. Another optional component is the Client Help Details tab in the Edit Module properties window (in MSD or MDD), described in Chapter 9.

Note that this utility produces rich text format (.RTF) files that need the MS Help compiler to generate finished .HLP files. You will find this compiler in most Windows software development kits, but be sure to read the online Designer/2000 System Release Bulletin (SRB) for the MS Help Generator for current limitations. The name of the compiler varies, but you can specify the name in the Win95 or Windows NT registry (using REGEDIT) under the HKEY_LOCAL_MACHINE\SOFTWARE\ORACLE\cgenh10 node. You need to add a new string value there (with a datatype of REG_EXPAND_SZ) with the name HelpCompiler and a data value of the full path and name of the help compiler executable (for example, C:\HELP\HC31.EXE). If you are running Windows 3.x, add a line to your ORACLE.INI file, in the CGENH10 section, that reads HelpCompiler=C:\HELP\HC31.EXE. (Substitute the appropriate path and filename for the help compiler.)

CAUTION
The short name of the module for which you generate help becomes the filename suffix. If this name exceeds six characters, the help generation process will fail.

Running the MS Help Generator

You can run the MS Help Generator from the Designer/2000 window application or the Utilities menu of various tools such as RON. If you use RON, be sure there are no modules selected in the hierarchy before selecting **Utilities→Generate Module** from the menu. You will see the Generator Type dialog box shown in the following illustration. Select Help System to go to the MS Help Generator.

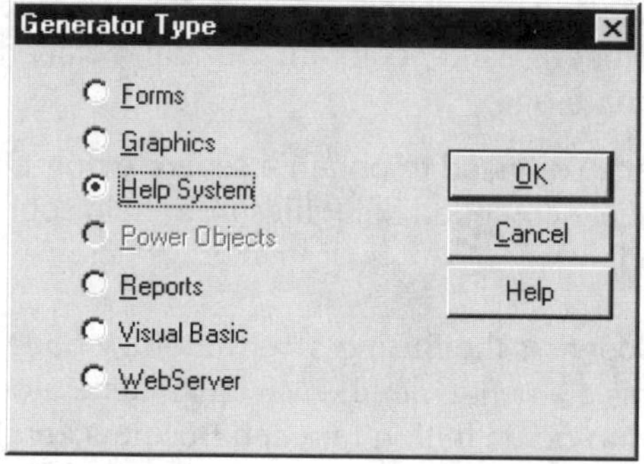

The Generate Help System window in Figure 10-13 will appear. In this window, you select the modules for which you want help text and the types of files you wish to generate. You can also choose to update the help tables themselves if you are using the help table system.

After the generator completes the help file generation, you will have an .HM file (that contains context ID numbers for the topics) and an .RTF file. At that point, you can click the Compile button in the final dialog window to compile the file. Once the file is compiled into an .HLP file, you can run it by clicking the Run button.

C++ Object Layer Generator

The objective of the C++ Object Layer Generator is to generate C++ classes and function code to manipulate and access the data structures in your application. Since the generated code handles data access, it allows you to concentrate in your C++ programs on the actual application-specific needs.

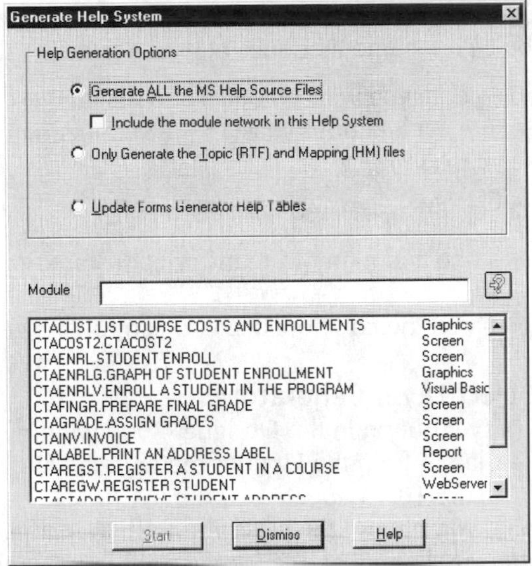

FIGURE 10-13. *Generate Help System window*

The code you produce from the C++ Object Layer Generator creates C++ classes that isolate your main application code from the data sources. Therefore, if the table model changes, you may only need to generate the new C++ class layer for the new structure, and the main C++ program may be able to access it in the same way as before. The generated code is compiled and linked with your other C++ application code and becomes part of the final application executable.

Since this generator produces code for tables, no module is needed or used. The definitions you use to produce the C++ classes and function code produces both the classes for the data object itself and the classes for the functions (such as select, insert, update, and delete) you perform on that data.

Required Steps

Perform the following steps to use the C++ Object Layer Generator:

1. Create C++ Generator class sets using the node of the same name in RON.
2. Associate entities with class sets using the Entity node under the C++ Generator Class Set node. Be sure there is a value in the C++ Class Name entity property. Note that you can type anything here, including a name

that does not identify a C++ Generator class set. However, the generator will fail if you type a name that does not exist as a C++ Generator class set.

3. Associate a C++ datatype with domains and assign these domains to all attributes. Be sure each attribute has a C++ member name, which is a unique, mixed-case string.
4. Ensure that tables are associated with each entity.
5. Remove one-to-one and many-to-many relationships.

Once you have prepared the components, you can run the generator utility.

Running the C++ Object Layer Generator

Click the C++ Object Layer button in the Designer/2000 window application or choose Generate C++ Classes from the Utilities menu in the ER Diagrammer or RON. The window in Figure 10-14 appears.

In the Class Sets tab, you choose the class you wish to load and click the Load button. If there are errors in the model, the Model Anomalies window will appear and describe the errors. Before moving on, you need to exit the generator, fix these errors, and restart the generator. After all errors are fixed, you can then access the other tabs: Classes (to see a list of the classes you can generate), Class Files (to

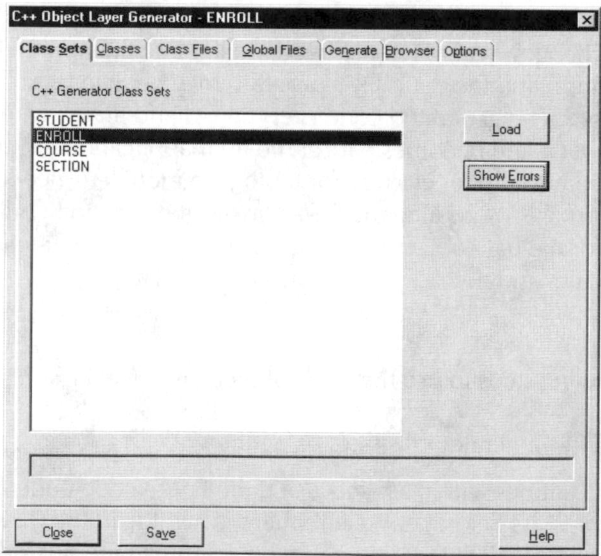

FIGURE 10-14. *C++ Object Layer Generator window*

specify the names and types of files to generate to), Global Files (to specify the files in which your global code is placed), Generate (to specify which global code you are generating and whether to generate or regenerate), Browser (to see the Object Browser display of the classes and class relationships), and Options (to specify the name suffixes and prefixes). When you click the Generate button on the Generate tab, the class code will be generated to the files you specified.

As with the VB, WebServer, and MS Help Generators, you need to do some work outside of Designer/2000. You use a separately purchased C++ compiler to compile your Designer/2000–generated classes with the rest of the C++ code you write elsewhere and link them to the appropriate libraries to create the finished application.

Repository Reports in the Build Phase

Other than the repository reports you will need for unit testing as discussed in Chapter 11, there are no repository reports that are crucial to the completion of module code in the Build phase. Your system documentation (one of the deliverables in the Build phase) consists of the repository itself and any of the element definition reports you feel are needed. There are also some reports that can be useful at this stage to check the database object and module definitions.

For the database side of the Build phase, you can run the Database Table and Index Size Estimate report in the Database Design group to recheck the estimated size of your complete database system. In addition, the Quality group contains reports you can use to check database objects for problems. You may want to run the following Quality reports before you create the DDL script for the database objects:

- *Database Trigger Quality Control* checks trigger definitions for potential inconsistencies.
- *Create Status Quality Control* lists problems with the Create flag of database objects.
- *Groups/Users Quality Control* lists users that have incorrect privileges for database objects.
- *Package/Procedure Quality Control* lists problems with function parameters and other problems with PL/SQL module definitions.

For the module side of the Build phase, you can run reports in the Module Design group to obtain full details of the finished module for documentation or cross-checking. The Module Definition report is an example of a report from this group that provides documentation on the module. If you make changes to table definitions after some modules are created, the reports from the Impact Analysis group, such as the Modules which Use a Given Table/View report, can tell you what modules will be affected by those changes. Other reports in this group that are useful if you change the module network are the Modules Used by a Given Module and Modules which Use a Given Module reports.

Conclusion

The system is nearly complete at the end of the Build phase. You have a database, migrated data, and unit-tested modules. All that remains to be done is to perform additional testing, finalize user and system documentation, and train users. The Build phase is probably the most complex from the Designer/2000 point of view. The true challenge in using Designer/2000 is the effective use of the generators.

There is a great temptation to generate applications and make all modifications using the client-side tool. However, this breaks the link to Designer/2000 and makes it impossible to regenerate the modules. In some cases, this strategy is necessary because of the complexity of the design. However, you should strive to use the Designer/2000 generators to build as many of your modules as possible. Where feasible, you should store any post-generation changes to those modules in module-specific templates and libraries. In this way, you can realize the full potential of Designer/2000.

Although you have used Designer/2000 as much as possible to create the finished application, the life cycle is not over. The next chapter details the Change control process, the post-Build phase steps in the life cycle, and the activities that you need to perform in the final step of the system before you place it in production. This next step is called the Test phase.

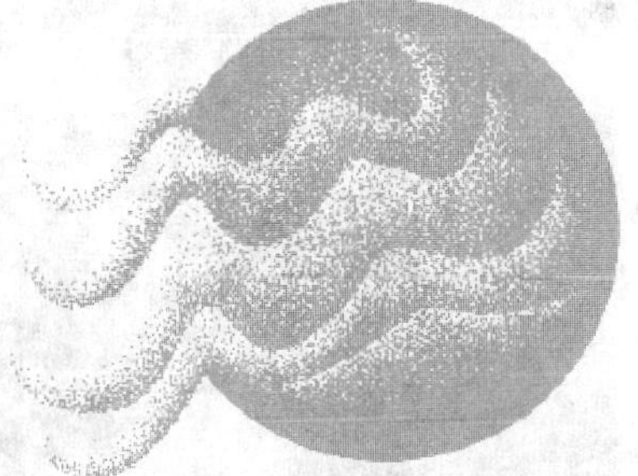

CHAPTER 11

Test and Change Control

This is a test of the Application Development System. Had this been an actual application, your data would already be corrupted and your organization would be plunged into chaos. This is only a test.

At this point, the system has been built, unit tested, and passed on from the developers to the test team. If you have followed the CADM process carefully, the Test phase should run smoothly.

Some of the activities and quality control executed during earlier phases that contribute significantly to the success of the Test phase include:

- Users approved the requirements document at the end of the Analysis phase.
- After the logical ERD was created in the requirements analysis portion of the Analysis phase, you worked with one or more senior modelers to carefully audit the logical model.
- The system storyboard went through a formal acceptance testing process with the users.
- Requirements were mapped to functions and modules.
- Column level usages were specified for each module and reviewed by senior team members.
- The design book was audited against the system requirements.

One of the most important features of CADM is that, as you move into the Test phase, you have a complete audit trail that allows you to logically follow a system requirement gathered in the Analysis phase all the way through to the completed system. Because of the way the system was built, you know that it meets the stated system requirements as you understand them. Every step in the process has been checked and audited throughout the system life cycle. Theoretically, all that is left in the final Test phase is to conduct integration, system-level performance tests, and user acceptance testing for the application.

However, as you have proceeded through the CADM process, everything undoubtedly has not gone completely smoothly. User requirements may have changed over time. Users may have changed. The scope may have changed. The business may have changed. In the course of the project, your thinking about how the requirements should be distilled into an analysis document may have changed. The design evolved as you moved through the Design and Build phases. For these reasons, many of your earlier audits and deliverables may not still be valid. In the development of the test plan, you need to carefully consider each of the major deliverables and decide what level of testing is appropriate.

This chapter discusses two very different topics. The first topic is change control throughout the CADM process. The development process included various quality control points and tests, but what happens when changes need to be made to steps that occurred in earlier phases of the system development process? This issue is discussed in the next section.

The second topic is system and user acceptance testing. Various system tests must be performed. Unit-level testing was already performed in the Build phase. However, you need to ensure that the new system interacts smoothly with existing systems, handles business transactions adequately, and performs adequately with the organization's full production load. The goal of user acceptance testing is to help uncover glitches in the user interface and inadequacies in the GUI design. User acceptance testing should not be performed until after the system testing is mostly complete and the development team is confident that the system is basically sound.

Change Control During Each Phase of the Process

A key feature of the CADM process has been the ongoing quality reviews. Sometimes quality reviews have been explicit, such as the audit of the logical ERD in the Analysis phase. At other times, the audit has been implicit, such as the automatic cross-checking of the physical database that occurred as a result of the migration of the legacy data. The point is that the CADM process is not linear; it can be spiral. At any phase in the process, you might discover information that, had you known it earlier, would have caused you to do something differently in an earlier phase. Unfortunately, if you tried to incorporate every new piece of information found throughout the CADM process into the new system, the system would never be built. Therefore, you need to carefully weigh the costs and benefits associated with the incorporation of each new piece of information into the application. In each phase, with the exception of the Strategy phase, you must consider what happens when new information is discovered that is relevant to prior phases. Keep in mind that the later in the process that a failure, new requirement, or change in scope is discovered, the more work that will be needed and the higher the cost of the change.

Who decides what will get done and when? Throughout the system life cycle, there should be a management team made up of the project leaders, a representative of upper-level management, one or more functional area users and, perhaps, a DBA (if no one else on the team has DBA experience). This small management team controls the CADM process and either performs all of the review tasks or delegates them to appropriate individuals. The process of review and quality assurance is critical to the success of the CADM process and should be handled by the best talent available. Of course, a key principle is that no one can perform a QA review of their own work.

As you progress through each phase of the CADM process, you have more and more to worry about with regard to changes to earlier phases. In the Analysis phase, you only have to worry about changes to the Strategy phase; whereas in the Design phase, you have to worry about changes to system requirements and changes in scope from the Strategy phase. At each phase, we will identify all the major deliverables from the earlier phases and discuss the impact of changes to any of those deliverables. Ideally, this information would be displayed in a giant matrix with all of the deliverables lined up on one axis and all the phases on the other in order to clearly see the impact of changing each deliverable for each phase. In the following section, we will move through the entire CADM process, one phase at a time. Within each phase, we will discuss how you should respond when information leads you to reassess how well the earlier phases were done.

Changes Discovered During the Pre-Analysis Phase

During the Pre-Analysis phase, any changes you discover should be relatively easy to make because the only stage completed thus far is the Strategy phase.

Strategy

If you discover changes in scope that affect the Strategy phase, little real work has been done yet; so changing the scope of the project at this point is not particularly costly. However, the modified strategy document will need to be reissued and the sign-off process for the strategy document repeated. If the organization in question is highly political, this may be a nontrivial cost.

One way to minimize the cost of amending the strategy document is not to reissue the entire document but instead to add an amendment that outlines the change in scope independently without opening up the entire strategy document for review.

Changes Discovered During the Analysis Phase: Information Gathering

The information gathering part of the Analysis phase is where you attempt to collect all of the system requirements through interviews, JAD sessions, questionnaires, and so on.

Strategy

As long as requirements are still being gathered, changes in scope do not have a particularly severe effect. You may even decide that many of the requirements that have already been gathered should be declared out of scope. At this point in the system development process, you should not hesitate to modify the scope of the project. The same issues apply here that applied to changes to scope in the Pre-Analysis phase.

Pre-Analysis

The two main goals of the Pre-Analysis phase are to set standards and formulate the analysis plan. Depending on how far you are in the requirements gathering process, the effects of changes to the requirements gathering standards can be quite severe. For example, changes to the document used for structuring interviews may require a great deal of repeated work. Do you go back and restructure all earlier information or leave the existing information and gather more in the new format? Another option is to reject the change in the standard altogether. The project leaders must carefully weigh the pros and cons of each alternative. However, given that at this point you are in the middle of requirements gathering, any decision that needs to be made should be made immediately.

Changes Discovered During the Analysis Phase: Requirements Analysis

In the requirements analysis part of the Analysis phase, requirements have mostly been gathered, so the cost of incorporating changes into the new system begins to increase.

Strategy

Once you are into requirements analysis, a change in scope may necessitate the reworking of the Analysis phase. You will need to go back to the users and ask more questions, even though information gathering was supposed to be finished. However, a change at this point may not be as bad as it may seem, since much of the thinking that goes into requirements analysis will not change. Depending on the nature of the scope change, the change may or may not have a serious impact at this point. Making a shift in scope during the requirements analysis portion of the Analysis phase won't have catastrophic effects; but the possibility of putting off any shift in scope until the next version of the system should be considered.

Pre-Analysis

At this point, you do not want to change standards regarding the gathering of information unless you fundamentally don't have the necessary information to complete the system. Changing standards at this point is a catastrophic analysis plan failure. Of course, if you are now finding that requirements are grossly inadequate, you will need to substantially redo the information gathering process. This will cost not only time and money, but your credibility with users may be lost. Analysts should never have to go back to users and ask them the same questions they were asked a month earlier.

On the other hand, if you need to change the requirements analysis method during the requirements analysis process, this is not a particularly large problem. For example, if it is decided that you need to deliver a dataflow diagram or state transition diagram as part of the analysis document, such modifications to the analysis plan can be made quite easily.

Analysis: Information Gathering

Discovering and incorporating new user requirements in the Analysis phase is not a particularly severe change and does not even require prior approval by the project leaders. Of course, modifications to the underlying requirements document must go through a small quality review, but this can easily be done in a group at the end of the requirements analysis process. All modifications to system requirements should be bundled together and go through a single review process at the end of requirements analysis.

Changes Discovered During the Pre-Design Phase

In the Pre-Design phase, standards are set, and the design plan is created along with the conceptual design of the application.

Strategy

Scope shifts in Pre-Design necessitate redoing the entire Analysis phase for the expanded scope. Any scope shift will require redoing some portion of requirements analysis. Such changes are not unusual since once requirements analysis is complete, you have a very clear picture of what is needed in the new system. The narrowing of scope, although a rare occurrence, merely means that you can ignore portions of the system requirements for version 1.

In fact, it might be worthwhile to include a quality check at this point in which the scope is reviewed to make sure that the development team's understanding of what is needed in the new system hasn't made the original strategy document obsolete. Some maturing of your understanding of the project scope is bound to take place as the project progresses. It is common to find that when the finalized requirements document is compared to the scope, the scope has already drifted. This is acceptable, but the strategy document needs to be amended to be consistent with the new and improved vision of the end product.

Pre-Analysis

Once Analysis is complete, changes to the whole structure of the analysis document should be made only if the project will otherwise fail.

Analysis: Information Gathering

Incorporating new requirements during the Pre-Design phase is more expensive than it may seem. Not only does each new requirement need to be documented, you must also ensure that it is appropriate and update all relevant portions of the requirements document. From this point forward, new system requirements cannot be added by the developers without authorization from the project leaders. New system requirements should be filed as "system modification requests" and periodically reviewed to either be included in the current design or deferred for a later version. This rule must be enforced. Developers must not be allowed to respond to user requests for additional requirements.

Not putting some controls on this process puts the entire project at risk. This is one of the primary reasons for "analysis paralysis." This is not to say that essential new system requirements will not arise throughout the CADM life cycle. However, it is crucial that the addition of new system requirements be handled in a controlled fashion. The process of adding new requirements should be made very clear to the users early in the CADM process so they are not surprised by the enforcement of new rules later on. The method for adding new requirements outlined here should remain in effect through the end of the project. However, because the cost of adding new system requirements increases exponentially as you move into the later phases of CADM, the rules for accepting new system requirements will become increasingly strict the farther along in the process new requirements are discovered or suggested.

A system modification request should contain an impact analysis section. Before approving or denying the inclusion of a new requirement, you need to analyze its cost.

Analysis: Requirements Analysis

Anything that requires you to modify the Analysis deliverables will not affect anything being done in Pre-Design. Thus, such changes should be allowed, if necessary, with relatively minor restrictions.

Changes Discovered During the Design Phase: Database Design

The database design part of the Design phase is where everything begins to be put into place in preparation for the Build phase.

Strategy

During the database design, modifying strategy is very costly. Scope changes at this late date should be allowed only if the system will fail if the scope is not allowed to change. Scope changes here will require the reworking of all previous phases and should be avoided whenever possible.

Pre-Analysis

Any changes affecting your work in the Pre-Analysis phase should be handled as described for the Pre-Design phase.

Analysis: Information Gathering

Any changes affecting your work in the information gathering part of the Analysis phase should be handled as described for the Pre-Design phase.

Analysis: Requirements Analysis

Changes to process flows have no effect on database design; but any changes to the logical ERD from this point forward are very costly and should be handled with the same system modification request process used for newly discovered system requirements. Physical database design is a very complex step. Changes in the ERD should be made only if they are truly necessary to avoid system failure.

Pre-Design

The area to avoid changing in database design is naming standards. It is necessary to closely audit how well naming standards are working early in the database design part of the Design phase so that any necessary changes to the design conventions can be made early. It is a good idea to hold a meeting early in the database design process to review the current level of comfort with the design method. Any changes that show up with conceptual design of the application done in Pre-Design have little impact during database design and should be freely allowed.

Changes Discovered During the Design Phase: Application Design

The Application Design part of the Design phase is where the detailed column usages are defined for each module and the database design is validated. Changes that are made during Design may appear simple and straightforward; however, they usually have a "ripple" effect. Each individual change may have a minimal cost or impact, but the overall effect of many such changes can be substantial. The project manager must evaluate the changes to determine if they could effect time, budget, or quality. Careful prioritization and impact on users/customer/client is paramount.

Strategy

Any changes affecting your work in the Strategy phase should be handled as described for the database design part of the Design phase.

Pre-Analysis

Any changes affecting your work in the Pre-Analysis phase should be handled as described for the Pre-Design phase.

Analysis: Information Gathering

Any changes affecting your work in the information gathering part of the Analysis phase should be handled as described for the Pre-Design phase.

Analysis: Requirements Analysis

At this point in the SDLC, the analysis document needs to be frozen. Any changes must now go through the same system modification request process used for changes that affect the Strategy phase and the information gathering part of the Analysis phase.

Pre-Design

Modifications to the database portion of the design plan need to go through the system modification request process. However, changes to the conceptual design of the application or the application part of the design plan can be made freely.

Design: Database Design

Changes to the database design during the application design process are to be expected. This is the main reason for creating the application design at this point in the CADM process. As column-level mapping is performed, columns that were omitted may be discovered, as well as columns that were never used which can be deleted.

Changes Discovered During the Build Phase

Making changes during the Build phase is something you want to avoid. The cost of change is very high and usually has an unpredictable "ripple" effect. If changes are made during Build, they should be documented and reflected as modifications or amendments to prior Analysis and Design phase deliverables.

Once you reach the Build phase, all potential changes to any phase, with the exception of the physical database and application design developed in the Design phase, must go through the system modification request process.

Design: Database Design

The database design needn't stay fixed during the Build phase. Indeed, the legacy system data migration will probably uncover some changes that need to be made to the database design.

Design: Application Design

The application design is still in flux as the application is being built. It is to be expected that there will be many changes. You need to make sure that changes don't cause individual modules to diverge from a consistent user interface. Constant monitoring during the unit testing of the modules is necessary.

Changes Discovered During the Test Phase

Any test failure should automatically initiate a system modification request. Just because a test failure occurs does not mean that this failure must be corrected in this system version. Changes can be very costly. Any change to the completed system should be thoroughly evaluated before it is incorporated into the new system.

Overview of the Test Phase

The Test phase is the point at which the new system is formally tested. In the Test phase, you develop a test plan that should describe not only tests to be run but also how test failures or variances will be handled. It is not necessarily true that every test failure or variance leads to modifications to the system prior to production. Within the Test phase, it will be necessary to re-audit the design process, perform system- and user-level tests, audit the quality of the documentation, test the internal controls and backup and recovery procedures, and in all ways ascertain the fitness of the system to move into a production environment.

Test Plan

The lead QA person needs to develop a test plan. Users need to be involved to identify the test cases, and they can write the test scripts and expected outcomes. There are two components to a test plan: the approach and the design. The approach includes the testing techniques, testing tools, roles and responsibilities, method of error detection and logging, change control process, retesting process, and testing environment. The design part of the test plan includes the test objectives, cases, and scripts. The test plan is the framework in which the different levels or types of testing are performed, i.e. system testing and user acceptance testing. You should develop a test plan for each type of testing.

The test plan must encompass the following elements.

System tests:

- **Audit of major CADM deliverables** Make sure early phases were completed correctly.
- **Integration tests** Make sure applications work together smoothly.
- **Transaction flow tests** Make sure business transactions meet business requirements.
- **Stress tests** Make sure the system can handle a realistic production environment.
- **Data migration validation** Make sure the legacy system data is moved accurately into the new system.
- **Backup and recovery tests** Make sure the system is adequately protected against potentially catastrophic system events.
- **Internal control evaluation** Make sure the new system is secure.

User acceptance tests:

- **Small pilot lab tests** Have a few users try out the applications in a controlled environment.
- **Training sessions** Conduct training sessions that also serve as user feedback sessions.

Training and documentation:

- **User training** Finalize the training material and train the trainer(s).
- **User documentation** Ensure that user documentation is accurate.
- **System documentation** Finalize the system operations manual and the disaster recovery manual.
- **Help desk** Make sure the help desk personnel have the documentation and training necessary to support customer problems.

System Testing

System testing must validate two aspects of the system: the database and the applications. However, there is not always a clear distinction between the two. For example, are database triggers part of the database or the application? For the purposes of this discussion, the database will be defined to include all tables, table structures, and database constraints. Some triggers will be considered part of the application.

Since the Analysis phase included a logical audit of the ERD and the Design phase included an audit of the physical ERD, you do not need to test the structure of the database at this point. The physical structure has already been checked. However, if modifications are made, these will have to be tested.

With regard to the application, several testing issues must be addressed. The integration of the applications must be clean and seamless. The most complex and failure-prone portions of the application are the interfaces between parts of the new application and the existing systems. Even though all systems have passed unit testing, you need to ensure that all of the interfaces are correct. The essence of system testing is not to test the individual modules; that has already been done. Instead, entire business transactions must be processed through the system.

You can probably assume that not all of the business rules have been implemented as triggers and constraints. Not all of them could be or the system would not run, would take years to code, and would never deliver adequate performance even if it were coded. It is therefore necessary to write some procedures that validate the business rules not implemented as constraints. For example, in an insurance company, a policy holder may not be allowed to have two policies in force for the same coverage at the same time. A business rule set up as a trigger to test for this condition would make any modifications to the insurance policy coverage table unacceptably slow.

The application must also be tested at full production loads—not just at today's production capacity but also at projected levels of capacity for the life of the system. There are many ways of checking the application portion of the system (that is, the code). The principle behind good testing is the one auditors use to find errors in large accounting systems. Many, many tests are run looking for the same errors in different ways. The logic is that if errors are not caught one way, they will be caught in another. Therefore, applications can be tested by running lots of little tests and looking for evidence that shows how well the system is working.

Auditing Major CADM Deliverables

During each stage of the CADM process, some tests will likely fail, new requirements will crop up, there will be scope creep, realignment of priorities, and new areas may need to be added to the system being built. Managing and controlling these changes in a thoughtful and systematic way can mean the difference between system success and failure.

At this point in the system development process, it is important to take another look at all of the major deliverables in the CADM process to decide what auditing is necessary.

Strategy Document If the system being delivered is significantly different from the proposed system, that difference needs to be documented. All that can really be done is to identify where objectives have not been met or where other valid objectives have been added. You may find that some portion of the system was overlooked and more work needs to be done. At this late point, anything missed will probably not be incorporated until the next version of the product.

Requirements Document A full audit of the requirements document was performed at the end of the Analysis phase. However, as mentioned earlier, the requirements document has probably changed significantly since the Analysis phase. There are two alternatives:

- Audit the process used to allow changes to the requirements document.
- Re-audit the requirements document in the same way as at the end of the Analysis phase.

If you were careful in your original audit of the requirements document and have controlled and documented all changes to the requirements document, you can be reasonably confident that your requirements document reflects your best current understanding of the system. The only part that would remain to be checked is whether or not the user requirements themselves have changed during the System Development Life Cycle. If they have, you may need to modify major portions of the system to make the system useful. One of the most difficult decisions to make is whether to go back and make substantive changes to the system before delivering version 1; however, it is better to delay a system than to deliver a grossly inadequate system. Of course, such an action should be undertaken only if absolutely necessary. In general, it is better to deliver something than nothing.

If your audit of the requirements document change procedure indicates that changes were not carefully controlled, it may be necessary to redo significant portions, if not all, of the requirements document audit as discussed at the end of Chapter 6. However, if such an action is necessary, the entire system is at risk. This is tantamount to acknowledging a lack of confidence in the foundation of the system. If the requirements document audit fails, everything done after Analysis may need to be redone.

Design Book Of course, the design book will change a lot over the project life cycle. It has had periodic reviews and updates and remains a working document from the Pre-Design phase through the Build phase. The most important point of your audit is to make sure that the design book is up-to-date. You cannot test the new system without an accurate, up-to-date design book.

The System The final deliverable is the system itself. Testing the system is what people traditionally think of as the work of the Test phase. As when testing other aspects of the CADM process, the key to good testing of the system is to perform multiple tests using different individuals and approaches to try to determine that the developers were careful and conscientious in conforming to standards and satisfying the system requirements.

Performing Integration Tests

As business transactions move through modules, they usually need to interact with other modules. For example, in a PO system, when a PO is initiated, it should show up in the approver's module for approval. To test this, you can enter a PO into the system to verify that it shows up in the approver's module.

You need to identify every such interface point in the system. In general, such interface points are easily identified through physical process flows. Modules naturally flow from one to the next. However, sometimes such interface points cannot be identified in this way. For example, some information may be gathered in a human resources system, and that same information may feed into an Equal Employment Opportunity (EEO) system that doesn't track human resource information but does report and manipulate it. Therefore, the interface between modules in the human resources system and the EEO system also needs to be identified and tested.

The testing of interface points involves the entry of information into one module and the retrieval or manipulation of that information by another module. The test should involve not only observation of the data through the modules, but also direct observation of the underlying database tables using SQL.

Performing Transaction Flow Tests

Transaction flow tests are an extension of integration tests. In this process, you walk entire business transactions through the whole new system. For example, in a PO system, you can follow the progress of a specific PO filled with sample data from its initiation through the approval process and the receipt and distribution of the goods. Transaction tests can be performed using only the interface with the modules, assuming that module-level tests and interface tests have been performed. The transactions must simply be walked through the entire process.

To adequately test the system, a small amount of sample data also needs to be used to test the entire process. This allows you to test not only the flow of transactions through the process flows, but also the interaction of those process flows with each other.

Performing Stress Tests

Just because a system works on sample data with one user on a dedicated machine does not mean that the same system will perform adequately in a true production environment. The system needs to be tested using realistic production loads to simulate the actual number of users in their actual locations, with production-level database sizes and realistic transaction rates (transactions per second). The stress testing should be done not only on current production loads but also on projected future loads.

Validating Data Migration

Making sure that data migration is accurate is a very complex step that should be performed table by table, subject area by subject area, as data migration takes place. This process was discussed in detail in Chapter 10.

Performing Backup and Recovery Tests

Backup and recovery procedures are crucial parts of any organization's system, and the testing of the backup and recovery system is just as crucial. If the system is supposed to support operation 24 hours a day, seven days a week, with no more than 20 minutes of consecutive down time, then a tester should be able to walk into the computer room and pull the plug, and the personnel on-site should be able to bring up the system again within the allotted time.

Realistic backup and recovery tests should be conducted without allowing the operations personnel to prepare for the tests. Real disasters rarely occur with prior warning. You can't realistically test a backup and recovery system by scheduling the test at a convenient time for systems people two weeks in advance. Each exposure that the backup and recovery system is supposed to protect against should be individually tested.

Evaluating Internal Controls

Testing the internal control system is much like testing the backup and recovery system except that there are many more exposures, most of which are, in general, less severe. The principle is the same: you should simulate each exposure, from incorrect data entry to fraudulent transactions, to make sure the system is protected.

Handing Test Results

Some of the results of the system tests will indicate that there are problems with the system. The test results that uncover problems should become system modification requests. Depending on the sophistication of the testers, you may or may not want to give the testers the authority to approve a system modification request for action before the new system goes into production. Only problems that prevent the system from going into production should be acted upon.

The most important point to remember is that only those requests that would prevent the system from going into production should be approved. It is easy to start making dozens of trivial formatting or data validation changes to each module that do not substantively affect the ability of the system to support the needs of the organization.

Determining Who Performs Testing

Testing can be done by people who do not have particular technical expertise. In fact, nontechnically oriented people are frequently better than systems professionals. Not only are they less expensive to hire, but they also better approximate the user population. In addition, automated testing tools are available that can help with many aspects of the testing process.

User Acceptance Tests

User acceptance testing involves putting the application in front of the users and making sure the users are satisfied. It also includes testing the documentation and training available. User acceptance testing helps identify any glitches in the user interface and inadequacies in GUI design. User acceptance testing should not be performed until the system testing is mostly complete and you are confident that the system is basically clean. The goal of user testing is not only to find any problems in the system; it also serves to generate user excitement. If the system has significant and obvious flaws, users will lose confidence in the quality of the system.

Performing Small Pilot Lab Tests

Small pilot lab tests involve bringing in a small number of users and extensively training them on the new system. The strategy here is largely the same as in transaction flow tests: the users should do real work on the system in a controlled environment. Users can identify problems and provide feedback.

Training and Documentation

The review of documentation, training, and help desk functions should first be done internally within the IS department. It is far too common to assign a technical writer to build a manual and then start making hundreds of copies before anyone reads it. After the IS review is complete, show the documentation to a small group of users for feedback. Also get a small group of users to provide feedback on training sessions and the help desk system. Then repeat these tests with a larger group as part of initial user training.

Good-quality documentation and training are critical factors in user acceptance of the new system. Testing this vital portion of the system should not be overlooked.

Conducting Training Sessions

At this point, if the system has passed all other tests and is close to implementation, users can begin real training on the new system prior to the Implementation phase. The first group of users of the new system brought in for training should be carefully observed. In addition, users should do real work to provide a full test run of the new system while they are under observation.

Modifications for Smaller Systems

For small systems, if the development team has a close enough relationship with the new system users, you can employ users as testers in the Test phase. This approach can also be taken if other testers are unavailable. However, users may not test as thoroughly as dedicated testers. What is required are individuals who will click every button, try every function, try every combination of buttons and functions, and find as many bugs as possible. Waiting until the system is in production to find bugs means those bugs might not show up for weeks or even months—certainly long after the people who developed the code are gone. Even if developers are still around, they may well have forgotten the intricacies of the code.

Of course, most of the process auditing, verifying of the strategy and requirements documents, and so on is irrelevant for small systems. Testing small systems may merely consist of making sure users are happy with the new system.

For medium-sized systems, careful verification of the early phases is not as important as for large systems. However, all system and user acceptance testing should be performed as described in this chapter.

The deliverables for small and medium systems are just as important as those for large systems. The reason that testing is less imperative for small and medium systems is that the time frame and number of system elements associated with the projects is small enough that there is a greater probability of doing it right the first time, perhaps making the final re-audit unnecessary. However, you may want to take small and medium systems through the entire Test phase for one of the following reasons:

- You have less confidence in the quality of the process due to test failures.
- The system is mission critical for the organization.
- A higher level of QA is desirable.
- Organizational policies and procedures mandate a quality review of the entire system upon completion.

When Is the Test Phase Complete?

The key to completing the Test phase is to not try to fix every little problem that comes up. As many as possible of the system modification requests generated by the Test phase should be shifted to version 2 of the system.

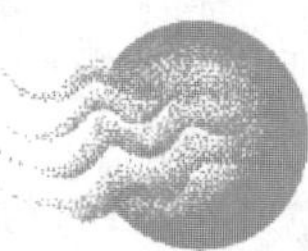

NOTE
One of the main deliverables of the Test phase is the version 2 specifications that address all the system modification requests.

To get the new system up and running, it is often necessary to "just say no" to more system modification requests. The system is complete when all type 1 bugs have been fixed. Type 1 bugs are bugs that prevent the system from going into production. For example, bugs that corrupt the data or prevent basic system functionality are type 1. Type 2 bugs represent a failure to meet a system requirement. Examples include inadequate performance or a bug in a noncritical system feature. Type 3 bugs represent previously undiscovered system requirements that would significantly improve the effectiveness of the system. Type 4 bugs are any other desirable modifications to the system. Whether type 2 bugs will be fixed for the first system production release or not is a decision to be made by the project leader. Type 3 and 4 bug fixes are typically deferred to later versions of the system.

Before the Test phase is complete, the strategy document, requirements document, and design book should be validated for correctness. Either amend or document any differences between the delivered system and the system proposed in the strategy document. This report must be signed by both the senior project leaders and the chief user.

System and user testing, documentation review, and training are complete when you have taken care of all type 1 bugs. Anything that is not a type 1 bug is deferred until version 2 of the system.

The Test Phase in Designer/2000

Most of the Test phase tasks are done outside the scope of Designer/2000. However, there are some key activities that the repository can help with. These are listed in Table 11-1 along with the supporting Designer/2000 tools and utilities.

This chapter focuses on how you can use the Designer/2000 tools and utilities for these specific activities in the Test phase. The Repository Object Navigator and Repository Reports tools were discussed fully in Chapter 4, and the Matrix Diagrammer was explained fully in Chapter 6; the Application Programmatic Interface is explored in detail in Chapter 14.

Unit and System Test Documentation

Generally, the test phase is handled by your quality assurance (QA) group. These people perform similar tests in both the Build and Test phases to ensure that the application performs correctly and as designed. The Build phase consists of unit or module-level tests that concentrate on each module, and the Test phase is concerned with system-level tests that check groups of modules or the interaction between modules.

Unit Testing

The objective of your finished application is to fulfill the business needs that were stated in the form of system requirements. In the Pre-Design phase, you attached these requirements to modules by creating a user-extended association type (as discussed in Chapter 7) and assigning individual requirements to each module. In the Build phase, you created the module code itself, and the QA group performs module-level unit tests to make sure the attached requirements are actually

Activity or Deliverable	Designer/2000 Tool
System test documentation	Matrix Diagrammer
Problem tracking	Repository Object Navigator Matrix Diagrammer, or the API
Database audit	Reconcile utility
Document problems and requirements mapping	Repository Reports

TABLE 11-1. *Test Phase Activities and Designer/2000 Tools*

implemented by that module. QA performs a requirements audit of the design document to ensure that all requirements stated in the Analysis phase are assigned to modules. QA also needs to revisit the mapping of requirements to modules and ask the question: "Does the module that now exists actually fulfill the requirements it was intended to fulfill?"

The tool used for this testing is the Matrix Diagrammer because you can set up a matrix of modules and requirements that provides, at a glance, a list of the requirements for all modules in the system. This utility makes it quite easy to look at a module in a particular row (or column, depending on how you set up the matrix) and quickly see which requirements are assigned to it. You can print this matrix or set up a repository report with the same information, as mentioned later in this chapter. QA uses this list as a reference when checking modules to determine if all requirements are indeed mapped to and fulfilled by modules.

System Testing: Module Design

The module-level requirements checking was done in the Build phase. All that is left in the Test phase are cross-module tests, also called system-level tests. These check whether requirements that use more than one module are fulfilled by the final code. The method used in this phase is the same as in the Build phase: check the requirements mapped to modules using the Matrix Diagrammer. In this case, however, since you have already tested the module-level requirements, you, as a QA person, need to concentrate on the cross-module requirements.

First, you need to know which requirements fall into the cross-module category. This is where the Matrix Diagrammer comes in. If you look at the Modules and Requirements matrix you created in the Pre-Design phase to assign this mapping, you can easily tell which requirements are fulfilled by more than one module. If you set up the matrix so the modules are rows and the requirements are columns, a cross-module requirement will have more than one intersection cell filled in for that column. You need to check all modules in that column to see if there is a dependency between them and to ensure that, together, they fulfill the requirement. For example, one requirement may state that a complete transaction needs actions from more than one module before it is considered complete. This kind of requirement cannot be tested on the unit level because one unit alone cannot fulfill the requirement. However, if you test all modules involved with the requirement by attempting to complete this transaction, you have a true test of the requirement and can verify that it is fulfilled.

System Testing: Database Design

In the Test phase, you also test the database design itself. First you have to ensure that the database objects that were actually created match corresponding definitions in the repository. A discrepancy may occur if a developer or someone else modified or added a database object without changing the Designer/2000 repository—which could easily happen in the heat of the Build phase. You can run the Reconcile utility discussed later in this chapter to check whether the database and repository are synchronized.

Another test you have to perform on the database in the Test phase consists of checking whether the requirements fulfilled by tables are truly fulfilled. Some system requirements may not be linked to modules but to tables. These would require another association type called Requirements to Tables that tracks the link between those two elements. You would create this association type in the Pre-Design phase and fill it in during the Design phase. The Test phase is the time to test whether these requirements are met properly by the tables. The Matrix Diagrammer is the tool to use to show a Requirements to Tables matrix.

The last category of database testing that is appropriate in the Test phase is the security test. You need to check whether the roles and user accounts in the actual database agree with the definitions in the repository. There is a repository report called Group Definition in the System Access group. If you run this report from the Repository Reports utility, you will see a list of all attributes of the group, including system privileges and database object privileges. You can compare this list to a list you get by querying the database data dictionary views ROLE_SYS_PRIVS and ROLE_TAB_PRIVS. Comparing the repository report and the data dictionary query results is largely a manual process, although you could automate it by querying both the data dictionary and repository with one SQL statement. The API views of the repository can assist in extracting the pertinent Designer/2000 information.

Problem Tracking

One of the activities you perform in the Test phase is ensuring that the modules work together with each other and fulfill the system requirements. During this activity, problems will surface that were not uncovered during the unit testing. You need to keep track of these problems so they can be fixed before the Implementation phase. In the Build phase, you performed unit testing to check whether the individual modules work, and you need to track problems that arise in that phase as well. You need a single system to handle problems revealed by the various tests in both the Build and Test phases. The ideal system would be contained in the repository so you can easily associate a problem with one or more modules.

Using the Repository Object Navigator for Problem Tracking

Designer/2000 has a Problems node that the help system states is for "...a business event or state that inhibits the progress of the enterprise towards its objective (e.g., personnel disputes, market moves, procedural or statutory changes, unresolved issues or unmade decisions)." This stated purpose is more a like a requirement: that is, it tracks a business problem rather than an application problem. Since you already defined a user extension for Requirements, you can use the Requirements element instead of the Problems element to track business problems. The Problems node is then available for you to use to track problems that are found in testing. Although Designer/2000 does not provide a specific tool to handle problems, you can use the Repository Object Navigator to enter and modify the problem definitions. Also, the Matrix Diagrammer lets you enter and access these elements because they are linked to other elements such as Modules. Figure 11-1 shows the Problem Properties window for a sample problem definition in RON.

The properties include normal tracking fields for the name of the person who uncovered the problem and the date, and you may want to define user extensions for Solved By—the person who solved the problem—and Solution—a description of the fix. The Problem Properties window also contains a number of descriptive fields—Comment, Opportunities, and Resolution Benefit—that you can use to organize the details of the problem. There are also flexibly defined properties for Type—a property that you could use as a priority level—and Cause Category—a classification of the problem. You can tailor these to your needs and use them to report on categories or types of problems. There is no input validation for these properties, although the fields force the entry into uppercase.

Once you define a problem, you can link it to the module or modules where that problem occurs through the Problems to Modules node under the specific

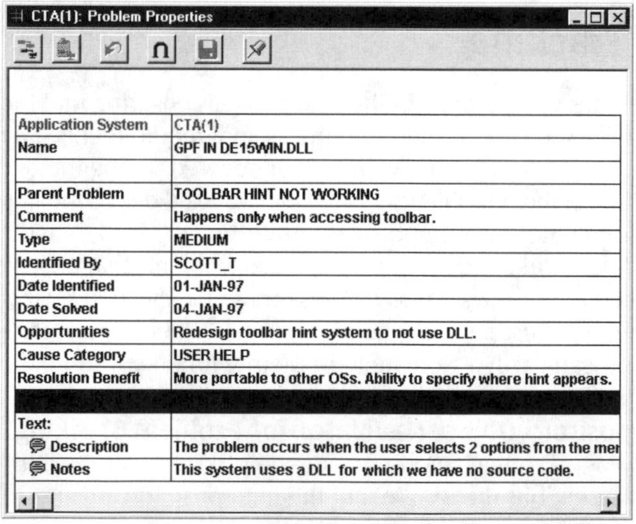

CTA(1): Problem Properties

Application System	CTA(1)
Name	GPF IN DE15WIN.DLL
Parent Problem	TOOLBAR HINT NOT WORKING
Comment	Happens only when accessing toolbar.
Type	MEDIUM
Identified By	SCOTT_T
Date Identified	01-JAN-97
Date Solved	04-JAN-97
Opportunities	Redesign toolbar hint system to not use DLL.
Cause Category	USER HELP
Resolution Benefit	More portable to other OSs. Ability to specify where hint appears.
Text:	
Description	The problem occurs when the user selects 2 options from the me
Notes	This system uses a DLL for which we have no source code.

FIGURE 11-1. *Problem Properties window*

problem instance, as the following illustration shows. This link gives you a way to create reports and matrix diagrams linking modules to problems.

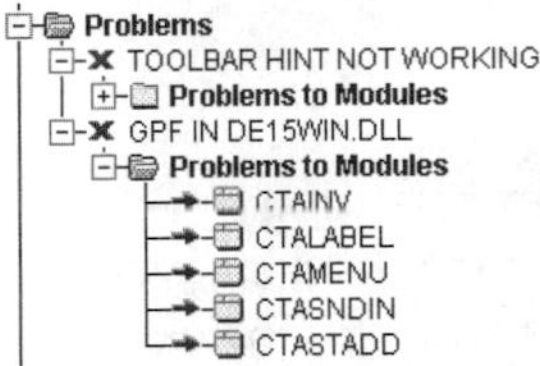

The Business Units to Problems node under Business units is another association element that links the problem to the business unit that experienced it. This association exists mainly to handle the intended concept of a problem as a business requirement. Since this is not the way you are using this element, you do not need to create these associations.

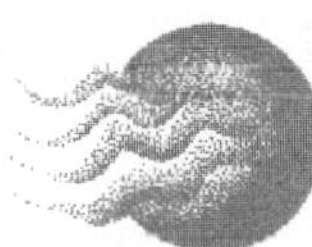

NOTE
Oracle has implemented the element type Problems, as well as the association types Business Units to Problems and Modules to Problems, as user extensions to the main set of types. This does not really affect you, although it does reduce the number of additional element and association types that you can create.

You can extend this problem tracking system to other repository elements such as tables, views, snapshots, and so on. This will allow you to track problems in those objects in the same way as you track problems in modules. You will need to define a new association type for each element type you want to link to Problems. These new associations are managed the same way as Problems to Modules: with the Repository Object Navigator.

The problem tracking system you use in the Build and Test phases of the life cycle is also suitable for tracking bugs or problems that arise in the system in the future. Inserting a problem definition in the repository can be the first step in the problem tracking procedure when bugs are detected. It can also be the first step in your system change request procedure when enhancements are needed. When the problem fix or enhancement is put into production, you fill out the applicable properties in the problem definition. This kind of tracking lets you store information on all bugs and problems in one place in the repository, whether they be from the Test, Build, or Maintenance phases.

Another utility that can assist in problem tracking is the Matrix Diagrammer. You can create a matrix of Problems and Modules to see which problems occur in which modules. This matrix is most useful if you have multiple modules in which multiple problems occur, or if you want to see all problems as rows or columns in a grid. If you want a "big picture" overview of problems and modules, the Matrix Diagrammer is the correct tool. Otherwise, RON is faster and more efficient to use for handling individual problems and their associated modules.

Using the API for Problem Tracking

Instead of using RON for problem tracking, you can write your own front-end system with Oracle Forms or another tool, as outlined in Chapter 14. You can use the Application Programmatic Interface to build your own front-end to insert, update, and delete problems and the associations of problems to modules. The drawback of this front-end is that it requires a bit of work to code, test, and maintain. The benefits of this front-end are that you can more easily enter and modify the problems and more easily associate modules to those problems. In addition, you can provide item-level validation in your code to restrict properties entries, for example, to the Type and Cause Category properties.

Reconcile Utility

As mentioned before, one of the tests you perform in the Test phase checks whether the database objects and repository definitions of those objects match in all respects. If there are differences either way (database to repository or repository to database), you need to correct one side or the other. The Reconcile utility assists with this task and eases what could be a quite tedious job. This repository utility is available on the Utilities menus of the Repository Object Navigator, Data Schema Diagrammer, Module Logic Navigator, Module Data Diagrammer, and Module Structure Diagrammer. Figure 11-2 shows the first tab of this utility. You will notice a similarity between this utility and the Reverse Engineer Database utility introduced in Chapter 5. Indeed, that utility as well as this one are in the same family as the Server Generator, and all three have a similar interface.

The Reconcile utility checks the database definitions against the repository definitions and writes a report in a file in the current working directory. The extension of this file depends on which of the two run options you choose. If you choose the Cross Reference option, the utility determines which elements in the repository are different from the database objects and lists them side by side in the CDRK55.LIS file. If you choose the Alter Database option, the utility determines which database objects are different from their repository definitions and produces the CDRK55.SQL file, which contains SQL statements to alter the database so it matches the repository.

Reconcile Repository Object Definitions

Options | Objects

Database CTA

Object Owner SCOTT

Remote Username SCOTT

Password *****

Connect String 2:

Selection

☑ Automatic Trigger Selection
☑ Automatic Index Selection
☑ Reconcile Constraints
☐ Reconcile private procedures
☐ Ignore Create Status
☑ Include unassigned objects

Options

◉ Cross Reference ○ Alter Database

OK | Save Options | Restore | Cancel | Help

FIGURE 11-2. *Options tab of the Reconcile utility*

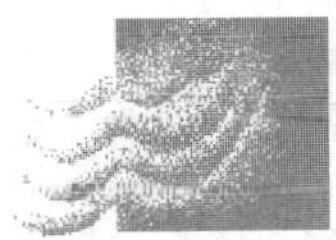

CAUTION

Remember that the utility uses only one file name for each of the two options. Therefore, if you run this utility more than once, you should rename the output file between runs if you want to keep the output from an earlier run. If you start the utility and forget to rename the file, Reconcile will ask if you want to delete the output file, and you can cancel at that point and rename the file before starting again.

Notice that there is no automatic synchronization of either side; the Cross Reference option just produces a report of the differences. It is up to you to change or delete repository elements as the report indicates. The following objects can be detected and reconciled using this option:

Cluster	Snapshot
Function	Synonym
Index	Table
Package	Trigger
Procedure	View
Sequence	

Note that only database procedures, functions, and packages that have a status of VALID in the USER_OBJECTS view will be reconciled. There are also certain limitations on PL/SQL code, sequences, views, and snapshots that are well described in the help system under the RON help topic **Utilities→Reconcile**.

The Alter Database option creates the SQL script with ALTER statements to change the database so it matches the repository definition, but this option does not automatically run the script. Only ALTER statements for cluster, index, sequence, table, trigger, and snapshot objects will be created. Other objects must be manually edited or deleted and re-created using the DDL generated by the Server Generator, but first you need to run the Cross Reference option to see which of these other objects are out of sync. Also, the Reconcile utility only creates supported ALTER statements. For example, if you delete a column definition in the repository, there will be no corresponding ALTER statement (although there will be comments explaining the situation) because the database does not support dropping a column.

Options Tab

The Options tab provides a field for entering the repository database definition that owns the objects to be reconciled. Only repository objects that have a database name as the Database property will appear in the list of available objects on the Objects tab. You can also enter the name of the database user account that owns the database objects as well as the remote user name, password, and connect string. Note that you can reconcile objects in only one physical database instance and one repository database definition at one time. If the user account you are logged in on is the one that owns the objects you want to reconcile, you do not need the remote information. You do always need the object owner, though, so Designer/2000 can construct the list of database objects on the next tab.

The Selection area on this tab has the following check boxes that determine some of the behavior of the utility:

- **Automatic Trigger Selection** If this box is checked, the Reconcile utility automatically reconciles all triggers attached to the tables selected on the Objects tab.
- **Automatic Index Selection** If this box is checked, the Reconcile utility automatically reconciles all indexes attached to the tables selected on the Objects tab.
- **Reconcile Constraints** If this box is checked, the Reconcile utility automatically reconciles all table-level constraints attached to the tables selected on the Objects tab.
- **Reconcile Private Procedures** If this box is checked, the Reconcile utility checks package procedures and functions with private scope (not known

outside the package). It always checks public procedures and functions regardless of the setting of this check box.

- **Ignore Create Status** If this box is checked, the Reconcile utility checks objects in the repository regardless of the value set for their Create property. If this box is not checked, the utility does not reconcile objects for which the Create status is set to False.
- **Include Unassigned Objects** If this box is checked, the Reconcile utility checks repository objects that have a database property value of null.

You can click the Save button to save the settings you made in the Selection items. The Restore button returns the settings to their state when they were last saved. When you have completed all areas of this tab, click the Objects tab to display that area.

Objects Tab

The Objects tab allows you to choose the database and repository objects you wish to reconcile, as Figure 11-3 shows. Note that when you select an object type in the Type box, both database objects and repository objects appear in the Name box on the right. You can then choose the objects themselves with click and CTRL-click (for more than one object) and click the down arrow button to move them to the Objects list at the bottom. If you want to move all objects from the top to the bottom, click the double-arrow down button. If you want to move objects from the Objects list back to the Name box, select them in the bottom list and click the up arrow button.

When you are done with the selection process, click OK to run the utility. It will run and, when it is done, it will display the results. If you do not see the message diaog box that indicates you are done, press ALT-TAB until you reach the message dialog box. The Cross Reference option shows the results in an editor window, and the Alter Database option displays a dialog box where you can run the SQL statement, as in the following illustration.

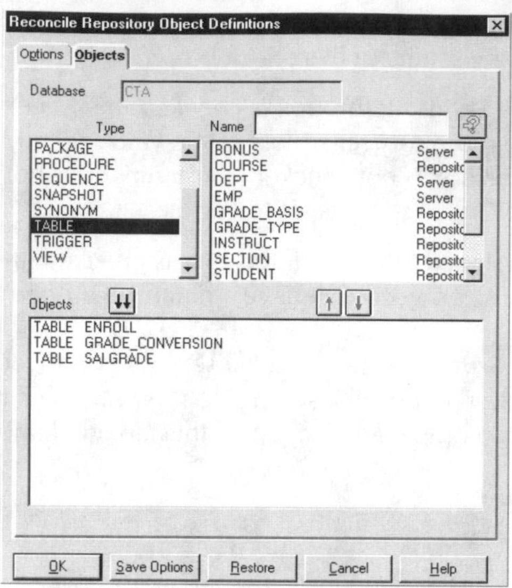

FIGURE 11-3. *Objects tab of the Reconcile utility*

If you press the Browse button in this dialog box, the editor will display the SQL script. This script may contain useful comments regarding objects for which there are no SQL statements (like the dropped column example mentioned before), so it is advisable to view this information before running the script. If you press the Execute button, SQL*Plus will run the script in the database.

TIP

If you have a large number (a hundred or more) of objects to reconcile, consider running the utility more than once on selected groups (of 50 or less). If a problem occurs in the middle of the run, you will not lose as much work as you would if you were working with a larger group. Also, you will have smaller files to examine at the end. Keep in mind that PL/SQL objects take longer to reconcile because of the additional parsing needed. In addition, if you use a remote database, the Reconcile utility may take longer because of the database link.

Repository Reports in the Test Phase

The elements you are using in this phase are modules and database object elements. The Repository Reports utility offers a standard set of reports in the

Module Design and System Design groups that can provide information on the application programs and database elements you are testing. In addition, the System Access group contains reports such as Access to Modules by User Groups, Group Definition, and User Definition. These reports show the security plan by listing database objects and the database roles that have access to them.

These reports are helpful to get a picture of what you are testing. You can run the Element to Element Matrix report to see the association of one element to another. This report is available in the User Extensibility group. You can set the parameters of this report to show associations such as Requirements to Modules and Problems to Modules. Both of these associations can also be displayed as matrices in the Matrix Diagrammer.

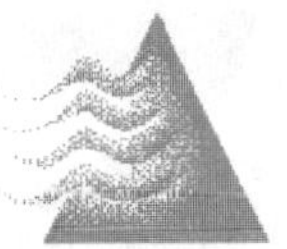

TIP

Although the Element to Element Matrix report is listed under the User Extensibility group, you can use it for any two elements that have an association type between them, such as Functions to Business Unit Usage. Many of the standard associations have reports already defined, but the user-extended elements, including the elements that Oracle created with user extensions, do not have special reports.

Conclusion

During the Test phase, you make the final necessary modifications to the system to prepare it for production. You perform a final review of the system deliverables to ensure that they reflect the system that was built. You present the system to the users for user acceptance testing to make sure they agree that it is ready to go into production. Documentation, training, and help systems are all in place. You are now ready to implement the system.

In the Test phase, Designer/2000 provides support for verification of database objects and system requirements. Since your system is made up of program modules and the database objects you created from definitions in Designer/2000, complete system design documentation is built in to the repository. From the repository definitions, you can check whether the application you have created fulfills the known business needs and other system requirements. The next steps in CADM are the Implementation and Maintenance phases, both of which are discussed in the next chapter.

CHAPTER 12

Implementation and Maintenance

Computer Thesaurus entry for "bug": see undocumented feature, unanticipated feature, unexplained behavior, uncooperative user.

Once the system is complete, it must be implemented and maintained. The concepts associated with implementation and maintenance are quite different, so each topic will be discussed separately.

Overview of the Implementation Phase

One of the most important factors in a successful implementation is adequate user support. If you roll out a system to an untrained, confused, or resistant user population, the system, no matter how good, is doomed to failure. Providing high-quality user training and documentation, maintaining positive public relations, and managing user expectations are frequently overlooked steps. Reducing user apprehension, fear, or distrust of a new system, however, cannot be done entirely during the Implementation phase.

The best way to overcome user fear or resistance is to adopt an approach that keeps users involved in the entire system development process. Users must believe that the system is being built to their specifications to meet their needs and improve their jobs. Ideally, the system belongs to the users. The absence of user involvement often results in resistance, which can manifest itself in sabotage. A number of years ago, the U.S. Postal Service attempted to implement a system without the support of the user community, and users went so far as to "accidentally" destroy electronic data gathering devices. Granted, usually user resistance to new systems is not so blatantly destructive; but a resistant user community makes system failure inevitable.

Another key to successful implementation is the ability of the project team to migrate the new application to the production environment. This process involves a transition period where the system is closely monitored and support is transferred from the project team to the system operation group.

You should have chosen an implementation strategy at the end of the Analysis phase: either to use phased implementation or to implement the entire system all at once (the "big bang" approach). Your strategy also should specify whether to keep the legacy system running in parallel with the new system for a trial period. It is important that you make these decisions before the Implementation phase begins.

Implementing the Entire System at Once

If the big bang approach is used, developers have to be very sure of the system. Any systematic bug is going to be multiplied by the amount of load on the system. Even trivial errors that don't show up in a controlled testing environment can become catastrophic when the big bang approach is used. The only rational justification for using a big bang approach is that the architecture of the new system demands it. For example, in a manufacturing environment, replacing one portion of an automated manufacturing process may not be feasible.

Frequently, the big bang approach is chosen for political reasons. It certainly can be cheaper, although much more dangerous, to implement the entire system all at once. Also, if the system is going to succeed, it will succeed much faster with this approach. There are certainly benefits to a big bang implementation. However, the question remains: Is a big bang approach worth the risk?

Phasing in the System

If phased implementation is used, you need to decide how the new system will be phased in. The first option for phasing is on a functional basis. If an application contains several functionally distinct groups of modules (for example, sales, purchasing, and human resources), then it may be possible to isolate those module groups and implement them individually. The second option is to phase in the new system organizationally, perhaps implementing the system for only a portion of the organization prior to rolling it out to all of the users. Phased implementation can be performed on a functional basis or an organizational basis, or both of these options can be used, and the new system can be implemented a portion at a time to a subset of the user community.

The longer the phase-in process, the more expensive the Implementation phase becomes, but the lower the risk. Whatever implementation strategy is employed should be carefully thought out and have the support of the user community prior to its initiation.

Paralleling

Another important decision made prior to the Implementation phase is whether or not to keep the legacy system running in parallel with the new system. Paralleling is a very expensive strategy. It requires all data entry to be performed twice. Users will have a sense that half of the work they are doing is a waste of time. If parallel implementation is chosen, it will be necessary to go to some lengths to support and help users get through this process. Hiring temporary help to reduce some of the burden of duplicate data entry on the users may be a wise investment.

If the organization cannot take the risk of any even temporary system shut down or failure, then paralleling may be the only option. Paralleling is frequently combined with a phased implementation. Also, it may be possible to parallel only key areas until the new system is performing adequately.

Developers may want to consider using a parallel implementation for a longer time with a small subset of the organization followed by a parallel implementation of the full system for the entire organization for a short period (one or two days) to verify that the new system can run with full production loads.

Handling Implementation Problems

Problems that arise in the Implementation phase should be handled in the same way as problems in the Test phase: documented, analyzed, prioritized, and resolved. System modification requests should be used to document problems and enhancements. Any serious problems may necessitate aborting implementation until the problems are corrected.

Implementation Modifications for Smaller Systems

Implementation issues of small and medium size systems are not greatly different from the issues associated with implementation of large systems. You still need to pay close attention to the effect of the implementation on the perception of the users. Flawed small and medium sized systems can harm organizations just as much as flawed large systems. However, because a smaller system is easier to test, you are more likely to be able to successfully implement a small system using a big bang approach.

If a phased implementation is necessary for a small system, the duration of the implementation period will likely be shorter and the implementation plan will be simpler than that of a large system. One of the great dangers of small systems is to underestimate the importance of a careful, well thought out implementation phase.

For medium-sized systems, you should use the same strategy as for large systems. For these systems, a shorter phase-in period is often used.

It is easier to support the users of small- and medium-sized systems. For these systems, running the legacy system in parallel for a limited period of time may be appropriate.

When Is the Implementation Phase Complete?

Implementation is complete when the following three criteria have been met:

- In phased implementation, the phasing has been completed and implementation has been done throughout the entire organization or whatever portion of the organization is appropriate for that application.
- All parallel processing with the legacy system has been discontinued.
- A suitable period of monitoring has passed that allows you to be confident the new system is up and running.

The last step is the most critical. Significant effort should be devoted to monitoring system performance, system resource usages, and user perceptions for the first few weeks after implementation. It is only after this intensive monitoring period is over that you can declare the Implementation phase complete.

Overview of the Maintenance Phase

Maintenance is a process that continues throughout the life of the system. A predefined process must be put into place to handle ongoing problems, modifications, and enhancements.

One interesting aspect of maintenance is the way requests are viewed. Many maintenance requests are not necessarily a bad thing. Some companies use the number of maintenance requests as a primary measure of system success or failure. Some companies may consider a large number of maintenance requests as an indication that the system is full of bugs and not meeting user requirements or expectations. Other companies may view a large maintenance queue as a sign that users want to fully exploit the system's potential.

Earlier chapters discussed how users log requests and problems through the system modification request process. In the Maintenance phase, these requests are ranked and decisions made as to when they will be addressed, if at all, and assigned to an appropriate version of the system.

Versioning

Changes to production systems should never be made on an ad hoc basis. Modifications need to be prioritized, grouped, approved, applied to the system, and then thoroughly tested before the next version of the system is implemented.

The approval and prioritization process should be handled by a steering committee made up of both developers and users. When requests are approved, they should be assigned to an upcoming version of the system to indicate when these modifications will be implemented. After all of the scheduled modifications for a version have been applied, the new version must be tested prior to implementation.

Of course, certain system modification requests cannot wait for a new version and must be implemented immediately. For example, a bug that corrupts underlying data cannot wait for a new software version but must go through an immediate testing and implementation process.

Version Testing

Version testing need not be as comprehensive as the original testing of the system. You are making changes to an already thoroughly tested system, so you do not need to repeat the full testing process for each new version release. However, you do need to perform incremental unit testing for each affected module. Not only should the changed portions of the module be checked, but a full retest of any affected module should be performed unless the modification was cosmetic.

In addition, all integration tests associated with all affected modules should be performed again, as should transaction flow tests for each physical process flow that includes an affected module.

Since this testing process is the same no matter how many changes are made to a module, it is much more cost effective to group as many system modification requests together as possible and implement them together.

Modifications Necessitated by Software Product Changes

When the underlying application software, DBMS, operating system, or platform changes, for example, when a new Developer/2000 version or the next version of any software is released, you must not assume that the system will still operate correctly. Whenever you want to change to a new product or version, the transaction flow and stress tests should be repeated prior to implementation to ensure that the system operates correctly with the new architecture. Coexistence testing is also necessary if new systems that interface with the existing system are brought online.

Maintenance Modifications for Smaller Systems

For small systems, versioning may not be necessary in the early phases of the project until the system is stable. After the initial Implementation phase, small systems should be versioned just like large systems.

For medium-sized systems, maintenance should be handled just as for large systems.

When Is the Maintenance Phase Complete?

Of course, the flippant answer to this question is that Maintenance is never complete. However, the reality is that systems do have a finite lifetime. One of the most difficult questions to answer is, "when it is time to stop all but essential modifications to the system and begin designing its replacement?"

There is an economically rational way to make this decision. You can carefully analyze the amount of money you are spending on maintenance versus the amount of money it would take to develop a new system. Of course, when you build a new system, you have the opportunity to re-engineer the business processes. In practice, systems frequently stay in production long after it is economically rational to keep them in production. Maintaining legacy systems remains a fixed, if not increasing, cost over time. As the business grows and changes, the ability of the system to keep pace with those changes decreases.

Systems are usually only replaced when failure to do so would cause great distress to the organization.

The Implementation Phase in Designer/2000

Although there are no Designer/2000 tools that uniquely support the Implementation phase, you can produce huge volumes of documentation of all sorts using the Repository Reports tool as well as reports you develop based on the Designer/2000 API views. This documentation from the repository can become part of the help desk reference material or even serve as part of the user documentation. The help table or files you produce in Designer/2000 can also be sources for material in this documentation. Suitable repository reports for this purpose are any that list the definitions of objects, such as the Module Definition report, or the associations between elements, such as the Module Data Summary report. These reports may be useful for help desk personnel when answering questions about the modules.

Activity or Deliverable	Designer/2000 Tool
Help desk reference material	Repository Reports
User documentation	Repository Reports, API view reports, help table, or help file printouts

TABLE 12-1. *Implementation Phase Activities and Designer/2000 Tools*

The Designer/2000 activities and deliverables for the Implementation phase are summarized in Table 12-1.

If you have gone to any level of detail when defining help text for various repository objects such as tables and modules, you can supplement user documentation with that text. This help text appears as part of various object definition reports; however, you may wish to write your own report of just help text using Oracle Reports or SQL*Plus to query the data in the CDI_HELP_TEXT view. You need to join this view with other object views to retrieve the name of the object that the text describes. This type of query is described in Chapter 14.

Depending on the level of knowledge of your users, descriptions of the tables and columns that hold the data may be of use in the user documentation. The Table Definition report and Column Definition report are appropriate for this purpose. As mentioned in Chapter 4, you may wish to add to or modify the reports that Designer/2000 provides to suit your needs. If you do this, you should give the task to someone who knows Oracle Reports well.

Reports on the Analysis phase elements are probably not as useful for user or help desk documentation, but you might want to maintain current sets as system documentation for designers and developers who do not have access to the repository. The only problem with those reports is that they become out of date once you make changes to the repository. The best documentation for the system is always the repository itself if it is well maintained.

Another set of reports that you probably do not need to run for the documentation purpose are the Quality Control reports. Otherwise, it is worth examining the full list of reports to see which ones might serve as documentation in the Implementation phase.

The Maintenance Phase in Designer/2000

Essentially, the Maintenance phase in Designer/2000 consists of the same kind of work as performed in the other phases. Depending on the particular change or upgrade, you may need to revisit each phase of the life cycle and work in the

Designer/2000 areas appropriate to those phases. The typical Maintenance activities and the tools that support them are shown in Table 12-2.

Versioning the Application System

The first step after you completely implement the system and before you make changes is to version the application system. This will freeze the version of the system that was implemented and create a new version you can use as the basis for upgrades and enhancements. The frozen version may not be changed, but you can, at any time, query the elements to see what the original system was like before changes were made in the Maintenance phase. Chapter 4 discusses how to perform versioning using the Repository Object Navigator.

Maintaining Repository Data

You should keep the repository up-to-date as you make changes or add new functionality to the system. This will ensure that the repository serves as detailed documentation for all aspects of the actual system. Changes to the system are easier to make if the repository is up-to-date because you can use Designer/2000 to drive them. That is, you can update or add the repository definitions needed for the change and generate the code required to implement it. If you use this tactic, the repository will always be in synch with the system. However, since you also will need to make manual changes on the fly, you need to employ the reverse engineering utilities to synchronize the repository with the database or application objects in the system. You can also use the Reconcile utility to identify any inconsistencies

Activity or Deliverable	Designer/2000 Tool
Version the application system.	RON
Maintain repository data.	RON, Reconcile utility, Reverse Engineer Database utility
Track module changes.	RON
Create new or modify existing elements.	Module Data Diagrammer, Reverse Engineer Forms and Reports utilities, and other tools appropriate to the element
Track problems.	RON

TABLE 12-2. *Maintenance Phase Activities and Designer/2000 Tools*

between the database and the repository. You can use this information as a basis for the work you do to synchronize the database design definitions in the repository.

An alternative to the reverse engineering utilities is making manual changes to the repository, an approach that is practical if you are making only a few minor changes. In general, you should use the Designer/2000 utilities whenever possible and consider writing an API utility if there is a job they cannot accomplish. Always weigh the potential work you intend to do manually against the development work needed for an API utility; you may find that the manual work is less time consuming. On the other hand, a well-written API utility can serve you well for future work.

Tracking Module Changes

You can use RON to assign module change information. RON provides a node called Module Change History where you can keep information on the different versions of a module. Each version or revision can have a separate element definition with properties such as the developer's name, date of revision, version number, directory name, and other change control information. This node is a good place to record details regarding the changes that you make to the modules during the Maintenance phase.

In addition, two text types, Release Notes and Module Generation History, are attached to the module and available in the MSD, MDD, and RON module properties windows. You can store free-form text here to describe the different releases or versions of the module as well as notes on the generation such as the date and changes made.

Creating New or Modifying Existing Elements

The Maintenance phase involves maintaining the system and making changes, fixing bugs, and even adding enhancements. You need to make these changes in the repository as well, either before or after you make changes in the system. Whenever you decide to make these changes, you should use the appropriate tool in Designer/2000.

For example, if you decide to add a function and a requirement to the system, you should insert the function using the appropriate function diagrammer and the requirement using RON or the Matrix Diagrammer. You will need to decide whether to follow a miniature version of the life cycle and go through all Designer/2000 tools to assign data usages to the functions and produce the modules from functions. You will need to add new modules to the menu hierarchy and generate the code. This process may be appropriate for some changes that need the analysis support of Designer/2000; however, minor changes are better done in the Designer/2000 design tools such as the Data Diagrammer, Module Schema Diagrammer, and Module Data Diagrammer.

If you implement the changes using the design tools, you have to decide whether the analysis elements are useful for full documentation of the system design. Since for full documentation purposes you should have both an accurate analysis model and an accurate design model, you should consider keeping these current. Remember that you can create entity definitions from existing table definitions using the Table to Entity Retrofit utility. There is no corresponding Module to Function utility, however, so keeping this information current will be a manual process.

Reports you might want to run before making changes to the existing modules are in the Repository Reports group Impact Analysis. This group contains such reports as Modules which Use a Given Module, Modules Used by a Given Module, Column Change Impact Analysis, and Modules which Use a Given Table/View. All of these are useful if you make changes to tables or modules and want to know the dependencies in other parts of the system.

Tracking Problems

The last category of activities that you perform in the Maintenance phase is problem tracking. You need to store information on problems that users experience with the system so you can map solutions to those problems and implement fixes. This activity is an extension of the problem tracking you did in the Build and Test phases and is discussed in Chapter 11.

Conclusion

Implementation marks the last of the CASE Application Design Method phases. However, once the system is complete, the developer's work is not finished. No system can succeed without competent maintenance. The ongoing satisfaction of the users depends upon how well the system can respond to requests for changes.

Following the CADM process does not guarantee that a project will proceed completely smoothly or that it will be on time or under budget. However, if you follow the CADM process throughout system development, you can be assured that your system requirements are coherently gathered, and that you can track any system requirement from its point of origin to its eventual system impact, if any. All of the audit and quality control portions of the CADM process virtually guarantee that the final system faithfully fulfills the system requirements as the developers understand them. By carefully following the methods outlined here, you will have sufficient documentation of the process to be able to defend your decisions throughout the process.

All of this does not guarantee that you will build a good system; however, CADM does guarantee that you will build the best system that can be generated by the development team. Good systems require not just a sound development process, but also skilled, creative developers and good luck.

Throughout all phases of system development, you need to perform tasks to administer the repository as well as its application systems. You also need to manipulate and query data in the repository in ways particular to your needs but not provided for by the Designer/2000 tools. The following chapters describe some of these other Designer/2000 activities performed throughout the phases.

PART 3

Other Designer/2000 Activities

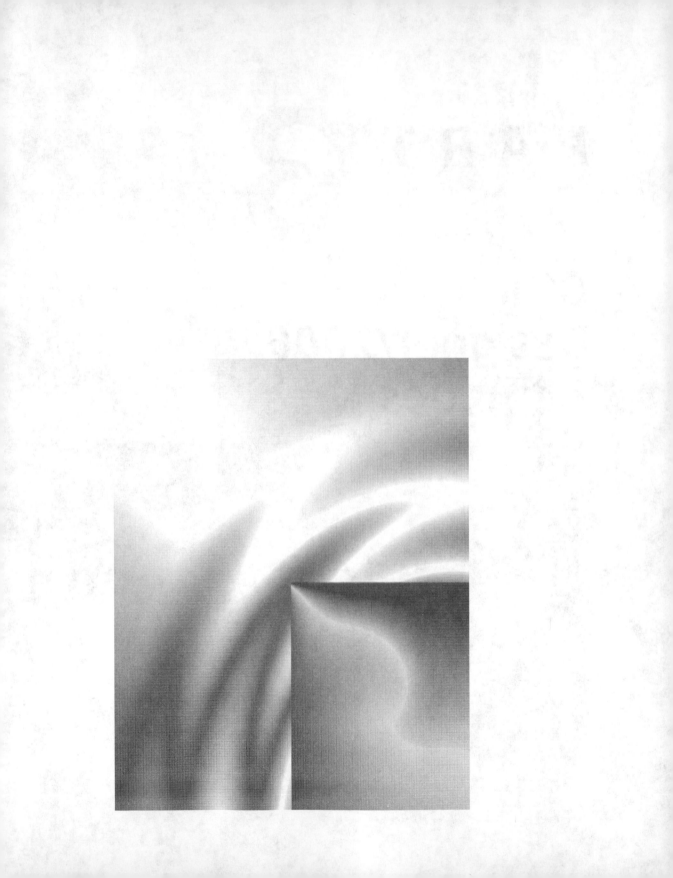

CHAPTER 13

Application System and Repository Administration

Do not administer this product without consulting your physician if you are currently taking prescription medication.

The goal of the work you do using the CASE Application Development Method life cycle is to produce a finished application that accurately meets business requirements. The Designer/2000 activities you perform to reach that goal are centered around entering information in the repository and getting output from the repository in the form of code and reports. While it is most important to complete the deliverables for a particular project, there is also essential work that you need to do to set up and maintain the application systems, and the repository itself, during the life cycle.

This chapter describes how to perform administrative activities on application systems such as versioning, sharing, copying, and transferring ownership. All application system administration occurs in the Repository Object Navigator (RON), which you used to create and manipulate the application system element definitions.

The other part of administration is for maintaining the repository itself. You or your Designer/2000 administrator needs to perform tasks to install and maintain the repository instance, set up repository user accounts, back up the repository, and perform upgrades when needed. All these activities and more are handled by the Repository Administration Utility (RAU). This chapter discusses the administration functions of RAU not mentioned in the preceding chapters.

Designer/2000 provides some repository reports not discussed in the other chapters that can help you administer and view the repository. These give you information on the repository itself, which you can use to document the setup of the repository at your particular site. This chapter also tells you how to find these reports for documentation on administrative matters. Last, this chapter tells you where to look for more information on Designer/2000.

Managing Application Systems with RON

The Repository Object Navigator (RON), introduced in Chapter 4, is the main tool you use to manipulate element definitions, and the application system is one of those elements. Therefore, the main tool you use to manage the application system itself is the Repository Object Navigator. RON has four main areas for managing the application system: the Properties window, the File menu, the Utilities menu, and the Application menu.

Properties Window

The Properties window for an application system appears when you select the top-level node that has the name of the application system. You can rename the application system by changing the Name property. You can also change or input any of the text and description properties such as Title, Priorities, Constraints, Authority, Summary, and Objectives. You can use the Status property to freeze an application system so no one can make changes to it. This property is handy if the application system stores information on a static set of elements that should not be changed. The Parent property specifies that another application system is the parent of this one. One parent application system can have many child application systems. This information appears in repository reports and documents you design.

File Menu

The File menu provides the best way to create a new application system: by choosing New from the File menu. The File menu also includes items for creating or loading separate files with repository objects using two different facilities: Load and UnLoad, and Check In and Check Out. It also provides menu items for Lock Set and Unlock Set.

Load and Unload

The load and unload utility allows you to move element definitions between repositories using a file. You select any number of elements in RON and choose **File→UnLoad** from the menu. The UnLoad utility will create a plain ASCII text file with a .DAT extension containing the definitions of those elements, applicable secondary access units (such as column definitions if you chose a table definition), associations from that element to other elements, and skeleton definitions (which have a name but no other details) for the associated elements if they are not selected in the unload set.

This file can then be loaded into another application system in another repository using the **File→Load** menu item and specifying the name of the unload file. Elements that are in the load file but not in the target application system will be loaded as is. You specify in the load process how you want Designer/2000 to handle element definitions that are in the file and also in the target application system. If you specify Insert mode, the load process will not load the conflicting definition but make an entry in the load log file that a conflict occurred. If you choose Update mode, the existing element will be modified to match the element definition in the file. It will update, but not delete, existing definitions based on the file element definition.

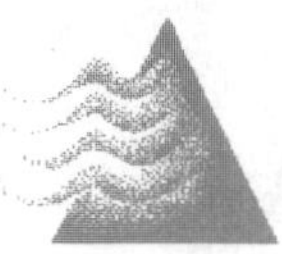

TIP
An Oracle white paper, "Oracle Designer/2000 Application Programmatic Interface," contains documentation on the structure and contents of the loader file. Check the Oracle Web site or contact your sales representative to obtain a copy of this white paper.

Check In and Check Out

The check in and check out utility uses a concept similar to the load and unload facility to store element definitions in a file. It is designed more for source control because it locks elements when they are checked out. The utility moves elements from a *source application system* (which owns the elements) to the *working application system* (where you work on the elements). This procedure is handy when an application developer needs some elements from the main application system. The developer can check out the elements, which locks them from changes in the source application, and check them into another application system in the same or a different repository. Then the developer can work on the elements, make changes as needed, check the elements back out of the working application system, and check them back in to the source application system, which unlocks them.

The Check In and Check Out utility employs another repository element, called a *User-Defined Set* (UDS), that is an element type (available in RON) used for the check-out process as well as for locking elements. You define a UDS and associate existing primary access controlled (PAC) elements with it. An element can be assigned to more than one UDS at a time. When you perform a check out operation, you first select a UDS in RON and choose **File→Check Out** from the menu. This displays the Check Out dialog window shown in Figure 13-1, where you specify whether this application system is the source or working application. When you click the Check Out button in this dialog window, the utility will create a repository check-out file with an .RCO extension that you can check in to the working application system. This file contains the ID numbers of all elements in the source application system that the utility will use to identify changes upon check in. This utility will also lock all elements in the UDS for the source application system. (Lock icons appear next to the element node in RON to flag this lock.)

After creating the file from the source application, you can check it in to another application system using the **File→Check In** menu item. In the dialog window that appears when you choose this item, you specify whether you are checking in to a working or source application system. You can also create an application system to hold the UDS you are checking in with a choice in that dialog window.

After making changes in the working application system, you check out the UDS to a repository check-in file which has an .RCI extension. When the check-in process occurs, the Check In utility matches the ID numbers of elements in the

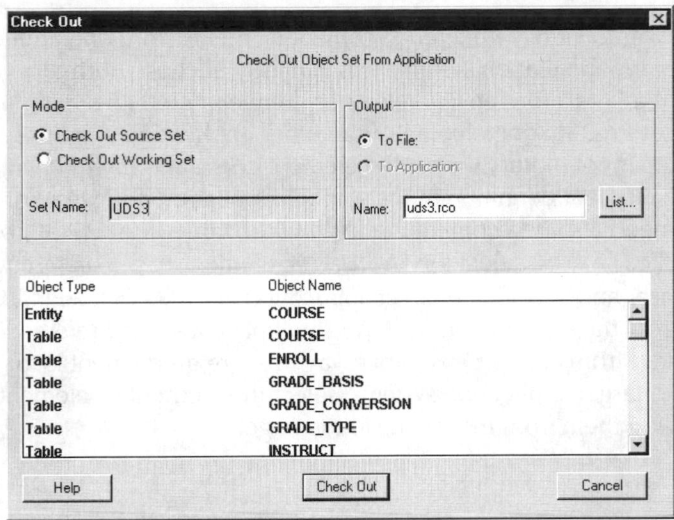

FIGURE 13-1. *Check Out dialog window*

UDS of the file with those in the working application system. If the file contains new elements, the utility creates definitions; if the elements in the file have been updated, the utility updates the repository definitions accordingly; if elements are missing because they were deleted in the UDS in the working application system, the utility deletes them from the source application system. Only the user who checked out the UDS can check it back in.

Lock Set and Unlock Set

The File menu also contains the Lock Set and Unlock Set options. You can lock a UDS without checking it out by using Lock Set to prevent others from making changes. To reverse the lock, you choose Unlock Set from the File menu. Unlock is also good if you check out a UDS by mistake or have a problem during the check-in process and need to unlock the UDS without checking it back in.

Utilities Menu

The Utilities menu includes the following five options: Share, UnShare, Transfer Ownership, Copy, and Force Delete. These functions work on individual elements or groups of selected elements in the application system.

Share

Share allows you to create a reference copy of elements from one application system to another application system. This is handy because normally you cannot create a link, such as a foreign key reference, between elements in different application systems. Sharing elements from other application systems solves this problem. You cannot modify the shared element copy, and it will change whenever the element definition in the source application changes. For example, suppose you need a shared copy of the EMPLOYEE table in APPSYS2, but it is owned by APPSYS1. You select the EMPLOYEE element in the hierarchy, choose **Utilities→Share**, and specify the target application as APPSYS2. APPSYS1 retains the ownership of the element, but APPSYS2 will have a shared reference copy (which is locked from changes). Another way to share an element is to open both the source and target application systems, select the element or elements to be shared, and drag them from the source to the target.

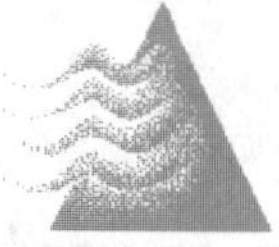

TIP

When you share an element, an open hand icon will appear on the shared copy to designate that it is shared. If you click that icon, the source application system will open and the source element will be selected.

UnShare

UnShare reverses the share process and removes the shared copy from the application system. Select the element, choose UnShare from the Utilities menu, and click UnShare in the confirmation dialog box that appears. You can also simply select the element and press the DELETE key.

Transfer Ownership

Transfer Ownership lets you move elements from one application system to another. Select the elements in the hierarchy, choose this menu item, and specify the target application system in the dialog window that appears. Note that the element will appear in the target application system but will leave a shared copy in the original application system. In addition, all SAC elements (such as columns for a table element) will be transferred, but any associated elements will be transferred only as shared elements.

For example, suppose application system APPSYS1 includes EMPLOYEE and DEPARTMENT table definitions, but APPSYS2 does not. EMPLOYEE has a foreign key that references DEPARTMENT. You want to transfer ownership of EMPLOYEE to APPSYS2, so you select EMPLOYEE in APPSYS1, choose **Utilities→Transfer Ownership** from the menu, and specify APPSYS2 as the target. EMPLOYEE will appear in APPSYS2 as an owned element with a shared copy in APPSYS1. DEPARTMENT will also be shared in APPSYS2, because the foreign key in

EMPLOYEE needs to refer to an element in the application system. The transfer results are summarized in the following table:

Step	EMPLOYEE	DEPARTMENT
Before the transfer ownership operation	Owned by APPSYS1	Owned by APPSYS1
After the transfer ownership operation	Owned by APPSYS2; shared copy in APPSYS1	Owned by APPSYS1; shared copy in APPSYS2

You can also transfer ownership by opening the source and target application systems, pressing and holding the SHIFT key and mouse button, dragging the element or elements from the source to the target application system, and releasing the mouse button.

Copy

Copy allows you to make an exact copy of an element in one application system and place it in another application system or, for some elements (such as tables), in the same application system. For example, you can copy the EMPLOYEE table from APPSYS1 to APPSYS2 by selecting it in APPSYS1, choosing **Utilities→Copy** from the menu, and specifying APPSYS2 as the target. You can also open both application systems in RON, select the element, hold down the CTRL key, and drag the element from APPSYS1 to APPSYS2. Copy creates a complete copy of the element and its SACs. With either method, a dialog window appears where you can enter the name of the new object.

Copying is trickier when the element you are copying has references or associations to it. In the previous example, the EMPLOYEE table has a foreign key reference to DEPARTMENT. When you copy EMPLOYEE, a shared copy of DEPARTMENT will also be copied so the reference is not left open. A problem occurs if the target location has an existing element with the same name as an associated element. You do not have a chance to rename the associated element, only the copied element, so the copy process will fail and a message will appear indicating that you tried to copy an element that has the same name as an existing element. You can avoid this problem by renaming the element with the duplicated name in one of the application systems before performing the copy operation.

Force Delete

Force Delete lets you delete an element whether or not it has associations to other elements. For example, suppose MODULE1 has a detailed table usage of TABLE1. If you try to delete TABLE1, an error message will appear indicating that deletion is not possible because detailed module table usages reference that table. You could open the definition for the module, but the error message did not tell you which module contained the references. Also, even if you know that MODULE1 includes references, there may be other references elsewhere. Instead of trying to find all usages of the table definition, you can select the table and choose **Utilities→Force Delete**. The element definition and all associations or references will be deleted. This menu option is quite powerful, and it is not reversible, so be careful when using it.

TIP
You can perform queries on the hierarchy nodes in RON to see a subset of the elements in that node. Select the node name and press F7. A query box (called the Add Where Clause Filter) will appear in which you can enter a SQL "where" clause to reduce the number of elements shown. For example, you can select the Entities node, press F7, and enter **el_name like 'GRADE%'** in the query box. When you click the OK button, the list of entities will contain only those whose names start with GRADE. Be sure to use correct SQL syntax and remember that the repository element name column is el_name. To remove the filter, just press F7 and delete the text in the query box.

Application Menu

The items on the Application menu allow you to manipulate the application system object itself. The user account you are logged into as must have the Manager role (as granted in the Repository Administration Utility) to enable the Application menu. The Application menu provides the following options: Freeze/Unfreeze, Rename, Transfer, Grant Access by Appl, Grant Access by User, New Version, Delete, Archive, Export, Restore, and Reset.

Freeze/Unfreeze

You can use the Freeze/Unfreeze option to protect an application system from changes or to remove that protection. Repository users can view, but not change, a frozen application system. Freezing has the same effect as changing the Status property in the application system Properties window, but the menu item allows you to freeze more than one application system at a time. To unfreeze an application system, choose the Freeze/Unfreeze menu item, select the frozen application system from the list and click the Freeze/Unfreeze button. To freeze an application system, follow the same steps, but choose an unfrozen application system from the list.

Rename

The Rename option displays a list of application systems so you can change their names. The results are the same as selecting the application system node and changing the Name property except that you can rename more than one application system at a time with this menu item.

Transfer

You can use the Transfer option to switch the ownership of an entire application system to another repository user. This option is useful if all your shared application systems are owned by the Designer/2000 administrator and you want to move an application system defined and owned by another user to the Designer/2000 administrator's account.

Grant Access by Appl

The Grant Access by Appl option lets you give other users access to application systems that you own or for which you have Admin rights. This menu item is helpful if you want to grant a number of users rights to a single application system. The dialog window contains a poplist of application systems and an area below to add and change user names and privileges. Select, Insert, Update, and Delete rights are the same access rights as in a standard SQL database and apply to all individual element definitions in the application system. Share rights allow the grantee to share elements from the application system with another application system. Admin rights apply only to users defined with the repository Manager role. Admin rights allow these users to grant access to the application system and perform all other operations on the Application menu.

Grant Access by User

The Grant Access by User option accomplishes the same task as the Grant Access by Appl option but in a slightly different way. This option displays a poplist for users and an area below to grant rights to more than one application system. This option is useful if you want to grant a particular user rights to more than one application system at the same time. This might be needed when, for example, you add a new repository user to the system.

New Version

The New Version option creates a copy of the application system or systems you select in the dialog box that appears when you choose this item. The new version will be a complete copy of the application system and will contain a version number to identify it. The old version will be frozen so it cannot be changed. This option was introduced in Chapter 4.

Delete

You can use the Delete option to delete an application system. Be aware that Designer/2000 checks all dependencies when you use this option, which can take a considerable amount of time for a large application system. This action is not reversible, so you may wish to archive and export the application system before deleting it.

Archive, Export, Restore, and Reset

The Archive, Export, Restore, and Reset options apply to operations you perform to create or load an external file containing all elements in one or more application system. This is described further in the following section, "More on Archive and Restore."

Most of these menu options display a dialog window like the one in Figure 13-2 in which you specify the application system you wish to affect. The dialog windows are self-explanatory and well documented in the help system. Some have a field for entering a rollback segment name. This is handy if the application system you are working on is large and the operation you are performing may exhaust your default set of rollback segments. If you specify the name of a rollback segment (that has a size of 5 megabytes, for example), the operation will use that as the rollback segment, and the "Out of extents" message should not appear.

More on Archive and Restore You can create a standard Oracle .DMP export file that contains one or more application system. This file serves as a backup of the application systems and can be loaded into any repository instance as a copy of the original application systems. You can also use it to make a copy of the application systems in the same repository instead of using the versioning facility. This type of copy is different from the copy you get when creating a new

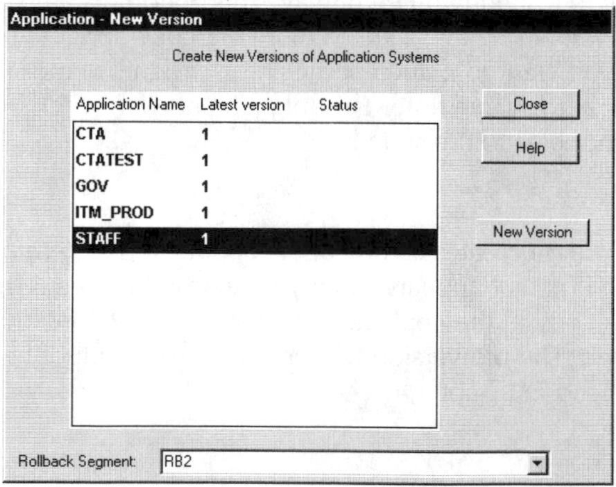

FIGURE 13-2. *Application - New Version dialog window*

version, because the original application system is not frozen and there is no version number link between the original and the copy. The archive process consists of choosing Archive from the Application menu and choosing the application system or systems to archive. This loads all the repository elements, including diagrams, from those application systems into a set of temporary archive tables, also called extract tables, that have names starting with XT_. The next step is to export the extract tables to a .DMP file that you can store or load in another application system. You choose Export from the Applications menu and fill in the fields in that dialog box to perform the export and create the file.

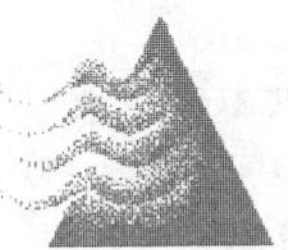

TIP
To make a copy of an application system in the same repository, archive it to the XT_ tables and restore it using a different name. If you need to copy it to another repository, you will have to export it to a .DMP file and then import it into the other repository.

The result of the Archive and Export steps is a .DMP export file that you can save or load into the same or another repository instance. To load the .DMP file, choose **Application→Restore** from the menu, and import the .DMP file by using the Import file field and Import button at the bottom of the Restore window. The file will be loaded into the extract tables. The last step is to choose the application system names you wish to restore (because the file may contain more than one) and supply the new name of the application system (which can be the same as the old name if you are restoring into a different repository). Be sure to select an application system by clicking it with the mouse cursor. Then press the Restore button, and the application system will be loaded from the extract tables into the main repository elements.

Use the Reset menu item to clear the XT_ tables, which will let you reuse their database space after you have restored an application system. Designer/2000 also automatically clears these tables when you select the Archive menu item.

Multiple Application System Projects

Your project or business setup may require multiple application systems. The best approach is to determine the number of application systems to use before entering data into the repository for a project, but you can partition the elements later, if necessary, by using a combination of copy and transfer ownership operations.

For example, you may have an application system that represents the current production environment, where all existing database objects and code modules have definitions. These definitions are maintained so that whenever a new object is put into production, the repository definition is also entered in the production application system. In this case, you will probably also have a development application system where you do your work on the objects before you put them into production.

You may also want multiple application systems if you have a common set of tables (for instance CUSTOMER or EMPLOYEE) that are shared by multiple applications and that are relatively stable. These tables could be contained in a separate application system, and new systems could reuse the definitions by sharing elements from this common application system. This would allow you to link new elements to existing elements and, at the same time, prevent modifications to the original element definitions. Although you can lock individual elements or sets of elements using the User-Defined Sets element, if you have a large group of elements that need to be locked, locking the entire application system will make management easier. You will also need multiple application systems if you want to specify a parent application that has elements shared by other application systems. The Parent property of the application system can store this hierarchy information, and you can share or transfer ownership to and from the children on a temporary or permanent basis. Separate application systems are needed to make up the hierarchy. There may be other considerations for your particular environment, so the best thing to do is budget some time in the Pre-Analysis phase to create a strategy for dividing up application systems.

Managing the Repository with RAU

When you install, upgrade, or make changes to the repository itself, you use the Repository Administration Utility (RAU). The repository consists of tables and PL/SQL code packages that are owned by a specific user. Therefore, when you are working in this utility, you must log in as the repository owner. Other users may have access to the screen, but they will not be able to perform most of the activities.

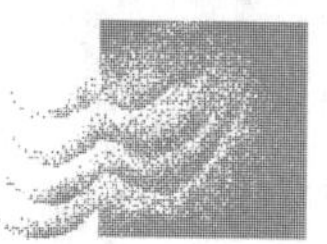

CAUTION
Anything you do to the repository will affect all existing and future application systems in that repository; therefore, you should be careful when using this utility.

The RAU is available from the Designer/2000 window application or the RON Tools menu. After you start it from one of these locations, the main RAU window appears as in Figure 13-3.

The easiest way to see how the RAU manages the repository is to examine the five main work areas, which correspond to groups of buttons in the RAU window: Repository Management, Backup, User Maintenance, Check, and User Extensions.

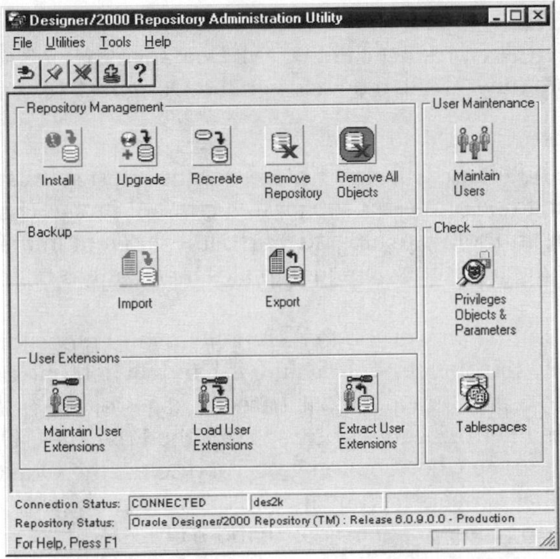

FIGURE 13-3. *Repository Administration Utility dialog window*

The User Extensions group was introduced in Chapter 4. The other groups are described here.

Repository Management

The Repository Management group of buttons contains procedures for working with the database objects for the repository. This group includes Install, Upgrade, Recreate, Remove Repository, and Remove All Objects buttons.

The Install button lets you create the repository tables, packages, and other database objects. You perform this installation after installing the Designer/2000 front-end software, because the scripts that this install process runs are part of the front-end software installation. When you run the RAU for the first time after installing the software, the Install button will be enabled, which signifies that you have not performed the repository installation. You click that button to install the repository database objects. Chapter 2 of the *Designer/2000 Installation Guide* provides more information on the installation process and the checks you need to perform before you perform the installation. It also gives routines to follow if you are upgrading or migrating repository data from older versions of Oracle CASE or Designer/2000.

NOTE
There is a product called CASE Exchange that lets you migrate data from other CASE products into the Designer/2000 repository.

The Upgrade button installs new features for the latest software upgrade of the repository. The upgrade process is similar to the install process because you need to install the front-end software (upgrade) first. It is different in that this button does not fully reinstall the repository, but just applies the changes or additions to the database objects.

The Recreate button allows you to recompile invalid repository database objects or re-create the objects. This feature is handy when unexplained errors occur that point to a problem in the database packages or views that compose the repository. If such an error occurs, you can click the Privileges, Objects and Parameters button in the Check button group and select the Object Status radio button. If the list that appears has any invalid or missing objects, you can use the Recreate function to recompile or re-create those objects.

The Remove Repository button lets you remove all repository database objects belonging to the repository owner. You can use this button to prepare to import data from a repository export file or to redo an aborted installation.

The Remove All Objects button also removes all repository database objects belonging to the repository owner, but, in addition, it removes other objects that were created outside of RAU, such as application tables or views created in SQL*Plus. You would use this button if, for example, you are preparing to import a .DMP file that contains both repository and non-repository objects.

Installation Considerations

Before installing Designer/2000, you should spend some time planning the administrative tasks that will be needed, as well as planning what your repository structure will be. For example, if you need multiple repository instances, will you create them in the same database in different user accounts or in different databases? The main issue to consider is that these repositories cannot share elements; although you can use the Archive facility to copy application systems, or the Unload facility to copy elements.

The installation manual contains some guidelines and strategies for repository setup, as does the RAU help file. (Look for the topic, "What Are the System Requirements for Installing a Repository?") In addition, you can consult bulletin number 10115748.6, "Data Administration (Versioning, Configuring, etc.)," which you can obtain from Oracle Support. This bulletin provides more information on different configurations of repositories and application systems.

Backup

The Backup group of buttons lets you export and import the repository database objects to a standard Oracle .DMP file. The Export button creates a file with the contents of the repository and the database structure definitions. You can use this file as a backup of the repository in case there is a database problem. You can also use this backup to move the repository to another database or user account. You can export either just repository database objects, such as the repository tables and views, or all objects owned by the repository user, which includes the repository in addition to other tables and objects created outside of the RAU, such as application-specific tables.

You can restore the repository .DMP file using the Import button after using the Remove All Objects or Remove Repository button in the Repository Management group.

User Maintenance

Once the repository database objects are installed, you have to grant access to users. The Maintain Users button lets you add, grant access to, and remove repository users. A repository user is an Oracle database account that also is allowed access to the repository. You or your DBA has to create the database account before you define it as a repository account. When you click this button, you will see a list of all current repository users, and you can add users by choosing an existing user account from the Oracle UserName poplist. The other required fields in this window are filled in by default, but you need to consider what role you want the user you are adding to have.

You can grant only one of two roles to a repository user: User (the default) or Manager. A repository user with the User role has access to all elements in the repository but cannot create application systems or access the Application menu in RON. A repository user with the Manager role can access all elements, as well as create new application systems and perform the functions on the RON Application menu. You can also restrict a user to read-only access to the repository by specifying the Mode field, which has a default value of Write.

After creating and defining a role for the repository user, you click the Save button to commit the changes. A dialog box will appear reminding you to click the Reconcile button in that dialog box to re-create or synchronize the synonyms and grants for the modified or added users. The last step in granting access to the repository is actually granting access to application systems using RON, as mentioned before.

Check

The check buttons allow you to verify the state of the repository database objects.

The Privileges, Objects and Parameters button in this group lets you check the status of the database objects in the repository. When you click this button and specify Object Status in the Check Options radio group, you will see a list like the one in Figure 13-4. You can use the same button to check the status of objects or system privileges, user privileges, user roles, object sizes, and RAU parameters.

The other button in this group is Tablespaces, which displays a window with information on the tablespaces (sizes, space used, allocation to the repository user, and other parameters). As with the other check button, you cannot change anything, but the data will give you an indication of potential problems in the repository that you may be able to fix with the Recreate button.

Repository Reports for Administration

Some repository reports can assist you in your administrative work. The Repository Reports Global group contains reports on the application system itself. The Application System Definition report in that group lists all properties and access rights for the application system or systems in the repository. This group also contains a set of reports on elements shared from one application system to another: for example, the Elements Shared into an Application System report. Other

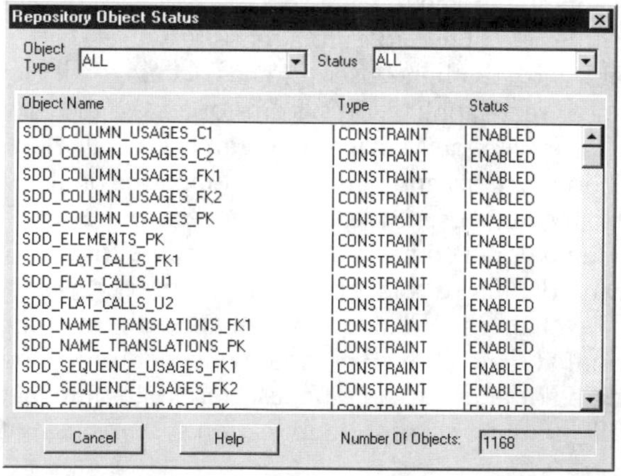

Repository Object Status

Object Type: ALL Status: ALL

Object Name	Type	Status
SDD_COLUMN_USAGES_C1	CONSTRAINT	ENABLED
SDD_COLUMN_USAGES_C2	CONSTRAINT	ENABLED
SDD_COLUMN_USAGES_FK1	CONSTRAINT	ENABLED
SDD_COLUMN_USAGES_FK2	CONSTRAINT	ENABLED
SDD_COLUMN_USAGES_PK	CONSTRAINT	ENABLED
SDD_ELEMENTS_PK	CONSTRAINT	ENABLED
SDD_FLAT_CALLS_FK1	CONSTRAINT	ENABLED
SDD_FLAT_CALLS_U1	CONSTRAINT	ENABLED
SDD_FLAT_CALLS_U2	CONSTRAINT	ENABLED
SDD_NAME_TRANSLATIONS_FK1	CONSTRAINT	ENABLED
SDD_NAME_TRANSLATIONS_PK	CONSTRAINT	ENABLED
SDD_SEQUENCE_USAGES_FK1	CONSTRAINT	ENABLED
SDD_SEQUENCE_USAGES_FK2	CONSTRAINT	ENABLED

Cancel Help Number Of Objects: 1168

FIGURE 13-4. *Repository Object Status screen*

reports list elements that do not easily fit into one of the other categories: for instance, the Document Definition and System Glossary reports. Another interesting report is the Changed Elements report, which shows which primary access controlled elements changed between one date and another.

The Repository Administration group contains reports on the repository itself, as well as shared elements between application systems. The System Glossary report in this group shows all entities, their synonyms, and business terminology definitions that you entered in RON. Another repository-specific report is the Repository User to Application System Access Rights report, which lists the repository users and the rights they have to all application systems in that repository. The Repository Administration group also includes some quality control reports, Create Status Quality Control and Invalid Database Objects Quality Control, which also appear in the Quality group and help you determine if there are problems in the database object definitions. The Area Metric report calculates a number for the application system that shows the complexity of the design. This number allows you to compare application system designs with one another.

The Function Point Analysis group gives you another method for evaluating the complexity and size of an application system. An example is the FPA MKI (Design Level) report, which examines the repository definitions in an application system and provides measurements of various aspects. Another example of this type of report is the FPA MkII (Design 2) report, which provides a measurement of the technical complexity of the system so you can determine the cost and time needed for a particular application system. The Area Metric report is related to the reports in this group, and, therefore, it appears in this group as well.

You can also run reports on some of the user-extended objects that Designer/2000 provides, such as Assumptions, Key Performance Indicators, and Critical Success Factors. These elements can track information that you determine early in the System Development Life Cycle and want to capture in the repository. For example, at any stage in the system development process, you might want to look at the Critical Success Factors report, which lists success factors with a property that indicates whether or not they are critical. To list Critical Success Factors, or any other element type, for that matter, you can run reports in the User Extensibility group. The <Element> Definition report shows the properties of the elements of a certain element type, and the Detailed <Element> Definition report provides more information on those elements, including their associations with other elements.

Bypassing the Designer/2000 Window

The Designer/2000 administrator may want to assist repository users by setting up faster methods for accessing the tools and utilities than those provided with the product. One limitation with running single-window utilities such as the ADW, DDW, and generators from the Designer/2000 window application, is that they run in the same session and disable the Designer/2000 window when they start. A solution is to always start these utilities from another tool, such as RON. Although that tool will be disabled while the utility runs, Designer/2000 will be enabled, so you can call other tools while the utility is active.

Another solution is to set up a program icon for the separate utility to bypass the Designer/2000 window. Most Designer/2000 tools and utilities have separate executable program files that you can use to create a program icon. If you are running Designer/2000 in Microsoft Windows 3.x, you should create a program group and add icons to the group. If you are using Windows NT (4.x) or Windows 95, you should add a folder to the desktop or to another folder and create program icons within that folder. Consult the operating system help file if you need information on how to do that; however, this file does not tell you the command line string to use when setting up the program icon.

You can determine the command line string for most of the Designer/2000 tools and utilities if you know the executable filename and the calling syntax. The executable filenames are listed in Table 13-1.

NOTE
The Designer/2000 Diagnostics utility listed in Table 13-1 is an undocumented program that lets you gather statistics about Designer/2000 sessions.

The calling syntax is actually available in an error message that appears when you run the program with the wrong syntax. Therefore, you can run the program with the wrong command line to get it to display its syntax. The easiest way to do this is to use the operating system file manager or file explorer utility. Navigate to the BIN directory under \ORAWIN95 or \ORANT or wherever your main Oracle directory is located. Then drag the program file to a new folder or program group. Open the properties for that new icon and type an entry for the command line like the following for the Process Modeller:

```
c:\orawin95\bin\bpmod13.exe scott/tiger@orcl /xxx
```

The "scott/tiger@orcl" is the necessary login information, and the "/xxx" is an invalid command line parameter that will cause an error message to state the correct syntax when you double-click the icon, as shown here:

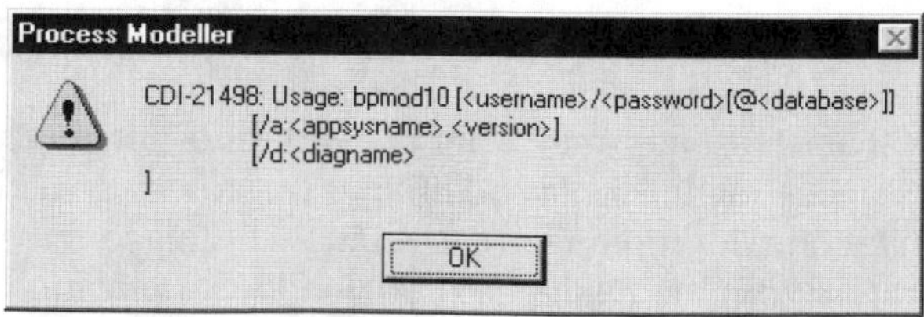

Designer/2000 Tool	Executable Filename
Data Diagrammer	dws13.exe
Dataflow Diagrammer	awd23.exe
Designer/2000 Diagnostics utility	ckndiag.exe
Designer/2000 window	des2k13.exe
Entity Relationship Diagrammer	awe23.exe
Forms Generator	cf45g32.exe
Function Hierarchy Diagrammer	afw23.exe
Graphics Generator	cg25g32.exe
Matrix Diagrammer	awm23.exe
Module Data Diagrammer	iwmdd13.exe
Module Logic Navigator	iwmln13.exe
Module Structure Diagrammer	dwm13.exe
MS Help Generator	cvhpg13.exe
Preferences Navigator	iwgpn13.exe
Process Modeller	bpmod13.exe
Reports Generator	cg25r32.exe
Repository Administration Utility	ckrau13.exe
Repository Object Navigator	ckron13.exe
Repository Reports	ckrpt13.exe
RON Load utility	ckld13.exe
Update Code Controls Table utility	cf45ct32.exe
Update Help Tables utility	cf45hp32.exe
Update Reference Codes Table utility	cf45rv32.exe
VB Generator	cvvbg13.exe
WebServer Generator	cvwsg13.exe

TABLE 13-1. *Executable Filenames of Some Designer/2000 Tools and Utilities*

Although the message states that the executable is bpmod10 (though it is really bpmod13), you can see that the calling syntax really is as follows:

bpmod13 ***user*/*password*@** *database* /a:*appsys,ver* /d:*drawing* where *bpmod13* is the name of the executable program, *user/password@database* is a standard Oracle login string, *appsys* specifies the application system name, *ver* denotes the version number, and *drawing* is the name of the drawing you want to load initially into the BPM. A sample runtime executable string might be the following:

```
c:\orawin95\bin\bpmod13.exe scott/tiger@orcl /a:CTA,1 /d:MAINFLOWS
```

Some of the utilities respond differently to this technique. For example, if you double-click the Forms Generator filename, cf45g32.exe, in the file manager or file explorer, you see a window such as the one in Figure 13-5. This message is a bit more helpful than the one for the Process Modeller because it contains a description of the parameters.

This technique lets you bypass the Designer/2000 window and is handy if you work in one tool frequently and want to load it directly without running the Designer/2000 window application.

CAUTION
This technique is undocumented and intended for "power users" only.

Oracle Forms Generator

Oracle Forms Generator (32bit) 4.5.9.0.0 - Production
Copyright © Oracle Corporation 1995, 1996. All rights reserved.

Format is: cgsf [option] ... [userid/password] [pref=value ...] [pfile=file]
Options are:

-i appl id Internal reference of application system
-a application Name of application system
-v version Version number of application system
-m module id Internal reference of module
-n module Short name of module
-c crt Use this terminal definition
-s Suppress feedback information
-q Quiet mode (i.e. use defaults)
-p Display/amend user preferences
-f flavor Use this flavor in place of default
Processing completed

Stop
Compile
Run
Design
Copy
More
Close
Help

FIGURE 13-5. *Syntax error window for the Forms Generator*

Additional Sources of Information

No matter how experienced you are with the various aspects of Designer/2000, there will be times when you have questions about how to perform a task. The more you know about the repository and the various strategies for using the tools, the better you will be able to handle these types of questions. There are, however, sources of information that you can use to assist you as you work and as questions arise.

Oracle-Supplied Documentation

As mentioned throughout this book, the most important way to obtain information is to take full advantage of the help system and cue card system. These online guides can get you started with Designer/2000 in general as well as with particular operations. They can also remind you about the meaning of seemingly obscure or forgotten properties. In addition, the help system contains a section for error messages and codes as well as a product overview (both available from the top level help topic). A handy help system facility you can employ with a 32-bit Windows operating system is the Find tab in the Help System window. This operating system facility allows you to create an index of words that appear throughout the document. It essentially lets you perform a word search on the whole help file and is useful if a keyword is not defined in the Index tab for the topic you are looking for. Also, don't forget to consult the Designer/2000 documentation set that ships in Oracle Book format on a documentation CD with the product. This documentation is also available in hard copy form as a separate purchase from Oracle Documentation Sales.

Another recommended source of information when you are learning Designer/2000 is the printed material included with the product—particularly the tutorial and the overview manuals. These will help you get a sense of the objectives and scope of the tools. The Release Notes are also critical reading material. These are printed pages that are included with the product and are last-minute supplements to the documentation and help system. They often contain information on installation, restrictions, and workarounds.

SRBs

Oracle ships System Release Bulletin (SRB) files with Designer/2000, and these will be installed when you install Designer/2000 on the client PC. There is a separate program group, or folder, for these bulletins. When you click one of the SRB icons, a text editor will open with the text of the file. The bulletins contain information not in the online help or other printed documentation, such as documentation available, dependent products, known restrictions (including bugs), bug fixes (from previous versions), and hints and tips. An example of a hint or tip is the following from the SRB for RON: "Use the Blue Arrow Icon in the Navigator window to navigate to the object definition." Often the SRBs contain information that is otherwise not easily found or just does not exist in the online help system.

The SRBs may also report existing limitations, such as functions that do not work as you might expect them to (or as they are supposed to). Sometimes the SRBs provide a workaround to enable you to do the work you need to do.

Getting Connected

Even if you have mastered all the material in the Designer/2000 help system and documentation, your education is not complete. You can take courses from Oracle and third-party vendors on Designer/2000 subjects. In addition, you may have mastered the basics, but you will be working in a void unless you get input from other people using the products.

One source for this information is Oracle Corporation itself. Oracle issues support bulletins like the one mentioned before on repository administration, and white papers such as "Oracle Designer/2000 WebServer Generator Technical Overview." These, like the SRBs, often contain information not in the manuals or help system. Some have been created in response to the most frequent user problems and questions addressed to the Oracle Support personnel. Others help get you started on new features or give hints on how to best use a product. In addition, Oracle Support personnel can look up bug fixes and workarounds if you run into problems.

The best source for detailed information on how people use the product for real-world system development are other Designer/2000 users. There are local, regional, and international Oracle user groups with special interest groups, or SIGs, for Designer/2000 and Oracle CASE technology. Membership in these groups gives you access to their list servers and conferences where you can network by e-mail and in person with other members. The conferences are also helpful because they give practical presentations on how designers and developers are using Designer/2000 as well as provide some advanced techniques that others have implemented.

As the popularity of Designer/2000 grows, so will these additional sources of information. The best advice is to tap in now and keep up with the flow of information. You will benefit from the experience of others and find yourself contributing your own advice.

Conclusion

You will use the application administration techniques throughout the system life cycle to manipulate and manage the application systems containing meta-data on your project. The Designer/2000 administrator will use the repository administration tools to install, change, and manage the repository instance itself so work on the system will not be slowed by database problems. As you do your work in the Designer/2000 tools, you will need information not supplied in the online documentation and will need to take advantage of other sources of information on Designer/2000, including other users and Oracle Corporation itself.

The next chapter discusses another Designer/2000 feature you use throughout the life cycle—the Application Programmatic Interface—and explains how you can employ it to extend the capabilities of the standard Designer/2000 tool set.

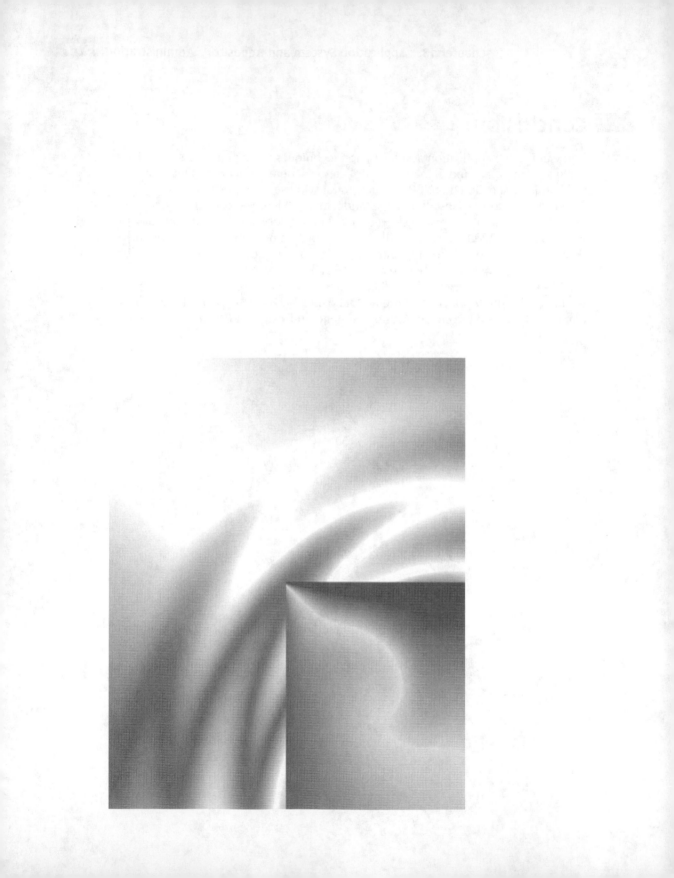

CHAPTER 14

The Application Programmatic Interface

Beneath the Planet of the APIs

Despite the sophistication and scope of the Designer/2000 tools, as you work in the CADM life cycle, you may discover activities you wish to perform that cannot be done with the supplied set of Designer/2000 tools and repository elements. One of the key benefits of Designer/2000 is its capability of storing all information regarding a system design in the repository, but you may find something particular in your situation that has no default place in the repository. The way to solve the problem of not being able to store a particular type of data is to employ the User Extensibility feature. However, once you add properties or elements to the repository, you need a way to put information into them and query them. While RON serves as a ubiquitous overseer of all repository data, including extensions you add to the default properties and elements, sometimes you want a faster or easier-to-use tool than RON to access the extensions you created.

No CASE tool could be written to handle all possible variations of requirements in all environments. However, Designer/2000 provides the Application Programmatic Interface (API) to help you handle these variations. The API opens the repository so you can write your own extensions to the tools and safely manipulate virtually any element in the repository. It allows you to input and output information from the base repository elements as well as the ones you add with the User Extensibility feature. Although you need to write some code (or have Designer/2000 write it for you) to access the repository through the API, you can use it to do almost anything with the repository elements. It allows you to manipulate the meta-data in a way that makes sense for your project and compensates for a wide range of problems that arise because of limitations in the built-in Designer/2000 functionality.

Thus, you may want to consider learning and using the API, although it may seem like an advanced feature. As you work with the Designer/2000 tools, you will surely need some functionality particular to your working environment or project that was not designed into the tool. In addition, you may be able to perform a task with the Designer/2000 tools, but the task may be extremely repetitive and prone to error. The API can help you here, too. For all these reasons, learning about the API is really a required step toward full understanding and maximum use of Designer/2000.

The first step toward using the API is to dig as deeply as you can in the documentation and other sources to determine whether the function you want to perform really is missing from Designer/2000. Working with the API is not difficult, but there is a learning curve, and you will have to spend time creating program code to access the repository. Therefore, planning not only what to do, but the best way to do it, will save time in the long run. Just as you would take time addressing any application development need, take time for analysis and design before you jump in and begin building an API routine.

This chapter explores the components of the API, how to get started using the API, and what the API can and cannot do. In addition, it presents a sample front-end application using Oracle Forms and the API to access and update repository elements.

What Is the API?

The API is a set of database views and PL/SQL packages in the repository owner's schema that allow safe access to the repository data (or meta-data). The repository consists of a relatively small number of tables that store the actual data. These tables have complex (undocumented) relationships, and Oracle does not support direct access to them using standard DML SQL statements. There are, however, many views of these tables that represent actual repository objects, such as entities and attributes. These views are an important part of the API because they allow you to examine the definitions you create in your application systems.

The API also consists of the PL/SQL packages that allow you to change the contents of the tables safely outside of the Designer/2000 front-end. These packages allow you to supplement the Designer/2000 diagrammers and utilities with your own front-end programs or code. The Designer/2000 tools also use the API to insert, update, delete, and select data from the repository. Therefore, when you use the API, you are using the same method Designer/2000 uses to manipulate the repository. Figure 14-1 shows how the API works with front-end tools to access

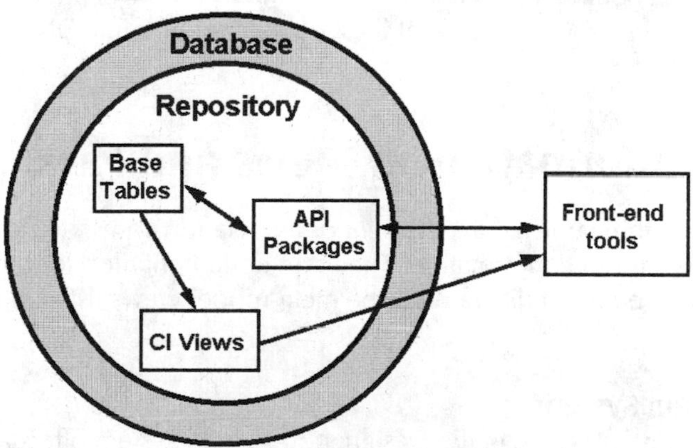

FIGURE 14-1. *API access to the repository*

and manipulate the repository data. Note that API packages provide the only method for writing to the repository, and all front-end tools use them, whether they are Designer/2000 tools or your own.

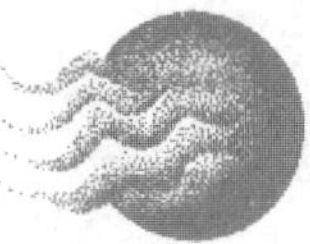

NOTE
To be most effective when using the API, you need to be relatively fluent with the SQL and PL/SQL languages. If you are using only the views component of the API, the SQL language SELECT statement will serve you well. If you intend to modify or store repository data with the API packages, you will also need a good understanding of PL/SQL control structures, packages, and record variables.

Getting Started with the API

In addition to an understanding of the SQL and PL/SQL languages, you need a good understanding of the elements and properties that you want to modify or manipulate. The steps you take when using the API are typically the following:

1. Identify the views and packages you need.
2. Obtain detailed information on those views and packages.
3. Create the API code.

After you get some experience with the API, the first two steps may take no effort at all if you know the details of the views and packages. With or without experience, the first step should be straightforward. If you have suitably analyzed your needs, you should already know what elements are involved in the activity you wish to perform, or you should at least be able to look in RON to find their names.

Detailed Information on Views and Packages

Once you know the names of the element or association types, you can consult the documentation for more information. The main documentation for the API is in the online help system and in diagrams of the meta-model views that are shipped with the product.

API in the Help System

The top-level contents topic of the Designer/2000 help system offers a help topic link called "Repository Application Programmatic Interface." Clicking this link displays the contents topic of the API help file, shown in Figure 14-2.

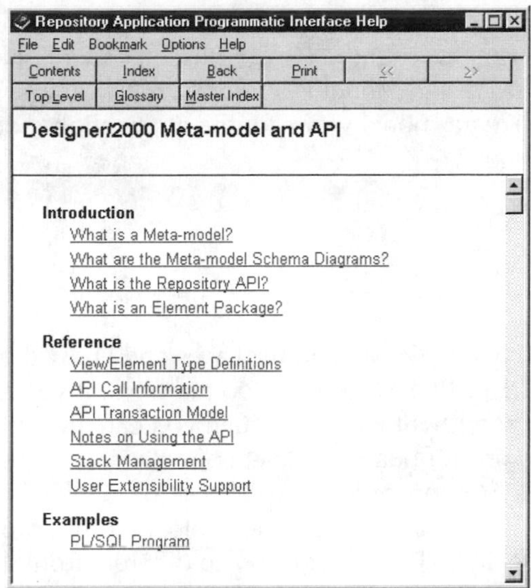

FIGURE 14-2. *API Help contents topic*

From this topic, you can load other topics that explain the meta-model in general and provide reference information as well as a sample program. The reference information contains topics on the API views, "View/Element Type Definitions," and packages, "API Call Information." Once you know the elements you are using, you can use these two topics to obtain detailed information on the calling syntax, view columns, and related views.

API in the Meta-Model Diagrams

Designer/2000 ships with a set of diagrams, in a package called "Repository Model," that shows the API views and their relationships. These are standard Data Diagrammer diagrams, with foreign key relationships between views and a notation of the view name and primary key. The views are grouped into the following subsets, with each of the subsets taking up one page:

- Business Planning Model
- Business Requirement Model
- Database Administrator Model
- Database Design Model
- Module Design Model

Which model you need to look at depends on the type of element you are manipulating. If you want to examine Design phase elements such as tables and columns, the Database Design Model is appropriate. If you want to view the relationships between meta-model views for the application modules, you consult the Module Design Model.

API Code

Once you have identified the views and packages and know the details of each, you can create the SQL or PL/SQL script to do the work. If you are just querying the views, a SQL SELECT script will work, although you can also use the API packages. If you are performing insert, update, or delete operations on a repository element, you need to write a PL/SQL procedure or package to do the work. This can be stored in the database or run as an anonymous block from any SQL front-end tool such as SQL*Plus. The SQL SELECT syntax is no different from that used for other purposes. However, special considerations and routines apply to the PL/SQL syntax, as described in the sections "API Packages" and "API Transaction Model," later in this chapter.

API Views

The repository base tables have names with prefixes such as SDD_ and CDI_: for example, SDD_ELEMENTS, SDD_STRUCTURE_ELEMENTS, and CDI_TEXT. These tables are highly normalized, and a handful of tables serves as the basis for many different element types. For example, table definitions are stored in the SDD_ELEMENTS table with a value of 'TAB' for the column EL_TYPE_OF and a value of 'TABLE' for the EL_OCCUR_TYPE. You can always look at the view definitions (in the USER_VIEWS data dictionary view) to see how the definitions for a particular element are stored in the SDD_ELEMENTS table, but all you really need to know is the name of the view.

Most API views have names starting with CI_ and containing the plural name of the element. For example, the view that shows entity definitions is called CI_ENTITIES, and the view that shows table definitions is called CI_TABLE_DEFINITIONS. Once you have determined the names of the views by looking in the help system topics as mentioned before, you can access the names of the columns in those views in the same help area. The column information consists of the datatype, size, and in most cases a brief description of the column and its valid values.

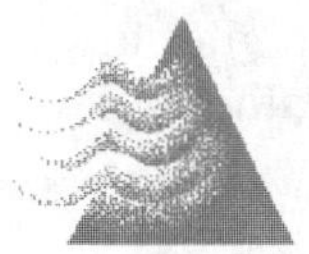

TIP
There are columns in all repository views called CREATED_BY and CHANGED_BY. You can use these to determine when the definition of a particular element was inserted or updated, and you can issue a query that lists, for example, all table definitions that have been created or changed in the last week.

View Columns and Sample Script

View columns correspond roughly on a one-to-one basis with the properties of the element that the view represents. Each view has an ID column containing a number that identifies the element uniquely within the repository. In addition, there are other columns that correspond with the properties of the element. Most element views also have a NAME column that holds the name you see in RON. For example, the CI_ATTRIBUTES view has such columns as FORMAT (for the datatype), OPTIONAL_FLAG (which indicates whether the attribute is nullable), MAXIMUM_LENGTH, and DEFAULT_VALUE. If you know the properties of an attribute, you will be able to interpret what these view columns display. In addition, the help system description of the columns can assist to some extent.

The CI_ATTRIBUTES view also contains a column called ENTITY_REFERENCE that contains a number acting as a foreign key that references the CI_ENTITIES view ID column. With this information, you can construct the following query to show details on all attributes in the EMPLOYEE entity:

```
SELECT a.name, a.format, a.maximum_length, a.optional_flag
  FROM ci_entities e, ci_attributes a
 WHERE e.id = a.entity_reference
   AND e.name = 'EMPLOYEE' ;
```

If you have an EMPLOYEE entity in more than one application system, you will need to work the CI_APPLICATION_SYSTEMS view into the query. This view displays information on the properties of the application systems themselves. The identifier is ID, as usual, but the foreign key column in CI_ENTITIES that refers to the application system is APPLICATION_SYSTEM_OWNED_BY. Therefore, the query for an application system called CTA, version 1, would become

```
SELECT a.name, a.format, a.maximum_length, a.optional_flag
  FROM ci_entities e, ci_attributes a,
       ci_application_systems s
 WHERE e.id = a.entity_reference
   AND s.id = e.application_system_owned_by
   AND s.name = 'CTA'
   AND s.version = 1
   AND e.name = 'EMPLOYEE' ;
```

You can use this same strategy—finding the element names and properties in the help system, checking for foreign key relationships, and constructing the SELECT statement with standard SQL syntax—for most API queries.

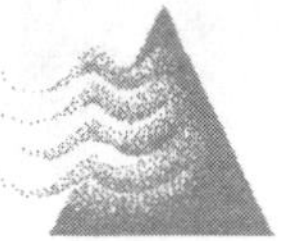

TIP
Although you cannot see the ID number for elements in RON, if you select an element in the hierarchy, click a property, and press F5, a Properties Details window will appear that contains the ID of the element along with the object type, base table name, and details of the property. This feature is extremely handy if you want to query an element using the view and need the ID.

API Packages

More than 300 PL/SQL packages make up the API. These are organized in a similar fashion to the views, so there is one package (prefixed with CIO) for each of the repository element types: for example, CIOCOLUMN, CIOTABLE_DEFINITION, CIO_VIEW_DEFINITION, CIOAPPLICATION_SYSTEM. You can think of the views as base tables that have a one-to-one relationship with the object types in RON, and the packages as the code you use to perform DML on those tables. Each package has procedures with the following names:

INS for insert operations
UPD for update operations
DEL for delete operations
SEL for select operations

NOTE
Some API packages and views support user-extended properties and elements as well as text types. These allow you to define and publish new extended properties and elements. Other packages contain procedures to update some user extensions and to delete user-extended elements that have not been published. More information on these packages and views is available in the API help system under the topic "User Extensibility Support."

For example, the CIOCOLUMN.INS procedure creates a new record in the repository tables as displayed through the CI_COLUMNS view. These API procedures perform validation checking, so if a value you are updating relates to or affects another object, the repository state will not be corrupted. For example, if you try to remove a primary key column that is referenced by a foreign key constraint, the API will stop you because the constraint would then be invalid.

Note that although you can select directly from the view, the package allows you to select from it as well (using the SEL procedure).

As mentioned, the help system for the API contains calling information for these packages.

Package Contents and Sample Code

The procedures in the API package use as parameters the ID number of the element you want to work on (for UPD, DEL, and SEL) and a record variable that contains the data (for INS, UPD, and SEL). Each package has a record variable called *data* (actually a record of records) that you can use to type a variable in your PL/SQL block. For example, if you want to change the optional property of a column definition, using a PL/SQL block of your own, you can declare a variable as follows:

```
DECLARE
   r_col   ciocolumn.data;
```

You then load a member of this record variable with the value you want to use to update the property of the element:

```
r_col.v.null_indicator := 'NOT NULL';
```

The "v" member indicates that this is a value. The "i" member acts as an indicator to the API that you changed this property:

```
r_col.i.null_indicator := TRUE;
```

The last step is to issue the update statement and pass the ID number of the column definition. You can query the CI_COLUMNS view to fetch this ID into a variable (for example, v_colid) before calling the package procedure with

```
cio_column.upd(v_colid, r_col);
```

Other API package calls are needed to create a transaction and close it correctly, but the essence of the operation is in loading the record variable and passing it to the API procedure. The next section discusses the transaction model and the code you need to write to implement it. For a complete example of a PL/SQL block that calls all necessary routines to access the API, click the "PL/SQL Program" topic link on the main contents page of the API help system.

API Transaction Model

In addition to the API calls already mentioned, there are API calls that implement a transaction model that handles the logical beginning and end of a unit of work.

This is somewhat like the standard SQL transaction model that uses COMMIT and ROLLBACK statements to mark and reverse transactions. However, the API transaction model uses a few more steps and methods to handle errors.

The intention of the transaction model is to provide a way to validate statements as a set rather than as individuals. During an API transaction, or *activity*, Designer/2000 constraints and rules defined for elements can be temporarily violated without aborting the operation. For example, when you enter the definition for a relationship between two entities, you have to make an entry for both ends of the relationship. However, if there is no concept of an activity and you enter the first relationship end without the second, an error state will occur, and the action will be rejected. The transaction model temporarily disables rule and validation checking until you state that the transaction is complete. This allows you to establish complex associations and dependencies as the transaction is taking place, but it still enforces the rules and validations at the end of the transaction.

The transaction model is handled mostly by the CDAPI package and consists of the steps listed in Table 14-1.

The two steps that load record variables may consist of multiple statements if you are inserting an element definition or updating more than one property at a time. In addition, you can choose to validate (close) the activity whenever you want. For example, you can loop through a number of records and update each before closing the activity. The validation will be deferred until the close, so if any of the records violate the constraints, the entire set will be rolled back. This behavior is similar to that of the SQL transaction model and should be familiar territory.

Limitations of the API

Despite the flexibility and support for all major element and association types in the repository, the API has some limitations. One of these is that you cannot manipulate text types such as Notes, Descriptions, Derivation Expressions, Select Text, PL/SQL Blocks, and Where clauses. You can directly access this text in the CDI_TEXT table, but the application of DML statements to this table, other than queries, is completely unsupported and discouraged by Oracle Corporation. You can, however, safely query the CDI_TEXT table, which has the following structure:

```
Name                 Null?    Type
-------------------- -------- ----
TXT_REF              NOT NULL NUMBER(38)
TXT_SEQ              NOT NULL NUMBER(6)
TXT_TYPE             NOT NULL VARCHAR2(6)
TXT_TEXT                      VARCHAR2(240)
```

Step	Sample Call	Notes
Initialize	`cdapi.initialize( 'APP1', 1);`	Declares which application system and version you are using. You need to perform this step only once each session for all statements in a particular application system.
Open	`cdapi.open_activity;`	Starts the activity (transaction).
Load record variable values	`r_col.v.null_indicator := 'NOT NULL';`	Inserts or updates a property value.
Load record variable indicator	`r_col.i.null_indicator := TRUE;`	Signifies that a particular property value is changing.
Perform the "DML"	`ciocolumn.ins(null, r_col);`	Inserts a repository definition.
Validate	`cdapi.validate_activity( v_status, v_warning);`	Checks whether the action succeeded.
Report errors	`cdapi.instantiate _message`	Returns an error message and takes as parameters values from the CI_VIOLATIONS view that is loaded automatically when an error occurs.
Close	`cdapi.close_activity( v_status);`	Validates the data and state at the end of the transaction.
Abort upon failure	`cdapi.abort_activity;`	Rolls back the transaction if an error occurs in the close process.

TABLE 14-1. *Steps in the API Transaction*

The TXT_REF column is the ID number of the element that this text describes. The TXT_TYPE is a code that designates the type of text. For example, a value of CDINOT means that this record contains notes for the element. CDIPLS is the text for the PL/SQL block. A block of text can consist of more than one record, and the TXT_SEQ column is the line number for this record. TXT_TEXT is the actual text. Using this information, you can construct a SQL statement to query the CDI_TEXT table and extract any text type for any element. For example, to extract the user help text for the STUDENT table in the version 1 CTA application system, you would issue the following SQL statement:

```
SELECT txt_text
  FROM cdi_text
 WHERE txt_type = 'CDHELP'
   AND txt_ref =
        (SELECT t.id
           FROM ci_table_definitions t,
                ci_application_systems a
          WHERE t.application_system_owned_by = a.id
            AND a.name = 'CTA'
            AND a.version = 1
            AND t.name = 'STUDENT')
 ORDER by txt_seq;
```

TIP
You can view a list of the text types and descriptions of those types by querying the RM_TEXT_TYPES view.

Another limitation of the API is that you cannot call the API packages directly from Oracle Forms because of the differences in PL/SQL between Forms (version 4.5) and the database. The section "Developing a Forms Front-End for the API," later in this chapter, addresses this issue and provides a solution.

Sample Uses for the API

While you can perform a large number of tasks with the Designer/2000 front-end tools, some things are not easy or possible with those tools. Also, even if a task is easy or possible, it may be repetitive or tedious if a large number of repository objects are affected. In addition, you may need to support access to and manipulation of a user-extended property or element. The API is the perfect facility to use in all these cases.

The following sections describe some possible uses for the API. Additional ideas are presented in the sections "Supplementing the Repository Reports" and "Developing a Forms Front-End for the API" later in this chapter.

Reverse Engineering Database Roles and Grants

You can insert data from another source, such as the data dictionary, for database roles that cannot be retrieved through the Reverse Engineering utility. Write a query for the data dictionary view DBA_ROLES and insert or update the group elements in the repository.

You can also get information on grants from the data dictionary views ROLE_SYS_PRIVS and ROLE_TAB_PRIVS. This information can be the seed for inserting associations for access rights to the Database User and Group repository elements.

Loading Legacy Report Definitions

The activities in the Analysis phase include creating module definitions for legacy reports and a value to a user-extended property to denote the status of the report. You can accomplish these tasks with the API by writing your own front-end in Forms or another tool that allows you to enter the definitions and mark the status more easily than you could using RON. An alternative is to create a non-Designer/2000 table or file with the information on the reports and read this into an API routine that creates the module definitions.

Supplementing the Reverse Engineer Database and Reconcile Utilities

Another Analysis activity, and one that occurs in other phases as well, is reverse engineering of existing database objects. The Reverse Engineer Database utility does not update existing repository definitions, but you can use the API to accomplish this after the utility runs. To do this, you need to query the data dictionary for the database objects, compare their properties with the existing elements of the same name in the repository, and update the repository definitions as necessary.

The Reconcile utility does not support some database objects that exist as repository definitions, such as tablespaces, databases, and rollback segments. You can write an API utility routine to query the data dictionary and compare the definitions of these objects with the definitions in the repository.

Creating Domains from Column Definitions

In the Analysis phase, you created domain definitions that were to be used in creating the attribute definitions for entities. If someone wanted to create an attribute for which there was no suitable domain, they would have to leave the domain name empty. An API routine can query for all attributes with null domain properties, create a domain definition for each, and attach the new domain definition to the attribute.

Making Global Changes to Column Names

In the Pre-Design phase, when the DDW creates columns from attributes, it uses the attribute name, substitutes underscore characters for spaces, and truncates the name to 30 characters. If you prefer to make your column names abbreviated versions of the attribute names, you can do this by storing the full name and abbreviation in an external table and writing an API routine to read the table, find columns with the full name, and update the definition using the abbreviated name.

Mapping Requirements to Modules

In the Pre-Design phase, you need to assign requirements to modules so you can ensure that all system requirements are being fulfilled, and track which modules or tables fulfill a specific requirement. This is a manual process of associating a requirement with a module, and you can use the Matrix Diagrammer for this purpose. The API can assist in this task, too. For this task, you need to copy the requirements mapping to the modules with an API routine that loops through all functions, finds the modules with which the functions are associated, finds the requirements that are mapped to those functions, and creates a requirements-to-modules association between the modules and requirements for that function. This can be a time-consuming task if performed manually or with the Matrix Diagrammer, but using the API will save time.

Tracking Problems

In the Test phase, and while performing unit tests in the Build phase, you need to track the problems for each module. You can write a front-end in Forms or another tool using the API so you can easily insert, update, and delete problem definition and the association of problems to modules.

Changing Free-Format View Text into Declarations

A limitation of the Reverse Engineer Database utility is that it loads view and snapshot definitions as free-format text. If you want the definition to be based on relations and columns already in your application system, you can write an API routine that reads the table names from the view text, finds the IDs for those table definitions in the repository, and adds a base relation association for each table. The API routine can also find the IDs of the columns and attach them to the Base Column property of the column definition. You also need to change the Free Format view property to False, but you cannot remove the FROM clause from the view text using the API. To do that, you go into RON and edit the Where/Validation Condition property for the view.

Loading Definitions from a File or Table

You can create a table or file that serves as a source for the definitions of any type you wish to insert or modify. An API routine you write can read the file or query the table and, based on the information in those sources, modify or insert definitions into the repository. This approach can be more convenient or faster than manual RON work when you have a large number of objects.

Supplementing User Documentation

You can query the CDI_HELP_TEXT view to obtain a listing of the user help text for a particular repository element. While this is not strictly an API view, it is accessible to repository users and offers a quick way to extract the text you wrote into the user help text property of various elements. You can use this text to supplement and provide a basis for the user documentation.

NOTE
Working with the API is straightforward once you understand the principles. However, no matter what your level of understanding is, the API routines will take time to write, which you should weigh against the time savings that the API potentially offers. Keep in mind also, though, that if the routine you are writing has a general-purpose use, you will be able to reuse it in future projects, so any extra time required to create it might be worthwhile in the long run.

Supplementing the Repository Reports

Before writing any reports on the repository elements, be sure that the Repository Reports facility does not already contain a report that can handle the job. Remember that the User Extensibility group contains flexible reports that allow you to see the definitions of most element types.

If you cannot find a predefined repository report, you can use the API views as described earlier in this chapter to query the database. Since repository access essentially involves standard SQL, you simply need to understand the contents of the views and their relationships and write a SELECT statement to return the desired results. The Designer/2000 software set includes SQL*Plus and the Oracle Reports Designer, and both may be used effectively to write these queries. You can also employ any other SQL reporting tool that connects to an Oracle database.

Using the Meta-Model Application System

Designer/2000 ships with an application system that contains the definitions of all meta-model views with their columns and relationships. You can load this application system into the repository from a .DAT load file or a .DMP archive file. The files are called MOD_1_3.DAT and MOD_1_3.DMP, respectively, and are located in the DES2_60\CREQ60\MODEL subdirectory of the directory where you installed the Designer/2000 software (for example, C:\ORAWIN95). You load the .DAT file into an empty application system using **File→Load** in RON. Alternatively, you can import the .DMP file using **Application→Restore** in RON. Either one will load the view definitions into the repository.

Once you have the view definitions loaded in an application system, you can create report modules based on them and use the Reports Generator to generate SQL*Plus or Oracle Reports code for the module. One benefit of creating the reports this way is that, if you are using Designer/2000 to generate code, you already know how to generate report modules and do not have to be concerned with the details of the Reports tool. In addition, the repository reports you write will have a standard appearance, and you can generate all supported report types, including matrix and drill-down reports.

Developing a Forms Front-End for the API

You may want a front-end program that interactively accesses the repository in the same way the Designer/2000 tools do. The API allows you to use a development tool you are comfortable with, such as Oracle Forms, to manipulate repository data. The following paragraphs outline the limitations and workarounds you need to consider when creating a Forms front-end program to access the repository. While this discussion is specific to Oracle Forms, you can translate the techniques into any other development tool that can connect to an Oracle database.

The main limitation with the current version of Developer/2000 (version 1.3) is that it uses PL/SQL version 1.2, which does not support record variables. Since record variables are an integral part of the API access, you have to write database packages to handle the record parameters needed by the API packages. The following explains a sample requirement and the Forms objects and code components needed to implement a Forms front-end for the API.

The Requirement

When you write code to perform work using the repository, it is important that you limit the scope. Completely generic programming can be time consuming, and if you never use the generalized part, it can be wasted effort. Suppose you run the Reconcile utility to cross-reference the repository to the data dictionary, and the resulting report has a number of differences in the Not Null properties of the database and repository definitions for some views. The database view definition may be based on tables that have the wrong Not Null constraint. What you really want is a utility that lets you see the data dictionary Not Null values side by side with the repository Not Null values. This utility can be a form you develop to show these properties side by side which will help you make up your mind about which values are wrong. At that point, you can click an item and change the value in the repository by issuing API calls to update the column definition.

The Components

The API is easy to call from SQL*Plus, but not as easy from Forms. The main parts of the solution are as follows:

- *PL/SQL database packages* that translate the record variables in the API packages to scalar variables that Forms can handle
- *An API form* with blocks to display the repository and database information
- *A Forms procedure* to issue the calls to the database packages

The PL/SQL Database Packages

The PL/SQL packages hide the PL/SQL version 2 specifics from Forms and call procedures in the API as would a normal PL/SQL version 2 routine. The first package to write is FORMS_CDAPI, which calls the standard transaction utilities such as initialize, validate, and close activity. Since these do not use record or table datatypes, although the CDAPI package spec itself does, you do not need any other logic than the call in each package. Here is an excerpt of a PL/SQL database package:

```
CREATE OR REPLACE package forms_cdapi
AS
   /*
   || This package provides calls which parallel
   || those in the CASE API CDAPI for use in
   || Forms PL/SQL
   */

   /*
   || initialize API variables
   */
   PROCEDURE initialize(
      p_app_sys_name VARCHAR2 DEFAULT NULL,
      p_app_sys_ver  NUMBER DEFAULT NULL,
      p_app_sys_ref  NUMBER DEFAULT NULL);
   -- more procedures defined
END forms_cdapi;
/

CREATE OR REPLACE package body forms_cdapi
AS
   PROCEDURE initialize(
      p_app_sys_name VARCHAR2 DEFAULT NULL,
      p_app_sys_ver  NUMBER DEFAULT NULL,
      p_app_sys_ref  NUMBER DEFAULT NULL)
   IS
   BEGIN
      cdapi.initialize(
         p_app_sys_name,
         p_app_sys_ver,
         p_app_sys_ref);
   END;
   -- more procedures defined
END forms_cdapi;
```

All procedures in this package are handled in the same way; that is, within the FORMS_CDAPI package, you create a procedure that mirrors the one in the CDAPI package. You can query the text of the CDAPI package from the database

USER_SOURCE view and copy some of those lines to get started. Notice that all these procedures do is call the corresponding CDAPI procedure.

The next package to write is FORMS_CIOCOLUMN, which calls the necessary INS, UPD, DEL, or SEL procedure in the CIOCOLUMN package. Since the API needs a record variable as a parameter for the CIOCOLUMN package, you pass elements of the record as parameters to the FORMS_CIOCOLUMN procedure and construct a record variable to call CIOCOLUMN. Here is an example:

```
CREATE OR REPLACE package forms_ciocolumn
AS
   /*
   || This package provides calls which parallel
   || those in the CASE API CIOCOLUMN for use in
   || Forms PL/SQL.
   */
   PROCEDURE upd(
      p_property IN VARCHAR2,
      p_colid    IN NUMBER,
      p_value    IN VARCHAR2);

END forms_ciocolumn;
/

CREATE OR REPLACE package body forms_ciocolumn
AS
   /*
   || update column value for property indicated
   */
   PROCEDURE upd (
      p_property IN VARCHAR2,
      p_colid IN NUMBER,
      p_value IN VARCHAR2) IS
      /*
      || Forms passes in the name of the property to update,
      || the column ID of the column you want to update,
      || and the new value of the property.
      */
      r_col     ciocolumn.data;
   BEGIN
      -- expand this to handle other properties if needed
      IF p_property = 'NULL_INDICATOR'
      THEN
         -- load the record structure
```

```
            r_col.v.null_indicator := p_value;
            -- indicate that we made a change
            r_col.i.null_indicator := TRUE;
            IF p_value = 'NULL'
            THEN
               r_col.v.initial_volume := 50;
               r_col.i.initial_volume := TRUE;
               r_col.v.final_volume   := 50;
               r_col.i.final_volume   := TRUE;
               -- the repository sets the values if NOT NULL

           END IF;

           -- update the repository

           ciocolumn.upd(p_colid, r_col);
        END IF;
     END;
  END forms_ciocolumn;
  /
```

Notice that this procedure handles only the NULL INDICATOR property, but you can easily expand it to handle other properties as the need arises. In addition, you can add the companion INS and DEL operations to insert and delete column records. A good starting point in creating these packages is to print to a file the repository specification of the package you wish to call (from the USER_SOURCE view). This will give you information on the parameters and return values as well as tell you what you need to do to construct the FORMS_CIOxxx package. You can use the following SQL*Plus query to list the package text for CIOCOLUMN in a file called CIOCOL.TXT:

```
set head off
set feed off
spool ciocol.txt
SELECT text
  FROM user_source
 WHERE name = 'CIOCOLUMN'
   AND type = 'PACKAGE'
 ORDER by line ;
spool off
set head on
set feed on
```

You can use this query to get other package specs by substituting the package name for CIOCOLUMN.

The API Form

You can develop a form that queries the data dictionary and the repository views to show the null indicator for a particular view definition. There are a few ways to do this. One way is to have a list of values from which the user can select a view definition name. You can then perform a query on a block based on the API view CI_COLUMNS using the selected view name. Naturally, you will need to have the user specify which application system this form is acting on. The columns block has a POST-QUERY trigger that looks up and displays the corresponding data dictionary property value in another nonbase-table item. You can have a mechanism (for example, double-clicking the null indicator) that indicates that the repository value is to be changed. If the user employs this mechanism, a value is written to a nondisplayed flag item that indicates a change.

If the repository and data dictionary are in separate databases or in different user accounts, you will also need database links and synonyms for those other databases.

The Forms Package

When the you click the Commit button, a package procedure checks the flag item of each record to determine if the record changed. If a record was changed, the procedure calls the API routines you wrote to make the change in the repository.

Part of the code to perform the update is shown here. It concentrates on the API calls and does not include some of the Forms mechanisms to perform a loop through the record or to check whether the record or the looping structure changed.

```
PROCEDURE fp_update_ci
IS
   -- ... indicates missing code
   v_act_status      VARCHAR2(255);
   v_act_warning     VARCHAR2(255);
BEGIN
   -- ... Check for anything changed. If nothing, exit
   -- initialize the application system access
   IF NOT forms_cdapi.initialized
   THEN
      -- the user chooses the app name into the :app.name item
      forms_cdapi.initialize(UPPER(:app.name),null, null);
   END IF;
   -- start the transaction
   forms_cdapi.open_activity;
```

```
-- ... do this in a loop through all records in the block
IF :col.changed = 'Y'          -- flag item
THEN
   -- Write the new value into the repository
   forms_ciocolumn.upd(:rel.dsp_property,
       :col.id, :col.dsp_property_value);
   v_changed_ct := v_changed_ct + 1;
END IF;
-- ... end of loop
-- Check for errors and display them
forms_cdapi.validate_activity(v_act_status, v_act_warning);
--
SELECT count(*)
  INTO v_recct
  FROM ci_violations;
--
IF v_act_status != 'Y'
THEN
   message(to_char(v_recct)||' errors. act_status = '||
      v_act_status||
      ' act_warning = '||v_act_warning||'. Messages follow.');
   -- loop through all errors
   FOR viol_rec IN (SELECT * FROM ci_violations)
   LOOP
      message(forms_cdapi.instantiate_message(
               viol_rec.facility, viol_rec.code,
               viol_rec.p0,  viol_rec.p1, viol_rec.p2,
               viol_rec.p3,  viol_rec.p4,  viol_rec.p5,
               viol_rec.p6,  viol_rec.p7) ) ;
   END LOOP;
   message('Aborting activity');
   forms_cdapi.abort_activity;
ELSE
   -- Close activity
   forms_cdapi.close_activity(v_act_status);
   IF v_act_status != 'Y'
   THEN
      message('act_status = '||v_act_status||
          ' after close activity. Aborting activity');
      forms_cdapi.abort_activity;
   END IF;
   message('Update successful.');
```

```
   END IF;
EXCEPTION
   WHEN others
   THEN
      message(SQLERRM);
      raise form_trigger_failure;
END;
```

Note that all the code to mark the start and end of the transaction is in the forms procedure. The values that are passed to the API are from the form, and the messages from the repository that indicate success or failure are handled by the form. Nevertheless, the form code follows the same model as code you would execute from another tool: for example, SQL*Plus. The only difference is that Forms requires an extra layer because it cannot call the API directly.

Although this form is limited to changes made to the Not Null property (also called Optional), other properties can be easily added to the logic to make the form generic to all column properties of all relation types. Some column properties will not have corresponding definitions in the data dictionary, so the comparison operation will not apply, but the repository update step will.

Conclusion

As you can see, the API provides a powerful way to access the repository. The main hurdle is learning about its design and how some specific objects work. The API help file, as mentioned, is the main source for documentation. Be sure to take advantage of the help system word search facility (the Find tab of the help window) offered by 32-bit Windows operating systems if you cannot find a keyword for a particular word. As mentioned in Chapter 13, you can also take advantage of Oracle Web sites, which contain white papers and, if you are an Oracle Support customer, Oracle Support Bulletins to learn more about the API.

The API, combined with the User Extensibility feature, can give you almost unlimited control over the repository. It provides access to otherwise hidden data and otherwise restricted methods for operating on that data. You will truly realize the power of Designer/2000 if you customize it for your working environment. You will gain the benefits of centralized information as well as control over the properties and associations of information that flows from the Strategy phase to the Implementation and Maintenance phases.

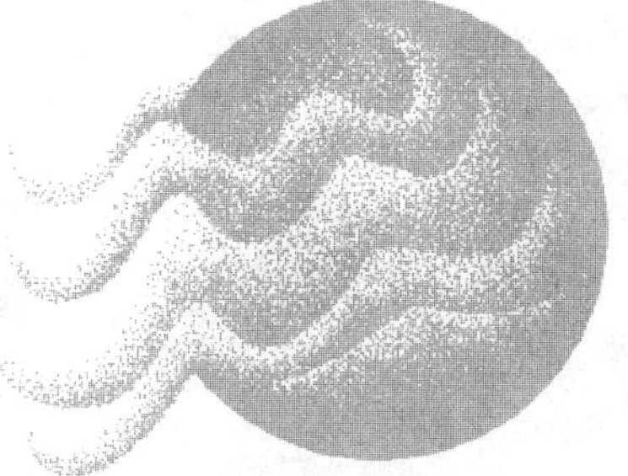

Index

A

E

L

M

N

O

P

Q

R

S

T

U

V

W

Get Your **FREE** Subscription to Oracle Magazine

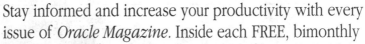

Stay informed and increase your productivity with every issue of *Oracle Magazine*. Inside each FREE, bimonthly issue, you'll get:

- Up-to-date information on the Oracle RDBMS and software tools
- Third-party software and hardware products
- Technical articles on Oracle platforms and operating environments
- Software tuning tips
- Oracle client application stories

Three easy ways to subscribe:

1 **MAIL:** Cut out this page, complete the questionnaire on the back, and mail to: *Oracle Magazine,* 500 Oracle Parkway, Box 659952, Redwood Shores, CA 94065.

2 **FAX:** Cut out this page, complete the questionnaire on the back, and and fax the questionnaire to **+ 415.633.2424.**

3 **WEB:** Visit our Web site at **www.oramag.com.** You'll find a subscription form there, plus much more!

If there are other Oracle users at your location who would like to receive their own copy of *Oracle Magazine,* please photocopy the form on the back, and pass it along.

☐ **YES! Please send me a FREE subscription to Oracle Magazine.** ☐ **NO, I am not interested at this time.**

If you wish to receive your free bimonthly subscription to *Oracle Magazine,* you must fill out the entire form, sign it, and date it (incomplete forms cannot be processed or acknowledged). You can also subscribe at our Web Site at **http://www.oramag.com/html/subform.html** or fax your application to *Oracle Magazine* at **+415.633.2424.**

SIGNATURE (REQUIRED) ✓ ________________ **DATE** ________

NAME ________________ TITLE ________________

COMPANY ________________

STREET/P.O. BOX ________________

CITY/STATE/ZIP ________________

COUNTRY ________________ TELEPHONE ________________

You must answer all eight of the questions below.

1 What is the primary business activity of your firm at this location? *(circle only one)*

01. Agriculture, Mining, Natural Resources
02. Communications Services, Utilities
03. Computer Consulting, Training
04. Computer, Data Processing Service
05. Computer Hardware, Software, Systems
06. Education—Primary, Secondary, College, University
07. Engineering, Architecture, Construction
08. Financial, Banking, Real Estate, Insurance
09. Government—Federal/Military
10. Government—Federal/Nonmilitary
11. Government—Local, State, Other
12. Health Services, Health Institutions
13. Manufacturing—Aerospace, Defense
14. Manufacturing—Noncomputer Products, Goods
15. Public Utilities (Electric, Gas, Sanitation)
16. Pure and Applied Research & Development
17. Retailing, Wholesaling, Distribution
18. Systems Integrator, VAR, VAD, OEM
19. Transportation
20. Other Business and Services ____

2 Which of the following best describes your job function? *(circle only one)*

CORPORATE MANAGEMENT/STAFF

01. Executive Management (President, Chair, CEO, CFO, Owner, Partner, Principal, Managing Director)
02. Finance/Administrative Management (VP/Director/Manager/Controller of Finance, Purchasing, Administration)
03. Other Finance/Administration Staff
04. Sales/Marketing Management (VP/Director/Manager of Sales/Marketing)
05. Other Sales/Marketing Staff ____

TECHNICAL MANAGEMENT/STAFF

06. Computer/Communications Systems Development/ Programming Management
07. Computer/Communications Systems Development/ Programming Staff
08. Computer Systems/Operations Management (CIO/VP/Director/ Manager MIS, Operations, etc.)
09. Consulting
10 DBA/Systems Administrator
11. Education/Training
12. Engineering/R&D/Science Management
13. Engineering/R&D/Science Staff
14. Technical Support Director/Manager
15. Other Technical Management/Staff

____

3 What is your current primary operating system environment? *(circle all that apply)*

01. AIX	12. Solaris/Sun OS
02. HP-UX	13. SVR4
03. Macintosh OS	14. Ultrix
04. MPE-ix	15. UnixWare
05. MS-DOS	16. Other UNIX
06. MVS	17. VAX VMS
07. NetWare	18. VM
08. OpenVMS	19. Windows
09. OS/2	20. Windows NT
10. OS/400	21. Other ____
11. SCO	____

4 What is your current primary hardware environment? *(circle all that apply)*

01. Macintosh
02. Mainframe
03. Massively Parallel Processing
04. Minicomputer
05. PC (IBM-Compatible)
06. Supercomputer
07. Symmetric Multiprocessing
08. Workstation
09. Other ________________

5 In your job, do you use or plan to purchase any of the following products or services *(check all that apply)*

	Use	Plan to buy
SOFTWARE		
01. Accounting/Finance	☐	☐
02. Business Graphics	☐	☐
03. CAD/CAE/CAM	☐	☐
04. CASE	☐	☐
05. CIM	☐	☐
06. Communications/ Networking	☐	☐
07. Database Management	☐	☐
08. Education	☐	☐
09. File Management	☐	☐
10. GIS	☐	☐
11. Image Processing	☐	☐
12. Laboratory Control	☐	☐
13. Materials Resource Planning (MRP, MRP II)	☐	☐
14. Multimedia Authoring Tools	☐	☐
15. Office Automation	☐	☐
16. Order Entry/ Inventory Control	☐	☐
17. Programming/Systems Development	☐	☐
18. Project Management	☐	☐
19. Scientific and Engineering	☐	☐
20. Spreadsheets/ Financial Planning	☐	☐
21. Systems Management Products	☐	☐
22. Workflow	☐	☐
HARDWARE		
23. Macintosh	☐	☐
24. Mainframe	☐	☐
25. Massively Parallel Processing	☐	☐
26. Minicomputer	☐	☐
27. PC (IBM-Compatible)	☐	☐
28. Supercomputer	☐	☐
29. Symmetric Multiprocessing	☐	☐
30. Workstation	☐	☐
PERIPHERALS		
31. Bridges/Routers/ Hubs/Gateways	☐	☐
32. CD-ROM Drives	☐	☐
33. Disk Drives/Subsystems	☐	☐
34. Tape Drives/Subsystems	☐	☐
35. Video Boards/Other Multimedia Peripherals	☐	☐
NETWORK/COMMUNICATIONS		
36. Communications Controllers	☐	☐
37. Local Area Networks	☐	☐
38. Modems	☐	☐
39. Wide Area Networks	☐	☐
SERVICES		
40. Computer-Based Training)	☐	☐
41. Education/Training	☐	☐
42. Maintenance	☐	☐
43. Online DatabaseServices	☐	☐
44. Support	☐	☐
45. **None of the above**	☐	☐

6 What Oracle products are in use at your site? *(circle all that apply)*

SERVERS

01. Oracle7
02. Oracle Media Server
03. Oracle7 Workgroup Server
04. Personal Oracle7
05. Oracle Rdb

TOOLS

06. Designer/2000 (CASE)
07. Developer/2000 (CDE, Forms, Reports, Graphics)
08. Oracle Media Objects
09. Oracle Power Objects

APPLICATIONS

10. Oracle Financials
11. Oracle Human Resources
12. Oracle Manufacturing
13. Other ________
14. **None of the above**

7 What other database products are in use at your site? *(circle all that apply)*

01. CA-Ingres	11. Progress
02. DB2	12. Sybase System 10
03. DB2/2	13. Sybase System 11
04. DB2/6000	14. Sybase SQL Serve
05. dbase	15. VSAM
06. Gupta	16. Other ________
07. IMS	17. SAP
08. Informix	18.Peoplesoft
09. Microsoft Access	19. BAAN
10. Microsoft SQL Server	20. **None of the abov**

8 During the next 12 months, how much do you anticipate your organization will spend on computer hardware, software, peripherals, and services for your location? *(circle only one)*

01. Less than $10,000
02. $10,000 to $49,999
03. $50,000 to $99,999
04. $100,000 to $499,999
05. $500,000 to $999,999
06. $1,000,000 and over

OM